INTEGRATED ADVERTISING, PROMOTION, AND MARKETING COMMUNICATIONS

SIXTH EDITION

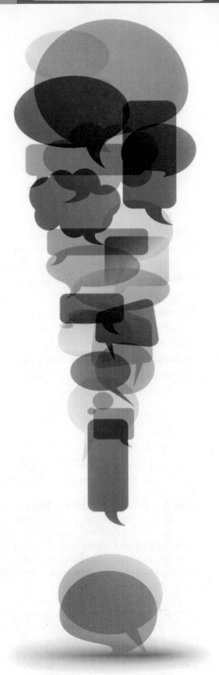

Kenneth E. Clow
University of Louisiana at Monroe

Donald Baack
Pittsburg State University

PEARSON

Boston   Columbus   Indianapolis   New York   San Francisco   Upper Saddle River
Amsterdam Cape Town   Dubai   London   Madrid   Milan   Munich   Paris   Montréal   Toronto
Delhi   Mexico City   São Paulo   Sydney   Hong Kong   Seoul   Singapore   Taipei   Tokyo

Editor in Chief: Stephanie Wall
Director of Editorial Services: Ashley Santora
Editorial Project Manager: Meeta Pendharkar
Editorial Assistant: Jacob Garber
Director of Marketing: Maggie Moylan
Executive Marketing Manager: Anne Fahlgren
Marketing Assistant: Gianna Sandri
Senior Managing Editor: Judy Leale
Production Project Manager: Jacqueline A. Martin
Operations Specialist: Cathleen Petersen
Creative Director: Blair Brown

Senior Art Director: Janet Slowik
Interior and Cover Designer: Laura Ierardi
Cover Images: Paintbrush: hfng/Shutterstock;
    Grunge: javarman/Shutterstock
Media Project Manager, Production: Lisa Rinaldi
Media Project Manager, Editorial: Denise Vaughn
Full-Service Project Management and Composition:
    PreMediaGlobal USA Inc.
Printer/Binder: R.R. Donnelley/Willard
Cover Printer: Lehigh-Phoenix Color/Hagerstown
Text Font: Times LT Std 10.5/12

Credits and acknowledgments borrowed from other sources and reproduced, with permission, in this textbook appear on the appropriate page within the text.

Library of Congress Cataloging-in-Publication Data

Clow, Kenneth E.
   Integrated advertising, promotion, and marketing communications / Kenneth E. Clow, University of Louisiana at Monroe, Donald Baack, Pittsburg State University.—Sixth edition.
      pages cm
   ISBN-13: 978-0-13-312624-2
   ISBN-10: 0-13-312624-2
 1. Communication in marketing.   2. Advertising.   I. Baack, Donald.   II. Title.
HF5415.123.C58 2014
659.1—dc23   2012049569

10 9 8 7 6 5 4 3 2 1

ISBN 10: 0-13-312624-2
ISBN 13: 978-0-13-312624-2

To my sons Dallas, Wes, Tim, and Roy, who provided encouragement, and especially to my wife, Susan, whose sacrifice and love made this textbook possible.

▶ **KENNETH E. CLOW**

I would like to dedicate my efforts and contributions to the book to my wife Pam; children Jessica, Daniel, and David; and grandchildren Tommy, Joe, Rile, Danielle, Andy, Emilee, and Jason.

▶ **DONALD BAACK**

BRIEF CONTENTS

CONTENTS

Part One
THE IMC FOUNDATION   2

3 BUYER BEHAVIORS 52

4 THE IMC PLANNING PROCESS 84

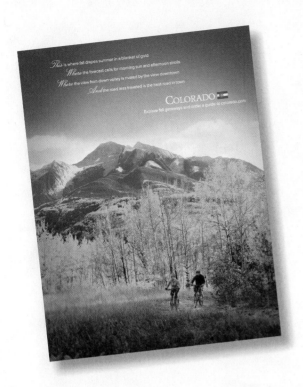

Part Two
IMC ADVERTISING TOOLS   116

7 ADVERTISING DESIGN: MESSAGE STRATEGIES AND EXECUTIONAL FRAMEWORKS 176

Part Three
IMC MEDIA TOOLS 206

8 TRADITIONAL MEDIA CHANNELS 206

Part Five
IMC ETHICS, REGULATION, AND EVALUATION   382

14 REGULATIONS AND ETHICAL CONCERNS   382

15 EVALUATING AN INTEGRATED MARKETING PROGRAM   410

PREFACE

Advertising, promotions, and marketing communications are integral components of marketing. If your students are marketing majors, understanding how companies can effectively communicate with customers and potential customers creates the foundation they need to develop effective marketing skills. This will help them succeed in their marketing careers.

If they are not marketing majors, consider all of the marketing communications around them. Any company or organization they work for will be involved in marketing its products or services. Understanding how marketing communications are developed and why will be valuable knowledge. It will help them comprehend the methods used by the people in the marketing departments where they will work and will provide them with better information to function as a consumer.

We created *Integrated Advertising, Promotion, and Marketing Communications,* in part, to help students understand the importance of integrating all marketing communications (IMC) and how they are produced and transmitted. When our first edition was written, almost all marketing communication textbooks focused exclusively on advertising. As your students know from their everyday experiences and the courses they have taken in college, marketing communications includes much more than that. It includes promotions, such as coupons, price discounts, and contests. Marketing has expanded to blogs on the Internet, customer reviews of products, messages delivered to mobile phones, and newer programs, such as buzz marketing. These venues are vital ingredients in effectively reaching consumers. These must also be carefully integrated into one clear message and voice for customers to hear.

We prepared this textbook and all of the additional materials in a way that will best help your students to understand integrated marketing communications. Students need opportunities to apply concepts to real-life situations. This helps them clearly understand and retain the ideas. As a result, we have prepared a variety of end-of-chapter materials that are designed to help them practice using the concepts. These materials include integrated campaigns in action, integrated learning exercises, discussion and critical-thinking exercises, creative exercises, and cases.

What's New in the Sixth Edition?

The sixth edition of *Integrated Advertising, Promotion, and Marketing Communications* offers some exciting new features. The most dynamic is the addition of the *Integrated*

Campaigns in Action series, which concludes nearly every chapter. These actual advertising and promotional programs are described by the people and advertising agencies involved in creating them. The professor's ancillary package provides additional materials for in-class presentations that should lead to a more dynamic and well-rounded learning experience. Other new features in this edition include:

- **MyLab Integrated Campaigns in Action.** Professors who adopt this text receive access to a the MyLab resource that was developed to support classroom teaching. Nearly every chapter contains at least one advertising and communications campaign, complete with power point slides, advertisements, collaterals, and other pieces of media that are designed to more fully explore the entire promotional process. Campaigns include Oscar Mayer, Skyjacker, Home Federal Bank, Philadelphia Cream Cheese, The Snoring Center, and Interstate Batteries. Each of these *Integrated Campaigns in Action* is mentioned at the close of the chapter text to draw student attention to them.

- **Interviews with advertising professionals.** At various points throughout the text, interviews and quotes from advertising professionals have been integrated into the chapters. A full description of the development of the Motel 6 advertising program by Stan Richards, founder of The Richards Groups is provided. Marketing professionals from the mcgarrybowen agency, The Richards Group, Spych Market Analytics, and Pink Jacket Creative add commentary and perspective on various marketing and promotions topics and will give your students an important perspective on real-world applications.

- **Increased emphasis on social media.** One of the most rapidly evolving aspects of advertising and promotion has been the demand for increased usage of social media. This edition presents a great deal of new material on these important changes. Coverage of social media has been added wherever it has impacted marketing communications.

- **New opening vignettes and cases.** Many of the chapter opening vignettes and cases are new to this edition. These materials keep the book fresh and current.

- **New advertisements.** Throughout the text, a significant number of new advertisements have been added. Many of these resulted from interactions with advertising agencies. Oscar Meyer, Philadelphia Cream Cheese, Chick fil A, Interstate Batteries, and other new advertisements are included, all helping to keep the content as fresh and current as possible.

- **Updated examples.** New examples of marketing communications principles have been incorporated to provide up-to-date information about companies students can relate to. New discussion and critical-thinking exercises have been created to help students understand and apply the materials presented in each chapter.

Integrated Learning Package

We have created several devices that are designed to help students learn the materials in this text. Advertising and marketing communications are interesting and enjoyable subjects, and these materials have been developed to make learning interactive and fun!

- **Integrated Campaigns in Action.** The most exciting and unique new feature in this textbook is a series of presentations about actual marketing programs, as created and designed by professional agencies, as provided in the MyLab resource center. These features are noted at the end of each chapter and in the instructor's PowerPoint materials.

- **Lead-in vignettes.** Each chapter begins with a vignette related to the presented topic. The majority of the vignettes revolve around success stories in companies most students will recognize, such as PetSmart. In this edition, new vignettes have been introduced, including stories about Miracle Whip, Applebee's, the mcgarrybowen agency, and Interstate Batteries. The vignettes introduce your students to the concepts presented throughout the chapter.

- **International marketing discussions.** Some of you have traveled to other countries. Most of you interact with students from around the globe. This book features international concerns that match the presented materials. Also, a section called "International Implications" is found at the end of every chapter.

- **Critical-thinking exercises and discussion questions.** The end-of-chapter materials include a variety of exercises designed to help your students comprehend and apply the chapter concepts. These exercises are designed to challenge students' thinking and encourage them to dig deeper. The best way to know that your students have truly learned a concept or theory is when they can apply it to a different situation. These critical-thinking and discussion exercises require them to apply knowledge to a wide array of marketing situations.

- **Integrated learning exercises.** At the end of each chapter, a set of questions guides students to the Internet to access information that ties into the subject matter covered. These exercises provide students an opportunity to look up various companies and organizations to see how they utilize the concepts presented in the chapter.

- **Creative Corner exercises.** Most students enjoy the opportunity to use their creative abilities. As a result, we feature a new exercise called the "Creative Corner," which asks students to design advertisements and other marketing-related materials. The exercises are designed to help students realize that they are more creative than they might think. Ken Clow has taught students who said they had zero creative ability. Yet these same students were able to produce ads that won ADDY awards in student competitions sponsored by the American Advertising Federation (AAF). If you don't know anything about the AAF student competition, go the organization's Web site at **www.aaf.org**. Entering the annual competition is exciting, and participating looks great on a student's resume.

- **Cases.** Two cases are provided at the conclusion of each chapter. They were written to help students learn by providing plausible scenarios that require thought and review of chapter materials. The short cases should help students conceptually understand chapter components and the larger, more general marketing issues.

Pearson MyMarketingLab

> **MyMarketingLab**
> - Check your understanding of the concepts and key terms using the mypearsonmarketinglab study plan for this chapter.
> - Apply the concepts in a business context using the simulation entitled *The Marketing Environment*.

Instructor's Resource Center

In addition to the MyLab access to *Integrated Campaigns in Action*, the following resources are also available:

PowerPoint BASIC. This simple presentation includes only basic outlines and key points from each chapter. No animation or forms of rich media are integrated, which makes the total file size manageable and easier to share online or via e-mail. BASIC was also designed for instructors who prefer to customize PowerPoint and want to be spared from having to strip out animation, embedded files, or other media-rich features. These files are available as a download from the Instructor's Resource Center.

Media-Rich PowerPoint Presentation. This PowerPoint presentation features print advertisements, slides that build concepts over several steps, discussion questions, Web links, and video snippets. The PowerPoint presentation not only includes ads from the text but also additional ads. The slides, Web site links, video clips, and questions form a coherent presentation for the class. The print advertisements are accompanied by questions or captions relating them to the concepts within the chapter. Integrated learning experiences take the class to Web sites referenced in the text. These files are available as a download from the Instructor's Resource Center.

Instructor's Manual. This resource provides support and suggestions for instructors. A complete outline is provided for each chapter, including key words and their definitions, important themes, references to text figures, and the material's implications for marketing professionals. Review questions, discussion questions, and application questions are all answered thoroughly by the authors, and the chapter-opening vignettes are also explained. Suggestions for classroom projects and presentations are also included. These files are available as a download from the Instructor's Resource Center.

Test Item File. The test file has been expanded to include approximately 3,500 true-false, multiple-choice, and short-answer questions. It includes page references and difficulty level so that instructors can provide greater feedback to students. These files are available as a download from the Instructor's Resource Center.

TestGen. The TestGen test-generation software is a computerized package that allows instructors to custom design, save, and generate classroom tests. The test program permits instructors to edit, add, and delete questions from the test bank; analyze test results; and organize a database of tests and student results. The new software allows for greater flexibility and ease of use. It provides many options for organizing and displaying tests, along with a search and sort feature. These files are available as a download from the Instructor's Resource Center.

Acknowledgments

We would like to thank the following individuals who assisted in the development of the first six editions through their careful and thoughtful reviews:

We are grateful to these reviewers for the sixth edition:

John Bennett, Univeristy of Missouri–Columbia
Donna Falgiatore, St. Joseph's University
Larry Goldstein, Iona College
Joni Jackson, Robert Morris University
Laurel Schirr, VA Polytech Institute/State University
Allen Smith, Florida Atlantic University
Debbie Campbell, Temple University
Rick Morris, University of North Texas
Steve Edwards, Southern Methodist University

We are grateful to these reviewers for the fifth edition:

Joni Jackson, Robert Morris University
Rick Morris, University of North Texas
Charles Larson, Northern Illinois University
Charlie Schwepker, University of Central Missouri
John Bennett, University of Missouri
Prema Nakra, Marist College
Linden Dalecki, Pittsburg State University
Kathleen Havey, University of Maryland
Bryan Johnson, Pennsylvania State University
Debbie Campbell, Temple University

We are grateful to these reviewers for portions of the fourth edition:

John Bennett, University of Missouri–Columbia
MaryEllen Campbell, University of Montana, Missoula
Donna Falgiatore, St. Joseph's University
Deanna Mulholland, Iowa Western Community College
Jim Munz, Illinois State University
Prema Nakra, Marist College
Allen Smith, Florida Atlantic University
Amanda Walton, Indiana Business College

We are grateful to these reviewers for the third edition:

Jeffrey C. Bauer, University of Cincinnati–Clermont
MaryElllen Campbell, University of Montana, Missoula
Sherry Cook, Missouri State University
Catherine Curran, University of Massachusetts–Dartmouth
Michael A. Dickerson, George Mason University
Donna Falgiatore, St. Joseph's University
Charles S. Gulas, Wright State University
Diana Haytko, Missouri State University
Al Mattison, University of California–Berkeley
Deanna Mulholland, Iowa Western Community College
Jim Munz, Illinois State University
Charlie Schwepker, University of Central Missouri
Eugene Secunda, New York University
Allen E. Smith, Florida Atlantic University
Bonni Stachowiak, Vanguard University
Rod Warnick, University of Massachusetts–Amherst
Patti Williams, Wharton Business School

We are grateful to these reviewers for the second edition:

Robert W. Armstrong, University of North Alabama
Jerome Christa, Coastal Carolina University
Stefanie Garcia, University of Central Florida
Robert J. Gulovsen, Washington University–Saint Louis
Sreedhar Kavil, St. John's University

Franklin Krohn, SUNY–Buffalo
Tom Laughon, Florida State University
William C. Lesch, University of North Dakota
James M. Maskulka, Lehigh University
Darrel D. Muehling, Washington State University
Esther S. Page-Wood, Western Michigan University
Venkatesh Shankar, University of Maryland
Albert J. Taylor, Austin Peay State University
Jerald Weaver, SUNY—Brockport

We are grateful to these reviewers of the first edition:

Craig Andrews, Marquette University
Ronald Bauerly, Western Illinois University
Mary Ellen Campbell, University of Montana
Les Carlson, Clemson University
Newell Chiesl, Indiana State University
John Cragin, Oklahoma Baptist College
J. Charlene Davis, Trinity University
Steven Edwards, Michigan State University
P. Everett Fergenson, Iona College
James Finch, University of Wisconsin–La Crosse
Thomas Jensen, University of Arkansas
Russell W. Jones, University of Central Oklahoma
Dave Kurtz, University of Arkansas
Monle Lee, Indiana University–South Bend
Ron Lennon, Barry University
Charles L. Martin, Wichita State University
Robert D. Montgomery, University of Evansville
S. Scott Nadler, University of Alabama
Ben Oumlil, University of Dayton
Melodie R. Phillips, Middle Tennessee State University
Don Roy, Middle Tennessee State University
Elise Sautter, New Mexico State University
Janice E. Taylor, Miami University
Robert L. Underwood, Bradley University
Robert Welch, California State University–Long Beach

Although there were many individuals who helped us with advertising programs, we want to thank a few who were especially helpful. We appreciate the owners and employees of advertising agencies Pink Jacket Creative, The Richards Group, mcgarrybowen, and Gremillion & Pou for providing us with a large number of advertisements. We want to thank Benny Black for his time explaining his highly successful company, Platinum Motorcars. Stan Richards, Mary Price, Dave Snell, Elena Petukhova, and Carrie Dyer (The Richards Group) were very generous with their time, as were Bill Breedlove and Elena Baca (Pink Jacket), Shama Kabini (Marketing Zen), Brian and Sarah Warren (Emogen Marketing Group), Charlie Brim (Interstate Batteries), Lee McGuire (Skyjacker), Paula Ramirez (1400 Words), Tim Clow and Jane Hilk (Oscar Mayer), Howard Friedman (Kraft), Tori Emery, Brittany Bowman, and Rick Thornhill (mcgarrybowen), Shauna McLean Tompkins (Boxcar Creative), Bo Bothe (Brand Extract) and Anne Gremillion (Gremillion & Pou).

On a personal note, we would like to thank Leah Johnson, who signed us for the first edition of the book. Thank you to Erin Gardner, Meeta Pendharkar, Ashley Santora, and Stephanie Wall for helping with this edition as it moved forward and to Jacqueline Martin and Jared Sterzer (PreMediaGlobal) for guiding the production process. We would also like to thank the entire Pearson production group.

Kenneth Clow would like to thank the University of Louisiana at Monroe for providing a supportive environment to work on this text. He is thankful to his sons Dallas, Wes, Tim, and Roy, who always provided encouragement and support.

Donald Baack would like to thank Mimi Morrison and Paula Palmer for their continued assistance in all his work at Pittsburg State University.

We would like to especially thank our wives, Susan Clow and Pam Baack, for being patient and supportive during those times when we were swamped by the work involved in completing this edition. They have been enthusiastic and understanding throughout this entire journey.

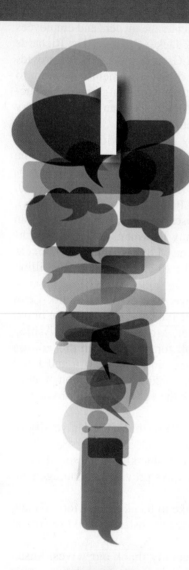

1 INTEGRATED MARKETING COMMUNICATIONS

CHAPTER OBJECTIVES

After reading this chapter, you should be able to answer the following questions:

1 How does communication take place?

2 What is an integrated marketing communications program?

3 What new trends are affecting marketing communications?

4 How does an integrated marketing communications program create value?

5 What are the components of an integrated marketing communications program?

6 What does the term *GIMC* mean?

MyMarketingLab™

⭐ **Improve Your Grade!**

Over 10 million students improved their results using the Pearson MyLabs.
Visit **mymktlab.com** for simulations, tutorials, and end-of-chapter problems.

MIRACLE WHIP

Advertising and promotion are experiencing a rapidly shifting landscape. The decline in traditional media viewing combined with the rise in Internet usage and the use of social media have created a new order. Effective advertising and promotion campaigns often now involve more than one well-made commercial. Recently, some advertisers have gone to greater extremes.

In early 2011, Miracle Whip was promoted in a surprising new way. In essence, consumers were asked if they "loved" or "hated" the product. The advertising agency, mcgarrybowen, directed the entire advertising and social media campaign. Using the concept, "We're not for everyone," the marketing acknowledges the inherent polarization of the product by inviting consumers to tell the world if they love the product or hate it.

Advertisements premiered on big primetime placements on *Glee* and *American Idol.* The work included a cast of celebrities and everyday people. Pundit James Carville proclaiming "Miracle Whip is America" alongside an unknown actor stating it "tastes like spreadable disappointment." Jersey Shore's Pauly D reported, "I'd never eat it. I'd never put it in my hair. It's just wrong." Comic actor Amy Sedaris offered, "It's always great in the bedroom." Soon, full page ads were used in major newspapers to support the launch with the tag line "Are you Miracle Whip?"

In conjunction with the effort, social media channels for people who both love and hate Miracle Whip were established. The campaign evolved urging the public to "Take a Side." A YouTube consumer promotion asked consumers to declare their love or hate, while the site tallied the numbers of "lovers" and "haters," creating a huge buzz about the page. As an attempt to reach a target market of nonusers and lapsed users, the site included a form for ordering a free sample, under the concept of, "it's okay if you don't like us, but give us a try." In all, 500,000 sample packets were sent out, quickly exhausting the supply.

Next, a Web-based consumer contest emerged under the concept of "Not for Every Relationship." This evolvement of the campaign included a priest and a lawyer pitching the contest in which entrants were asked to tell the world how Miracle Whip impacts their relationships. The winning 60-second video submitted to the YouTube site received a prize of $25,000.

The buzz grew quickly, as did a wave of criticism. The critics suggested the brand was trivializing both marriage and divorce. The *National Review* called for the contest and campaign to end, and a social media petition was circulated with the same goal. The discussion became a trending topic on Twitter. None of these efforts was successful in breaking up the campaign. Instead, Miracle Whip continued the conversation tying the

SOME SWEAR BY US. OTHERS SWEAR AT US. ARE YOU MIRACLE WHIP?

Used with the permission of Kraft Foods Inc.

themes of either loving or hating Miracle Whip with its impact on marital and family relationships. In the summer of 2011, marketers took to the streets asking people to talk about their relationships, even reaching out to some just married in Las Vegas. In the end, the buzz lasted for more than half a year.

The Miracle Whip campaign has been criticized and condemned, hailed and praised, with comments ranging from "genius" to "mad men." In the end, Miracle Whip's honesty with the public combined with this innovative advertising and promotional campaign turned an ordinary condiment into an extraordinary national conversation.[1]

OVERVIEW

The global marketplace consists of a complex set of competitors battling for customers in a rapidly changing environment. New companies form on a daily basis. Small businesses, Internet-based operations, and global conglomerates are all part of the worldwide marketing environment.

A wide variety of media are available to the leaders of these companies. Advertising and marketing methods range from simple stand-alone billboard advertisements to complex, multilingual global Web sites. The number of ways to reach potential customers continually increases while alternative methods expand and become increasingly popular.

In the face of these sophisticated and cluttered market conditions, firms try to be heard. Marketing experts know that a company's communications must speak with a clear voice. Customers must understand the essence of a business and the benefits of its goods and services. The vast variety of advertising and promotional venues combined with a multitude of companies bombarding potential customers with messages makes the task challenging.

This first chapter explains the nature of an integrated advertising and marketing communications program. The first section describes communication processes. Understanding how communication works builds the foundation for an integrated marketing program. Next, an integrated marketing communications program is described. Finally, the integrated marketing communications process is applied to global or international operations, creating a globally integrated marketing communications (GIMC) program.

The Nature of Communication

OBJECTIVE 1.1

How does communication take place?

Communication is transmitting, receiving, and processing information. When a person, group, or organization attempts to transfer an idea or message, communication occurs when the receiver (another person or group) comprehends the information. The model of communication shown in Figure 1.1 displays the pathway a message takes from one person to another.[2]

Communication plays a key role in any advertising or marketing program. Consider a person planning to dine at a quick-serve chicken restaurant. In the communications model (Figure 1.1), the **senders** include the chains KFC, Chick-fil-A, Poppeye's, Church's Chicken, Bojangles, and Raising Cain's Chicken Fingers. Each one tries to capture the customer's attention. Most of these firms hire advertising agencies. Some utilize in-house marketing groups.

Encoding is forming verbal and nonverbal cues. In marketing, the person in charge of designing an advertisement takes an idea and transforms it into an attention-getting message. The commercial consists of cues being placed in various media, including television, magazines, and billboards. The message may also be encoded on the firm's Web site, a social media page, or a Twitter account.

Messages travel to audiences through various **transmission devices**. Marketing communications move through various channels or media. The channel may be a television station carrying an advertisement, a Sunday paper with a coupon placed in it, the Internet, or a billboard placed along the interstate.

Decoding occurs when the message reaches one or more of the receiver's senses. Consumers both hear and see television ads. Others consumers handle (touch) and read (see) a coupon offer. It is even possible to "smell" a message. A well-placed perfume sample might entice a buyer to purchase both the magazine containing

▶ **FIGURE 1.1**
The Communication Process

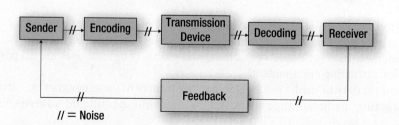

// = Noise

the sample and the perfume being advertised. Hungry people tend to pay closer attention to advertisements and other information about food.

Quality marketing communication takes place when customers (the **receivers**) decode or understand the message as it was intended by the sender. In the case of Chick-fil-A, effective marketing communications depend on receivers encountering the right message and responding in the desired fashion, such as by making a trip to the local Chick-fil-A restaurant or becoming loyal fans on the company's social media page.

Chick-fil-A's approach to social media provides an example of a successful communication strategy that integrates the Web site with both online and off-line advertising to build a loyal customer base.[3] Before launching a social media site, Chick-fil-A's third-party digital agency discovered that more than 500 Facebook profiles mentioned Chick-fil-A, and that one particular fan page had 25,000 "fans." Engaging consumers constituted the goal of the social media program. John Keehler, director of interactive strategy at ClickHere, noted that, "One of the mistakes we'd seen is brands would gather a lot of friends but wouldn't get people to interact with them."

The Facebook page allows fans to interact with Chick-fil-A. The company holds a "Cow Appreciation Day" each July in which customers are encouraged to dress like cows and post their photos on the Facebook fan page. To build the base of members, in the past coupons have been offered as part of a "Chicken Wave" during the kickoff of the college football season. Other promotions through Twitter and Facebook resulted in a Facebook community with more than 1 million members. Currently, any new Chick-fil-A store opening is first announced on Facebook, and customers are invited to visit the restaurant and participate in grand-opening festivities.

A compatible offline program represents one key to the social media utilization. Successfully-integrated communications employ multiple channels providing a consistent message. Many Chick-fil-A commercials urge people to "Eat Mor Chikin." All advertising and promotional venues present the same tagline and theme, thereby increasing the chances that consumers will encounter and perceive the same message. The result can be a stronger brand presence over time.

 In the communication process, **feedback** takes the form of the receiver's response to the sender. In marketing communications, feedback includes purchases, inquiries, complaints, questions, store visits, blogs, and Web site hits.

Noise consists of anything that distorts or disrupts a message, including marketing communications. It can occur at any stage in the communication process, as shown in Figure 1.1. The most common form of noise affecting marketing communications is **clutter**. Examples of noise that can affect the advertising messages are provided in Figure 1.2.

The marketing professionals involved in the communication process pay attention to each aspect of the communications model to ensure that all audiences receive a consistent message. They try to be sure the message cuts through noise and clutter. In the case of quick-serve chicken restaurants, increases in market share, sales, and brand loyalty constitute common objectives the marketing team attempts to achieve.

Permission granted by CFA Properties, Inc.

▲ This Chick-fil-A advertisement encourages young customers to dress like a cow.

Permission granted by CFA Properties, Inc.

▲ A Chick-fil-A contest winner.

▶ Opening page of the
"Eatmorchikin" Web site.

▶ **FIGURE 1.2**
Communication Noise

- Talking on the phone during a commercial on television
- Driving while listening to the radio
- Looking at a sexy model in a magazine ad and ignoring the message and brand
- Scanning a newspaper for articles to read
- Talking to a passenger as the car passes billboards
- Scrolling past Internet ads without looking at them
- Becoming annoyed by ads appearing on a social media site
- Ignoring tweets on Twitter because they are not relevant
- Being offended by the message on a flyer for a local business

Communicating with consumers and other businesses requires more than simply creating attractive advertisements. The upcoming section describes the nature of integrated marketing communications. An effective program integrates all marketing activities into a complete package designed to effectively reach the target market or audience.

Integrated Marketing Communications

OBJECTIVE 1.2

What is an integrated marketing communications program?

The communications model provides the foundation for an advertising and marketing program. **Integrated marketing communications (IMC)** is the coordination and integration of all marketing communication tools, avenues, and sources in a company into a seamless program designed to maximize the impact on customers and other stakeholders. The program covers all of a firm's business-to-business, market channel, customer-focused, and internally directed communications.[4]

Before further examining an IMC program, consider the traditional framework of marketing promotions. The **marketing mix** provides the starting point. As shown in Figure 1.3, promotion constitutes one of the four components of the mix.

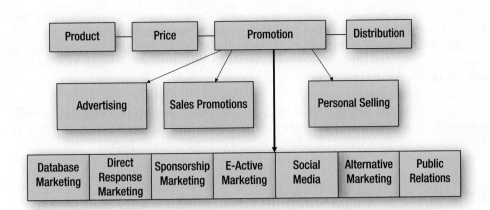

For years, the traditional view was that promotional activities included advertising, sales promotions, and personal selling activities. This view has expanded to incorporate online and alternative methods of communication. It also includes activities such as database marketing, direct response marketing, sponsorships, online marketing, social media, guerrilla marketing, alternative marketing, and public relations programs.

A complete IMC plan reaches every element of the marketing mix: products, prices, distribution methods, and promotions. While this textbook primarily deals with the promotions component, it should be noted that, in order to present a unified message, the other elements of the marketing mix will be blended into the program.

An Integrated Marketing Communications Plan

A strategic marketing plan forms the basis for integrated marketing communications. The plan coordinates every component of the marketing mix in order to achieve harmony in the messages and promotions relayed to customers and others. Figure 1.4 lists the steps required to complete a marketing plan.

A *current situational analysis* is the process of examining the firm's ongoing market situation. Next, marketers conduct a *SWOT analysis* by examining factors in the organization's internal and external environments. SWOT identifies internal company strengths and weaknesses along with the marketing opportunities and threats present in the external environment.

Defining primary *marketing objectives* establishes targets such as higher sales, an increase in market share, a new competitive position, or desired customer actions, such as visiting the store and making purchases. Marketing objectives are identified along with key target markets. A comprehensive understanding of these markets helps the marketing team prepare effective integrated marketing communications.

◀ **FIGURE 1.4**
Steps of a Marketing Plan

- Current situational analysis
- SWOT analysis
- Marketing objectives
- Target market
- Marketing strategies
- Marketing tactics
- Implementation
- Evaluation of performance

Based on the marketing objectives and target market, *marketing strategies* are produced. These strategies apply to all the ingredients of the marketing mix, plus any positioning, differentiation, or branding strategies. Based on the strategies, *marketing tactics* guide the day-by-day activities necessary to support marketing strategies. The final two steps in the marketing plan consist of stating how to *implement* the plan and specifying methods to evaluate *performance*.

The steps of the strategic marketing plan help pull together all company activities into one consistent effort. These steps provide guidance to company leaders and marketing experts as they coordinate the firm's overall communications package.

Emerging Trends in Marketing Communications

OBJECTIVE 1.3

What new trends are affecting marketing communications?

Many forces impact the field of marketing communications. Financial pressures have caused the company leaders who hire advertising agencies to recognize that they cannot pay out unlimited dollars for marketing programs. Emerging social trends affect marketing messages and means of communication. New technologies also influence the field. As a result, new trends have emerged (see Figure 1.5).

EMPHASIS ON ACCOUNTABILITY AND MEASURABLE RESULTS

Company leaders expect advertising agencies to produce tangible outcomes. They spend promotional dollars carefully. Any coupon promotion, contest, rebate program, or advertising campaign should yield measurable gains in sales, market share, brand awareness, customer loyalty, or other observable results to be considered successful.

The increasing emphasis on accountability and measurable results has been driven by chief executive officers (CEOs), chief financial officers (CFOs), and chief marketing officers (CMOs). According to Martyn Straw, chief strategy officer of the advertising agency BBDO Worldwide, corporate executives and business owners are tired of "funneling cash into TV commercials and glossy ads" that keep increasing in cost while appearing to do less and less.

Many companies rely less on 30-second television spots and instead pursue alternative communication venues. Marketing messages can be tied to special events where names, profiles, and addresses of prospective customers are collected and tracked. Straw suggests that marketing should not be viewed as an expense, but rather as an investment in which promotional dollars generate sales and profits.[5]

CHANGES IN TASKS PERFORMED

The tasks performed by the players in advertising programs are changing. An *account executive* works the advertising agency (see Figure 1.6), seeking to sell, direct, and manage advertising and promotional programs for client companies. The account manager develops overall strategic communication plans for client companies while at the same

---

- Emphasis on Accountability and Measurable Results
- Changes in tasks performed by key players
- Explosion in the use of alternative media

▲ **FIGURE 1.5**
Trends affecting marketing communication

- Account executive
- Brand or product manager
- Creatives
- Account planners

▲ **FIGURE 1.6**
Key individuals in an ad program

time overseeing individual promotional activities. Growing demand for accountability means this individual closely examines each marketing campaign seeking evidence of success to show prospective clients.

The *brand* or *product manager* oversees a specific brand or line of products for the client company. The brand manager works with the advertising agency, specialists in trade and consumer promotions along with other individuals and agencies involved in conveying brand image to customers. The brand manager organizes the activities of multiple individuals and agencies while integrating each marketing campaign. The goal of ensuring customers encounter the same consistent voice remains.

Creatives are the individuals who develop the actual advertisements and promotional materials. Most are employed by advertising agencies. Some work for individual companies; others are freelancers.

The *account planner* represents the voice of the consumer within the agency to the agency's creative staff. An account planner will be involved in the development of an advertising campaign. In this new era in which attracting attention to a company, good, or service is difficult, creatives and account planners are being asked to contribute ideas about the firm's strategic marketing direction and the types of communication that will best reach each target audience.

A new partnership has emerged among account executives, brand managers, account planners, and creatives. Most advertising and marketing agencies do more than create ads. The companies assist clients with building the entire integrated communications program.

EMERGENCE OF ALTERNATIVE MEDIA

Internet-based marketing communications have evolved from simple Web advertisements to interactive Web sites, blogs, and social networks. Smartphones and text-messaging systems have created a new landscape and, in some cases, nearly a new language. Alternative interactive marketing techniques can create experiences with a brand and rather than mere purchases.

Many companies have cut traditional media expenditures, moving to nontraditional or alternative media. Procter & Gamble (P&G), AT&T, Johnson & Johnson, Kraft Foods, Verizon, and Toyota spend less on television advertising and have shifted funds to digital media. Unilever recently increased its digital spending by 15 percent.[6] As a General Motors executive noted, "Some 70 percent of consumers who shop for a new car or truck do Web research."[7] The same holds true for many other products.

Currently, younger consumers with considerable amounts of purchasing power may be less inclined to watch television. Instead, they engage in technology-based interactions with friends around the world through various social media sites. Finding ways to reach such consumers who are increasingly sophisticated at blocking out traditional advertising messages constitutes the key challenge. Capturing their attention is not enough. Marketers seek to find ways to engage and interact with consumers in ways that create positive, long-term experiences and bonds.

The Value of IMC

Advances in technology and communications have dramatically changed marketing.[8] Engaging consumers requires an entirely new, carefully integrated approach. Figure 1.7 identifies reasons for the shift to greater integration of advertising and marketing communications programs.

OBJECTIVE 1.4

How does an integrated marketing communications program create value?

◀ **FIGURE 1.7**

Reasons for Integrating Advertising and Marketing Programs

- Advances in information technology
- Changes in channel power
- Increase in global competition
- Increase in brand parity
- Emphasis on customer engagement
- Increase in micro-marketing

▲ Technologies such as smartphones and texting have changed the landscape of advertising and marketing.

ADVANCES IN INFORMATION TECHNOLOGY

Technology enables instant communications among business executives, employees, channel members, and customers around the world, creating both opportunities and threats for marketing communications. Consumers hold access to a wealth of information about companies, products, and brands. They can communicate with each other, sending favorable or unfavorable ratings and information. Messages travel almost instantaneously. Marketers are adapting methods to communicate and vend products effectively in this new communication-rich age. They also monitor what consumers are saying in blogs and online forums.

Advances in information technology allowed self-styled makeup maven Lauren Luke to sell cosmetics around the world. She started by offering them on eBay and then began posting videos that she recorded in her bedroom on YouTube. The videos have been viewed 50 million times. Her YouTube channel now contains over 250,000 subscribers. It is not just entrepreneurs such as Lauren Luke who have taken advantage of the opportunities present in today's information and technology-rich environment. In just 6 months. Dell generated $1 million in sales from individuals who contacted the firm using Twitter.[9]

CHANGES IN CHANNEL POWER

A marketing channel consists of a producer or manufacturer vending goods to wholesalers or middlemen, who, in turn, sell items to retailers who sell the items to consumers. Recent technological developments alter the levels of power held by members of the channel.

Retailers seek to maintain channel power by controlling shelf space and purchase data which allows them to determine which products and brands are placed on store shelves. Through checkout scanners, retailers know what products and brands are selling. Many retailers share the data with suppliers and require them to ensure that store shelves remain well stocked. The size and power of mega-retailers mean manufacturers and suppliers have no choice but to follow the dictates of "mega" stores.

At the same time, the growth of the Internet and other methods of communication shifts some channel power to consumers.[10] Consumers obtain information about goods and services and purchase them using the Internet and other resources. The Visa advertisement on the next page encourages consumers to book hotel rooms, air travel, and car rentals online. Internet-driven sales have grown at a tremendous rate. According to Forrester Research, online retail sales have grown from $31 billion in 2001 to $252 billion in 2013 and are projected to reach $327 billion by 2016. Online purchases now account for 8 percent of all retail purchases.[11]

To illustrate the effects of technology on channel power, consider an individual in the market for a mobile phone provider. First, she completes an Internet search. She identifies several possible brands and narrows them down to three. Next, she travels to a local mall to investigate the carriers. Asking questions of the salespeople helps her gather additional information. After returning home, she logs onto the Web sites of the three brands to learn about warranties, the types of phones being offered, and about company policies, such as ease in changing calling plans, plus other details about rollover minutes and other services. She then goes to various forums and blogs to read what other consumers say about the three brands.

After gathering sufficient information to make a decision, the customer can use Internet sources, the telephone, or a personal visit to the carrier's store to finalize the purchase. She might even play one carrier off against another to negotiate a better price. Soon, she has a new phone and new service. The buyer remained in charge of the entire process. Although individuals still purchase the majority of products in brick-and-mortar stores, many now use these technology-driven methods of gathering information.

The same principles apply to business-to-business purchasing activities. Buyers who shop on behalf of organizations and other company members seeking business-to-business products also tap into these resources (i.e., Web sites, databases). Consequently, a similar shift in channel power has taken place in the business-to-business sector.

INCREASES IN GLOBAL COMPETITION

Information technology and communication advances influence the marketplace in other ways. Competition no longer comes from the company just down the street—it may be from a firm 10,000 miles away. Consumers desire quality along with low prices. The company that delivers both quality and value makes the sale, regardless of location. Advancements in delivery systems make it possible for purchases to arrive in a matter of days.

▲ This VISA advertisement encourages consumers to book vacations online.

In this environment, integrating advertising and other marketing communications becomes increasingly important. Advertising alone cannot maintain sales. The situation is further complicated for manufacturers when retailers hold stronger channel power and control the flow of merchandise to consumers. In that circumstance, manufacturers invest in trade promotions (dealer incentives and discounts) to keep products displayed in various retail outlets. Encouraging retailers to promote a manufacturer's brand or prominently display it for consumer viewing requires an even greater expenditure of promotional dollars. Manufacturers also spend money on consumer promotions (coupons, contests, sweepstakes, bonus packs, and price-off deals) to retain customers, seeking to keep a brand attractive to the retailer.

The global mobile phone market provides a model of this new global marketplace. Figure 1.8 displays market shares for the top brands in the industry, with Nokia as the

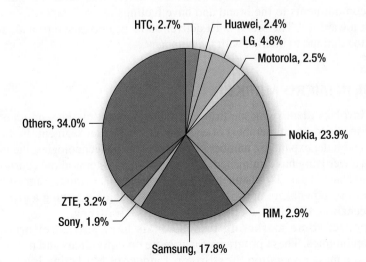

▶ **FIGURE 1.8**
Global market share of mobile phones

▲ To minimize brand parity effects, brands such as Asics use advertising to create a strong brand name.

market leader, Samsung number two, LG as the number three brand. The primary way these companies gain market share is by taking it away from other brands. As the market leader, Nokia often becomes the main target of such efforts and as a result experienced a shrinking market share, from 40.47 percent in 2009 to 23.9 percent today.[12]

INCREASE IN BRAND PARITY

Many currently available products offer nearly identical benefits. When consumers believe that most brands provide the same set of attributes, **brand parity** results. When it occurs, shoppers select from a group of brands rather than one specific brand.[13] Brand parity means quality becomes less of a concern, because consumers perceive only minor differences between brands. Consequently, on other criteria, such as price, availability, or a specific promotional deal impact purchase decisions. The net effect may be a steady decline in brand loyalty.[14] Brand loyalty has also been reduced by the growing acceptance of private brands.

A recent survey revealed that consumers are willing to switch brands in most product categories and do not have one specific brand they must buy or believe is significantly superior.[15] In response to this trend, marketing teams tried to create messages that suggest a company's products were different. Although these messages were designed to convince consumers that the company's brand was superior and not the same as the competition, they often did not move consumers from the perception of brand parity. As a result, some companies have changed to new and innovative marketing tactics.

EMPHASIS ON CUSTOMER ENGAGEMENT

The expanding number of available brands perceived to be roughly equivalent leads to another response. To build loyalty, many marketing efforts have been made to engage customers with the brand at every contact point. A **contact point** is any place where customers interact with or acquire additional information about a firm. Customer engagement programs often utilize digital media and should become part of the total integrated marketing approach.

Effective engagement provides a venue for two-way communication. It can be built by offering incentives and reasons for the consumer to communicate with the company. For customers to take advantage of these initiatives, however, they must develop emotional commitments to the brand and have feelings of confidence, integrity, pride, and passion toward it.[16] The brand must deliver on its promises and provide reasons for consumers to continue to interact with the company.

INCREASE IN MICRO-MARKETING

Marketing involves identifying the firm or product's target market and identifying the appropriate media to reach members of each particular market segment. In this information age and with the expanding number of communication technologies, the influence of mass-media advertising has diminished. DVRs and other systems allow consumers to use the remote to channel surf TV channels and watch programs without commercials. Many television advertisements are not seen, even by those people watching a given program. The same scenario takes place in other forms of mass advertising.

In response, some marketing professionals have shifted efforts to micro-marketing techniques. These programs focus more on individuals and micro-segments rather than the mass population. Rex Briggs, founder of Marketing Evolution, stated

◀ Nonprofits such as Salvation Army must understand how to engage donors to ensure sufficient funds when disasters strike.

that ". . . going into the future you're going to see more fragmentation of the media mix and more digital."[17]

Advertising agencies assist in these marketing efforts. Until 1970, almost all agencies focused solely on advertising. Now, many agencies help clients in develop and refine IMC programs.[18] In addition to advertisements, agencies design Web content, create special events, and look for opportunities to build two-way communication systems with customers.

IMC Components and the Design of This Text

Figure 1.9 presents an overview of the IMC approach featured in this textbook. As shown, the foundation of an IMC program consists of a careful review of the company's image, the buyers to be served, and the markets in which the buyers are located. Advertising programs are built on this foundation, as are the other elements of the promotional mix. The integration tools located at the peak of the pyramid help the company's marketing team make certain all of the elements of the plan are consistent and effective.

OBJECTIVE 1.5

What are the components of an integrated marketing communications program?

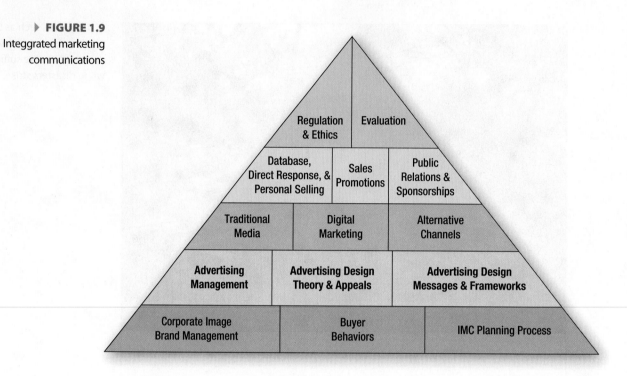

THE IMC FOUNDATION

The first section of this text builds the foundation for an IMC program. Chapter 2 examines the elements of corporate image and brand management. Strengthening the firm's image and brands answers the question, "Who are we and what message are we trying to send?" Branding includes the development of packages and labels that speak with the same voice as other marketing messages.

Chapter 3 describes buyer behaviors. The steps of the consumer purchasing process explain how individuals make choices. Marketers identify the motives leading to purchases and factors affecting those decisions. Then, the IMC program can be designed to influence consumer thinking. Business-to-business buyer behaviors are also examined. Discovering viable business-to-business marketing opportunities by reaching purchasing managers and other decision makers in the target business plays a vital role in overall company success.

Chapter 4 explains the IMC planning program. This includes identifying all target markets, most notably consumer and business-to-business market segments. The plan is complete when communications budgets have been developed and all appropriate media have been identified.

ADVERTISING TOOLS

Advertising issues are noted in the second section of this text. Advertising management, as described in Chapter 5, addresses the major advertising activities, the general direction the company takes, and the selection of an advertising agency. The functions performed by various advertising agency personnel are also explained.

Several advertising theories, which are explored in Chapter 6, help creatives design advertisements. The various advertising appeals that can be used, including those oriented toward fear, humor, sex, music, and logic, are highlighted in the chapter.

Chapter 7 reveals the ingredients involved in creating effective message strategies. Various executional frameworks, Creating successful message strategies involves various executional frameworks, which are various ways to construct the actual commercial or advertisement, deliver the messages. Creatives and other advertising professionals know that effective advertising includes the use of effective sources or spokespersons and following well-established principles of success.

IMC MEDIA TOOLS

The third section of this book contains information regarding both traditional and cutting-edge methods of reaching potential customers. First, the traditional media channels, including television, radio, outdoor, magazines, and newspapers, are described in Chapter 8, along with the advantages and disadvantages of each medium. The roles provided by media planners and media buyers are also explained.

Chapter 9 examines digital marketing efforts designed to integrate e-commerce programs with recent trends in online interactive marketing. These include social networks, blogs, and customer reviews. In these forums, consumers play interactive communications roles.

Many communication channels are available beyond both the traditional networks and the Internet. Chapter 10, titled "Alternative Marketing," describes methods such as buzz marketing, guerrilla marketing, product placements, branded entertainment, and lifestyle marketing. Brand communities are also featured.

PROMOTIONAL TOOLS

The next level of the IMC pyramid adds database and direct response marketing programs, personal selling, trade promotions, consumer promotions, public relations efforts, and sponsorship programs. When marketing managers carefully design all of the steps taken up to this point, the firm can integrate these activities. Messages presented in the advertising campaign can be reinforced through a variety of communication promotions.

Personal selling, database, and direct response marketing programs are outlined in Chapter 11. Personal selling involves contacts with retail customers and other businesses. The chapter describes effective data collection and analysis. Then, the information gained can be used to develop data-driven marketing programs, including permission marketing, frequency programs, and customer relationship management systems as well as personal selling activities.

Chapter 12, which has the general title of "Sales Promotions," describes consumer and trade promotions. Trade promotions include trade incentives, cooperative advertising, slotting fees, and other promotions and discounts that help the manufacturer or channel member to push the product through the distribution channel. Consumer promotions are directed at end users and include coupons, contests, premiums, refunds, rebates, free samples, and price-off offers.

Chapter 13 focuses on public relations programs that connect with consumers in positive ways. This involves emphasizing positive events and dealing with negative publicity. In many cases, the marketing team utilizes public relations efforts to help a sponsorship program achieve the greatest impact.

INTEGRATION TOOLS

The top level of the IMC program adds the integration tools needed to make sure the company effectively serves all customers. Chapter 14 begins with a presentation of the many legal and regulatory issues that are part of the advertising and promotions environment. Ethical issues in marketing communications are also discussed.

▼ Advertising is an important integrated marketing component for Interstate Batteries.

REFUSES TO LET YOU ROUGH IT

INTRODUCING THE INDUSTRY'S FIRST DEDICATED 6-VOLT RV BATTERY.
Featuring our QuickCaps™ for easy maintenance, a peel-away care and installation tips booklet and an 18-month consumer warranty, this battery is ready to hit the road. Find out more at interstatebatteries.com/rvdealer.

INTERSTATE BATTERIES
Outrageously Dependable

Recreational Vehicle
DEEP CYCLE

© 2011 Interstate Battery System International, Inc.

Advertisement furnished by Interstate Batteries

▶ Companies often utilize the expertise of marketing research firms such as ReRez to evaluate IMC programs.

The final chapter of this textbook, Chapter 15, explains the evaluation of integrated marketing communications programs. Evaluations can begin prior to any promotional campaign and continue during the campaign to post-campaign evaluations. These evaluations generate valuable information to alter campaigns before they are commercially introduced. They also provide input to modify programs that have already run. A promotions evaluation process holds everything together and drives the entire IMC process. Fully integrated marketing requires a well-defined linkage between planning and evaluation processes.

International Implications

The same trends that exist among advertising agencies in the United States occur in the international arena. Instead of IMC, international programs are called *GIMC*, or a *globally integrated marketing communications programs*.[19] The goal remains the same—to coordinate marketing efforts across all platforms. The challenges become greater due to larger national and cultural differences in target markets.

Marketers employ two different strategies for global companies. **Standardization**, in which a company features a uniform product and message across countries, represents one option. The approach involves generating economies of scale in production while creating a global product using a more universal promotional theme. The language may be different, but the basic marketing message stays the same.

The second approach, **adaptation**, results in the creation of products and marketing messages designed for and adapted to individual countries. The manner in which a product is marketed in Mexico will be different the methods used in Italy, India, or Australia.

The standardization method is in many ways easier to apply; however, GIMC can and should be used with either adaptation or standardization.[20] To reduce costs, careful coordination of marketing efforts should occur across countries. Even when a firm uses the adaptation strategy, marketers from various countries learn from each other. Synergies take place between countries and regions. More important, learning can occur.

Recently, Adrian Hallmark, global brand director of Jaguar, commented that "for too many luxury consumers there is awareness of the Jaguar brand, but not consideration and modern relevance." To restore its iconic status, Jaguar launched a multinational ad campaign created by Spark 44, a London ad agency. The campaign debuted on Web sites JaguarUSA.com, Facebook, and YouTube with a 45-second version of a 30-second TV ad. Jaguar then introduced print, digital and outdoor advertising in the United States, Austria, Spain, France, Germany, Italy, Russia, Korea, Japan, Australia, and South Africa. The campaign included an 18-city road show in the United States to allow prospective buyers to try the new Jaguar. The ads were adapted to individual markets in each country using the central theme of the campaign "How alive are you?" which was featured in every print, digital, outdoor, television, and video ad.[21]

INTEGRATED CAMPAIGNS IN ACTION

In the upcoming chapters of this book, this section presents basic information about various integrated advertising and marketing campaigns. The insights resulted from personal interviews by the authors with members of the advertising agencies and client companies. Some of the brands include

- Argent Financial
- Skyjacker
- Philadelphia Cream Cheese
- Just Curb It

Each features a PowerPoint presentation that professors can use as well as copies of collateral materials featured in the campaigns, such as print ads, photos, television ads, and radio spots.

Ouachita Independent Bank

The campaign for the Ouachita Independent Bank revolves around the theme of local people, local trust. The campaign consists of 15 and 30 second television ads, out-of-home materials, magazine ads, and newspaper ads. Many of these collateral materials will be available to students to access through QR codes within the textbook, such as the television ad available through the QR code below. The entire campaign, including a PowerPoint, can be found at the Pearson Instructor's Resource Center (www.pearsonhighered.com). The campaign was produced by Newcomer, Morris, and Young advertising agency.

▶ A billboard ad for Ouachita Independent Bank.

Advertisement provided by Newcomer, Morris, and Young

SUMMARY

Communication consists of transmitting, receiving, and processing information. It represents a two-way street in which a sender establishes a connection with a receiver. Effective communication forms the basis for a solid and successful marketing program.

The components of the communication process include the sender, an encoding process, the transmission device, the decoding process, and the receiver. Noise is anything that distorts or disrupts the flow of information from the sender to the receiver.

In the marketing arena, senders are companies seeking to transmit ideas to consumers, employees, other companies, retail outlets, and others. Encoding devices provide the means of transmitting information and include advertisements, public relations efforts, press releases, sales activities, promotions, and a wide variety of additional verbal and nonverbal cues sent to receivers. Transmission devices are the media and spokespersons that carry the message. Decoding occurs when the receivers (customers or retailers) encounter the message. Noise takes many forms in marketing, most notably the clutter of an overabundance of messages in every available channel.

Integrated marketing communications (IMC) takes advantage of the effective management of the communications channel. Within the marketing mix of products, prices, distribution systems, and promotions, firms that speak with one clear voice are able to coordinate and integrate all marketing tools.

The fields of advertising, promotions, and marketing communications have experienced several new trends. Marketing departments and advertising agencies, as well as individual account managers, brand managers, and creatives, encounter strong pressures. They are being held accountable for expenditures of marketing communications dollars. Company leaders expect tangible results from promotional campaigns and marketing programs. As a result, new partnerships are forming among account executives, creatives, and the companies that hire them.

IMC plans are vital to achieving success. The explosion of information technologies strongly influences IMC programs. Channel power has shifted from manufacturers to retailers and now to consumers. Company leaders adjust in order to maintain a strong market standing and IMC programs can assist in this effort. New levels of competition drive marketers to better understand customers and be certain that those end users are hearing a clear and consistent message from the firm. As consumers develop a stronger sense of brand parity, wherein consumers perceive no real differences in product or service quality, marketers seek to create situations in which company brand hold a distinct advantage over others. This may be difficult, because consumers collect and integrate information about products from a wide variety of sources, including technological outlets (Web sites) and interpersonal (salespeople) sources. Quality IMC programs help maintain the strong voice a company needs to ensure customers hear its message. The decline in effectiveness of mass-media advertising constitutes an additional challenge. IMC helps company leaders find new ways to contact consumers with a unified message and to engage them in long-term relationships.

When a firm conducts business internationally, a GIMC, or globally integrated marketing communications system, can be of great value. By developing one strong theme and then adapting that theme to individual countries, the firm conveys a message that integrates international operations into a more coherent marketing package.

This text explains the issues involved in establishing an effective IMC program. The importance of business-to-business marketing efforts is noted, because many firms market items as much to other companies as they do to consumers. Successful development of an IMC program should help firms remain profitable and vibrant, even when the complexities of the marketplace make these goals more difficult to reach.

Key Terms

communication Transmitting, receiving, and processing information.

senders The person(s) attempting to deliver a message or idea.

encoding The verbal (words, sounds) and nonverbal (gestures, facial expressions, posture) cues that the sender utilizes in dispatching a message.

transmission devices All of the items that carry a message from the sender to the receiver.

decoding What occurs when the receiver employs any of his or her senses (hearing, seeing, feeling) in an attempt to capture a message.

receivers The intended audience for a message.

feedback The information the sender obtains from the receiver regarding the receiver's perception or interpretation of a message.

noise Anything that distorts or disrupts a message.

clutter What exists when consumers are exposed to hundreds of marketing messages per day, and most are tuned out.

integrated marketing communications (IMC) The coordination and integration of all marketing communication tools, avenues, and sources in a company into a seamless program designed to maximize the impact on customers and other stakeholders.

marketing mix The elements of a marketing program, including products, prices, places (the distribution system), and promotions.

brand parity What occurs when there is the perception that most goods and services are essentially the same.

contact points The places where customers interact with or acquire additional information about a firm.

standardization A program in which a firm features uniform products and market offerings across countries with the goal of generating economies of scale in production while using the same promotional theme.

adaptation What takes place when products and marketing messages are designed for and adapted to individual countries.

Review Questions

1. Define communication. How does it play a crucial role in marketing and business?

2. What are the parts of an individual communications model?

3. Who are the typical senders in marketing communications? Who are the receivers?

4. Name the transmission devices, both human and nonhuman, that carry marketing messages.

⭐ 5. Define clutter. Name some of the forms of clutter in marketing communications.

6. Define integrated marketing communications (IMC).

7. What are the four parts of the marketing mix?

8. What steps are required to write a marketing plan?

9. How has the job of an advertising account executive changed? How has the job of a brand manager changed? How has the job of a creative changed? How has the job of account planner changed? How do the four jobs interact in the new marketing environment?

10. What reasons were given to explain the growth in importance of IMC plans in this chapter?

11. How has the growth of information technology made IMC programs vital to marketing efforts?

12. What is channel power? How has it changed in the past few decades?

13. What is brand parity? How is it related to successful marketing efforts?

14. What is a contact point? How are contact points linked to customer engagement?

15. What is micro-marketing?

16. What are the components of an integrated marketing communications program, as outlined in this textbook?

17. What is a GIMC? Why is it important for multinational firms?

18. What is the difference between standardization and adaptation in GIMC programs?

Critical Thinking Exercises

DISCUSSION QUESTIONS

⭐ 1. Do you use Miracle Whip? Ask five people how they feel about the product. Using YouTube and the Web site from this book, view the 2011 campaign. Evaluate its impact and explain whether you believe the campaign was a good idea. Defend your answer.

⭐ 2. The marketing director for a furniture manufacturer is assigned the task of emphasizing the furniture's natural look in the company's integrated marketing communications program. Discuss the problems the director might encounter while developing this message and in ensuring that consumers understand the message

correctly. Refer to the communication process outlined in the chapter for ideas. Explain how noise or clutter interferes with the communication process.

3. What do you typically do during commercials on television? What percentage of the time do you watch commercials? What makes you watch? Ask these same questions of five other people. What type of activities do people engage in during commercials?

4. Brand parity has become a major issue for companies. Identify three product categories where the brand you purchase is not very important. Why is the brand not important? Identify three product categories where the

brand is important. What brand or brands do you typically purchase in each category?

5. The marketing director for a manufacturer of automobile tires has been asked to integrate the company's global marketing program. Should the director use a standardization or adaptation approach? How could the company be certain that its marketing program will effectively be integrated among the different countries in which it sells tires?

Integrated Learning Exercises

1. Access the Web site of Chick-fil-A at www.chickfila. com. Access the Web sites of Chick-fil-A's competitors: KFC (www.kfc.com), Popeye's (www.popeyes. com), Church's Chicken (www.churchschiken.com), and Bojangles (www.bojangles.com). Which sites have a link to Facebook, Twitter, or other social media site? Compare and contrast the information available and the design of each company's Web site. Which Web site did you like the best? Why? Which one did you like the least? Why?

2. Information is one key to developing a successful integrated marketing communications program. Access each of the following Web sites and examine the information and news available on each site. How would this information help in developing an integrated marketing campaign?

a. *Brandweek* (www.brandweek.com)
b. *Adweek* (www.adweek.com)
c. *Mediaweek* (www.mediaweek.com)
d. *Branding Asia* (www.brandingasia.com)

Student Project

CREATIVE CORNER

One of Procter & Gamble's primary products is Febreze. The product targets individuals who do not like washing laundry and has been positioned by P&G as an alternative method of completing this chore. An ideal target market would seem to be the 18 million college students in the United States. With busy class schedules, work, and social events, they may believe they do not have enough time to do laundry. For jeans and other clothes that are not quite dirty yet, Febreze offers the chance to "refresh" the clothes and kill any possible odors. John Paquin, Executive Vice-President at the advertising agency WPP Grey Worldwide, which handles the Febreze product, states that "washing is not a convenient part of the lifestyle at college." He also recognizes that "mainstream media buys [such as television] are not effective for the 18- to 22-year-olds."[22] For more information about Febreze, access the Febreze Web site at www.febreze.com.

1. Identify alternative media you would use to reach 18- to 22-year-old college students.

2. Design an advertisement for Febreze aimed at the college demographic. Where would you place your ad? Why?

CASE 1   TWITTER

The language of Twitter has become part of our cultural lingo. Tweets are reported on the national news, via traditional media, and on various Web sites. Celebrities, sports figures, businesspeople, and politicians use this new social networking forum. When the site first gained notoriety, two questions emerged. First, is it only a flash in the pan? Second, can the company generate profits?

To combat concerns that Twitter would only be viewed as the latest fad, the company's cofounder Biz Stone states that, "We are building a company to last." To do so, the company's leaders have tried to "…focus on value before we optimize profits." Value can be delivered to two important segments: individual users and businesses. Stone notes that the company's goal is to deliver value at what he terms, "both ends of the spectrum," which means for both small and large businesses. The common link is that small and large firms can both use Twitter to create a better customer experience.

Stone offered examples of how small businesses create positive customer experiences through Twitter. One local bakery sends out a tweet when its cookies are fresh and warm out of the oven. Local fans of the bakery quickly descend to buy up the inventory. Another bakery tweets the "pie of the day" to its enthusiasts.

At the other extreme, Best Buy created the Twelpforce, consisting of 700 employees who are available to answer customer questions and inquiries using Twitter, to make almost instant connections while shopping. Stone believes the model allows Best Buy to effectively engage with current and potential customers. Twitter also assists Dell in selling computers over the system. The employees at Twitter developed Twitter 101, or a "Suite of Education," according to Stone, designed to show other companies how to effectively use the system.

The second question remains—can the company generate profits? Some analysts speculate that Twitter may well be worth over $1 billion, but the actual cash flow and profit figures have not yet been realized. Biz Stone and cofounder Evan Williams are working on methods to generate those profits, but argue that building the base of the company remains more important.

As with any new and growing company, obstacles have appeared. Hackers were able to access some of Twitter's planning documents and then posted them online. Security

▲ Twitter can be an effective means of reaching consumers.

concerns remain for many users. At the same time, optimism abounds among the company's 55 employees, who are located in a single building in San Francisco. "We have a lot of growing still to do," Stone notes, adding, "We are thinking big."

Social networking sites and other forms of instant communication are changing the face of business. At the forefront will be marketing communications. Although traditional advertising methods remain the cornerstone of many promotional programs, these new methods of interaction and communications with customers simply cannot be ignored as the world becomes increasingly interconnected. There is, as Biz Stone has noted, value to be gained by enhancing the customer's experience through these unique new communication channels.[23]

1. How do customers use Twitter as part of the shopping experience? How can companies take advantage of this trend?

2. Identify five examples of the use of Twitter in a retail and a business-to-business marketing experience. Explain how this format can enhance an integrated marketing communications program.

3. Will Twitter remain a primary form of social media in the future? Defend your answer.

A NEW SALSA SENSATION

Hector Fernandez created a salsa that became legendary within just a few years. Hector operated a successful restaurant, El Casa Grande, in Taos, New Mexico, for many years. A new chapter in his life opened when he was approached by two of his best customers, who offered to help him produce and market his salsa throughout the state, with the goal of reaching regional distribution in 5 years.

As a first step, Hector located the home office of a major advertising agency in Albuquerque. The agency positioned itself as being a "full-service" organization. Hector wondered exactly what that meant. He was introduced to Matt Barnes, who was to serve as his marketing and promotions consultant.

Matt's first questions were about Hector's salsa: "What makes your salsa better?" and "Is there a way we can convince people of the difference?" Hector responded that his customers often commented about both the taste and the texture of the salsa. He had a secret formula that had a few unusual seasonings that made his salsa burst with flavor. Hector also believed that it was less "runny" than others.

The next item the two discussed was potential customers. Hector noted that Tex-Mex was a popular form of dining in New Mexico as well as across the country. He believed that his salsa would appeal to a wide variety of people who enjoy Tex-Mex cuisine.

Matt's next question was simple: "Who do you think are your major competitors?"

Hector responded, "That's easy, Pace and Old El Paso."

Matt then asked what Hector thought of the two companies and their products. He suggested an investigation on both a personal and competitive basis. For example, Matt asked, "What do you think of when you hear the name Pace? How about Old El Paso?" He noted that both brands were solid and that Hector's company would need a compelling brand in order to compete.

The next step was a visit to the Web site of each company (www.pacefoods.com and www.oldelpaso.com). They noticed that the two companies offered some products that were the same and others that were not.

Matt asked Hector what he thought about the advertising and promotions for each company and its products. Hector replied, "Well, to tell you the truth, I only remember one television ad. It said something about one of the two companies was located in New York City instead of near Mexico, but I can't remember which was which." They concluded that it was possible that these companies do not engage in a great deal of traditional media advertising or that Hector was simply too busy with his own company to notice. Hector noted that he used a DVR to watch television and that he listened to satellite radio in both his restaurant and his car.

Matt suggested that Hector should look in Sunday papers for the past several weeks to see if either company

▲ Hector had a great salsa, but no brand name and no marketing communication plan.

Yantra/Fotolia

was offering price-off coupons or other promotions, such as a contest or sweepstakes. He told Hector it would be a good idea to attend events where salsa was being sampled or sold, such as at county fairs, Mexican heritage events, and at ballparks and other sports stadiums where nachos were on the menu.

The two then discussed a crucial issue: How could Hector's new company convince grocers and others to designate some shelf space for his salsa, thereby taking space away from some other product?

Finally, Matt handed Hector a package of materials (see Figure 1.10 on the next page). He asked Hector to consider how to reach every possible type of customer for his product, including grocery stores, other restaurants, and individual consumers shopping for salsa. He suggested that Hector would need to think about what type of sales tactics to use, which promotional programs were most important, and how the company should look—from its logo, to its letterhead, to the business cards handed out by sales representatives. Remember, Matt stated, "Everything communicates."

1. Can you think of a brand name that could be used not only for salsa, but for any other product related to salsa that Hector's company might sell?

2. How can Hector's company compete with Pace and Old El Paso? Is there a market niche the company can locate?

3. What kinds of advertising and promotions tactics should the company use? Will the tactics be the same in 5 years?

- Company logo
- Product brand name and company name
- Business cards
- Letterhead
- Carry home bags (paper or plastic)
- Wrapping paper
- Coupons
- Promotional giveaways (coffee mugs, pens, pencils, calendars)
- Design of booth for trade shows
- Advertisements (billboards, space used on cars and busses, television, radio, magazines, and newspapers)
- Toll-free 800 or 888 number
- Company database
- Cooperative advertising with other businesses
- Personal selling pitches
- Characteristics of target market buyers
- Characteristics of business buyers
- Sales incentives provided to salesforce (contests, prizes, bonuses, and commissions)
- Internal messages
- Company magazines and newspapers
- Statements to shareholders
- Speeches by company leaders
- Public relations releases
- Sponsorship programs
- Web site

FIGURE 1.10
Items to Be Included in an IMC Program

MyMarketingLab

Go to **mymktlab.com** for Auto-graded writing questions as well as the following Assisted-graded writing questions:.

1-1. For years, Nike's advertising tagline was "Just do it." What meaning was conveyed by the tagline? Do you think this conveys a clear message about the company's operations?

1-2. Find each of the following companies on the Internet. For each company, discuss how effective its Web site is in communicating an overall message. Also, discuss how well the marketing team integrates the material on the Web site. How well does the Web site integrate the company's advertising with other marketing communications?

a. Revlon (www.revlon.com)
b. J.B. Hunt (www.jbhunt.com)
c. United Airlines (www.united.com)
d. Steamboat Resorts (www.steamboatresorts.com)

1-3. Mymktlab Only—comprehensive writing assignment for this chapter.

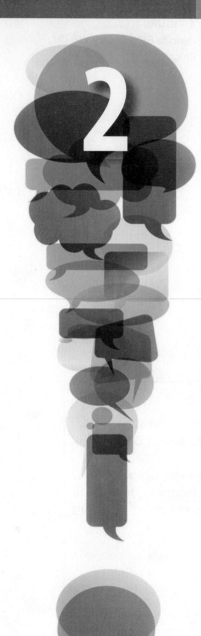

2

CORPORATE IMAGE AND BRAND MANAGEMENT

CHAPTER OBJECTIVES

After reading this chapter, you should be able to answer the following questions:

1 How does a corporate image affect consumers, other businesses, and the company itself?

2 What elements are involved in identifying, creating, rejuvenating, or changing a corporation's image?

3 What are the different types of corporate names?

4 What are the characteristics of effective logos?

5 What different kinds of brands can firms offer?

6 How are brands developed, built, and sustained in order to build brand equity and fend off perceptions of brand parity?

7 What current trends affect private brands?

8 How can packages and labels support an IMC program, domestically and in foreign settings?

MyMarketingLab™

⭐ **Improve Your Grade!**

Over 10 million students improved their results using the Pearson MyLabs.
Visit **mymktlab.com** for simulations, tutorials, and end-of-chapter problems.

APPLEBEE'S

BRAND REJUVENATION IN A TOUGH ECONOMY

The 2008 recession brought substantial challenges to the casual dining industry. As unemployment rates rose and many families cut back on certain types of spending, non-fast food chains including Applebee's Neighborhood Bar and Grill, T G I Fridays, Chili's and others experienced declining sales. Just prior to these new events, Dine-Equity, which owns IHOP (formerly the International House of Pancakes), approved the purchase of Applebee's.

IHOP CEO Julia A. Stewart labeled the Applebee's purchase, "Make the minnow swallow the whale." After all, IHOP had only 1,400 locations where Applebee's maintained 2,000 units. Stewart, who labels herself the "food server made good," ("we called it 'waitress' back then," she noted) first worked in an IHOP restaurant at the age of 16. She then moved on into the Applebee's chain and rose through the ranks to the point where many believed she would become the company's CEO; however, Stewart was passed over for the position. At that point, she returned to IHOP, becoming its CEO in 2001.

Concerns were raised that Stewart and DineEquity were purchasing the Applebee's chain as an act of retribution. She countered, "Sweet vengeance? No. I would never borrow $2.3 billion for ego." Instead, Stewart pointed to her success at rejuvenating the IHOP brand, where she had concentrated efforts in two main areas: improving the employment experience and making the restaurants better.

Stewart employed much of the same model upon arriving at Applebee's, emphasizing product quality, pricing, promotion, the dining experience, and a quality employment environment. In the area of product quality, Stewart and her executives personally tasted the menu offerings at numerous restaurants. Some food items were removed and others were added. Newer, fresher hamburgers were added to the menu along with sliders and other food innovations.

In terms of pricing, Applebee's developed the 2 for $20 purchasing option, in which patrons received an appetizer and two full sized entrees. The program met with immediate success. By 2010, sales were again on the rise.

In the area of promotion, in 2011, Applebee's relaunched its "Girl's Night Out" social media campaign. The Applebee's Facebook Fan Page allows guests to send a GNO invite, with time, date, Applebee's location—and even a personalized message. The tool also lets Fans keep track of events they're hosting, attending or both. "Applebee's is convinced that girls STILL want to have fun, so we're doing all we can to make it easier to have 'girl time' happen at Applebee's," said Rebeca Johnson, senior vice president, marketing and culinary for Applebee's Services, Inc.

To enhance the dining experience, Stewart concentrated on helping employees. At Applebee's, Stewart often leaves sealed notes on the chairs of employees at the end of the day explaining how she believes the person has done good work. She also leaves voice mail messages of appreciation.

© Robert Kneschke/Fotolia

Stewart hires executives over meals in restaurants. "I want to see your ability to interact with a server," she reports. She watches for eye contact and whether the meal companion thanks the server. "You wouldn't be successful with us unless you were really able to interact with a server."

Not content with maintaining the status quo in advertising and promotion, DineEquity changed advertising agencies in 2012. The Crispin Porter agency was retained. Rebeca Johnson noted that, Crispin Porter's creative staff members, ". . . really excel at retail," she added, "and they are knowledgeable about food and beverage and restaurant brands, big, iconic American brands that have large, loyal followings."

The success stories at IHOP and Applebee's indicate that brand building and rejuvenation are possible, even in difficult situations. Quality marketing communication programs, working in conjunction with other managerial efforts, can help a stagnant company turn the corner and once again become a major player in an industry.[1]

OVERVIEW

Managing an organization's image continues to be a critical ingredient in the successful development of an integrated marketing communications plan. A **corporate image** reflects the feelings consumers and businesses have about the overall organization and its individual brands. Advertising, consumer promotions, trade promotions, personal selling, the company's Web site, and other marketing activities all affect consumer perceptions. A strong brand creates a major advantage for any product or service. When the image of an organization or one of its brands becomes tarnished, sales revenues and profits can plummet. Rebuilding or revitalizing the image then becomes difficult.

The marketing team seeks to understand the firm's image and the strengths of individual brands in order to make solid connections with consumers and business-to-business customers. A strong IMC foundation combines an analysis of the firm's image and brands with assessments of consumer and business buyer behaviors. The marketing team prepares consistent messages designed to reach every individual that might purchase a company's products.

The first part of this chapter examines the activities involved in managing a corporation's image, including its name and logo. The second part addresses ways to develop and promote the various forms of brand names. Brand equity and brand parity are described. Finally, packages and labels, which should be part of a marketing communications program, are assessed. Ethical and international considerations are noted.

OBJECTIVE 2.1

How does a corporate image affect consumers, other businesses, and the company itself?

▼ A State Farm advertisement stressing driver safety.

Courtesy of State Farm Insurance Companies.

Corporate Image

A corporate image summarizes what the company stands for as well as how it is known in the marketplace. Whether it is the "good hands" of Allstate Insurance or the "good neighbors" at State Farm Insurance, creating a specific impression in the minds of clients and customers should be the goal of image management. Insurance companies often accomplish this by stressing helpfulness, safety, and security as elements of a strong image.

Consumer beliefs about a firm are more important than how company officials perceive the image. Corporate names such as Bank of America, Toyota, Kraft Foods, and BP (British Petroleum) create impressions in the minds of clients and customers. Although the specific version of the image varies from consumer to consumer or for each business-to-business buyer, the combined views of all publics determine the overall image of a firm, which can be positive or negative.

COMPONENTS OF A CORPORATE IMAGE

A corporate image contains invisible and intangible elements (see Figure 2.1). Consumers encounter many elements as they interact with a company. A recent study suggested that the quality of a company's goods and services ranks as the most important component of corporate image. The willingness of a firm to stand behind its goods and services when something went wrong was second. Third were perceptions of how the firm dealt with customers, such as by being pleasant, helpful, or professional.[2]

Negative publicity can stain or damage consumer perceptions of a corporation's image. Examples include the damaged reputations of financial

Tangible Elements	Intangible Elements
1. Goods and services sold	**1.** Corporate, personnel, and environmental policies
2. Retail outlets where the product is sold	**2.** Ideals and beliefs of corporate personnel
3. Factories where the product is produced	**3.** Culture of country and location of company
4. Advertising, promotions, and other forms of communications	**4.** Media reports
5. Corporate name and logo	
6. Packages and labels	
7. Employees	

◀ **FIGURE 2.1**
Elements of Corporate Image

institutions, such as Bank of America, Toyota after quality control problems, and Domino's after poor customer evaluations of its pizza.

Each firm's image consists of a unique set of features. The corporate image of an automobile manufacturer such as Porsche, Mazda, Toyota, or General Motors might be based on the following: (1) evaluations of vehicles, (2) whether the company is foreign or domestic, (3) customer views of each company's advertisements, and (4) reactions to the local dealership. A corporation's image often includes consumer assessments of company employees. In fact, the mechanic trying to repair a vehicle at a local Mr. Goodwrench garage might become the dominant factor that shapes a customer's perception of General Motors.

Recently, Subaru and Mazda created programs emphasizing the importance of the dealership as an influence on consumer assessments of the company's image. Both firms launched aggressive remodeling plans for local dealerships with the goal of providing a more pleasant shopping environment. These new-look dealerships helped boost the images of both Subaru and Mazda, resulting in higher sales. Subaru dealers that remodeled using the new retail format sold 54 percent more vehicles in the following year. Mazda dealers that adopted the new retail design sold 30 percent more vehicles.[3] Toyota, recognizing that many women purchase automobiles and that an even greater number have a significant influence on the purchase decision, launched "Image USA II." The program recommended that every Toyota dealer provide a children's play area in the showroom, a coffee bar in the service area, and nicely decorated restrooms to make the showroom more inviting to women.[4]

THE ROLE OF A CORPORATE IMAGE—CONSUMER PERSPECTIVE

From a consumer's perspective (or business customer perspective), corporate image serves several useful functions including those displayed in Figure 2.2. A well-known corporation offers customers *positive assurance* about what to expect. A can of Coke or Pepsi purchased in Anchorage, Alaska, features a comparable taste to one purchased in Liverpool, England, or Kuala Lumpur, Malaysia. Products ordered online from Bed Bath & Beyond are the same as those purchased in the retail store.

Positive assurance generates greater value when customers purchase goods or services with which they have *little experience*. Consider families on vacation. A family visiting Brazil might normally not stay at the Holiday Inn, but the familiar name makes it a lower-risk option. Purchasing from a familiar corporation seems "safer" strategy than

- Provides confidence regarding purchase decisions
- Gives assurance about the purchase when the buyer has little or no previous experience
- Reduces search time in the purchase decision
- Provides psychological reinforcement and social acceptance of the purchase

◀ **FIGURE 2.2**
Corporate Image: Benefits to Consumers

The PORSCHE CREST, PORSCHE, 911 and the distinctive shape of PORSCHE 911 automobile are registered trademarks in the United States of Dr. Ing. h. c. F. Porsche AG. Used with permission of Porsche Cars North American, Inc. Copyrighted by Porsche Cars North America, Inc. Photographer: Erik Chmil.

▲ Porsche maintains a strong and positive corporate image that influences consumer purchase decisions.

buying something from an unknown company. Taking a room at an unfamiliar hotel feels riskier than utilizing a recognizable name.

Purchasing from a familiar firm *reduces search time* and saves effort. An individual or company loyal to Ford spends fewer hours searching for a new car than does someone without such loyalty. The same holds true when purchasing low-cost items such as groceries or office products.

Purchasing from a highly recognized company often provides psychological reinforcement and social acceptance. *Psychological reinforcement* comes from feeling that a wise choice was made, and the belief that the good or service will perform well. *Social acceptance* results from knowing that other individuals, such as family and friends, have purchased from the same firm and are likely to accept the choice. The Porsche advertisement in this section illustrates the power of psychological and social forces on the purchase of an expensive automobile.

Interbrand produces a yearly list of the top 100 corporate brands. Companies offering portfolios of products and brands, such as Procter & Gamble, were not included. In addition, companies that are privately held, such as VISA, or companies that operate under different names in different countries, such as Wal-Mart, were not included. The list only notes corporations that provide products under one name. Using these criteria, Interbrand ranked Coca-Cola as the top global corporate brand. IBM (International Business Machines) was second.[5] Figure 2.3 provides a complete listing.

THE ROLE OF A CORPORATE IMAGE—COMPANY PERSPECTIVE

From the viewpoint of the firm itself, a highly reputable image generates many benefits, as noted in Figure 2.4. A quality corporate image provides the basis for the development of *new goods and services*. When potential customers are familiar with the corporate name and image, the introduction of a new product becomes much easier. Long-term

▶ **FIGURE 2.3**
Top 10 Corporate Global Brands

Source: Based on "2011 Ranking of Top 100 Brands," *Interbrand*, www.interbrand.com/en/knowledge/best-global-barnds, accessed October 5, 2011.

Rank	Company	Brand Value (Billions)	Country
1	Coca-Cola	$71.8	United States
2	IBM	$69.9	United States
3	Microsoft	$59.0	United States
4	Google	$55.3	United States
5	General Electric	$42.8	United States
6	McDonald's	$35.5	United States
7	Intel	$35.2	United States
8	Apple	$33.4	United States
9	Disney	$29.0	United States
10	Toyota	$27.7	Japan

customers are willing to try something new and transfer trust in and beliefs about the corporation to new products.

Most customers believe they "get what they pay for." Better quality is often associated with a higher price. A strong corporate image allows a company to *charge more for goods and services*. This can lead to improved markup margins and profits for the firm.

Firms with well-developed images have more loyal customers, which results in patrons *purchasing products more frequently*. Loyal customers are less inclined to make substitute purchases when other companies offer discounts, sales, and similar enticements.

Heightened levels of customer loyalty often results in *positive word-of-mouth* endorsements. Favorable comments help generate additional sales and attract new customers. Consumers and business buyers have more faith in personal references than other forms of advertising or promotion.

Positive customer attitudes create corporate equity, which provides *greater channel power*. Retailers offer the brands that are viewed positively by customers. Retailers need brands that pull customers into stores. A company with a high positive image retains control and channel power.

Attracting quality employees can become another advantage of a dominant corporate image. Just as consumers are drawn to strong firms, potential workers apply for jobs at companies with solid reputations, thereby reducing recruiting and selection costs. Employee turnover may also be lessened.

A strong corporate reputation often results in *more favorable ratings* by Wall Street analysts and other financial institutions, which can help a company raise capital. Legislators and governmental agencies tend to act in a more supportive manner toward companies with strong and positive reputations. Lawmakers may be less inclined to pursue actions that might hurt the business. Members of regulatory agencies are less likely to believe rumors of wrongdoing.

Building a strong corporate image provides tangible and intangible benefits. Both customers and organizations benefit from a well-known firm with an established reputation. Organizational leaders devote considerable amounts of time and energy to building and maintaining a positive organizational image. Client companies expect advertising account managers and creatives to help design marketing programs that take advantage of the benefits of a strong corporate image.

Advertisement furnished by Interstate Batteries

▲ The strong Interstate Batteries brand makes the introduction of new products easier.

• Extension of positive customer feelings to new products

• Ability to charge a higher price or fee

• Consumer loyalty leading to more frequent purchases

• Positive word-of-mouth endorsements

• Higher level of channel power

• Ability to attract quality employees

• More favorable ratings by financial observers and analysts

◀ **FIGURE 2.4**
Corporate Image: Benefits to Companies

Identifying the Desired Image

OBJECTIVE 2.2

What elements are involved in identifying, creating, rejuvenating, or changing a corporation's image?

A corporation's image can be a major part of its success. To promote the desired image, the marketing team first evaluates the nature of the company's current image. Future communications can be tailored to promote the proper image. These communications should reach every constituency, including customers, suppliers, and employees.

Company leaders study the firm's image to identify the firm's strengths and weaknesses. A strong image can be combined with an opportunity present in the external environment to create a strategic advantage.

As the advertising team examines a company's image, other consumers, especially noncustomers of the firm, should be approached to discover their views. Once the marketing team understands how others see the company, decisions can be made regarding how to correct any misperceptions and/or build on the image that customers currently hold.

Creating the Right Image

In each industry, the right image sends a clear message about the unique nature of an organization and its products. A strong image accurately portrays what the firm sells, even in large corporations, such as Kraft Foods, that offer multiple brands. Recently, top management at Kraft Foods developed the phrase "Make today delicious" in an effort to unite the corporation and its various brands by focusing its employees in a cohesive direction. Kraft's leadership team established seven core values to reinforce the Kraft Foods image across all brands.[6]

In a business-to-business operation, creating the right image can be challenging. Calumet faced that situation, because most consumers and businesses only knew the firm as a petroleum company. The company's advertising agency, Gremillion & Pou, established the goal of creating a different corporate image for Calumet. Recognizing that people knew little about the company, an advertising campaign called "All things Calumet" with the tagline, "Products you every day" was created. The Calumet advertisement in this section attempts to change the organization's image from a petroleum company to one that produces important ingredients used in everyday products, such as lipstick, candles, gum, and crayons.[7]

Courtesy of Gremillion & Pou.

▲ An advertisement conveying the message that Calumet ingredients are in products used every day by consumers.

Rejuvenating An Image

Rejuvenating an image helps a firm sell new products and can attract new customers. At the same time, reinforcing previous aspects of an image enables the company to retain loyal patrons and those who are comfortable with the original image. Successful image reengineering requires the company to remain consistent with a previous image while at the same time incorporating new elements to expand the firm's target audience.

Successful rejuvenation includes attention to four key areas (see Figure 2.5).[8] First, former customers need to rediscover the brand. For these individuals, the brand experience will be nostalgia. For other consumers, usually the younger age groups, the brand represents

▶ **FIGURE 2.5**
Keys to Successful Image Rejuvenation

- Help former customers rediscover the brand
- Offer timeless consumer value
- Stay true to original, but contemporize
- Build a community

a totally new experience. Connecting the nostalgic and new consumer groups requires attention to some timeless value, such as authenticity, simplicity, or a compelling brand story or heritage. When making this connection, the message should stay true to what originally made the brand great. Then the brand can be contemporized. Successful rejuvenation involves building a brand community through social media, mobile, and other interactive marketing techniques. Energizing brand advocates and influencers to spread the word about the "new and improved" version of the brand becomes the goal. As was noted in the opening vignette to this chapter, both IHOP and Applebee's were able to rejuvenate brand images by focusing on numerous aspects of the marketing program that went beyond mere changes in advertising.

L'eggs represents a once highly-visible brand that recently achieved rejuvenation. Twenty years ago, the slogan "Nothing beats a great pair of L'eggs" was well known, as was the jingle that went with it. When the fashion industry changed, and fewer females wore hosiery, L'eggs brand name and market share almost vanished. Angela Hawkins of HanesBrands (corporate owner of L'eggs), said, "We wanted to move on, contemporize, and modernize [the L'eggs brand]. We needed to speak to a new generation, [but] we wanted to stay true to our brand positioning and personality, which is fun and kind of flirty." In addition to a new Web site, L'eggs developed a strong presence in social media and developed a new slogan "You're in luck. You're in L'eggs." In addition to social media, L'eggs used television and print advertising to reach its target market, women ages 18 to 34.[9]

Changing An Image

Completely changing the image people hold regarding a company may not be possible. Attempting to change an image becomes necessary when target markets have begun to shrink or disappear, or the firm's image no longer matches industry trends and consumer expectations. At

▲ These Maxwell House coffee advertisements seek to change consumer perceptions that they can purchase and enjoy gourmet coffee at home.

that point, company leaders carefully consider what they wish to change, why, and how they intend to accomplish it.

The retailer Target faced a unique situation when the companied tried to buy advertising space in *Vogue* magazine. Target was told "no." Tom Novak, President of Target's advertising agency (Peterson Milla Hooks), said the company received a letter from *Vogue* stating "We don't want your money, because including a brand like Target would diminish the quality of our advertising." As a result, Target and its advertising agency realized that the company had an image of being a "dowdy Midwestern discounter." The challenge for Peterson Milla Hooks was to design an advertising campaign that would change that image for media outlets such as *Vogue* as well as current and new customers.

Target attacked its image problem on two fronts. First, company leaders changed the product mix by including designer labels, such as a collection from the Italian fashion house Missoni. Second, Target's advertising agency created a campaign entitled "Signs of the Times" that was designed to elevate the Target brand rather than sell merchandise. Target was positioned as a place where consumers could purchase high-end designer lamps, clothes, and other merchandise for less. The Peterson Milla Hooks agency created the now famous red and white red bull's-eye image that consumers instantly recognize as Target. The efforts changed the image of Target among consumers as well as with media outlets. In a recent issue, Target placed a 20-page insert as well as an advertisement on the back cover of *Vogue*.[10]

At times, changing an image requires trying to influence views of the product or service category. The previous page contains two advertisements created by the mcgarrybowen agency for Maxwell House coffee. The campaign sought to persuade individuals that gourmet coffee is available at grocery stores and not just from coffee shops.

Corporate Names

OBJECTIVE 2.3

What are the different types of corporate names?

A corporate name provides the overall banner for operations. David Placek, president and founder of Lexicon, Inc., said, "The corporate name is really the cornerstone of a company's relationship with its customers. It sets an attitude and tone and is the first step toward a personality."[11] Corporate names can be divided into the following four categories based on their actual, implied, or visionary meaning (see Figure 2.6).[12]

Overt names include American Airlines, Kraft Foods and BMW Motorcycles USA. *Implied names* include FedEx and IBM. *Conceptual names*, such as Google, Twitter and Krispy Kreme, take a different approach. The name "Google" evokes a vision of a place where an endless number of items can be found, and "Krispy Kreme" suggests confectionaries filled with tasty crème. Monster.com, Nabisco, and Calumet are examples of *iconoclastic names*.

The first two categories (overt and implied) are easier to market, because they will be recalled by consumers. The other two categories (conceptual and iconoclastic) require greater marketing efforts to ensure that consumers connect the corporate name with the goods and services. Figure 2.7 provides backgrounds for some well-known company names.

More than 1,000 Kraft employees from around the world submitted over 1,700 names for the new high-growth snack business spun off from Kraft Foods. The name chosen, Mondelez, combines "monde" the Latin word for "world" with "delez," a new

▶ **FIGURE 2.6**
Categories of Corporate Names

- Overt names. Reveal what a company does.
- Implied names. Contain recognizable words or word parts that convey what a company does.
- Conceptual names. Capture the essence of what a company offers.
- Iconoclastic names. Represent something unique, different, and memorable.

- Google—name started as a joke about the way search engines search for information. Word googol is one followed by 100 zeros.
- Lego—combination of Danish phrase "leg godt" which means "play well" and Latin word lego which means "I put together."
- Reebok—alternative spelling of "rhebok" which is an African antelope.
- Skype—original name was "sky-peer-to-peer," which was changed to "skyper" then to "skype."
- Verizon—combination of Latin word "veritas" which means "truth" and horizon.
- Volkswagen—created by Adolph Hitler as a car for the masses that could transport 2 adults and 3 children at speeds up to 62 mph. Name means "people's car."
- Yahoo—word from Jonathan Swift's book *Gulliver's Travels,* which represented a repulsive, filthy creature that resembled Neanderthal man. Yahoo founders, Jerry Yang and David Filo considered themselves yahoos.

◀ **FIGURE 2.7**

Origins of Some Unique Corporate Names

Source: Based on "How 16 Great Companies Picked Their Unique Names," www.openforum.com/idea-hub/topics/innovation/artile/how-16-great-companies-picked-their-unique-names, July 12, 2010.

word that conveys "delicious." According to Kraft CEO Irene Rosenfeld, "we wanted to find a new name that could . . . reinforce the truly global nature of this business and build on our higher purpose—to make today delicious." She further suggests that the name Mondelez is "unique and captures a big idea—just the way the snacks we make take small moments in our lives and turn them into something bigger, brighter, and more joyful."[13]

FINALLY...a man who doesn't snore!

CALL US TODAY | The Snoring Center

snoringcenter.com

Courtesy of Pink Jacket Creative A Creative Factory.

▲ The Snoring Center is an overt name because it reveals what a company does.

Corporate Logos

A logo contributes an additional aspect to a corporation's image. A **corporate logo** is the symbol used to identify a company and its brands. It should be designed to be compatible with the corporation's name. Organizations have spent millions of dollars selecting and promoting corporate names and logos. A strong corporate name featuring a well-designed logo helps consumers remember specific brands and company advertisements. Search time is reduced when consumers look for specific product names that are identified by effective logos. Quality logos and corporate names should meet the four tests identified in Figure 2.8.[14]

Logos assist in-store shopping. The mind processes visuals faster than it does words. A corporate logo may be more quickly recognized by shoppers. Logo *recognition* can occur at two levels. First, a consumer might remember seeing the logo in the past. It is stored in memory, and when it is seen at the store that memory is jogged. Second, a *familiar* logo may remind the consumer of the brand or corporate name. This reminder can elicit *positive* (or *negative*) *feelings* regarding either the corporation or branded item.

Successful logos *elicit shared meanings across consumers*, a process known as **stimulus codability**. Logos with high stimulus codability evoke consensual meanings

OBJECTIVE 2.4

What are the characteristics of effective logos?

- Recognizable
- Familiar
- Elicits a consensual meaning among those in the firm's target market
- Evokes positive feelings

◀ **FIGURE 2.8**

Four Tests of Quality Logos and Corporate Names

▲ Sartor Associates designed five different logos for Achievers, Inc.

within a culture or subculture (such as the Prudential Rock). Logos with a high degree of codability are readily recognized, such those used by Apple, McDonald's, and Pepsi. Companies using logos with a low degree of codability spend more money on advertising. At first, Nike spent a considerable amount of funds to make the "swoosh" more recognizable, because, at first, the swoosh, by itself, did not conjure any specific image.

A company's marketing team may modify a logo, as was the case with Pepsi. Pepsi vice president Frank Cooper noted that a change was needed as the company moved, "out of traditional mass marketing and mass distribution," and that a "more dynamic and alive" logo was needed to engage consumers. The new logo took 5 months to create and cost over $1 million. Additional costs were incurred when the company placed the new logo on delivery trucks, vending machines, stadium signage, and point-of-purchase materials.[15]

Branding

OBJECTIVE 2.5

What different kinds of brands can firms offer?

Many of the benefits of a strong corporate image apply to brands. The primary difference between the two is that of scope. **Brands** are names assigned to individual goods or services or to a group of complementary products. A corporation may own multiple brands. For instance, Hormel Foods carries several brands, including Dinty Moore, Jennie-O Turkey Store products, Chi-Chi's Mexican products, Valley Fresh, Farmer John, and SPAM.

An effective brand name allows a company to charge more for products. Strong brands provide customers with assurances of quality and reduce search times while shopping. Transference might occur to other brands sold by the same company. For the first time in 119 years, Hormel Foods ran a television and print advertising campaign highlighting the entire portfolio of Hormel brands. The campaign tagline "Life Better Served" was aimed at consumers who purchased one or two of Hormel's brands, but were not aware of Hormel's other products. The advertising agency BBDO suggested it involved "pulling the blanket off of the brand" so that consumers could see the other quality Hormel brands and products.[16]

Types of Brands

Brands develop histories. They have personalities. They include strengths, weaknesses, and flaws. Figure 2.9 identifies several types of brands.

▶ **FIGURE 2.9**
Types of Brands

- **Family brands.** A group of related products sold under one name.
- **Brand extension.** The use of an established brand name on products or services not related to the core brand.
- **Flanker brand.** The development of a new brand sold in the same category as another product.
- **Co-branding.** The offering of two or more brands in a single marketing offer.
- **Ingredient branding.** The placement of one brand within another brand.
- **Cooperative branding.** The joint venture of two or more brands into a new product or service.
- **Complementary branding.** The marketing of two brands together for co-consumption.
- **Private brands.** Proprietary brands marketed by an organization and sold within the organization's outlets.

FAMILY BRANDS

Many brands produce family trees. A **family brand** means a company offers a series or group of products under one brand name. The Campbell's brand applies to various lines of soups and other vegetable products. Consumers seeing the Campbell's brand expect a certain level of quality in existing products and any product line addition or modification, such as Healthy Choice soups. These transfer associations occur as long as the new product remains within the same product category. When the additional products added that are not related to the brand's core merchandise, the transfer of loyalty does not occur as easily.

BRAND EXTENSIONS

Brand extension is the use of an established brand name on new goods or services. The extension may not be related to the core brand. Nike has been successful in extending its brand name to a line of clothing. Black & Decker has effectively extended its brand name to new types of power tools, but did not succeed in extending the brand to small kitchen appliances.

FLANKER BRANDS

As an alternative to brand extensions, a **flanker brand** is the development of a new brand by a company in a good or service category in which it currently has a brand offering. Procter & Gamble's primary laundry detergents are Cheer and Tide. Over the years, P&G introduced a number of additional brands, such as Ivory, Dreft, and Gain. In total, P&G offers eight different brands of detergents in North America (see Figure 2.10). The company's marketing team creates flanker brands to appeal to target markets a brand does not reach. This helps the company to offer a more complete line of products and reach a higher percentage of customers. It also establishes barriers to entry for competing firms.

A flanker brand may be introduced when company leaders believe that offering the product under the current brand name might adversely affect the overall marketing program. Hallmark created the flanker brand Shoebox Greetings to sell cards in discount stores as well as Hallmark outlets. At first, the Hallmark brand was only sold in retail stores carrying the Hallmark name. The marketing team discovered that although Shoebox Greeting cards are lower priced, they allowed Hallmark to attract a larger percentage of the market, even in its own stores. Firms operating in high-end markets may use flanker brands to compete in low-end markets. They are also used in international expansion. Procter & Gamble sells Ariel laundry detergent in Latin America, Europe, the Middle East, Asia, and Africa, but not in the United States. Offering different brands for specific markets helps a firm to operate in international markets.

◀ **FIGURE 2.10**
Brands Sold by Procter & Gamble

Cosmetics	Laundry & Fabric Care	Hair Care
• Covergirl	• Bounce	• Aussie
• Max Factor	• Cheer	• Head & Shoulders
Body Wash & Soap	• Downy	• Herbal Essences
• Camay	• Dreft	• Pantene
• Ivory	• Era	**Dish Washing**
• Olay	• Febreze Air Fresheners	• Cascade
• Old Spice	• Gain	• Dawn
• Safeguard	• Ivory	• Ivory
• Zest	• Tide	• Joy

▶ **FIGURE 2.11**
Forms of Co-Branding

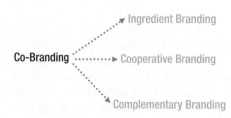

Co-Branding ⋯⋯⋯➤ Ingredient Branding

Co-Branding ⋯⋯⋯➤ Cooperative Branding

Co-Branding ⋯⋯⋯➤ Complementary Branding

CO-BRANDING

Co-branding, or the combination of two brands, takes three forms: ingredient branding, cooperative branding, and complementary branding (see Figure 2.11). **Ingredient branding** involves the placement of one brand within another brand, such as Intel microprocessors in Dell computers. **Cooperative branding** is a joint venture in which two or more brands are placed in a new good or service, such as the Gillette Venus and (Oil of) Olay razor. The advertisement in this section features a cooperating branding venture by Citibank that combines American Airlines and MasterCard. **Complementary branding** is the marketing of two brands together to encourage co-consumption or co-purchases, such as Velveeta Cheese being marketed with Rotel Tomatoes and Diced Green Chilies.

Co-branding succeeds when it builds brand equity in both brands. When Monsanto created NutraSweet, consumer trust was generated by placing the NutraSweet logo on venerable and trusted brands including Diet Coke, Wrigley's Chewing Gum (Wrigley's Extra), and Crystal Light. The strategy worked. NutraSweet remains as the standard of quality in the sweetener industry.[17]

Co-branding involves some risk. If the relationship fails to do well in the marketplace, both brands may suffer. To reduce the risk, co-branding is normally undertaken only with well-known brands. Co-branding of goods and services that are highly compatible generally will be less risky. Ingredient and cooperative branding tend to be less risky than complementary branding, because both companies have more at stake and devote greater resources to ensure success.

For small companies and brands that are not as well known, co-branding can be an effective strategy. Finding a well-known brand willing to co-brand with a lesser-known product may be difficult. When such an alliance forms, the co-brand relationship often builds brand equity for the lesser-known brand, as was the case for NutraSweet. Co-branding also provides access to distribution channels that may be otherwise hard to obtain.

▼ An example of a cooperative branding.

Developing Brands

Developing a strong brand begins with discovering why consumers buy a brand and why they rebuy the brand. In assessing a brand, marketing professionals ask the following questions:

OBJECTIVE 2.6

How are brands developed, built, and sustained in order to build brand equity and fend off perceptions of brand parity?

- Where does your brand stand now?
- What are your objectives?
- What are you doing in terms of building your brand and business?
- What are your brand's strengths? Weaknesses?
- Which opportunities should be pursued first? Where are the pitfalls?[18]

The answers to these questions assist the company's marketing team or its agency in developing a plan that cultivates a stronger brand position.

A primary feature that keeps a brand strong occurs when it contains something that is **salient** to customers, which can come from several sources. A product or brand that has benefits consumers consider important and of higher quality than other brands enjoys salience. The view that the brand represents a good value also creates this advantage. The brand may be deemed superior to others because its image leads to customer loyalty based on such salient properties.[19]

Building Powerful Brands

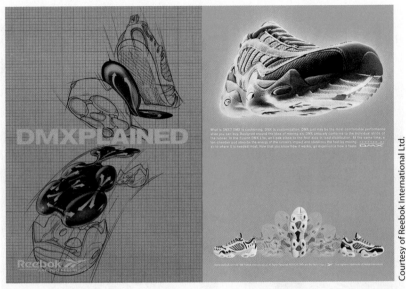

▲ Reebok has built a strong brand name in the athletic shoe market.

Powerful brands result from careful planning. Figure 2.12 identifies the ingredients required to build powerful brands such as Google, IBM, Apple, Microsoft, Coca-Cola, and McDonald's. As shown, strong brands require substantial investments. These expenditures create the communications needed to effective portray the brand to consumers and businesses.

Branding begins with awareness, which may be achieved by featuring the brand name prominently in repeated advertisements. Repetition captures the buyer's attention. It increases the odds that a brand and the accompanying message will be stored in long-term memory and recalled.

Brands should be authentic or unique in some manner. The brand name should be associated with the product's most prominent characteristic that makes it stand out from competitors. Many consumers connect Crest with "cavity prevention." Coca-Cola seeks to associate its name with a product that is "refreshing." For BMW, it is "performance driving," and for 3M it is "innovation." Marketers seek to identify the "one thing" the brand stands for, that consumers recognize, and that will be salient to them. When these are present, more powerful brand recognition occurs. In the marketplace for automotive suspension systems, the Skyjacker brand is well-known to many consumers, distributors, and automobile manufacturers.

Business and retail customers trust powerful brands. **Trust** represents the customer's belief in the efficacy and reliability of the brand. It can be established over time through personal experiences. Trust results from a brand performing consistently and fulfilling its promise, its authenticity, and its uniqueness. For decades, Tide has consistently kept its promise to consumers. To sustain that trust, the marketing team at Tide continues to pay attention to the brand's image. Recent advertisements note how well Tide cleans clothes, using themes such as "Tide knows fabrics best," "Dirt can't hide from Tide," "If it's got to be clean, it's got to be Tide," and "Style is an option. Clean is not." To make sure the message will be seen and heard, Tide employs traditional mass media advertising; alternative media including YouTube and Facebook; posts signs known as *wild postings* in urban locations; sponsors events in South Beach, Florida and other resort areas; and

- Invest in the brand
- Create awareness
- Offer authenticity, uniqueness
- Build trust
- Deliver an experience

- Offer value
- Utilize soda media
- Utilize mobile
- Act responsibly

◀ **FIGURE 2.12**
Building Powerful Brands

Courtesy of Reebok International Ltd.

▲ Skyjacker has built a high level of brand equity through domination in the vehicle suspension market.

delivers cleaning products to victims in disaster areas such as those affected by tornadoes and hurricanes.[20]

Powerful brands go beyond delivering functional features. They focus on providing an experience that involves the opportunity to be to customized and personalized. The iPhone, with over 100,000 apps, allows users to customize the phone to fit their personalities. The brand becomes a central part of their lives and who they are. When delivered effectively, the experience creates a strong emotional bond between the consumer and the brand. Apple, Nike, Harley Davidson, and Jeep are brands that have built strong communities of followers.

Similar experiences can be built by retailers. Tom Novak of Peterson Milla Hooks, the advertising agency for Target, states "A lot of retailers focus on the transaction, but we really believe that an emotional connection trumps selling. Because you like Target, you feel better buying your toothpaste there even though you could buy it at Wal-Mart."[21]

Recent economic conditions caused many consumers and businesses to re-evaluate brands they have long purchased. Value has become the current buzz word in the marketplace. Consumers and businesses look for brands that offer the best value, which is a balance between quality and price. Only 7 percent of consumers focus entirely on price while discarding quality considerations. Even fewer individuals focus on quality without any price considerations.

Building powerful brands requires the effective use of social media. It should be authentic and in-tune with the brand. Merely creating a Facebook page or posting videos to YouTube does not suffice. The social media strategy must engage consumers and enrich their experiences with the brand.

Building brands includes the use of mobile advertising. Marketers for more powerful brands have discovered ways to use mobile to enhance the customer's experience with the brand through personalization and customization of content. Mobile advertising offers brands that the opportunity to interact with customers anywhere at any time; however, the interaction must be enhance the customer's experience and not be an intrusion. A text or an ad every time the user turns his or her phone on will quickly alienate even a brand loyal customer.

The final ingredient of powerful brands results when the company acts responsibly. Consumers want brands that understand the importance of not harming the earth or people. Using sweat shops to produce products alienates customers. Consumers tend to prefer brands care for the earth and its resources.

Brand Loyalty

Brand loyalty constitutes the ultimate objective of building powerful brands. Brand loyalty means customers purchase only one brand. They consider no other brand, regardless of price differences. The Brand Keys Customer Loyalty Engagement Index (CLEI) suggests that emotion and value are the core drivers of brand loyalty, rather

Soft drinks	Quick Serve Restaurants	Pasta Sauce
• Coca-Cola	• McDonald's	• Barilla
• Pepsi	• Subway	• Ragu
• Mountain Dew	• Wendy's	• Progresso
Ice Cream	**Breakfast cereals**	**Casual Dining Restaurants**
• Haagen Dazs	• Cheerios	• Ruby Tuesday
• Ben & Jerry's	• Special K	• Outback
• Blue Bell	• Honey Nut Cheerios	• Chili's

◀ **FIGURE 2.13**

Top performing brands in select product categories based on Brand Keys Customer Loyalty Engagement Index (CLEI)

Source: Based on "Comeback Kids: Haggar, KedsStage Brand Revival," *Advertising Age*, October 30, 2011. http://adage.com/print/230721.

than rational thought based on functional product attributes. Loyalty results from the consumer's experience with the brand and emotional connection she has with it. In essence, loyalty represents what a "brand stands for or means to the consumer on an emotional level."[22]

The degree to which the brand has established a clear unique or authentic proposition determines the value of the brand. Value depends heavily on the "delight factor," or the degree to which the brand exceeds basic expectations by delivering benefits or an emotional connection that enhances a consumer's day-to-day life." Using the Customer Loyalty Engagement Index, Brand Keys identified the top performing brands in 83 different product categories. Figure 2.13 identifies some of the top brands in select categories.

Brand Equity

Many companies encounter the *brand parity* problem, which occurs when there are few tangible distinctions between competing brands in mature markets. Customers see only minor product differences, and, in many product categories, even minor variations are difficult to identify.

In contrast, **brand equity** represents a set of characteristics that are unique to a brand. Equity helps to fight the brand parity problem. The perception of brand equity means that a good or service with a given brand name is different, better, and can be trusted. Figure 2.14 displays the benefits of brand equity.

In business-to-business markets, brand equity influences selections in the buying decision-making process. Products with strong brand equity are often selected over products with low brand equity or brands that firms know less about. The same scenario occurs in international markets. Brand equity opens doors to foreign firms, brokers, and retailers and provides privileges that products with low brand equity cannot obtain.

Brand equity often dissuades consumers from looking for cheaper products, special deals, or other incentives. It prevents erosion of a product's market share, even when a proliferation of brands is coupled to promotional maneuvers by those competitors.

◀ **FIGURE 2.14**

Benefits of Brand Equity

1. Allows manufacturer to charge more for products
2. Creates higher gross margins
3. Provides power with retailers and wholesalers
4. Captures additional retail shelf space
5. Serves as a weapon against consumers switching due to sales promotions
6. Prevents erosion of market share

- Financial value
- Stock market value
- Revenue premium
- Consumer value

▲ **FIGURE 2.15**
Methods of Measuring Brand Equity

▼ Kraft enjoys a high level of brand equity.

MEASURING BRAND EQUITY

Measuring brand equity can be difficult. To do so, marketing experts apply **brand metrics**, which measure of the return on branding investments. According to Millward Brown Optimor, a strong brand constitutes one of the most valuable assets a company holds and accounts for about one-third of shareholder value.[23]

Unfortunately, no concrete, scientific or quantitative method exists, because brand equity is an abstract concept. In response, marketers have developed four different methods to measure it (see Figure 2.15). Arguments can be made in favor of each. The personal preference of the company's CEO or the one that yields the highest value often dictates method selection.

Brand equity based on *financial value* estimates the future cash flows of a brand based on its unique strength and characteristics, which will then be discounted to determine a net present value. With the *stock market* approach, the financial value of the company is determined through stock valuation. Then an estimate of the portion of the value allocated to brand equity and not physical assets is made.

The third approach, *revenue premium* compares a branded product to the same product without a brand name. To calculate a brand's revenue premium, the revenue generated by a particular brand will be compared to a private label brand. The difference is the revenue premium, or value of that brand and would equate to the brand equity that has accrued.

The final method, *consumer value*, attempts to measure the value of a brand based on input from consumers. Typical measures include familiarity, quality, purchase considerations, customer satisfaction, and willingness to seek out the brand. The difficulty with this approach is that all of the measures are based on consumer attitudes. No concrete financial or accounting numbers are calculated.[24]

Private Brands

Private brands (also known as private labels and store brands) are proprietary brands marketed by an organization and normally distributed exclusively within the organization's outlets. Private brands have experienced a roller-coaster ride in terms of popularity and sales. To some individuals, private brands carry the connotation of a lower price and inferior quality. Historically, the primary audiences for private labels were price-sensitive individuals and low-income families. This may no longer be the case. Retailers invest significant dollars to develop private brands, which now account for approximately 23 percent of all unit sales in the United States.[25]

MAKE SOMETHING GOOOOOOOOD

Always MADE *with* MILK, *and* NO ARTIFICIAL *flavors*

KRAFT CHEESE make something amazing

KRAFT Singles American

SCAN FOR INSPIRATION
kraftsingles.com

• Improved quality	• Used to differentiate retail outlets
• Perceived as a value purchase	• Increased advertising of private brands
• Higher loyalty toward retail outlets and lower loyalty toward specific brands	• Increased quality of in-store displays and packaging of private brands

◀ **FIGURE 2.16**
Changes in Private Brands

Many consumers report that they cannot tell the difference in quality between national brands and private brands. In a Nielsen survey of consumers, two-thirds said private brands are equivalent to national brands. Another survey suggested that only 19 percent of consumers believe national brands are worth paying more money for.[26] These changes, as well as others that have occurred in the private-brand arena, are summarized in Figure 2.16.[27]

Private brands tend to fare better in recessions and slow economic times as consumers try to save money. Sales for national brands often decline during slow economic cycles. Retailers offering private brands can reduce the impact of slow economic times by offering store brands.[28]

ADVANTAGES TO RETAILERS

Although private labels still tend to be priced between 5 and 20 percent lower than national brands, they also generate higher gross margins than national brands because middlemen are not used. Higher margins enable retailers to earn higher profits on private brands or, alternatively, to reduce the prices of the private brands to make them more attractive to price-sensitive consumers. Retailers that maintain the higher markup on private labels have the opportunity to use some of the margin for advertising and promotions of the brands.

One emerging trend in retailing indicates that loyalty toward retail stores has been growing while loyalty toward individual brands has been on the decline. Rather than going to outlets selling specific brands, many shoppers visit specific stores and buy from the brands offered by those stores. The increase in loyalty to retailers has caused several department and specialty stores to expand the number of private-brand products offered. This requires the retailer to develop private brands that are congruent with consumer images of the company.[29]

Savvy retailers recognize the value of private labels and how they can be used to differentiate the store from competing retailers and from national brands. These stores promote these labels as distinctive brands aimed toward specific market segments. Retailers can emphasize meeting consumer needs with a quality product rather than simply focusing on price.

JCPenney has been successful utilizing private branding in apparel lines. JCPenney offers more than 30 private labels, accounting for more than 40 percent of sales.[30] Liz Sweeney of JCPenney stated, "We are dedicated to creating and managing winning private brands that develop customer loyalty. This means managing and marketing our key private brands as true brands versus labels."[31]

Emerging trends in the use of private labels include retailers spending marketing dollars on improving the label, on designing noticeable in-store displays, and on packaging. Retailers without large national ad budgets rely more on displays and attractive packaging. A drab, cheap package does not convey the message that the private brand represents the equivalent or better alternative to a national brand. Many consumers blur the distinction between private labels and national brands. Unless a customer is familiar with the store's private brand labels, the individual might believe she is purchasing a national brand.[32]

Some retailers go one step further by designing the advertising of private brands apart from the store's regular advertising program. Recently, Sears launched a series of advertisements featuring its Kenmore and Craftsman brands. Sears was only mentioned

▶ **FIGURE 2.17**
Tactics Used by Manufacturers to Combat Gains Made by Private Labels

Source: Based on Vanessa L. Facenda, "A Swift Kick to the Privates," *Brandweek 48*, no. 31 (September 3, 2007), pp. 24–28.

- Focus on core brands.
- Increase advertising.
- Introduce new products.
- Focus on in-store selling and packaging.
- Use alternative methods of marketing.

in the context of being the place to purchase Kenmore and Craftsman products. A similar approach was used for Lands' End. Kmart's private labels include Martha Stewart, Jaclyn Smith, Route 66, Structure, and Joe Boxer. The company promotes these private brands separately in order to establish the names as bona fide brands, competing head-to-head with national brands and to distance the brands from the retail parent.

RESPONSES FROM MANUFACTURERS

Manufacturers respond to the inroads made by private labels in various ways. Figure 2.17 lists some common tactics.[33] A manufacturer can *focus on a few core brands* rather than split advertising dollars among a large number of brands. The core brands are *advertised heavily*, which helps the manufacturer maintain its brand name and reinforces the message that consumers are making the right decision when they purchase the manufacturer's national brand. Creating bonds with consumers both before and after purchases will be the goal.

Manufacturers may attempt to reduce the impact of private labels on sales by *expanding product offerings*. By aggressively introducing new products and new versions of current products, a manufacturer can maintain the loyalty of its current customers and be seen as an innovator. Hanesbrands, Inc. owns a number of well-known brands, such as Bali, Playtex, Champion, L'eggs, Barely There, Outerbanks, Duofold, and Hanes. The company expanded into the active sports underwear market with the Hanes Sport underwear collection. The surge in popularity of active lifestyles created an increase in sales of other related products, such as the sports underwear featured in the Hanes ad in this section. Hanes Sport now manufactures products for women, men, and children.

To further combat the impact of private brands, manufacturers can *focus on in-store selling* to emphasize core brands. Also, *alternative methods of marketing*, such as brand communities and social networks, might increase loyalty to a brand rather than a private label.

OBJECTIVE 2.8
How can packages and labels support an IMC program, domestically and in foreign settings?

▼ Private labels are often displayed in retail store windows and made to look as attractive as manufacturers' brands.

Packaging

A product's package represents the final opportunity to make an impression on a consumer. Packaging constitutes a marketing activity as much as television and social media advertising. Marketing surveys reveal that only 31 percent of purchases are planned prior to reaching a retail outlet. This means 69 percent of consumers make purchase decisions while in the store. Other research indicates that when an individual walks within 10 to 15 feet of a product, the item has as little as 3 seconds to catch the person's attention.[34]

The primary purposes of packaging are shown in Figure 2.18. Now, however, packages and labels are increasingly viewed as a key part of a company's integrated

- Protect product
- Provide for ease of shipping and handling
- Provide for easy placement on shelves
- Prevent or reduce theft
- Prevent tampering (drugs and food)
- Meet consumer needs for speed, convenience, and portability
- Communicate marketing message

◀ **FIGURE 2.18**
Primary Purposes of Packaging

marketing communications program. It makes little sense to spend millions of dollars on advertising only to lose the sale in the store because of a lackluster, unattractive, or dull package.

Most retail purchase decisions are made based on familiarity with a brand or product at a retail store. Consequently, a unique and attractive package that captures the buyer's attention increases the chances the product will be purchased, sometimes as an impulse buy. In the grocery market, customers prefer foods that are fast, convenient, portable, and fresh. A consumer who experiences inferior packaging will be more likely to switch to another brand the next time.[35]

The marketing team at Alcoa Rigid Packaging watched consumers as they purchased groceries and stocked refrigerators. The team noticed that the standard 3-by-4-can (12-pack) beverage box was too large for the refrigerator, and consumers would only take out a few cans at a time to cool. It seemed logical that if more cans were cold, consumers might drink more. This observation led to the design of a box that was easier and more convenient to use, the longer and slimmer 6-by-2-can box. The newly designed self-dispensing 12-pack fits into the refrigerator door or on a shelf. As a can is taken out, a new one automatically slides down to the front of the box. The innovation improved sales for both Alcoa and soft-drink manufacturers, who embraced the new package.[36]

▼ Hanes Sport offers products in the active lifestyle underwear market.

Labels

Labels on packages serve several functions. First, they must meet legal requirements. This includes identifying the product contained in the package and any other specific information about content, such as nutritional information on foods. The Food and Drug Administration (FDA) regulates food labels in the United States. Also, many times warranties and guarantees are printed on the label.

The label represents another marketing opportunity. It can make the difference in whether a particular brand is purchased. Simple, yet powerful, changes can be made that makes a difference in purchase behavior. For Honest Tea it was just a matter of the label for the peach tea showing the peach cut open rather than a whole peach. The same approach was applied to pomegranate tea; a picture of a cut pomegranate instead of a whole one was featured on the label.[37]

A typical label contains the company's logo and the brand name. Labels may reveal special offers and other tie-ins, such as a box of cereal with a toy contained inside. Labels often carry terms designed to build consumer interest and confidence in making the purchase. Words such as "gourmet," "natural," "premium," "adult formula," and "industrial strength" help make the product appear to be a better buy. A company's image, brand, logo, and

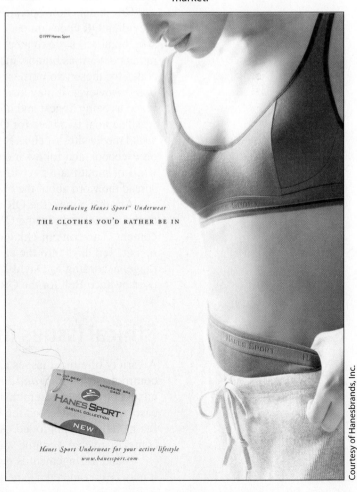

©1999 Hanes Sport

Introducing Hanes Sport™ Underwear
THE CLOTHES YOU'D RATHER BE IN

Hanes Sport Underwear for your active lifestyle
www.hanessport.com

▶ **FIGURE 2.19**
Ways QR Codes are Used
on Packaging

Source: Based on Heidi Tolliver-Walker,
"The Top Five Most Effective Ways to Use
QR Codes on Packaging." *Seybold Report
Analyzing Publishing Technologies,* Vol. 12,
No. 1 January 9, 2012, pp. 2–6

- Access product information
- Access videos on product use
- Access recipes and nutritional information
- Compare sizes, brands, and styles

- Access to product reviews and ratings
- Provide links to social media and entertainment sites

theme extend to the design of the package and label, which allows the marketing team the opportunity to make the sale when the consumer is in the store making a purchasing decision.

QR CODES

The placement of QR codes for consumers to access with mobile devices represents a new trend in packaging and labeling. Figure 2.19 identifies the various ways companies use QR codes on packages and labels. Two common uses are to access product information and videos or instructions on how to use the product. While in a retail store, consumers can access via the QR code information about the product to see if it fits their particular needs. The information can also help to ensure that customers are purchasing the right size, kind, or style of particular product to meet their particular needs. When it comes to how to use the product, videos can be useful. They may be posted on YouTube or on the manufacturer's Web site. Either way, consumers can access information from the QR code For food information, QR codes take consumers to sites providing nutritional information, which can be valuable to people on special diets or those with allergies to certain foods, such as peanuts or shellfish.

Consumers now operate smartphones while in retail stores to make comparisons. By providing QR codes on packages and labels, companies help customers choose the right size, brand, or style to meet their needs. Shoppers can also access product reviews and ratings of various brands, including the brand being considered. The danger in using QR codes for these two purpose is that they could lead consumers to choose an alternative brand; however, it may also strengthen the relationship with a customer who views the brand as being honest and not afraid to share information, both good and bad.

The final two uses for QR codes are strictly for marketing purposes. By linking to social media sites, such as Facebook, companies hope the consumer will "like" the brand on Facebook and follow it on Twitter or other social media sites. Realizing the power of word-of-mouth and peer-to-peer recommendations, the goal is to have consumers help spread the word about the brand.

At other times, the QR code links to an entertainment site. Taco Bell developed a campaign around placing QR codes on its cups and boxes that took customers to MTV content. The content changed every week to keep it fresh to encourage customers to revisit. Ten days into the campaign, the scans of the QR code were into the six-figure range, according to David Javitch, vice president of marketing at Scanbuy, the agency used by Taco Bell for the QR campaign.[38]

Ethical Issues in Brand Management

A variety of ethical issues are associated with brand management. For years, the most common problem *brand infringement*, occurred when a company created a brand name that closely resembled a popular or successful brand, such as Korrs beer. In that case, the courts deemed the brand an intentional infringement on the Coors brand, and the name was abandoned. Another brand-infringing company that was forced by the courts to give up its name was Victor's Secret.

Brand infringement is more complex when a brand becomes so well-established that it may be considered a generic term, such as a Kleenex tissue or a Xerox copy. Band-Aid encountered the problem in the 1970s, forcing the marketing team to make sure the product was identified as "Band-Aid Brand Strips" rather than simply "band aids," to keep the competition from being able to use the name. The most vulnerable new brand names might be Google and Twitter, because the names have entered everyday conversation, as in "I googled myself" or "I tweeted you."

According to many sources, *cyber squatting*, or *domain squatting,* constitute another form of unethical behavior. The practice involves buying domain names (e.g., *barnesandnoble.com, kohls.com, labronjames.com*, etc.) that are valuable to specific people or businesses in the hopes of making a profit by reselling the name. Any new company trying to build a presence in the online marketplace might find itself stifled by domain squatters. Names matter. Cyber squatters take advantage of that to make profits at someone else's expense.

International Implications

In international markets, product development, branding, and maintaining an image are more complex. As noted previously, firms employ either an *adaptation* strategy or a *standardization* strategy in promotional programs. These two approaches are applied to the products themselves as well as to brand names. With standardization, the same brand name and product are sold in all countries. With adaptation, the brand and/or the actual product may be different in each country or region. This can mean a product may be viewed as a local brand. Mr. Clean uses the adaptation brand approach for the same products. Items are sold under the names of Mr. Proper and Maestro Limpio, as well as other names in various countries.

Using a standardized global brand reduces costs. Instead of advertising each local brand with a separate communication strategy, one standardized message can be sent. Standardized global brands also allow for the transference of best practices from one country to another. Further, purchasing a standardized global brand may be viewed as a better choice than buying a local brand. The global brand might have a higher perceived quality. The consumer's self-concept of being cosmopolitan, sophisticated, and modern can be enhanced when buying a global brand.[39] As the world continues to shrink through advances in telecommunications, consumers are becoming increasingly similar, displaying comparable consumer characteristics and purchase behaviors. This may lead to greater use of standardized global brands.

Despite all of the advantages of global brands, some efforts to standardize brand names have met with resistance. A number of recently-introduced global brands were not received with enthusiasm. Although consumer behavior might have converged somewhat throughout the world, local idiosyncrasies still exist. Global brands enjoy the most success in high-profile, high-involvement products. Local brands have performed the best in low-involvement everyday products. Automobiles and computers have achieved success as global brands. Food, candy, and some soft drinks have done better using a local-brand approach.[40]

A common GIMC strategy is to "think globally, but act locally." This approach applies to branding. Developing global brands might be the ultimate goal; however, the marketing team still considers each local market's unique features and be sensitive to supporting and developing local brands. The success of

global brand largely depends on the brand's ability to adapt to local needs and tastes or as Eileen Campbell, CEO of Millward Brown Group noted, "Cultural relevance is important." For example, the "Real Beauty" campaign developed by Ogilvy and Mather for Unilever's Dove featured images of women in underwear in Western countries, but was modified to reveal a face behind a woman's veil for the Middle East.[41]

Packaging and labeling issues are complex for global firms. The label must meet the legal requirements of the country in which the product is sold. An attractive label can be an attention-getting device that draws the consumer to the product. Labels remain vitally important ingredients in the United States as well as Asian countries where purchases, in part, are driven by the appeal of the label.[42] At the same time, some culturally sensitive items, such as lingerie and other personal products, carry labels that basically disguise or hide the contents. Packages must also be able to withstand the rigors of being shipped longer distances, meet any legal restrictions, and be as cost-effective as possible.

INTEGRATED CAMPAIGNS IN ACTION

Home Federal Bank

Home Federal Savings and Loan opened its doors in 1924. A strong, responsible institution, it weathered the Great Depression, World War II, and the savings and loan crisis of the 1980s. In 2009, Home Federal celebrated its eighty-fifth anniversary; hired a new president and CEO, James R. Barlow; and received a charter to become Home Federal Bank (HFB).[3]

Gremillion & Pou had been Home Federal's advertising agency since 1988. When the institution moved from being a savings and loan to a bank, Gremillion & Pou was asked to:

- Refresh the brand and create a new logo that was progressive, without losing the equity of the 85-year-old logo
- Introduce and reinforce a new brand promise
- Introduce Home Federal as a bank
- Create market awareness of the new HFB brand
- Work closely with HFB and its partners to ensure that the brand promise is consistently communicated across all customer touch points

A Web link to the entire campaign created by Gremillion & Pou for Home Federal Bank can be found at the Pearson Instructor's Resource Center (www.pearsonhighered.com) by instructors who adopt this textbook. The campaign has a PowerPoint presentation outlining the details of the campaigns and examples of the collaterals developed by Gremillion & Pou.

STRONG. STABLE. SECURE.

Locally managed and headquartered in Shreveport for 85 years, Home Federal is not only strong enough for these difficult times, but we also successfully weathered the Great Depression, World War II and the Savings and Loan Crisis of the '80s. Prudent and responsible business practices have always kept us strong, stable and fully capitalized.

Now, as a full-service bank, we are proud to say we stand well-prepared to provide peace of mind for all your family's financial needs. It's really simple. Home Federal Bank has money to loan and you'll be sitting at the table with the same people who can make decisions and make them quickly! Together, we will weather this current recession just fine.

HOME FEDERAL BANK
A Better Way

Courtesy of Gremillion & Pou.

▲ The Gremillion & Pou advertising agency faced the challenge of creating a new brand for a company that was already well-known and respected.

SUMMARY

An effective integrated marketing communications program emphasizes a strong and positive company or corporate image. An image consists of the feelings consumers and business-to-business customers have toward the organization and each individual brand. An image contains both tangible and intangible components. Tangible elements include products, advertisements, names, logos, and services provided. Intangible elements consist of policies and practices that change or enhance the company's image in the consumer's mind.

A corporate name provides the overall banner under which all other operations occur. The corporate logo accompanying the name is the symbol used to identify a company and its brands, helping to convey the overall corporate image. The firm's name and image are important to general customers as well as other firms that might purchase from or conduct business with a manufacturer or service provider.

Brands are names given to goods or services or groups of complementary products. Effective brands present the firm with an advantage, especially in mature markets containing fewer actual products or where service differences exist. Strong brands convey the most compelling benefits of the product, elicit proper consumer emotions, and help create loyalty. Various versions of brands include family brands, flanker brands, and co-brands. In each, marketers build brand equity through domination, or the recognition that the brand has one key advantage or characteristic.

Creating an effective image constitutes a difficult task. It requires understanding of how various publics view the firm before seeking to build or enhance an image. Rejuvenating the image involves reminding customers of their previous conceptions of the company while at the same time expanding into a closely related area of concern. A strongly established image becomes difficult, if not impossible, to change.

Private brands, or private labels, have become important components in the success of both producers and retailers. Consumers now view private brands as having quality equal to or close to that of more famous manufacturer brand names. At the same time, customers expect price advantages in private label products. Effective brand management includes creating a mix of offerings that both end users and retailers recognize as a beneficial range of choices.

Company leaders remain aware of legal and ethical brand challenges. Brand infringement remains both a domestic and international problem. The generic problem may also influence a new generation of products and services.

International marketers utilize both standardization and adaptation tactics with regard to brands and products. Packages and labels must meet the legal and cultural needs of individual countries.

Key Terms

corporate image The overall consumer perceptions or end-user feelings toward a company along with its goods and services.

corporate logo The symbol used to identify a company and its brands, helping to convey the overall corporate image.

stimulus codability Feelings attached to items that evoke consensually held meanings within a culture or subculture.

brands Names generally assigned to a good or service or a group of complementary products.

family brand A strategy in which a company offers a series or group of products under one brand name.

brand extension The use of an established brand name on goods or services not related to the core brand.

flanker brand The development of a new brand by a company in a good or service category in which it currently has a brand offering.

co-branding What occurs when marketers offer two or more brands in a single marketing effort.

ingredient branding A form of co-branding in which the name of one brand is placed within another brand.

cooperative branding A form of co-branding in which two firms create a joint venture of two or more brands into a new good or service.

complementary branding A form of co-branding in which the marketing of two brands together encourages co-consumption or co-purchases.

salient A situation in which consumers are aware of the brand, have it in their consideration sets (things they consider when making purchases), regard the product and brand as a good value, buy it or use it on a regular basis, and recommend it to others.

trust A customer's belief in the efficacy and reliability of a brand.

brand equity A set of brand assets that add to the value assigned to a product.

brand metrics Measures of returns on brand investments.

private brands (also known as *private labels*) Proprietary brands marketed by an organization and normally distributed exclusively within the organization's outlets.

Review Questions

1. Define the term "corporate image." What are the tangible aspects of a corporate image?

2. How does a corporation's image help customers? How does it help the specific company?

⭐ 3. How will company leaders know when they have created the desired image for their firm?

4. What four areas require attention when seeking to rejuvenate a firm's image?

⭐ 5. What is a corporate logo? What are the characteristics of an effective corporate logo?

6. What is meant by the term "stimulus codability?"

⭐ 7. What is a brand? How is a brand part of a corporation's overall image?

8. Describe the use of brand extension and flanker-brand strategies.

9. Identify and describe three types of co-brands.

10. What are the characteristics of a strong and effective brand name?

11. Explain the role of trust in creating a strong brand.

12. What is the difference between brand equity and brand parity?

13. What methods can be used to measure brand equity?

14. How has private branding, or private labeling, changed in the past decade?

15. What role does a product's package play in the marketing program?

16. How can a label support an IMC program or advertising campaign?

17. What ethical issues are associated with brand management?

18. How do the concepts of standardization and adaptation apply to products, brand names, and marketing strategies?

Critical Thinking Exercises

DISCUSSION QUESTIONS

1. Dalton Office Supply Company has been in business for over 50 years and has been the predominant office supply company in its region during that time. Approximately 85 percent of Dalton's business is based on providing materials to other businesses. Only 15 percent comes from walk-in customers. Recently, low-cost providers such as Office Depot have cut into Dalton's market share. Surveys of consumers indicate that Dalton has an image of being outdated and pricey. Consumers did report that Dalton's customer service was above average. What image should Dalton project to regain its market share? Outline a plan to rejuvenate the company's image.

⭐ 2. Henry and Becky Thompson plan to open a new floral and gift shop in Orlando, Florida. They want to project an image of being trendy, upscale, and fashionable. They are trying to decide on a name and a logo. What should be the name of the company? What kind of logo should be developed?

⭐ 3. Brand and corporate image affect purchase decisions. What brands or corporations do you consider to have a positive image? Why? Which brands or corporations should attempt to change images? Why? Explain how to accomplish this task. Name brands that you believe need rejuvenation. How can it be accomplished for each brand?

4. Identify five different brands for which you have a high level of brand loyalty. Describe your level of loyalty and discuss why you are loyal. How important is brand equity in your loyalty?

5. What is your opinion of private brands or labels? Compare your purchase behavior of private labels in contrast to national or manufacturers' brands. What private labels do you purchase regularly? Why do you purchase those particular private labels instead of national or manufacturers' brands?

6. Go to a local retail store. Choose five packages that are effective. Describe why they are effective. Choose five labels that are effective at capturing attention. What are the attention-getting aspects of each label?

7. Go to a local retail store. Look at packaging and locate five packages with QR codes. Access the code through a smartphone. Which of the purposes discussed in the chapter does the QR code serve? Evaluate the QR code and the information or site that was accessed.

Integrated Learning Exercises

1. Web sites constitute an essential element of a company's image. Access the Web sites of the following companies to get a feel for the image each company tries to project. Is the image projected on the Web site consistent with the image portrayed in the company's advertisements?

a. Bluenotes (**www.blnts.com**)

b. Portillo's Restaurants (**www.portillos.com**)

c. BMW Motorcycles (**www.bmwmotorcycles.com**)

d. McDonald's (**www.mcdonalds.com**)

e. HP (**www.hp.com**)

2. A leading consulting firm that has been a leader in extending marketing knowledge and in the area of brand development is the Boston Consulting Group. Other companies that have actively been involved in brand development include Lexicon Branding and Corporate Branding. Access each firm's Web site. What kinds of services does each provide?

   a. Boston Consulting Group (**www.bcg.com**)

   b. Lexicon Branding, Inc. (**www.lexicon-branding.com**)

   c. Corporate Branding (**www.corebrand.com**)

3. Brand extension and flanker branding are common strategies for large corporations. Access the following Web sites. Identify the various brand extension strategies and flanker brands used by each company.

   a. Marriott Hotels (**www.marriott.com**)

   b. Procter & Gamble (**www.pg.com**)

   c. Sara Lee Corporation (**www.saralee.com**)

   d. VF Corporation (**www.vfc.com**)

   e. Kraft Foods (**www.kraftfoods.com**)

4. Private labels provide a significant source of revenue for many retail stores and manufacturers. The Private Label Manufacturers' Association promotes manufacturers that produce private labels. Visit the organization's Web site at www.plma.com and identify the press updates, store brands, and upcoming events that illustrate the importance of private labels for both retailers and manufactures.

5. Look up one of the following companies on the Internet. Discuss the image conveyed by each company's Web site. What positioning strategy does it use? What changes or improvements could these companies make?

   a. Scubaworld (**www.scubaworld.com**)

   b. Union Pacific Railroad (**www.uprr.com**)

   c. Bicycle Museum of America (**www.bicyclemuseum.com**)

   d. Metropolitan Transportation Commission (**www.mtc.ca.gov**)

   e. Canyon Beachwear (**www.canyonbeachwear.com**)

Student Project

CREATIVE CORNER

The brand name and logo are critical elements a marketing manager considers when introducing a new product. Pick one of the products from the following list. Assume that you are the new product manager and that your company has introduced a new brand within the product category. Your first task is to choose a brand name. Using the Internet, identify three key competitors and make a case for how the brand name you select will help the item stand out in the marketplace. Once you have created your brand name, create a logo that you think will fit well with the brand name and will be distinctive on your product or the product's packaging.

PRODUCTS

1. A new brand of skis for recreational boating

2. A new line of eyeglasses

3. A new chocolate candy bar

4. A new line of jeans

5. A new energy drink

6. A new perfume or cologne

CASE 1 BARBIE VERSUS BRATZ

Mattel general manager and senior vice president for the Barbie doll brand, Richard Dickson, faced a significant problem. The Barbie collection experienced a dramatic decline in sales. In essence, the buzz shifted to newer, seemingly more twenty-first century doll lines, especially the Bratz line from outside Mattel and the American Girl brand from within the company. The Bratz line was viewed as being "edgier" and more ethnically diverse. The American Girl line appealed to older girls.

Barbie dolls and accessories enjoyed a rich tradition of popularity and status as a cultural icon. The first edition, produced in 1959, became a coveted for young girls. The companion Ken doll was launched in 1961. Christie, an African American doll, emerged in 1968. In 2000, the Barbie line held an astonishing 80 percent market share. The Barbie line's peak year of sales, 2002, was the financial pinnacle.

Barbie's market share began to drop dramatically and reached bottom in 2009, when it fell to less than 50 percent of dolls sold to girls. Richard Dickson was assigned the task of rejuvenating the line. In the attempt to restore some of the glamour of the brand, Dickson created a team of in-house brand managers and sent them to the mod-baroque, Kelly Wearstler–designed Viceroy hotel in Santa Monica, California. "I wanted people to see what it was like to be surrounded by a signature style," Dickson reported.

The team responded with a new model, the "Generation of Dreams" Barbie line. They also mandated that all Barbie products be consistent with the brand's identity. For several years, powerful retailers such as Wal-Mart had influenced the doll's specs, creating what Dickson called "brand goulash." Further, the number of licensees of Barbie products was significantly reduced.

Additional changes were made. A real-life Barbie dream home was designed and built in Malibu, California. Fashion giant Diane von Furstenberg created life-size Barbie apparel for Fashion Week magazine. To pay for the programs, the number of traditional 30-second television advertising spots was reduced. The Barbie Web site was expanded to include contests, games, videos, and a virtual world. Initial results of these efforts were promising. In 2009, sales rose by 18 percent in one quarter, the largest increase in 3 years. The new line created additional publicity and buzz, which also generated greater interest.

Mattel directly confronted Bratz with a copyright infringement lawsuit, which it won. The essence of the lawsuit was that Mattel is the legal owner of the Bratz dolls, which are manufactured by archrival MGA Entertainment. The ruling by a federal judge was reached, in part, because Bratz's creator Carter Bryant was working at Mattel under an exclusive contract when he came up with the idea for the doll. The jury's

Pavel Losevsky / Fotolia

▲ Social media has changed the way companies now market dolls to young girls.

$100 million judgment did not include punitive damages. Both sides claimed victory based on the jury's decision.

The future of the doll industry remains clouded. One trend, known as "age compression marketing," dramatically affects all traditional toy manufacturers and retailers. Children simply abandon certain toys, including dolls, at much younger ages. Both the Barbie and Bratz lines continue to adapt, with more mature clothing options for dolls combined with more mature marketing presentations. Although the Mattel brand remains strong, the company continues to face challenges as the world of children and toys continues to evolve.

1. Provide an analysis of the Mattel Barbie brand. What factors shape perceptions of the brand in the eyes of parents and young girls?

2. What brand problems did the Bratz line of dolls create for the Barbie brand?

3. How might social media affect perceptions of both the Bratz and Barbie doll lines?

4. Do you think the efforts made by Richard Dickson were the most effective ways to restore the brand? Defend your answer.

5. Going forward, what tactics would you use to maintain and build the Barbie brand?

Sources: "Jury Awards Mattel $100 in Barbie-Bratz Lawsuit," WCCO. (http://wcco.com/business/barbie.bratz.lawsuit.2.803672.html, accessed August 10, 2010); Jeremy Deutchman, "After 50 Years, Barbie's Still a Living Doll," USE News, (http://uscnews.usc.edu/business/after_50_years_barbies_still_a_living_doll.html accessed August 10, 2010).

CASE 2 A HEALTHY IMAGE

Mary Wilson was both nervous and excited as she opened her first staff meeting in the marketing department of St. Margaret's General Hospital. Mary's new role was Director of Marketing and Communications. Her primary task was to increase the visibility of St. Margaret's Hospital in order to raise the image of the institution in the eyes of the many publics served. The long-term goal was to attract the best possible physicians while increasing use of the hospital's facilities and attracting more patients.

The world of health care changed dramatically in the past decade. Government regulations and support, concerns about lawsuits, evolving and expensive technologies, and changes in health insurance provisions affected hospitals of all sizes. In addition, St. Margaret's faces strong competition. The hospital's primary location is in a major metropolitan area in Minnesota. Two other large hospitals also offer comparable services in the same city. Each seeks to sign physicians to exclusive contracts in which they will only provide care with one organization.

The other significant challenge to St. Margaret's is its proximity to the Mayo Clinic. Clearly, Mayo holds the highest level of prestige in the state and even in the region. Most physicians are inclined to think of Mayo first when making referrals for patients with difficult medical problems. Mayo would be viewed by most publics as the "best" care possible.

The key issues in the image of any health organization include developing trust and a feeling of confidence in the quality of care that will be received. Beyond technological advantages, other, more subtle elements of an image could have an influence. Mary noted that the nurse plays a primary role in determining how patients view hospitals An uncaring and inattentive nurse is likely to drive away both the patient who encountered the nurse and all of the patient's family and friends. Negative word-of-mouth, Mary said, must be held to an absolute minimum.

Mary believed St. Margaret's needed to overcome two problems. First, the name "Margaret" is not commonly used anymore.

▲ How important is image for a medical institution?

Some publics may view it as an "old-fashioned" name. Second, there was nothing distinctive about the hospital's image. The overlap in services provided (heart care, cancer treatment) made it difficult to differentiate St. Margaret's from other providers.

If there was any advantage, Mary believed it was that St. Margaret's was affiliated with the Catholic Church. It was the only nonprofit hospital of the three major competitors. This attracted both Catholic patients and some Catholic physicians. Also, the hospital was able to utilize the services of a wide variety of volunteers.

As the marketing meeting opened, the agenda was to discuss all of the ways St. Margaret's could build its client base. The task would not be easy, but everyone in the room believed the hospital offered high-quality services in a caring atmosphere.

1. What are the image issues in this case?
2. What are the brand-name issues? Should the brand name be changed? If so, to what?
3. What types of advertisements should Mary develop for St. Margaret's General Hospital?
4. What other types of activities could St. Margaret's pursue to build a strong and positive corporate image?

MyMarketingLab

Go to **mymktlab.com** for Auto-graded writing questions as well as the following Assisted-graded writing questions:.

2-1. Brand and corporate image are important in purchase decisions. What brands or corporations do you consider to have a positive image? Why? Which brands or corporations should attempt to change images? Why? Explain how to accomplish this task. Name brands that you believe need rejuvenation. How can it be accomplished for each brand?

2-2. Look up one of the following companies on the Internet. Discuss the image conveyed by each company's Web site. What positioning strategy does it use? What changes or improvements could these companies make?
   a. Scubaworld (www.scubaworld.com)
   b. Union Pacific Railroad (www.uprr.com)
   c. Bicycle Museum of America (www.bicyclemuseum.com)
   d. Metropolitan Transportation Commission (www.mtc.ca.gov)
   e. Canyon Beachwear (www.canyonbeachwear.com)

2-3. Mymktlab Only—comprehensive writing assignment for this chapter.

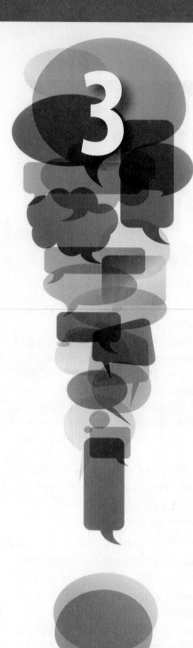

BUYER BEHAVIORS

CHAPTER OBJECTIVES

After reading this chapter, you should be able to answer the following questions:

1. What elements are involved in internal and external information searches by consumers, as part of the purchasing process?

2. What three models explain how individuals evaluate purchasing alternatives?

3. What trends are affecting the consumer buying environment?

4. How do the roles played by various members of the buying center and the factors that influence them impact business purchases?

5. What types of business-to-business sales are made?

6. What are the steps of the business-to-business buying process?

7. How does dual channel marketing expand a company's customer base and its sales?

8. How can a company overcome international differences when adapting to buying processes?

CHIPOTLE MEXICAN GRILL
A NEW DIMENSION IN DINING

One simple buying decision many consumers make every day is the choice of where and what to eat for breakfast, lunch, or dinner. Those who crave Mexican food review a variety of possibilities, including fast-food operations, such as Taco Bell and Del Taco; locally owned establishments; and dine-in chains, such as El Chico and On the Border. In this competitive marketplace, a new option emerged.

A chipotle is a ripened, dry, smoked jalapeno contains a smoky, hot flavor that is often added to Mexican and Southwestern dishes. In 1993, Steve Ells based a new business as well as the original company name on this single ingredient, and the Chipotle Mexican Grill was born. He notes, "I had a very simple idea: Offer a simple menu of great food prepared fresh each day, using many of the same cooking techniques as gourmet restaurants. Then serve the food quickly, in a cool atmosphere. It was food that I wanted, and thought others would like too. We've never strayed from that original idea. The critics raved , and customers began lining up at my tiny burrito joint," which was in Denver, Colorado.

Chipotle Mexican Grill food items may be purchased in a variety of ways, including dine-in, call-in, or online. The relatively simple menu offers a series of options for each item. The choices include burritos, fajitas, and tacos featuring pork, shredded beef, chicken, steak, and vegetarian fillings along with side dishes such as salads, chips, and pinto or vegetarian black beans. Drinks include margaritas, beers, and soft drinks. Ordering is quick and easy. As one marketing expert noted, "The menu is kind of like a Subway—only for Mexican food."

Early rave reviews about the generous portions and the quality of the meals helped the original restaurant to add a second location within 3 years. Seeing the potential for growth, McDonald's purchased a minority interest in Chipotle, which made it possible for the company to quickly expand the number of units. By 2003, 300 new restaurants were open. Later in the decade, the company began to add nearly 100 new locations per year, now topping 800 units.

Chipotle restaurants feature artistic, classy, and brightly lit interiors. The stores have an open-kitchen design. Customers interact directly with the staff and watch as orders are processed.

The chain's corporate governance follows a unique approach to selecting ingredients. In an effort to upgrade its foods, the company switched from yellow corn, which could contains genetically modified corn, to organic white corn, which does not. Chipotle purchases organic beans whenever possible. Chipotle offers naturally raised, antibiotic-free chicken from Bell & Evans in more than 50 restaurants in Washington, D.C., New York, and Ohio. Eight restaurants in Chicago and New York use naturally raised beef. Recently, ABC News *Nightline* presented a free-range pig farm from which Chipotle acquires

Garren/Shutterstock.com

some of its pork. Ells reported, "You have to be concerned where your food comes from and how the animals were raised. I call it 'Food with Integrity.'"

McDonald's recently acquired majority ownership of the company, although Steve Ells remained the operational manager. The link to McDonald's increased Chipotle's buying power, leading to, for example, a better supply of avocados as well as to more rapid expansion of locations.

Chipotle maintains a relatively limited advertising budget. Most of its advertisements draw on humor. An online presence and word-of-mouth have supported the company's growth and success for over a decade.

Which factor leads a customer to purchase food at Chipotle? Is it the organic ingredients, the quick-and-simple ordering methods, the quality interiors of the restaurants, the large portions, or some other element? Regardless of the decision variable, the success and growth of the chain suggests a well-designed integrated marketing communications program.[1]

OVERVIEW

 One primary goal of many integrated marketing communications program continues to be enticing people to buy goods and services. Understanding how buyers make purchase decisions helps the marketing team achieve this goal. Two types of buyer

OBJECTIVE 3.1

What elements are involved in internal and external information searches by consumers, as part of the purchasing process?

behaviors—consumer buyer behaviors and business-to-business buyer behaviors—receive attention in this chapter. Comprehending the steps consumers use to make purchase decisions assists the marketing team in creating quality communications.

This chapter first examines consumer purchasing processes. Two stages of the process are the key to marketing communications. In the *information search* stage, the customer reviews previous memories and experiences looking for acceptable ways to meet a need by buying a product. During the *evaluation of alternatives* stage, the individual compares various purchasing possibilities. An effective IMC program targets potential buyers involved in these activities. This chapter provides a review of the traditional factors affecting consumers, along with discussion of the newer trends present in the consumer buying environment.

Business-to-business buyer behaviors create the focus for the second part of this chapter. First, a review of the five major roles played in the buying center takes place. Next, the chapter notes the types of purchases companies, along with the steps involved in the purchasing process. Finally, dual channel marketing, which involves selling the same product to both consumers and business buyers, is discussed. Effective IMC programs identify potential customers from both markets. This leads to increased sales and helps a company maintain a strong presence in the marketplace.

▼ This advertisement for Skyjacker might trigger a search for additional information about truck suspensions and lift kits.

Furnished by Skyjacker Suspensions

Consumer Purchasing Process

Finding ways to influence the consumer purchasing process continues to be a vital marketing communications activity. Figure 3.1 models the consumer buying decision-making process. Two of the stages are the most directly related to integrated marketing communications: the information search and the evaluation of alternatives. Discovering how customers seek out product information and then evaluate the information are keys to creating effective marketing messages.

The first step of the buying decision-making process shown in Figure 3.1 occurs when the consumer notices a need or want. A problem or gap exists between an individual's current state and desired state. The need can be physical, such as hunger or thirst. It can be social, such as when a consumer visits a friend's apartment and sees his new HDTV and wants one in order to "keep up." Needs may be psychological in nature, including feelings for love, self-efficacy, or protection from fear.

Consumer needs can be triggered by marketing communications. The advertisement for Skyjacker suspensions in this section may act as a catalyst for an individual to want a lift kit for his vehicle. Once this occurs, consumers enter the next phase of the process.

▶ **FIGURE 3.1**
Consumer Decision-Making Process

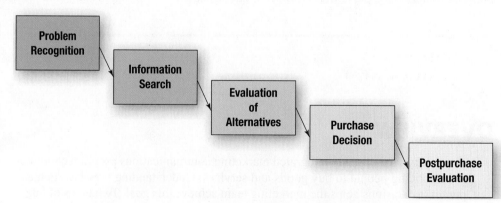

Information Search

Once a need emerges, the consumer begins an internal search, mentally recalling products that might satisfy it. Often, the individual remembers how the need was met in the past. If a particular brand was chosen and the experience was positive, the consumer repeats the purchase decision, and the information search ends. When a previous purchase did not work out, or the consumer wishes to try something else, a more complete internal search may result.

INTERNAL SEARCH

During an internal search, the consumer thinks about the brands she is willing to consider. This group may not contain every brand the consumer has experienced, because she removes brands associated with negative experiences. Brands she knows little about are also eliminated. In other words, the consumer quickly reduces the number of potential brands.

Making sure a company's brand becomes part of the consumer's set of potential purchase alternatives in an internal search should be a key marketing communication objective. A product with a high level of brand awareness or brand equity will likely be included in the consumer's set of alternatives. The Neutrogena advertisement shown in this section uses "#1" four times to persuade consumers that Neutrogena is the number-one anti-wrinkle cream and should be considered. The ad seeks to cause consumers who want an anti-wrinkle cream to consider Neutrogena as the first and best choice.

EXTERNAL SEARCH

Following an internal search, the consumer makes a mental decision regarding an external search. When the customer has sufficient internal information, she moves to the next step of the decision-making process: evaluating the alternatives. A consumer who remains uncertain about the right brand to purchase undertakes an external search.

External information can be gathered from a variety of sources, including friends, relatives, experts, books, magazines, newspapers, advertisements, in-store displays, salespeople, and the Internet. The amount of time a consumer spends on an external search depends on three factors: ability, motivation, and costs versus benefits (see Figure 3.2).[2]

▲ A Neutrogena advertisement designed to convince consumers that the product should be the first choice when selecting an anti-wrinkle cream.

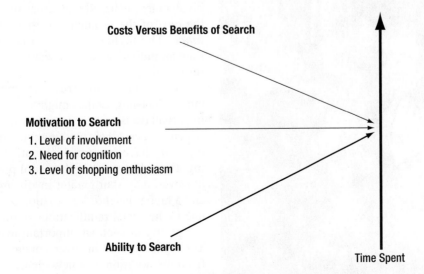

Costs Versus Benefits of Search

Motivation to Search
1. Level of involvement
2. Need for cognition
3. Level of shopping enthusiasm

Ability to Search

Time Spent

◀ **FIGURE 3.2**
Factors that affect the amount of time a consumer will spend conducting an external search

Ability to Search   The extent of an information search will be partially determined by the ability to search. Ability consists of a person's educational level combined with the specific knowledge he has about a product and the brands in a given category. Educated individuals are more inclined to spend time searching for information. They are more willing to visit stores or search online prior to making decisions. Consumers possessing extensive knowledge about individual brands and product categories are better able to conduct a more involved external search. Thus, someone who knows a great deal about digital cameras has a more sophisticated ability to examine information than does someone who knows little about the technology. In addition, a person with more comprehensive knowledge of a product area often collects additional information, even when she is not in the market for the product.[3]

In terms of the amount of time an individual devotes to the external search process, an unusual phenomenon occurs. Although extensive product category knowledge means an individual has greater ability to search for external information, the consumer normally spends less time on the external search process because of the extensive knowledge he already possesses. Consumers at the other end of the spectrum also spend less time in the external search process, but for the opposite reason. They do not have knowledge about the product category and do not know what type of information to ask for or what type of information is needed, which means they lack the ability to search for information. Individuals in the middle, who have some knowledge of a product category but feel additional information is needed to make intelligent decisions, typically spend the most time searching for external information.

Level of Motivation   The degree to which an external search takes place further depends on the customer's level of motivation. The greater the motivation, the more time spent on an external search. Motivation is determined by the consumer's:

- Level of involvement
- Need for cognition
- Level of shopping enthusiasm

▼ Enthusiasm for shopping has an impact on the amount of time spent on an external search.

iofoto / Fotolia

Individuals experience greater motivation to search for information when involvement levels are high. **Involvement** reflects the extent to which a stimulus or task is relevant to a consumer's existing needs, wants, or values. When a consumer deems a product to be important, it becomes more likely she will engage in an external search. The amount of involvement is based on factors such as the *cost* of the product and its *importance*. The higher the price, the more time an individual spends searching for information.

The same holds true for importance. Choosing clothes might not be an important decision to some young males, which suggests their clothing purchases typically have low involvement. Picking a tuxedo for the high school prom, however, may spur greater involvement and a higher level of information search due to the social ramifications of dressing poorly at such an important event. The higher level of involvement emerges from the addition of a new element—a major occasion in the person's life.

The **need for cognition** personality characteristic identifies individuals who engage in and enjoy mental activities. Mental exercises have a positive impact on the information search process. People with high needs for cognition gather more information and search more thoroughly. The search also depends on a person's **enthusiasm for shopping**. Customers who enjoy shopping undertake a more in-depth search for goods and services.[4]

Costs Versus Benefits The final factors that influence an information search are the perceived costs versus the perceived benefits of the search. Higher perceived benefits increase the tendency to search.

The ability to reduce purchase risk becomes a benefit that many consumers seek while examining external information. Additional information lowers the chances of making a mistake in the purchase selection. The cost of the search consists of several items:

- The actual cost of the good or service
- The subjective costs associated with the search, including time spent and anxiety experienced while making a decision
- The opportunity cost of foregoing other activities to search for information (e.g., going shopping instead of playing golf or watching a movie)

Higher perceived subjective costs associated with collecting external information search decrease the likelihood that the consumer will conduct a search.[5]

The three factors that make up an external search (ability, motivation, costs versus benefits) are normally considered simultaneously. When the perceived cost of a search is low, and the perceived benefit is high, a consumer has a higher motivation to search for information. A consumer with a minimal amount of product knowledge and a low level of education will be less likely to undertake an external search, because the consumer lacks the ability to identify the right information.

From a marketing communications perspective, the search process represents an important time to reach the consumer. The consumer's objective during an external search is to acquire information leading to a better, more informed decision. The marketing team provides information that leads consumers to the company's products. One ideal time to attempt to influence the decision-making process occurs when the consumer has not yet made up his mind. Marketing experts utilize three models of the information search process: attitudes, values, and cognitive mapping.

CONSUMER ATTITUDES

Effective marketing communications influence consumer attitudes. An **attitude** is a mental position taken toward a topic, a person, or an event that influences the holder's feelings, perceptions, learning processes, and subsequent behaviors.[6] Attitudes can drive purchase decisions. A consumer holding a positive attitude toward a brand becomes more likely to buy it. Someone who enjoys an advertisement also will be more inclined to purchase the product.

Attitudes consist of three components: affective, cognitive, and conative.[7] The *affective* component consists of the feelings or emotions a person has about the object, topic, or idea. The *cognitive* component refers to a person's mental images, understanding, and interpretations of the person, object, or issue. The *conative* component contains an individual's intentions, actions, or behavior. One common sequence of events that takes place in attitude formation is:

$$\text{Cognitive} \rightarrow \text{Affective} \rightarrow \text{Conative}$$

Most of the time, a person first develops an understanding about an idea or object. In the case of marketing, these ideas center on the benefits of the good or service. Thoughts about the product emerge from watching or reading advertisements. Other thoughts may result from exposures to information from other sources, such as the Internet or a friend's referral. Eventually, these ideas become beliefs the consumer holds about a particular product. A consumer seeing the Centric Federal Credit Union advertisement on the next page might notice the emphasis on fewer fees and better rates for banking.

Advertisement for Centric Federal Credit Union furnished by Emogen Marketing

▲ This advertisement for Centric Federal Credit Union is designed to influence a person's beliefs about the financial institution's fees and rates.

The affective part of the attitude carries the general feeling or emotion a person attaches to the idea. In the case of goods and services, the product, its name, and other features can all generate emotions. Consider your emotional reactions to the following goods and services:

▼ What emotions does this advertisement for Pampers Wipes elicit?

Courtesy of D'Arcy Masius Benton & Bowles Inc. © Procter & Gamble Productions, Inc. 1999. Photograph by Penny Gentjeu.

- Cough medicine
- Diaper wipes
- Motorcycles
- Children's toys made in China
- *Sports Illustrated*'s annual swimsuit issue
- Condoms

What emotions and thoughts did you associate with diaper wipes? The Pampers diaper wipe advertisement shown in this section attempts to influence emotions. When considering the items listed here, note that some emotions or attitudes about them seem relatively benign. Others are more strongly held. Cough medicine does not typically evoke an emotional response; however, the swimsuit issue or condoms may generate stronger reactions.

Decision and action tendencies are the conative parts of attitudes. Therefore, when a person feels strongly enough about the swimsuit issue, she might cancel a subscription to *Sports Illustrated*. Most attitudes are not held that strongly. Some people might feel favorably about a topic, such as green marketing, but this does not necessarily change their purchasing behaviors.

Attitudes develop in other ways. An alternative process is:

$$Affective \rightarrow Conative \rightarrow Cognitive$$

Advertisements and other marketing communications can first appeal to the emotions or feelings held by consumers in order to move them to "like" a product and make the purchase (the conative component). Cognitive understanding of the product comes after the purchase. A woman viewing the ad for Platinum Motorcars in this section may be drawn to the idea of being "pampered" in a luxury car. Emotionally, she has a desire to rent the car and takes action. Cognitive reasoning about renting the luxury car follows the emotional experience.

Some attitudes result from a third combination of the components, as follows:

Conative → Cognitive → Affective

Purchases that require little thought, that have a low price, or do not demand a great deal of emotional involvement might follow this path. For instance, while shopping for groceries a customer may notice a new brand of cookies on sale. The person may have never seen the brand or flavor before, but, because it is on sale, decides to give the cookies a try. As the consumer eats them, he develops a greater understanding of the product's taste, texture, and other qualities. Finally, the consumer reads the package to learn more about contents, including how many calories were present in each bite. He finally develops feelings toward the cookies that might affect future cookie purchases.

No matter which path a consumer takes to develop attitudes, each component will be present, to some extent. Some attitudes are relatively trivial (e.g., "I like ping pong, even though I hardly ever get to play"). Others are staunchly held, such as "I hate cigarette smoke!" Both are associated with feelings toward things, including products in the marketplace.

This advertisement for Platinum Motorcars focuses on the affective component of an attitude.

CONSUMER VALUES

Attitudes reflect an individual's personal values. **Values** are strongly held beliefs about various topics or concepts. Values frame attitudes and lead to the judgments that guide personal actions. Values tend to endure. They normally form during childhood, although they can change as a person ages and experiences life.

Figure 3.3 identifies some of the more common personal values. Individuals hold them to differing degrees. Factors that affect a person's values include the individual's personality, temperament, environment, and culture. By appealing to basic values, marketers try to convince prospective customers that the company's products align with their values.

In terms of consumer decision-making processes, both attitudes and values are influential. A good or service tied to a relatively universal value, such as patriotism, helps the firm take advantage of the linkage and present the product in a positive light. Levi Strauss attempted to do this with its recent "Go forth" campaign replete with American imagery. The campaign was based on research by Levi Strauss that discovered teenagers and individuals in their twenties were more patriotic and optimistic about the United

• Comfortable life	• Pleasure
• Equality	• Salvation
• Excitement	• Security
• Freedom	• Self-fulfillment
• Fun, exciting life	• Self-respect
• Happiness	• Sense of belonging
• Inner peace	• Social acceptance
• Mature love	• Wisdom
• Personal accomplishment	

◀ **FIGURE 3.3**
Personal Values

INVEST IN FUTURES.

They come from humble beginnings. But even in the face of poverty, thousands of children across the country still hope for a better life. Which is why The Salvation Army's youth programs offer the physical, mental, and spiritual enrichment they need to break free. All thanks to your donations at 1-800-SAL-ARMY or salvationarmyusa.org.

THE SALVATION ARMY

YOUTH SERVICES   SOCIAL SERVICES   REHABILITATION   UTILITY ASSISTANCE   EMERGENCY RESPONSE   EVANGELISM

DOING THE MOST GOOD

 This advertisement for Salvation Army appeals to personal values of individuals to invest in the future of children.

States. The goal was to transfer positive feelings of patriotism to Levi's products.[8]

COGNITIVE MAPPING

The manner in which individuals store information further affects decisions, because it impacts recall. Knowing how people store, retrieve, and evaluate information assists the company's marketing team in developing advertisements and marketing communications. Understanding how various thought processes and memories work constitutes the first step.

Cognitive maps simulate the knowledge structures and memories embedded in an individual's brain.[9] These structures contain a person's assumptions, beliefs, interpretation of facts, feelings, and attitudes about the larger world. These thought processes interpret new information and determine a response to fresh information or a novel situation. Figure 3.4 depicts a simplified hypothetical cognitive map of an individual thinking about a Ruby Tuesday restaurant.

Based on the cognitive structures illustrated, when this customer thinks about Ruby Tuesday, she connects images of it with other restaurants offering fast food and others providing dine-in services. The individual recognizes Ruby Tuesday as a dine-in establishment. The consumer believes that Ruby Tuesday offers excellent food, but that the service is slow. Next, when the person thinks of slow service, her thoughts turn to Mel's Diner. When she thinks of excellent service, she recalls Applebee's.

Cognitive Linkages   Cognitive structures contain many linkages and exist on several levels. For instance, one level of cognition may be the map shown in Figure 3.4.

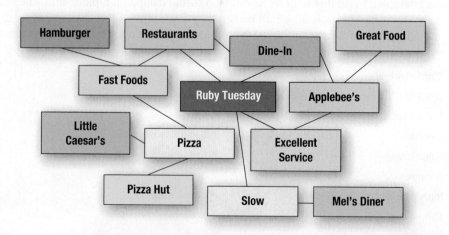

▶ **FIGURE 3.4**
A Cognitive Map for Ruby Tuesday

At another level, the cognitive map is more spatial and conjures images of the actual physical location of Ruby Tuesday and the surrounding businesses. A third cognitive level related to Ruby Tuesday may be the person's recall of the interior of the restaurant along with other linkages that occur at that level. The consumer may have thoughts about Ruby Tuesday that focus on employees, including a relationship she had with a friend who was a server. Therefore, cognitive processing occurs on several levels using highly complex mechanisms.

Processing New Information In terms of cognitive mapping, when a consumer receives information or sees an advertisement, it is processed in several ways. New information that stays consistent with current information tends to strengthen an existing linkage. For example, when a consumer views a Applebee's advertisement promoting great service, the result might be that the ad will strengthen an existing belief, because the consumer already reached that conclusion.

A different response occurs when a message has no current linkages. A consumer who sees an advertisement featuring Ruby Tuesday's seafood selection and does not know that Ruby Tuesday offers seafood experiences a different reaction. In order for this information to remain in the consumer's mind and to become linked to Ruby Tuesday, the customer must create a new linkage between previous Ruby Tuesday images and other images of seafood.

Retaining Information Hearing something once usually does not cause it to be retained in a person's long-term memory, due to differences between short-term recall and long-term memories. The cognitive mapping process explains the knowledge structures embedded in a person's long-term memory. Ordinarily, information will be retained in short-term memory for only a few seconds. As stimuli reach an individual's senses, short-term memory processes them. Short-term memory retains only five to nine pieces of information, meaning new messages are either soon forgotten or added to long-term memory. A repeated message may cause an individual to become more likely to remember it, because the message will be processed into long-term memory and placed into previously developed cognitive maps.

As a result, when a company attempts to introduce consumers to a new brand, advertisements and other marketing messages repeat the name of the brand several times during the presentation. The repetition improves the chances of recall at a later time. To illustrate how this works, consider what happens when a person gives a phone number to a friend. To help remember it, the individual repeats the number over and over.

New Concepts Another way a consumer can process information is to link the message to a new concept. For example, if a consumer sees an advertisement from Ruby Tuesday emphasizing that it has great food but has never thought about the restaurant in terms of quality food, that linkage is not currently present. If the advertisement persuades the consumer, she might construct a linkage between Ruby Tuesday and good food without even traveling to the restaurant. If she does not believe the message, she will ignore or forget the information, and no new linkage results. A third possibility is that the consumer recalls the advertisement at a later time and decides to try Ruby Tuesday. If the food is great, then the link is established at that point. If it is not, the consumer continues thinking that Ruby Tuesday does not offer good food.

Marketing Messages From a marketing perspective, strengthening linkages that

▼ This Sunkist advertisement is designed to establish a new linkage between Sunkist lemon juice and a salt substitute.

Courtesy of Sunkist Growers.

▶ **FIGURE 3.5**
The Roles of Marketing Messages in
Cognitive Mapping

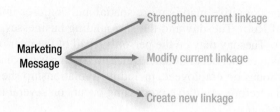

already exist will be easier. Adding new linkages or modifying linkages will be more difficult (see Figure 3.5). Regardless of how information is presented, repetition remains important due to the limitations of short-term memory. Consumers are exposed to hundreds of marketing messages daily. Only a few become processed into long-term memory.

Cognitive mapping and persuasion techniques designed to change attitudes or tap into strongly held values are two key ingredients of any IMC program. When the marketing team understands the needs and attitudes of the target market, messages can be structured to meet those needs. The message should capture the consumer's attention by exposing him to messages that travel effectively through a core mental processing channel or peripheral channels, either through logic or alluring emotional appeals.

Creatives attempt to design ads that reach the linkages consumers have already made between a product and other key ideas. For instance, for a long time a linkage existed between Cadillac and quality, as witnessed by the advertising and promotional phrase "This product is the *Cadillac*...[of all products in the market]." Common linkages exist between products and ideas such as quality, value, low cost, expense, fun, sex, danger, practicality, exoticness, and others. Carefully planned marketing campaigns identify linkages that entice the consumer to buy a brand and to believe in or be loyal to that brand in the future. This advantage remains as the consumer considers various purchasing alternatives.

Evaluation of Alternatives

OBJECTIVE 3.2

What three models explain how individuals evaluate purchasing alternatives?

Evaluation of alternatives constitutes the third step in the consumer buying decision-making process (see Figure 3.6). Three models portray the nature of the evaluation process: the evoked set approach, the multiattribute approach, and affect referral. Understanding how consumers evaluate choices helps the firm's marketing team develop more effective materials.

THE EVOKED SET METHOD

A person's **evoked set** consists of the brands the individual considers in a purchasing situation. An evoked set might be reviewed during both the information search and evaluation stages of the buying decision-making process. Two additional brand sets become part of the evaluation of purchase alternatives: the inept set and the inert set. The **inept set**

▶ **FIGURE 3.6**
Methods of Evaluating Alternatives

contains the brands that are part of a person's memory that are *not considered* because they elicit negative feelings. These negative sentiments are normally caused by a bad experience with a vendor or particular brand. They can also originate from negative comments made by a friend or by seeing an advertisement that the potential customer did not like.

The **inert set** holds the brands that the consumer is aware of but the individual has neither negative nor positive feelings about them. Using the terms from cognitive mapping, these brands have not been entered into any map, or they only have weak linkages to other ideas. The lack of knowledge about these brands usually eliminates them as alternatives. In other words, in most purchase situations the only brands considered are those in the evoked set.

Placing a brand name in the evoked sets of consumers may be the primary goal of a marketing message. Doing so requires promoting the brand name and that brand's primary benefit extensively and consistently using multiple media and other venues. The consumer should see the brand name frequently in as many locations as possible. Then, to make sure the name becomes part of an evoked set, the concepts described related to cognitive mapping can be employed. By tying the brand with its primary benefit, the the marketing team seeks to embed the brand's name in the consumer's long-term memory. The message establishes or reinforces linkages between benefit and the brand name. When a consumer evaluates alternatives using his evoked set and the company's brand becomes the part of the set being considered, the advertisement succeeds.

THE MULTIATTRIBUTE APPROACH

The multiattribute approach may be most useful for understanding high-involvement types of purchases. Consumers often examine sets of product attributes across an array of brands. The multiattribute model suggests that a consumer's attitude toward a brand is determined by:[10]

- The brand's performance on product or brand attributes
- The importance of each attribute to the consumer

The higher a brand rates on attributes that are important to the consumer, the more likely it becomes that the brand will be purchased. Figure 3.7 notes various products, along with some of the characteristics that affect their selection. Each has potentially a lesser or greater value to individual consumers.

From an integrated communication standpoint, providing consumers with information about a brand's performance on criteria that are likely to be used becomes the key. This can be achieved on a brand's Web site, where consumers often gather information about high-involvement decisions. Brochures and print ads can also be prepared; however, getting them into the hands of consumers just as they desire information presents the greatest challenge.

In advertising, creatives often feature a product with multiple benefits by designing a series of messages. Advertisements highlight price, style, service contracts, software, memory, storage, or other product features. Only one or two of these benefits should be presented in each message. Otherwise, the advertisement becomes overloaded with information. Consumers who see commercials featuring one or two benefits are able to

▲ This advertisement for Dark Chocolate Philadelphia Cream Cheese seeks to move the product into consumers' evoked sets as they consider chocolate snacks.

Courtesy of Scott + Cooner Inc. Creative by Gina Cotroneo.

▶ **FIGURE 3.7**
The Multiattribute Model

Product	Characteristics				
Computer	Price	Style	Service contract	Software	Memory storage
Telephone	Price	Style	Speed dial	Caller ID	Cordless feature
Car	Price	Style	Safety	Room	Other features
T-bone steak	Price	Age	Fat content	Degree cooked	Seasonings
Sunglasses	Price	Style	UV protection	Durability	Prescription lenses
Sofa	Price	Style	Foldout bed	Stain resistance	Color
Credit card	Interest rate	Fees	Billing cycle	Access to ATM	Credit limit

Consider each item. Which characteristic is most important to you personally? Least important?

learn about a brand's characteristics. Over time, consumers obtain sufficient information to evaluate the product.

▼ The multiattribute model can be used in the purchase of high-involvement products, such as furniture sold by Scott + Cooner.

From the Paola Lenti Aqua Collection - the Cove modular sofa featuring Aquatech yarn.

THE RIGHT SPOT FOR THOSE OLD **WICKER** PATIO CHAIRS? **THE FIREPIT.**

SCOTT + COONER

Dallas 1617 Hi-Line Dr. Ste. 100 214.748.9838 Austin 115 W. 8th St. 512.814.8702
terrapass *Proud member of the TerraPass carbon offset program.*

AFFECT REFERRAL

The concept of **affect referral** suggests that consumers choose brands they like the best or the ones with which they have emotional connections. The individual does not evaluate brands or think about product attributes. Instead, he buys the brand he likes the best or the one that incites positive feelings. Toothpaste, chewing gum, soft drinks, and candy are some of the products consumers normally select in this way. These purchases typically have low levels of involvement. They also tend to be frequently-purchased products.

The affect referral model also explains purchases of higher priced and "socially visible" products. The emotional bond that has been established between the consumer and the brand leads to a purchase under those circumstances.

The affect referral model explains three things. First, using this approach to product evaluation saves mental energy. A quick choice is easier than going through the process of evaluating every alternative. Some purchases do not deserve much effort, and the affect referral model fits those situations.

Second, a multiattribute model approach might have been used previously when making a purchase. The person already spent a great deal of time considering various product attributes, deciding which are most critical, and reaching a decision. Going through the process again would be "reinventing the wheel." A teenager buying jeans may have already spent considerable time evaluating styles, prices, colors, durability levels, and "fit" of various brands. After making the purchase, the teen continues to purchase the same brand as long as the experience remains positive. The affect referral model explains this buying behavior. Making a repurchase becomes simple and convenient.

Third, consumers often develop emotional bonds with brands. In terms of the purchase decision, an emotional bond with a product can be the strongest and most salient factor in the decision.[11] It can be more important than any attribute or benefit the product can offer. Successful brands establish emotional bonds with consumers. A bond generates brand loyalty, enhances brand equity, and reduces brand parity. Consequently, consumers do not evaluate alternatives because of the bond with the brand. Harley-Davidson has developed such a bond with many of its customers. These individuals hold feelings toward Harley-Davidson that are so strong they would not even consider other alternatives. Affect referral explains this outcome.

Trends in the Consumer Buying Environment

Studying the steps consumers take while making purchasing decisions helps create effective marketing communications. The environment in which purchases are made continually changes and evolves. Several trends in the consumer buying environment affect purchasing patterns (see Figure 3.8).

OBJECTIVE 3.3
What trends are affecting the consumer buyer environment?

AGE COMPLEXITY

Technology has changed the way children grow up. Children are bombarded with advertisements, video games, television shows, movies, and a myriad of other images from an early age. Most become fashion conscious as preteens. Many social observers believe children "grow up" at a much earlier age.

At the other end of the spectrum, some adults refuse to grow old. They wear fashions that resemble those worn by college students. They drive sports cars or convertibles. Many middle-aged adults apparently do not want to grow old, acting like younger people and buying products normally purchased by them. This trend challenges marketers to create messages that reflect these behaviors but do not offend or confuse more traditional middle-aged persons.

GENDER COMPLEXITY

Gender complexity means that the traditional roles, lifestyles, and interests of men and women have become blurred. Many women attend college, delay marriage, and wait to start families. Some choose to focus on moving up the corporate ladder instead of other options.

Men have become more likely to play an active role in parenting, help with household chores, and do more of the shopping. Since 1985, a shift in the number of men who are the primary household shopper has occurred. Almost one-third of men are now the principal shopper. Males spend 38 percent of all grocery dollars.[12] The percentage of men who do the household cleaning is almost as high, 31 percent. According to Alexandra Smith, editor of Mintel Inspire, "The next generation of men is coming of age in an era when gender roles are less rigidly defined."[13] Whether groceries or household cleaning supplies, companies now consider men in terms of what they buy and how they shop. In the past, an automaker such as Ford would target ads to men. Such an approach no longer works. Women either purchase the vehicle or have a major influence on the one the choice.

ACTIVE, BUSY LIFESTYLES

Active lifestyles impact consumer behaviors. In one survey, 47 percent of respondents stated that they would prefer additional free time over more money. The recent recession caused many individuals to work longer hours in order to protect their jobs. Many

- Age complexity
- Gender complexity
- Active, busy lifestyles
- Diverge lifestyles
- Communication revolution
- Experience pursuits
- Health emphasis

◀ **FIGURE 3.8**
Trends Affecting Consumer Buying Behavior

Courtesy of Guess Inc.

Courtesy of Guess Inc.

▲ Understanding the issues created by age and gender complexities, Guess created these two advertisements.

people concentrate less on material possessions and more on experiences with friends and family.[14]

Time pressures account for increases in sales of convenience items, such as microwave ovens, drive-through dry-cleaning establishments, and one-stop shopping outlets, most notably large superstores. People on the go use mobile phones, Blackberries, and social media to make sure they stay in touch with others and do not miss any messages during busy days. The demand for convenience products continues to increase.

DIVERSE LIFESTYLES

The percentage of young people growing of age, marrying, and having children is now the minority. A wide diversity exists in the adult paths individuals take and the living arrangements. More college kids are moving back home to live with parents. Those that do not may live with roommates of mixed genders and ethnicities. Many put off marriage to later in life or choose to remain single or co-habitate.

Divorce and remarriage alter many family units. Remarried divorcees represent about 10 percent of the population. Divorcees tend to develop a new outlook on life. This group, called *second chancers*, is usually between the ages of 40 and 59 and has a higher household income. Second chancers are more content with life than are average adults. They tend to be happy with their new families but also have a different life focus. Second chancers spend less time trying to please others and more time seeking fuller, more enriching lives for themselves and their children or spouse. Although the home and family continue to be a major emphasis, entertainment and vacation services also appeal to this group.[15]

The number of openly lesbian, gay, bisexual, and transgender (LGBT) has grown to approximately 5 percent to 10 percent of the population. These consumers tend to purchase products that feature gay themes in advertising and support causes that are important to them. Wes Combs, President of Witeck-Combs Communication, notes that, "LGBT consumers express an unmistakable and stronger sense of brand loyalty to companies that support their communities." Digital ads are especially effective with this group because they have a higher than average ownership of smartphones.[16]

COMMUNICATION REVOLUTION

Advances in telecommunications, primarily social media and smartphones, have impacted consumers all over the world and have created significant changes in the way individuals communicate with each other, with brands, and with companies. Social media and smartphones have created cultural changes as well. Individuals now communicate with one another through social media, such as Facebook, or through Twitter, instead of talking in person or even calling on the phone. An individual in Florida can communicate with someone in Alaska or in Japan instantaneously. Smartphones allow these individuals to take the Internet with them, which means they do not even have to phone someone to talk. Instead, they can send text messages, or access the Internet and correspond through email, Skype, or another social media platform.

These technologies have changed the way brands and firms are influenced by word-of-mouth communication. If consumers have a bad experience with a brand, they are not limited to telling just a few of their friends and family members. They can use social media and Twitter and instantly be "heard" by thousands of consumers all over the world within hours and many times within minutes. The potential for negative word-of-mouth can be devastating to a brand.

These same technologies can be used to engage consumers and stimulate positive endorsements. Companies now monitor social media. Marketers listen to what consumers say and respond to them. Social media can be used to engage consumers in two-way communication, at the point of purchase in a retail store, in their homes, or at their place of business.

EXPERIENCE PURSUITS

Some people handle the stress of a hectic, busy lifestyle through occasional indulgences or pleasure binges such as expensive dinners out and smaller luxury purchases. Pleasure pursuits include getaway weekends in resorts and on short cruises. These self-rewarding activities make the consumer feel that all the work and effort is "worth it." Instead of buying "things" the current trend is to purchase "experiences," which can vary from theme parks to virtual reality playrooms. It may be visiting a gambling establishment or taking an exotic vacation.

Recognizing that consumers often prefer experiences over things, companies can provide customers with moments to remember rather than more things to put in their homes. Ritz-Carlton used the theme "Let us stay with you" in a recent campaign to emphasize the memories of staying in a Ritz-Carlton luxury property rather than the usual campaign requesting consumers to "Please stay with us." Similarly, Orient-Express Hotels created a campaign with the theme "Embark on a journey like no other." The commercial emphasized a positive consumer experience that would be remembered.[17]

HEALTH EMPHASIS

The U.S. population continues to age, leading to two trends: a blossoming interest in health and maintaining youthful appearance. Many consumers try to develop a balanced lifestyle with an emphasis on nutrition, exercise, and staying active.[18]

Sodium intake has become a concern for health insurance companies, government entities, and many consumers. Producers face the of reducing salt content when most consumers still like the taste or have little concern about daily salt intake. Approximately 77 percent of the typical American's salt intake comes from processed foods. The challenges have led food companies including Kraft, Campbell's, and General Mills to reduce the salt content in some foods. Companies and giant retailers such as Wal-Mart set the

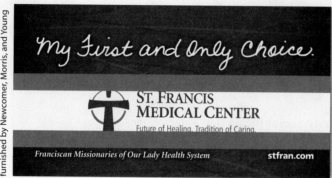

▲ With the emphasis on health, St, Francis Medical Center promotes itself as the first and only choice for medical care.

goal of reducing the sodium content in products by 25 percent before 2015. ConAgra has been slowly reducing the salt content its Hunt's diced tomatoes 10 percent per year since 2008. By reducing it slowly, ConAgra believes consumer will not notice a difference in taste. Other food manufacturers are taking a similar approach.[19]

Consumers desire healthier foods but also want convenience. Busy lifestyles mean consumers are less willing to cook from scratch. They prefer prepared foods that can be assembled easily and cooked quickly. Products that combine health attributes with convenience are likely to sell well.

In sum, these new trends in the consumer buying environment create several challenges for marketing experts, as shown in Figure 3.9. Company leaders will continue to monitor changes so their organizations are not surprised by them. Second, companies can create goods and services that match changing values. Third, marketing messages can be designed to reflect and build on the values people express. Incorporating new trends into the marketing program may be undertaken while at the same time being careful not to alienate any current customers who might not like those trends.

▶ **FIGURE 3.9**
Marketing Responses to Changing Trends in the Consumer Buying Environment

- Monitor consumer environment for changes.
- Create goods and services that are compatible with the changes.
- Design marketing messages that reflect the changes.

Business-to-Business Buyer Behavior

OBJECTIVE 3.4

How do the roles played by various members of the buying center and the factors that influence them impact business purchases?

In business-to-business purchases, *people* still make the decisions. At the same time, when selling to a business organization, the marketing team knows that normally several individuals are involved. Further, corporate policies create restrictions and decision rules that affect purchasing activities. Factors such as costs, quality, and profit considerations also influence the final choice.

The **buying center** consists of the group of individuals making a purchase decision on behalf of a business. This complicates buying decisions. The buying center contains five different purchasing roles shown in Figure 3.10. The five roles are:

- **Users**—Members of the organization who actually use the good or service
- **Buyers**—Individuals given the formal responsibility of making the purchase
- **Influencers**—People who shape purchasing decisions by providing the information or criteria utilized in evaluating alternatives, such as engineers
- **Deciders**—Individuals who authorize the purchase decisions
- **Gatekeepers**—Individuals who control the flow of information to members of the buying center

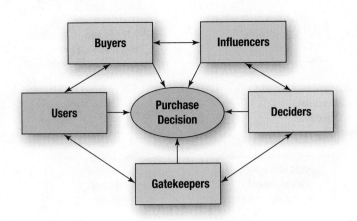

These roles often overlap. Also, several individuals can occupy the same role in a buying center, especially for large or critical purchases. A variety of members of the organization may serve as influencers, because the roles usually are not fixed and formal.

The purchasing process will be unique in each organization. It also varies within an organization from one purchase decision to the next. Salespeople calling on a business seek to locate members of the buying center and understand their roles in the process. When these roles change from one purchase situation to another, the marketing and selling task becomes more complicated.[20]

Factors Affecting Business Buying Centers

A series of organizational and individual factors influence the behaviors of members in the buying center.[21] These influences change the manner in which decisions are made and often affect the eventual outcome or alternative chosen.

ORGANIZATIONAL INFLUENCES

Several organizational factors affect the ways employees make purchasing decisions for a company. The factors include the company's goals and its operating environment (recession, growth period, lawsuits pending, etc.). Decisions are further constrained by the organization's finances, capital assets, market position, the quality of its human resources, and the country in which the firm operates.

Studies of organizational decision making indicate that employees tend to adopt *heuristics*, which are decision rules designed to reduce the number of viable options to a smaller, manageable set. Company goals, rules, budgets, and other organizational factors create heuristics. One decision rule often employed is *satisficing*, which means that when an acceptable alternative has been identified it is taken and the search ends. Rather than spending a great deal of time looking for an optimal solution, decision makers tend to favor expedience.[22]

INDIVIDUAL FACTORS

At least seven factors affect each member of the business buying center (see Figure 3.11).[23] Each impacts how the individual interacts with other members of the center.

Personality   Many facets of personality exist. A decisive person makes purchase decisions in a manner different from someone who vacillates. Confidence, extroversion, shyness, and other personality traits affect both the person performing the decision-making role and others in the process. An aggressive "know-it-all" type affects the other members of a decision-making team. Such a personality feature does not always benefit

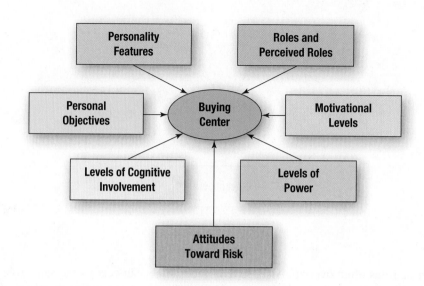

▶ **FIGURE 3.11**
Individual Factors Affecting
Members of the Buying Center

the organization. An extrovert tends to become more involved in the buying process than a more introverted individual. The extrovert spends more time talking while the introvert spends more time listening to sellers. The introvert might be too timid with salespeople and consequently might not ask important questions.

Roles   An individual's age, heredity, ethnicity, gender, cultural memberships, and patterns of social interaction influence the roles the person plays. Roles are socially constructed, which means people define how they intend to play roles as part of a negotiation process with others. A person's perception of how the role fits into the buying center process and the overall organization affects how the individual becomes involved in the purchase.

A buying center member who views his role as merely giving approval to decisions made by the boss (the decider) does not actively participate. Members who believe their inputs are valued and are being solicited become more active. One person might believe that his role is to provide information. Another might perceive her role as being the person who synthesizes information provided by vendors and then relating the information to the buying center to save time. Roles and perceptions of roles are crucial factors that determine how members of the buying center engage in the decision.

Motivation   A person's degree of motivation depends on the match of the individual's goals to the organization's objectives. A factory foreman with a personal goal of becoming the vice president of operations will be more likely to become involved in the purchasing decisions that affect his performance and that of his department. A purchasing agent who has been charged by the CEO to reduce expenses will take a more active role to ensure that cost-cutting selections are made. The need for recognition motivates many individuals. Then the goal of making successful purchasing decisions becomes to ensure that others recognize the effort, because the person believes a link exists between recognition and promotions or pay raises.

Level of Power   A person derives her level of power in the buying process from the role

▼ An advertisement for Sub-Zero directed toward business buyers for refrigeration units, containing the message "Fresh is everything".

Courtesy of Sub-Zero and Wolf, The Richards Group, Photography
Credit: Robb Debenport

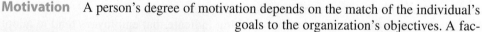

in the buying center, official position in the organization, and the impact of the purchase decision on a specific job. When a particular purchase decision directly affects an employee, she may try to gain more power through the buying process. For instance, a factory foreman has greater power within the buying center in the purchase of raw materials, whereas the maintenance foreman has more power in the purchase of maintenance supplies. In these situations, each strives to influence the decision that affects his or her area.

Risk   Many vendors are chosen because buyers believe the choice represents the lowest risk. Risk avoidance leads buyers to stay with current vendors rather than switching. In marketing to businesses, reducing risk remains a priority, especially when signing large contracts or when a purchase might affect company profits. People tend to believe that taking risks, especially when a failure follows, affects performance appraisals, promotions, and other outcomes.

Levels of Involvement   Both consumer and business buying behaviors are influenced by levels of cognitive involvement. Individuals with higher levels of cognitive capacity seek more information prior to making decisions. They ask more questions when interacting with a salesperson. They spend more time deliberating prior to making decisions. Clearly-stated message arguments help persuade both consumers and business buyers with higher cognitive levels.

▲ A 3M advertisement directed to businesses for Premium-Performance Packaging Tape.

Personal Objectives   Motives, personality types, perceptions of risk, and the other individual factors influence personal objectives. These objectives can lead buyers to make purchases that help them politically in the organization, even when they are not the best choice. For example, if someone knows his boss is friends with a particular vendor, the buyer might choose that vendor even when others offer higher quality, lower prices, or both. Personal objectives in buying decisions can be tied to getting promotions, making rivals look bad, "brown-nosing" a boss, or the genuine desire to help the organization succeed.

In sum, a buying center consists of a complex set of relationships. Members can serve different roles and may play more than one role. Understanding these dynamics helps when marketing to businesses. The marketing team identifies who will make the decision, how the decision will be made, and any forces or factors that might affect the decision-making process. Examining the organizational and individual influences makes it possible to design a communications program that reaches the key people at the right time.

Types of Business-to-Business Sales

Business buyers make different types of purchasing decisions. The marketing team adapts to the type of decision being made. Three categories of buying activities are: straight rebuy, modified rebuy, and new task.[24]

A **straight rebuy** occurs when the firm has previously chosen a vendor and places a reorder. This routine process involves only one or a few members of the buying center. Often the purchasing agent (buyer) and the users of the product are the only persons aware of a rebuy order. The user's role in this purchase situation is to ask the buyer to

OBJECTIVE 3.5

What types of business-to-business sales are made?

▶ **FIGURE 3.12**
Reasons to Make a Modified Rebuy

- Dissatisfaction with current vendor.
- A different vendor makes an attractive offer.
- End of contractual arrangement with current vendor.
- Individuals involved in decision process have no or little experience with the product.

replenish the supply. The buyer then contacts the supplier and places the order. Little or no evaluation of alternatives or information takes place. These purchases often take place electronically.

When making a **modified rebuy**, the buying team considers and evaluates alternatives. As identified in Figure 3.12, a modified rebuy purchase can be made for four different reasons. First, when a company's buyers are *dissatisfied with the current vendor*, they look for new options. A greater level of dissatisfaction creates a strong enticement to examine new possibilities. Second, if a new company offers what is perceived by a member of the buying center to be a *better buy*, the purchase decision may be revisited.

A third type of modified rebuy occurs at the *end of a contractual agreement*. Many organizations, as dictated by corporate policy, must ask for bids each time a contract is written. This situation often occurs when governmental and nonprofit organizations make purchases. The final reason for a modified rebuy is that the people in the company assigned to make the purchase might have only *limited or infrequent experience with the good or service*. When a company purchases delivery trucks, the typical time between decisions may be 5 to 7 years. This creates a modified rebuy situation, because many factors change over that amount of time. Prices, product features, and vendors (truck dealerships) change rapidly. Also, in most cases the composition of the buying group will be different. Some may have never been part of the decision to purchase delivery vehicles.

In **new task** purchasing situations, the company considers a good or service for the first time or it has been a long time since the last purchase. Further, the product involved is one with which organizational members have no or extremely little experience. This type of purchase normally requires input from a number of buying center members. A considerable amount of time will be spent gathering information and evaluating vendors. In many cases, vendors are asked to assist in identifying the required specifications.

The Business-to-Business Buying Process

OBJECTIVE 3.6

What are the steps of the business-to-business buying process?

The steps involved in the business-to-business buying process are similar to those made by individual consumers. In new task purchasing situations, members of the buying center tend to go through each of the seven steps as part of the buying decision-making process. In modified rebuy or straight rebuy situations, one or more of the steps may be eliminated.[25] Figure 3.13 compares the consumer buying process to the business-to-business buying process.

IDENTIFICATION OF NEEDS

Just as consumers identify needs (hunger, protection, social interaction), businesses also make purchases because of needs ranging from raw materials to professional services. The manner in which business needs are determined is often different.

Derived demand creates many business needs. **Derived demand** is based on, linked to, or generated by the production and sale of some other good or service.[26] The demand for steel used in automobile frames results from the number of cars and trucks sold each year. When the demand for vehicles goes down during a recession or downturn, the demand for steel also declines. Steel manufacturers find it difficult to stimulate demand because of the nature of derived demand. Purchases of raw materials used in the production of goods and services, such as steel, aluminum, concrete, plastic, petroleum products (e.g., jet fuel for airlines), construction materials, and others

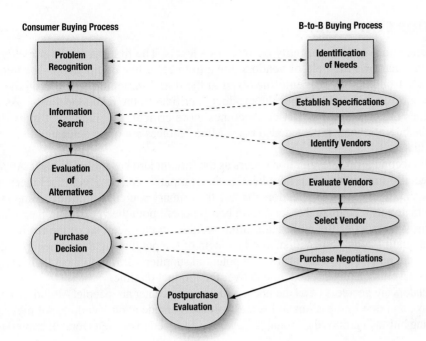

Consumer Buying Process

- Problem Recognition
- Information Search
- Evaluation of Alternatives
- Purchase Decision

B-to-B Buying Process

- Identification of Needs
- Establish Specifications
- Identify Vendors
- Evaluate Vendors
- Select Vendor
- Purchase Negotiations

Postpurchase Evaluation

◀ **FIGURE 3.13**
A Comparison of the Business to-Business Buying Process to the Consumer Buying Process

create derived demand. It also exists for services. Most of the demand for mortgages depends on housing sales.

Once a need has been recognized, the order will be placed with the current vendor, in a straight rebuy situation. When the purchase constitutes a modified rebuy or new task, members of the buying center move to the next step.

ESTABLISHMENT OF SPECIFICATIONS

In a new task purchase, the most complete specifications are spelled out. Many times, various vendors assist the buyer in developing clear specifications. In modified rebuy situations, managers examine specifications to ensure that they are current and that they still meet the company's needs. While they occasionally change, normally most are minor alterations.

▼ ReRez provides quality marketing research for business clients.

IDENTIFICATION OF VENDORS

Once specifications have been identified, potential vendors are located and asked to submit bids. In most business situations, written, formal bids are required. A vendor's ability to write a clear proposal often determines whether the company will present a successful bid. Effective proposals spell out prices, quality levels, payment terms, support services, and other conditions requested by the company.

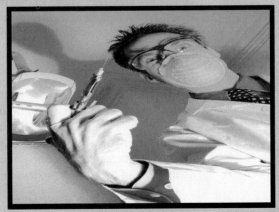
Advertisement furnished by ReRez

VENDOR EVALUATION

Evaluations of vendors normally occur at two levels. The first, an *initial screening* of proposals, narrows the field of vendors down to three to five competitors. The number of people from the buying center involved in the initial screening depends on the dollar value of the bid and whether the product is critical to the firm's operation. As dollar values increase and the product becomes more critical, the number of individuals from the buying center involved also rises. Minor choices are often delegated to a single individual.

The second level of evaluation occurs as the firm undertakes a *vendor audit*. An audit is especially important when members of the company seek to develop a longer-term relationship with a supplier. Vendors that are the primary sources for critical components or raw materials recognize that long-term bonds benefit both the vendor and the purchasing firm. Members of the audit team often include an engineer, someone from operations, a quality-control specialist, and members of the purchasing department. An audit services the purposes of evaluating each potential supplier's ability to meet demand, provide the level of quality needed, and deliver the product on time.

Vendors are people, just as members of the buying center are people. Attitudes, values, opinions, and first impressions influence evaluations made about vendors. All messages, including bids and proposals, should be carefully designed to create favorable impressions.

VENDOR SELECTION

Once company officials have studied all of the vendors and the bids have been considered, the final choice can be made. In the decision-making process, members of the buying center experience the individual and organizational pressures presented earlier. The selection criteria used include quality, delivery, performance history, warranties, facilities and capacity, geographic location, technical capability, and per-dollar value.[27] A single vendor rarely will be deemed superior across all selection criteria. Consequently, the marketing team for each seller emphasizes the company's specific strengths as part of its presentation. In reality, however, politics and other similar forces often impact the final decision.

NEGOTIATION OF TERMS

In most purchasing situations, negotiation of terms will be a formality because the conditions have already been worked out. Occasionally, however, changes are made at this point in a contract or purchase. These tend to be minor and are normally negotiated by the purchasing agent. When the final agreement is set, goods are shipped or services provided. Assuming no further complications, the buying process is complete until the next cycle begins.

POSTPURCHASE EVALUATION

In the business-to-business arena, the postpurchase phase represents a marketing opportunity. Vendors that provide high-quality products, make follow-up calls, and offer additional services often move into a straight rebuy situation. They avoid going through the process again, because they are the chosen vendor unless something changes. Even for products that are purchased occasionally, the firm that gives attention to the postpurchase component of the selling process gains an edge the next time a purchase is made.

Dual Channel Marketing

OBJECTIVE 3.7
How does dual channel marketing expand a company's customer base and its sales?

Firms sell virtually the same goods or services to both consumers and businesses in **dual channel marketing**.[28] The approach fits several situations. Perhaps the most common scenario occurs when a product sold in business markets is then adapted to consumer markets. New products often have high start-up costs, including R&D expenditures, market research, and other tasks. Businesses tend to be less price-sensitive than retail consumers, which makes it logical to approach them first.

As sales grow, economies of scale emerge. Larger purchases of raw materials combined with more standardized methods of production make it possible to enter consumer markets. The benefits of economies of scale entice manufacturers to sell products previously supplied to the business sector in the retail markets. Products including digital cameras, calculators, computers, fax machines, and mobile phones were first sold to businesses and then later to consumers.

To make the move to the retail arena possible, prices must come down and products need to be user-friendly. For example, consumers can now have their photos put on a CD rather than obtaining prints. The imaging technology developed by Kodak and Intel was first sold to various businesses and now is offered to retail customers. By forming an alliance with Intel, Kodak brought the cost down and developed the economies of scale necessary for consumer markets.

SPIN-OFF SALES

Another type of dual channel marketing—spin-off sales—occurs when individuals who buy a particular brand at work have positive experiences and, as a result, purchase the same brand for personal use. This situation often takes place with computers and computer software. Favorable feelings about more expensive items can also result in spin-off sales. A salesperson who drives a company-owned Buick for work might like it so well that she purchases one for personal use. Holiday Inn's marketing team discovered that many of its private stays come from business-related spin-offs. Approximately 30 percent of Holiday Inn's business customers also stay with the chain on private vacations.[29]

MARKETING DECISIONS

In dual channel marketing, a primary decision will be made about how to represent the product in each channel. The firm can either emphasize similarities between the two markets or focus on differences. Consumers and businesses looking for the same benefits and product features receive similar marketing messages. When consumers and business buyers value different product attributes or desire different benefits, the marketing strategy team customizes messages for the separate markets. Figure 3.14 identifies three approaches companies can use in marketing products to dual channels.

In some instances, the product attributes are the same, but the value or benefit of each attribute differs. Messages then focus on the benefits each segment derives from the product. Mobile phones marketed to businesses stress area coverage and service options. For consumers, mobile phone marketing messages may center on the fashionable design of the product, ease of use, or price.

To avoid confusing individuals who might see both messages from the same producer, companies may apply dual branding. For instance, when Black & Decker launched a professional line of power tools, the DeWalt brand name was chosen. This avoided confusion with the Black & Decker name.

▼ 3M Post-It Sortable Cards are sold to retail customers and in business-business markets

- Use different communication messages
- Create different brands
- Use multiple or different channels

▲ **FIGURE 3.14**
Dual Channel Marketing Strategies

In most cases, business customers and consumers seek the same basic benefits from products. In these situations, a single approach for both markets will be used. Tactics include:

- Integrating communications messages
- Selling the same brand in both markets
- Scanning both markets for dual marketing opportunities

In addition to creating economies of scale, integrating consumer markets has another advantage: the potential to create the synergies that arise from increased brand identity and equity. An image developed in the consumer market can then be used to enter a business market, or vice versa. Using one brand makes it easier to develop brand awareness and brand loyalty. A business customer who uses a company-owned American Express Card may obtain a card from the company for personal use.

Scanning both types of customers for new opportunities is part of dual channel marketing. For example, the firm Intuit, which sells Quicken software, discovered that individuals who use Quicken at home were willing to use a similar version for their small businesses. Capitalizing on this advantage, Quicken added features including payroll and inventory control to its business software package while maintaining the easy-to-use format. By identifying business use for a consumer product, Quicken adapted the product and captured 70 percent of the small-business accounting software market.[30]

Dual channel marketing can create a major competitive advantage as products are sold in both markets. A complete IMC planning process includes the evaluation of potential business market segments as well as consumer market segments. Firms that integrate messages across these markets take major steps toward reaching every potential customer.

International Implications

OBJECTIVE 3.8

How can a company overcome international differences when adapting to buying processes?

Selling to consumers and businesses requires the marketing team to understand cultural differences related to products, messages, and selling techniques. A *cultural assimilator* will be a valuable member of the marketing team in international projects. Individual buyers and members of companies from other countries exhibit cultural differences as they consider purchasing alternatives.

Understand the nuances of the purchasing process for transactions that take place in foreign countries can be helpful. For example, at domestic U.S. trade shows actual purchases are normally not finalized. Instead, information is collected and transferred between the buyer and the seller. At international trade shows, however, sales are often completed. Higher-ranking members of the purchasing company attend the shows and want to complete transactions. Knowing these kinds of differences helps a company succeed in international trade.

Building a powerful brand represents an important activity in any IMC program. A strong brand means the product becomes part of the consumer's initial set of brands to consider when making a purchase. A powerful brand crosses national boundaries and becomes part of an effective GMIC program. Successful global brands are built over time. It takes a combination of high-quality products and effective marketing communications to reach that point.

In business-to-business marketing, a visible global brand presence is equally crucial. The existence of multiple vendors, increasing perceptions of brand parity, and growing use of the Internet make it impossible for a company to succeed using only price differentiation. To combat such situations, a strong brand is a necessity in the global environment. A strong brand increases the chances of being selected. As Robert Duboff writes, "It is no longer sufficient to be a great company; *you must be a great brand*."[31]

INTEGRATED CAMPAIGNS IN ACTION

Argent Financial

Argent Financial Group provides comprehensive financial services and products to individuals, families, and friends. Argent is growing into a large corporation, but it still operated as a smaller organization. As a result, its marketing efforts were reactive rather than strategic and planned. Little coordination across subsidiaries and between offices took place.

The objective for the marketing agency, Emogen Marketing Group, was to define and promote a single brand that would increase Argent's brand recognition and value. After brainstorming with the client, Emogen suggested the following brand identity statement: "Argent is a wealth management firm comprised of highly qualified professionals helping clients manage, grow and protect assets."

Based on the brand identity statement, Emogen suggested that the new campaign stress: high values, trust, and expertise; relationships, not performance; and that client satisfaction grows when using a single advisor. From these ideas came the new campaign tagline "Be informed, not sold."[32]

A Web link to the entire campaign created by Emogen Marketing for Argent can be found at the Pearson Instructor's Resource Center (www.pearsonhighered.com) for instructors who adopt this textbook. The campaign has a PowerPoint presentation outlining the details of the campaigns and examples of the collaterals developed by Emogen.

▼ The value proposition for the new Argent campaign was "Be informed, not sold".

Courtesy of Argent Financial

MyMarketingLab

Go to **mymktlab.com** to complete the problems marked with this icon .

SUMMARY

Buyer behaviors are part of the purchasing process in both consumer markets and business-to-business transactions. An effective IMC program accounts for the ways in which goods and services are purchased in both markets. The consumer buying decision-making process consists of five steps. Marketing experts are aware of each step and prepare effective communications that lead most directly to the decision to buy. For the purposes of creating effective marketing communications, two of the most important are the information search stage and the evaluation of alternatives stage.

After recognizing a want or need, a consumer searches for information both internally and externally. Marketing messages attempt to place the product or service in the consumer's evoked set of viable prospects. Three factors that influence search behaviors include involvement, needs for cognition, and enthusiasm for shopping. Customers consider the benefits and costs of searches and make decisions regarding how extensively they will seek information. Evoked sets, attitudes and values, and cognitive maps explain how an individual evaluates various purchasing choices.

Marketers face an evolving buying decision-making environment. New cultural values and attitudes, time pressures, and busy lifestyles influence what people buy, how they buy, and the manner in which they can be enticed to buy. Many consumers try to escape through indulgences and pleasure binges, by finding excitement or fantasy, and by planning to meet social needs. An aging baby boom population concentrates more on lasting values and on health issues. Marketing experts can address these needs and lead customers to purchases based on them.

By understanding business buyer behaviors, the marketing team constructs a more complete and integrated marketing communications program. Business purchases are driven by members of the buying center. These members include users, buyers, influencers, deciders, and gatekeepers. Members of the buying center are influenced by both organizational and individual factors that affect various marketing decisions.

Business-to-business sales take three forms. A straight rebuy occurs when the firm has previously chosen a vendor and intends to place a reorder. A modified rebuy occurs when the purchasing group is willing to consider and evaluate new alternatives. This decision is usually based on dissatisfaction with a current vendor. A new task purchase is one in which the company buys a good or service for the first time, and the product involved is one with which organizational members have no experience.

The business-to-business buying process is similar to the consumer purchase decision-making process. A more formal purchasing process includes formal specifications, bids from potential vendors, and a contract finalizing the purchasing agreement.

Dual channel marketing means that the firm sells virtually the same goods or services to both consumers and businesses. Dual channel marketing creates both economies of scale and synergies for the vendor company. It also enhances the chances that a product will be sold to every available customer. The challenge to the marketing team is to create strong and consistent marketing messages to every potential buyer, accounting for how buyer behaviors are present in purchasing processes.

Key Terms

involvement The extent to which a stimulus or task is relevant to a consumer's existing needs, wants, or values.

need for cognition A personality characteristic an individual displays when he or she engages in and enjoys mental activities.

enthusiasm for shopping Customers who like to shop will undertake a more in-depth search for details about goods and services.

attitude A mental position taken toward a topic, person, or event that influences the holder's feelings, perceptions, learning processes, and subsequent behaviors.

values Strongly held beliefs about various topics or concepts.

cognitive maps Simulations of the knowledge structures embedded in an individual's brain.

evoked set Consists of the set of brands a consumer considers during the information search and evaluation processes.

inept set The part of a memory set that consists of the brands that are held in a person's memory but that are *not considered*, because they elicit negative feelings.

inert set The part of a memory set of brands that hold the brands that the consumer has awareness of but has neither negative nor positive feelings about.

affect referral A purchasing decision model in which the consumer chooses the brand for which he or she has the strongest liking or feelings.

buying center The group of individuals who make a purchase decision on behalf of a business.

straight rebuy What occurs when the firm has previously chosen a vendor and intends to place a reorder.

modified rebuy The company buying team considers and evaluates new purchasing alternatives.

new task A purchase in which the company buys a good or service for the first time, and the product involved is one with which organizational members have no experience.

derived demand Demand based on, linked to, or generated by the production and sale of some other good or service.

dual channel marketing Selling virtually the same goods or services to both consumers and businesses.

compensatory heuristics A purchasing decision model that assumes that no one single brand will score high on every desirable attribute and that individual attributes vary in terms of their importance to the consumer.

conjunctive heuristics A purchasing decision model that establishes a minimum or threshold rating that brands must meet in order to be considered.

phased heuristics A purchasing decision model that is a combination of the compensatory and conjunctive heuristics models.

Review Questions

1. What are the five steps of the consumer buying decision-making process? Which two steps are the most important with regard to developing quality integrated marketing communications?

2. Describe the natures of an internal search and an external search in a purchasing decision.

3. Define attitude. What are the three main components of attitude, and how are they related to purchasing decisions?

4. How do values differ from attitudes? Name some personal values related to purchasing decisions.

5. Explain what a cognitive map models.

6. What is an evoked set? Why are evoked sets, inept sets, and inert sets important to the marketing department?

7. What are the key features of the multiattribute approach to evaluating purchasing alternatives?

8. What is meant by affect referral? When is a person likely to rely on such a cognitive approach to evaluating purchasing alternatives?

⭐ 9. What new trends in the consumer buying environment affect consumer purchasing decisions?

10. Name and describe the five roles played in a buying center.

11. What organizational and individual factors affect members of the business buying center?

12. Describe the three main forms of business-to-business sales.

13. Name the steps in the business-to-business buying process.

14. Describe dual channel marketing and explain why it is important to a company's well-being.

Critical Thinking Exercises

DISCUSSION QUESTIONS

1. For college students and other individuals with compulsive buying behaviors, a primary influence is the family. Often one or both parents are compulsive shoppers. Families that display other forms of dysfunctional behaviors, such as alcoholism, bulimia, extreme nervousness, or depression tend to produce children who are more inclined to exhibit compulsive shopping behaviors. Why do dysfunctional behaviors among parents produce compulsive shopping behavior among children? Another component of compulsive buying behaviors is self-esteem. Again, self-esteem is partly inherited, but it also develops in the home environment. How would self-esteem be related to compulsive shopping behaviors? What influences other than family might contribute to compulsive shopping behaviors? If an individual has a tendency to be a compulsive shopper, what can (or should) be done?

⭐ 2. Think about the way you purchase products and consider a recent purchase that involved an external search. Discuss your ability to search, the need for cognition, your personal level of shopping enthusiasm, and the perceived costs versus the perceived benefit of the search. How much time did you spend in the external search, and what was the outcome?

3. Study the list of personal values presented in Figure 3.3. Identify the five most important to you. Rank them from first to last. Beside each value, identify at least one product you have purchased to satisfy those values.

Then, gather into small groups of three to five students. Using the information from your list of values, discuss differences among members of the group. Identify a way to send a marketing message that will appeal to the top value from each person's list.

⭐ 4. Identify the last brand of clothing you purchased. Create a cognitive map similar to the one illustrated in the text for Ruby Tuesday in Figure 3.4. Discuss the linkages. Identify which linkages are strong. Which linkages are loosely held?

⭐ 5. Review the three methods of evaluating alternatives. For each method, discuss a recent purchase you made using that method. Which method did you tend to use the most? Why?

6. A member of the buying center for a large shoe manufacturer tries to purchase soles for shoes from an outside vendor (or vendors). Study the individual and organizational factors that affect buying center members. Discuss the effect of each factor on the roles of members in the shoe company's buying center. How does the factory foreman's role differ from that of the purchasing agent? How do these roles differ from the company president's role?

⭐ 7. A purchasing agent for a clothing manufacturer is in the process of selecting a vendor (or vendors) to supply the materials to produce about 30 percent of its clothes. The clothing manufacturer employs about 300 people. As the audit nears completion, what factors are most important to the purchasing agent?

Integrated Learning Exercises

1. Consumers and businesses conduct external searches when they lack sufficient internal knowledge to make a wise decision. Assume you have $80,000 to $100,000 to spend on a sailboat. Locate four Web sites that sell sailboats. Select one in your price range. Why did you select that particular brand? What features are attractive to you? Would you want any additional information before making a final purchase decision? Would you purchase a used boat or new boat? Why?

2. Almost everyone has an opinion about tattoos. Some attitudes are positive whereas others are negative. Few are neutral. Go to www.tattoos.com and examine the material that is on the Web site. Did this information modify your attitude toward tattoos? What factors on the Web site influenced your attitude? Find at least one additional Web site of a company that offers tattoos. Discuss the components of the Web site in terms of which components of attitude it is trying to influence: cognitive, affective, or conative.

3. United Raw Material Solutions, Inc. is a business-to-business marketplace that brings together buyers and sellers of textiles, petrochemicals, plastics, and electronics. Access the Web site at www.urms.com. Which members of the buying center would be most interested in this site? What services and benefits do you see for buyers? For suppliers?

4. Examine the following Web sites. What kind of information is provided? Which component of attitude is the site designed to affect: cognitive, affective, or conative?
   a. Kenneth Cole (www.kennethcole.com)
   b. Starbucks (www.starbucks.com)
   c. Cadillac (www.cadillac.com)
   d. IKEA (www.ikea.com)
   e. Oscar Mayer(www.kraftbrands.com/OscarMayer)

5. A member of the buying center has been asked to gather information about possible shipping companies for international shipments. Visit the following Web sites. What companies have the most appealing Web sites? Beyond online materials, what additional information do they need to supply to the buying center in order to win the contract?
   a. ABC India Limited (www.abcindia.com)
   b. SR International Logistics, Inc. (**www.srinternational .com**)
   c. Falcon Transportation & Forwarding Corp. (**www .falcontrans.com**)
   d. Global Freight Systems (**www.globalfreightsystems .com**)

Student Project

CREATIVE CORNER

A local travel agency decides to advertise in the student newspaper on your campus to promote spring break packages. The company hires you to perform the creative work. The marketing department is not sure which type of advertising approach to use. The agency knows that attitude consists of three parts: cognitive, affective, and conative. They also know that an advertisement can appeal to any one of the attitude components. The agency's management team is also not sure which component to use. Consequently, they have asked you to design three advertisements, with one designed to appeal to the cognitive component of attitude, the second to the affective component, and the third to the conative component. After you have finished designing the ads, discuss the pros and cons of each and make a recommendation to the travel agency about which one to use. The ads should be for a 5-day spring break vacation on the beach in Fort Lauderdale, Florida.

CASE 1 THE CHOICE

The Planter's Insurance Company's home office operations are located in Kansas City, Missouri. The agency provides health insurance packages to other businesses. The company's reputation has been built on professional service delivered at competitive prices. Currently, the agency's contract with its office supply company is about to expire. Planter's Insurance purchases paper and other materials and leases copiers and printers on a 3 year cycle. The members of the buying center include five individuals: Martin Garza, Suzette Simon, Jason Talley, Paul Johnson, and Rose Knotts.

Martin Garza serves as the purchasing agent for the company. He is actively seeking to be promoted into a vice presidential role in the area of support staff. Martin's outgoing personality has made him friends and rivals. His approach to managing the purchasing function has been to save the company money whenever possible, believing this approach will help when the next promotion decision will be made. Martin is willing to use political tactics to achieve his personal and organizational goals.

Suzette Simon manages the copy center. She believes taking the offer from the lowest bidder is normally not a wise choice. When reviewing the bids, Suzette noticed that the lowest offer came from a company that had been retained previously. The company did a poor job; its service was inadequate, and its copiers regularly broke down. Suzette has a strong personality and does not back down in a disagreement, even with higher-ranking and male employees.

Jason Talley, the vice president of finance, is the highest ranking member of the buying center. He will make the final decision because of his position. Jason is an introvert who listens, seldom takes a stand, and tries to get the group to make a decision that is unanimous. If not, he normally goes with the lowest risk solution – which in this case would be the current vendor.

Paul Johnson manages the IT department, which maintains the computers and printers. He wants to exclude printers from the contract and purchase them instead of leasing, which he believes will save the company money. He sees this purchasing decision as a chance to demonstrate his power. He dislikes Martin Garza and believes Garza has secret motives in pursuing the low cost bidder.

Rose Knotts is the administrative assistant to the president. She is the lowest ranking member of the buying center. Rose sees her role as providing information and keeping peace. She is reluctant to voice an opinion and almost always defers to the Jason Talley, the vice president of finance.

The company received four bids for the contract. Basic information about each is as follows:

Company 1: the current vendor, $123,000 for the copier and printer lease contract. Suzette says the company delivers "acceptable" quality but is often slow to respond when a repair is needed.

Company 2: has an excellent reputation for quality service. The company's salesperson is a friend of Suzette

▼ A buying center meets to discuss copier and printer contract.

© auremar/Fotolia

Simon. She argues that his company will save Planter's Insurance money in the long run due to fewer instances of down time and the best quality equipment. The bid was $139,000 for the copier and lease contract.

Company 3: is new to Kansas City. No one in the buying center has knowledge about the company. Its bid was $115,000 with the notation that repairs are made within 24 hours and that a repair person is on duty at all times, including overnight.

Company 4: was the company that Suzette noted was of poor quality. The company's bid was $114,000, making it the low offer. Paul Johnson believed that Martin Garza revealed the bid of Company 3 to this company, so that it could make an offer that was lower.

Jason Talley opening the final meeting of the buying center team. He asked each member to name the company they thought should receive the bid. The opinions were as follows:

Martin Garza: Company 4
Suzette Simon: Company 2
Paul Johnson: Company 3
Rose Knotts: Company 1

Jason favored Company 3 for two reasons. First, he respected the opinion of Paul Johnson. Second, he thought the 24 hour service feature made the company stand out.

Questions

1. Discuss the reasoning behind each person's choice based on the information provided and the individual factors outlined in this chapter.

2. Identify the factors that favor each vendor and the factors that are the company's weaknesses.

3. How should Jason make the final choice, given there is such a great divergence in opinion?

4. What should Jason say to the members of the buying center whose favorite companies are not chosen?

CASE 2 CHOOSING A PHONE COMPANY: OPTIONS AND ALTERNATIVES

The past two decades have witnessed a dramatic shift in the ways people can talk on the phone. Landline phones, while still in common use, are being challenged by new and different technologies. AT&T, a major landline provider, has expanded to compete in areas such as mobile phones, texting, and Internet access using handheld devices.

Also, a new type of telephone technology has emerged, Voice over Internet Protocol (VoIP). This new technology allows a customer to make voice calls using a broadband Internet connection instead of a regular (analog) phone line.

Some VoIP services allow users to make calls to people who use the same service. Others allow users to call anyone who has a telephone number, including local, long-distance, mobile phone, and international numbers. Some VoIP services only work over a computer or a special VoIP phone. Others can be used with a traditional phone connected to a VoIP adapter.

▲ VoIP services can work with just a computer or with traditional phones.

Sources: HowStuffWorks, "Skype vs. Vonage" (http://electronics. howstuffworks.com/ skype-vonage2.htm, accessed November 24, 2009); Skype (www.skype.com/intl/en/ getconnected/, accessed November 24, 2009); FCC, "Voice-Over-Internet Protocol" (www.fcc.gov/voip/, accessed November 24, 2009); Vonage (www.vonage.com/how_ vonage_works/?refer_id=WEBHO0706010001W&lid=main_nav_how_works, accessed November 24, 2009).

In addition, wireless "hot spots" in locations such as airports, parks, and cafes allow callers to connect to the Internet and use VoIP service wirelessly.

A customer owning a special VoIP phone or a regular telephone connected to a VoIP adapter will have a phone that rings like a traditional telephone. If the person's VoIP service requires him to make calls using a computer, the software supplied by the service provider alerts the user when he has an incoming call.

VoIP services do have some disadvantages. First, some VoIP services do not work during power outages unless the service provider offers backup power. Second, not all VoIP services connect directly to emergency services through 911. Third, VoIP providers may not offer directory assistance or white page listings.

The two major VoIP providers are Skype and Vonage. Skype allows customers to make calls to other Skype members free of charge. The service includes free text messaging and video calls as well. Skype offers low rates for calls of other types. A customer can use Skype on a computer or on a mobile device. Skype works on a wide range of mobile phones, as well as on devices such as PlayStation Portable. Instant messages can be directed at individuals or group chat rooms. Skype users can also make conference calls. Skype offers customers pay-as-you-go or monthly payment options. No special equipment purchase is required in order to use Skype.

Vonage emphasizes that it provides lower-cost options when compared to AT&T. The company features international calling at greatly reduced rate. Vonage does require users to install special hardware. After signing up for an account, Vonage ships an adapter or other equipment to the customer, who must then install it and set it up. Complete instructions are provided, and setup is relatively simple. Vonage service can be purchased at Best Buy, Wal-Mart, and Target. The systems offer unlimited local and long-distance calling, call waiting, call forwarding, automatic redial, and voice mail for a single monthly fee.

Kelli is evaluating the two VoIP services and two mobile phone services. Figure 3.15 provides the multiattribute

◀ **FIGURE 3.15**

Example of a Multiattribute Evaluation Approach for a Phone Service

Attribute	Importance	AT&T	Vonage	Skype	Verizon
Sound quality	10	10	8	5	8
Special services	9	6	9	8	9
Mobile device access	8	8	8	5	6
Setup difficulty	6	7	5	2	8
Phone style	5	8	4	9	4
Compensatory score		300	275	219	277

evaluation approach she has developed. She is considering the attributes of sound quality, special services available, access to mobile devices, and difficulty in set up. Each attribute receives a score on a scale of 1 to 10 in terms of importance to Kelli, with 10 being the most important and 1 the least important. The four companies are then evaluated with a 10-point scale for each attribute, with 10 indicating the highest performance.

Using a compensatory heuristics method, Kelli assumes that no one single brand scores high on every attribute and that individual attributes vary in importance. With this model, Kelli will purchase the brand with the highest compensatory score, which is calculated by multiplying each attribute score by its importance, and then summing the total, as shown at the bottom of Figure 3.15.

Using the conjunctive heuristics method, a threshold or minimum rating is established. A brand is eliminated if an important attribute is rated lower than a certain number. For example, Kelli has rated "sound quality" as very important (rating of 10). She may decide any service with a rating lower than 8 will be eliminated. In her situation, Skype would be eliminated because it scored only a 5. This process is followed until one brand is left.

The phased heuristic approach combines the two methods. Any brand with a low score on any criterion is eliminated first. Then, if a tie exists, the conjunctive heuristics method is used to decide between the two remaining contenders.

Consumers make purchase decisions using one of these methods, or some other approach. Each competitor seeks to highlight the advantages of its approach in order to maintain current customers and attract new ones.

1. Use Figure 3.15 to explain the purchase decision Kelli will make using the following methods: (a) conjunctive heuristics, (2) compensatory heuristics, and (3) phased heuristics. Elaborate on which brand is chosen and which brands are not and explain why.

2. Create a similar table for two of the following products that you have recently purchased. Explain which method of evaluation could be used for each purchase decision.

   a. An automobile
   b. A dinner at a high-end restaurant
   c. A life insurance policy
   d. A new pair of jeans

3. How would the multiattribute model be expanded to include paging services?

4. If a customer bases a purchase on affect referral rather than a multiattribute method for mobile phone service, which of the companies may have an advantage? Why?

MyMarketingLab

Go to **mymktlab.com** for Auto-graded writing questions as well as the following Assisted-graded writing questions:.

3-1. Consumers and businesses conduct external searches when they lack sufficient internal knowledge to make a wise decision. Assume you have $80,000 to $100,000 to spend on a sailboat. Locate four Web sites that sell sailboats. Select one in your price range. Why did you select that particular brand? What features are attractive to you? Would you want any additional information before making a final purchase decision? Would you purchase a used boat or new boat? Why?

3-2. United Raw Material Solutions, Inc. is a business-to-business marketplace that brings together buyers and sellers of textiles, petrochemicals, plastics, and electronics. Access the Web site at www.urms.com. Which members of the buying center would be most interested in this site? What services and benefits do you see for buyers? For suppliers?

3-3. Mymktlab Only – comprehensive writing assignment for this chapter.

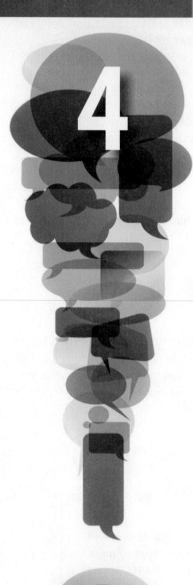

4

THE IMC PLANNING PROCESS

CHAPTER OBJECTIVES

After reading this chapter, you should be able to answer the following questions:

1 How can the three Cs of the IMC planning context form the basis for an effective advertising program?

2 What categories are used to identify consumer target markets or market segments?

3 What categories are used to identify business-to-business market segments?

4 How do the various approaches to positioning influence the selection of target markets?

5 How do the marketing communications objectives interact with the other elements of an IMC planning process?

6 What are the relationships between communications expenditures and company sales?

7 What types of marketing communications budgets may be used when developing the IMC planning program?

8 In addition to advertising, what other IMC components are selected as part of the IMC planning process?

MyMarketingLab™

⭐ **Improve Your Grade!**

Over 10 million students improved their results using the Pearson MyLabs.
Visit **mymktlab.com** for simulations, tutorials, and end-of-chapter problems.

PETSMART

IT'S A DOG'S LIFE (WHICH AIN'T HALF BAD)

Not so many years ago, pets kept in homes and on farms were there to serve a purpose, which typically was either to provide companionship or to serve as protective watchdogs. It wasn't unusual for a dog to sleep outdoors (no matter what the weather), to dine on the scraps that fell from the table at night, and to endure the aches and pains that accompany the aging process in silence, or with the occasional moan.

Today, the world of pet ownership consists of an entirely new form of "parent." No longer is a dog, cat, fish, potbellied pig, or snake just a diversion—the critter is considered part of the family. The pet industry has grown from simple dog and cat food, plus a few toys along the way, to a $51 billion per year industry. Companies vending products to pet owners have shifted with the times.[1]

PetSmart serves as an example of a company prospering in this environment of animal indulgence. In 1986, founders Jim and Janice Dougherty created Pacific Coast Distributing, Inc. The primary company business, a pet owner superstore, was vending food and other basic pet supplies. As time passed, the scope of company operations grew dramatically.

By 1988, PetSmart sold pet sweaters and emphasized cutting down on pet overpopulation. Soon after, fish and birds were added to the original line of pets for sale and the company launched a new doggie salon. It wasn't long until the company's original tagline, "Where high prices have been housebroken," was outdated. The most dramatic change introduced, a new corporate vision statement, appeared in 2000. PetSmart now operates, "To provide Total Lifetime Care for every pet, every parent, every time—which means that we offer solutions, superior products, unmatched services and superb customer service."

Why the change? The market continues to evolve along with the types of pet owners in the marketplace. Many pets now have different types of owners, including empty nesters, single professionals, and couples who have decided to delay starting a family. These new, more passionate pet lovers have a great deal of income to spend on their "babies." American families spend more annually on buying, feeding, and caring for pets than they do on movies, video games, and recorded music in any form.

The range of pet-related goods and services continues to expand. The list of items available in store and online includes indoor potties, pet perfumes, trench coats for dogs, and even a patented testicular implant for dogs that have been neutered, so as to not hurt the animal's self-esteem following the surgery.

Pet psychology opens up an entirely new realm. Many find relief from the troubles and woes of a dog's life through psychotherapy and animal antidepressants. More shallow pets can rely on cosmetic procedures to keep up their self-image. Harley-Davidson branded products are available for bikers wanting their pets to live on the edge.

PetSmart's competitors take animal pampering to the extreme. Doggie spas offer pedicures, professional dog walkers provide exercise, and massage therapy for those aching doggie muscles. The market is also filled with specialty pet foods with vegetables and other healthy nutrients in the products. At the other end of the spectrum, entire companies have formed to

Courtesy Kenneth Clow

take care of end-products, including service agencies named Doody Duty, Scoopy-Poo, and Pooper Trooper.

PetSmart offers vet clinics for ailing animals and adoption centers to find homes for pets (over 200,000 are placed each year). The company also sponsors charities associated with animal well-being. Today's owner wants an animal to have an excellent quality of life, from beginning to end. The net result is services oriented to ailing and dying pets along with their grieving parents.

PetSmart continues to adjust to changing conditions. The company features a strong emphasis on brand recognition and has adjusted selling techniques to meet the needs of various product lines. The company also opened distribution centers to make product delivery to each store more efficient. In 2005, PetSmart opened a series of pet hotels. Fifty have been built, with an eventual goal of 435 hotels across the United States. A traveling pet owner has new options available, which means less guilt about leaving a pet behind.

In general, a major shift in the marketplace took place. Pets are treated not in pet terms, but rather in human terms. This means that the number of marketing opportunities continues to increase and the nature of the competition continues to grow as the animal kingdom becomes more human-like each year. PetSmart vows to identify each new trend and respond accordingly, keeping pace in the dog-eat-dog world of animal comfort.[2]

OVERVIEW

The integrated marketing communications planning process requires careful oversight by the company's marketing personnel and any agencies the firm employs. Decisions are made with regard to matching products to marketing messages and communications tactics. Successful marketing efforts occur when the company's marketing team identifies every opportunity to make quality contacts with customers or potential customers.

This chapter describes the nature of the IMC planning process. As illustrated in Figure 4.1, it begins with an analysis of the company's context, including a review of customers, competitors, and communications. This allows the marketing team to identify potential target markets and positioning strategies that match those markets. Next, communications objectives are specified. Finally, a budget designed to achieve the communication objectives is matched with the IMC components to be employed. In addition, any international considerations are taken into account.

The IMC Planning Context

OBJECTIVE 4.1

How can the three Cs of the IMC planning process form the basis for an effective advertising program?

Developing an integrated marketing communications plan requires the analysis of the three Cs: customers, competitors, and communications. Understanding the firm's current situation and context within the industry makes it possible to specify target markets and positioning strategies. The other steps of the planning process can then be completed.

CUSTOMERS

Every product or service meets the needs of a set of customers. When conducting an analysis of customers for the purposes of IMC planning, the marketing department examines current customers, former customers, potential new customers, and competitor's customers.

Current Customers   The easiest group to study will be current customers; however, the other three groups are of equal if not greater importance. Members of the other groups may think in other ways or make decisions differently from a firm's current customers. They might also apply other standards to evaluate products and advertisements.

An analysis of current customers helps identify the type of message that will effectively reach this group. Discovering how current customers think constitutes the first step. This includes an assessment of what they buy, why, when, where, and how they evaluate products, both while making purchases and upon completion of those purchases. In

▶ **FIGURE 4.1**
The IMC Planning Process

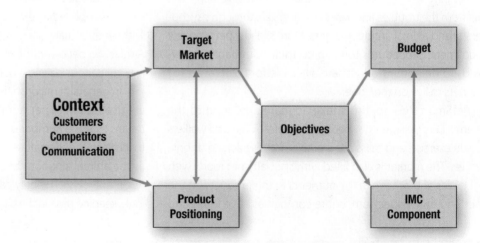

essence, the marketing team finds out what works for this group. The consumer and business buying behavior processes presented in the previous chapter may serve as a guide.

Former Customers   Marketers seek out customers who no longer purchase the company's products. Understanding why they defected may reveal valuable information, including whether a competitor's product enticed them away or if it was marketing tactics such as advertising, consumer promotions, or personal selling that made the difference. Then, the marketing team can identify methods to reconnect with former customers.

Potential New Customers   When seeking out potential new customers, the marketing team determines which customers the firm should seek to win. They may form a new target market or target markets. The advertisement for Philadelphia Dark Chocolate Cream Cheese shown in this section was based on the observation that chocolate lovers could be persuaded to enjoy cream cheese. The advertising department creates messages and utilizes media that matches this group's interests and preferences.

Competitor's Customers   An analysis of the processes that lead the competitor's customers to choose the competition's offering assists the marketing team in modifying the company's approach and/or its products to better meet their needs. Alternatively, company marketers may conclude that members of this group cannot be persuaded to switch or are not attractive because of purchase patterns or other factors. Convincing them to switch may be too costly, especially when they are brand loyal.

▲ One goal of this advertisement is to encourage people who love chocolate to try a special version of Philadelphia Cream Cheese.

COMPETITORS

The second phase of an analysis of the company's context involves examining competitors. The company's marketing professionals study the methods and strategies competitors employ to interact with consumers. Consumers integrate information from many sources. It helps to know what potential customers see, hear, and read about the competition.

Every domestic and foreign competitor should be identified. After listing the competing firms, an analysis can be conducted using primary research. In retailing, this includes visiting competing stores to study merchandise displays and observing the store's employees as they interact with customers. Members of the marketing department talk to vendors and suppliers that have relationships with the competition, as well as wholesalers, distributors, and agents. For businesses other than retail, marketers can contact salespeople in the field to obtain additional information about the competition.

Next, the competitive analysis includes gathering secondary data about those companies. The first items to look at are statements competitors make about themselves. These can be found in:

- Advertisements
- Promotional materials
- Annual reports
- Web sites

▲ Intense competition in the fashion industry makes a competitive analysis important for Daniel Taylor Clothier.

OBJECTIVE 4.2

What categories are used to identify consumer target markets or market segments?

▼ This ad for Ouachita Independent Bank was developed after an analysis of customers, competition, and communications revealed the importance of trust in choosing a financial institution.

By collecting as much information as possible about competitors, including messages to customers, the marketing team can respond more effectively.

The third task involves studying what *other people* say about the competition. Marketers often read trade journals. The library might yield additional news articles and press releases about competitor activities. The marketing team also tries to discern how competing companies view the organizations. This provides a sense of how others view a company in comparison with its competition.

An analysis of the competition assists the marketing manager in understanding the company and product's situation relative to the competition. When the situation appears to be viable, the company can build on this strength. When the company is incorrectly perceived or encounters a disadvantage, marketing efforts are made to reposition the product or brand.

COMMUNICATIONS

An analysis of the company's context by examining communications constitutes the third step. It includes the firm's current communications at all levels and in all channels. Marketers study messages to current and potential customers, employees, and channel members to find out what works and what does not. A further examination focuses on the communications used in the industry and by competing firms. This provides an important backdrop when making decisions about the IMC components.

A communications analysis provides information that assists marketing personnel and advertising creatives in developing marketing messages and selecting the best IMC components. Marketing communications materials, including advertisements, blogs, sponsorships, and others are designed to integrate what is known about the firm's customers, target markets, competitors, and the product's position with a consistent message.

Target Markets

When the analysis of the company's context has been completed, the marketing group moves on to delineate the target markets to be served as well as the company's approach to product positioning. As shown in Figure 4.1, these two activities take place concurrently. In this chapter, target markets and market segmentation approaches are described first, followed by product-positioning issues.

Target markets exist in two areas: consumer markets and business-to-business markets, which may be termed market segments. A **market segment** consists of a set of businesses or group of individual consumers with distinct characteristics. For a market segment to be considered viable, it should pass the following tests:

- The individuals or businesses within the market segment should be similar in nature, having the same needs, attitudes, interests, and opinions. This means that persons or businesses within the segment are *homogenous*.

- The market segment differs from the population as a whole. Segments are distinct from other segments and from the general population.
- The market segment must be large enough to be financially viable to target with a separate marketing campaign.
- The market segment must be reachable through some type of media or marketing communications method.

Market researchers spend considerable resources and time working to discover viable market segments. This process, known as **market segmentation**, consists of identifying specific consumer and business groups based on their needs, attitudes, and interests.

Market Segmentation by Consumer Groups

Consumers, or end users, are often the primary target market for a firm's offerings. Effective IMC programs identify sets of consumers who are potential buyers. The most common consumer market segmentation approaches are listed in Figure 4.2.

SEGMENTS BASED ON DEMOGRAPHICS

One primary method of segmentation employs **demographics**, or population characteristics. Typical demographic variables include gender, age, education, income, and ethnicity. Companies create goods and services to meet the needs of individual demographic segments.

Gender   Men and women purchase different products, buy similar products with different features (e.g., deodorants), desire products for dissimilar reasons (stereos, televisions), and buy the same products after being influenced by different kinds of appeals through different media. A recent study suggested that women control 66 percent, or $12 trillion, of the world's annual consumer spending. Women now influence or make purchases in product categories that were traditionally controlled by men.[3] For instance, in the United States:

- 96 percent of women are involved in purchasing high-priced electronics.
- 90 percent of women deal with financial advisors.
- 80 percent of women buy and sell stocks to make money.
- 70 percent of women are their household's primary "accountant."

Figure 4.3 offers suggestions for marketing to women. Some companies that have done well include Olay, Paige Premium, and OfficeMax. Olay advertises skin care

• Demographics	• Geodemographics
• Psychographics	• Benefits
• Generations	• Usage
• Geographic	

◀ **FIGURE 4.2**
Methods of Segmenting Consumer Markets

- Be helpful. Focus messages on how the brand can improve a woman's life.
- Engage them. Women are excellent brand ambassadors, so involve them with the brand.
- Focus on practical, not trivial.
- Tell a story that will resonate with females.
- Provide details.
- Be positive. Don't focus on female insecurities, focus on how the brand will help women.

◀ **FIGURE 4.3**
Tips for Marketing to Women

Source: Adapted from Nancy Pekala, 'Marketing to Today's Women: Focus on Life Stages, Not Ages," *Marketing Matters Newsletter*, American Marketing Association, November 11, 2009.

products for all women and tells women that the company wants to help them enjoy beautiful skin. Paige Premium encourages women to love their bodies and places a card in each pair of denim jeans that reads "I want you to love your body. Feel comfortable in your skin. Feel comfortable in your jeans. Thanks for believing in our product." Office-Max has created a fashion brand of office products targeted specifically at women.[4]

Mothers represent a group of women that have become increasingly attractive to marketers. This target segment is the fastest growing buyers of iPhones. They tune in more often and for longer periods of time to media Web sites such as Pandora. They are more likely to share photos and news on Facebook via a smartphone as well as a computer. Moms represent 20 percent of online users and an even higher percentage of mobile device users. They are the biggest Web spenders either directly through a mobile app or researching a product online then purchasing it later at a retail store. Many moms now use smartphones to access product and brand information rather than calling a relative or friend.[5]

Other marketing programs target men. Researchers have discovered that men are shopping more, whether for their own clothes or for groceries. To reach males shoppers, marketers seek to understand how males differ from females. Males tend to focus on product performance. Dyson has done well reaching males with this approach by focusing on the powerful suction and the design that creates it.

Men like doing things that they can do well and dislike things they cannot. They do not enjoy browsing and instead prefer looking for specific information. Amazon.com meets both of these needs by helping men purchase books and music online. Consumer lists, reviews, and suggestions provide concise information that males desire in order to feel confident about their purchases. Men prefer products that reflect their status in the world that demonstrate "I have good taste." As a result, they tend to purchase well-known brand names and look for other indicators of quality.[6]

Gender presents the opportunity to match a product with a large category of individuals. Careful thought should be given as to whether it should be aimed at only one sex, because gender roles have shifted over the past half-century.

Age Marketing programs often concentrate on persons of a certain age, such as children, young adults, middle-age adults, and senior citizens. Age can be combined with another demographic, such as gender. Consequently, older women may be primary targets for specific types of vitamins and medical products, such as those that combat osteoporosis. Young working women with children are more likely to notice advertisements for conveniences, including ready-made foods and snacks and even quick oil and lube facilities. Sexual dysfunction products and other medicines target middle-aged and older men.

In the past the focus of orthodontists was on adolescents. Today, a large number of adults are getting braces or other teeth straightening treatments. Since 2010, the number of adults seeking these types of procedures increased by 58 percent. The increase can partially be attributed to a national advertising campaign utilizing print, radio, and online ads focused on adults. One advertisement features a woman saying that straightening her teeth gave her confidence. Another says her pearly white teeth has allowed

▼ Ad advertisement for Bijan targeted to females.

her to date again and a man in his 30s states "It is never too late." According to Dr. Michael B. Rogers, President of the American Association of Orthodontists, "We're trying to emphasize the adult market and show how good they're going to look and how much self-confidence it's going to create."[7]

At the other end of the age spectrum are infants to 3-year-olds. A study by the Campaign for Commercial-Free Childhood revealed that by 6 months of age babies are forming mental images of brand logos and mascots. Other studies indicate by the time children reach 3 years of age, they recognize as many as 100 brand images. Reaching babies is easier now than ever before, primarily because of technology and parent use of technology. A Joan Ganz Cooney Center study indicates that 80 percent of children age 5 and under use the Internet weekly and 60 percent of children 3 and younger now watch online videos. In 2010, the average age children could have their own cell phone was 13 years old. Today, 1 in 4 parents allow children to interact with a mobile phone or iPad by the age of 2. Infants now have their own TV show, called Baby-FirstTV.com. Some content is free, other content charges a fee. Despite criticisms from parental and other watchdog groups, advertising to children (even babies) generates big business. If brand loyalty can be obtained at a young age, a company might have a customer for an entire lifetime.[8]

Income Closely related to educational attainment is an individual's or family's income. Lower-income homes focus primarily on *necessities* such as food, clothing, and housing needs; however, members of these households also purchase cell phones, automobiles, and other, more costly products. As income increases, household members can purchase from a greater selection of expensive items. The products, or *sundry* items, include vacations, more expensive automobiles, more fashionable clothes, and meals at higher-end restaurants. They are purchased occasionally by those who can afford them, but not on a routine basis. At the extreme, *luxury* items such as yachts and private planes target the wealthy.

The furniture industry uses income segmentation to create products and advertisements. One demographic group that has received attention recently is the "exhausted affluent." Individuals in this group generate household incomes from $100,000 to $150,000. They are affluent but identify with the working class. They bridge the gap between, "the haves and the have nots." In furniture, they desire style and quality rather than something overly fancy. Members of this segment want furniture to be right for them; that lets them stand out, but not so much that it says "I've been too extravagant and spent money foolishly."[9] In contrast, many furniture sellers focus on price, appealing to lower-income consumers, while another group offers high-end furniture to the wealthy.

Ethnic Groups The United States is becoming increasingly diverse. Ethnic minorities now represent $2.5 trillion in buying power. This increase represents both an opportunity and a threat: an opportunity for companies able to adapt their messages to other cultures and heritages. It threatens those that do not. Seventy percent of ethnic minorities state that ethnicity constitutes a significant part of their personal identities. Ethnic marketing succeeds

My first and only choice.

"When my child is ill, if I need a blood test or a prescription filled— St. Francis Community Health Center is my first and only choice."

Our team of healthcare professionals are here for you—including physicians, registered x-ray techs, cardiac rehab nurses, nutritionists, therapists, pharmacists, nurse practitioners to nurses and more!

ST. FRANCIS
COMMUNITY HEALTH CENTER
Franciscan Missionaries of Our Lady Health System
Future of Healing. Tradition of Caring.

920 Oliver Road, Monroe • (318) 966-6200
stfran.com

▲ A St. Francis advertisement targeted to women making health care provider choices.

Pavel Losevski/Fotolia

▲ Children are an attractive segment of consumers because they influence more than $500 billion in purchases.

in some, but not all, product categories. 62 percent of African Americans want health and beauty products marketed specifically to them, 53 percent of Hispanics said ethnicity is important for consumer packaged goods, entertainment, and clothing, and 50 percent of Asians said ethnicity was important for entertainment services.[10]

Chrysler Group LLC created a campaign targeted towards Hispanic involving television, radio, print, newspaper, and digital media in the top 15 Hispanic markets. The campaign spots were not trans-created or translated from English spots. They were produced for the Hispanic audience, although the ads were in Spanish and English. Large pickups are historically one of the best-selling trucks among Latinos, so the campaign focused on the Ram 1500 and Ram 2500. The creative focused on unscripted, real-life testimonies from Hispanic truck owners talking about the values that are essential to them and how the Ram truck is an extension of their lives. The campaign theme "A Todo Con Todo" is translated "To everything, with everything" was designed to capture the consumer mindset and "true essence" of the Ram truck for the Hispanic target market.[11]

A recent advertising campaign for the Ford Focus included print, radio, and digital messages targeted at African-American consumers. The idea for the campaign came from focus groups and consumer reactions to driving the car. Shawn Lollie, manager of multicultural marketing for Ford, reported "Some of what we heard is that it brought back good childhood memories and sparked a lot of emotions. We wanted to tap into those feelings – how you felt when you were a kid riding a bike. At the end of the day our goal was to show the driving experience in a way that sparked an emotional connection to the vehicle." The ad starts with a young girl learning how to ride a bicycle then quickly transforms to a new Focus with a friend in the passenger seat. The person still has the enthusiastic voice of a child as she talks about the car's features.

To market effectively to ethnic groups, marketing experts look for creative approaches that respect America's ethnic differences while also highlighting its similarities. Achieving this requires advertising and marketing agencies that understand the subtleties of multiculturalism.

▼ This Thomasville furniture advertisement appeals to the "exhausted affluent" and the desire for style and quality.

PSYCHOGRAPHICS

Demographics are relatively easy to identify. They do not, however, fully explain why people buy particular products or specific brands or the type of appeal that works to reach them. To assist in the marketing effort while building on demographic information, psychographic profiles have been developed. **Psychographics** emerge from patterns of responses that reveal a person's activities, interests, and opinions (AIO). The measures can be combined with demographic information to supply marketers with a more complete understanding of the target market.[12]

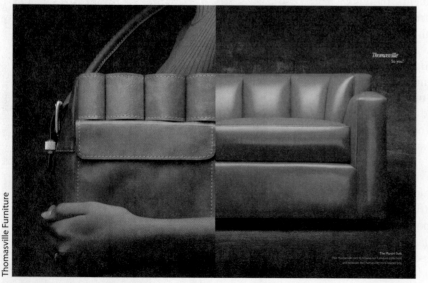

Thomasville Furniture

Strategic Business Insights provides a popular classification of lifestyles using psychographic segmentation. The VALS typology categorizes respondents into eight different groups based on resources and on the extent to which they are action-oriented.[13] The VALS typology includes the following segments:

- **Innovators**—Successful, sophisticated, and receptive to new technologies. Their purchases reflect cultivated tastes for upscale products.
- **Thinkers**—Educated, conservative, practical consumers who value knowledge and responsibility. They look for durability, functionality, and value.
- **Achievers**—Goal-oriented, conservative consumers committed to career and family. They favor established prestige products that demonstrate success to peers.
- **Experiencers**—Young, enthusiastic, and impulsive consumers who seek variety and excitement and spend substantially on fashion, entertainment, and socializing.
- **Believers**—Conservative, conventional consumers who focus on tradition, family, religion, and community. They prefer established brands and favor American-made products.
- **Strivers**—Trendy, fun-loving consumers who are concerned about others' opinions and approval. They demonstrate to peers their ability to buy.
- **Makers**—Self-sufficient consumers who have the skill and energy to carry out projects, respect authority, and are unimpressed by material possessions.
- **Survivors**—Concerned with safety and security, focus on meeting needs rather than fulfilling desires. They are brand loyal and purchase discounted products.

This type of information helps marketers design more effective communications. For instance, reaching Strivers requires advertisements that convey fun and trendy products. Ads for Believers should focus more on traditional and patriotic values.

Revel, the $2.4 billion resort casino in Atlantic City, developed an advertising campaign targeted to the VALS "experiencer" group. The target market was defined as "leisure and lifestyle consumers among the 47 million people age 21 and over who live within a 5-hour drive of Atlantic City." The emphasis of the campaign was not on gambling, but on "elevationism," which according to Revel meant "when you go to Revel, you experience something you've never experienced before—you feel elevated as a result of it. The TV, radio, print, and digital ads focused on presenting an elevated experience and featured the resorts concerts, cabanas, beaches, and bonfire—all of the amenities except gambling. The campaign and resort was built "on the belief that the more fun we have, the more fun we have!"[14]

▼ This Skechers ad is directed to the VALS group "strivers."

SEGMENTS BASED ON GENERATIONS

Many marketing efforts target generational cohorts, because the approach does not require the use of psychographic information, but does possess some of the richness of psychographics. Marketing to generational cohorts relies on the common experiences and events that create bonds between people who are about the same age.

Generational segmentation proponents suggest that people experience significant events during late adolescence or early adulthood. These events create an impact on social values, attitudes, and preferences, based on shared experiences. This may lead to common preferences for music, foods, and other products. A cohort group may respond favorably to the same type of marketing appeal. Figure 4.4 identifies six generational cohorts along with basic characteristics.

▶ **FIGURE 4.4**

Characteristics of Generation Segments

Source: Based on dana-nicoleta Lascu and Kenneth E. Clow, *Marketing Principles* (Cincinnati, OH: Textbook Media Press, 2012).

Adapted from Zenith Optimedia, March 14, 2012, http://printinthemix.com/fasfacts/show/543

Name of Segment	Year of Birth	Characteristics
Millennials	1978–2002	Spend money on clothes, automobiles, college, televisions, and stereos. Ninety percent live at home or in a dorm or rent an apartment.
Generation X	1965–1977	Focus on family and children. Spend on food, housing, transportation, and personal services.
Younger Boomers	1954–1964	Focus on home and family. Spend on home mortgage, pets, toys, playground equipment, and large recreational items.
Older Boomers	1952–1953	Spend on upgrading homes, ensuring education and independence of their children, and luxury items, such as boats.
Seniors	Up to 1951	Most have fixed incomes. Spend heavily on health care and related medical items.

SEGMENTATION BY GEOGRAPHIC AREA

Marketing appeals made to people in a geographic area or region is **geo-targeting**. Retailers often seek to limit marketing communications programs to specific areas where primary customers live in order to maximize the impact of advertising dollars. The increased ownership of smartphones with built-in GPS devices allows marketers to expand geo-targeting programs. For instance, during a snow storm along the East Coast, consumers in that area can receive Home Depot ads related to snow removal while other areas of the country getting ads related to fall lawn care or other topics of relevance. With geo-targeting, advertisements can be aimed to specific regions with messages that fit consumers, the region, and specific events.

▼ Med Camps of Louisiana could use geo-targeting to increase support for its work with disabled children.

GEODEMOGRAPHIC SEGMENTATION

A hybrid form of geographic segmentation allows companies to enrich geographic approaches to segmentation. Geodemographic segmentation identifies potential customers using demographic information, geographic information, and psychographic information.

Geodemographic segmentation may be beneficial for national firms conducting direct-mail campaigns or using sampling promotions. Mailing a sample to every household in a geographic area can be expensive and unproductive. Through geodemographics, samples are only sent to households matching the profile of the target market. For instance, colleges and universities use geodemographics to locate ZIP codes of communities that match particular student profiles.

One firm, PRIZM (Potential Rating Index by Zip Marketing) specializes in geodemographics. PRIZM has identified 62 different market segments in the United States. The company has categorized every U.S. ZIP code. The PRIZM concept is that ZIP codes contain neighborhoods of people with relatively uniform characteristics. Consumers tend to be attracted to neighborhoods consisting of people who are similar to them. Recognizing that more than one market segment might live within a ZIP code; however, PRIZM identifies the top market segments within each ZIP code.[15]

A PRIZM-coded map of downtown Jackson, Mississippi, identifies two primary clusters. The more predominant is the "Southside City" residents. This cluster contains mainly young and elderly African Americans employed in low-paying blue-collar jobs. They tend to have lower levels of formal education, rent apartments, and read sports and fashion magazines. The second cluster within downtown Jackson holds the "Towns and Gowns" neighborhoods. Towns and Gowns inhabitants also rent apartments, but members tend to be college graduates with better-paying white-collar jobs. This group likes to ski, reads beauty and fitness magazines, and frequently uses ATM cards.[16]

Monkey Business / Fotolia

▲ The fitness industry is often segmented based on the benefit each segment seeks from exercise.

Geodemographic marketing has expanded to the Internet. The Adfinity program designed by Intelligent Interactions allows an advertiser to direct specific ads to Web users based on user-defined demographics. When users visit Web sites, they often provide their names and addresses along with other demographic information. While the user is surfing a site, Adfinity's software can access the user's file in order to place a targeted ad on the page. To extend its power and effectiveness, Adfinity formed a strategic alliance with PRIZM. When a user accesses a Web site, the user is matched with data from the 62 PRIZM clusters. Based on the lifestyle and interests of that cluster, messages are sent that match the user. A person from the cluster "Executive Suites" will see advertisements about jazz or business books, because people in this cluster tend to enjoy those items.

BENEFIT SEGMENTATION

Benefit segmentation focuses on the advantages consumers receive from a product rather than the characteristics of consumers themselves. Demographic and psychographic information can be combined with benefit information to identify segments. Then the marketing team will then further analyze each segment's consumers.

Benefit segmentation appears in the fitness market. Regular exercisers belong in one of three benefit segments. The first group, "Winners," do whatever it takes to stay physically fit. This segment tends to be younger, upwardly mobile, and career-oriented. The second group, "Dieters," exercise to maintain their weight and enhance physical appearance. This group tends to be females over the age of 35. They are primarily interested in reliable wellness programs offered by hospitals and weight-control nutritionists. The third group, "Self-Improvers," exercise to feel better and to control medical costs.[17] The understanding that individuals exercise for different reasons provides excellent material for designing marketing programs.

USAGE SEGMENTATION

The final type of consumer segmentation examines groups based on usage or purchases, including the company's best customers or heavy users, average users, casual or light customers, and non-users. The objective becomes to provide the highest level of service to the best customers while promoting the company to the other two usage groups in the attempt to move them up to the next usage group.

Marketing teams identify heavy users with internal databases. Bar-code scanners, point-of-sale systems, and data from credit, debit, and in-house transaction cards provide marketers a wealth of information about customers. Many companies experience a situation in which 10 to 30 percent of a company's customers generate 70 to 90 percent of total sales. Instead of using firms such as PRIZM to create customer clusters, firms develop customer clusters from in-house databases. Customers are then placed in clusters based on common attitudes, lifestyles, and past purchase behaviors. This technique offers a business the following advantages:[18]

1. A meaningful classification scheme to cluster customers based on a firm's actual customers.
2. The ability to reduce large volumes of customer data down to a few concise, usable clusters.
3. The ability to assign a cluster code number to each customer in the database. Each number is based on the customer's actual purchases and other characteristics (e.g., address, amount spent, spending potential, demographics, etc.).
4. The capacity to measure the growth and migration of customers over time and from one cluster to another, which allows for the evaluation of marketing programs.
5. The ability to develop different marketing programs for each cluster that matches the characteristic of the clusters.

Occasionally, a company will try to develop a communications program for non-users. Such was the case of Carnival Cruise Lines and its campaign aimed at the 76 percent of Americans that had never taken a cruise. A dozen humorous ads were prepared with the theme of "land versus sea." Scenes compared disastrous land vacations to peaceful and calm moments on the cruise ship. Along with the humorous scenes, the ads pointed out the prices were competitive with the costs of land vacations dispelling the myth that cruises are expensive. Passengers were shown in roomy cabins and relaxing on deck to dispel beliefs that cruise rooms are small and cramped and that schedules were too structured to just relax and enjoy some private time.[19]

Business-to-Business Market Segmentation

OBJECTIVE 4.3

What categories are used to identify business-to-business market segments?

Another set of target markets may be found by identifying business-to-business market segments (see Figure 4.5). The primary goals of business segmentation efforts are to group similar organizations into meaningful clusters in order to provide better service.

SEGMENTATION BY INDUSTRY

When segmenting by industry, many marketers use the NAICS (North American Industry Classification System) coding system. NAICS allows the marketing team to examine specific industries, such as construction (23) or wholesale trade (42). There are also segments within specific categories. For example, NAICS codes health care and social assistance services as 62. A manufacturer of health-related products may find four segments, based on these subsections:

- Industry (NAICS code)
- Size of business
- Geographic location
- Product usage
- Customer value

▲ **FIGURE 4.5**

Methods of Segmenting Business-to-Business Markets

621	Ambulatory Health Care Services
622	Hospitals
623	Nursing and Residential Care Facilities
624	Social Assistance

The segments can be broken down into smaller subcomponents. For example, Ambulatory Health Care Services includes physicians, dentists, chiropractors, and optometrists.

The NAICS system divides the economy into 20 broad sectors using a six-digit code. The six-digit code allows for stratification of industries and provides flexibility in creating classifications. The federal government records corporate information and data using the NAICS, making it a useful system for identifying market segments.

▲ Scott Equipment can use the NAICS codes to target this advertisement to specific industries.

SEGMENTATION BY SIZE

Some market segments may be based on a company's sales volume or number of employees. Large firms with 100,000 employees experience needs that are different from mid-size firms and smaller companies with 100 or fewer employees. Marketing approaches will vary based on the size of a target prospect. For instance, for a large prospect firm a selling company may utilize outside sales staff to make sales calls. For mid-size corporate prospects, contacts are made by outside sales people after a company has shown initial interest through digital and telephone inquiries. For smaller firms, e-mail and surface mail may be used with inbound telemarketing. A salesperson would not make a sales call on the customer, because the revenue generated would be too small to warrant the expense.

SEGMENTATION BY GEOGRAPHIC LOCATION

Identifying market segments by geographic location can be a successful tactic. The approach benefits businesses with customers concentrated in geographic pockets, such as the Silicon Valley area of California. It works for other firms as well.

▼ An advertisement for Reynolds Protection targeted to businesses requiring protection services.

When the Applied Microbiology firm developed a new antimicrobial agent, the goal was to market the product to dairy farmers. The traditional agricultural marketing and distribution channel required for a national launch was estimated to be $3 million. Such a traditional marketing plan involved national advertising in agriculture magazines plus recruiting sales agents and brokers to introduce the product. Instead, Applied Microbiology used geodemographics. The marketing team identified areas with dairy herds consisting of 1,000 or more cows per ranch. These farmers were contacted for two reasons. First, large dairy farmers who adopted the product would purchase greater quantities. Second, the company's leaders believed that the larger farmers were the opinion leaders who could influence smaller farmers, thereby causing them to adopt the product as well.

Several separate direct-response pieces offering discounts for and samples of Applied Microbiology's new product were sent to larger farms. After sales started rising, farmers were asked for testimonials. The most powerful testimonials were incorporated into new direct-marketing pieces. One brochure contained three testimonials and validation of the product by Cornell University. After a dairy farmer adopted the product, direct-marketing pieces were sent to farmers in the surrounding area. The method yielded excellent sales figures and reduced marketing costs to one-third of the traditional approach. Using geodemographics, marketing costs were $1 million rather than the proposed $3 million.[20]

SEGMENTATION BY PRODUCT USAGE

Business markets can be segmented based on the manner in which the good or service is used. Many services (financial, transportation, shipping, etc.) have a variety of uses for distinct customers. For example, many times companies require protection services for various individuals. The Reynolds Protection advertisement featured on the previous page targets services for three different situations – hostile meetings, workplace threats, and employee terminations. The company also provides protection services in other circumstances. By segmenting the market based on the specific service needed, Reynolds can prepare marketing materials for the various client types.

SEGMENTATION BY CUSTOMER VALUE

Customer value offers one final method of business segmentation. Business-to-business firms are more likely to use this approach than consumer-oriented businesses, due to the availability of in-depth data about each business customer. A more precise value can be assigned to each individual business through sales records and other sources of data and information, placing them into low-, medium-, and high-value groups.

In summary, consumer and business-to-business market segments are identified many ways. In choosing market segments to approach, a marketer looks for groups that best match the company's goods and services, as well as the overall marketing message. Then the message can be structured to meet the needs of the various market segments and will be aligned with the company's positioning strategy.

OBJECTIVE 4.4

How do the various approaches to positioning influence the selection of target markets?

▼ To prevent cannibalization of its other teas, Celestial Seasonings positions each version for a different target market.

Courtesy of Celestial Seasonings.

Product Positioning

Each target market or market segment will be selected, in part, because the company, product, or brand position matches the segment. **Product positioning** summarizes the perception in the consumer's mind of the nature of a company and its products relative to competitors. Positioning features variables such as the quality of products, the price, methods of distribution, packaging, image, and other factors. Typically, however, two elements stand out: customer perceptions of the product along with the product's standing relative to the competition.

Consumers ultimately determine the position a product holds. Marketing programs attempt to help position the product or brand effectively. Marketing communications either reinforce what consumers already believe about a product and the brand or try to shift consumer views. The first outcome will be easier to accomplish. It also facilitates selection of target markets. When attempting to reposition a product, consideration will be given as to whether the new position continues to match existing market segments.

Positioning enables companies such as Procter & Gamble, VF Corporation, Sara Lee Corporation, and Campbell's Soups to prevent cannibalism among various brands within a product category. Campbell's produces five different types of V8 juice. Each one targets a different market segment.

- Attributes
- Competitors
- Use or application
- Price–quality relationship

- Product user
- Product class
- Cultural symbol

◀ **FIGURE 4.6**
Product Positioning Approaches

Celestial Seasonings offers several types of tea. The company's advertisement shown on the previous page is for health-conscious consumers.

APPROACHES TO POSITIONING

Effective positioning can be achieved in seven different ways (see Figure 4.6). Although companies might try two or three approaches, such efforts generally only manage to confuse customers. Using one approach consistently represents the best approach.

Product Attributes   Any product trait or characteristic that sets a brand apart from other brands may be considered an attribute. The Sony ad in this section targets business customers. The advertisement promotes the attribute of quality, because the projector provides stronger light. The message also suggests that the featured attribute outperforms the competition.

Competitors   Using competitors to establish position can be accomplished by contrasting the company's product against others. For years, Avis ran advertisements comparing itself to Hertz. Avis admitted it was not number one, but turned that position into an advantage, because Avis was willing to "try harder" for business.

▼ A business-to-business advertisement positioned based on the projector's attributes.

Use or Application   Positioning that involves creating a memorable set of uses for a product emphasizes the use or application approach. Arm & Hammer has long taken this approach by convincing consumers to use baking soda in other ways, such as a deodorizer in the refrigerator. Arm & Hammer is a co-brand in toothpaste, creating another use for the product and enhancing its position.

Price–Quality Relationship   Businesses that offer products at the extremes of the price range may position by price–quality relationships. At the high end, the emphasis will be on quality. At the low end, price is emphasized. Hallmark cards cost more but are for those who "only want to send the very best." Other firms seek to be a "low-price leader," with no corresponding statement about quality. Instead of focusing solely on low prices, Wal-Mart's tagline "Save Money, Live Better" highlights the importance of price and how it can improve the customer's quality of life.

Product User   Another positioning strategy distinguishes a brand or product by specifying who might use it. Kraft has reintroduced the SnackWells line of nonfat and low-fat snacks and positioning it for weight-conscious women. Ads in magazines such as *People*, *Cosmopolitan*, and *Glamour* featured the headline "Deliciously indulgent, perfectly portioned" copy that reads "at 130 calories, they let you be bad, and still be good." In addition to the 130 calorie snacks,

Exactly how bright is Sony's new projector?
Let's just say, your presentation definitely won't go unnoticed.

SONY

Courtesy of J.B. Stetson Company.

▲ An advertisement for Stetson using the cultural symbolism of cowboys as the positioning strategy.

SnackWell also has 100 calorie and 150 calorie packages – all positioned for the weight-conscious female.[21]

Product Class　Position can be based on product class. In the beverage category, soft drinks compete with energy drinks and others, such as breakfast drinks. Recently, Denny's repositioned its restaurant as a diner. Focus groups were not calling Denny's a family restaurant. According to Frances Allen, chief marketing officer for Denny's, "People think of the brand as a diner, with great comfort food at a great price, and they feel that incredible warmth and connection to the servers. There's a soul to a diner that is very authentic, very warm, and very accepting."[22]

Cultural Symbol　Positioning a product as a cultural symbol will be difficult. When the position is successfully achieved, the company holds a strong competitive advantage. For many years, Chevrolet enjoyed such a position. Chevrolet was advertised as being as American as baseball and apple pie. In its advertisement shown in this section, Stetson cologne is tied to the American cowboy and the spirit of the West. The ad copy reads that "The attraction is legendary." The purpose of placing this ad in *Glamour* magazine was to entice women to purchase the product for the men in their lives.

OTHER ELEMENTS OF POSITIONING

A brand's position is never completely fixed. It can be altered if market conditions change over time or a brand's target market shrinks. Competitors can enter a market and usurp a brand's position. Company leaders must then decide whether to fight for the position through strong advertising or seek an alternate position.

International Positioning　In the international arena, effective positioning remains vitally important. Plans are made to establish an effective position when a firm expands into new countries. Often the positioning strategy present in one country will not work as well in another. Marketing experts analyze the competition as well as the consumers or businesses that are potential customers. After this analysis, the marketing team chooses a positioning approach. Although the positioning strategy might need to be modified for each country, the company's overall theme and the brand image should remain as consistent as possible.

Image and Brand　Positioning constitutes a critical part of image and brand-name management. Consumers have an extensive set of purchasing options and can try products with specific advantages or attributes. Effective positioning, by whatever method chosen, should increase sales and strengthen the long-term position of an individual brand and the total organization.

Marketing Communications Objectives

OBJECTIVE 4.5

How do the various marketing communications objectives interact with the other elements of the IMC planning process?

An effective IMC planning process requires quality communication objectives. These objectives tie the organization's context, target markets, and positioning approaches to the ultimate selection of budget figures and IMC components, as depicted in Figure 4.1. Further, communications objectives guide account executives and advertising creatives

- Develop brand awareness
- Increase category demand
- Change customer beliefs or attitudes
- Enhance purchase actions
- Encourage repeat purchases

- Build customer traffic
- Enhance firm image
- Increase market share
- Increase sales
- Reinforce purchase decisions

◀ **FIGURE 4.7**
Communication Objectives

in designing the actual advertising messages. Communication objectives are derived from overall marketing objectives. Marketing objectives tend to be general because they are for the entire company. Some examples of marketing objectives include:

- Sales volume
- Market share
- Profits
- Return on investment

In contrast, a communications plan may emphasize a specific communications objective. Figure 4.7 lists some of the more common objectives. A large firm may establish different objectives for each brand within a product portfolio. Oftentimes, a communications plan for an individual brand emphasizes a single objective.

Some programs can accomplish more than one communication objective at a time. This occurs when logical combinations of communication objectives are identified. For example, the same advertisement can develop brand awareness and enhance a brand's image. Increasing sales can be accomplished through price changes, contests, or coupons. Matching the objective to the medium and the message remains the key.

Many marketing professionals believe that benchmarks are helpful tools. A **benchmark measure** represents the starting point that has been established in relation to the degree of change following a promotional campaign. In other words, the benchmark constitutes the baseline from which future outcomes can be assessed.

When market research revealed that a dry cleaning company's name was only known by 20 percent of the community's population and that the company held a 3 percent share of the city's total market, a benchmark was present. In response, the primary communications objective for the next advertising cycle became to increase awareness and market share to 30 percent awareness and a 5 percent share. Then a campaign featuring advertisements, coupons, and discounts for certain days of the week (Tuesday specials) and to senior citizens was designed by establishing a budget that matched these IMC components. If the company achieved the desired target, this would indicate a level of success based on the previously specified benchmarks.

◀ Benchmark measures can provide Ouachita Independent Bank with an indication of the success of the advertising campaign.

An OIB Welcome!

We are pleased to announce that Kathy Boykin has joined our team. She will lead the Hwy 165 North branch in Monroe. Customers will benefit from Kathy's years of experience in personal banking, lending and other banking services.

Kathy Boykin
Branch Manager

It's nice to rely on my bank. **OIB**
OUACHITA INDEPENDENT BANK

FDIC

OIBank.com

Advertisement provided by Newcomer, Morris, and Young

Establishing A Communications Budget

OBJECTIVE 4.6

What are the relationships between communications expenditures and company sales?

The final two steps in the IMC planning process include preparing a communications budget and selecting the IMC components to be utilized (Figure 4.1). Once again, these two activities occur concurrently. In this section, budgets are described first, followed by the IMC components.

Budgets are based on communication objectives as well as marketing objectives. Communications budgets and IMC components will be different in consumer markets as compared to business-to-business markets. Normally, a much larger percentage of the budget for business-to-business markets will be allocated to trade journals and telemarketing. Consumer markets are more likely to feature use of media such as television, magazines, and the Internet.

Many times, unrealistic assumptions guide the communications budgeting process. This occurs, for example, when a manager assumes a direct relationship exists between expenditures on advertising communications and subsequent sales revenues. For years, it was generally believed that a 10 percent increase in advertising would lead to a 2 percent increase in sales. Recent studies, however, show that increase will be closer to 1 percent; however, the actual amount varies widely.[23] Figure 4.8 displays a more realistic relationship between marketing expenditures and advertising. The factors present in the relationship include:

- The goal of the promotion
- Threshold effects
- Diminishing Returns
- Carryover effects
- Wear-out effects
- Decay effects
- Random events

Communication goals differ depending on the stage in the buying process. The hierarchy of effects model suggests that prior to making a purchase a consumer goes through

▶ **FIGURE 4.8**

Relationships Between Advertising and Marketing Expenditures and Sales and Profit Margins

An unrealistic assumption about the relationship between promotional expenditures and sales

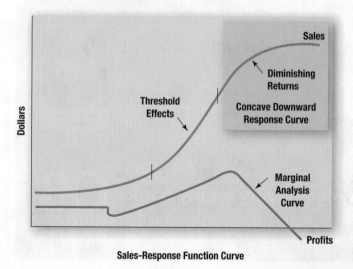

Sales-Response Function Curve

the stages of awareness, knowledge, liking, preference, and conviction. The objective and stage in the hierarchy of effects model influences the objectives, budget, IMC components, and advertising message that will be sent. For example, an early advertising campaign for the Sun Life Financial company highlighted the fact that people had not heard of the company, but would. Several humorous commercials developed awareness of the brand. Over time, other aspects of the company's services and comparative advantages were featured. The entire campaign began at one place (awareness) and ended at another (encouraging action). It would not be logical to expect that early marketing expenditures would create a dollar-for-dollar relationship with sales as the campaign moved to new communication goals.

THRESHOLD EFFECTS

As shown in Figure 4.8, the early effects of advertising are minimal. The same holds true for all communication expenditures. At first, few behavioral responses occur, especially when only advertising is used. Over time, a consumer who is exposed repeatedly to a company's marketing message recalls the company or brand and eventually becomes willing to make an inquiry or purchase.[24] Coupons, free samples, and other marketing tactics can help a good or service reach the threshold point sooner. **Threshold effects** are present at the point where the advertising program begins to affect consumer responses.

Threshold effects may be relatively easy to achieve in some circumstances. For instance, a new good or service may be so innovative that consumers become quickly aware of its advantages and are willing to buy the item immediately. Such was the case with the first iPhone. Also, when new products are introduced carrying an established, strong brand name, the threshold point will be reached more quickly.

DIMINISHING RETURNS

A point exists at which a promotional campaign has saturated the market. At that point, further expenditures have a minimal impact. The S-shaped curve displayed in Figure 4.8 represents a **sales-response function curve** and the diminishing returns from additional advertising expenditures. Diminishing returns are part of the **concave downward function**, in which incremental increases in expenditures in advertising result in smaller and smaller increases in sales. A **marginal analysis** reveals that further advertising and promotional expenditures adversely affect profits, because sales increases are less than what is spent on marketing or advertising.

CARRYOVER EFFECTS

Many products are only purchased when needed, such as washing machines and refrigerators. Promotions for these products must be designed to create brand recall. This occurs when the consumer has been exposed to the company's message for so long that, when the time comes to buy, the individual remembers the key company, which indicates that **carryover effects** are present. In other words, when a washing machine breaks down and requires a replacement, remembering Maytag brand will be the company's goal. Consequently, Maytag's products will be considered and the advertisements have effectively carried over.

▼ For products such as boats, it is important for advertising to create carryover effects.

▶ **FIGURE 4.9**
A Decay Effects Model

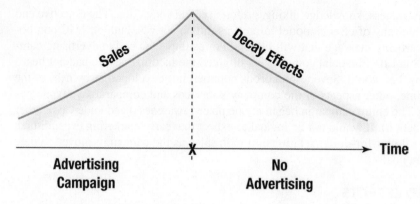

WEAR-OUT EFFECTS

An additional complication to the advertising budgeting process may emerge. At a certain point, an advertisement or particular promotional campaign simply becomes "old" or "boring." Consumers tend to ignore the advertisement or tune it out.[25] Some consumers may even develop negative attitudes toward the brand if they become annoyed at the marketing communication and believe the advertisement should be discontinued. This indicates **wear-out effects**.

Research regarding advertising campaigns over the last 50 years indicates about half of all campaigns last too long and experience wear-out effects. On the other hand, the same research indicates that the long-term effect of advertising remains twice as high as the short-term effect. As a result, marketers try to continue a campaign long enough to capture that long-term effect, but not so long that wear-out sets in.[26] Finding the balance between wear-out and long-term impact remains challenging.

DECAY EFFECTS

When a company stops advertising, consumers begin to forget the message, indicating **decay effects** (see Figure 4.9). In some instances, the degree of decay is dramatic. In others, the carryover effects are strong enough that some time can lapse before the brand drops out of the consumer's consciousness. The presence of decay effects means that companies should continue to engage in some form of marketing communications to keep the brand in people's minds.

OBJECTIVE 4.7

What types of marketing communications budgets may be used when developing the IMC planning program?

Types of Budgets

A communications budget can be prepared in a number of different ways. Figure 4.10 provides a list of the various methods that are used.[27]

PERCENTAGE OF SALES

With the **percentage-of-sales budget**, allocations are derived from either sales from the previous year or anticipated sales for the next year. Simplicity provides the major reason for using this method. A percentage-of-sales budget is relatively easy to prepare.

The approach also encounters problems. First, it tends to change in the opposite direction of what is typically needed; that is, when sales go up, so does the communications budget. When sales decline, the communications budget also declines. In most cases, when sales are declining the communications budget should be increased to help reverse the trend. Further, during growth periods the communications budget may not need to be increased. The method also experiences the disadvantage of failing to allocate money for special needs or to combat competitive pressures. Therefore, many marketing experts believe the disadvantages of the percentage of sales method tend to outweigh its advantages.

- Percentage of sales
- Meet the competition
- "What we can afford"
- Objective and task
- Payout planning
- Quantitative models

▲ **FIGURE 4.10**

Methods of Determining a Marketing Communications Budget

Auto Insurer	Ad Spending (millions)	Brand Recognition	Market Share
Geico	$600	98%	8.2%
Progressive	$506	92%	7.5%
State Farm	$455	76%	18.6%
Allstate	$369	63%	10.5%
Farmers	$203	59%	6.4%

◀ **FIGURE 4.11**

Ad Spending, Brand Recognition, and Market Share of Top Auto Insurance Companies

Source: Adapted from Gregory Bresiger "It's Ad Infinitum". *New York Post*, May 1, 2011, www.nypost.com/f/print/news/business/it_ad_infinitum_3ThF9xodhiknskcljdTPK.

MEET THE COMPETITION

The **meet-the-competition budget** seeks to prevent loss of market share. Expenditures are raised or lowered to match those of the competition. This method may be found in highly competitive markets where intense rivalries exist between competitors.

The potential drawback to meet-the-competition budgeting is that marketing dollars might not be spent efficiently. Matching the competition's spending does not guarantee success. Market share can still be lost. Rather than *how much* is spent, *how well* money has been allocated and how effectively the marketing campaign works at retaining customers and market share is the key.

The overall spending in the auto insurance industry has grown dramatically in the last decade. It is now over $5 billion. Each company encounters pressures to increase its advertising budget to match the competition, because the level of brand recognition often corresponds with the level of spending. Market share, however may not be affected quite as much since exposure and recognition of an insurance brand do not always equate to purchases. It takes time. Figure 4.11 displays the level of spending of the top five insurance companies, the level of brand recognition, and the market share.[28]

"WHAT WE CAN AFFORD"

The **"what we can afford" budget** sets the marketing allotment after all of the company's other budgets have been determined or while determining the other budgets. Money will be allocated based on what company leaders feel they can spend. Use of this method suggests that management may not fully recognize the benefits of marketing. Instead, company leaders view marketing expenditures as non-revenue-generating activities. Newer and smaller companies with limited finances often use the "what we can afford" approach.

OBJECTIVE AND TASK

To prepare an **objective-and-task budget**, management lists the communication objectives to pursue during the year and then calculates the cost of accomplishing each objective. The communications budget represents the cumulative sum of the estimated costs for all objectives.

Many marketing experts believe that the objective-and-task method represents the best budgeting approach because it relates dollar costs to achieving specific objectives. Unfortunately, a large company, such as Procter & Gamble, may find it difficult to apply. With hundreds of products on the market, producing a budget based on objectives for each brand and product category is time consuming. Despite the challenge, some form of the objective-and-task method of setting marketing budgets is used by about 50 percent of the firms.[29]

PAYOUT PLANNING

With a **payout-planning budget**, management establishes a ratio of advertising to sales or market share. This method normally allocates greater amounts in early years to yield payouts in later years.[30] Allocating larger amounts at the beginning of a new product introduction helps build brand awareness and brand equity. As the brand becomes accepted and sales build, a lower percentage of advertising dollars will be needed to maintain a target growth.

▲ The objective-and-task method of budgeting is effective because it matches specific advertising dollars to specific advertising objectives.

OBJECTIVE 4.8

In addition to advertising, what other IMC components are selected as part of the IMC planning process?

The payout-planning approach is based on threshold effects and diminishing returns concepts. A company that has reached the maximum threshold point should not continue pouring money into advertising that only results in diminishing returns. Instead, a company can maintain awareness and brand equity by more effective expenditures of marketing dollars. Future promotions and advertisement target specific market segments and consumer groups rather than simply increasing the volume of marketing dollars spent.

QUANTITATIVE MODELS

In some instances, computer simulations can be developed to model the relationship between advertising or promotional expenditures with sales and profits.
These models are far from perfect. They do offer the advantage of accounting for the type of industry and product in the model. In most cases, quantitative models are limited to larger organizations with strong computer and statistics departments.

Therefore, as the marketing team constructs a budget, the assumptions that drive the process should be considered. The newness of the product, the economy, and other complicating factors must be considered during the process of tying budgeting expenditures to marketing and communication objectives. A budget is finalized when the company marketing team specifies how funds will be spent on each of the major communications tools.

IMC Components

As has been noted, marketing communications consists of much more than traditional advertising. In fact, advertising expenditures may not make up the major portion of a marketing communications budget. In terms of dollars spent, media advertising normally accounts for about 41 percent of a marketing communications budget. Trade promotions receive about 28 percent and consumer promotions average about 28 percent of overall marketing expenditures (see Figure 4.12).[31] These percentages vary considerably from

▶ **FIGURE 4.12**
Breakdown of Marketing Communication Expenditures

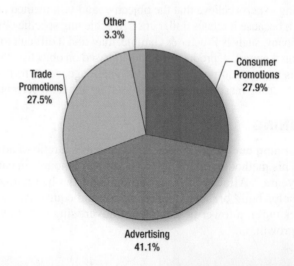

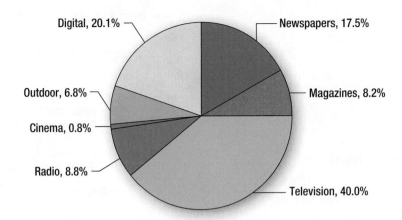

◀ **FIGURE 4.13**
Global Ad Spending by Media

Source: Adapted from Zenith Optimedia March 14, 2012. http://printinthemix. com/fasfacts/show/543.

industry to industry. Consumer product manufacturers spend more on trade promotions directed toward retailers. Service companies tend to spend more on media advertising.

Budgets also vary by product type. For example, for dolls and stuffed toys the average expenditure on media advertising as a percentage of sales is 11.2 percent, whereas for men's clothing expenditures on media advertising represent only 3.3 percent of sales.[32]

Selecting IMC components and media takes place in conjunction with preparation of the budget. Figure 4.13 highlights the ways global advertising dollars are allocated among the various media. Television ranks first, primarily because of the high cost of advertising time. Digital expenditures now rank second and are the fastest growing component.[33]

The clutter among the major advertising media has caused many marketing professionals to shift communication dollars to alternative methods. Figure 4.14 displays the breakdown of alternative media spending in the United States. Online and mobile advertising make up the largest category. This category includes lead generation, online display and video ads, online yellow pages, and mobile phone advertising. Branded entertainment includes paid product placement along with event sponsorships. The entertainment/digital category consists of local pay TV, video-on-demand, DVR advertising, and video games. Almost $12 billion was spent in interactive marketing, which involves direct marketing by e-mail and word-of-mouth marketing. The smallest category, but one of the fastest growing, is social media advertising.[34] It includes social media pages such as Facebook, Twitter, and numerous smaller, targeted social sites.

Decisions regarding business-to-business IMC components are different than for consumer products. Figure 4.15 on the next page indicates the ways companies allocate business-to-business marketing funds. The top categories of spending are for trade shows, TV advertising, inside sales/telemarketing, and direct mail. Trade journals used to be the mainstay of business marketing but now make up only 13 percent of marketing budgets, which includes b-to-b ads in consumer magazines and trade journals. The IMC components used in business-to-business markets vary from those chosen for consumer markets.

Choosing the best IMC components remains the challenge. IMC components are selected to reach the target audience and achieve the objectives that are set while

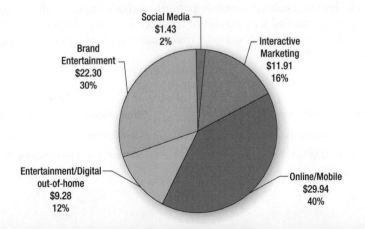

◀**FIGURE 4.14**
U.S. Alternative Media Spending

Source: Adapted from "U.S. Alternative Media spending," 2008 *Marketing Fact Book, Marketing News* July 15, 2008, p. 18, 22.

▶ **FIGURE 4.15**
Business-to-Business Marketing
Spending

Source: Adapted from B-to-B marketing
in 2009; Trends in Strategies
and Spending *Marketing Profs
Research, Inc.*, p. 18.

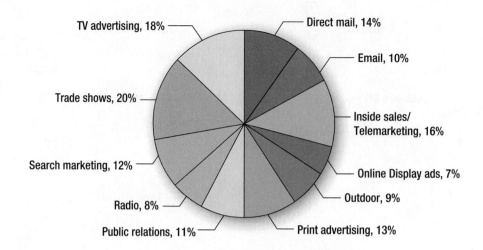

operating within the constraints imposed by budgetary concerns. Marketing personnel with a company and its external agencies analyze the firm's context, including customers, competition, and communication within the industry (the 3Cs) to provide the background for choosing IMC components.

International Implications

Globally integrated marketing communications (GIMC) programs are vital for international firms. Each message should fit a country's language and culture. Brand names, marketing ideas, and advertising campaigns designed for one country do not always translate correctly to another. Consequently, understanding the international market is essential. Figure 4.16 highlights the ingredients of successful GIMC plans.

Marketing campaigns do not necessarily require a unique program for each country and each cultural group within a country. It is important to make sure the company's products and marketing messages will be *understood in the region*. When needed, the message is tailored to an individual area. The goal is to *create a borderless marketing plan* that uses the same basic marketing approach for all of a company's markets. This allows each subsidiary the freedom to determine how to implement that marketing plan, in essence, to *think globally but act locally*. It also presents the opportunity to maintain a theme while targeting the message to a given region.

Another key to a successful GIMC is developing *local partnerships*. Local partners can be marketing research firms or advertising firms that are familiar with the local language and culture. These partnerships sometimes are formed by hiring a **cultural assimilator**. This individual will have an understanding of the market and speak both the language of the parent company and the local region.

Communication segmentation means creating a communications package that effectively reaches all possible target markets in another country. Many times both consumer and business-to-business segments are present.

A well-designed *market communications analysis* begins with the marketing team identifying strengths and weaknesses of local competitors and places in which opportunities exist. They must also develop an understanding of how the firm is perceived in the international marketplace.

▶ **FIGURE 4.16**
Successful Globally Integrated
Marketing Tactics

- Understand the international market
- Create a borderless marketing plan
- Think globally but act locally
- Local partnerships
- Communication segmentation strategies
- Market communications analysis
- Solid communication objectives

Finally, *solid communication objectives* should be established. Linguistics is a major hurdle. Translating an English advertisement into another language requires expertise, because exact word translations often do not exist. For example, the slogan of Ruth's Steak House, "We sell sizzle as well as steaks," could not be translated into Spanish, because there is no equivalent word for "sizzle." Therefore, the translator found a Spanish idiom conveying a similar meaning in order to solve the problem.

The IMC planning process becomes more complicated in international settings; however, it is crucial in creating an effective GIMC. Language, culture, norms, beliefs, and laws all must be taken into consideration. Literal translation of a commercial's tagline might not be acceptable within a given culture. Laws concerning advertising and promotions vary by country. Cultures view ideas and objects differently. These differences should be considered when designing a communications program.

INTEGRATED CAMPAIGNS IN ACTION

Skyjacker

Skyjacker was established in 1974 in West Monroe, Louisiana. The company manufactures suspension lift kits and shocks for four-wheel-drive trucks, SUVs, and Jeeps. The kits and shocks are sold to warehouse distributors and distributed internationally. Skyjacker provides retailers and jobbers with point-of-purchase displays and a strong integrated marketing campaign to pull the products through the various channels.

Skyjacker engages in both consumer and trade advertising. Skyjacker uses television and print advertising to sell the products to consumers. The company sponsors drivers and various off-road events. To support the retailers who sell the products, Skyjacker budgets money for trade advertising and trade support. The consumer and trade marketing materials can be found at the Pearson Instructor's Resource Center (www.pearsonhighered.com). The campaign includes a PowerPoint presentation outlining the details of the campaigns and examples of the collaterals developed by Skyjacker.

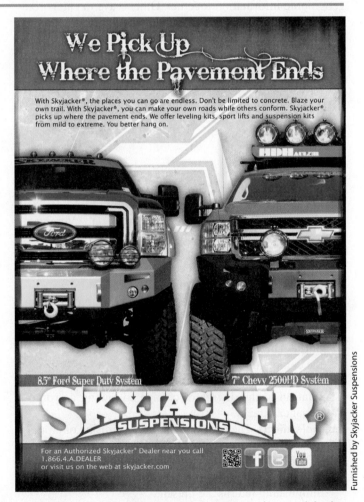

▲ Skyjacker uses an integrated marketing approach to reach both consumers and channel members.

SUMMARY

A marketing communication planning program begins with the analysis of the organization's context, including customers, competitors, and communications. When the analysis is complete, target markets may be selected in conjunction with product-positioning tactics.

Market segmentation identifies sets of business or consumer groups with distinct characteristics. Segments must be clearly different, large enough to support a marketing campaign, and reachable through some type of media. Consumer groups that can be segmented include those identified by demographics, including gender, age, income, and ethnicity. Markets can also be identified using psychographic, generational, and geographic delineations. Geodemographic segmentation combines demographic, psychographic, and geographic information together. Other ways to categorize consumers are by the benefits they receive from goods or services and by the ways they use products.

Business-to-business segmentation can be accomplished by targeting business customers by industry, business type, the size of the company, geographic location, usage, and customer-value calculations. Marketing managers specify the company's consumer and business market segments. All other promotions opportunity analysis processes are tied to the identification of key customers.

Product positioning represents the perceptions in consumer minds of the nature of a company and its products relative to the competition. Positioning may be based on product attributes, competitors, product uses or applications, the price–quality relationship, product class, or through the association with a cultural symbol.

Marketing objectives lead to the development of communications objectives that are matched to the product, target market, and product positioning. These objectives form the basis for developing communications budgets and selecting IMC components for actual marketing campaigns.

Globally integrated marketing communications efforts are guided by the IMC planning process. National differences, cultural concerns, language issues, and other challenges must be viewed in light of the target markets an individual company intends to serve.

Key Terms

market segment A set of businesses or group of individual customers with distinct characteristics.

market segmentation Identifying specific groups (target markets) based on their needs, attitudes, and interests.

demographics Population characteristics such as gender, age, educational levels, income, and ethnicity.

psychographics Patterns of responses that reveal a person's activities, interests, and opinions (AIO).

geo-targeting Marketing appeals made to people in a geographic area or region

product positioning The perception in the consumer's mind of the nature of a company and its products relative to the competition.

benchmark measures Starting points that are studied in relation to the degree of change following a promotional campaign.

threshold effects The point at which an advertising or promotional program has begun to affect customer responses.

sales-response function curve An S-shaped curve that indicates when threshold effects are present and when diminishing returns are present.

concave downward function A model of the diminishing returns of advertising expenditures on sales.

marginal analysis A model that shows when additional expenditures on advertising and promotions have an adverse affect on profits.

carryover effects The point at which a consumer has been exposed to the company's message for so long that,

when the time comes to buy, the individual remembers the company.

wear-out effects Declines in advertising effectiveness that occur when an ad or marketing communication becomes "old" or "boring."

decay effects Declines in advertising effectiveness that occur when advertising stops and consumers begin to forget about the company.

percentage-of-sales budget A form of communications budgeting in which budgeting is based on sales from the previous year or anticipated sales for the next year.

meet-the-competition budget A communications budget in which expenditures are raised or lowered to match the competition.

"what we can afford" budget A communications budget that is set after all of the company's other budgets have been determined or while the other budges are being set and communications money is allocated based on what company leaders feels they can afford to spend.

objective-and-task budget A communications budget in which management first lists all of the communications objectives to pursue during the year and then calculates the cost of accomplishing those objectives.

payout-planning budget A budgeting method that establishes a ratio of advertising to sales or market share.

cultural assimilator A person who is familiar with the local language and culture of a given country who is employed to help marketing efforts in that particular region.

Review Questions

1. What are the three components of analysis of the IMC planning context?

2. What four categories of customers are examined when analyzing the IMC planning context?

3. What three types of research are used when analyzing the competition?

4. Define market segment and market segmentation.

5. Define demographics. How are they used to segment consumer markets?

6. How can firms take advantage of target markets by gender?

7. What generational cohorts have marketing experts identified?

8. What problems are associated with markets segmented according to geographic areas?

9. What are geodemographics? How can they be successfully used to define market segments?

10. Describe usage segmentation and benefit segmentation.

11. What are the common business-to-business market segments?

12. Describe the NAICS approach to business market segmentation.

13. Describe a usage segmentation approach in a business-to-business setting.

14. Describe a segmentation approach based on company size.

15. Define product positioning and identify the types of positioning approaches that can be used in the IMC planning process.

16. What is a benchmark measure?

17. What common marketing communications objectives do firms establish?

18. Describe the natures of threshold effects, carryover effects, wear-out effects, decay effects, and random event with regard to communications budgets.

19. Describe the methods that can be used to establish a communications budget.

20. Which IMC components are more likely to be used in business-to-business marketing communications programs, as compared to consumer markets?

21. What is a cultural assimilator?

Critical Thinking Exercises

DISCUSSION QUESTIONS

1. Pick a product that you have recently purchased and that you have considerable knowledge about. Conduct a context analysis. Examine the customers, competition, and communications of the product and brand.

2. An analysis of movie theaters revealed the primary moviegoers tend to be between 18 and 24 years of age. Twenty years ago, 44 percent of the individuals in this age bracket went to movies frequently. Today, less than 34 percent are frequent moviegoers.[35] Conduct a customer analysis by interviewing five individuals between the ages of 18 and 24. Based on their responses, what suggestions would you make to movie theaters to reverse this declining trend?

3. Pick one of the following industries. Discuss the types of marketing communications used in the industry by various firms or brands. What are the similarities and differences in the communication approaches being used?
   a. Tanning salons
   b. Local night clubs
   c. Local dine-in restaurants around your university or in a specific area of town
   d. Soft drinks
   e. Bottled water

4. Make a list of five consumer goods or services segmented on the basis of gender but sold to both genders. Are there any differences in the product or service attributes? Are there differences in how they are marketed?

What are those differences? Do you think using a different marketing approach has worked?

5. Examine the list of demographic segmentation variables. For each demographic variable listed in the text, identify two products that are marketed to a specific demographic segment. Identify the specific demographic segment and explain why the product is aimed at that particular market segment. Identify one brand that has been especially successful at reaching a specific demographic segment.

6. For each of the following goods or services, identify the various benefits that consumers may derive from the good or service. Can you think of an advertisement or marketing communication that has featured the benefit as the central part of the appeal?
   a. Seafood restaurants
   b. Auto insurance
   c. Optometrist or eye-care clinics
   d. Soft drinks
   e. Aspirin or other pain relievers

7. For each of the product-positioning strategies discussed in this chapter, identify two brands that feature the strategy and explain how the strategy is used to successfully market the brand.

8. Locate five ads in a magazine. Either tear out the ads or scan them. For each ad, identify the target market of the ad, the communications IMC objective, and the product-positioning strategy that you think is being used.

Integrated Learning Exercises

⭐ 1. Use a search engine to locate five companies on the Internet that sell swimwear. For each company, discuss the types of products sold, the types of promotional appeals that are used, and the types of special offers used to entice buyers. From looking at each Web site, describe the type of customer you think the company is trying to reach. Of the five companies, which one do you think does the best job of marketing itself? Why?

2. A brand's product positioning strategy should be an integral part of the company's advertising and marketing strategy, including its Web site. Examine the following Web sites and identify the product-positioning strategy that you think is being used. Explain your choice.

   a. Polaris (www.polarisindustries.com)

   b. Edgewater Beach & Golf Resort (www.edgewater-beachresort.com)

   c. Celestial Seasonings (www.celestialseasonings.com)

   d. Sony (www.sony.com)

   e. Stetson cologne (www.stetsoncologne.com)

3. VALS psychographic segmentation can be a valuable tool for marketers as they prepare their marketing materials. Access VALS through the Strategic Business Insights (SBI) Web site at www.strategicbusinessinsights.com/vals and examine the characteristics of each of the groups. Then take the test to determine which group you belong to. How can VALS help marketers develop advertising messages?

4. A current trend for many companies is the development of marketing messages for specific demographic, ethnic, or lifestyle groups. This allows for a more targeted message than is possible for the mass audience. Go to the following Web sites. What types of marketing messages are on each site? How could the information on these Web sites be used to develop integrated marketing communication plans?

   a. Women (www.ivillage.com)

   b. Hispanics (www.hispaniconline.com)

   c. African Americans (www.targetmarketnews.com)

   d. Gays and lesbians (www.planetout.com)

5. Choose two of the following companies. Examine the company's Web site to determine what segmentation strategy the firm uses. Describe the intended target market for the Web site. What communication objective(s) do you think the company is trying to accomplish? What product-positioning strategy is being used? Explain your responses.

   a. Sports Spectrum Greeting Cards (www.sportsgreetingcards.com)

   b. Ty Beanie Babies (www.ty.com)

   c. Sara Lee (www.saralee.com)

   d. Skeeter boats (www.skeeterboats.com)

   e. Gold Bond (www.goldbond.com)

Student Project

CREATIVE CORNER

The VALS typology has been used by a number of companies and advertising agencies to create marketing materials. Your task is to design two advertisements for Yamaha boat. Pick one of the following pairs of VALS segments and design an advertisement promoting Yamaha for each segment. When you are finished, write a paragraph explaining how the ads you created will appeal to their respective VALS segment and how the two ads are different. Before

you begin work on the ads, go to the Strategic Business Insights (SBI) Web site at www.strategicbusinessinsights.com/vals to obtain more information about the two segments you will be targeting with your ads.

Pair 1: Innovators and Survivors

Pair 2: Thinkers and Makers

Pair 3: Believers and Achievers

Pair 4: Strivers and Experiencers

CASE 1 PLATINUM MOTORCARS: MARKET SEGMENTATION AND REPEAT PURCHASES

Benny Black drove up to his Platinum Motorcars location to begin another day's work in his 1997 Mercury Sable with 198,000 miles on the odometer. He calls the car, which he purchased on craigslist, "Goldie." Benny doesn't believe in using his own money to buy and drive fancy cars.

At the same time, he wore a high-end black suit. As he explained, "I'm always going to be dressed to the nines. I always have the matching pocket square with the same color tie. I'm letting you know where my brand is. I'm not going to be cheap. You know that right from the get-go. You know it's going to be expensive, but you're going to get the value in what it is that you're trying to do."

Platinum Motorcars grew out of a unique entrepreneurial experience. Benny said, "I had 2 years experience in the limo business. I told the wife one day that I wanted to start a limo company. I always had the affinity for wanting to serve people of wealth, with means, because I thought, 'If you can serve the masses, great, but if you can find a niche, and just reach a certain type of clientele, I always thought the easy one would be people with money.' My motto has always been 'a rich man will always be rich.' That's the ones you want to try to get to."

He continued, "I had that (limo service) for 2 years. I had already built a clientele base, but I thought there was too much competition, because I wasn't using my own limousine. What I was doing was borrowing a limo from my friends, pay them for the limo, get paid for my time, and then just try to give that great service to the client.

"I had to figure out a different way. I could utilize the same clientele but in something that nobody else is doing. So that's where I had the idea that I needed to figure out how I can drive nice cars and not have to pay for them.

"My biggest catalyst for that was that I got a call from one of the larger hotels, and they had a ballplayer in town that wanted to be driven around in a limousine. I picked him, and while I was driving I actually said to him, 'If you ever need a nice car while you're in Dallas, let me see what I can do for you.'

"And he said, 'Can you get me a Bentley tomorrow after the game?' This was in 2000.

"So I said, 'Yeah, I think I can make that happen.' I just got on the phone with some of the clients I'd been servicing, I called one client in particular and I said, 'I need to borrow one of your Bentleys.'

"They said, 'What have you got going on?'

"I said, 'I've got an athlete that wants to rent one to drive tomorrow after the game.'

"He said, 'What will you give me?'

"I said, 'I'll give you a thousand.'

"He said, 'Give me a thousand and an autographed jersey, and it's yours.'"

Benny completed the deal, making a handsome profit.

From there, Black developed the business model that has expanded to include rental services for high-end luxury vehicles, chauffeur services, and sales/leasing arrangements. His exotic rental cars include Aston Martin, Bentley, Rolls Royce, Ferrari, and Lamborghini. Sports cars are also available, with Mercedes, BMW, Porsche, and Maserati vehicles for rent.

Renters must meet high standards, including a $1,000 hold on a credit card, a $250 nonrefundable reservation fee, proof of insurance, and a significant charge for cancellation. Drivers must be 25 years old for some cars and over 30 for others. Platinum Motorcars serves an impressive client list, including major sports stars, celebrities, local business leaders, and even foreign dignitaries and tourists. As Black puts it, "I became 'The Exotic Car Guy.' I'm the guy you call when you come into Dallas. My tagline is 'We provide the lifestyle you deserve.'"

Bennie noted that several similar auto rental businesses had come and gone in the Dallas area. His explanation was that

Courtesy of Platinum Motorcars

▲ Benny Black turned his vision into a lucrative exotic car rental business.

the businesses catered to people who would drive a luxury car as a "once in a lifetime experience," such as for a prom, wedding, or some other major event. Instead, his company focuses on individuals who might desire a luxury driving experience on an ongoing (even if sporadic) basis. These customers, rather than buying a single car, are able rent from a wide selection for various events during the course of the year, including simply taking a weekend to drive a luxury vehicle.

Through connections with a variety of people of wealth, including the "new" and the "old" rich, and effective combinations of the Internet, social media, word-of-mouth, and exciting events and offers, the future looks bright for Benny Black and Platinum Motorcars. Most recently, the company expanded to a second location using the same marketing and business model.[36]

1. Provide an analysis of the following groups as they relate to Platinum Motorcars: current customers, former customers, potential new customers, and competitor's customers.

2. Define the consumer market segments served by Platinum Motorcars. Define the potential business-to-business market segments Platinum Motorcars could serve.

3. Explain the product positioning of the Platinum Motorcars rental service.

4. Using the Internet, locate Platinum Motorcars. What new businesses has the company entered? Do these make sense given the company's target markets and product positioning? Defend your answer.

5. Consider Benny's target market of individuals who could afford to purchase one of his exotic cars, but realizes the investment is not wise for the few times they would drive it. Design a print ad for the Dallas magazine aimed at individuals with incomes of $300,000 plus.

CASE 2 BOSE: HIGH-END SOUND REPRODUCTION

A case can be made that sound reproduction has become one of the areas in which technological innovations have made the most profound leaps forward. Leading the way are major competitors such as Sony, Philips, Tivoli Audio, and Bose. Many forms of sound delivery exist, some featuring earphones and headphones, and others through stand-alone speakers.

The Bose Corporation began operations in 1964. Amar G. Bose, a professor of electrical engineering at the Massachusetts Institute of Technology, became frustrated during his attempt to purchase a high-quality stereo system. He believed that the speakers that were available had impressive technical specifications but failed to reproduce the realism of a live performance.

Four years later, the first Bose product reached the market. In a very short time, Bose has delivered a series of innovations in sound.

Currently, the Bose Wave products are at the forefront of quality sound, including the Wave radio, Wave music system, and Acoustic Wave music system. Each is designed to deliver the most realistic sound through a compact, attractive device that will fit in any room in the home or office. The product can be linked with a dock that both plays and recharges an iPod. Another product allows the user to wirelessly play and store music from an Internet radio station. Other Bose products include headphones, home theater systems, speakers, and sound systems for various locations, including boats and businesses.

Bose systems are on the high end in terms of price. For example, the most widely purchased Wave music system had a list price of $499.95 in November 2009. To entice buyers, product discounts are routinely offered, including a $100.00 price reduction when the Wave is purchased with the accompanying multi-CD changer. Also, Bose offers 1-year, interest-free financing.

The Bose marketing program includes use of traditional media, most notably television, newspaper, and magazine advertising. The company's Web site allows buyers to find and purchase all items online. The company employs a limited number of retail stores that feature the Bose line. The primary marketing emphasis remains focused on quality. For example, Fortune rated the Bose QuietComfort headset, which cancels outside noise, as the best-quality option for headphones.

Although a company's reputation for quality may help to drive sales, outside factors can interfere. The recession which began in 2008 and continued into 2009 led many shoppers to cut back purchases, especially for more expensive luxury items. Bose was not immune to this trend. The company was forced to lay off nearly 1,000 workers, or 10 percent of its labor force, during the decline.

At the same time, Bose forged ahead, seeking to develop new technologies in areas other than sound. As the economy continues to recover, business analysts expect Bose to build on its core products while moving into new areas, furthering the growth of this innovative, energetic organization.

1. Explain how the IMC planning process would apply to future marketing efforts for Bose Wave products.
2. Identify the market segments that the Bose Wave products should continue to maintain.
3. Should Bose continue to compete based on high-price/high-quality positioning, or should it develop programs to reduce prices and entice a wider variety of shoppers?
4. What should be the primary marketing communications objectives for Bose?
5. What type of budget should be used for the Bose promotional program?
6. Which IMC components best match the target market, position, objectives, and budget for Bose products?

Sources: "Bose Confirms Layoffs," Boston.com (www.boston.com/business/ticker/2009/01/bose_confirms_l.html, accessed November 10, 2009), January 20, 2009; Peter Lewis, "Sounds of Silence Noise-Canceling Headphones Make Air Travel Quiet," Fortune (http://money.cnn.com/magazines/fortune/fortune_archive/2002/05/13/322899/index.htm, accessed November 10, 2009), May 13, 2002.

MyMarketingLab

Go to **mymktlab.com** for Auto-graded writing questions as well as the following Assisted-graded writing questions:.

4-1. Pick a product that you have recently purchased and that you have considerable knowledge about. Conduct a context analysis. Examine the customers, competition, and communications of the product and brand.

4-2. Use a search engine to locate five companies on the Internet that sell swimwear. For each company, discuss the types of products sold, the types of promotional appeals that are used, and the types of special offers used to entice buyers. From looking at each Web site, describe the type of customer you think the company is trying to reach. Of the five companies, which one do you think does the best job of marketing itself? Why?

4-3. Mymktlab Only—comprehensive writing assignment for this chapter.

5 ADVERTISING MANAGEMENT

CHAPTER OBJECTIVES

After reading this chapter, you should be able to answer the following questions:

1. What are the essential ingredients in advertising campaign management, including the role of advertising?

2. When should a company employ an external advertising agency rather than completing the work in-house?

3. How do companies choose advertising agencies?

4. What roles are played within advertising agencies and client companies?

5. What steps are completed as part of advertising campaign management?

6. What are the primary goals of advertising?

7. What are the key elements of an advertising budget?

8. What are the issues in the media-selection process?

9. How does a creative brief facilitate effective advertising?

MyMarketingLab™

⭐ **Improve Your Grade!**

Over 10 million students improved their results using the Pearson MyLabs. Visit **mymktlab.com** for simulations, tutorials, and end-of-chapter problems.

THE RICHARDS GROUP

"Some companies push products. Some sell ads. We sell the truth." This guiding principle appears on the Web site for The Richards Group, America's largest independent advertising agency, based in Dallas, Texas; an agency so distinguished that it has been listed as one of the six most influential agencies in the United States by Graphic Design USA.

The firm, which at one point consisted of fewer than 60 employees, all located on one floor of an office building, has expanded to a major office building on the North Central Expressway. The company has received many awards, including *Adweek* magazine's "Agency of the Year" numerous times.

The Richards Group generates billings exceeding $1 billion annually. The organization employs more than 650 marketing professionals. Its list of current and former clients includes a variety of well-known companies, Orkin, Fruit of the Loom, T.G.I. Friday's, Zales, Red Lobster, Farmer's Insurance, and others.

Beyond these simple statistics rests a story that owner-founder Stan Richards once described as "a rocket ride," which has taken him to being named as one of *The Wall Street Journal's* "Giants of Our Time." Many of the tactics employed by The Richards Group have been emulated by other agencies. Richards notes that his company did them first and does them best.

Richards prefers hiring new employees straight out of college, because, he says with a smile, "We don't want them picking up bad habits in other agencies, before they join us." These individuals quickly discover that the offices are all completely open, with no doors or walls. More significant, Richards notes, "What we do is commingle all the disciplines, so that in every cluster of spaces we will have an art director who sits next to a brand manager, who, for example, sits next to a print production manager, so that, in those interdisciplinary villages that everyone here occupies, nobody's next door neighbor does the same thing that he or she does. What you don't get is all the creative people sitting on this floor, then all the account management people on the next floor, and the media people on the floor above that."

"The reason I did that in the first place," Richards continues, "was that when we were 50 or 60 people, there was an extraordinary level of energy and electricity that just flowed through the place. You could just walk in and feel it. A lot of it was created by the casual contact people had with each other. When you have 50 or 60 people packed into a tight space, you see everybody every day."

"What agencies have always done, is when they reach that 120- to 130-person size, they then have to move to multiple floors. And the minute they do, they take a tight-knit bunch of people who really liked each other and understood each other, because they saw each other every day, and divide them up into tribes. These tribes don't always get along."

"There are lots of occasions where a creative will butt heads with a planner, because they have a different point of view. When you are packed into a tight space, and when you have a great deal of casual contact going on all day, every day, you get over that stuff, because they are your

Courtesy of The Richards Group

▲ Stan Richards

friends. When you're on a different floor, you seldom see them, and you decide, 'That's a different tribe up there, and they drive me crazy.'"

Richard's approach clearly works. "When we are hired by a client," Richards notes, "it's not just to make ads. We do so

Courtesy of The Richards Group

▲ Employees of The Richards Group

many things that are extremely important. That ad is what the consumer ultimately sees, but in order to get there, you have to have a dead-on strategy, if you're going to be successful. You go through the strategic process, you get to the right answer, and then you can execute against that answer."

Some of the success stories created by The Richards Group are relayed in various places in this textbook, including the long-standing Chick-fil-A cow campaign, the fascinating "ride" with Motel 6 described in this chapter, the company's 2010

Super Bowl commercials, and its relationships with Firestone and The Home Depot.

In the meantime, the next time you view a commercial for Corona Beer, featuring a laid-back setting on a beach in the Caribbean somewhere, and you leave the cares of the world behind you, Richards suggests, you are viewing another company success story. Corona has become the number one imported beer in the United States, passing Heineken, due, in part, to a successful advertising management program assisted by The Richards Group.[1]

OVERVIEW

OBJECTIVE 5.1

What are the essential ingredients in advertising campaign management, including the role of advertising?

The average person encounters more than 600 advertisements per day, delivered by an expanding variety of media. Television and radio have long been the advertising staples, along with newspapers, magazines, and billboards. More recently, Internet advertisements, social networks, and mobile phones apps offer additional ways to contact and interact with customers.

Today's marketers face several challenges. A company simply cannot afford to prepare advertisements for every medium. Further, each message should create a marketing advantage in a highly cluttered world in which people are increasingly adept at simply tuning ads out.

To be effective, an advertisement first must be noticed. Next, it must be remembered. Then, the message of the advertisement should incite an action, such as a purchase, a shift in brand loyalty, or, at the very least, find a place in the buyer's long-term memory.

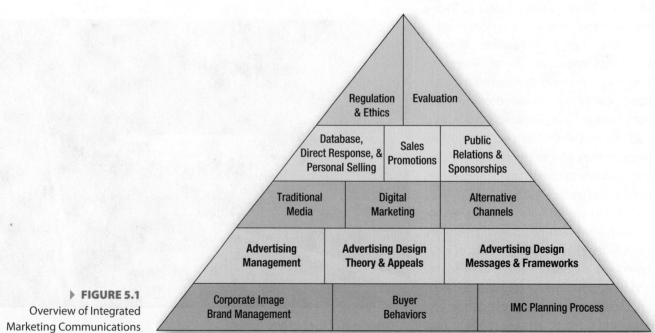

▶ **FIGURE 5.1**
Overview of Integrated Marketing Communications

Part 2 of this textbook describes the role advertising plays in an integrated marketing communications program. Figure 5.1 portrays the overall IMC approach. The three chapters in this section focus on developing an effective IMC advertising program.

Three ingredients create effective advertisements: development of a logical advertising management scheme for the company, thoughtful design of advertisements, and careful media selection. Media tools and media-selection processes will be described in the next section of this textbook (Part 3); however, media selection and advertising design go hand in hand: One cannot be performed without the other. Although they are presented separately in this textbook, they occur at the same time.

This chapter focuses on advertising management, which lays the groundwork for the total advertising program. One element is developing the **message theme**, or the outline of the key idea(s) the advertising campaign conveys.

Chapters 6 and 7 describe advertising design processes. The primary issues include choosing a leverage point, the major appeal in the advertising campaign, and the type of executional framework to use. A **leverage point** presents the key element in the advertisement that taps into, or activates, a consumer's personal value system (a value, idea, or concept). The **appeal** constitutes the approach used to design the advertisement that attracts attention or presents information to consumers through the use of humor, fear, sex, logic, or emotions. The **executional framework** explains how the message will be delivered. Methods include the slice-of-life approach, fantasies, dramatizations, and ads featuring animation. Figure 5.2 displays the advertising design elements.

Overview of Advertising Management

An **advertising management program** is the process of preparing and integrating a company's advertising efforts with the overall IMC message. The program consists of four activities:

1. Review the role of advertising in the IMC effort.
2. Select an in-house or external advertising agency.
3. Develop an advertising campaign management strategy.
4. Complete a creative brief.

Consistency constitutes the guiding principle of these four efforts. The company's goods or services and methods of doing business should match the advertising

◀ FIGURE 5.2
Advertising Design Overview

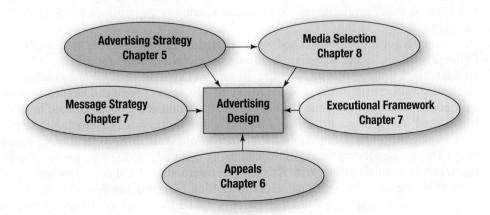

▶ Creating eye-catching ads plays a vital role in advertising management.

Courtesy of Volkswagen.

agency chosen, the strategy of the campaign, and the work of the advertising creatives. The result should be a coherent message stating the theme of the entire IMC program.

Advertising and the IMC Process

Advertising continues to be a major component of integrated marketing communications. It represents one part of the "traditional" promotions mix of advertising, consumer and trade promotions, and personal selling. These functions, along with other activities, such as direct marketing, digital content, public relations efforts, and alternative marketing strategies, form the basis for communicating with customers.

The role advertising plays varies by company, product, and the firm's marketing goals. For some products and companies, advertising remains the central focus, and the other components (trade promotions, consumer promotions, and personal selling) support the advertising program. In other situations, advertising plays a secondary role, such as supporting the national sales force and a firm's trade promotion program. In the business-to-business sector, advertising often assists other promotional activities, including trade shows and personal sales calls. In the consumer sector, the reverse is often true. Advertising constitutes the primary communication vehicle with other promotional tools (contests, coupons, sampling) reinforcing the campaign.

Oscar Mayer recently launched an integrated campaign entitled "It Doesn't Get Better Than This." The campaign featured new advertisements for all Oscar Mayer products (Deli Fresh, Bologna, Deli Creations, Hot Dogs, and Bacon) and emphasized an altruistic effort called "Good Mood Mission." Consumers were encouraged to share their good moods. For each one shared, Oscar Mayer donated 1 pound of food to families in need. The goal was to donate a total of 2 million pounds. Advertising launched the campaign through TV spots on the *Golden Globe Awards* as well as sponsorship of the show. The message was reinforced using print ads, video ads, package redesigns, public relations efforts with Kristin Chenoweth, digital and consumer-generated content on the Internet, and local event marketing featuring the Wienermobile (see Figure 5.3). The campaign illustrates the key role advertising continues to play in communications.

◀ **FIGURE 5.3**
Oscar Mayer's "Mission to Spread
Good Mood Food" Campaign

Source: Adapted from Tom Lopez, Senior
Director of Marketing, Oscar Mayer, Good
Morning Headquarters, January 16, 2010.

In-House Versus External Advertising Agencies

When beginning an advertising program, deciding whether to use an in-house advertising group or an external advertising agency constitutes the first issue. Figure 5.4 compares the advantages of an in-house facility to an outside agency.

Approximately 40 percent of companies use some type of in-house facility, due to its potential advantages. Managers believe the approach *lowers cost*s and retains better control of the message, which can be *aligned* with the brand and other company communications.[2] The CEO can *work closely* with the marketing team to make sure this occurs. Consequently, members of the marketing department may conclude they have a *better understanding of the firm's products and mission* and more *quickly produce* advertisements. An in-house program will be more consistent because of a *lower turnover rate in the creative team*.

Firms including CareerBuilder and Skyjacker perform all advertising functions in-house. Others hire marketing and advertising experts to assist in the effort. Some contract specific functions, such as writing, filming, recording, and editing advertisements. Most utilize media companies to plan and purchase media time (on television and radio) and space (in magazines, in newspapers, and on billboards).

An outside agency often *reduces costs* when compared to less efficient in-house facilities. This occurs when in-house employees spend more time on campaigns and ad designs than would an agency. The agency provides *greater expertise* and may have *access to top talent* in the industry. Advertising agencies offer an *outside perspective* not influenced by internal corporate politics and personal biases. Agency professionals often have a better understanding of consumers and trends, because they work with a number of clients over an array of products. Often knowledge gained from one product can be transferred to other, even unrelated products.

OBJECTIVE 5.2

When should a company employ an external advertising agency rather than completing the work in-house?

Advantages of In-House	Advantages of Outside Agency
• Lower costs	• Reduce costs
• Consistent brand message	• Greater expertise
• Better understanding of product and mission	• Outsider's perspective
• Faster ad production	• Access to top talent
• Works closer with CEO	
• Lower turnover rate in the creative team	

◀ **FIGURE 5.4**
Advantages of In-House versus
Outside Agencies

Source: Adapted from Rupal Parekh, "Thinking of Pulling a CareerBuilder? Pros and Cons of Bringing an Account In-House," *Advertising Age*, http://adage.com/print?article_id136701, May 18, 2009.

▲ Skyjacker is one of a number of firms that perform all advertising functions in-house.

BUDGET ALLOCATION CONSIDERATIONS

The size of the account affects the choice between an in-house team versus an external advertising agency. A small account may not be attractive to an advertising agency and often generate lower revenues. If the agency charges a higher fee to compensate, it becomes too costly for the small firm. Smaller accounts create other challenges. Less money can be spent on media time and space purchases, because the majority of the advertising budget is spent on production of the advertisement.

One rule of thumb marketers consider is the *75–15–10* breakdown, where 75 percent of the money spent on advertising should be used to purchase media time or space, 15 percent to the agency for the creative work, and 10 percent for the actual production of the ad. In contrast, for smaller accounts, the breakdown may be 50–30–20. Only 50 percent of expenditures are for media purchases. The other 50 percent of the funds goes to the creative and production work.

Unless the majority of the company's advertising budget can be spent on media purchases, it may be wise either to perform the work in-house or to develop contracts with smaller specialty firms to prepare various aspects of an advertising campaign.

CROWDSOURCING

Crowdsourcing involves outsourcing the creative aspect of an advertisement or campaign to the public. It offers an alternative to creating commercials in-house or hiring an external advertising agency. Crowdsourcing can create a viral buzz as users view advertisements online, recommend or send favorites to friends, and post links.

Doritos used crowdsourcing to create Super Bowl ads for the last five years. Fans are invited to submit ideas for ads. Doritos ads have been voted as some of the best of the Super Bowl. Although it may seem that crowdsourcing would be a cheaper method of creating a Super Bowl commercial, in reality the total cost stays about the same as for hiring a professional agency. The costs of running the contest, paying prize money, creating the microsite to host the contest, and producing the commercial combined with the time spent by Doritos and the agency in choosing from the thousands of entries are nearly equal to what would have been spent on an agency. Crowdsourcing yields the advantage of involving fans and generating the subsequent buzz that surrounds the contest for the consumer-generated advertisement.[3]

Consumer-generated ads are not always created for television. One January morning several hundred commuters greeted travelers by dancing instead of getting onto the train. The dance was captured by hidden cameras, and a day later it played during a commercial break on the *Celebrity Big Brother* television program. T-Mobile sponsored the entire episode as part of for its "Life for Sharing" campaign. Even though the ad ran only one time on television, it spread via e-mail messages, blogs, social networks, and Twitter until it had been watched more than 15 million times on YouTube.[4]

Harley-Davidson employs an extreme approach to crowdsourcing. The company obtains all creative work through crowdsourcing with agencies only being responsible for producing the ads. According to Harley-Davidson CMO Mark-Hans Richer, "We made a decision to turn over the major creative to owners because we have a passionate customer base who wants to engage with us." The creative comes through Facebook. Harley-Davidson has about 3 million Facebook fans. About 8,000 have signed up to be part of the Fan Machine, the creative forum for Harley. The Fan Machine group reviews advertising briefs, submits ideas, and votes on ideas from members. While the company offers some branded products according to Richer "it's really about the spirit and creativity and passion of the brand than the financial reward." A recent project received 300 idea submissions, with 20,000 votes for the best ideas. "What really shocked me was how good the ideas actually were. There were a lot of surprising insights. It's like a focus group and creative wrapped into one," he said.

Critics of crowdsourcing, including Stan Richards (see the opening vignette to this chapter), argue that while the approach may lead to innovative and eye-catching advertisements, no consistent message or theme results over time. The commercials may or may not reinforce the brand's major selling points or elements. Richards suggests that without a strategic approach, a key component of the overall communications effort can be lost.

External Advertising Agencies

Most companies hire advertising agencies to perform some or all of the advertising functions. When a company retains an external advertising agency, leaders commit substantial resources to the goal of expanding its audience.

Advertising agencies provide a variety of options. All sizes and types of agencies exist. At one end of the spectrum are the highly specialized, boutique-type agencies offering one specific service (e.g., making television ads) or serving one type of client. G+G Advertising of Albuquerque, New Mexico, specializes in advertising to Native Americans, a market of an estimated 10 million people.[5]

At the other end of the spectrum are full-service agencies such as The Richards Group that provide every type of advertising and promotional activity. These companies offer advice and assistance in working with the other components of the IMC program, including consumer and trade promotions, direct-marketing programs, digital programs, and alternative media (see Figure 5.5.)

Two other closely associated types of firms operate. *Media service companies* negotiate and purchase media packages (called *media buys*) for companies. *Direct-marketing agencies* handle every aspect of a direct-marketing campaign, through telephone orders (800 numbers), Internet programs, and by direct mail. Some companies focus on *consumer promotions*, *trade promotions*, or both. These companies assist in developing promotions such as coupons, premiums, contests, and sweepstakes. A new group of agencies specialize in developing *online and digital services*. Boxcar Creative designs *interactive Web sites* and widgets that can be used on multiple sites. Other companies offer *social media services* to reach consumers and businesses through a wide array of Internet techniques. *Public relations* firms provide experts to help companies and individuals develop positive public images and for damage control responses when negative publicity arises.

▲ Creatives at advertising agencies tend to have greater expertise and objectivity in creating ads, such as this one designed by Crispin, Porter & Bogusky for Volkswagen.

OBJECTIVE 5.3

How do companies choose advertising agencies?

- Advice about how to develop target markets
- Specialized services for business markets
- Suggestions about how to project a strong company image and theme
- Assistance in selecting company logos and slogans
- Preparation of advertisements
- Planning and purchasing media time and space

◀ **FIGURE 5.5**
Services Provided by Full-Service Agencies

Advertising management systems have moved from developing ads to sell a client's products to helping the client achieve total success in the marketplace. Doing so requires a more fully integrated marketing approach that includes a wider array of services. As client companies began to move to more integrated marketing approaches, full-service agencies such as Young & Rubicam, The Richards Group, and mcgarrybowen (see Chapter 6) have captured more accounts.[6]

Choosing an Agency

Choosing an agency begins with developing effective selection criteria. Figure 5.6 lists the steps involved in selecting an agency.

▶ **FIGURE 5.6**
Steps in Selecting an Advertising Agency

1. Set goals.
2. Select process and criteria.
3. Screen initial list of applicants.
4. Request client references.
5. Reduce list to two or three viable agencies.
6. Request creative pitch.

GOAL SETTING

Prior to making any contact with an advertising agency, company leaders identify and prioritize corporate goals. The goals provide a sense of direction and prevent personal biases from affecting selection decisions. Goals guide company leaders by providing clear idea of what is to be accomplished. They also help the marketing team as they make requests for proposals for campaigns.

Kraft Foods changed agencies for 20 of the company's iconic brands including Maxwell House, Crystal Light, Kraft singles, Cadbury, Fig Newtons, Planters, Oreo, and Kraft Macaroni & Cheese, in 2010. Dana Anderson, Senior VP of Marketing Strategy and Communications stated that, "More than ever, we're focusing on contemporizing and making our iconic brands more relevant to today's consumers. We're raising the bar with our agencies in order to deliver more creative and engaging campaigns. Our ultimate goal is to heighten the profile and performance of Kraft Foods brands." By determining the goal in advance, Kraft's marketing team was better able to select the best agency for each of the brands under review.[7]

SELECTION CRITERIA

Even firms with experience set selection criteria in advance in order to reduce any biases that might affect decisions. Emotions and other feelings can lead to poor choices. Figure 5.7 identifies some of the major issues to be considered during the process. The list can be especially useful during the initial screening, when the field narrows to the top five (or fewer) agencies.

▶ **FIGURE 5.7**
Evaluation Criteria in Choosing an Advertising Agency

- Size of the agency
- Relevant experience of the agency
- Conflicts of interest
- Creative reputation and capabilities
- Production capabilities
- Media purchasing capabilities
- Other services available
- Client retention rates
- Personal chemistry

Agency Size As noted earlier, the size of the agency should be considered, most notably as it compares to the size of the company hiring the agency. A good rule of thumb to follow is that the account should be large enough for the agency so that it is important to the agency but small enough that, if lost, the agency would not be badly affected.

Relevant Experience When an agency has experience in a given industry, the agency's employees are better able to understand the client firm, its customers, and the structure of the marketing channel. At the same time, the client company makes sure the agency does not have any *conflicts of interest*. An advertising firm hired by one manufacturer of automobile tires would experience a conflict of interest if another tire manufacturer attempted to hire the agency.

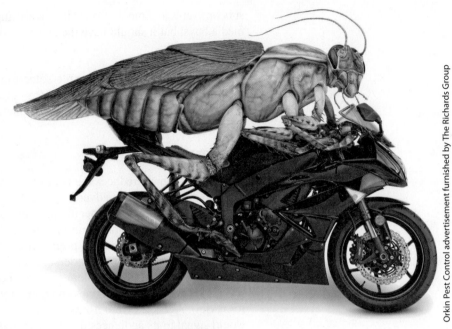

An advertising agency can have relevant experience without representing a competitor. Such experience can be gained when an agency works for a similar company operating in a different industry. For example, when an agency has a manufacturer of automobile batteries as a client, the experience is relevant to selling automobile tires.

The agency should also have experience with the business-to-business program, so that retailers, wholesalers, and any other channel party are considered in the marketing and advertising of the product. A number of advertisements in this textbook were created by The Richards Group. In addition to the Orkin advertisements in this section, The Richard's Group's clients include Home Dept, Sub-Zero, and Bridgestone. Note that the list does not include competing firms within the same industry.

▲ Orkin Pest Control is just one of the accounts being handled by The Richards Group.

Orkin Pest Control advertisement furnished by The Richards Group

Creative Reputation and Capabilities One method of assessing an agency's creativity would include asking for a list of awards the company has received. Although awards do not always translate into creating effective advertisements, in most cases there a positive relationship exists between winning awards and writing effective ads. Most creative awards are given by peers. As a result, they are good indicators of what others think of the agency's creative efforts.

Production and Media-Purchasing Capabilities These capabilities should be examined if these services are needed. A firm that needs an agency to produce a television commercial and also buy media time should check on these activities as part of the initial screening process. Many agencies either employ subsidiary companies to perform the media work or subcontract it to a media firm. The advertising agency does not necessarily need to make media buys, but it should have the capacity to make sure they are made to fit with the ads being designed.

Other Criteria   The final three selection criteria—*other services available*, *client retention rates*, and *personal chemistry*—are utilized during the final steps of selection. These criteria help make the final determination in the selection process.

CREATIVE PITCH

When the company reduces the list to two or three finalists, the selection team asks each for a creative pitch. The advertising agencies chosen to compete provide a formal presentation that addresses a specific problem, situation, or set of questions, a process also called a *shootout*. The presentations reveal how each agency would deal with specific issues that might arise during preparation of a campaign. This helps a client company choose the agency that best understands the issues at stake and offers a comprehensive approach to solving the problem or issue. For instance, after Bank of America suffered several years of corporate crises and publicity missteps, it put its $380 million account up for review. Agencies were asked "to create a new positioning for Bank of America" that would signal to its audiences that the bank was addressing its challenges.[8]

Preparing a pitch takes time and creates expenses for advertising agencies; therefore, they only want to prepare pitches that have a decent chance of being accepted. Spending time preparing a pitch only to find out later that the company had no desire to switch agencies, but were told by upper management to solicit pitches, is frustrating.[9] A company seeking to retain an advertising agency should provide sufficient time for the competing finalists to prepare the pitch. Pink Jacket Creative's Bill Breedlove reports, "I would prefer at least 30 days to prepare a pitch. Even 45 to 60 days would be wonderful sometimes, and for some companies."

Recently, Oscar Mayer, a brand under the Kraft umbrella, sought ways to unify its portfolio of products and contemporize its image with consumers. The mcgarrybowen agency demonstrated how Oscar Mayer could contemporize the brand and build emotional ties with customers. The agency's ideas were fresh, contemporary, and had the emotional spark the organization desired.[10]

When Kraft launched its Oscar Mayer Deli Creations sandwiches, the initial print ad developed by the brand's previous agency depicted a woman in a suit, standing with her arm bent eating one of the Deli Creation sandwiches. Karen Adams, senior director of advertising at Kraft Foods, stated, "People don't eat sandwiches that way." Instead, new ads were created showing real people in real-life situations eating sandwiches.[11] The Oscar Mayer ad in this section depicts a construction worker ready to enjoy a Deli Creation sandwich with the tagline "Oh goody, it's Monday."

Successful creative pitches result from hard work and thorough planning. Figure 5.8 highlights some of the "dos" and "don'ts" for advertising agencies in making pitches.

▼ Selecting the right media ensures that consumers who are the most likely to purchase Gold Bond Body Lotion will see this advertisement.

Courtesy of Chattem, Inc.

AGENCY SELECTION

During the presentation phase, company marketers meet with agency creatives, media buyers, account executives, and other people who will work on the account. *Chemistry* between employees of the two different firms becomes critical. The client company's leaders should be convinced that they will work well together. Chemistry can break or make the final decision.[12]

- Do listen. Allow the client to talk.
- Do your preparation. Know the client and its business.
- Do make a good first impression. Dress up, not down.
- Do a convincing job of presenting. Believe in what you are presenting.
- Don't assume all clients are the same. Each has a unique need.
- Don't try to solve the entire problem in the pitch.
- Don't be critical of the product or the competition.
- Don't overpromise. It will come back to haunt you.
- Don't spend a lot of time pitching credentials and references.

◀ **FIGURE 5.8**
Pitching Do's and Don'ts

Source: Based on Heather Jacobs, "How to Make Sure Your Pitch Is Heard," *B&T Weekly* 57, no. 2597 (February 2, 2007), pp. 14–16.

After completing the selection process, the agency and the company work together to prepare the advertising campaign. The account executive, account planner, and advertising creative all plays key roles in the process.

Roles of Advertising Personnel

Advertising agency employees perform a wide variety of roles. In small agencies, an individual may perform multiple roles. In a large agency, multiple individuals will be employed in the various departments and perform similar functions. The primary roles within the agency consist of the account executives, creatives, traffic managers, and account planners.

OBJECTIVE 5.4

What roles are played within advertising agencies and client companies?

ACCOUNT EXECUTIVES

The account executive serves as the go-between for the advertising agency and the client company. The executive will be actively involved in soliciting the account, finalizing details of the contract, and working with personnel within the agency to make sure the advertisements meet the client's specifications. The account executive often helps the company define the theme of the overall IMC program and provides other support, as needed.

CREATIVES

Creatives develop and design advertisements. They are either members of advertising agencies or freelancers. Some smaller companies provide only creative advertising services without becoming involved in other marketing programs and activities. Creatives may appear to hold the "glamour" jobs in agencies, because they get to actually create ads and marketing materials. At the same time, creatives work long hours and face enormous pressures to design effective advertisements that produce tangible results.

TRAFFIC MANAGERS

The traffic manager works closely with the advertising agency's account executive, creatives, and production staff. The manager's responsibilities include scheduling the various aspects of the agency's work to make sure it is completed on time. During production, the traffic manager will be responsible for making sure props, actors, and make sure that all other items needed have been ordered and are in place at the time of the filming or recording.

Maxwell House/Kraft Foods Inc.

▲ The account planner represents the consumer's viewpoint so that creatives can design effective advertisements, such as this one for Maxwell House coffee.

ACCOUNT PLANNERS

The account planner provides the voice and will be the advocate for the consumer within the advertising agency. The planner makes sure the creative team understands the consumer (or business). Account planners interact with the account executive and the client to understand the target audience of the ad campaign. The planner then works to make sure creative messages reach the right customers.

The account planner assists the client in developing long-term communication strategies and provides direction for individual advertising campaigns. In small agencies, the role may be performed by the account executive. Larger firms employ separate individuals and or departments to conduct the account planning role.

THE ROLE OF QUALITY COMMUNICATION

Quality communication will be a vital part of the relationship between a client company and an advertising agency. A recent survey of 250 senior executives of marketing and advertising agencies revealed that these managers believed that at least 30 percent of their staff's time was wasted or used ineffectively because of poor communication with clients. Issues such as poor competitive information and lack of clarity about the company or brand's position in the marketplace were common. More disturbing was that 75 percent of the ad agencies indicated that clients go through at least five significant changes in the directions they give to agencies and about what they want the agencies to do. The agencies reported that, on average, they dealt with five different individuals from the client company, each with a different agenda and different directions for the agency.[13]

The company's marketing department manager works closely with the advertising agency's account manager to overcome these obstacles. The manager remains aware that missteps and changes to an advertising program are costly in terms of additional advertising agency fees as well as the less effective campaign that might result.

Clients want to know if they are getting a good value. Many clients worry that they do not understand the relationship between an agency's cost and the actual value it renders. *Stewardship reports* help clients review the creative process as well as the outcome. Updating clients will be critical, especially when large amounts of money are spent on advertising.[14]

Advertising Campaign Management

OBJECTIVE 5.5

What steps are completed as part of advertising campaign management?

Advertising campaign management is the process of preparing and integrating a specific advertising program. Whether an in-house employee or an external agency performs the work, the marketing manager oversees the development of the advertising campaign. An effective campaign consists of five steps:

1. Conduct and review the advertising research.
2. Establish advertising objectives consistent with the overall IMC program.
3. Review the advertising budget.

4. Select the appropriate media based on the viewing habits of the target market.

5. Prepare a creative brief.

The advertising program should be consistent with every part of the IMC program as well as the company's mission and make sure the firm presents a clear message to key target markets. Advertising efforts are refined to gain the maximum benefit from promotional dollars.

Advertising Research

After being hired, the advertising agency's, team immediately seeks to understand the client's company and products. Clients try to provide accurate and timely information that assist the agency in the preparation of the campaign. To create an effective advertising program, the advertising agency's creative personnel requires information about customers, why they purchase the product, and what exactly they seek to purchase.

Products are not typically purchased solely for attributes. Customers also consider other benefits the product provides. Individuals purchasing makeup, cologne, perfume, and other beauty products may not care about the ingredients, but care a great deal about how these items will make them look or smell. Advertising research goes beyond identifying demographic profiles or target markets. It identifies the brand's competitors and the communications used in the industry.

To best understand a company's customers, their purchasing habits, and the other key ideas about them, various agencies employ various forms of advertising research. Key insights about how products are used, when they are used, and why can emerge from effective research. Two primary approaches exist.

Product-specific research involves identifying key product characteristics that become selling points. For example, the marketing team might try to discover the most desirable features are "apps" for a cell phone. The team may find that certain apps are used when customers are bored and are just passing time, whereas others provide specific functional information, such as the location of a restaurant while the customer drives to dinner. One feature or the other becomes the focal point of a commercial.

Consumer-oriented research helps marketers understand the context of a product's use. An *anthropological* approach involves direct observation of consumers using the good or service. Other customer-oriented research may feature a *sociological* analysis of social class issues, trends, and family life cycle changes. A third customer-oriented approach analyzes *psychological* motives for product purchases, such as feeling sexy, powerful, or intelligent.

Before developing the campaign for Scotts Miracle-Grow lawn fertilizer, The Richards Group turned to marketing

▼ Consumer-oriented research provides valuable information, such as why consumers could be enticed to use Philadelphia Cream Cheese in their cooking recipes.

pheel **refreshed**

PHILADELPHIA Summer Potato Salad

Prep Time: 30 min. plus refrigerating
Total Time: 1 hour 30 min. (incl. refrigerating)
Makes: 22 servings, about ½ cup each

What You Need

- 3 lb. baby red potatoes, quartered
- ½ cup water
- ¼ cup KRAFT Zesty Italian Dressing
- 1 tub (10 oz.) PHILADELPHIA Reduced Fat Italian Cheese & Herb Cooking Creme
- ¼ cup KRAFT Shredded Parmesan Cheese
- 1½ cups cherry tomatoes, halved
- 2 stalks celery, sliced

Make It

Place potatoes in 2-qt. microwaveable dish. Add water; cover. Microwave on HIGH 12 to 15 min. or until tender; drain. Place in large bowl. Toss with dressing. Refrigerate 1 hour until cooled. Add remaining ingredients; mix.

Spoon it in and make an ordinary dish, anything but. **pheel the moment**

cookphilly.com

When you're sleeping, we look
just like those big fancy hotels.
Motel 6

▲ The ad for Motel 6 was inspired by a focus group and a comment made by one of the participants: "If my eyes are closed, all hotel rooms look alike."

research. The company interviewed 4,000 consumers and gained the valuable insight that "people would change their behavior if an expert spoke to them about lawn care." The research revealed that many people reported that usually someone in the neighborhood is "knowledgeable about lawn care." Using this information, The Richards Group made the expert Scottish, a mnemonic play on the Scotts brand. Early evaluations of the campaign show it resonates well with consumers.[15]

Sometimes a company's marketing team becomes so close to products and customers that they do not see these issues. Consequently, agencies often seek out more information clients provide. One common approach used by agencies to understand a client's customers is a **focus group**, which consists of consumers who are retained to talk about a particular topic, product, or brand.

MOTEL 6 AND THE RICHARDS GROUP

During the interview with Stan Richards conducted for the opening vignette in this chapter, he talked about a "perfect example" of understanding a client's customers using focus groups. "We've worked with Motel 6 for 24 years," he said, "and the beginning of that relationship was a remarkable insight."

"The insight came out of our research, which was primarily qualitative. We sat behind a glass window in a focus room setting. Our account planner sat at the head of the table, moderating the session. We've got a dozen people in the room whom we recruited by phone. They don't know why they're in the room. We know that they all use Motel 6. The moderator asks, 'Where do you stay when you're on the road?' They go around the table and nobody says, 'Motel 6.'"

"The moderator pushes further and says, 'Well, where else do you stay?' They go around the table again, and nobody says, 'Motel 6.' Now, why is that? They didn't know who the other people in the room were, and they didn't want to be perceived as being poor or cheap."

"Now, finally, you get somebody, by going around the table again, to say, 'You know, if it's late at night, I'll stop at a Motel 6, and I can save enough money to buy a tank of gas.' And then, somebody else across the table would say, 'I do the same thing, and I save enough money to bring a gift home to the grandkids.' And all of a sudden, the character of the room changed, because everybody had a story like that. What happened was a move from embarrassment to pride in the benefits of frugality.

"That's what the insight was all about. I am a frugal person, and if my eyes are closed, all hotel rooms look alike. I don't see any reason to overspend for lodging, when I can find a perfectly good place like Motel 6."

From this insight, The Richards Group developed the theme, tagline, and advertising approach for Motel 6 that are still used today. Richards noted that the phrase, "A clean, comfortable room, at the lowest price of any national chain," appears in every spot.[16]

Richards argues that this approach highlights the difference between crowdsourcing and conducting the type of quality research that leads to a better outcome. "Let's suppose that Motel 6 has cast a wide net; that 1,000 people are working on creative, and then we're going to run the one they like best. Just run a contest. It is so unlikely that they would have gotten to the insight that really propelled their business. The insight was a really simple one, but it wouldn't have come out if people were simply just trying to sell Motel 6."

Advertising Goals

Establishing and clarifying the advertising goals that are derived from the firm's overall communication objectives constitutes the second step of the advertising process. Several advertising goals are central to the IMC process (see Figure 5.9).[17]

BUILDING BRAND AWARENESS

A strong global brand and corporate image should be a key advertising goal. Building a brand's image begins with developing brand awareness. *Brand awareness* means the consumers recognize and remember a particular brand or company name when they consider purchasing options. Advertising can increase brand awareness.

In business-to-business marketing, brand awareness leads to being considered by members of the buying center, because business customers recognize the brand name of the goods or services the company offers. Brand awareness becomes especially important in modified rebuy situations, when a firm looks to change to a new vendor or evaluates a product that has not been purchased recently. In new buy situations, members of the buying center spend more time seeking prospective vendors than they will for modified rebuys. Consequently, brand equity creates a major advantage for any company with such recognition.

Successful brands possess two characteristics: the top of mind and the consumers' top choice. When consumers are asked to identify brands that quickly come to mind from a product category, one or two particular brands are nearly always mentioned. These names are the **top-of-mind brands**. For example, when asked to identify fast-food hamburger restaurants, McDonald's and Burger King almost always head the list. The same may be true for Nike and Reebok athletic shoes, and may occur both in the United States and in other countries.

The term **top choice** suggests what the term implies: A top-choice brand is the first or second pick when a consumer reviews her evoked set of possible purchasing alternatives. Many products become top-of-mind or top choice due to brand equity. Advertising can strengthen brand equity.

PROVIDING INFORMATION

Advertising serves other goals, such as providing information to both consumers and business buyers. Typical information for consumers includes a retailer's store hours, business location, or sometimes more detailed product specifications. Information may make the purchasing process appear to be simple and convenient, which can entice customers to travel to the store to finalize a purchase.

In business-to-business situations, information from some advertisements may lead various members of the buying center to consider a particular company. Information that reaches members of the buying center during the search stage of the purchasing process will be the most valuable. For high-involvement purchases, in which members of the buying center have strong vested interests in the success of the choice, informative advertisements are the also beneficial. Low-involvement decisions usually do not require the same level of detail.

PERSUASION

Persuasion takes place when an advertisement convinces consumers of particular brand's superiority. Changing consumer attitudes and persuading them to consider a new purchasing choice can be a

▼ **FIGURE 5.9**
Advertising Goals

- To build brand awareness
- To inform
- To persuade
- To support other marketing efforts
- To encourage action

OBJECTIVE 5.6

What are the primary goals of advertising?

▼ This advertisement informs consumers that GameStop workers are also players and can provide tips on how to get out of a jam.

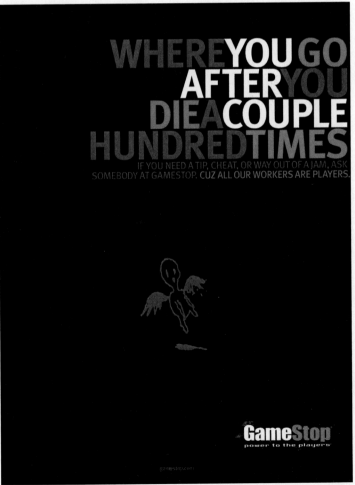

WHERE **YOU** GO AFTER **YOU** DIE **A COUPLE** HUNDRED TIMES

IF YOU NEED A TIP, CHEAT, OR WAY OUT OF A JAM, ASK SOMEBODY AT GAMESTOP. CUZ ALL OUR WORKERS ARE PLAYERS.

GameStop
power to the players

challenging task. Advertisers can utilize several persuasion methods persuasion. One involves showing consumers the negative consequences of failing to use a particular brand. Persuasive advertising more often targets consumers rather than business-to-business situations.

SUPPORTING MARKETING EFFORTS

Advertising supports other marketing functions. Manufacturers use advertising to accompany trade and consumer promotions, such as theme packaging or combination offers. Contests, such as the McDonald's Monopoly game, require additional advertising to be effective.

Retailers also advertise to support marketing programs. Any type of special sale (white sale, buy-one-get-one-free, pre–Christmas sale) requires effective advertising to attract customers to the store. Manufacturers and retail outlets both run advertisements in conjunction with coupons or other special offers. Del Monte placed a 30-cent coupon in the advertisement shown in this section. The ad highlights a smaller-size container with a pull-top lid. These features match the advertisement's target market: senior citizens. The first magazine featuring this advertisement was *Modern Maturity*. Manufacturer coupons are regularly redeemed at grocery stores and in-store coupons are part of many retail store print advertisements. When ads are combined with other marketing efforts into a larger, more integrated effort revolving around a theme, the program is called a **promotional campaign**.

ENCOURAGING ACTION

Many firms set behavioral goals for advertising programs. A television commercial encouraging viewers to take action by dialing a toll-free number to make a quick purchase serves as an example. Everything from ShamWow to Snuggies has been sold using action tactics. Infomercials and home shopping network programs rely heavily on immediate consumer purchasing responses.

Action-oriented advertising can be used in the business-to-business sector. Generating leads becomes the primary goal. Many business advertisements provide Web addresses or telephone numbers buyers can use to request more information or make a purchase.

The five advertising goals of building image, providing information, being persuasive, supporting other marketing efforts, and encouraging action are not separate from each other. They work together in key ways. For instance, awareness and information are part of persuasion. The key is to emphasize one goal without forgetting the others.

OBJECTIVE 5.7

What are the key elements of an advertising budget?

▼ A Del Monte advertisement directed to senior citizens offering a smaller can with a pull-off lid.

Courtesy of Del Monte Foods.

The Advertising Budget

Once the major goals of the advertising campaign have been established, a review of the advertising budget follows. Chapter 4 described the various methods for developing marketing communication budgets. After establishing the total amount of dollars to be allocated to advertising, the challenge becomes choosing the proper media approach to reach the advertising goal. Three basic tactics used to allocate advertising funds are:

- Pulsating schedule
- Flighting schedule
- Continuous schedule

A **pulsating schedule of advertising** involves continuous advertising during the year with bursts of higher intensity at specific times (more ads in more media). Companies can also select a **flighting** approach or schedule, whereby ads are presented only during peak times, and not at all during other times of the year.

Firms often advertise more during peak seasons such as Christmas, seeking to send messages during the times when customers are most inclined to buy, or when they are *on the hot spot*. Weight Watchers, Diet Centers, and others advertise heavily during the first weeks of January. Many New Year's resolutions include going on a diet.

Advertising during slow sales seasons focuses on "drumming up business" when people do not regularly buy. In retail sales, slow seasons occur during January and February. Some companies advertise more during these months to sell merchandise left over from the Christmas season and to encourage customers to shop. Manufacturers also realize that many retailers are not advertising and hope that the ads will capture greater attention as a result.

Many marketing experts believe advertising in level amounts keeps the brand name repetitively in front of consumers, which is a **continuous campaign schedule**. Durable goods, such as dishwashers and refrigerators, are purchased on an "as needed" basis. A family ordinarily buys a new dishwasher only when the old one breaks down or when they build or remodel a home. Level advertising increases the odds that the buyer will see an advertisement or remember a given name (Kenmore, Whirlpool, or General Electric) at the right time.

Matching the pacing of advertisements with the message, the media, and the nature of the product should be the objective. Some media make it easier to advertise for longer periods of time. Contracts for billboards are normally for a month or a year. They can be rotated throughout a town or city to present a continuing message. At the same time, budgetary constraints can influence the strategies and tactics used in any advertising program.

▲ Weight loss companies such as Weight Watchers tend to budget more for advertising after the Christmas holidays, when individuals make New Year's resolutions to diet.

Media Selection

Selecting the appropriate media requires an understanding of the media usage habits of the target market and then matching that information with the profile of each medium's audience. Volkswagen positioned the Tiguan crossover as a fun vehicle aimed at young, active individuals who love the outdoors. Although the campaign featured television commercials, the more unique component of the campaign was the outdoor segment. The theme "people want an SUV that parks well with others" was featured in a series of outdoor ads placed at bike racks and trail heads at 150 national parks and resorts. Brian Martin, CEO of Brand Connections Active Outdoor, which placed the ads, noted that over 30 million impressions were made with hikers, bikers, and other outdoor-lovers.[18]

The advertising team identifies the media a target market uses. Teenagers surf the Web and watch television. Only a small percentage reads newspapers and news magazines. Various market segments exhibit differences in when and how they view various media. Older African Americans watch television programs in patterns that are different from those of older Caucasians. Males watch more sports programs than females, and so forth.

In business-to-business markets, knowing the trade journals or business publications that various members of the buying center most likely read assists in the development of

OBJECTIVE 5.8

What are the issues in the media-selection process?

Trust & Wealth Management

PROGRESSIVE BANK

Progressive Bank offers:

• A Private Banking & Trust Division to address specifically your individual wealth management needs.

• Expert financial advice and investment management services.

• A team of credentialed financial planning professionals who work diligently to help you achieve your dreams.

Call today and let's discuss the benefits of a professionally managed personal financial plan.
(318) 651-5056 • progressivebank.com

Investment products are not FDIC insured, and are not obligations of or guaranteed by Progressive Bank or its affiliates. Investments are subject to market risk, including the possible loss of principal.

▲ Selecting the right media ensures that consumers who are the most likely to use Progressive Bank will see this advertisement.

a print advertising campaign. Engineers, who tend to be the influencers, often have different media viewing habits than do vice presidents, who may be the deciders.

Although media buys are guided by the advertising agency and the client company, media companies typically make the purchases. A trend toward involving media companies at an earlier stage in the campaign process has evolved in recent years. Previously, most media companies were contacted after a campaign became ready or was nearly complete, with the specific task of purchasing media space or time. Now, companies such as Procter & Gamble, Johnson & Johnson, Clorox, Kimberly-Clark, Verizon, and HP enlist media companies as strategic partners in developing advertising and marketing campaigns.[19] Media companies are invited to participate in the strategy development stage because many have a good understanding of the target audience. They are able to provide valuable information to the creative staff about how to best reach the client's target market employing the primary media that target consumers use.

In some cases, media companies actually create commercials. Joe Kuester, senior brand manager for Kimberly-Clark, stated, "It doesn't matter to us where the idea comes from or who champions that idea." That statement was in response to Kimberly-Clark's media company, Mindshare Entertainment, creating a series of webisodes involving Whoopi Goldberg for its Poise brand. Another media company, MEC Entertainment worked with its client Ikea to produce a campaign for A&E called "Fix this Kitchen." This trend to involve media companies in all facets of advertising campaign development is quickly gaining momentum with companies.[20]

The Creative Brief

OBJECTIVE 5.9

How does a creative brief facilitate effective advertising?

Typically, creative work with a document prepared by the client and account executive called the *creative strategy* or *creative brief*. Although various forms exist, the basic components of a standard creative brief are provided in Figure 5.10. The creative takes the information provided to produce advertisements and use it to convey the desired message. A quality creative brief, when prepared properly, saves the agency considerable time and effort and results in a stronger advertising campaign for the client.

As mentioned earlier, ineffective communications with clients represent a common difficulty agencies experience. The creative brief may constitute part of the problem. A survey of senior executives of advertising agencies suggested that fewer than 40 percent of client briefs are clear.[21] Agency leaders reported that many briefs are weak in the areas of providing competitive information and statements about brand positioning within the competitive landscape. Consequently, attention should be given to clarifying these issues before creating advertisements.

THE OBJECTIVE

A creative brief identifies the objective of the advertising campaign, such as those common objectives that were noted in Figure 5.9. The creative reviews the main objective (or goal) before designing specific ads or the advertising campaign. The objectives guide the advertising design and the choice of an executional framework. For instance, for an increased brand awareness goal, the *name* of the product will be prominently displayed in the advertisement. Building brand image normally results in the *actual product* being more prominently displayed in the ad.

• The objective
• The target audience
• The message theme
• The support
• The constraints

▲ **FIGURE 5.10**
The Creative Brief

THE TARGET AUDIENCE

A creative then examines the target audience. An advertisement designed to persuade a business to inquire about new computer software differs from a consumer advertisement created for the same company. The business advertisement focuses on the type of industry and a specific member of the buying center. The more detail available regarding the target audience, the easier it becomes for a creative to design an effective advertisement.

Overly general target market profiles are not helpful. Rather than specifying "males, ages 20 to 35," more specific information will be needed, such as "males, ages 20 to 35, college educated, and professionals." Other information, including hobbies, interests, opinions, and lifestyles, make it possible to more precisely develop an advertisement. The Playtex advertisement in this section was prepared for young females who enjoy playing sports and have active lifestyles. The additional information helped the creative design an advertisement that appealed to the right group of females.

THE MESSAGE THEME

The message theme presents an outline of key idea(s) that the advertising program conveys. The message theme represents the benefit or promise the advertiser uses to reach consumers or businesses. The promise, or *unique selling point*, describes the major benefit the good or service offers customers. A message theme for an automobile could be oriented toward luxury, safety, fun, fuel efficiency, or driving excitement. A message theme for a hotel could focus on luxury, price, or unusual features, such as a hotel in Paris, France, noting the ease of access to all of the nearby tourist attractions. The message theme matches the medium selected, the target market, and the primary IMC message.[22] In the advertisement for Sub-Zero refrigerators on the next page, the message theme features the "freshness of food" being kept in the Sub-Zero refrigerator. The message targets consumers, but also may influence managers of restaurants, cafeterias, and catering services.

Message themes can be oriented toward either rational or emotional processes. A "left-brain" ad oriented toward the logical, rational side informs individuals using numbers, letters, words, and concepts. Left-brain advertising features a logical, factual, rational appeal. A number of logical features (size, price, special features) influence the decision to buy a car. At the same time, many cars are purchased for emotional reasons. The right side of the brain contains emotions. It works with abstract ideas, images, and feelings. A car may be chosen for its color, sportiness, or other less rational reasons.

Most advertising targets either the right brain or the left brain. Advertising can also be effective by balancing the two sides. Rational, economic beings have difficulty defending the purchase of an expensive sports car such as a Porsche. Many product purchases are based on how a person feels about the good or service, combined with rational information.[23]

THE SUPPORT

Support should be provided in the fourth component of the creative strategy. **Support** takes the form of facts that substantiate the message theme. When Aveeno products won "Best of Beauty" awards from *Allure* magazine, its "Best of Beauty" seal was placed on the company's products. Company advertising mentioned the award to support Aveeno's claims of superiority.

In the Pearle Vision advertisement in this section, various statements provide support. These include the idea that microTHINS are 30 percent thinner, 40 percent lighter, 4

▼ This advertisement for Playtex used additional target market profile information to help design a message directed to active teenagers and young women.

▲ An advertisement for Sub-Zero illustrating the message theme of keeping foods fresh.

▼ The advertisement for Pearle Vision presents support to substantiate the message claim.

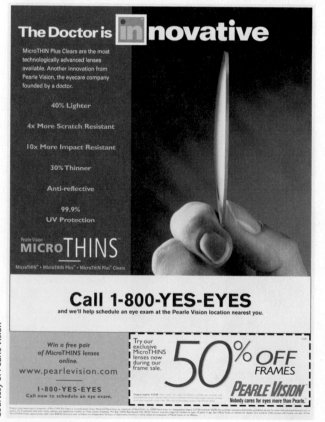

times more scratch resistant, 10 times more impact resistant, antireflective, and have 99.9 percent UV protection. Supporting evidence allows creatives to design advertisements that attract attention to the materials that substantiate claims made about products.

THE CONSTRAINTS

Constraints are any legal and mandatory restrictions placed on advertisements. Constraints include legal protections for trademarks, logos, and copy registrations. Constraints also spell out disclaimers about warranties, offers, and claims. For warranties, a disclaimer specifies the conditions under which they will be honored. Tire warranties, for example, often state that they apply *under normal driving conditions with routine maintenance*. A person cannot ignore tire balancing and rotation and expect to get free new tires when the old ones quickly wear out. Disclaimer warranties notify consumers of potential hazards associated with products. Tobacco advertisements contain statements and images regarding the dangers of smoking and chewing tobacco. Disclaimers about offers specify the terms of financing agreements, as well as when bonuses or discounts apply. Claims identify the exact nature of the statement made in the advertisement. This includes nutritional claims as well as statements about serving sizes and other information describing the product.

After these steps have been completed, the creative brief is ready. From this point forward, the message and the media match, and actual advertisements can be produced. Effective creative briefs take the overall IMC message and tailor it to a specific advertising campaign. This, in turn, gives the company a better chance of reaching customers with messages that return measurable results and help guarantee success. Recent research suggests that campaigns designed in 2 months or less have the greatest likelihood of being "highly effective." Those that take longer tend not to be as effective. Marketers try to move forward without rushing. A campaign designed in 2 weeks or less is also likely to be ineffective.[24]

International Implications

Advertising management now involves major expenditures overseas. The top 100 global advertisers spent an average of 62 percent of advertising budgets outside the United States. Figure 5.11 compares the non-U.S. advertising budget to non-U.S. sales revenue for six major corporations. As illustrated, Coca-Cola spends 83.5 percent of company advertising dollars outside the United States, where 74.9 percent of its total revenues are generated. Colgate-Palmolive spends 85.6 percent of its advertising dollars on non-U.S. ads and generates 76.7 percent of its revenues outside the United States. Data for Ford, Mattel, McDonald's, and Procter & Gamble are also provided.[25]

Two major differences emerge when considering advertising management in an international perspective. The first is in regard to the process itself. The second concerns preparing international advertising campaigns.

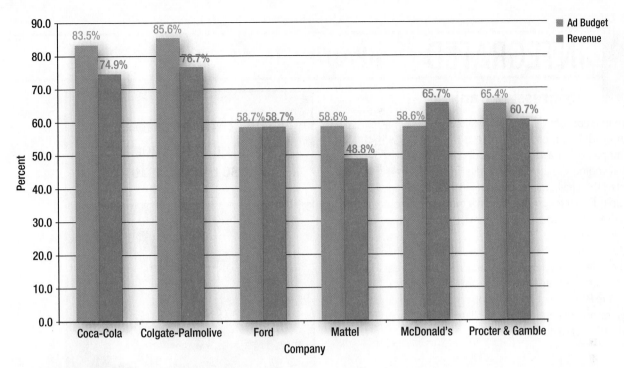

▲ **FIGURE 5.11**

Non-U.S. Ad Budgets and Sales Revenues for Major Corporations

Source: Adapted from Laurel Wentz and Bradley Johnson, "Top 100 Global Advertisers Heap Their Spending Abroad," *Advertising Age*, http://adage.com/print?article_id=140723, November 30, 2009.

The general processes used to prepare advertising campaigns remain fairly uniform. Some of the most important differences are in the areas of availability of qualified advertising agencies and how those agencies are selected. For example, in many Asian cultures the beginning of a face-to-face meeting would include an exchange of gifts. Also, business cards have differing uses and meanings across cultures. In some countries, cards are only presented to highly trusted allies. In others, they are freely passed out. The marketing team in any company should carefully study the nuances of business meetings, including the use of formal titles, eye contact, who speaks first, and other variables, before beginning a relationship with an advertising agency in another country.

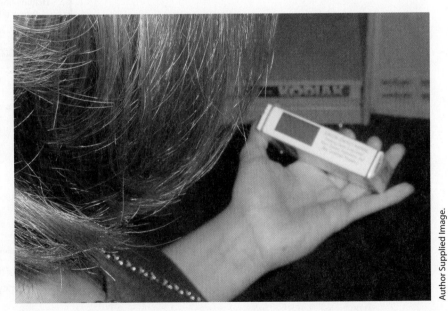

▲ The Surgeon General's warning is an example of a constraint.

Agencies in other countries might not follow typical procedures such as a shootout or the preparation of a creative brief. Forms of preplanning research may also vary. In some countries, it is not possible to conduct the same types of research as in the United States and other Western cultures.

Advertising campaigns designed for an international audience require an understanding of the various languages and cultures that might be involved. In Europe, French, Spanish, Portuguese, Italian, and other languages need translation and back-translation of advertising themes and messages to make certain the idea can be clearly presented in various countries. Media-selection processes may also require adjustment; some countries have state-run television networks and others place restrictions on what can be shown in an advertisement.

INTEGRATED CAMPAIGNS IN ACTION

Progressive Bank

Banks operate in a competitive market. Make one standout can be difficult, especially through an advertising campaign. For a local bank, it becomes even more challenging. French Creative advertising agency accepted this challenge with Progressive Bank. The agency developed a unique campaign that not only highlighted some of the bank's strengths but also brought a human into the campaign to make the bank personal.

Information about the Philadelphia Cream Cheese campaign and the Progressive Bank campaign is available at the Pearson Instructor's Resource Center (www.pearsonhighered.com). The campaigns feature PowerPoint presentations outlining the details of the campaigns and examples of the collaterals developed by each of the advertising agencies.

▲ One part of the Progressive campaign focused on the local community and the involvement of its employees.

SUMMARY

Effective advertising requires matching the mess age with the appropriate media. This chapter reviews the advertising management process. Effective advertising occurs when the firm has a well-defined mission statement and targets its energies in the direction of creating goods or services to meet the needs of a target market.

Advertising management begins with deciding whether an in-house department should develop advertisements or whether an external advertising agency should be retained. When choosing an external agency, the company's leaders establish clear steps to lead to the selection of optimal agency. The steps include: spelling out and prioritizing organizational goals, establishing quality selection criteria, screening firms based on those criteria, requesting references from firms that are finalists, performing background checks, requesting creative pitches, making on-site visits to get to know those in the agencies, and offering and finalizing a contract.

Common selection criteria used in selecting agencies include: the size of the agency matching the size of the company, relevant experience, no conflicts of interest, production capabilities, quality creative capabilities, suitable media-purchasing skills, other services that can be rendered as needed, client retention rates, and a good chemistry between those in the company and those in the agency. Carefully utilizing these criteria increases the odds of a successful match between the company and the agency will exist, which increases the chance of success.

Within the advertising agency, the account manager performs the functions of soliciting accounts, finalizing contracts, and selecting creatives to prepare advertising campaigns. Account executives are go-betweens who mediate between the agency and the client company. Account executives also help client organizations refine IMC messages and programs.

Creatives prepare advertisements and are guided by the creative brief. The document spells out: the objective of the promotional campaign, the target audience, the message theme, the support, and the constraints. The message theme presents an outline of the key idea(s) that the program seeks to convey. The constraints include logos, warranties, disclaimers, or legal statements that are part of various advertisements.

The creative, account executive, and company should agree about which media to use in a campaign. Media are selected based on costs, types of messages, target market characteristics, and other criteria. The creatives then complete the final elements of the ad, and the campaign is prepared.

Advertising management constitutes an important ingredient in the success of an integrated marketing communications program. A quality ad that garners the attention of people in the target audience, makes a key memorable point, and moves buyers to action is difficult to prepare. At the same time, company officials and market account executives know that designing effective ads with tangible results is a challenging but necessary activity. Every step of the process should be examined carefully to help the company achieve its short and long-term marketing goals.

Key Terms

message theme An outline of key idea(s) an advertising campaign conveys.

leverage point The key element in the advertisement that taps into, or activates, a consumer's personal value system (a value, idea, or concept).

appeal The approach used to design the advertisement that attracts attention or presents information to consumers, through the use of humor, fear, sex, logic, or emotions.

executional framework The method used to deliver the advertising message.

advertising management program The process of preparing and integrating a company's advertising efforts with the overall IMC message.

crowdsourcing The process of outsourcing the creative aspect of an advertisement to the public.

advertising campaign management The process of preparing and integrating a specific advertising program in conjunction with the overall IMC message.

product-specific research Research that identifies key product characteristics that become selling points.

consumer-oriented research Research used to understand the context of a product's use.

focus group A set of consumers or businesspeople who are retained to talk about a particular topic, product, or brand.

top-of-mind brands The brands that quickly come to mind when consumers are asked to identify brands from a product category.

top choice The first or second pick when a consumer reviews his or her evoked set of possible purchasing alternatives.

promotional campaign The process of combining advertisements with other marketing efforts into a larger, more integrated effort revolving around a central idea or theme.

pulsating schedule of advertising Featuring continuous advertising with bursts of higher intensity (more ads in more media) during the course of the year.

flighting schedule of advertising A schedule whereby companies present ads only during specific times and not at all during other times of the year.

continuous campaign schedule of advertising An advertising program in which the company advertises in level amounts throughout the year.

support The facts that substantiate the unique selling point of a creative brief.

constraints The company, legal, and mandatory restrictions placed on advertisements which include legal protection for trademarks, logos, and copy registrations.

Review Questions

1. Describe the following terms: message theme, leverage point, appeal, and executional framework.

2. Define advertising management. What are the four main steps involved?

3. What four main company activities are involved in the advertising management process?

4. What is the relationship between advertising and the overall IMC process?

5. What factors influence the decision of whether to use an in-house advertising group or an external advertising agency?

6. Besides advertising agencies, what other types of organizations play roles in the communication process?

7. What steps should be taken in selecting an advertising agency?

8. What evaluation criteria should be used in selecting an advertising agency?

9. What is a creative pitch?

10. Describe the role of an advertising agency account executive.

11. Describe the role of the advertising creative.

12. Describe the role of a traffic manager.

⭐ 13. Describe the role of an account planner.

14. What are the steps of an advertising campaign management process?

15. What are the two main forms of research for the purposes of creating advertisements?

16. What is a focus group, and how can such a group help to create more effective advertisements?

17. Describe the terms top-of-mind and top choice.

18. What elements are included in a creative brief?

Critical Thinking Exercises

DISCUSSION QUESTIONS

⭐ 1. Pick up a magazine that you read on a regular basis. Examine five advertisements and identify the major selling point in each. Was the major selling idea clear, or was it difficult to ascertain?

2. Look through the ads in this chapter. Which ad to you like the best? Why? Which ad is the least appealing to you? Why? Discuss what makes a print ad appealing and what creates the opposite effect.

3. Review the responsibilities of each of the jobs under "Roles of Advertising Personnel." Which one most appeals to you? Why? Which is least appealing? Why?

4. Print off or open the textbook to the list of advertising goals. Create a table with three columns. In the first column, you will record the brand being advertised. In the second column, you will write down

which advertising goal you think the ad was designed to meet. In the third column, you will assign a score based on your evaluation of each ad's effectiveness, with 10 being effective and 1 being completely ineffective. Once you have created the table, watch a 30 minute television program and record and evaluate every commercial you see. When you are finished, write a paragraph discussing which goals were used the most and which ads were the most effective at accomplishing their goal.

5. Follow the instructions given in Question 4, but instead of a television program gather a group of five advertisements from a magazine. Make sure the ads are in a sequence and not ones that you randomly picked or chose.

⭐ 6. Follow the instructions given in Question 4, but instead of a television program gather a group of five banner ads from the Internet. Make sure the ads are in a sequence and not ones that you randomly picked or chose.

7. Choose one of the following. Using the information in this chapter, prepare a creative brief. You can pick a brand from within the product category.

a. Energy drink
b. Frozen apple juice
c. Fast-food restaurant
d. Museum
e. Dress shoes

Integrated Learning Exercises

1. Making the decision to use an external advertising agency as opposed to an in-house program for advertising or some other aspect of the advertising function is difficult. Access the American Association of Advertising Agencies Web site at www.aaaa.org. From the "News and Views" section, examine articles that might help identify benefits of using an advertising agency. What type of information is available at this Web site?

2. A number of agencies assist business organizations with integrated marketing communication programs. Whereas some firms try to provide a wide array of services, others are more specialized. Access the following association Web sites. What type of information is available on each site? How would the information provided be useful in building an IMC program?

   a. International Social Media Association (**www.ismaconnects.org**)
   b. Promotion Marketing Association (**www.pmalink.org**)
   c. Outdoor Advertising Association of America (**www.oaaa.org**)
   d. Direct Marketing Association (**www.the-dma.org**)

3. Part of a communication marketing analysis includes understanding the media usage habits of consumers and their attitudes toward various media. An excellent source of information in Canada is the Media Awareness Network at www.media-awareness.ca. Review the types of information available at the Web site. Examine the news articles. What type of information is available at this Web site and how could it be used in developing an advertising campaign?

4. Many advertisers direct ads toward the right side of the brain and develop advertisements based entirely on emotions, images, and pictures. Companies often advertise auto parts and tools with a scantily clad woman to attract the attention of men. The woman has nothing to do with the product, but garners attention. The rationale for using a sexy woman is that if consumers like her, they will like the product and then purchase that brand. Effective advertisements integrate elements from both the left side of the brain as well as the right. They contain elements that appeal to emotions but also have rational arguments. A laundry detergent can

be advertised as offering the rational benefit of getting clothes cleaner but also contain the emotional promise that your mother-in-law will think of you more favorably. For each of the following Internet sites, discuss the balance of left-brain versus right-brain advertising appeal.

   a. Pier 1 Imports (**www.pier1.com**)
   b. Pig O' My Heart Potbellies (**www.potbellypigs.com**)
   c. Volkswagen of America (**www.vw.com**)
   d. Discount Cheerleading.com (**www.discountcheerleading.com**)
   e. Backcountry.com (**www.backcountry.com**)

5. You have been asked to select an advertising agency to handle an account for Red Lobster, a national restaurant chain. Your advertising budget is $30 million. Study the Web sites of the following advertising agencies. Follow the selection steps outlined in the chapter. Narrow the list down to two agencies and justify your decision. Then choose between the two agencies and justify your choice.

   a. The Richards Group (**www.richards.com**)
   b. Leo Burnett (**www.leoburnett.com**)
   c. BBDO Worldwide (**www.bbdo.com**)
   d. Lucas Design & Advertising (**www.aladv.com**)
   e. mcgarrybowen (**www.mcgarrybowen.com**)
   f. DDB Worldwide Communications Group (**www.ddb.com**)

6. A marketing manager has been placed in charge of a new brand of jeans to be introduced into the market. The company's corporate headquarters are in Atlanta, and the firm's management team has already decided to use one of the local advertising agencies. Two primary objectives in choosing an agency are: the agency must have the capability to develop a strong brand name, and the agency must be able to help with business-to-business marketing to place the jeans into retail stores. Type "advertising agencies in Atlanta" into a search engine. Identify an initial list of six ad agencies. Follow the steps outlined in the chapter to narrow the list to two agencies. Then design a project for the agencies to prepare as part of an oral and written presentation to the company's marketing team.

Student Project

CREATIVE CORNER

Use the following creative brief for this exercise.

Product:	Porsche
Objective:	To change consumers view that the Porsche can be driven every day
Target Audience:	30 to 55-year-old consumers, slightly more male, college educated, with annual incomes of approximately $100,000. Psychographically, the targeted market is a group known as individualists. They tend not to buy mainstream products. In automobile selection, they place greater emphasis on design elements, distinctiveness, and utility. Social status is important.
Background Information:	Market research found that potential customers balked at the idea of buying a car just to sit around. When asked what kept them from driving the car every day, they said, "I don't feel comfortable driving in city traffic. It doesn't have the technology that I need to manage my everyday life. It doesn't have space for passengers."
Message Theme:	The Porsche can be driven every day for normal activities. It does not have to sit in the garage and only driven on weekends. It has the newest technology and can comfortably carry passengers
Constraints:	All ads must contain the Porsche logo.

1. As an account executive for an advertising agency, discuss the creative brief in terms of the completeness of the information provided and whether the objective is realistic. What additional information should Porsche provide before a creative can begin working on the account?

2. The media planner for the Porsche account suggests a media plan consisting of cable television, print advertising, Internet ads, and network advertising on *Family Guy*, *CSI*, *Monday Night Football*, *Big Bang Theory*, and *American Idol*. Evaluate this media plan in light of the creative brief's objectives. Can these shows reach the target audience? What information does a creative and the account executive want from the media planner before starting work on actual commercials?

3. From the viewpoint of the creative assigned to this account, do the creative brief and the media plan (see Question 2) contain sufficient information to design a series of advertisements? What, if any, additional information is necessary?

4. Using the information provided in the creative brief, prepare a magazine advertisement. Which magazines might match the target audience?

CASE 1 ADVERTISING JEANS TO TEENS

If there is one nearly common denominator among teens around the world, it may be the desire to impress peers and potential romantic partners. A variety of enticing adornments assist in the process, including choices regarding hair style, cosmetics, jewelry, and clothing. In many cultures, designer jeans allow younger consumers to look sleek and sassy.

In the United States, top name designer jeans include Citizens of Humanity, Rockstar, Bluelab, Superfine, Dylan George, Stitch's, Current/Elliot, Red Engine, Rich and Skinny, Chip & Pepper, Mavi, Monarchy, HA-67, and Diesel. These companies compete with more established Lee and Levi jeans. In Brazil, Butt Lift products have gained an edge in the marketplace, competing with Moleton and Blue Monster. French products include 2Leep and German companies sell Trewano.

The market for jeans remains lucrative. Teens with disposable income may spend a great deal of time and effort choosing the brand they will wear. Influences include the price and fit, but also social and peer pressure, jeans worn by celebrities, and parental limitations. Social media allows them to consider a variety of brands, discussing the options with friends while seeking to discover the most popular new hot item.

Each year, jean styles change. The elements in jeans may move from looking old and torn, to those stitched with special designs, and then to multi-fabric entries. Length can be Capri, full, straight-legged, or flared. Pockets may be small or large. They may be closed using zippers or buttons. Trend-setters dictate the new fads and fashions.

To complicate matters further, jeans may be worn for style or for work. Besides teenagers, young children and older adults also buy these items. Some marketers, such as Levi and Lee try to develop brands and lines with staying-power. Others focus solely on one segment, such as young women or work jeans for older men.

You have just been placed in charge of the advertising program for a jean company. It can be one of the firms mentioned in this case or one of your own. Select the type of jean you will try to sell and then complete the following creative brief.

Product: Designer blue jeans for ….

Objective:

Target Audience:

Background Information:

Message Theme:

Constraints:

Jason Stitt / Fotolia

▲ Teens are an attractive market for brands of jeans.

1. What companies provide the primary competition for your jeans?
2. Which media will you select for the next campaign, given the information provided in the creative brief?
3. How do you plan to deliver the message theme in the advertising campaign?
4. Describe your advertising program in detail.
5. What tagline will you choose for your advertisements?

CASE 2 NAME YOUR HERO

During a recent holiday season, the crowded fantasy and gaming world gained several products designed to entice new sets of buyers. The entire Guitar Hero brand faced stiff competition from other gaming products. One highly touted release was the new The Beatles: Rock Band game released early in the season. Other competitors included the Madden NFL product line and the Halo 3: ODST product.

In response, three new Guitar Hero titles were released: Guitar Hero 5, Band Hero, and DJ Hero. Each focused on a specific set of players.

Guitar Hero 5, the most recent version of the original product released in 2005, expands on the innovative technology that allows users to play real songs, real chords, and an almost-real guitar, integrating music, interactivity, and gameplay in a totally new way. The game offers the opportunity to play lead guitar, bass guitar, or drums or to sing the vocals of a variety of tunes. The primary attraction remains the ability to play great guitar riffs from the past. Guitar Hero 5 drew grumbles from Nirvana and Kurt Cobain fans, who did not like the intrusion into the band's well-established image.

Band Hero is a more family-oriented product. The music was selected to attract females and younger "tween" users. At one point, the opening page of the Guitar Hero Web site featured a music video by the youthful Taylor Swift, a recent CMA Music Awards "Best Artist" winner. Many industry observers believe that Band Hero's design is an obvious response to The Beatles: Rock Band, which has many similar features.

The final new entry, DJ Hero, seeks to capture the hip-hop/rap connoisseur. The game features a turntable. According to Game Hero CEO Dan Rosensweig, "It's really cool. It's got 100 songs and 94 mixes that no one has ever mixed before. This is going to be one of those transformational games. You have this generation's iconic piece of equipment—the turntable—and some fantastic mixes that really give you a chance to release your inner DJ. I think that's going to be one of the hottest selling games this holiday season."

Additional trends should also be considered. When asked about mobile gaming on handheld devices, Rosensweig replied, "We're going to focus on making sure that our consumers can access games wherever it makes sense for them to access it—mobile is one of those environments which is always with you. And obviously, we're taking a look at that."

Part of the challenge in promoting both ongoing and new games is finding ways to capture the attention of the target audience. In the case of the Guitar Hero brand, consumers have somewhat differing viewing and media habits. Guitar Hero 5's audience is likely to be more of a classic music, hard

laurent hamels / Fotolia

▲ Guitar Hero allows users to play real songs, real chords, and an almost real guitar.

rock crowd; Band Hero needs to reach younger females and families; and DJ Hero should find ways to access the hip-hop crowd.

Rosensweig notes, "Like anything else, we have to continue to remain fresh. You have to really understand that technology makes the game more interesting, more expansive, and more fun." He believes the future is bright. "I think we have an opportunity to redefine the way people interact with music. They want to listen to music, they want to play music, they want to contribute music, they want to create music. The more people and consoles are connected, the more opportunity we have to remain in consumers' lives."

1. Should Guitar Hero retain an advertising agency or develop its own ads in-house? Justify your answer.

2. If Guitar Hero's marketing team retains an advertising agency, what type should it be, and which decision variables should guide the choice?

3. Search online for five advertising agencies that you think would be a good fit for Guitar Hero. Choose the best one. Justify your choice.

4. What type of advertising planning and research should be used for each Guitar Hero product?

5. Should the marketing team develop one set of advertisements for each Guitar Hero product, or an overall campaign for the entire company?

6. Should the company use a pulsating, flighting, or continuous schedule of advertising? Explain.

Sources: Kim Thai, "'Guitar Hero' Amps up for the Holidays," CNNMoney com (http://money.cnn.com/2009/10/23/technology/guitar_dj_hero_activision.fortune/index.ht, accessed November 17, 2009), October 23, 2009; www.guitarhero.com (accessed November 17, 2009); Seth Colter Wells, "Nirvana Heaven and Hell," Newsweek.com (www.newsweek.com/id/220978, accessed November 17, 2009), November 3, 2009.

MyMarketingLab

Go to **mymktlab.com** for Auto-graded writing questions as well as the following Assisted-graded writing questions:.

5-1. Look through the ads in this chapter. Which ad to you like the best? Why? Which ad is the least appealing to you? Why? Discuss what makes a print ad appealing and what creates the opposite effect.

5-2. You have been asked to select an advertising agency to handle an account for Red Lobster, a national restaurant chain. Your advertising budget is $30 million. Study the Web sites of the following advertising agencies. Follow the selection steps outlined in the chapter. Narrow the list down to two agencies and justify your decision. Then choose between the two agencies and justify your choice.

a. The Richards Group (www.richards.com)

b. Leo Burnett (www.leoburnett.com)

c. BBDO Worldwide (www.bbdo.com)

d. Lucas Design & Advertising (www.aladv.com)

e. mcgarrybowen (www.mcgarrybowen.com)

f. DDB Worldwide Communications Group (www.ddb.com)

5-3. Mymktlab Only—comprehensive writing assignment for this chapter.

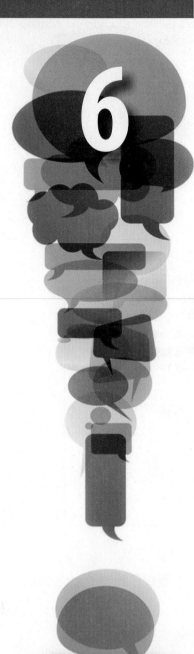

6

ADVERTISING DESIGN
Theoretical Frameworks and Types of Appeals

CHAPTER OBJECTIVES

After reading this chapter, you should be able to answer the following questions:

1 How can the hierarchy of effects model and a means–ends analysis help an advertising creative design better commercials?

2 How can leverage points and taglines increase advertising effectiveness?

3 What roles do visual and verbal images play in advertisements?

4 What are the seven main types of advertising appeals?

5 How can fear be used to create an effective advertisement?

6 How can humor be used to create an effective advertisement?

7 Why does sex play such a prominent role in advertising?

8 How can music, rationality, emotions, and scarcity be used to increase advertising effectiveness?

9 What are the primary areas of concern in international advertising?

MyMarketingLab™

⭐ **Improve Your Grade!**

Over 10 million students improved their results using the Pearson MyLabs. Visit **mymktlab.com** for simulations, tutorials, and end-of-chapter problems.

---

mcgarrybowen

A POWERFUL FORCE IN INTEGRATED MARKETING COMMUNICATIONS

n 2002, three partners came together to form a new competitor in the advertising and communications world, the mcgarrybowen agency. John P. McGarry, Jr., Gordon Bowen, and Stewart Owen designed an organization that would be "gracious" and "tenacious" at the same time. Instead of one distinct style with a predetermined media solution, the agency delivers a strategic approach focused on the client's business and brand.

Over the past decade, a series of marketing triumphs emerged, some of which are documented in this textbook. The agency's impressive client list includes Chevron, Canon, Disney, J. P. Morgan, Kraft, Marriott, Oscar Mayer, Pfizer, Sharp, *The Wall Street Journal*, and Verizon.

Specific products advertised and marketed through mcgarrybowen include 7UP, Advil, Miracle Whip, Philadelphia Cream Cheese, Snapple, and Viagra. Most recently, the agency recaptured the Reebok account and added several new clients, including Sears, Burger King, United Airlines, and Bud Light. *Advertising Age* named mcgarrybowen Agency of the Year in 2009, #2 on its A-List in 2010 and Agency of the Year in 2011.

Mcgarrybowen Chicago

◀ Chicago Office of mcgarrybowen

Mcgarrybowen Chicago

Mcgarrybowen Chicago

Three primary locations house the agency's activities: New York, Chicago, and London. The company's full service approach includes nearly every marketing and communications activity. Among them, advertising, naming, brand strategies, digital messages, mobile, social networks, data and analytics, direct marketing, sponsorships and entertainment marketing, media planning and buying, and multicultural marketing are featured.

The principles that guide the selection and utilization of marketing professionals within the agency include: "A belief in belief," in which "Conviction makes a brand great." Further, the company emphasizes "taking things personally," believing in people, an emphasis on collaboration, the goal of "decency" and the desire to inspire personal growth in employees. The net result has been a motivated and inspired work force that delivers high-quality, creative solutions for clients.

The company's hiring process involves finding a "cultural fit" between the applicant and the company. The agency seeks out individuals that are "collaborative" and "spontaneous." Those chosen "expect to work hard on ideas and put your ego aside," according to Assistant Account Executive Nicole Marriott.

To achieve key marketing goals, as one creative noted, "We pride ourselves on storytelling. The foundations of those stories come out as a product truth." This strategic approach at times stands in contrast to marketing programs based primarily on market research. Another stated, "Research can result in report and react . . . a reactive approach. Our account planning has more fluidity. Planning becomes most crucial when strategy is the first chapter of the story. The premise of our brand strategy is how we are going to connect the brand story on a human level." In essence, storytelling involves "getting to a single insight that interprets the brand and makes a personal connection." Such stories are readily evident in the Philadelphia Cream Cheese campaign noted in this text.

On its Web site, the agency proclaims that it has moved past "mere integration." Now the concept of "unification" applies to a company that was built from the ground up. The organization delivers "An equally adamant focus on delivering those ideas anywhere and everywhere that customers interact with our brands has resulted in a nimble agency model with global reach."

OVERVIEW

Which advertising message made the biggest impression on you in the past 5 years? Was it funny, sexy, or emotional? Was it something shown during the Super Bowl? In a recent Adweek Media and Harris Interactive survey, the majority of consumers (55 percent) said that advertisements were somewhat or very interesting. Only 13 percent replied that ads were not interesting at all. When making purchase decisions, 6 percent of the respondents said advertisements were "very influential," and 29 percent viewed them as "somewhat influential." Contrary to popular opinion, advertising does influence younger consumers. Nearly half of 18- to 34-year-olds in the survey reported that they were influenced in some way by advertising, compared to 37 percent for 35- to 44-year-olds, and 28 percent for consumers age 45 and older.[1]

This poll emphasizes the importance of designing an compelling and influential advertising campaign, which can be one of the most challenging elements of an integrated marketing communications program. A successful advertising campaign results when people do more than merely enjoy what they see; it also changes their behaviors and attitudes. At the least, viewers should remember the good or service, so that the next time they make purchases the company or brand comes to mind.

Chapter 5 described the overall advertising management program. The advertising agency is led by an account executive who works with creatives, media planners, and media buyers. In this chapter and the next chapter, the focus turns to the actual message design. This work will be completed by the agency's creative staff.

A message design process will be based on the creative brief that was prepared by the client in conjunction with the account executive. It takes into consideration the media to be utilized. By combining all of these elements, the creative can design effective advertisements.

This chapter covers two major topics. The first part details three theoretical approaches to advertising design: the hierarchy of effects model, means—ends theory, plus visual and verbal imaging.

The second part reviews the major advertising appeals. Many of these may seem familiar. The advertising agency's creative team selects the appeal with the best chance of conveying a message that achieves the desired outcome. Several steps are taken before beginning the process of creating an advertising campaign. The activities are summarized by the creative brief.

Advertising Theory

In developing an advertising campaign, three theoretical approaches might aid in the design process. The hierarchy of effects model and a means–end chain can both assist in developing the leverage point. A leverage point moves the consumer from understanding a product's benefits to linking those benefits with personal values. A third theoretical perspective involves the visual and verbal images present in an advertisement.

HIERARCHY OF EFFECTS

The **hierarchy of effects model** helps to clarify the objectives of an advertising campaign. The model outlines six steps a consumer or a business buyer moves through when making a purchase:

1. Awareness
2. Knowledge
3. Liking
4. Preference
5. Conviction
6. The actual purchase

These steps are sequential. A consumer spends a period of time at each one before moving to the next. Thus, before a person develops a liking for a product, she must first know about the product. Once the individual has the knowledge and develops liking for the product, the advertiser tries to influence the consumer to favor a particular brand or company.

The hierarchy of effects approach helps a creative understand how a consumer reaches a purchase decision. Some of the theory's assumptions have been questioned. For one, these six steps might not always constitute the route taken by a consumer. A person may make a purchase (such as an impulse buy) and then later develop knowledge, liking, preference, and conviction. Also, a shopper could purchase products when little or no preference is involved, because a coupon, discount, or purchase incentive caused him to choose one brand instead of another. At other times, the individual might not even remember the name of the brand he purchased. This may be the case with commodity products such as sugar or flour or even clothing purchases such as socks and shirts.

The hierarchy of effects model's primary benefit involves its ability to identify the typical steps consumers and businesses take when making purchases. Building brand loyalty requires all six steps. Logically, a customer cannot be loyal to a brand without first being aware of it. The customer typically also will not be loyal to a brand without sufficient knowledge. Then, the purchaser must like the brand and build a strong

Courtesy of Bozell Worldwide, Inc.

I never get bent out of shape over a few vampires. And with fat free milk on my tray, there's a good chance I never will. It has calcium to help prevent osteoporosis. So have a nice tall glass. It's easier to keep your neck out of a vampire's reach if you can stand up straight.

got milk?

▲ By featuring a celebrity, this advertisement seeks to convince consumers of the importance of drinking milk.

OBJECTIVE 6.1

How can the hierarchy of effects model and a means-end analysis help an advertising creative design better commercials?

preference for it. Finally, the customer experiences the conviction that the particular brand is superior to the others on the market. The components of the hierarchy of effects approach highlight the responses that advertising or marketing communication should stimulate, in both consumers and business-to-business customers.

The hierarchy of effects model features similarities with theories about attitudes and attitudinal change, including the concepts of cognitive, affective, and conative elements. As presented in Chapter 3, the cognitive component refers to the person's mental images, understanding, and interpretations of the person, object, or issue. The affective component contains the feelings or emotions a person has about the object, topic, or idea. The conative component consists of the individual's intentions, actions, or behavior. The most common sequence that takes place when an attitude forms is:

$$\text{Cognitive} \rightarrow \text{Affective} \rightarrow \text{Conative}$$

Any combination of these components is possible, which parallel the six-step hierarchy of effects process. Advertising may follow the steps or be different and highly successful because of how it captures an individual's attention in some unique way. As a general guideline, cognitive-oriented ads work best for achieving brand awareness and brand knowledge. Affective-oriented advertisements are better at inspiring liking, preference, and conviction. Conative-oriented ads are normally best suited to facilitating product purchases or other buyer actions.

MEANS-END THEORY

The second theoretical approach available to creatives, a **means-end chain**, suggests that an advertisement should contain a message, or *means*, that leads the consumer to a desired end state. These *end* states are personal values (see Figure 6.1 on the next page). A means-end chain should start a process in which viewing the ad leads the consumer to believe that using the product will help achieve one of the personal values.

Means-end theory forms the basis of the **Means-End Conceptualization of Components for Advertising Strategy (MECCAS)** model.[2] The MECCAS model suggests using six elements in creating ads:

◀ This is a conative-oriented advertisement for Cub Cadet, because it offers consumers a $50 appreciation bonus.

◀ **FIGURE 6.1**
Personal Values

- Comfortable life
- Equality
- Excitement
- Freedom
- Fun, exciting life
- Happiness
- Inner peace
- Mature love
- Personal accomplishment
- Pleasure
- Salvation
- Security
- Self-fulfillment
- Self-respect
- Sense of belonging
- Social acceptance
- Wisdom

▼ A "Got Milk?" advertisement illustrating the use of a means-end chain.

- The product's attributes
- Consumer benefits
- The leverage point
- A tagline
- Personal values
- The executional framework

The MECCAS approach moves consumers through the six elements. The attributes of the product are linked to the specific benefits consumers can derive. These benefits, in turn, lead to the attainment of a personal value. Using the elements in Figure 6.2 and the milk advertisement shown in this section, the product attribute calcium connects to the benefits of being strong and healthy. The personal value the consumer obtains from healthy bones may be feeling wise for using the product. The leverage point in the advertisement arises from the connection between the benefit of health and the personal value of feeling wise. The white mustache and the text in the advertisement remind the viewer of the healthy aspects of drinking milk. In this case, preventing osteoporosis in women becomes the key selling point.

The MECCAS approach can be applied to business-to-business advertisements. Members of the buying center may be influenced by personal values, organizational values, and corporate goals. In the advertisement for Greenfield Online on the next page and the means–end chain in Figure 6.3, each attribute leads to the benefits business customers can obtain. Although not explicitly stated, the personal

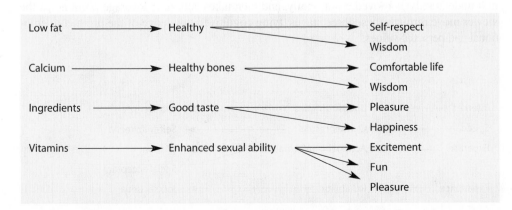

◀ **FIGURE 6.2**
Means–End Chains for Milk

ARE YOU STILL BUYING MARKETING RESEARCH DONE THE OLD-FASHIONED WAY?

Do it better on the Internet with the company that pioneered online marketing research.

Our panel of more than one million consumers from all across the Internet is the largest of its kind. It produces robust samples of any demographic or lifestyle you choose. You'll get richer, more actionable information quicker than you can say dot com.

Join the Research Revolution!™ Contact the world's most experienced Internet marketing research company for studies online, on time, on target and on budget.

www.greenfield.com   888.291.9997

Greenfield Online
Leading the Research Revolution®

▲ A Greenfield Online business-to-business advertisement illustrating the use of a means-end chain.

OBJECTIVE 6.2

How can leverage points and taglines increase advertising effectiveness?

values of members of the buying center choosing Greenfield Online might include job security for making good decisions, self-fulfillment, wisdom, and social acceptance by other members of the buying group.

LEVERAGE POINTS

The hierarchy of effects model and the means–end chain approach both include leverage points. A leverage point moves the consumer from understanding a product's benefits to linking those benefits with personal values. To construct a quality leverage point, the creative builds the pathway that connects a product benefit with the potential buyer's value system.

In terms of the hierarchy of effects model, the initial level of awareness begins the process of exposing consumers to product benefits. As the viewer moves through the six stages, she eventually develops the conviction to buy the product. At that point, the benefit has indeed been linked with a personal value. In the milk advertisement used to illustrate the means–end chain, the leverage point presented in the phrase "There's one person I won't be" is tied to the copy message "a woman with osteoporosis." The copy explains that because milk contains calcium (the product attribute), it helps women maintain health bones (the product benefit). Making the decision to drink milk to prevent osteoporosis connects to the personal values of wisdom and seeking a healthy lifestyle.

In the Greenfield Online business-to-business advertisement, the leverage point is the picture of an old-fashioned woman using an old telephone sandwiched between the headline "Are you still buying marketing research done the old-fashioned way?" and the first sentence of the copy explaining that companies can "Do it better on the Internet." The picture presents an excellent mental image of marketing research conducted the old-fashioned way and the opportunities Greenfield Online can provide.

The means–end chain and MECCAS approaches accentuate the product's attributes and its benefits to the consumer. The leverage point message links these attributes and benefits to consumer values. In the ad itself, the executional framework provides the plot or scenario used to convey the message designed to complete the linkage. Chapter 7 presents executional frameworks in detail.

An effective leverage point can be associated with an attitudinal change, especially when the cognitive → affective → conative sequence exists. As the attitude forms, the individual first understands, is moved emotionally, and then takes action. A leverage point helps the viewer move through these three stages, tying cognitive knowledge of the product to emotional and personal values.

▶ **FIGURE 6.3**
B-to-B Means–End Chain for Greenfield Online

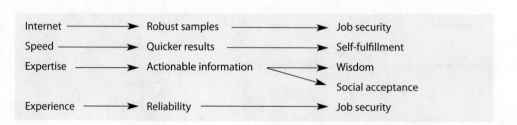

Creatives spend considerable amounts of time designing ads with powerful leverage points. Various types of appeals become the tools creatives use to help consumers make the transition from awareness of a product's benefits to incorporating them with personal values.

TAGLINES

The key phrase in an advertisement, the **tagline**, should be something memorable that identifies the uniqueness of a brand or conveys some type of special meaning. "Just Do It" has been Nike's tagline for many years. Figure 6.4 identifies other well-known taglines.

Taglines carry over from one advertisement to others. They provide consistency across various advertising platforms. Consumers often remember taglines and identify them with specific brands. A catchy tagline identifies a brand and then stays with it over successive campaigns. In order to bring freshness to a campaign, company marketers occasionally tweak or modify a tagline every few years. With shorter attention spans, taglines have been shrinking from short sentences to just two or three words. L'Oreal Paris has used the shortened tagline "Because I'm Worth It" for over 40 years. Other taglines that have been shorted include BMW's "ultimate driving machine," Lucozade"s (British energy drink) "Yes" and Wal-Mart's "Save money, live better."

In other instances, a completely new version may be developed. To make the Oscar Mayer brand more contemporary, the company's marketing personnel and its agency, mcgarrybowen, created a new tagline. Oscar Mayer was known for trust, nostalgia, heritage, jingles, bologna, hot dogs, and kids. The image needed to be freshened, made more contemporary, and reach adults as well as kids. The Oscar Mayer marketing team wanted to take the brand to a place that was energetic, culturally relevant, and that captured the spirit of everyday food making people feel good. Real joy, real moments, real friendship, real emotion, and real people were at the forefront. The idea was that Oscar Mayer is "good mood food." One Oscar Mayer ad conveys the good mood feeling that resulted from marketing brainstorming sessions and music collaborations and led to the campaign tagline "It doesn't get better than this."[3]

VERBAL AND VISUAL IMAGES

Another theoretical approach to advertising design focuses on the decision the creative makes about the degree of prominence given to the visual part of an advertisement versus the verbal element. Most major forms of advertising contain both visual and verbal or written elements. A visual ad places the greatest emphasis on the picture or visual element of the ad. A verbal or written ad places more emphasis on the copy.

Visual images often lead to more favorable attitudes toward both the advertisement and the brand. Visuals tend to be more easily remembered than verbal copy. They are stored in

OBJECTIVE 6.3

What roles do visual and verbal images play in advertisements?

◀ **FIGURE 6.4**

Taglines Used by Various Brands

- American Express—"Don't leave home without it."
- Avis—"We try harder."
- Bounty—"The quicker picker-upper"
- Capital One—"What's in your wallet?"
- CNN—"The most trusted name in news"
- Energizer—"It keeps going, and going, and going."
- Hallmark—"When you care enough to send the best"
- John Deere—"Nothing runs like a Deer."
- Maxwell House—"Good to the last drop"
- Nokia—"Connecting people"
- Office Depot—"Taking care of business"
- Target—"Expect more. Pay less."
- UPS—"What can Brown do for you?"
- Wal-Mart—"Save money. Live better."

▲ This advertisement features a strong visual appeal.

the brain as both pictures and words. This dual-coding process makes it easier for people to recall the message. Further, verbal messages tend be stored in the left side of the brain only; images are usually stored in both the left and right sides of the brain.

The advertisement for the Nicole Chair by Thomasville on the next page illustrates the power of visual imagery. Created by The Richards Group, it conveys the chair is "so you" that the design of the chair would be something you would be proud to wear as clothes. The imagery of the chair fabric matching a dress makes the message more powerful.

Visual images range from concrete and realistic to highly abstract. A concrete visual displays something recognizable, such as a person, place, or thing. In an abstract image, the subject becomes more difficult to recognize. Concrete pictures instill a higher level of recall than abstract images. Concrete pictures are dual-coded, allowing the image to be stored in the brain with both a visual and verbal elements. Viewers process an advertisement with a picture of spaghetti as both a picture and as a verbal representation of the restaurant. Ads with concrete images also tend to lead to more favorable attitudes than those with no pictures or abstract pictures.[4]

Radio advertisers often seek to create visual images for the audience. Pepsi produced a commercial in which listeners could hear a can being opened, the soft drink being poured, and the sizzle of the carbonation—an excellent example of creating a visual image. If consumers visualize a picture in their imaginations, the effect may be greater than an actual visual. A visual image requires less brain activity than using one's imagination. The secret is getting the person to think beyond the advertisement and picture the scene being simulated.

Visual Esperanto   Visual imagery is widely used in international marketing. Global advertising agencies try to create **visual Esperanto**, the universal language that makes global advertising possible for any good or service. *Visual Esperanto* advertising recognizes that visual images are more powerful than verbal descriptions. Visual images can transcend cultural differences.[5] To illustrate the power of a visual image compared to a verbal account, think of the word *exotic*. To some, exotic means a white beach in Hawaii with young people in sexy swimsuits. To others, it may be a small cabin in the snow-capped mountains of Switzerland. To others still, exotic may be a close-up of a tribal village in Africa. The word exotic can vary in meaning. At the same time, a picture of a couple holding hands in front of Niagara Falls has practically the same meaning across all cultures. The image conveys a similar meaning across multiple cultures.

Finding the appropriate image constitutes the most important task in creating *visual Esperanto*. The creative looks for the image that conveys the intended meaning or message. Brand identity can be emphasized using visuals rather than words. Then the creative uses words to support the visual image. For example, the creative may decide that a boy and his father at a sports event illustrate the priceless treasure of a shared family moment. In Mexico, the setting could be a soccer match instead of a baseball game in the United States. The specific copy (the words) can then be adapted to another country. Identifying an image that transcends cultures is the difficult part of inspiring *visual Esperanto*. Once a universal image has been found, creatives in each country represented take the image and modify it to appeal to the local target audience.

Business-to-Business In the past, creatives designing business-to-business advertisements relied heavily on the verbal or written element rather than on visuals. The basis of this approach was the belief that business decisions are made in a rational, cognitive manner. In recent years, more business ads have incorporated strong visual elements to heighten the emotional aspects of making a purchase.

In summary, the three theoretical models provide useful ideas for the advertising creative. Each suggests a sequence to be followed as during the preparation of an advertisement. The endpoint will be reached when the viewer remembers the products, thinks favorably about it, and looks for that product when making a purchase decision. Various kinds of advertising messages, or appeals, can be utilized to reach such key advertising objectives.

Types of Advertising Appeals

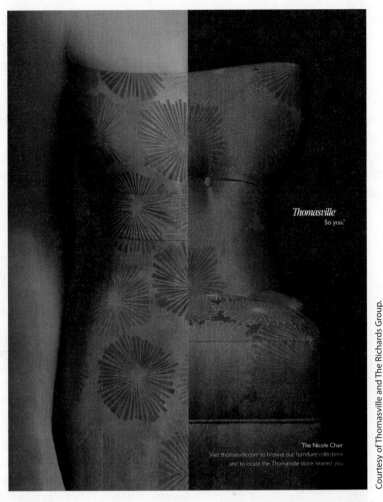

Courtesy of Thomasville and The Richards Group.

▲ This advertisement for the Nicole Chair by Thomasville illustrates the power of visual imagery.

OBJECTIVE 6.4

What are the seven main types of advertising appeals?

Throughout the years, advertisers have employed numerous advertising approaches. Of these, seven **advertising appeals** have achieved the most success. Normally one of these types of appeals will be featured in an advertisement (see Figure 6.5).

The type of appeal chosen should be based on a review of the creative brief, the objective of the advertisement, and the means–end chain to be conveyed. Advertisers consider a number of factors, including the product being sold, the personal preferences of the advertising creative and the account executive, as well as the wishes of the client. The team also identifies appeals that are *inappropriate*. Advertising experts know that certain appeals are less successful in certain circumstances. For example, sexual appeals are not very effective for items not related to sex. The advertising team tries to ensure that the appeal represents the best option for the brand, target audience, and the message, to whatever degree is possible.

Fear

Advertisements featuring fear appeals are commonplace. Life insurance companies focus on the consequences of not having a life insurance policy when a person dies. Shampoo and mouthwash ads invoke fears of dandruff and bad breath, which can make a person a social outcast. Advertisements feature fear more often than most realize.

Advertisers employ fear appeals because they work. Fear increases viewer interest in an advertisement and the ad's persuasiveness. Many individuals remember commercials with fear appeals better than they do warm, upbeat messages.[6] Consumers pay more

OBJECTIVE 6.5

How can fear be used to create an effective advertisement?

- Fear
- Humor
- Sex
- Music
- Rationality
- Emotions
- Scarcity

▲ **FIGURE 6.5**
Advertising Appeals

attention to ads using fear and are more likely to process the information it presents, which makes it possible to accomplish the advertisement's main objective.

The *behavioral response model* explains the way fear works (see Figure 6.6 on the bottom of this page) in advertising.[7] As shown, various incidents can lead to negative or positive consequences, which then affect future behaviors.

SEVERITY AND VULNERABILITY

In developing fear advertisements, the creative includes as many aspects of the behavioral response model as possible. A business-to-business advertiser offering Internet services tries to focus on the **severity** of downtime if a company's Internet server goes down or is hacked. Another ad describes the firm's **vulnerability** by showing the probability that a company's server will crash or can be hacked into and customer data stolen. The ReRez advertisement on the next page for marketing research services features a picture of a man hanging to illustrate the danger of poor marketing research. The advertisement attempts to cause business leaders to believe low quality decisions would result from inadequate research. ReRez can help them identify these potential problems before they turn into disasters.

REWARDS TO RESPONSE EFFICACY

To further understand the behavioral response model, consider a young smoker who sees an ad for the Nicoderm CQ patches, which help a person quit. The man considers three things in evaluating the advertisement and making a decision to purchase Nicoderm CQ.

Intrinsic and extrinsic rewards are the first factor. Intrinsic rewards come from gaining social acceptance by quitting and feeling healthier. Extrinsic rewards may include saving on the cost of cigarettes as compared to the price for Nicoderm CQ.

The smoker then considers the second factor, *response costs*. When smoking leads to peer acceptance, it becomes rewarding less incentive to quit exists, because smoking creates intrinsic value, which makes quitting more difficult. A man who quits smoking becomes more likely to gain weight and lose the friends that continue to smoke. The higher the perceived costs, the less likely the decision to quit smoking becomes.

Self-efficacy constitutes the third factor. In this situation, self-efficacy relates to the man's confidence in his ability to stop smoking. Many individuals have tried and failed. Thus they have little hope Nicoderm CQ will work. The smoker must believe that Nicoderm CQ can truly help him quit before he will purchase it.

▶ **FIGURE 6.6**
The Behavioral Response Model

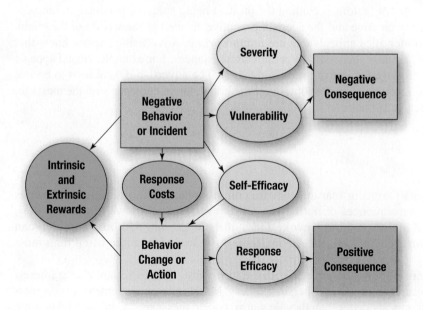

◀ A fear appeal in a business-to-business advertisement.

The combination of intrinsic and extrinsic rewards, response costs, and the degree of self-efficacy contribute to the smoker's *response efficacy*. The decision to purchase Nicoderm CQ with the idea of stopping smoking will be based on the conclusion that doing so will have net positive consequences. The person concludes he will fit in with family and friends, feel better, improve his health, and that he is capable of quitting smoking.

APPEAL STRENGTH

When using fear, another factor will be the strength of the appeal. Most advertisers believe a moderate fear level will be the most effective. A low level of fear may not be noticed, and the fear level may not be convincing in terms of severity or vulnerability. An advertisement with a fear level that is too strong can also backfire, because the message only generates feelings of anxiety. This leads the viewer to avoid watching the commercial, by changing the channel or muting the sound.[8] Consequently a fear appeal's goal should be to make it powerful enough to capture a viewer's attention and to influence her thinking, but not so scary that she avoids the advertisement.

Fear ads match well with certain types of goods and services, especially products that eliminate problems or threats to a consumer's sense of personal security. Account executives, creatives, and company leaders decide when fear represents the best approach or whether some other type of appeal offers greater promise.

Humor

Clutter presents a significant problem in every advertising medium. Capturing a viewer's attention continues to be difficult. Even after grabbing the audience's attention, keeping it becomes even more challenging. Humor has proven to be one of the best techniques for cutting through clutter, by getting attention and keeping it. Consumers, as a whole, enjoy advertisements that make them laugh. A funny message offers intrusive value and attracts attention.[9]

OBJECTIVE 6.6

How can humor be used to create an effective advertisement?

Humor appears in about 30 percent of television and radio advertisements.[10] Humorous ads often win awards and tend to be favorites among consumers. In a *USA Today* consumer survey of the most likeable advertising campaigns, humor was a key ingredient.[11]

For years, Anheuser-Busch chose humor to advertise the Bud Light brand. Humorous ads included "Spuds McKenzie," "Yes I am," "I love you man," and "Real Men of Genius." As Bud Light's target market began to grow older, the marketing department decided to attract a new set of younger consumers. The decision was made to depart from humorous commercials and show young consumers that Bud Light was not your dad's beer. The "Drinkability" campaign was born. Sales dropped by 3 percent. It was the first decline in Bud Light's history in over 30 years. As a result, Anheuser-Busch dropped the "Drinkability" theme for Bud Light and returned to humor.[12]

Humorous ads achieve success for three reasons. Humor causes consumers to: watch, laugh, and, most important, remember. In recall tests, consumers most often remember humorous ads. The best results occur when the humor connects directly with the product's benefits. The advertisement should link the product's features with the advantage to customers and personal values in a means–end chain.

ADVANTAGES OF HUMOR

Humorous ads pique viewer interest, which makes gaining consumer consideration of the advertisement's message easier. A funny ad captures the viewer's attention, leading to improved comprehension and recall of the advertising message and tagline. Advertising research indicates that humor elevates people's moods. Happy consumers often associate a good mood with the advertiser's products. In essence, humor helps fix the brand in the consumer's cognitive structure with links to positive feelings.

PROBLEMS WITH HUMOR

Although a funny advertisement can capture the viewer's attention, cut through clutter, and enhance recall, humorous ads can also go wrong. A Snickers commercial that ran during a recent Super Bowl featured two mechanics eating from opposite ends of the same candy bar until they accidentally ended up kissing. The two men responded in disgust by ripping out their own chest hairs. The outcry from some groups was loud enough that it was immediately pulled.[13]

Advertisers should not allow the humor to overpower the message. Humor fails when consumers remember the joke but not the product or brand. In other words, the advertisement was so funny that the audience forgets or does not catch the sponsor's name. Humorous advertisements can also fail to accomplish advertising objectives.

To avoid these problems, the humor in an advertisement should focus on a component of the means–end chain. The humor can relate to a product's attributes, a customer benefit, or the personal value obtained from the product. The most effective ads are those in which the humor incorporates all three elements.

INTERNATIONAL USAGE

Some evidence suggests that while enjoying humor is universal there are particular executions of humor that may not be effective. Forms of humor are often rooted in various cultures and humor may not transfer from one culture to another. Further, not all audiences experience a humorous ad in the same way. Advertisers should pre-test commercials before they are launched in other countries to ensure the message will be liked and will be considered funny rather than offensive.

A humorous ad developed for McDonald's in Singapore had the highest recall rate (90 percent) of all other commercials released during the month it ran. In Germany, Ford deviated from traditional ads that concentrated on promoting product quality and value to humor. One advertisement features a pigeon sitting on tree branch with a Ford Ka parked nearby. The bird swoops down to bomb the car, but at the last minute the car hood springs up and knocks the bird out. The advertisement was first shown on Ford's U.K. Web site.

• Captures attention.	• High recall scores.
• Holds attention.	• Consumers enjoy ads that make them laugh.
• Often wins creative awards.	• Evaluated by consumers as likeable ads.

◀ **FIGURE 6.7**
Reasons for Using Humor in Ads

Word about the ad quickly spread until more than 1 million people had visited the Web site to see the ad. German dealers requested the ad so they could show it on television. The feedback and popularity of the ad in the United Kingdom caused Ford's marketing managers to agree to run the ad in Germany. The ad resonated with young, affluent buyers, which Ford had been trying to reach. The new ad was seen as witty, gutsy, and edgy, which worked well with Ford's theme of projecting the Ka as a stylish car.[14]

Humorous ads can be difficult to design. One cynic noted that there are only 12 funny people in the United States. Humor that does not work often creates a negative image for the company. Effective humor can generate success and provide dividends in terms of brand equity. Figure 6.7 summarizes the major reasons for using humor.

Sex

Sexual appeals are often used to break through clutter. Advertisements in the United States and other countries contain more visual sexual themes than ever. Nudity and other sexual approaches are common. Sexual themes in ads, however, do not always work. Sex no longer has shock value. Today's teens grow up in societies immersed in sex. One more sexually-oriented ad captures little attention. Currently, many advertisers prefer more subtle sexual cues, suggestions, and innuendos.[15] Figure 6.8 lists the ways sexuality has been employed in advertising.

OBJECTIVE 6.7

Why does sex play such a prominent role in advertising?

SUBLIMINAL APPROACHES

Placing sexual cues or icons in advertisements in an attempt to affect a viewer's subconscious is the subliminal approach. In an odd paradox, truly subliminal cues are not noticed, which means they do not create any effects. Consumers already pay little attention to ads. A subliminal message that registers only in the viewer's subconscious will not be effective. If it worked, there would be no need for stronger sexual content in advertising.

SENSUALITY

Many women respond more favorably to a sensual suggestion than an overtly sexual approach. An alluring glance across a crowded room can be sensual and draw attention to a product. Many view sensuality as being more sophisticated, because it relies on the imagination. Images of romance and love can be more enticing than raw sexuality.

SEXUAL SUGGESTIVENESS

A sexually suggestive advertisement hints that sex is about to take place. Recently, Pine-Sol used suggestiveness to advertise a household cleaner. In several television ads, shirtless, muscular men are shown mopping the floor while the female watches or fantasizes. Diane Amos, who has been featured in Pine-Sol ads for the last 16 years and also appears in this new series of ads featuring men, says "We would all like our husbands to mop. . . . It can be fun, it can be sexy, and women like it clean."[16]

▼ **FIGURE 6.8**
Sexuality Approaches Used in Advertisements

NUDITY OR PARTIAL NUDITY

Products that contain sexual connotations or elements, such as clothing, perfume, and cologne, may feature a degree of nudity. Some ads are designed to solicit a sexual response. Others are not. In 1987, underwear companies were first allowed to use live models in television advertisements. The first commercials were modest and informational, emphasizing the

• Subliminal techniques
• Sensuality
• Sexual suggestiveness
• Nudity or partial nudity
• Overt sexuality

Forever on the lips, never on the hips.

▲ An advertisement for Old Orchard featuring sensuality.

▼ An advertisement for Benetton featuring partial nudity.

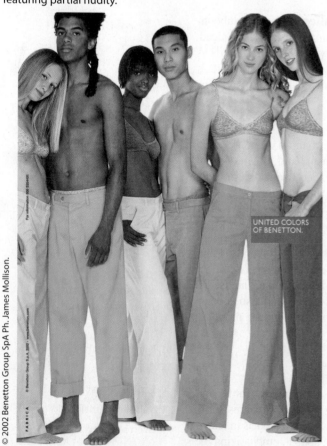

design or materials used in the undergarment. The first Playtex bra commercials using live models drew strong criticism from organizations such as the American Family Association. Currently, advertisements for undergarments go much further and involve superstars, such as actress Jennifer Love Hewitt who appeared in television and print ads for the Hanes All-Over Comfort bra and the Perfect Panty. The campaign even included an online element with footage from the photo shoots, a "bad bra toss" game, and a blog about bad bra moments.[17]

Decorative Models   A common sexual approach in advertising involves placing **decorative models**, or individuals in advertisements to adorn products as a sexual or attractive stimuli. The models serve no other purpose than to attract attention. In the past, commercials for automobiles, tools, and beer often used female models dressed in bikinis standing by the products. A number of studies were conducted to determine the effectiveness of decorative models. The basic conclusions are provided in Figure 6.9.[18]

OVERT SEXUALITY

Using overt sexuality in ads for sexually-oriented products is normally accepted, but it often becomes controversial when used for other types of products. When Procter & Gamble launched a television advertising campaign for Dentyne, eyebrows were raised. The commercial showed two teens in a living room. The girl pops a piece of Dentyne Fire bubble gum into her mouth and then rips off her blouse and jumps on her boyfriend. At first the parents stare in shock. Then, the mom tries a piece of Dentyne Fire and promptly jumps on the dad. The controversy centered on whether the ad promoted teenage sexuality by suggesting that parents should openly display sexual feelings and desires.[19]

ARE SEX APPEALS EFFECTIVE?

Numerous studies have examined the effectiveness of sexual appeals and nudity in advertising. Almost all of them conclude that sex and nudity do increase attention, regardless of the gender of the person in the advertisement or the gender of the audience. Normally, the attention will be greater for opposite-sex situations than same-sex situations, for both males and females viewing the opposite gender. To encourage both genders to pay attention to its ads, Guess often features a male and female in a sexually provocative setting in an advertisement.

Attracting Attention   Although sexually-oriented ads attract attention, brand recall for ads using a sex appeal might be lower than those using other types of appeals. It appears that although people watch the advertisement, the sexual theme distracts them from noticing the brand name.[20]

Observers often rate sexually-oriented advertisements rated as more interesting. Those ads deemed to be highly controversial in terms of sexual content are rated as more interesting by both males and females. The paradox, however, is that although the controversial ads are more

- The presence of female (or male) decorative models improves ad recognition, but not brand recognition.
- The presence of a decorative model influences emotional and objective evaluations of the product among both male and female audiences.
- Attractive models produce a higher level of attention to ads than do less attractive models.
- The presence of an attractive model produces higher purchase intentions when the product is sexually relevant than if it is not sexually relevant.

interesting, they fail to increase the transmission of information. Respondents are less likely to remember any more about the message.[21]

Physiological Arousal   Advertisements featuring overt sexual stimuli or containing nudity produce higher levels of physiological arousal responses. These arousal responses have been linked to the formation of both affective and cognitive responses. If the viewer is male and the sexual stimulus is female, such as a nude female in an ad for cologne, then the viewer tends to develop a strong feeling toward the ad based on the arousal response his body experiences. Female viewers of male nudity in an advertisement often experience the same type of response, although the arousal response may not be as strong.

Cognitive Impressions   The cognitive impression made on viewers of a sexually-oriented ad depends on whether the viewer sees the advertisement as pleasant or offensive. When the viewer likes the ad, it results in a positive impression of the brand. When the viewer thinks the ad exhibits poor taste, negative feelings and beliefs about the brand often emerge. When sex works, it increases sales. An ad that does not may inspire negative feelings toward the brand.[22]

▼ A Guess advertisement with a male and a female model.

Societal Trends   In determining the level of sex appeal to feature in an advertisement, the advertising team considers society's view and level of acceptance.[23] Just as economies go through cycles, attitudes toward sex in advertising experience acceptance fluctuate.

The use and acceptance of sexual themes in advertising had swung to a high level of tolerance in the early part of the 2000s, until the Super Bowl of 2004. The public reaction to Janet Jackson's breast-baring halftime show sent ripples all the way to Madison Avenue. Shortly afterward, Victoria's Secret dropped its TV lingerie fashion show. Abercrombie & Fitch killed the company's quarterly catalog, which had been strongly criticized for featuring models in sexually suggestive poses. Anheuser-Busch dropped some of its risqué ads.[24]

The pendulum may now be slowly swinging back toward greater acceptance of sexually—oriented ads, but it has not reached the pre-2004 level yet. A recent Calvin Klein ad featuring actress Eva Mendes in the nude in a provocative pose for its Secret Obsession fragrance was rejected by the major networks in the United States, but accepted by television stations in Europe. A less-provocative version was created for the United States, and it was not shown until after 9:00 p.m.[25]

Although the use of sex in advertising has regained acceptance in main stream society, it is still not very

Courtesy of J.B. Stetson Company.

▲ An Stetson advertisement directed to women using a sex appeal.

well accepted for the Super Bowl. Recent studies suggest that Super Bowl ads with sexual imagery were 10 percent less likeable than ads without sexual imagery. Instead of sex, most viewers of the Super Bowl prefer ads with kids or animals. Chuck Tomkovick, the marketing professor who conducted the studies, concluded "The more you put sex in an ad, the less it is liked."[26]

The use of sex in advertising will continue. Advertisers should carefully determine the level and the type of sexuality to use and the target audience. What will work at one particular point in time may not work at another.

DISADVANTAGES OF SEX APPEALS

One major criticism of sexually based advertising is that it perpetuates dissatisfaction with one's body. Females in print advertisements and models in television advertising are often thin. The key to success seems to be the thinner the better. As advertising models have gotten thinner, body dissatisfaction and eating disorders among women have risen. Research indicates that women feel unhappy about their own bodies and believe they are too fat after viewing advertisements showing thin models. Still, ads with thin models are more likely to convince women to purchase a product.[27]

Thin male models have an effect on men, but in reverse. Many men worry they are not muscular enough and are too thin or too fat. It does not make any difference whether the male views a male model or a female model in advertisements.[28]

Some companies have begun to feature real women of different shapes and sizes, such as Dove's "Campaign for Real Beauty." The campaign has garnered international attention, won several major advertising awards, and achieved a healthy growth in sales. The approach struck a responsive chord with many women.

SEX APPEALS IN INTERNATIONAL ADVERTISING

What is deemed appropriate or acceptable in terms of sexual appeal varies across countries. In Chile, a campaign featuring nude celebrities touting the benefits of drinking milk was launched. The ad's producers stated, "Chile is a country of stuffed shirts, so this campaign is going to shake them up, and at a relatively low cost, thanks to nudity." The Chilean Dairy Federation believed that the ads would promote the idea of rebellion to Chilean youth. As more Chilean kids travel the world and see teens with green and blue hair and body piercings, public nudity becomes associated with freedom. Despite opposition by conservatives, the "naked" milk campaign aroused the attention of Chilean young people, and milk sales grew.[29]

Religions, cultures, and value systems determine the levels of nudity, sexual references, and gender-specific issues that are permitted in a country. Muslim nations tend to reject any kind of nudity and any reference to sexuality and other gender-related issues. They also do not permit any type of advertising for personal goods, such as female hygiene products, contraceptives, or undergarments. Many Muslim countries forbid any hint of sexuality or display of the female body.

In many Middle Eastern countries, sex and gender issues are taboo subjects. Sexual appeals are not used in advertising, and even sexually-related products are difficult to advertise. In response, Procter & Gamble hosted a call-in TV show directed toward young girls in Egypt. The show's panel contained health experts, and topics ranged from marriage to menopause. The call-in show was followed up with a TV talk show called *Frankly Speaking* about feminine hygiene. The show's goal was to tackle some of the more sensitive issues facing young Egyptian girls. Although the show discussed what happens during puberty, it was P&G's policy not to discuss sexuality. P&G sponsored the show, and the primary product advertised was P&G's Always feminine sanitary pads.[30]

In other countries, standards regarding sexually—oriented advertising are more permissive but sometimes confusing. In France, sex appears everywhere. Advertisers can feature seminude or completely nude models in advertisements if they can be justified; a relationship must exist between the product and the nude model. It does not take much of a justification in France, where citizens view sex as healthy, innocent, and natural. One difference in France, however, is that sex and humor are not mixed. The French do not consider sex to be silly or funny.[31]

The problem with the stereotyping of females in ads takes a different twist in other countries. For example, in Saudi Arabia and Malaysia women must be shown in family settings. They cannot be depicted as being carefree or desirable to the opposite sex.[32]

In general, the use of sex to make products more appealing provides a legitimate tactic for many companies, products, and advertising firms. The goal should be to use sex in an interesting manner that is germane to the product, and within the ethical standards of the region. From there, taste and other more personalized standards serve as guides. The U.S. milk industry advertisement shown in this section has been effective. Although the model wears a swimsuit, it is germane to the product. The advertisement seeks to persuade women that milk not only is good for healthy bones, but that it also enhances one's appearance. By telling women that bones continue to develop until the age of 35, the ad reinforces a reason to consume milk.

▲ An example of an effective sexual appeal promoting milk.

Musical Appeals

Music oftens adds an important ingredient to an advertisement. It connects with emotions, memories, and other experiences. Music can be intrusive; it gains the attention of someone who previously was not listening to or watching a program. It may provide the stimulus that ties a particular musical arrangement, jingle, or song to a certain product or brand. As soon as the tune begins, consumers recognize product being advertised because they have been conditioned to tie the product to the music. For example, numerous consumers recall the Intel "tune."

Music gains attention and increases the retention of information when it becomes intertwined with the product. Even when consumers do not recall the ad message argument, music can lead to a better recall of an advertisement's visual and emotional aspects. Music can increase the persuasiveness of an argument. Subjects who compared ads with music to identical ads without music almost always rated those with music higher in terms of persuasiveness.[33]

OBJECTIVE 6.8

How can music, rationality, emotions, and scarcity be used to increase advertising effectiveness?

▲ The song "It Doesn't Get Better Than This" was written and sung by Joy Williams for the television ads in the Oscar Mayer campaign.

Several decisions are made when selecting music for commercials, including the following:

- What role will music play in the ad?
- Will a familiar song be used, or will something original be created?
- What emotional pitch should the music reach?
- How does the music fit with the message of the ad?

Music plays a variety of roles in advertisements. Sometimes the music is incidental. In others, it becomes the primary theme. An important decision involves selecting a familiar tune as opposed to creating original music. Writing a jingle or music specifically for the advertisement occurs more often and has become the current trend. Background or mood-inducing music is usually instrumental, and advertisers often pay musicians to write music that matches the scenes in the ad. A number of advertising agencies are now forming in-house recording labels for the sole purpose of writing jingles, songs, and music for ads.[34]

As an alternative, some advertising agencies send the creative brief to interested musicians and ask them to compose and pitch a song. The mcgarrybowen advertising agency used the approach when selecting a song for the new Oscar Mayer campaign. The creative brief was sent to approximately 60 musicians. Each was asked to compose a song he or she felt expressed the emotions conveyed in the brief. Both the Oscar Mayer marketing team and mcgarrybowen decided that the song "It Doesn't Get Better Than This" composed and sung by Joy Williams best brought the emotions of the new Oscar Mayer campaign to life.

ADVANTAGES OF USING WELL-KNOWN SONGS

In the 2000s, using a well-known song in an advertisement was common. A popular, well-known song creates certain advantages. The primary benefit is that consumers already have developed an affinity for the song. Brand awareness, brand equity, and brand loyalty become easier to develop when consumers are familiar with the music. This occurs when consumers transfer an emotional affinity for the song to the product. Some companies purchase an existing song and adapt the ad to the music.[35] Using popular songs may be expensive. The price for the rights to a very popular song can be in the range of six to seven figures.[36] The Internet company Excite paid $7 million for the rights to Jimi Hendrix's song "Are You Experienced," and Microsoft paid about $12 million for "Start Me Up."[37]

ALTERNATE METHODS

An alternative method of developing music has emerged, primarily because of the Internet. More cooperation now exists between musicians and marketers. Some musicians view advertisements as a way to get their songs heard. Marketers see an opportunity to tie a new, exciting song to a product. This has spurred a new type of company, such as Artists & Brands, an organization with the goal of developing songs for commercials. Many consumers are interested in finding out who performs the music in various ads so it is a way of breaking into the music industry for an unknown singer. The Internet provides the opportunity not only to find out, but also to post it for others to enjoy on sites such as YouTube. When an ad only contains part of the song, many firms place entire tunes on company Web sites or on YouTube so that individuals can download them.

Occasionally, a song written for a commercial will crack Billboard's Top 100 list. Jason Wade, a singer in the band Lifehouse, had never written a song for a commercial before. After viewing a copy of the 60-second commercial for Allstate Insurance produced by Leo Burnett Agency, Wade wrote a song entitled "From Where You Are." The commercial promoted Allstate's safe-driving program for teenagers. After the commercial aired, the song was made available on iTunes. Within 2 weeks, sales were high enough for the song to reach number 40 on Billboard's charts.[38]

Rational Appeals

A rational appeal follows the hierarchy of effects stages of awareness, knowledge, liking, preference, conviction, and purchase. A creative designs the advertisement for one of the six steps. An ad oriented to the knowledge stage transmits basic product information. In the preference stage, the message shifts to presenting logical reasons that favor the brand, such as the superior gas mileage of an automobile. A rational advertisement should lead to a stronger conviction about a product's benefits, so that the purchase eventually will be made.

Rational appeals rely on consumers actively processing the information presented in the advertisement. The consumer must pay attention to the commercial, comprehend the message, and compare the information to knowledge embedded in a cognitive map. Messages consistent with the current concepts in the cognitive map strengthen key linkages. New messages help the person form cognitive beliefs about the brand and establish a new linkage from her current map to the new product.

A business customer who sees a Kinko's advertisement about videoconferencing services already may have the company in his cognitive structure. The customer may have used Kinko's in the past but was not aware that the company offers videoconferencing. When Kinko's has been established in this person's cognitive map, creating a new linkage to entice the customer to try its videoconferencing services becomes easier.

MEDIA OUTLETS

Print media and the Internet offer the best outlets for rational appeals. Print and Internet ads allow readers greater opportunities to process copy information. They can pause and take time to think about the written content. Television and radio commercials are short, which makes it difficult for viewers to process message arguments. Also, if television viewers miss a television commercial, they do not have the opportunity to see it until the ad is broadcast again.

BUSINESS-TO-BUSINESS

Print media are used extensively for business-to-business messages. These advertisers take advantage of print's ability to feature rational appeals. Many advertising account executives believe trade publications offer the best method of reaching members of the buying center. Those in the industry often subscribe to trade publications. Placing an advertisement in a trade publication means the firm has a better chance of hitting its primary target market. Further, trade publications allow advertisers the opportunity to convey more details to potential buyers.

Buying center members who scan trade journals while in the information search stage of the buying process are likely to notice the ad, read it, and process the information. Buying center members who are not looking for information about the particular product will probably ignore the same ad. Magazines do not have intrusion value and

▲ This Colorado advertisement features visual elements that create an emotional appeal of serenity and peace.

readers can easily skip or ignore an advertisement. A rational appeal usually presents a primary appeal with no strong peripheral cues to attract the reader's attention.

PRODUCT ATTRIBUTES

Conventional advertising wisdom suggests that rational appeals are well suited to high-involvement and complex products. High-involvement decisions require considerable cognitive activity, and consumers spend more time evaluating the attributes of the individual brands. Thus, a rational appeal should be the best approach to reach them. For some consumers, however, emotions and feelings even influence high-involvement decisions. For instance, life insurance involves both rational and emotional elements. Various insurance companies can use both in seeking to influence consumers.

In general, rational appeals are effective when consumers have high levels of involvement and are willing to pay attention to the advertisement. Message arguments and product information should be placed in the copy. Consumers can then more fully absorb information.

A rational appeal often works better than other appeals in developing or changing attitudes and establishing brand beliefs. This will be mainly true when a consumer has a particular interest in the product or brand. Otherwise, the consumer often ignores an ad with a rational appeal.

Emotional Appeals

Emotional appeals are based on three ideas (see Figure 6.10). First, consumers ignore most advertisements. Second, rational appeals go unnoticed unless the consumer is in the market for a particular product at the time it is advertised. Third, and most important, emotional advertising can capture a viewer's attention and create an attachment between the consumer and the brand.

BRAND LOYALTY

Most creatives view emotional advertising as the key to brand loyalty. Creatives want customers to experience a bond with the brand. Visual cues in advertisements are important in emotional appeals. The visual elements in the ad for Colorado contribute to a feeling or mood of serenity. The female in the ad for State Farm elicits feelings of happiness. Also, peripheral cues, such as the music and the actor, are crucial. Although individuals develop perceptions of brands based largely on visual and peripheral stimuli,

▶ **FIGURE 6.10**
Reasons for Using Emotional Appeals

- Consumers ignore most ads.
- Rational appeals generally go unnoticed.
- Emotional appeals can capture attention and foster an attachment.

- Trust
- Reliability
- Friendship
- Happiness
- Security
- Glamour-luxery
- Serenity
- Anger

- Protecting loved ones
- Romance
- Passion
- Family bonds
- with parents
- with siblings
- with children
- with extended family members

it does not happen instantly. With repetition, perceptions and attitudinal changes emerge. Figure 6.11 displays some of the more common emotions presented in advertisements.

Godiva employed an emotional appeal in its latest advertising campaign entitled "the golden moment." Created by Lipman Agency, the campaign focused on the emotional appeal of giving, sharing, or eating Godiva chocolates. Laurie Len Kotcher, Chief Marketing Officer and Senior Vice President for Global Brand Development of Godiva Chocolatier, said "When you give the gold box, receive the gold box, eating something from the gold box, there is something special about that moment."[39]

BUSINESS-TO-BUSINESS

Emotional appeals have begun to appear more frequently in business-to-business advertising. In the past, only 5 to 10 percent of all business-to-business ads featured emotional appeals. Today, the figure has risen to nearly 25 percent. A magazine advertisement created by NKH&W Advertising Agency for a product to treat racehorses switched from a rational appeal to an emotional appeal. The target market was veterinarians. In the past, an advertisement would have opened with such ad copy as "For swelling in joints use…" The emotional ad shows the horse thinking, "I will prove them wrong. I will run again. I will mend my spirits."[40] *Business Week* magazine had always focused on the functional benefits of the magazine in its advertising. With declining subscriptions, *Business Week* created an emotional campaign that focused more on the magazine's identity and personality along with the individuals that read it.[41]

The underlying principle for changing to more emotional business-to-business ads is that emotions can be part of every type of purchase decision. Members of the buying center consider product information in making decisions but, at the same time, they are can be affected by emotions. Although a member of the buying center may try to minimize the emotional side of a purchase, it still provides an influence. The affective component of attitudes is as important as the cognitive component. In the past, business-to-business advertisers tended to ignore the affective element.

▲ An advertisement for State Farm generating the emotion of happiness.

If you could hold onto
any moment in time,

which?

pheel
the moment

KRAFT
PHILADELPHIA
REGULAR

▲ An advertisement for Philadelphia Cream Cheese with an emotional appeal.

MEDIA OUTLETS

Television remains one of the best media for emotional appeals. Television offers advertisers intrusion value and can utilize both sound and sight. Models in the ads can be real people. Facial expressions convey emotions and attitudes. Consumers learn about a particular product and develop attitudes based on these experiences. Television ads also are more vivid, lifelike, and often create dynamic situations that pull viewers in. Music can be incorporated to make the commercial more dramatic. Peripheral cues constitute important components of emotional appeals. The cues, such as music and background visuals, help capture the viewer's attention.

Emotional ads are widely featured on the Internet. Many of the same benefits for television are found online. The use of streaming video, animation, and software such as Photoshop make it possible to create engaging emotional ads.

Emotions are tied with humor, fear, music, and other appeals to make a compelling case for a product. The same ad can influence a consumer both emotionally and rationally. The creative selects the most appropriate emotional appeal for the product and company.

Scarcity Appeals

Scarcity appeals urge consumers to buy a particular product because of a limitation. It can be a limited number of the products available or that the product will be made available for only a limited time. When consumers believe only a finite supply of a product will be available, the perceived value of the product may increase. For the Olympics, General Mills introduced USA Olympic Crunch cereal and Betty Crocker Team USA desserts for a limited time.[42] McDonald's, Wendy's, and Burger King offer sandwiches (McRib, Hot N' Spicy Chicken, Dollar Whoppers) for limited-time periods throughout the year. The scarcity concept applies to musical compilations, encouraging consumers to buy a CD because of its restricted availability. By making sure it is not available in retail stores, marketers increase its scarcity value.

A scarcity appeal may be tied to other promotional tools. For example, a manufacturer will advertise a limited price discount offer to retailers who stock up early for Christmas or some other holiday season. Contests and sweepstakes also run for limited times. The approach yields the benefit of encouraging consumers to take action. Creatives normally receive information about scarcity issues in the creative brief or from the account executive who has consulted with the company.

International Implications

Many of the international implications of both advertising theory and the various types of appeals have already been described in this chapter. In summary, leverage points lead to customer values. These values may be influenced by the culture or country in which the consumer lives. Therefore, advertisements should be constructed in ways that express those values.

Advertising appeals should be adapted to cultural differences. As a small example, fear of body odor often sells products in the United States. In other cultures, body odor does not carry the same meaning. Sexual appeals, as noted, must be adjusted to fit the laws and customs of a region. Musical tastes vary, as do perceptions of rationality and scarcity. Emotions may be stronger in some cultures, whereas in others people are much more reserved.

An international company or a firm seeking to expand into additional countries should adapt and adjust both the theoretical approach and type of appeal in order to create effective advertisements. Finding universal themes, such as *visual Esperanto*, may be a great help to the international advertising creative.

INTEGRATED CAMPAIGNS IN ACTION

Philadelphia Cream Cheese

Sales of Philadelphia Cream Cheese had been stagnant for several years, because most United States consumers only use the product to spread on bagels or as the main ingredient in cheesecake. To spur sales in the United States, Kraft Vice President of Marketing Howard Friedman worked with the advertising agency mcgarrybowen to create a new campaign.

One component of the campaign targeted women who cook. In addition to the print and broadcast ads, the campaign focused on providing recipes online submitted by consumers through a contest entitled "Real Women of Philly." The grand prize was $125,000 and an appearance on television on a cooking show.

▲ An Philadelphia Cream Cheese advertisement developed by the mcgarrybowen agency.

MyMarketingLab

Go to **mymktlab.com** to complete the problems marked with this icon .

SUMMARY

Developing effective advertisements represents a key ingredient in integrated marketing communications efforts. The advertising team defines the objective of the ad, the target audience, the message theme used, the type of support needed, and any constraints that apply. Then, a creative works within the context of key advertising theories in selecting the correct media and designing the leverage point and message appeal that work effectively within each medium.

Three important theoretical approaches drive the development of many advertisements. The hierarchy of effects model suggests consumers move through a series of stages as they are persuaded to make a purchase: awareness, knowledge, liking, preference, conviction, and the actual purchase. Although the process probably is not a lock-step model that every buyer follows, the hierarchy of effects approach provides important information about which mental issues to account for in various advertising campaigns. The hierarchy of effects model can be combined with the three main elements present in attitudes: cognitive, affective, and conative components. Ads are designed to influence affective feelings, cognitive knowledge, or conative intentions to act or behave based on an attitude. A means–end chain displays the linkages between a means to achieve a desired state and the end or personal value at issue. Advertisers can select personal values that mesh with the key characteristics of the target market and then construct ads designed to provide them the means to achieve these ends by purchasing the good or service. These ideas help the creative develop a leverage point to move the buyer from understanding the product's benefits to incorporating those benefits with his or her personal values.

Visual and verbal issues should also be considered in the formation of an ad. Concrete visual images are easily recognized and recalled. Abstract images may be linked with values or emotions the product creates or the feeling the buyer should experience that may be associated with the product or company. Visual elements are key components in almost every form of advertising. Verbal elements must reach the more rational, central route of the audience's mental processing procedures.

Beyond these components, advertising creatives must form messages using one (or more) of the seven major appeals: fear, humor, sex, music, rationality, emotions, or scarcity. Just as there are logical combinations of media, there are logical combinations of these appeals for various messages. Often, music provides the backdrop for messages invoking fear, humor, sex, and emotions. Humor can be linked with sex, music, rationality (by showing how being illogical is silly or funny), and scarcity. Rationality combines with fear in many commercials. Designing a message argument that takes advantage of the various characteristics of these appeals breaks through clutter, and convinces the audience to buy the item involved will be the creative's goal. Mismatches of message tactics are to be avoided, such as combining sex with humor in France, as was mentioned earlier.

Business-to-business ads often appear in print and many times include rational approaches in the copy because the purchase decision variables are more complex. At the same time, many advertisers have recently discovered that emotional ads can be effective, which expands business-to-business advertising into other venues, such as television, radio, and the Internet.

The process of designing ads for international markets is similar to that for domestic ads. The major difference is careful consideration of local attitudes and customers, with due care given to the language, slang, and symbols of the area. For example, Sega recently discovered that its product's name is slang for "masturbation" in Italian, after a major advertising campaign had started. These types of mistakes are to be avoided.

Key Terms

hierarchy of effects model A marketing approach suggesting that a consumer moves through a series of six steps when becoming convinced to make a purchase: awareness, knowledge, liking, preference, conviction, and the actual purchase.

means–end chain An advertising approach in which the message contains a means (a reasoning or mental process) to lead the consumer to a desired end state, such as a key personal value.

Means–End Conceptualization of Components for Advertising Strategy (MECCAS) An advertising approach that suggests using five elements in creating ads: the product's attributes, consumer benefits, leverage points, personal values, and the executional framework.

tagline A catchy, easy-to-remember phrase in an ad used to make the key point and reinforce the company's image to the consumer.

visual Esperanto A universal language that makes global advertising possible for any good or service by recognizing that visual images are more powerful than verbal descriptions.

advertising appeals Advertising approaches to reaching consumers with ads, featuring an element of fear, humor, sex, music, rationality, emotions, or scarcity.

severity The part of the fear behavioral response model that leads the individual to consider how strong certain negative consequences of an action will be.

vulnerability The part of the fear behavioral response model that leads the individual to consider the odds of being affected by the negative consequences of an action.

decorative models Models in an advertisement whose primary purpose is to adorn the product as a sexual or attractive stimulus without serving a functional purpose.

Review Questions

1. What are the six stages of the hierarchy of effects model? Do they always occur in that order? Why or why not?

2. How are the three components of attitude related to the hierarchy of effects model?

3. In a means–end chain, what are the means? The ends? How do they affect advertising design?

4. What is a leverage point? How are leverage points related to the hierarchy of effects model, attitudinal changes, and means–end chains?

5. What is a tagline?

6. Why are visual elements in advertisement important? What is the relationship between visual and verbal elements? Can there be one without the other?

7. What is *visual Esperanto*?

8. What are the seven most common types of advertising appeals?

9. What are the advantages and disadvantages of fear appeals in advertising?

10. When does humor work in an ad? What pitfalls should companies avoid in using humorous appeals?

11. What types of sexual appeals can advertisers use?

12. When are sexual appeals most likely to succeed? To fail?

13. What should international advertisers consider when thinking about using sexual appeals?

14. Name the different ways music can play a role in an advertisement. Explain how each role should match individual appeals, media, and other elements in the design of the ad.

15. What are the advantages and disadvantages of rational appeals? Which media do they best match?

16. How can emotions accentuate advertisements? Why are they being used more often in business-to-business advertisements?

17. What is scarcity? How do scarcity ads lead to buyer action?

Critical Thinking Exercises

DISCUSSION QUESTIONS

1. Pick one of the following brands. Develop a means–end chain similar to the two that are shown in this chapter.
   a. Benetton clothes
   b. Stetson cologne
   c. New Balance shoes
   d. Oscar Mayer deli meats

2. Evaluate the balance of visual and verbal elements of five advertisements shown in this chapter. Which is predominant? Which images are considered appropriate for international advertising because they display visual Esperanto characteristics?

3. Watch one of your favorite television shows. Record all of the television commercials in one commercial break (at least seven ads). Identify the appeal used in each one. Were the ads effective? Why or why not?

4. Locate a print ad or television ad that features a fear appeal. Using the behavioral response model shown in this chapter, identify various elements in the ad that correspond with the components in the model. Some of the elements will require thinking beyond what is visually or verbally present in the ad itself.

5. Hardee's and Carl's Jr. recently used a television commercial featuring a schoolteacher dancing on top of her desk while a room full of guys performed a rap song entitled "I Like Flat Buns." The song seemed appropriate because the ad was for the Patty Melt on a flat bun. Instead, the ad received considerable flack because the sexy blonde schoolteacher was wearing a short, tight skirt. Teachers' associations complained that it was inappropriate because it was a "sexually exploitive assault" on teachers, students, and schools.[43] Do you agree or disagree?

⭐ 6. Using magazines that you normally read, locate at least one print ad for each of the appeals, except music. Discuss the quality of each advertisement and its best and worst aspects. For each ad, present another possible appeal and how it could be used. What personal values and customer benefits does each advertisement present?

7. Locate five television commercials or find five print advertisements that use sex appeals. Identify which of the five ways sexuality was used. Evaluate each ad in terms of the appropriateness and effectiveness of the sex appeal.

8. For each of the following products and target markets, discuss which appeal you think would be the best. Explain why you think it would be effective. Briefly describe a print or television ad that you think would be effective.
   a. Senior citizens—soup
   b. Females, ages 25–40, with children—hot dogs
   c. College students—jeans
   d. Males, ages 25–40, married with children—life insurance

Integrated Learning Exercises

1. Toluna Group, LTD is one of the leading online research firms. Access the Web site at http://www.toluna-group.com. What types of products does the company offer? How would this information help a creative in developing an advertisement for Toluna? How would this information assist an advertising agency in understanding the target audience for an advertisement?

2. Examine the means-end chain shown in this chapter about milk and then access the following Web sites for the milk industry. What differences do you see in the Web sites? Who do you believe is the intended audience for each Web site? Why would the milk industry have different URLs?
   a. www.gotmilk.com
   b. www.whymilk.com
   c. www.bodybymilk.com
   d. www.milkmustache.com

3. Visit the following Web sites. Identify which type of appeal each site uses. Evaluate the quality of that appeal. What other appeals can be used to make the site more appealing? Discuss the balance of visual and verbal elements on the Web site and ad.
   a. Service Metrics (www.servicemetrics.com)
   b. Hyundai Motors, USA (www.hyundaiusa.com)
   c. Skechers (www.skechers.com)
   d. Bijan Fragrances (www.bijan.com)
   e. Guess (www.guess.com)
   f. Oscar Mayer (www.oscarmayer.com)
   g. Liz Claiborne (www.lizclaiborne.com)

4. Access an online database search engine through your library. Pick one of the appeals listed in the chapter. Find at least three different articles that discuss the appeal. Write a report based on your findings.

Student Project

CREATIVE CORNER

It is time to try your creativity with a television advertisement. Borrow a camcorder and develop a 30- or 45-second television spot for one of the following products, using the suggested appeal. Be sure to develop a means–end chain prior to creating the advertisement. If you do not have access to a camcorder, then develop a magazine ad.

a. Denim skirt, sex appeal
b. Tennis racket, humor appeal
c. Ice cream, emotional appeal
d. Vitamins, fear appeal
e. Golf club, rational appeal
f. Spring break trip package, scarcity appeal
g. Restaurant, music appeal

CASE 1 **ECKO ENTERPRISES**

It is a safe bet to guess that the majority of people over 40 years old have not heard of Marc Ecko or Ecko Enterprises. He was born as Marc Milecofsky and grew up south of New York City in Lakewood, New Jersey. His parents were real estate agents. Ecko has two sisters, one of whom is his twin, Marci. The name Ecko is the result of a family story. When Ecko's mother was pregnant with Marci, the doctor informed her of an "echo" on an ultrasound, which turned out to be Marc.

The world of hip hop belongs to a new generation, one with its own unique form of clothing, known to many as "urban apparel." Ecko Enterprises was formed in 1993 when three friends began creating T-shirt fashions using cans of spray paint. By 2004, the company reported sales of nearly $1 billion. Items from Ecko Enterprises and the Ecko Unlimited brand are sold in more than 5,000 department and specialty stores domestically and in over 45 countries internationally. There are now 30 Ecko Unlimited full-price company annex stores, 16 of which are located outside of the United States. The Ecko Unlimited clothing line often features the stark silhouette of a rhinoceros on T-shirts, baggy jeans, and other products.

Ecko's company competes with firms that rely on the "cred" (credibility) that comes from being a performer, such as the Sean John line featuring P. Diddy, Rocawear from Jay-Z and Damon Dash, and Phat Fashions offered by Russell Simmons. Marc Ecko, in contrast, is simply a fan of the music who grew up living in suburban neighborhoods. Although he is sometimes described as a "former graffiti artist," the reality is that his company was formed while he was studying at Rutgers University to become a pharmacist.

A variety of products are featured through Ecko Unlimited, Marc Ecko Formalwear, and Eckored Kids, including outerwear, footwear, watches, eyewear, underwear, belts, bags, hats, small leather goods, and formal wear. The Marc Ecko Cut & Sew brand is a contemporary menswear line consisting of casual and dress separates designed to blend street-inspired edginess with more sophisticated designs and fabrics. Cut & Sew offers semi-tailored separates, sweaters, urban spa-inspired active wear, woven shirts, and premium denim.

A newer brand, the G-Unit Clothing Company, is an independent venture operated by Ecko and multiplatinum-selling artist 50 Cent. The G-Unit line includes items for men, women, boys, and girls. It features denim, T-shirts, fleece, outerwear, hats, and sportswear. Also, Marc Ecko Enterprises formed an exclusive U.S. and Canadian licensing agreement with Avirex Ltd. to introduce a sportswear collection. The line carries a full collection of apparel, including fashion denim, tees, knits, and outerwear. Other licensing agreements have been formed with Geoffrey Allen, Skechers, Paul D'Avril, Inc., Kid Headquarters, and Viva International.

The company also offers skateboards and skater-influenced clothing and accessories through the Zoo York label. The brand was launched in 1993 and is now part of the MEE line, which is the East Coast's largest action sports company. Ecko also publishes *Complex Magazine*, a bimonthly urban lifestyle publication with a circulation of 325,000. Another new venture is

Andrey Kiselev / Fotolia

▲ Ecko Enterprises began by selling its unique form of clothing, known as "urban apparel".

Contents Under Pressure, a game developed in partnership with Atari, Inc. The game features stories and characters in a futuristic universe in which graffiti plays a key role.

Urban apparel can be viewed as a form of "lifestyle merchandising." Ecko was able to translate his own enthusiasm for hip hop into something new and different in the fashion world. By placing ads in hip-hop magazines such as *The Source* and *Vibe*, the Ecko rhino grew based on relationships with a wide range of maverick recording artists, including Talib Kweli and the Beatnuts. Although many retailers feared the urban look, Federated Department Stores, the owner of Macy's and Bloomingdale's, became an enthusiastic seller of Ecko Unlimited.

Russell Simmons, founder of Phat Fashions and the godfather of hip-hop culture, was quoted as saying, "Marc is a very, very creative designer. He's got more edge than most." Simmons describes Ecko's line as having an "alternative" quality or a "more suburban edge." In other words, the Ecko brands were able to gain market among the hip-hop audience. The next issue becomes, as the hip-hop generation ages and new fads and fashions emerge, will Ecko Enterprises be able to continue to grow and succeed?[44]

1. Which of the models presented in this chapter best explains a consumer's purchase of a fashion product created by Ecko Enterprises? Explain.

2. Examine Ecko Enterprises' Web site at www.marceckoenterprises.com. Pick one of the brands and develop a means–end chain that could be used by a creative to develop an advertising campaign.

3. Of the seven advertising appeals, which would work best for Ecko Enterprises' products? Why? Would combinations of appeals be useful for this company? If so, which ones?

4. Pick one of the appeals discussed in the chapter and one of the brands sold by Ecko Enterprises and then develop a print advertisement. Describe your target audience in terms of demographics and psychographics.

CASE 2 LIGHTING UP KINDLE

The world of book publishing and book reading is currently undergoing radical changes that are largely being driven by new technologies. Authors who previously found themselves shut out of traditional publishing can now use the Internet to distribute their books on topics ranging from self-help to political ideology.

After the initial wave of e-book releases, including one by well-known author Stephen King, changes in consumer book-purchasing patterns slowed. Noted New York literary agent Peter Rubie believed that the secret was mobility. He stated that "as soon as someone can carry an e-book to the beach without needing a laptop, the industry is going to change."

That day may have arrived. In late 2007, Jeff Bezos, the founder and CEO of Amazon.com, announced the release of a revolutionary new product—the Kindle. The Kindle is a wireless, portable reading device that offers instant access to more than 90,000 books, blogs, magazines, and newspapers. The technology behind the Kindle is the same as that contained in cell phones, which means that users do not need to find a wi-fi hotspot to use it. The Kindle weighs 10.3 ounces and can carry 200 books at any time. Readers can download books, magazines, blogs, and newspapers from any location.

The device offered a variety of new features. For example, if a person does not know the meaning of a word in a text, the word can be highlighted and then found in an instant dictionary. Links to other sources, such as Wikipedia, are also available.

The great benefit of Kindle to authors is that their books remain available in perpetuity. No longer will a book go "out of print." Each book download costs the reader about $10.00, and the author receives a royalty, just as in the past. For some authors, an additional benefit is the ability to revise a book over time, because the entire content is digital rather than print.

The Kindle debuted with some buzz, despite its hefty price tag ($400). Bezos appeared on Charlie Rose, and several newspaper and magazine articles about the product created some publicity. The company will need to build on that early momentum, because it clearly did not generate the same kind of interest as the MP3 player or the iPhone. Further, competition soon became available in the form of the Sony Portable Reading System.

Author Kevin Maney summarized the Kindle this way: "It's too early to tell whether this is the book's future. The Kindle isn't even set up to do all that just yet. But it is the first e-book reader built to be wirelessly connected to the Internet at all times. It's the first system that shows that living, connected books—some combination of traditional books and Wikipedia—are possible. And, in fact, that's the first reason to think that e-books could

Marcel Mooij / Fotolia

▲ Portable readers can download books, magazines, blogs, and newspapers from any location.

evolve into something other than paper books." Consumers will undoubtedly decide the rest.[45]

1. As an advertising executive who is working with a creative, which advertising theory do you think best fits the release and subsequent advertising for Kindle?

2. What should be the leverage point in a commercial for Kindle?

3. What type of advertising appeal, or sets of appeals, should be used in promoting Kindle?

4. What should be the headline of a Kindle ad? Why?

5. Design a print ad promoting Kindle. Identify which appeal you used and explain why you chose it.

MyMarketingLab

Go to **mymktlab.com** for Auto-graded writing questions as well as the following Assisted-graded writing questions:.

6-1. Watch one of your favorite television shows. Record all of the television commercials in one commercial break (at least seven ads). Identify the appeal used in each one. Were the ads effective? Why or why not?

6-2. Hardee's and Carl's Jr. recently used a television commercial featuring a schoolteacher dancing on top of her desk while a room full of guys performed a rap song entitled "I Like Flat Buns." The song seemed appropriate because the ad was for the Patty Melt on a flat bun. Instead, the ad received considerable flack because the sexy blonde schoolteacher was wearing a short, tight skirt. Teachers' associations complained that it was inappropriate because it was a "sexually exploitive assault" on teachers, students, and schools. Do you agree or disagree? Explain your response.

6-3. Mymktlab Only—comprehensive writing assignment for this chapter.

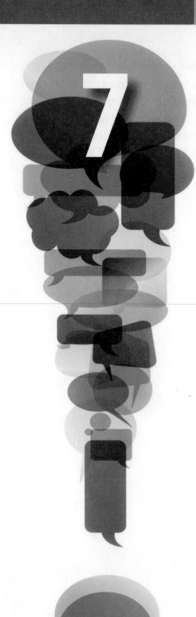

7

ADVERTISING DESIGN
Message Strategies and Executional Frameworks

CHAPTER OBJECTIVES

After reading this chapter, you should be able to answer the following questions:

1. How do the three main types of message strategies increase advertising effectiveness?

2. What types of executional frameworks help to deliver quality advertising messages?

3. What types of sources or spokespersons can be featured in advertisements or commercials?

4. Which characteristics are most important when selecting a source or spokesperson?

5. What process is used to create advertisements?

6. What are the principles of advertising effectiveness?

7. How are advertising programs adjusted to fit international circumstances?

MyMarketingLab™

⭐ Improve Your Grade!

Over 10 million students improved their results using the Pearson MyLabs.
Visit **mymktlab.com** for simulations, tutorials, and end-of-chapter problems.

DOVE'S CAMPAIGN FOR REAL BEAUTY

Advertising and marketing to women and girls may be at a crossroad. For women, models and marketing messages constantly emphasize body image and seeking a type of perfection in appearance that is clearly unattainable for large numbers of females. For young girls, pressures to grow up more quickly, to look older at a younger age, and to fit in socially drive a great deal of product design and what is called *age-compression marketing*. Some responsible parents and those who offer social commentary are pushing back with the essential message, "Let girls be girls."

Complaints about the overemphasis on body image are not new. In the 1960s, a young supermodel named Twiggy captured international attention by looking girlish and paper thin, leading some to argue her appearance would cause young girls to see her as the ideal size. Pressures on models and women of all ages to achieve such unrealistic looks have been well-documented and denounced by many social critics.

In response, marketers for the Dove line of products began the "Campaign for Real Beauty." The program originally launched in England and then moved to the United States and Canada. Over the next several years, the campaign created buzz, applause, and criticism each step of the way.

One of the initial advertisements that ran in print media featured women who were not the standard, size two, beautiful models. Instead, women of various shapes and sizes were shown reveling in their natural state. Part of the program included the "Dove Pro-Age" for older women with a page on the company's Web site along with additional commercials. These women were seen proclaiming "Wrinkled? Wonderful," "Gray? Gorgeous," "Oversized? Outstanding," and "Flawed? Flawless."

Bob Garfield of *Advertising Age*, who was eventually swayed to see the positive side of the campaign, first criticized Dove, calling the approach self-righteous and hypocritical. The models, he said " . . . are all still head-turners, with straight white teeth, no visible pores, and not a cell of cellulite . . . they represent a beauty standard still idealized and, for the overwhelming majority of consumers, still pretty damn unattainable." Not long after the advertisements appeared, an additional problem emerged. Pascal Dangin, a professional photo employee, admitted that he had retouched the images of the women, stating, " . . . it was great to do, a challenge, to keep everyone's skin and faces showing the mileage but not looking unattractive." The revelation went viral, because the effort appeared to be "hypocritical" and counter to exactly what the advertisements claimed to find objectionable.

A second feature, the "Dove Evolution" campaign displays the methods used to enhance the looks of a female model through make-up, hair care, and photo retouching, with the tag line, "No wonder our perception of beauty is so distorted." Consumers were then presented with the admonition to take part in the Real Beauty Workshops for Girls sponsored by the Dove Self-Esteem Fund, a program aimed at helping females feel good about themselves, in part by turning away from a constant emphasis on physical appearance.

Another advertisement entitled "Onslaught" opens with the words "A Dove film" and shows a close-up of a smiling, innocent, red-headed girl for nearly 20 seconds. With music featuring a modern sound and the words "Here it comes" frequently repeated in the background, cuts from various

Galina Barskaya/Fotolia

pseudo-advertisements display slinky, fashionable, beautiful models. The attributes needed to reach such a status are mentioned, among them "younger, smaller, lighter, thinner, tighter, softer." "It works" is highlighted again and again by the advertising pitchwomen. The inevitable pathway to yo-yo dieting, eating disorders, and various forms of cosmetic surgery follows. Finally, as a group of young girls around the age of 10 cross a street, the commercial closes with the words, "Talk to your daughter before the beauty industry does." The compelling message does not mention Dove soap or any of its product features. Instead, it

CandyBox Images/Fotolia

offers a strong indictment of the social pressures young girls and young women face. Dove's "Onslaught" campaign also linked to the Dove Self-Esteem Fund.

These commercials and the Campaign for Real Beauty merited discussion on programs such as *Oprah Winfrey*, *The View*, and *Good Morning, America* among others. Many commentators hailed the efforts as tackling the problem of self-esteem in a new and valuable way. The program achieved success in terms of bringing the Dove line or products into the minds of its target audience through an integrated advertising and

marketing communications program that for the most part had generated a great deal of positive buzz.

Some critics complained that male body image issues were being ignored, and that these deserved similar attention. And *Time* magazine noted that Unilever also markets the Axe line of products. The commentary reminds readers the company "advertises its Axe Body Spray to men using a lingerie-and-stiletto-clad rock band called Bom Chicka Wah Wahs," The writer asks, "What do we tell our daughters about that?"[1]

OVERVIEW

Designing messages to effectively reach a target audience constitutes the essence of integrated marketing communications. Many of these messages are highly personal. They are designed to change or shape attitudes. They should be remembered and lead to some type of action.

Marketing messages travel in two ways. First, a personal message can be delivered through a personal medium. A sales representative closing a deal, shaking the hand of the buyer, giving a reassuring tap on the shoulder, and smiling while talking delivers a message in an intimate, warm, personal fashion. Clearly, personal media (e.g., sales reps, repair department personnel, customer services representatives) contribute to the overall IMC program.

Marketing messages also travel through the various forms of advertising media. Most of these are *impersonal*. Televisions are indifferent as to what appears on the screen. Radios deliver any sound that can be transmitted. Computer screens are nothing more than special-purpose television screens. The challenge to the advertising agency, the company, and especially the creative is to design a personal message, even one being delivered by an impersonal medium. The message should engage the buyer and influence her to recall and purchase the product. Also, many marketers and advertising agencies seek tangible, measurable results.

This chapter first focuses on the main three types of message strategies. Each may be used to help convince the consumer to make a purchase, either through reason, emotion, or an action-inducing advertisement. Second, the major types of executional frameworks are explained. These forms of advertising presentations help the creative prepare original, convincing, and memorable messages. Third, the four types of sources or spokespersons that appear in various advertisements are described, and the criteria used to select them are reviewed. Finally, the principles of effective advertising campaigns are presented. Advertisements that are effectively combined with other elements of the promotions mix can lead to a strong company image reflecting a clear IMC theme.

Message Strategies

OBJECTIVE 7.1
How do the three main types of message strategies increase advertising effectiveness?

The **message theme** outlines the key ideas in an advertisement. It should be the central part of the creative brief. A message theme can be created by using a **message strategy**, the primary tactic or approach used to deliver the message theme. The three broad categories of message strategies are: cognitive, affective, and conative.[2] The categories represent the components of attitudes, as described earlier. Figure 7.1 identifies the various forms or approaches from each category.

COGNITIVE STRATEGIES

A **cognitive message strategy** presents rational arguments or pieces of information to consumers. The ideas require cognitive processing. The advertisement's key message describes the product's attributes or benefits customers can obtain by purchasing the product.[3]

A cognitive message strategy advertisement influences a person's beliefs and/or knowledge structure by suggesting any one of a variety of potential product benefits. Foods may be described as healthy, pleasant tasting, or low calorie. A tool can be shown as durable, convenient, or handy to use. A drill press machine used in a manufacturing operation may be portrayed as being more reliable or faster than the competition's machines. Cognitive message strategies clearly present these benefits to customers. The five major forms of cognitive strategies are generic messages, preemptive messages, unique selling propositions, hyperbole, and comparative advertisements.

Generic Messages An advertisement that directly promotes the product's attributes or benefits without any claim of superiority transmits a **generic message**, which works best for a brand leader firm or one that dominates the industry. A generic message makes the brand synonymous with the product category. Campbell's can declare "Soup is good food" without making any claim to superiority. The company leads the industry. When most consumers think of soup, they think of Campbell's, which sells 69 percent of all cans sold each year.[4] Nintendo employs a similar approach because the company dominates the game-console category with a 47 percent market share.[5]

Generic message strategies seldom appear in business-to-business advertisements because few firms dominate an industry to the extent of Campbell's or Nintendo. Intel is the major exception. The company controls 80 percent of the microchip market.[6] The generic message "Intel inside" has been repeated for years.

Generic message strategies can stimulate brand awareness. The advertiser may try to develop a cognitive linkage between a specific brand name and a product category, such as Skechers and sporty footwear. The advertisement might contain little information about the product's attributes. Instead, it attempts to place the brand in a person's cognitive memory and cognitive map.

Preemptive Messages A claim of superiority based on a product's specific attribute or benefit with the intent of preventing the competition from making the same or a similar statement is a **preemptive message**. Crest toothpaste's reputation as "the cavity fighter" preempts other companies from making similar claims, even though all toothpastes fight cavities. An effective preemptive strategy occurs when the company states the advantage first. Competitors that say the same thing become viewed as "me-too" brands or copycats.

Unique Selling Proposition An explicit, testable claim of uniqueness or superiority that can be supported or substantiated in some manner is a **unique selling proposition (USP)**. The Bonne Bell advertisement shown on the next page features a unique selling proposition aimed at teenagers. The message that Bonne Bell Lipshade is "your 1 and only, 1 handed, sleek sweep flipstick!" stresses a unique product feature.

Hyperbole An *untestable* claim based on some attribute or benefit is **hyperbole**. When NBC states that it has America's favorite comedies, the claim is hyperbole. It does not require substantiation, which makes this cognitive strategy quite popular.

Comparative Advertising The final cognitive message strategy, a **comparative advertisement**, allows an advertiser to directly or indirectly compare a product to the competition

- Generic
- Preemptive
- Unique selling proposition
- Hyberbole
- Comparative
- Resonance
- Emotional
- Action-inducing
- Promotional support

▲ **FIGURE 7.1**
Message Strategies

▼ An advertisement for Marion State Bank using a cognitive message strategy.

100 Years of Growing
by Helping Others Grow

MARION
● STATE BANK ●

FDIC   Marion • Farmerville • Sterlington • www.MarionStateBank.com

Courtesy of Newcomer, Morris & Young, Inc.

▲ An advertisement for Bonne Bell featuring a unique selling proposition.

on some product attribute or benefit. The advertisement may or may not mention the competitor by name. An advertiser can simply present a "make-believe" competitor with a name such as "Brand X." The approach may not be as effective as making a comparison using the actual competitor's name. To provide legal protection, marketers make sure any claim concerning the competition can be clearly substantiated.

AT&T and Sprint compare rates. VISA notes that many merchants will not accept American Express. In the business-to-business sector, shipping companies compare delivery times and accuracy rates.

Comparative ads offer the advantage of capturing the consumer's attention. When comparisons are made, both brand awareness and message awareness increase. Consumers tend to remember more of what was said about a brand than when a noncomparative format presents the same information.

Believability and consumer attitudes represent the negative side of comparative ads. Many consumers consider comparative ads to be less believable. They view the information about the sponsor brand as exaggerated and conclude that the advertisement probably misstates information about the comparison brand to make the sponsor brand appear superior.

Another danger with comparative ads occurs when consumers develop negative attitudes toward the advertisement, which can then be transferred to the sponsor's product. This becomes more likely when the sponsor runs a *negative comparative ad* about the competition's product. Research suggests that negative comparative ads typically result in lower believability of the advertising claim and may result in less favorable attitudes toward the brand.[7] In psychology, the concept of *spontaneous trait transference* suggests that when a comparative advertisement criticizes the competition's brand based on a particular attribute, it may lead viewers to also attribute the deficiency to the sponsor brand. The transference becomes more likely when the consumer purchases the comparative brand, not the sponsored brand.[8]

Company leaders should carefully choose an appropriate comparison firm and use cautious when using a negative comparison format. The comparison brand must be viewed as a viable competing brand. Actual product attributes and customer benefits are noted, without stretching the information or providing misleading information. When actual differences exist, comparative advertising works well. Comparisons consisting of hype and opinion with no substantial differences are less likely to succeed. Misleading comparisons can cause the Federal Trade Commission (FTC) to investigate. The majority of complaints filed with the FTC are about potentially misleading comparison advertisements.

Comparing a brand with a low market share to the market leader works well, because viewers concentrate more carefully on the advertisement's content and message. Comparing a high-market share brand with another high-market share brand may not be as effective. In these cases, a better strategy may be to simply make the comparison without naming the competitor.

Several years ago Avis ranked tenth in market share in the rental car industry. A series of commercials compared Avis to the market leader, Hertz, mentioning the Hertz name specifically. Most consumers now believe Avis provides the same level of quality as Hertz.[9]

The five cognitive message strategies are based on rational logic. Advertisers design messages that lead consumers pay attention to the ad and take the time to cognitively process the information. In terms of attitudes, the sequence of *cognitive → affective → conative* represents the rational approach. The cognitive message strategy first presents consumers with rational information about a good, service, or company, and then leads them to develop positive feelings about the same product or company.

AFFECTIVE STRATEGIES

Advertisements that invoke feelings or emotions and match those feelings with the good, service, or company display **affective message strategies**. These messages attempt to enhance the likeability of the product, recall of the appeal, or comprehension of the advertisement. Affective strategies elicit emotions that, in turn, lead the consumer to act, preferably by buying the product, and subsequently affecting the consumer's reasoning process.

An emotion such as love can be featured in order to convince consumers that Cheerios is a superior breakfast cereal for loved ones. Consumers can be told that Cheerios offers a rational choice. Company advertisements then mention the cereal's positive effect on cholesterol levels, as shown in the Cheerios ad in this section that states, "Your heart has better things to do than deal with heart disease." Family memories and emotions are combined with the product's heart-smart feature. Affective strategies fall into two categories: resonance and emotional.

Resonance advertising connects a product with a consumer's experiences in order to develop stronger ties between the product and the consumer. The use of music from the 1980s takes Echo Boomers back to that time. Any strongly held memory or emotional attachment becomes a candidate for resonance advertising.

Subaru used this approach in an online marketing effort that tapped into a person's nostalgia for his first car. Subaru used an animation generator at a microsite called FirstCarStory.com for a consumer to recreate the look and feel of her first car. The program used technology that transferred words into custom images. Alan Bethke, director of marketing communications at Subaru, noted, "The First Car Story campaign provides a creative outlet for reliving those unique, funny, unforgettable care experiences anyone who had a first car can relate to."[10]

A new form of resonance advertising, **comfort marketing**, has emerged as marketers look for ways to encourage consumers to purchase branded products rather than generic versions. The approach reassures consumers looking for value that a branded product has stood the test of time. Comfort marketing involves bringing back vintage characters, themes and jingles from the past to evoke fond memories when times were better. To ensure the brand does not look old-fashioned, most are refreshing the mascot, music, taglines, and other aspects of the ad to the twenty-first century. Brands that have used this approach include StarKist tuna, Alka-Seltzer, Bacardi, Doritos, Dr. Pepper, Pepsi-Cola, and Planters. Robert Furniss-Roe of Bacardi North America, said, "People, particularly in this environment, are looking for substance and authenticity."[11]

Emotional advertising attempts to elicit powerful emotions that eventually lead to product recall and choice. Many emotions can be connected to products, including trust, reliability, friendship, happiness, security, glamour, luxury, serenity, pleasure, romance, and passion. Companies employ emotional appeals in both consumer-oriented and business-to-business advertisements. Members of the buying center in a business are human. They do not make purchasing decisions based solely on rational thought processes. Emotions and feelings also affect choices. When an advertisement presents product's benefits using an emotional framework, it will normally be more effective, even in business-to-business ads.[12]

Affective strategies may help build a stronger brand name. Affective advertisements guide consumers to like the brand, develop positive feelings towards it, and eventually purchase the item. Cognitive beliefs about the brand then follow. This approach relies on the attitude development sequence of *affective → conative → cognitive*. For some products, affective advertisements are successful because there are few real tangible differences among the brands. St. Francis Medical Center features an affective strategy in the advertisement on the next page by depicting a warm mother daughter relationship.

Your Heart Has Better Things To Do Than Deal With Heart Disease

Eating heart-healthy whole grain oat foods like Cheerios as part of a low-fat diet, may be a good way to lower your cholesterol and reduce your risk of heart disease. So make health a habit for your heart, body and soul. And let your heart do something it's better at...holding your family together.

Cheerios

"The One and Only Cheerios"

Courtesy of General Mills.

▲ A Cheerios advertisement utilizing an affective message strategy approach.

▲ An advertisement for St. Francis Medical Center using an emotional message strategy.

CONATIVE STRATEGIES

Conative message strategies are designed to lead directly to some type of consumer response. They can support other promotional efforts, such as coupon redemption programs, in-store offers such as buy-one-get-one-free, or encourage consumers to access a Web site. Any advertisement for old television programs that seeks to persuade viewers to call a toll-free number to purchase the DVDs contains the goal of eliciting behaviors. The ads typically encourage quick action by stating that the DVD cannot be purchased in stores and will be available for only a limited time.

Action-inducing conative advertisements create situations in which cognitive knowledge of the product or affective liking of the product may come later (after the actual purchase) or during product usage. For instance, a point-of-purchase display can be designed (sometimes through advertising tie-ins) to cause people to make *impulse buys*. Making the sale constitutes the goal, with cognitive knowledge and affective feelings forming as the product is used. The attitude sequence for conative message strategies is *conative → cognitive → affective*.

Promotional support conative advertisements are tied in with other promotional efforts, including coupons, phone-in promotions, or a sweepstakes that a consumer enters by filling out the form on the advertisement or by going to a particular retail store.

Cognitive, affective, and conative strategies can be matched with the hierarchy of effects approach, which suggests that consumers pass through a series of stages, from awareness to knowledge, liking, preference, conviction, and, finally, to the purchase. As shown in Figure 7.2, each message strategy highlights a different stage of the hierarchy of effects model.

Choosing the right message strategy often becomes the key ingredient in creating a successful advertising program. To be effective, the message strategy should match the leverage point and executional framework. These should mesh with the media to be utilized. The creative and the account executive remain in constant contact throughout the process to be certain all of these advertising ingredients remain consistent.

▶ **FIGURE 7.2**
The Hierarchy of Effects Model and Message Strategies

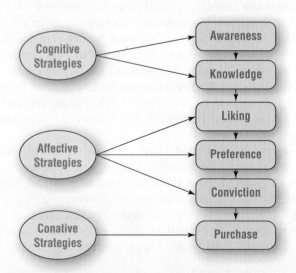

Executional Frameworks

An **executional framework** signifies the manner in which an ad appeal will be presented. Framework selection takes place in conjunction with an advertising appeal and message strategy. The common types of advertising appeals include fear, humor, sex, music, rationality, emotions, and scarcity. Each can be matched with the appropriate executional framework. Figure 7.3 displays the various frameworks.

ANIMATION

Animation has become an increasingly popular executional framework, and its use has risen dramatically. The growing sophistication of computer graphics programs makes new and exciting animation technologies available. Successful animated movie films such as *Up*, and *Dr. Seuss' The Lorax* continue to generate interest in animation advertising, which can be featured in television spots, on the Internet, and in movie trailers. Single shots of animated characters, such as *Dora the Explorer*, are placed in print ads.

The *rotoscoping* process facilitates digitally painting or sketching figures into live sequences, which makes it possible to present both live actors and animated characters in the same frame.[13] The creative can also merge or modify various live scenes. Advertising executive Stan Richards noted, "The opportunities are great, because, we are at a point where, anything that we can think of, we can do. We've never had that before. There is a cost consequence. A lot of that digital production is expensive, but those costs are coming down. Within a few years, those costs will be half of what they are now."[14]

For years, animation was rarely found in business-to-business advertising. Many advertising leaders viewed it negatively, believing animation appealed to children but not to businesspeople. These opinions have changed. Business ads shown on television now take advantage of high-quality graphics to illustrate a product's uses with animation.

SLICE-OF-LIFE

In slice-of-life commercials, advertisers provide solutions to the everyday problems consumers or businesses face. The format was made famous by Procter & Gamble during the early days of television advertising in the 1950s. Slice-of-life commercials depict the common experiences, and especially the problems people encounter, and a product is introduced to solve the problem. The most common slice-of-life format has four components: encounter, problem, interaction, and solution (see Figure 7.4). In some ads, the actors portray the dilemma or problem and solve the problems themselves. In others, a voice-over explains the benefits or solution to the problem that the good, service, or company provides.

Slice-of-life executions also appear in business-to-business advertisements, such as the MessageMedia shown on the next page. The encounter begins with the potential female customer's problem that the "average single female breaks up with 4.3 men, avoids 237 phone calls, and ignores approximately 79 red lights per year." The interaction occurs through the copy "What are the chances she'll read your e-mail message?" MessageMedia's "E-messaging campaign" provides the solution.

Business-to-business advertisements often utilize the slice-of-life method because it allows the advertiser to highlight the ways a product can meet business needs. A typical business-to-business ad begins with a routine business experience, such as a sales manager making a presentation to the board of directors. Then, a projector being used does not have a clear picture. The ad offers the solution: a projector from Sony. The presentation resumes with great clarity, and the board of directors accepts the customer's bid for the account. As with all slice-of-life commercials, a disaster has been avoided and a happy ending results instead.

OBJECTIVE 7.2

What types of executional frameworks help to deliver quality advertising messages?

- Animation
- Slice-of-life
- Testimonial
- Authoritative
- Demonstration
- Fantasy
- Informative

▲ **FIGURE 7.3**
Executional Frameworks

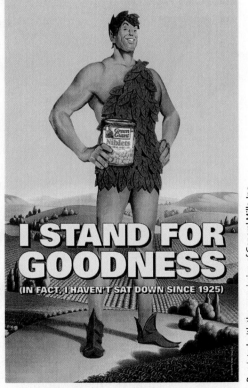

Reprinted with the permission of General Mills, Inc.

▲ A Green Giant advertisement using animation.

► **FIGURE 7.4**
Components of a Slice-of-Life Ad

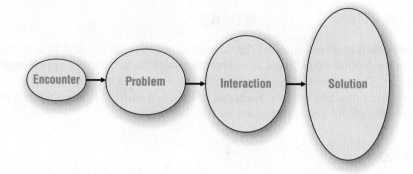

Slice-of-life executions are possible in most media, including magazines or billboards, because a single picture can depict a normal, everyday situation or problem. Finding an image that tells the entire story, with the product being the solution, will be the challenge. An alternative approach is to use a type of storyboard, such as the one on the next page for the Snoring Center created by the Pink Jacket advertising agency.

TESTIMONIALS

The testimonial type of executional framework has been successful for many years, especially in the business-to-business and service sectors. A customer relating a positive experience with a product offers a testimonial. In the business-to-business sector, testimonials from current customers add credibility to the claims. In many business buying situations, prospective vendors are asked for references. Testimonials provide references in advance. Further, most buyers believe what others say about a company more than they believe what a company says about itself. Testimonials offer greater credibility than self-proclamations.

Testimonials offer an effective method for promoting services. Services are intangible; they cannot be seen or touched, and consumers cannot examine them before making decisions. A testimony from a current customer provides a succinct description of the benefits or attributes of the service. Choosing a dentist, an attorney, or an automobile repair shop employee often leads customers to ask friends, relatives, or coworkers. A testimonial advertisement simulates this type of word-of-mouth recommendation.

▼ A business-to-business advertisement for MessageMedia containing a slice-of-life execution.

Testimonials can enhance company credibility. Endorsers and famous individuals do not always have high levels of credibility, because consumers know they are being paid for their endorsements. The same holds true for paid actors who look like everyday consumers. The most believable testimonies are from everyday people, actual customers. Retailer Stein Mart featured real customers talking about their favorite merchandise in a recent TV campaign. The customers were recruited through the company's Facebook page. The TV spots encouraged customers to create videos about their favorite merchandise at Stein Mart and upload them to the Web site. The goals were to reach a younger target market, women between 35 and 55, and to create an online community of avid customers who found something they love at Stein Mart.[15]

AUTHORITATIVE

When using the authoritative executional framework, the advertiser seeks to convince viewers regarding a product's superiority. **Expert authority** constitutes one form. The ads employ a physician, dentist, engineer, or chemist to state the particular brand's advantages compared to other brands. Firms also can feature less recognized experts such as automobile mechanics, professional

Courtesy of Message Media.

house painters, nurses, and aerobics instructors. These individuals talk about the attributes of the product that make the brand superior.

Many authoritative advertisements include scientific or survey evidence. Independent organizations such as the American Medical Association undertake a variety of product studies. Quoting the results generates greater credibility. Survey results are less credible. Stating that four out of five dentists recommend a particular toothbrush or toothpaste may be less effective, because consumers do not have details about how the survey was conducted or even how many dentists were surveyed (5 or 500). In contrast, an American Medical Association statement that an aspirin a day reduces the risk of a second heart attack is highly credible. Bayer can take advantage of the finding by including the information in the company's ads. The same holds true when a magazine such as *Consumer Reports* ranks a particular brand as the best.

Authoritative advertisements have been widely incorporated into business-to-business sector advertisements, especially when scientific findings support a company's product claims. Independent test results often exhibit a more profound influence on buying center members, especially those actively looking for rational information to help them make decisions.

The authoritative approach assumes consumers and business decision makers rely on cognitive processes when making purchase decisions and that they will pay attention to an ad and carefully think about the information conveyed in it. The approach works well in print ads, because the buyers take the time to read the claim or findings presented in the advertisement.

Authoritative advertisements often appear in specialty magazines and on specific Web sites. In a hunting magazine, an expert sportsman can discuss the superiority of a particular gun, as the readers are individuals with an interest in hunting. Brides observe the endorsements of wedding experts in bridal magazines and Web sites. Readers notice these specialized messages, and the claims have greater credibility. The same will be true in business-to-business magazines. Trade journals in the business world are similar to specialty magazines in the consumer world.

DEMONSTRATION

A demonstration execution shows how a product works. It offers an effective way to communicate the product's benefits to viewers. One recent advertisement featured a new form of dust cloth that could be attached to a handle or used separately. The demonstration highlighted the product's multiple uses by cleaning a television screen, a wooden floor, a saxophone, and light fixtures. Consumers were being shown how to use the product while at the same time hearing about its advantages.

Business-to-business ads often present demonstrations. They allow a business to illustrate how a product meets the specific needs of another business. For example, GoldTouch, Inc. can demonstrate the InstaGold Flash System, which deposits a bright and uniform gold surface finish on products, such as jewelry, through a nonelectrical current process of immersion plating. Such demonstrations can be offered via television ads or flash media ads on the Internet.

Demonstration ads are well-suited to television and the Internet. To a limited extent, the print media can feature

Pink Jacket Creative: A Creative Factory.

▲ An advertisement created by Pink Jacket Creative for the Snoring Center using animated characters and a slice-of-life approach.

▼ An authoritative execution combined with a humor appeal.

Courtesy of 3M/SPD.

IF I RULED THE WORLD>I'D LIVE ON AN
ISLAND WHERE THE SUN WOULD ALWAYS
SHINE. ALL THE SWIMSUITS WOULD COME
IN TANGERINE. AND THE MARTINIS WOULD
BE SERVED BY JAMES BOND...SHAKEN, NOT
STIRRED.

jantzen®

▲ A Jantzen advertisement utilizing a fantasy execution.

▼ This advertisement contains an informative execution to convey the message that products people use every day are made with petroleum ingredients processed by Calumet.

ALL THINGS CALUMET
PRODUCTS YOU USE EVERY DAY
⟲ CALUMET ⟳

demonstrations, especially when a series of photos outlines the sequence of product usage.

FANTASY

Fantasy executions lift the audience beyond the real world to a make-believe experience. Some are meant to be realistic. Others are completely irrational. Viewers often more clearly recall the most irrational and illogical ads. Fantasies can deal with anything from a dream vacation spot or cruise ships to a juicy hamburger or an enticing DiGiorno pizza. The Jantzen advertisement in this section encourages people to share their fantasies by contacting the company.

The most common fantasy themes involve sex, love, and romance. Some marketing experts believe raw sex and nudity in advertising have lost their impact. Instead, advertisers feature a softer, more subtle presentation. Fantasy fits with target audiences that have a preference for a tamer presentation. Instead of raw sexuality, fantasy takes them into a world of romantic make-believe.

The perfume and cologne industries often employ fantasy executions. In the past, a common theme was that splashing on the cologne caused women to flock to a man. For women, the reverse was suggested. Although used extensively, these ads were not particularly effective because people did not believe them. Currently, perfume advertisers tend to portray the product as enhancing a couple's love life or making a man or woman feel more sensuous.

Television fantasy ads for cruise lines portray couples enjoying romantic, sensuous vacations together; swimming; jet skiing; and scuba diving. The cruise becomes more than just a vacation—it is a romantic fantasy trip. Fantasy ads also can show people experiencing the thrill of winning a major sports event or sharing a common product (e.g., beer, pizza) with a beautiful model. The Biltmore advertisement on the next page features a different kind of fantasy—an escape to a serene castle with beautiful gardens. Effective fantasies can inspire both recall and action.

Business-to-business advertising ordinarily does not employ fantasy, primarily because of fear that members of a buying center will not take it seriously. Some advertising creatives have been able to feature a fantasy in a business-to-business advertisement by showing a product helping the buyer achieve an unrealistic result or outcome. For example, being promoted from janitor to president because of the correct choice of a cleaning product would be a fantasy aimed at people using or purchasing janitorial supplies.

INFORMATIVE

Informative advertisements present information to the audience in a straightforward manner. Agencies prepare informative messages extensively for radio commercials, where only verbal communication takes place. Informative ads are less common in television and print, because consumers tend to ignore them. With so many ads bombarding the consumer, it takes more than just the presentation of information to capture someone's attention.

Consumers who are highly involved in a particular product category pay attention to an informational ad. Business buyers in the process of gathering information for either a new buy or a modified rebuy will notice an informative advertisement. When a business does not need a particular product, buying center members pay less attention to the advertisement. Thus, informative ads tend to work best in high-involvement situations. Many advertisers believe that business buyers desire detailed information to make intelligent buying decisions. As a result, the informative framework continues to be a popular approach for business-to-business advertisers.

Correct placement of an informative advertisement is vital. An informative advertisement about a restaurant placed on a radio station just before noon will be listened to more carefully than one that runs at 3:00 p.m. An informative ad about a diet product in an issue of *Glamour* that has a special article on weight control or exercising will be noticed more than if it is placed in the fashion section of the magazine. An informative business ad featuring a new piece of industrial equipment works well next to an article about the capital costs of equipment. Informative ads may have limited uses but become more effective when placed properly.

Beyond these executional frameworks, the creative selects the other ingredients, including music, copy, color, motion, light, and the size of a print ad. Almost any of these executional frameworks can be used within the format of one of the various appeals. A slice-of-life can depict fear. Informative ads may be humorous, but so can animations. Testimonials or demonstrations are rational or emotional, and so forth. As the advertisement comes together, one element remains: the choice of a source or spokesperson.

▲ This advertisement for Biltmore uses a fantasy approach of an escape to a romantic castle.

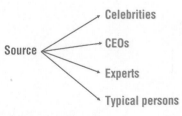

Sources and Spokespersons

One final issue remains for the creative, the company, and the account executive. Selecting the ideal **source** or **spokesperson** to appear in an advertisement will be critical. Figure 7.5 identifies four types of sources and spokespersons.

CELEBRITY SPOKESPERSONS

Of the four types, celebrity spokespersons are the most common, even though their appearances in ads have been declining. The research firm Millward Brown notes that only around 6 percent of advertisements feature celebrity endorsements.[16] The high cost of celebrity endorsements represents a primary reason for the decline. Many ask for millions of dollars and want multi-year deals. Others may sign on for only a single campaign. It cost the high-end fashion label Louis Vuitton $10 million for actress Angelina Jolie's appearance in a single advertising campaign.[17]

An advertiser employs a celebrity endorser when the person's stamp of approval enhances the product's brand equity. Celebrities can also help create emotional bonds with brands. Transferring the bond that exists between the celebrity and the audience to the product being endorsed is the objective. A bond transfer will often be more profound for younger consumers. A MediaEDGE survey revealed that 30 percent of 18- to 34-year-olds would try a product promoted by a celebrity. The survey also indicated that younger people are 50 percent more likely than older consumers to recommend a celebrity-endorsed product to others. Older consumers are less likely to be influenced by celebrity endorsements. Fewer than 14 percent reported that they would try a celebrity-endorsed product. Still, many advertisers believe that celebrity endorsements improve brand awareness and help define the brand's personality.[18]

OBJECTIVE 7.3

Which types of sources or spokespersons can be featured in advertisements?

▲ **FIGURE 7.5**

Types of Sources and Spokespersons

▲ Interstate Batteries features Kyle Busch in some of its advertisements.

Athletes constitute a significant component of the celebrity endorsers. Some, such as Danica Patrick, earn more from endorsements than they do from their sports. Top athletic endorsers include Phil Mickelson, Roger Federer, Lebron James, David Beckham, Cristiano Ronaldo, Alex Rodriguez, and, until recently, Tiger Woods. The top two female athletic endorsers are Danica Patrick and Maria Sharapova.[19]

Agencies also feature celebrities to help establish a brand "personality." The objective is to tie the brand's characteristics to those of the spokesperson. A brand personality emerges after the brand has been established. The celebrity helps to define the brand more clearly. Using celebrities for new products does not always work as well as for already established brands.

Additional Celebrity Endorsements   Four additional variations of celebrity endorsements are: unpaid spokespersons, celebrity voice-overs, dead-person endorsements, and social-media endorsements. *Unpaid spokespersons* are celebrities supporting a charity or cause by appearing in advertisements. These types of endorsements are highly credible and can entice significant contributions to a cause. Politicians, actors, musicians, and athletes all appear in these ads. A few years ago, a campaign featured a number of musicians plus former Presidents Bush and Clinton in an effort to raise money for Haiti after its devastating earthquake.

Many celebrities also provide *voice-overs* for television and radio ads without being shown or identified. Listeners often respond to the ads and try to figure out who is reading the copy, which adds interest. Agencies may use a voice-over because the celebrity provides a quality voice to the advertisement even when individuals listening to the ad do not recognize the voice. Advertising executive Stan Richards noted, "We use Hollywood actors quite a bit. It's largely not for their celebrity; we're not interested in that. Our voice for Home Depot is Ed Harris, who is a terrific actor. I don't think anybody in the world knows it's him, but he can take a script and bring it to life."[20] One negative of voice-overs is that they can be a distraction if the consumer becomes focused on identifying the speaker rather than hearing the content of the ad.

A *dead-person endorsement* occurs when a sponsor uses an image or past video or film featuring an actor or personality who has died. Dead-person endorsements are somewhat controversial but are becoming more common. Bob Marley, Marilyn Monroe, John Wayne, John Lennon, Elvis Presley, and many others have appeared in ads and have even become spokespersons for products after dying.

The newest form of endorsements is through *social media*. Firms now pay celebrities to send promotional tweets for them. Most of these tweets are not cheap, costing between $200 and $10,000 per tweet. Snoop Dog was recently paid to tweet about the Toyota Sienna, which he called a "swagger wagon." Kathy Ireland has been hired by Therapedic International to endorse their mattresses through social media and Twitter.[21]

CEO SPOKESPERSONS

Instead of celebrities, advertisers can employ a CEO as the spokesperson or source. Michael Dell has appeared as the spokesperson for Dell. A highly visible and personable CEO can become a major asset for the firm and its products. Many local companies succeed, in part, because their owners are out front in small-market television commercials. They then begin to take on the status of local celebrities.

EXPERTS

Expert sources include physicians, lawyers, accountants, and financial planners. These experts are not celebrities or CEOs. Experts provide backing for testimonials, serve as authoritative figures, demonstrate products, and enhance the credibility of informative advertisements.

TYPICAL PERSONS

Typical persons are one of two types. The first includes paid actors or models that portray or resemble everyday people. The second is actual, typical, everyday people. Wal-Mart has featured store employees in freestanding insert advertisements. Agencies also create "man-on-the-street" types of advertisements. For example, PERT shampoo recently prepared ads showing an individual asking people if they would like to have their hair washed. Dr. Scholl's interviews people about foot problems that might be resolved with cushioned shoe inserts.

Real-people sources are becoming more common. One reason may be the overuse of celebrities. Many experts believe that consumers have become bored by celebrity endorsers and that the positive impact today will be less than in the past. One study conducted in Great Britain indicated that 55 percent of the consumers surveyed reported that a famous face was not enough to hold their attention.[22]

▲ An advertisement for the U.S. Marines with a typical person spokesperson.

Courtesy of U.S. Marines.

SOURCE CHARACTERISTICS

In evaluating sources, most account executives and companies consider several characteristics. The effectiveness of an advertisement that utilizes a spokesperson depends on the degree to which the person has one or more of the characteristics listed in Figure 7.6.

Credibility   The composite of attractiveness, similarity, likeability, trustworthiness, and expertise creates credibility, which in turn affects the receiver's acceptance of the spokesperson and message.[23] A credible source is believable. Most sources do not score highly on all four attributes, yet they need to score highly on multiple characteristics to

OBJECTIVE 7.4

What characteristics are most important when selecting a source or spokesperson?

◀ **FIGURE 7.6**
Characteristics of Effective Spokespersons

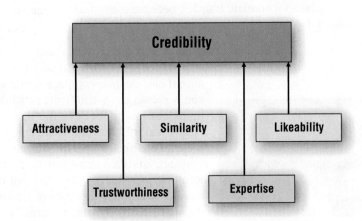

be viewed as credible. Celebrities may be more likely to possess at least an element of all characteristics. A CEO, expert, or typical person probably lacks one or more of them.

Attractiveness   Two forms of attractiveness include physical and personality characteristics. Physical attractiveness contributes an important asset for an endorser. Advertisements with physically attractive spokespersons fare better than advertisements with less attractive people, for both male and female audiences. The attractiveness of the spokesperson's personality will also be important to many consumers, because it helps viewers form emotional bonds with the spokesperson. When the spokesperson has a sour personality, even if physically beautiful, consumers become less likely to develop an emotional bond with the individual and the product.

Similarity   Closely related to attractiveness is the concept of similarity. Consumers are more inclined to be influenced by a message delivered by a similar person. A "stay-at-home" mom may be more influenced by an advertisement that starts out with a woman saying, "Since I made the decision to stop working and care for my family full-time . . ." Similarity leads the viewer to identify with the spokesperson. Dove recently launched a series of ads featuring male athletes, but the focus was on them and their families, not sports. Individuals such as Magic Johnson, Drew Brees, and Shaquille O'Neal talk about being "comfortable in their own skin."

At other times *identification* comes from the belief that the source has similar beliefs, attitudes, preferences, or behaviors or faces the same or a similar situation as the customer. Female fans are able to identify with Anna Roberts as the "new face of horse racing" because many females have enjoyed horseback riding and have dreamed of winning a famous horse race. Identification was also gained because most jockeys are males. Anna Roberts immediately gained similarity and identification with female fans.

Likeability   Attactiveness and similarity are closely linked to likeability. Consumers respond positively to spokespersons they like. Viewers may like an actor or the character played by the actor in a movie. La-Z-Boy signed a multi-year agreement with Brook Shields to serve as its celebrity spokesperson. The campaign targeted females ages 35 to 64 who report a high degree of likeability for her.[24] An athlete gains likeability when he plays on the consumer's favorite team. Other individuals are likeable because they support the favorite charities of consumers.

Consumers who do not like a particular spokesperson are inclined to transfer that dislike to the product. This explains why many companies who retained Tiger Woods quickly dropped him as an endorser in 2010 after his extramarital affairs became public. The worry was that his endorsement would result in a negative impact on attitudes toward the brand. In other situations it may not be an automatic transfer, because consumers recognize that endorsers are paid spokespersons.

Trustworthiness   A celebrity may be likeable or attractive but may not be viewed as trustworthy. Trustworthiness represents the degree of confidence or the level of acceptance consumers place in the spokesperson's message. A trustworthy spokesperson helps consumers believe the message. Likeability and trustworthiness are connected. People who are liked tend to be trusted, and people who are disliked tend not to be trusted. A Reuters/Ipsos survey revealed that celebrities ranking the highest in terms of trustworthiness included Betty White, Denzel Washington,

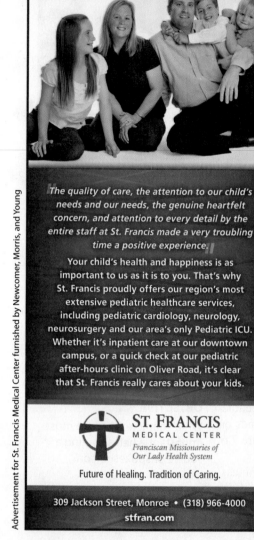

The quality of care, the attention to our child's needs and our needs, the genuine heartfelt concern, and attention to every detail by the entire staff at St. Francis made a very troubling time a positive experience.

Your child's health and happiness is as important to us as it is to you. That's why St. Francis proudly offers our region's most extensive pediatric healthcare services, including pediatric cardiology, neurology, neurosurgery and our area's only Pediatric ICU. Whether it's inpatient care at our downtown campus, or a quick check at our pediatric after-hours clinic on Oliver Road, it's clear that St. Francis really cares about your kids.

ST. FRANCIS
MEDICAL CENTER
Franciscan Missionaries of Our Lady Health System

Future of Healing. Tradition of Caring.

309 Jackson Street, Monroe • (318) 966-4000
stfran.com

▲ Attractiveness is an important source characteristic.

▼ An advertisement for Louisiana Downs featuring the female jockey Anna Roberts.

A Girl on a Horse?
YOU BET!
Watch her race Thursday - Sunday
LOUISIANA DOWNS
Anna Roberts — *Jockey*

1. Betty White
2. Denzel Washington
3. Sandra Bullock
4. Clint Eastwood
5. Tom Hanks

6. Harrison Ford
7. Morgan Freeman
8. Kate Middleton
9. Will Smith
10. Johnny Depp

◀ **FIGURE 7.7**
The 10 Most Trusted Celebrities

Source: Adapted from "Betty White Voted America's Most Trusted Celebrity: Poll," *Reuters*, August 18, 2011, www.reuters.com/assets/print?aid=USTRE77H2WE20110818

Sandra Bullock, and Clint Eastwood (see Figure 7.7 for a complete list). The most unpopular personalities included Paris Hilton, Charlie Sheen, Britney Spears, Arnold Schwarzenegger, and Tiger Woods.[25]

Expertise Spokespersons exhibiting higher levels of expertise are more believable. Kyle Bush and Jeff Gordon are experts when advertising automobile products and lubricants. Often when a commercial requires expertise the advertising agency opts for the CEO or a trained or educated expert in the field. American Express features Maria Barraza, a small-business owner and designer, to promote its Small Business Services. Expertise can be valuable in persuasive advertisements designed to change opinions or attitudes. Spokespersons with high levels of expertise are more capable of persuading an audience than someone with zero or low expertise.[26]

MATCHING SOURCE TYPES AND CHARACTERISTICS

The account executive, ad agency, and corporate sponsor, individually or jointly, may choose the type of spokesperson. They can choose a celebrity, CEO, expert, or typical person, and the specific individual should have the key source characteristics.

Celebrities In terms of trustworthiness, believability, persuasiveness, and likeability, celebrities tend to score well. These virtues increase when the match between the product and celebrity consists of a logical and proper fit. Phil Mickelson endorsing golf merchandise offers a good fit, as does Anna Roberts in horse racing. Companies can be creative when making matches. The match of boxer George Foreman to his Lean Mean Grilling Machine achieved great success.[27] Some celebrities have become almost as famous for their advertising appearances as for an acting or athletic career. Danica Patrick has signed endorsement contracts with Honda, Secret, Boost Mobile, Pepsi, and Go Daddy, possibly gaining as much notoriety from endorsements as she has from competing in races.[28]

Several dangers exist when using celebrities. Any negative publicity about a celebrity caused by inappropriate conduct may damage credibility. Michael Vick's arrest and conviction for dog fighting created considerable negative press. Before his conviction, Vick earned about $7 million per year in endorsements. All of those stopped. When Vick returned to football, a small unknown company called Unequal decided to take a chance on him when he got hurt. Wearing Unequal's chest protector, Vick returned to action sooner than expected and performed successfully. He gave credit to Unequal. As a result, Unequal signed him to an endorsement contract knowing of the high risk. Any further negative publicity would destroy the small company, but positive publicity could move it into becoming a major player in protective gear marketing in the NFL and other leagues.[29]

The potential for negative publicity has led some advertisers to use deceased celebrities. Companies have concluded that there is no need to risk bringing embarrassment or injury to themselves or the brand. It is also a reason that more ads use cartoon characters. Many consumers enjoy cartoons.

▼ Michael Jordan is a rare celebrity who can endorse multiple products and maintain a high level of credibility.

A second danger of using celebrities occurs when they endorse too many products, which can tarnish their credibility. Consumers know celebrities are paid, which detracts from believability. When a celebrity endorses a large number of products, evaluations of credibility decline. Some advertising research indicates that when a celebrity endorses multiple products, it tends to reduce likeability as well as consumer attitudes toward the brand.[30]

A third danger that rarely occurs, but must be considered, is when the celebrity becomes the face of a brand and overshadows the brand. Such was the case of Priceline.com spokesperson William Shatner. He became so well known as The Negotiator that it was virtually impossible for Priceline to advertise one of its other services, fixed-price discount, which was the fastest growing segment. In order to get the attention of consumers about the fixed-price discount and other services, the company had to kill off The Negotiator as part of a campaign.[31]

As a result of these dangers, careful consideration should be given to the choice of a celebrity. The individual cannot simply be famous. The person should possess as many of the key source characteristics as possible, match the good or service being advertised, not be "spread too thin" or overexposed, and promote a positive image that can be transferred to the good, service, or company.

CEO   A CEO or other prominent corporate official may or may not possess the characteristics of attractiveness and likeability. CEOs should, however, appear to be trustworthy, have expertise, and maintain a degree of credibility. A CEO is not a professional actor or model. It might be difficult for the CEO to come across well in a commercial.

One CEO who scores high in sports endorsements is the charismatic Mark Cuban, owner of the NBA Dallas Mavericks. He has an endorsement deal with Samsung. He has appeared on several TV shows, such as *Dancing with the Stars* and HBO series *Entourage*. The risk associated with Cuban, however, is his brashness. Despite this drawback, some companies view him as being worth the risk. Convincing a billionaire to be an endorser could pose a challenge.[32]

Advertising creatives and account executives should carefully consider asking a CEO or business owner to serve as a source. They first must believe that the individual sufficient source characteristics to promote the product and gain the consumer's interest and trust.

Experts   First and foremost, experts should be credible. The advertising agency seeks an attractive, likeable, and trustworthy expert. Experts are helpful in promoting health care products and other high-involvement types of products. Recent research indicates that experts are more believable than celebrities for high-technology products. As a result, the use of an expert reduces a consumer's level of perceived risk in purchasing the product, which means they are the most helpful when consumers or businesses perceive high levels of risk involved in a purchase.[33] When selecting an expert spokesperson, agency leaders make certain that the person has valid credentials and can clearly explain a product's benefits. Doing so will reduce the level of perceived risk.

Typical Persons   Advertisements with typical persons are sometimes difficult to prepare, especially when they use real persons. Typical-person sources do not have the name recognition of celebrities. Consequently, advertisers often use multiple sources within

◀ Showing the partners, Ronquillo and Godwin, in this ad for litigation services, adds credibility.

one advertisement to build credibility. Increasing the number of sources makes the ad more effective. Hearing three people talk about a good dentist will be more believable than hearing it from only one person. By using multiple sources, viewers are motivated to pay attention and process its arguments.[34]

Real-person ads present a double-edged sword. On the one hand, trustworthiness, similarity, and credibility rise when the source is bald, overweight, or has some other physical imperfections. This can be especially valuable when the bald person promotes a hair replacement program or the overweight source talks about a diet program. On the other hand, attractiveness and likeability may be lower.

For the first time in its history, Pizza Hut, decided to go with servers, bartenders and franchise executives in their advertisements rather than celebrities. Dan Howard, a marketing professor at Southern Methodist University noted, "With an actor, there's an inherent loss of persuasiveness because they are paid. Employees are not viewed in the same way as paid actors. They have greater credibility." One of the employees, 28 year-old Ashlie Marquez, who was featured in an ad further stated, "We're real employees who know what the customer likes and we can talk more passionately about it." Not only are the employees seen as more credible, it has had a positive effect on the company's culture. It involves recognizing employees make a difference, team building, and celebrating the work of employees.[35]

Featuring customers in commercials can be difficult, because they will flub lines and look less natural on the screen. These difficulties with actual customers and employees lead many advertising agencies to turn to professional models and actors to portray ordinary people. Professional actors make filming and photographing much easier. Also, the agency can choose a likeable, but plain, person. The desired effects (trustworthiness, similarity, and credibility) are often easier to create through professional actors and models.

In general, the advertising agency wants to be certain that the source or spokesperson has the major characteristics the advertisement requires. Likeability would be important when creating a humorous appeal. In a rational or informational ad, expertise and credibility are crucial, especially in business-to-business ads. In each case, trying to include as many of the characteristics as possible when retaining a spokesperson will be the goal.

Courtesy of Alliance One Advertising

▲ An advertisement for Richland State Bank using typical persons.

Creating an Advertisement

Figure 7.8 illustrates the process a creative uses in preparing an advertisement. The work begins with the creative brief, which outlines the message theme of the advertisement, as well as other pertinent information. With the creative brief as a blueprint, the creative develops a means–end chain, starting with an attribute of the product that generates a specific customer benefit and eventually produces a desirable end state. This means–end chain forms the foundation for all other decisions.

Following the development of the means–end chain, the creative selects a message strategy, the appeal, and the executional framework. The creative suggests or chooses a source or spokesperson at this point, because the choice usually affects other creative decisions. Development of the leverage point that moves the consumer from the product

OBJECTIVE 7.5

What process is used to create advertisements?

▶ **FIGURE 7.8**
Creating an Advertisement

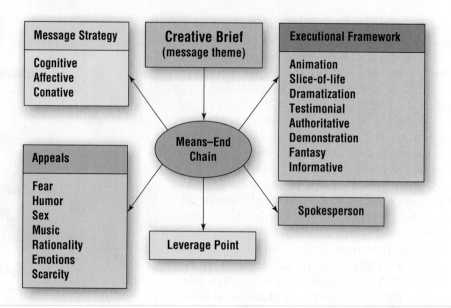

attribute or consumer benefit to the desired end state occurs after the creative begins work on the advertisement. The type of leverage point depends on the message strategy, appeal, and executional framework.

Although certain combinations tend to work well together, the creative has numerous options when preparing an advertisement or campaign. For example, if the creative wants to present a cognitive message strategy, normally rationality provides the most logical approach. The creative could, however, use fear, humor, sex, music, or even scarcity. An emotional approach probably would not work, because the emotion might overpower the cognitive message being sent.

When the creative decides to employ humor with a cognitive strategy, other logical and illogical combinations emerge. In terms of an executional framework, the authoritative approach tends not to work as well with humor. The other executional frameworks are viable. This flexibility allows a variety of advertisements to emerge from a single means–end chain. The best combination depends on the creative's expertise and experience, as well as her judgment regarding the ideal way to accomplish the client's advertising objectives.

Advertising Effectiveness

OBJECTIVE 7.6

What are the principles of advertising effectiveness?

Producing effective ads requires the joint efforts of the account executive, creative, account planner, and media planner. Working independently might produce some award-winning ads, but often they may not achieve the client's objectives. Advertising agencies seek to produce commercials that stand out among the competing messages. An advertisement that breaks through the clutter wins half the battle. Finding ways to lead consumers to react to the ad in the desired manner still remains. An effective advertisement accomplishes the client's objectives. To do so, advertisers follow the seven basic principles of advertising effectiveness (see Figure 7.9).

VISUAL CONSISTENCY

Repeatedly seeing a specific image or visual display helps to embed it in long-term memory. Visual consistency helps, because most customers spend very little time viewing an advertisement. In most cases, an individual makes just a casual glance at a print advertisement or a cursory glimpse at a television commercial. Visual consistency leads the viewer to move the message from short-term to long-term memory. Consistently used logos and other long-standing images help place the brand or company in the consumer's mind. People remember Nike because of the visually consistent use of Swoosh. The Prudential Rock emblem has been established in the minds of many consumers.

- Visual consistency
- Campaign duration
- Repeated taglines
- Consistent positioning—avoid ambiguity
- Simplicity
- Identifiable selling point
- Create an effective flow

CAMPAIGN DURATION

The length or duration of a campaign should be identified. Using the same advertisement for an appropriate period of time allows the message to embed in the consumer's long-term memory. Account executives consider how long to run an advertisement. It should be changed before it becomes stale, and viewers lose interest; however, at the same time changing ads too frequently impedes retention. Reach and frequency affect a campaign's duration. Higher frequency usually leads to a shorter duration. Low reach may be associated with a longer duration. Typical campaigns last about 6 months, but there are exceptions.

The image that can be created through a campaign constitutes a key facet of campaign duration. A recent advertising campaign featuring Jennifer Lopez cruising New York City Streets in a Fiat 500 convertible was a powerful campaign. The danger with the running the campaign too long was that the Fiat would be viewed as a car for women, and the company might lose sales to males.[36] Yet, because of the high cost of using a celebrity, it was necessary to run the campaign longer. Fiat followed with a more male-oriented campaign, but it did not yield the same type of impact as the JLo campaign.

REPEATED TAGLINES

Visual consistency combined with consistent taglines can provide an effective approach. The advertisement may change, but either the visual imagery or the tagline remains the same. The U.S. Army has promoted the tagline "Be all that you can be" for many years, and the Marines are known as "The few. The proud. The Marines." Taglines help consumers tie the advertisement into current knowledge structure nodes that already exist in their minds. Figure 7.10 contains some well-known taglines.

CONSISTENT POSITIONING

Maintaining consistent positioning throughout a product's life makes it more likely that a consumer will place the product in a cognitive map. When the firm emphasizes quality in every advertisement, it becomes easier to tie the product into the consumer's cognitive map than if the firm stresses quality in one ad, price in another, and convenience in a third campaign. Inconsistency in positioning makes the brand and company more difficult to remember. Consistent positioning avoids ambiguity, and the message stays clear and understandable.

SIMPLICITY

Simple advertisements are easier to comprehend than are complex ads. A print ad with a short tagline and limited copy will be easier to read than an overloaded and complex message. Consequently, advertisers should resist the temptation to describe all of a product's attributes in a single commercial. Such a practice may be more prevalent

1. Finger Lickin' Good
2. Think Small
3. Between Love and Madness Lies Obsession
4. Save Money, Live Better
5. Innovation
6. Connecting People
7. I'm Lovin it
8. A Diamond is Forever
9. Have it Your Way
10. Buy It. Sell It. Love It.

in business-to-business print advertising; however, it should be avoided there as well. Also, consumer ads on radio or television spots can be verbally overloaded, forcing the announcer to talk faster. Doing so may be ineffective, because the listener receives too much information in a short time period.

The principle of simplicity applies to Internet advertising. Load time constitutes the primary reason. Individuals surfing the Internet will not wait more than a few seconds for something to load; if it does not, they will move on.

IDENTIFIABLE SELLING POINT

An identifiable selling point places emphasis on three words: identifiable, selling, and point. The advertisement should stress a readily *identifiable* feature, such as price, quality, convenience, or luxury. The advertisement should then *sell* a product's benefits as much as the product itself. Also, the concept is a selling *point*, not selling points. The best advertisements emphasize one major point and do not confuse the viewer by presenting too many ideas. Fixing the product into the viewer's cognitive map through establishing new linkages or strengthening current linkages should be the goal. An identifiable selling point helps achieve that objective.

CREATE AN EFFECTIVE FLOW

In order to create an effective flow, a print ad should move the reader's eye to all of the key points in the advertisement. In a television ad, the points to be made should flow in a manner that leads the consumer to the appropriate action or conclusion. Ads without flow confuse the consumer or are simply tuned out.

BEATING AD CLUTTER

Overcoming clutter constitutes a major challenge when seeking to create an effective advertising campaign. The presence of a competitor's advertisement within the same medium or time slot makes the ad clutter problem worse. A recent survey of television advertising revealed that during prime-time programming, 42 percent of the ads shown had one or more competitors advertised during the same hour. Research suggests that an advertisement's effectiveness will be significantly reduced when a competitor's advertisement runs during the same time slot.[37]

One method advertisers use to overcome this brand interference is repetition. Repeating an ad can increase brand and ad recall. In advertising studies, repetition effectively increases recall when no competitor ads are present. When competitor ads are present, repetition does not help the competitive ad interference problem and does not stimulate greater recall.

Variability Theory Mere repetition of an advertisement does not always work. Some advertisers emphasize the principles present in **variability theory**,[38] which suggests that variable encoding occurs when a consumer sees the same advertisement in different environments. These varied environments increase recall and effectiveness by encoding it into the brain through various methods. Creatives can generate the effect by varying the situational context of a particular ad. For example, the MasterCard campaign uses various settings to convey the same basic message, "There are some things money can't buy. For everything else, there's MasterCard." Varying the context of the ad increases recall and offers an effective method for overcoming competitive ad interference.[39]

Using a Second Medium Selecting two media to convey a message generally can be more effective than repeating an advertisement in the same medium. An advertisement placed in more than one medium reduces competing ad interference. In other words, a message presented on television and in magazines works better than one that appears only on television. Consumers seeing an advertisement in a different medium are more likely to recall the ad than when it appears in only one medium.

Clutter remains a difficult problem in advertising. Creatives who are able to capture the attention of the audience and transmit messages successfully are in great demand.

◀ These two advertisements for St. Patrick's use variability theory concepts to help beat clutter.

Companies constantly experiment with various approaches to reach audiences. When a program works, the advertising firm and its client have a great deal to celebrate.

International Implications

Many common themes and messages translate well across cultures. Making sure that the message strategy and form of executional framework match the tendencies and preferences in a region represents the primary challenge. For example, some cultures tend to be more rational in terms of decision-making processes, whereas others favor more emotional approaches. This may, in turn, affect the selection of a message strategy in a given nation.

Comparison advertisements are less common in other countries, due to both social and cultural differences, as well as legal restrictions. Marketers should be aware of these issues. Many European countries have made comparative advertising illegal. Japan does not prohibit comparisons, but they run against the society's cultural preferences. In Brazil, the advertising industry is so powerful that any attempt to create a comparative advertisement has been challenged and stopped. Often, international consumers not only dislike the advertisements, but often transfer that dislike to the company sponsoring the ad.[40]

The message strategy chosen affects the execution. The slice-of-life execution has become popular in Japan in recent years, because it matches Japan's soft-sell approach to marketing. A more hard-sell attitude may be used in the United States. Japanese advertising tends to be more indirect, and the slice-of-life approach allows advertisers to present a product in a typical everyday situation. Benefits can be presented in a positive light without making brazen or harsh claims and without directly disparaging the competition.[41]

Other patterns and changes in preferred forms of executions can be discovered by watching local media and reading about trends in magazines and trade journals in the country involved. While maintaining an overall message and idea, the advertiser adjusts to social customs present in a region.

OBJECTIVE 7.7

How are advertising programs adjusted to fit international circumstances?

INTEGRATED CAMPAIGNS IN ACTION

The Soap Opera

The Soap Opera is a one-location laundry that offers 24/7 self-service washers and dryers, as well as a fluff and fold service. With the fluff and fold service, customers drop off their laundry and The Soap Opera's staff wash, iron, and fold the clothes. The Soap Opera is located in Ruston, Louisiana, near the campus of Louisiana Tech University.

The owners of The Soap Opera met with Emogen Marketing to discuss the feasibility of a marketing campaign. The objective of the campaign was to increase awareness of the fluff and fold service, particularly among college students. With limited funds, Emogen Marketing crafted a campaign entitled "Why do your own laundry?" that involved a one-day, on-campus event; creation of a Facebook page; posters on campus bulletin boards; an in-store registration for a $50 gift card; and a series of newspaper ads in the student newspaper.[42]

St. Francis Medical Center

Newcomer, Morris, and Young advertising agency was retained to develop a marketing campaign for St. Francis Medical Center. The medical facility has three locations and a rich history of providing medical care in the area. From dialog with the client and agency staff, the tagline "My first and only choice" was born. To present this idea, the agency recruited patients that had experienced the excellent care provided by St. Francis.

Information about the Soap Opera campaign and the St. Francis campaign is available at the Pearson Instructor's Resource Center (www.pearsonhighered.com). The campaigns feature a PowerPoint presentation outlining the details of the campaigns and examples of the collaterals developed by Emogen Marketing and Newcomer, Morris, and Young, respectively.

Courtesy of Emogen Marketing Group.

▲ Animation was a key component of the Soap Opera campaign.

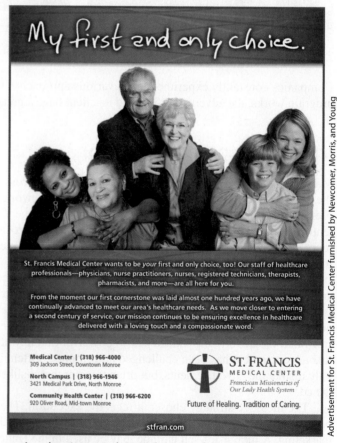

Advertisement for St. Francis Medical Center furnished by Newcomer, Morris, and Young

▲ An advertisement designed as part of the "My first and only choice" campaign.

MyMarketingLab

Go to **mymktlab.com** to complete the problems marked with this icon

SUMMARY

Advertising transmits a personal message through one or more impersonal media. The message reflects the image that occurs throughout an IMC program. Three types of message strategies are possible. Cognitive strategies emphasize rational and logical arguments to compel consumers to make purchases. Affective strategies are oriented toward buyer emotions and feelings. Conative strategies link to more direct responses, behaviors, and actions. These strategies should be integrated with various types of appeals through the media selected for the campaign.

Executional frameworks tell the story in the ad. Animation has become more sophisticated and provides many new creative approaches in the design of ads. The slice-of-life approach and dramatizations are problem-solving types of ads, leading the consumer to something better by using the product. Testimonials are rendered by individuals who have realized the benefits of a product. An authoritative expert can build consumer confidence in a product or company. Demonstrations show how products can be used. A fantasy takes people away from the real world to a make-believe place. This makes the product more exotic and desirable. Informative ads provide basic information about the product. Each execution can be used effectively to persuade consumers and business-to-business buyers to consider a company's offerings.

Celebrities, CEOs, experts, and typical persons can be chosen to be "out front" in the advertisement. Each has advantages and disadvantages. The marketing team selects sources or spokespersons based on the individual's attractiveness, similarity, likeability, trustworthiness, expertise, or credibility. The more of these characteristics that are present, the better off the advertiser will be.

Effective advertising campaigns are based on the seven principles of visual consistency, sufficient campaign duration, repeated taglines, consistent positioning, simplicity, presentation of an identifiable selling point, and creation of an effective flow. Creatives and account executives incorporate these principles into the advertising campaign to enhance the odds of success. Clutter can be overcome by repeating ads and showing them in various media.

Many consider advertising design to be the most glamorous part of the advertising industry, and in many ways it is. The other side of the glamour coin is hard work and the constant pressure to perform. Many people believe a creative position is a burnout-type of job. At the same time, those who have proven track records are well rewarded for their efforts. Utilizing the principles presented in this chapter can be a key to success in the highly competitive and exciting business of advertising design.

Key Terms

message theme The outline of the key idea(s) that the advertising program is supposed to convey.

message strategy The primary tactic used to deliver the message theme.

cognitive message strategy The presentation of rational arguments or pieces of information to consumers.

generic messages Direct promotions of product attributes or benefits without any claim of superiority.

preemptive messages Claims of superiority based on a specific attribute or benefit of a product that preempts the competition from making the same claim.

unique selling proposition (USP) An explicit, testable claim of uniqueness or superiority that can be supported or substantiated in some manner.

hyperbole Making an untestable claim based upon some attribute or benefit.

comparative advertisement The direct or indirect comparison of a good or service to the competition.

affective message strategies Advertisements designed to invoke feelings and emotions and match them with the good, service, or company.

resonance advertising An advertisment that attempts to connect a product with a consumer's experiences to develop stronger ties between the product and the consumer.

comfort marketing An advertising effort designed to reassure consumers that are looking for value that a branded product has stood the test of time

emotional advertising An advertisement that attempts to elicit powerful emotions that eventually lead to brand recall and choice.

conative message strategy Advertisements that are designed to lead directly to some type of consumer response.

action-inducing conative advertisements Advertisements that create situations in which cognitive knowledge of the product or affective liking of the product follow the actual purchase or arise during usage of the product.

promotional support conative advertisements Advertisements that are designed to support other promotional efforts.

executional framework The manner in which an ad appeal is presented.

expert authority When an advertiser employs a spokesperson with expertise in order to convince viewers that a given product is superior to other brands in some authoritative manner.

sources and spokespersons Persons in the advertisement who make the actual presentation.

variability theory A theory stating that when a consumer sees the same advertisement in different environments, the ad will be more effective.

Review Questions

1. Name the three types of message strategies creatives can use. How are message strategies related to the message theme?

2. What types of goods or services best match cognitive message strategies? List the five types of cognitive approaches.

3. When will an affective message strategy be most effective? What two types of affective messages can creatives design? Give an example of each.

4. What is the primary goal of a conative message strategy?

5. How is an executional framework different from an ad appeal? How are they related?

6. List as many uses of animation-based advertisements as possible. What forms of animation are possible with the available technology?

7. Describe the components of the slice-of-life execution.

8. How are authoritative and informational executional frameworks similar? How are they different?

9. What types of testimonials can advertisers use? Give an example of each.

10. Which media are best for demonstration-type ads?

11. What kinds of products or services are best suited to fantasy-based executional frameworks? What products or services are poor candidates for fantasies?

12. Identify the four main types of sources or spokespersons. What are the advantages and disadvantages of each?

13. List the key criteria used when selecting a spokesperson.

⭐14. Identify the tactics available to overcome clutter. How does variability theory assist in this process?

15. What issues are present when adapting an advertising program to an international audience?

Critical Thinking Exercises

DISCUSSION QUESTIONS

⭐ 1. Select five advertisements from a magazine. Identify the message strategy, appeal, and executional framework in each. Did the creative select the right combination for the advertisement? What other message strategies or executional frameworks could have been used?

2. Watch five television advertisements. Identify the message strategy, appeal, and executional framework each uses. Did the creative select the right combination for the advertisement? What other message strategies or executional frameworks could have been used?

3. Studies involving comparative advertisements versus to noncomparative advertisements produced the following findings.[43] Discuss why you think each statement is true. Try to think of comparative ads you have seen that substantiate these claims.

   a. Message awareness was higher for comparative ads than for noncomparative ads if the brands were already established brands.

   b. Brand recall was higher for comparative ads than for noncomparative ads.

   c. Comparative ads were viewed as less believable than noncomparative ads.

   d. Attitudes toward comparative ads were more negative than those toward noncomparative ads.

⭐ 4. The marketing team for Charles Schwab wants to develop an advertisement with the message theme that Charles Schwab understands the needs of individual consumers and can design an investment strategy to meet each person's particular needs. Which type of message strategy should Schwab choose? Why? Based on the message strategy chosen, which executional framework should the company use? Why? What type of source or spokesperson should Schwab use? Why? Would the type of media being used for the advertisement affect the message strategy choice? Explain your answer.

⭐ 5. A resort in Florida wants to develop an advertisement highlighting scuba diving classes. The target market will be college students. Discuss the merits of each of the following approaches. In your opinion, which one would be the best? Why? Describe a television ad that could be created using the strategy you chose.

a. Hyperbole cognitive message strategy, humor appeal, and demonstration execution

b. Emotional message strategy, emotional appeal, and slice-of-life execution

c. Conative message strategy, scarcity appeal, and informative execution

d. Emotional or resonance message strategy, sex appeal, and fantasy execution

e. Comparative message strategy, fear appeal, and testimonial execution

6. Refer to Question 5. Pick one of the combinations (a through e). Design a magazine print ad for the resort. The ad will be for the Karianga Dive Resort.

7. Name three influential commercial spokespersons. For each one, discuss the five characteristics used to evaluate spokespersons and their overall level of credibility. Next, make a list of three individuals who are poor spokespersons. Discuss each of the five evaluation characteristics for each of these individuals. What differences exist between an effective and a poor spokesperson?

8. Find a copy of a business journal, such as *Business-Week* or *Fortune*, or a trade journal. Also locate a copy

of a consumer periodical such as *Glamour*, *Time*, *Sports Illustrated*, or a specialty magazine. Look through an entire issue. What differences between the advertisements in the business journal and consumer journals are readily noticeable? For each of the concepts that follow, discuss specific differences you noted between the two types of magazines. Explain why the differences exist.

a. Message strategies

b. Executional frameworks

c. Sources and spokespersons

9. Identify an advertisement that uses each of the following executional frameworks. Evaluate the advertisement in terms of how well it is executed. Also, did the appeal and message strategy fit well with the execution? Was the ad memorable? What made it memorable?

a. Animation

b. Slice-of-life

c. Testimonial

d. Authoritative

e. Demonstration

f. Fantasy

g. Informative

Integrated Learning Exercises

⭐ 1. Current as well as past Super Bowl ads are available at www.superbowl-ads.com. Access the site and compare Super Bowl ads for the last several years. What types of message strategies were used? What types of executions were used? Who and what types of endorsers were used? Compare and contrast these three elements of ads.

2. Most advertising agencies provide examples of advertisements on company Web pages. The goal is to display the agency's creative abilities to potential clients. Using a search engine, locate three different advertising agencies. Locate samples of their work. Compare the ads produced by these three agencies in terms of message appeals, executions, and spokespersons. What similarities do you see? What differences do you see? Which agency, in your opinion, is the most creative? Why?

3. Access the following Web sites. For each, identify the primary message strategy used. Does the site use any sources or spokespersons? What type of appeal is being used? For each Web site, suggest how the site could be improved. Explain how the change would improve the site.

a. Georgia–Pacific (**www.gp.com**)

b. Playland International (**www.playland-inc.com**)

c. MGM Grand (**www.mgmgrand.com**)

d. Anderson's Furniture (**www.andersonsfurniture.com**)

e. CoverGirl (**www.covergirl.com**)

f. Dove (**www.dove.com**)

g. Skechers (**www.skechers.com**)

4. Access the following Web sites. For each, identify and evaluate the primary executional framework used. Is it the best execution, or would another execution work better? Does the site use any sources or spokespersons? What type of appeal is being used? For each Web site, suggest how the site could be improved. Explain how the change would improve the site.

a. Kellogg's Frosted Flakes (**www.frostedflakes.com**)

b. Bonne Bell (**www.bonnebell.com**)

c. MessageMedia (**www.message-media.com.au**)

d. Jantzen (**www.jantzen.com**)

e. Jockey International (**www.jockey.com**)

Student Project

CREATIVE CORNER

For a number of years, LendingTree.com featured the tagline "When banks compete, you win." In the mid-2000s, when the housing market tumbled, mortgage companies faced financial problems, and consumers defaulted on home mortgages, LendingTree.com changed its approach. The company developed new ads and modified the Web site to educate consumers about "smart borrowing." Other financial and mortgage companies followed suit. JPMorgan Chase asserted "Whether you are saving money, looking for a loan, or managing a business, you can always depend on Chase." Astoria Federal Savings promoted its longevity, telling consumers it had been in business "more than 118 years" and using phrases such as "We're part of your community" and "We're here when you need us."[44]

The marketing department for First National Bank intends to promote its home mortgage business. They are not sure about which creative message strategy to use, which execution would work best, and which appeal to use. They would also like to use some type of spokesperson, but they are not sure which of the four types would be the most effective. They also realize they cannot afford a celebrity.

Based on the information provided, design a print advertisement for the local newspaper for First National Bank. Describe a television campaign for the bank. Before launching into these two creative assignments, identify and justify your choice of creative message strategy, executional framework, appeal, and spokesperson.

CASE 1 PEERLESS MARKETING

In the United States, the majority of homes have indoor plumbing. Sinks, faucets, toilets, and other pieces of hardware are largely taken for granted. Only in two circumstances are they prominently in the minds of customers. The first is when a plumbing product is being purchased for the first time, such as when a home is being built or an area is being refurbished. The second is when an item is defective and must be replaced.

Manufacturers try to make certain consumers will remember a company's brand and that it will be preferred by builders and plumbers. The products must be placed in stores such as Home Depot or Lowes in ways that makes them easy to find and always accessible.

One of the major players in the plumbing fixture marketplace is Delta Faucet Company. A strange path brought the company to prominence. In the 1920s, an immigrant named Alex Manoogian founded Masco Company, which provided auto parts. Twenty-five years later, Manoogian was contacted by an inventor who had created the first washerless faucet. Although it was not related to his current business, Manoogian saw the potential and refined the item, which was first sold out of the trunks of salesmen's cars, as the first Delta Faucet. The name was chosen because a key part of the product resembled the shape of the Greek letter delta.

The Delta Faucet Company became a separate part of the original Masco Company and relocated. Over the next two decades, it expanded quickly to an entire line of products. Currently, Delta Faucet Company is a multinational firm with four primary locations: Indianapolis, Indiana; Jackson, Tennessee; London Ontario, Canada; and Panyu, China. It sells over 1 million faucets per month. The overall Masco Company now sells door hardware and locks, cabinets, and glass products in addition to faucets.

The Delta line includes two other names: Brizo and Peerless. Brizo is the high-end line of faucets, Delta is the flagship and primary brand, and Peerless is the lower-end line of items.

The primary advertising challenges appear to exist in four main areas. First, company leaders must make sure that one brand does not cannibalize the others. The brands must remain as distinct products offered to separate sets of consumers. Second, the brands must be viewed as the primary choices and must be remembered by consumers when the time comes to buy a plumbing fixture. Third, there cannot be brand confusion. Builders and plumbers must believe that the fixtures are distinct along several lines, including quality and durability, ease of installation, and strong warranties, but they must also be perceived as being fashionable. Fourth, innovation has become a new part of the plumbing fixture industry. A wide variety of options exist. Delta's products must compete with all the new faucet variations and retain its position as a manufacturer.

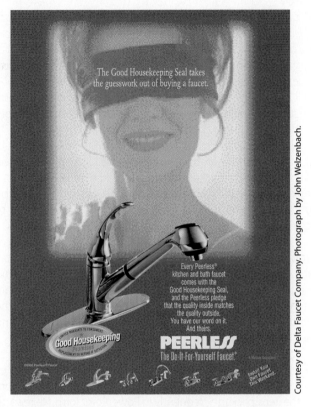

Courtesy of Delta Faucet Company. Photograph by John Welzenbach.

▲ The Delta Faucet Company offers the Peerless brand.

Complications occur due to differences in markets and customers. Many contractors and builders are simply looking for a low-cost option, especially when lower-end rental properties and similar units are being developed. Plumbers may be willing to install a wide variety of products. They will consider the costs of a product but also want something that will be easy to install and that will be durable. Individual consumers are the most likely to be interested in other product qualities, such as novel features and the look of the product.

1. What type of message strategy should Delta Faucet Company utilize? Should it be the same for all of the brands and in all of the markets (builders, plumbers, consumers)?

2. What leverage point makes the most sense for Delta Faucet Company advertising?

3. What type of executional framework should be used in traditional advertisements aimed at consumers?

4. What type of executional framework should be used for print advertisements aimed at contractors, builders, and plumbers? Why might it be different (or the same) from ads aimed at consumers?

5. Should the company use a spokesperson? If so, which one of the four types should be used? Justify your answers.

Source: www.deltafaucet.com (accessed April 20, 2012).

CASE 2   **BLACK-EYED MARKETING**

If Black Eyed Peas band member will.i.am wasn't in music, "He'd be the best ad executive on Madison Avenue," says Randy Phillips, president and CEO of the concert promoter AEG Live. "I've never seen anyone more astute at dealing with sponsors' and companies' needs and understanding their brands." The Black Eyed Peas have been able to move beyond the status as a high-energy band into the world of corporate sponsorship without missing a beat.

Marketers love the Black Eyed Peas for the diverse ethnicity of the band's members, writes the Wall Street Journal. The band's corporate backers include Coors, Levi's, Honda, Apple, Verizon, and Pepsi. The advertisement featuring the group's song "Hey Mama" and dancing silhouettes that was used to help launch Apple's iTunes store gained almost iconic status.

What makes this group of musicians such an effective set of spokespeople? Part of the appeal is the group's global fan base and the Pea's fetching party anthems, with powerful dance beats, crazy special effects, and repetitive hooks that are integrated into numerous party mixes. As one critic noted, the band achieves the nearly impossible—making both kids and their parents feel cool at the same time.

Beyond the glitz and glitter of the shows, the group gives careful thought to its marketing. Oftentimes, will.i.am pitches concepts to corporate sponsors himself, using "decks" that sum up the Peas' package, frequently in PowerPoint form. He reports, "I consider us a brand. A brand always has stylized decks, from colors to fonts. Here's our demographic. Here's the reach. Here's the potential. Here's how the consumer will benefit from the collaboration."

There was a time when rock and roll was nearly synonymous with rebellion. Bands with corporate ties would be viewed as sell outs. For companies such a move would seem too risky; especially if the band's fans felt betrayed. Over the years, music has become less threatening, as Baby Boomers near retirement age.

The economics of music have also changed. Downloading and pirating CDs is commonplace. Bands can no longer count on record sales to make money. Many younger bands now look for other sources of income and publicity. The Peas were among the fastest learners of the industry's new math. Even now, however, the band hears complaints that they are merely shills. "You have to take the criticism, and sometimes it hurts a lot," says band member Stacy Ferguson, who is also known Fergie.

Currently, many top-name musicians and groups have corporate sponsors. Cooperative advertisements promote the brand, the band, and often a tour. The Rolling Stones began the movement when the group's "Tattoo You" tour was sponsored by Jovan Musk cologne. Even groups that at first resolutely avoided corporate tie-ins, such as U2, have changed. U2 developed a relationship with Apple that included commercials featuring the song "Vertigo." The band helped with BlackBerry commercials and had a sponsored tour with the brand.

▲ The Black Eyed Peas use marketing to enhance the band's image and presence.

DWP/Fotolia

The Black Eyed Peas continues to expand their corporate connections. A concert in Times Square promoted Samsung's new line of 3D televisions, which led to a meeting with Avatar director James Cameron, who agreed to direct a feature film about the Peas. The 3D film incorporates concerts, travel footage, and narrative themes about technology, dreams, and the brain.

According to will.i.am, all corporate partnerships are equally important. The band lends its music at relatively small charges in exchange for exposure. "It wasn't about the check," says former manager Seth Friedman.

The efforts have paid off. The Black Eyed Peas have performed at an NFL season-kickoff show and at half time of the Super Bowl, New Year's Eve in Times Square, the Grammys, a Victoria's Secret fashion show, and the season opener for The Oprah Winfrey Show, for which they summoned a flash mob of synchronized dancers to downtown Chicago. As will.i.am puts it, "I get the credit from the brands. They know. I used to work with the marketing people and the agencies, now I work with the CEOs of these companies."

1. Discuss each of the source characteristics in terms of the Black Eyed Peas serving as a spokesperson for a product. Would it make a difference as to what type of product the Black Eyed Peas were endorsing? Explain.

2. What types of brands or products are best suited to endorsements by the Black Eyed Peas? By rock bands in general? What about country music artists?

3. If you were going to design a television advertisement for a concert for the Black Eyed Peas, what would be your target market? What message strategy and executional framework would you use? Why? Describe your concept of an effective television ad.

4. Suppose the Black Eyed Peas were contracted to perform at your university. Design a print ad for your local student newspaper. Discuss the message strategy and execution you used and why you used it.

5. What types of brands or products would not be suited to endorsements by groups such as the Black Eyed Peas?

Source: John Jurgensen, "The Most Corporate Band in America," *Wall Street Journal Online* (www.wsj.com, accessed April 14, 2010).

MyMarketingLab

Go to **mymktlab.com** for Auto-graded writing questions as well as the following Assisted-graded writing questions:.

7-1. Name three influential commercial spokespersons. For each one, discuss the five characteristics used to evaluate spokespersons and their overall level of credibility. Next, make a list of three individuals who are poor spokespersons. Discuss each of the five evaluation characteristics for each of these individuals. What differences exist between an effective and a poor spokesperson?

7-2. Current as well as past Super Bowl ads are available at www.superbowl-ads.com. Access the site and compare Super Bowl ads for the last several years. What types of message strategies were used? What types of executions were used? Who and what types of endorsers were used? Compare and contrast these three elements of ads.

7-3. Mymktlab Only—comprehensive writing assignment for this chapter.

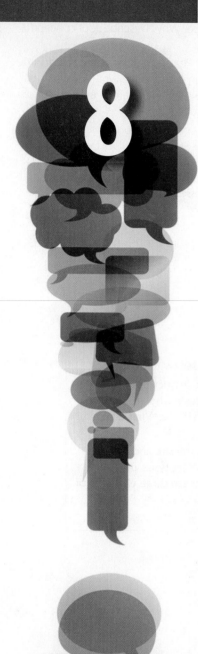

8

TRADITIONAL MEDIA CHANNELS

CHAPTER OBJECTIVES

After reading this chapter, you should be able to answer the following questions:

1 What is a media strategy?

2 What elements and individuals are involved in media planning?

3 How do the terms used to describe advertising help the marketing team design effective campaigns?

4 What are some of the primary advertising objectives?

5 What are the advantages and disadvantages associated with each traditional advertising medium?

6 How can the marketing team use the media mix to increase advertising effectiveness?

7 What are the key issues associated with media selection for business-to-business markets?

8 What issues are associated with media selection in international markets?

MyMarketingLab™

⭐ **Improve Your Grade!**

Over 10 million students improved their results using the Pearson MyLabs. Visit **mymktlab.com** for simulations, tutorials, and end-of-chapter problems.

GODADDY.COM

SUPER BOWL BUZZ

f you ask just about anyone where to go to register a domain name on the Internet, the answer will likely be, "Go Daddy." The iconic company developed a strong brand and marketplace presence through its Web site and Internet advertising. In 2012, the company's Super Bowl commercial went one step further, placing a QR code on the screen for anxious viewers to access the newest racy, tantalizing Web site message.

Go Daddy advertisements have built a strong legacy in attracting interest and buzz. In 2005, the company's commercial entitled "Proceedings" appeared the year after Janet Jackson's infamous half-time wardrobe malfunction. "Go Daddy Girl" Nikki Cappelli appears to testify before a shocked Congress, as her tank-top strap keeps breaking. One of the questioners finally has to grab for an oxygen mask.

From the attention that grew out of that advertisement, plus the one network executives would not allow to be shown, a new form of Super Bowl commercial emerged, because Go Daddy discovered a novel way to create buzz. The company's marketing team submits suggestive and highly provocative advertisements to appear on the Super Bowl that they know will not be allowed to be shown. Word spreads about the prohibited ads on Web sites and in forums and news articles. This buzz helps drive inquisitive customers to the Go Daddy Web site to watch the more controversial ads.

Brocreative/fotolia

Go Daddy advertising has often featured race car driver Danica Patrick. The 2010 "Lola" commercial features a former football player who becomes a lingerie designer and makes his fortune with Go Daddy's assistance, with Patrick as the narrator. In another, Ms. Patrick is portrayed in sexy situations as a "Hot Smoking" dancer and entertainer.

To maintain interest, Go Daddy annually follows up the initial buzz with 30-second spots that tell viewers that to see the entire "unedited" version of the ad they need to visit the Web site. Over the years, these methods have allowed Go Daddy to benefit from substantial amounts of free publicity, which also increases brand awareness. The commercials provide a new method of creating Web site traffic through traditional media.

Super Bowl advertising represents one of the most powerful venues for reaching customers. Television audiences totaling around 100 million viewers in the United States and nearly 1 billion people worldwide watch at least part of the game. The 2-week buildup, the 4- to 6-hour pregame shows,

and the massive media attention paid to the teams and players have been rewarded with a series of exciting games over the past decade.

Go Daddy's marketing team recognizes that Super Bowl ads generate a great deal of buzz. Of the 38 brands presented during the recent Super Bowl, 75 percent experienced nearly twice as many blog posts on the Internet as compared to the average online mentions in the 6 months prior. About one-third of the brands had a threefold increase in online mentions. The additional buzz is not limited to the Internet. One study revealed that 22 percent of word-of-mouth recommendations, whether in person or online, were directly tied to a Super Bowl commercial.

The Go Daddy sequence of provocative advertisements may draw criticism for some individuals for the use of decorative models and sexuality to sell a non-sexual product. At the same time, it would be difficult to argue with the overall success the campaigns have achieved in a relatively short period of time.[1]

OVERVIEW

f a tree falls in the forest and no one is present, does it make a sound? This philosophical question has been posed for many years. In the world of advertising, far too many "trees" fall as unheard and unseen advertisements. Successful marketing involves

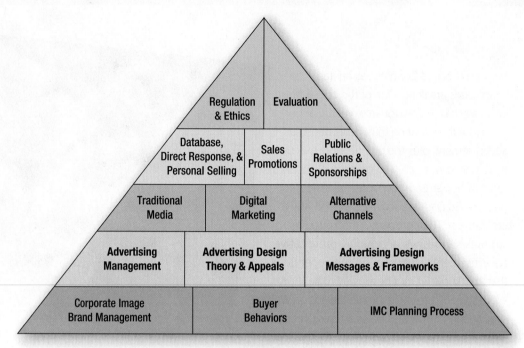

▶ **FIGURE 8.1**
Overview of Integrated
Marketing Communications

identifying target markets and finding media that reach the members of those markets. Once they identify the right media, creatives can design clever, memorable, exciting, and persuasive advertisements.

The third part of this textbook covers the IMC media tools, including both traditional media channels and newer approaches. The concepts of digital marketing and alternative channels are explained in the upcoming chapters (see Figure 8.1).

Traditional media continue to play an important role in developing a fully integrated marketing program. This chapter explains the various traditional media channels, including:

- The media strategy
- Media planning processes and the roles of the media planner and buyer
- Advertising objectives
- Media choices based on the advantages and disadvantages of each medium
- Media selection in business-to-business and international settings

Advertising agencies design a campaign within the framework of the overall integrated marketing communications program. Client companies depend on effective advertisements to attract customers and entice them into purchasing various goods and services. This helps build the firm's image and creates a larger customer base. Advertising media selection remains an important element in the process.

The Media Strategy

OBJECTIVE 8.1

What is a media strategy?

A **media strategy** involves analyzing and choosing media for an advertising and promotions campaign. The average consumer examines only nine of the more than 200 consumer magazines on the market. A radio listener usually tunes in to only three of the stations available in an area. Television viewers watch fewer than eight of the stations available via cable or satellite. Average network prime-time ratings have declined by more than 30 percent over the last decade. Choosing the best media to speak to potential customers creates challenges.

- A favorite wake-up radio station or one listened to during the commute to work
- A favorite morning news show or newspaper
- Trade or business journals examined while at work
- A radio station played during office hours at work
- Favorite computer sites accessed during work

- Favorite magazines read during the evening hours
- Favorite television shows watched during the evening hours
- Internet sites accessed during leisure time
- Shopping, dining, and entertainment venues frequented

◀ **FIGURE 8.2**
Examples of Times Consumers Are Exposed to Advertisements

To make the account executive and media buyer's jobs more difficult, prices for advertising time and space have risen. Client budgets for advertising have not gone up as quickly, even as stronger demands for results and accountability emerged. The marketing team faces difficulties in locating cost-effective media outlets. After developing a media strategy, other aspects of media selection can proceed.

Media Planning

Media planning begins with an analysis of the target market. It involves understanding the processes customers use in making purchases and what influences the final decisions. One method of addressing media planning is to study the media choices that members of a specific, defined target market might make at different times during the course of a day (see Figure 8.2).

Details of this type are valuable when developing a media strategy. Demographics such as age, sex, income, and education do not explain the media habits of consumers. Information about the listening and viewing patterns of groups helps the marketing team design messages that appeal to them. These can then be placed at the best times and in the best places. No two media plans are alike. The components of a media plan include the elements identified in Figure 8.3.

A *marketing analysis* provides a comprehensive review of the marketing program. It includes a statement about current sales, current market share, and prime prospects to be solicited (by demographics, lifestyle, geographic location, or product usage). These elements should reflect a compatible pricing strategy based on the product, its benefits and distinguishing characteristics, and an analysis of the competitive environment.

An *advertising analysis* states the primary advertising strategy and budget to be used to achieve advertising objectives. The *media strategy* spells out the media to be used and the creative considerations. The *media schedule* notes when ads will appear in individual vehicles. The *justification and summary* outlines the measures of goal achievement. It also explains the rationale for each media choice.[2]

Several individuals take part in media planning. In addition to account executives, account planners, and creatives, most agencies utilize media planners and media buyers. In smaller agencies, the media planner and media buyer can be the same person. In larger companies, they are usually different individuals. Some agencies employ media firms to handle the media planning and buying, or hire a subsidiary agency.

MEDIA PLANNERS

The **media planner** formulates a media program stating where and when to place ads. Media planners work closely with creatives, account executives, account planners, agencies, and media buyers. The creative should know which media will be used to help design effective messages. Television commercials are constructed in different ways than radio or newspaper ads.

Media planners provide valuable services and are in high demand. The issue of accountability for advertising results combined with the need to create a "return on

OBJECTIVE 8.2
What elements and individuals are involved in media planning?

- Marketing analysis
- Advertising analysis
- Media strategy
- Media schedule
- Justification and summary

▲ **FIGURE 8.3**
Components of a Media Plan

When does a jogger become a runner?

On a day like this.

achieve new balance

© 1999 New Balance Athletic Shoe, Inc.

▲ An advertisement featuring New Balance that was placed in Runner's World magazine.

investment" on marketing dollars has caused greater power to be held by the media buying side of an agency.

Media planning impacts strategic planning. Marketing experts at companies such as Procter & Gamble and Unilever consider media planning to be at the heart of a communications strategy. In both companies, setting brand priorities and objectives constitutes the first step.[3] The challenge for media buyers in this environment, according to Carl Fremont of the media services company Digitas, is "to integrate marketing messages across a range of media, and sometimes this involves working with several agencies to accomplish the client's goals."[4]

The media planner conducts research to help match the product with the market and media. A target market consisting of 18- to 25-year-old males with college degrees who love the outdoors leads to media that match those characteristics. The New Balance running shoe ad in this section was placed in *Runner's World* near an article about running and was targeted to avid runners.

The media planner gathers information about various media. This includes newspaper and magazine circulation rates along with the characteristics of those who use them. The audience for a television show may be different from those of a radio station or a magazine. Careful research improves the chances of selecting the appropriate media.

MEDIA BUYERS

After the media are chosen, the **media buyer** purchases the space and negotiates rates, times, and schedules for the ads. Media buyers remain in contact with media sales representatives. They know a great deal about rates and schedules. Media buyers watch for special deals and tie-ins between media outlets (e.g., radio with television, magazines with the same owner, etc.).

Placement in a television show or magazine continues to be an important consideration, both in terms of price and effectiveness. Recently, the Pink Jacket Creative advertising agency purchased magazine space for The Snoring Center consisting of the outer sides of adjacent pages containing an article. The slender ads on the edges of the two pages bracketed the article. As individuals read the article, they first noticed the ad on the left side of the article and the second half on the right side as they held the magazine open. Not only was the ad space cheaper, it turned out to be more effective in conveying the two-part message.

Some research indicates that little connection exists between the size of an advertising firm and the prices it can negotiate. Differences in media costs are based on the time of the actual purchase (closer to the day the ad is to run) rather than the size of the agency.[5] A media plan costing one firm $10 million can cost another $12 million. Other major factors in cost differences are knowledge of the marketplace and the ability to negotiate package deals.

A **spot ad** is a one-time placement of a commercial in a medium. Rates are negotiated individually by the number of times the ads appear. Spot television prices fluctuate by as much as 45 percent for the same time slot. Radio time slot prices vary by as much

I said for better or worse...

DALLAS | 214.369.2345
FORT WORTH | 817.737.5678

as 42 percent and national print ads by as much as 24 percent.[6] Negotiation skills affect media purchase outcomes.

Differences in effectiveness of advertising are related to the quality of media choices, creativity, financial stewardship, the agency's culture and track record, and the relationship between the agency and the medium's sales representative. Advertising effectiveness will be determined by quality of the media selections made combined with the advertisement's content.

Advertising Terminology

As with many subjects, advertising has its own unique set of terms and measures (see Figure 8.4). **Reach** represents the number of people, households, or businesses in a target audience exposed to a media vehicle or message schedule at least once during a given time period, which normally consists of 4 weeks. In other words, how many targeted buyers did the ad reach at least once during a 4-week period?

FREQUENCY

The average number of times an individual, household, or business within a particular target market is exposed to a particular advertisement within a specified time period, again, usually 4 weeks, represents **frequency**. It specifies how many times the person saw the ad during a campaign. A regular viewer sees the same ad shown daily on *Wheel of Fortune* more frequently than an ad shown once on *CSI*, even though the program has a greater reach.

OPPORTUNITIES TO SEE

In media planning, instead of frequency, opportunities to see (OTS) can be used. **Opportunities to see** refers to the cumulative exposures achieved in a given time period. When a company places two ads on a weekly television show, there are 8 OTS (4 shows × 2 ads per show) during a 4-week period.

GROSS RATING POINTS

Gross rating points (GRPs) measure the impact or intensity of a media plan. Gross rating points are calculated by multiplying a vehicle's rating by the OTS, or number of insertions of an advertisement. GRPs give the advertiser a better idea of the odds that members of the target audience actually viewed the commercial. By increasing the OTS or frequency, the chances of a magazine reader seeing the advertisement rise. An advertisement featured in each weekly issue of *People* during a 4-week period is more likely to be seen than one appearing in a monthly periodical.

COST

Cost measures the overall expenditures associated with an advertising program or campaign. To be able to compare how cost effective one medium or ad placement is to another, a measure called **cost per thousand (CPM)** can be calculated. CPM is the dollar

Not for snoring!

Make bedtime better for your better half.

▲ Ads for the Snoring Center placed strategically on a two-page article spread on the outer edges.

OBJECTIVE 8.3

How do the terms used to describe advertising help the marketing team design effective campaigns?

- Reach
- Frequency
- Opportunities to see (OTS)
- Gross rating points (GRP)
- Cost per thousand (CPM)
- Cost per rating point (CPRP)
- Ratings
- Continuity
- Gross impressions

◀ **FIGURE 8.4**
Advertising Terminology

cost of reaching 1,000 members of the media vehicle's audience. It is calculated using the following formula:

$$CPM = (\text{Cost of media buy}/\text{Total audience}) \times 1,000$$

Figure 8.5 displays cost and readership information for a campaign for a 35 mm digital camera. The first three columns of the figure provide the name of the magazine, the cost of a four-color full-page advertisement, and the magazine's paid and verified circulation. The fourth column contains a measure of the CPM of each magazine. The CPM for *Better Homes and Garden* is $66.21and has a circulation of 7.6 million. *Sports Illustrated* has a smaller circulation, 3.2 million, but the CPM is $122.69. In terms of cost per thousand readers, *Reader's Digest* offers the best buy, at $26.04 per thousand.

RATINGS AND COST PER RATING POINT

A critical concern is the number of readers that fit the target market's profile, in this case for a 35 mm digital camera. **Ratings** measure the percentage of a firm's target market that is exposed to a television show or the number of readers of a print medium. In order to compare media, a measure called the **cost per rating point (CPRP)** may be used. The cost per rating point formula that measures the relative efficiency of a media vehicle relative to a firm's target market is:

$$CPRP = \text{Cost of media buy} / \text{Vehicle's rating}$$

The number of potential buyers of the 35 mm digital camera is 20 million. The figure shows the rating for *Better Homes and Garden* is 5.2, which means that 5.2 percent of the defined target market for 35 mm digital cameras read the *Better Homes and Garden*. Backing up a step, 13.51 percent, or 1.033 million, of *Better Homes and Garden's* readership fits the target profile for the 35 mm digital camera. The 5.2 rating is then obtained by dividing the 1.033 million *Better Homes and Garden* readers that fit the target profile by the 20 million total in the target market. The CPRP for *Better Homes and Garden* become $98,041. This is the average cost for each rating point, or of each 1 percent of the firm's target audience (35 mm digital camera buyers) that can be reached through an advertisement in *Better Homes and Garden*. Not all readers of a magazine are part of the firm's

Publication	4C Base Rate	Total Paid & Verified Circulation	CPM	Target Market (20 Million)			
				Percent of Readers Fit Target Market	Number of Readers Fit Tareet Market	Rating (Reach)	Cost per Rating Point (CPRP)
Better Homes and Garden	$506.380	7,648,600	$566.21	13.51%	1,033,000	5.2	$98,041
Glamour	$219,190	2,320,325	$94.47	24.65%	572,000	2.9	$76,640
Good Housekeeping	$387,055	4,652,904	$83.19	10.81%	503,000	2.5	$153,899
National Geographic	$225,455	4,495,931	$50.15	26.96%	1,212,000	6.1	$37,204
Reader's Digest	$185,300	7,114,955	$26.04	18.62%	1,325,000	6.6	$27,970
Southern Living	$198,800	2,855,973	$69.61	10.57%	302,000	1.5	$131,656
Soorts Illustrated	$392,800	3,201,524	$122.69	16.77%	537,000	2.7	$146,294
Time	$320,100	3,376,226	$94.81	18.60%	628,000	3.1	$101,943

▲ **FIGURE 8.5**
Hypothetical Media Information for Select Magazine

Publication	4C Base Rate	Total Paid & Verified Circulation	CPM	Target Market (20 Million)		
				Percent of Readers Fit Target Market	Number of Readers Fit Target Market	Weighted (Demographic) CPM
Better Homes and Gardens	$506,380	7,648,600	$66.21	13.51%	1,033,000	$490.20
Glamour	$219,190	2,320,325	$94.47	24.65%	572,000	$383.20
Good Housekeeping	$387,055	4,652,904	$83.19	10.81%	503,000	$769.49
National Geography	$225,455	4,495,931	$50.15	26.96%	1,212,000	$186.02
Reader's Digest	$185,300	7,114,955	$26.04	18.62%	1,325,000	$139.85
Southern Living	$198,800	2,855,973	$69.61	10.5%	302,000	$658.28
Sports Illustrated	$392,800	3,201,524	$122.69	16.77%	537,000	$731.47

▲ **FIGURE 8.6**
Calculating Weighted (or Demographic) CPM

target market. The CPRP more accurately measures an advertising campaign's efficiency than does CPM. Notice that the CPRP is the lowest for *National Geographic* and *Reader's Digest*. It is the highest for *Good Housekeeping*.

CPRP provides a relative measure of reach exposure in terms of cost. It costs $37,204 to reach 1 percent, or 200,000, of the 20 million in this firm's target market using *National Geographic*. It costs $146,294 to reach 1 percent, or 200,000, using *Sports Illustrated*. To reach 1 percent, or 200,000, using *Reader's Digest* costs only $27,970. *Reader's Digest* is the most efficient, which raises the question, "Why wouldn't a media planner just do all of the advertising in that magazine?" The answer lies in *Reader's Digest*'s rating. Advertising in only that magazine reaches just 6.6 percent (or 1,325,000) of the target audience; 93.4 percent of the target market does not read *Reader's Digest* and would not see the ad. Another magazine or media outlet is needed to reach them. This explains why diversity in media is essential to reach a large portion of a firm's target market.

An alternative method of determining whether an ad has reached the target market effectively is a **weighted (or demographic) CPM** value, which can be calculated as:

$$\text{Weighted CPM} = \frac{\text{Advertisement cost} \times 1,000}{\text{Actual audience reached}}$$

Referring to Figure 8.6, the cost of an advertisement in *Good Housekeeping* is $387,055. Although it has a circulation of 4,652,904, only 503,000 of the readers fit the target profile for the 35 mm digital camera. Using the formula for weighted CPM, the cost to reach 1,000 readers of *Good Housekeeping* that fit the target profile is $769.49. As with CPRP, marketers can compare the various magazines to determine which offer the best buy in terms of reaching the target demographic. The difference in the numbers is that CPRP measures the cost of reaching 1 percent of the target market, whereas the weighted CPM measures the cost of reaching 1,000 members of the target market.

CONTINUITY

The exposure pattern or schedule used in a campaign is its **continuity**. The three types of patterns are continuous, pulsating, and discontinuous. A *continuous campaign* uses media time in a steady stream. The Skechers ad shown on the next page could be presented on a continuous schedule. The media buys would be for ad space in specific

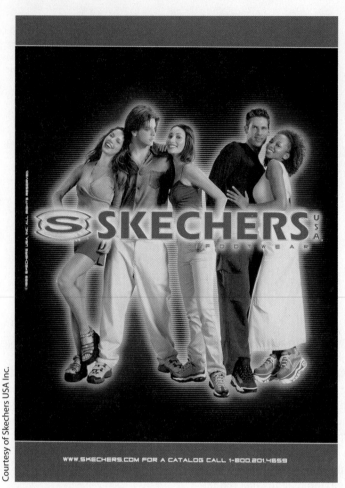

▲ An advertisement promoting the Skechers brand.

magazines for a period of 1 to 2 years. By using different ads and rotating them, readers will not get bored, because they will see more than one advertisement for the same product.

A retailer such as JCPenney might try a *pulsating schedule* by placing ads in various media throughout the entire year, but then increasing the number of advertisements in small, short bursts around holidays, including Christmas, Thanksgiving, Memorial Day, Labor Day, Mother's Day, Father's Day, and Easter. Pulsating advertising should reach consumers when they are most likely to make purchases or buy special merchandise, such as during the holidays. A Barnes & Noble advertisement just prior to Christmas can encourage consumers to purchase gift cards.

A *flighting (or discontinuous) campaign* schedule would be more likely to be used by a ski resort that runs ads during the fall and winter seasons but none during the spring and summer.

IMPRESSIONS

The final advertising objective is impressions. The number of **gross impressions** represents the total exposures of the audience to an advertisement. It does not account for the percentage of the total audience that sees the advertisement. Figure 8.5 indicates that *National Geographic*'s total circulation at 4.6 million. If six insertions were placed in *National Geographic,* multiplying the insertions by the readership would yield a total of 27.6 million impressions.

Achieving Advertising Objectives

OBJECTIVE 8.4

What are some of the primary advertising objectives?

Advertisers consider the number of times a person will be exposed to an advertisement before it creates an impact. Most agree that a single exposure will not be enough. The actual number inspires a great deal of debate. Some argue it takes three. Others say as many as 10 or more.

THE THREE-EXPOSURE HYPOTHESIS

With regard to exposures, most media planners believe it takes a minimum of three for an advertisement to be effective. The three-exposure hypothesis, as developed by Herbert Krugman, suggests that advertisements can make an impact on an audience regardless of individual needs or wants.[7] Further, the **intrusion value** of an advertisement represents the ability of a medium or an advertisement to capture the attention of a viewer without her voluntary effort. This theory suggests that it takes at least three exposures to capture and keep a viewer's attention.

RECENCY THEORY

Currently, many advertisers believe that clutter has diminished the viability of the three-exposure hypothesis. Another concept, **recency theory**, notes that a consumer's attention is selective and focuses on his individual needs and wants, and the consumer has selective attention processes as he considers advertisements.[8] A consumer pays attention to messages that might meet his needs or wants. The closer or more recent an ad is to a purchase, the more powerful the ad becomes. Further, when a consumer contemplates a future purchase of the product being advertised, the consumer will be more likely to notice and react favorably toward an ad. A member of a buying center from a business in the market for a new copier will more readily notice copier advertisements. Someone who is not in the market for a copier ignores the same ad. The same holds true in consumer markets: An individual needing a new pair of jeans notices clothing ads, especially ones that feature jeans.

Recency theory proposes that *one ad exposure* may actually be enough to affect an audience when that person or business needs the product being promoted. Additional exposures may not be necessary. Therefore, companies must advertise almost continually to ensure an advertisement reaches a buyer when she thinks about making a purchase.

The advertising approach that matches recency theory would be to spread the message around using a variety of media, each type providing limited exposure per week or time period. In the case of selling supplemental health insurance to the elderly, magazines such as *Senior Living*, television spots on local news and weather programs, and newspaper ads can quickly reach the target audience in a cost-effective manner. This method, which maximizes reach, accomplishes more than increasing frequency.

In the business-to-business arena, recency theory argues that advertisements should appear in a number of outlets and over a longer period of time rather than running a series of ads in one trade journal. Many times, buying centers consist of several members, each with different responsibilities. Making sure each one sees an advertisement would mean placing ads in every journal that might be read by buying center members. To facilitate the purchasing process for a company seeking to acquire an audio-conferencing system, the media buyer purchases space in trade journals, human resource journals, sales journals, and business journals. This increases the odds that the message will reach buying center members. One exposure might be enough for each, because the member actively looks for information and is ready to make a decision.

EFFECTIVE REACH AND FREQUENCY

Seeking to discover the minimum number of exposures needed to be effective may be based on two concepts: effective frequency and effective reach. **Effective reach** identifies the *percentage of an audience* that must be exposed to a particular message to achieve a specific objective. **Effective frequency** refers to the *number of times* a target audience must be exposed to a message to achieve a particular objective. The concept of effective frequency implies that a minimum number of exposures is needed.

Effective frequency and effective reach are crucial. Too few exposures means the advertiser will fail to attain its intended objectives. In contrast, too many exposures waste resources. Discovering the optimal reach and frequency mix to accomplish the intended objectives without experiencing diminishing returns from extra ads should be the goal. The optimal mix for an objective dealing with brand recognition will be different than when brand recall serves as the objective.

Courtesy of Scott and Cooner Inc. Creative by Gina Cotroneo

▲ Based on recency theory, a person looking for designer home furnishings is likely to notice this advertisement.

▼ Effective reach and effective frequency are important measures to evaluate ads, such as this one for Keepsake.

Courtesy of Keepsake American Achievement Corporation AAC Group Holding Corp.

▶ **FIGURE 8.7**
Brand Recognition versus
Brand Recall

Objective	Brand Recognition	Brand Recall
Goal	Create or strengthen mental linkages	Place brand in evoked set
Method	Increase reach	Increase frequency (repetition)
Best media	Television	Television
	Billboards	Radio
	Magazines	Newspapers
	Internet	Internet
	Direct mail	

Other elements can also enhance effective frequency and effective reach. They include the size and placement of an advertisement. A small magazine advertisement does not create the same impact as a larger ad. If a firm uses 15-second television ads, effective frequency may require six exposures. In comparison, a longer 45-second spot may require only four exposures to be remembered. In television advertising, a spot in the middle of an ad sequence usually has less of an impact than the ads shown at the beginning and end of the series.

The number of different media used in an advertising campaign also influences effectiveness. In general, a campaign featuring ads in two types of media, such as television and magazines, has greater effective reach than a campaign in only one medium, such as magazines only.

In recent years, numerous media companies have designed computer models to optimize reach and frequency, such as Nielsen SAVE or Adware. The programs that evaluate effective reach and frequency are based on probability theory. They are designed to help the marketing team effectively allocate advertising dollars. The interaction between an attention-getting television commercial and a magazine ad with copy explaining the product's features may create a more potent synergistic effect than either ad would alone.

BRAND RECOGNITION

Brand recognition requires an emphasis on the visual presentation of the product and/or logo. Strengthening or creating links between the brand and other nodes of information that exist in the person's knowledge structure becomes the goal. Rather than having the individual recall the brand name from memory, the advertiser wants the person to recognize the brand name and logo at the retail store or in the advertisement. Media that are effective at maximizing reach include television, billboards, magazines, the Internet, and direct mail.[9]

BRAND RECALL

To increase brand recall, frequency becomes more important than reach. Repetition helps embed a brand in the consumer's cognitive memory. Repetition increases the odds that a particular brand will come to mind. When a 30-second commercial repeats the name of a restaurant seven times, it becomes easier to remember than when it is stated only once or twice. In terms of media selection, television, radio, newspapers, and the Internet offer the potential for higher frequency.[10] Figure 8.7 compares brand recall with brand recognition.

Once the media buyer, media planner, account executive, and company leaders agree about basic objectives of the advertising campaign, they select the actual media, seeking to identify logical media combinations. The next section examines traditional advertising media.

OBJECTIVE 8.5

What are the advantages and disadvantages associated with each traditional advertising medium?

Media Selection

Effectively mixing the advertising media continues to be a vital part of designing a quality advertising campaign. To do so, the advantages and disadvantages of each individual medium should be understood.

TELEVISION

Deloitte Research noted that 71 percent of Americans still rate television as their favorite medium. In terms of impact on buying decisions, 86 percent stated that TV advertising exerts the greatest influence.[11] While the power of television has declined, for many brands and companies it remains a viable advertising option. Figure 8.8 lists the pros and cons of television advertising.

Advantages of Television Advertising Television provides the most extensive coverage and highest reach of any medium. A single advertisement can reach millions. Television offers a low cost per contact, which justifies spending as much as $3.5 million for a 30-second spot on the Super Bowl, where a vast audience of over 110 million households may be watching. The cost per person reached by the commercial is low.

Television has intrusion value. Television commercials featuring a catchy musical tune, sexy content, or humor can quickly grab a viewer's attention. Television offers opportunities to be creative in designing advertisements. Visual images and sounds can be incorporated in a commercial. Products and services can be demonstrated on television in a manner not possible in print or using radio advertisements. Segmentation may be achieved by targeting specialty shows and networks, such as *The Food Channel* or *ESPN*.

Disadvantages of Television Advertising Clutter continues to be the primary problem for television advertising. Many programs include 31 commercials per hour and they take as long as 19 minutes to run. Four- and 5-minute commercial breaks are common.[12] As a result, many viewers switch channels during commercial breaks. Often, low recall exists, especially for commercials in the middle of an advertising segment. Messages at the beginning or near the end of the break have a better chance at recall. Also, ads near the beginning of a television show or during the last commercial break have a higher recall since individuals want to catch the beginning of a show and also make sure they see the last part of a show for its climax or conclusion.

Some viewers cope with clutter by using a DVR, recording favorite programs and watching them later. Advertisers fear the DVR users will skip over the commercials. Recent research indicates, however, that fewer than half fast-forward through commercials. Also, the majority watches the television show the same day it is recorded, and 75 percent have watched it by the end of the next day. This means that time-sensitive ads are being seen close to when they first were run. Consequently, the fear that DVRs cause viewers to skip commercials may be somewhat unjustified.[13]

HIKING BOOTS, A BOTANY TEXTBOOK, AND AN OLD PICK-UP.
THIS WAS VENTURE CAPITAL FOR A TEA COMPANY IN 1969.
We may have had an unorthodox business plan when we started making tea in 1969, but we worked hard to create the most delicious blends of herbs the Rocky Mountains had to offer. Today our operation is a little more sophisticated, but we still create our tea the old-fashioned way: hand-blended from the finest ingredients in the world.

celestialseasonings.com

▲ The placement of this ad by Celestial for Sleepytime Tea will depend on whether the objective is brand recognition or brand recall.

Courtesy of Celestial Seasonings.

Advantages	Disadvantages
• High reach	• High level of clutter
• High frequency potential	• Low recall due to clutter
• Low cost per contact	• Channel surfing during ads
• High intrusion value	• DVRs skipping ads
• Quality creative opportunities	• Short amount of copy
• Segmentation through cable	• High cost per ad

◀ **FIGURE 8.8**
Television Advertising

▶ In addition to this billboard, the advertising agency for Louisiana Downs considers other media that might be used to effectively reach the horse racing target market.

NEW FACE OF HORSE RACING

Anna Roberts —*Jockey*

LOUISIANA DOWNS RACETRACK

Television airtime is expensive, as are the costs of producing ads. The average cost of production for a 30-second national ad is $358,000. Production fees account for the largest portion of the cost, an average of $236,000. Other costs include director fees ($23,000), fees for editing and finishing the ad ($45,000), and creative/labor fees and music ($34,000).[14]

Ratings To gain a sense of how well an advertisement fared in terms of reaching an audience, a given program's rating can be calculated. The typical ratings formula is:

$$\text{Rating} = \frac{\text{Number of households tuned to a program}}{\text{Total number of households in a market}}$$

In the United States, approximately 109.7 million households have television sets. To calculate the rating of an episode of *American Idol*, if the number of households tuned to the season finale was 17.8 million, the rating would be:

$$\text{Rating} = \frac{17,800,000}{109,700,000} = 16.2$$

▼ A storyboard produced for Interstate Batteries for a television commercial.

INTERSTATE ALL BATTERY CENTER

Outrageously Dependable

Next, if the advertiser were interested in the percentage of households that actually were watching television at that hour, the program's share could be calculated. Assuming 71 million of the 109.7 million households had a television turned on during the hour in which *American Idol* aired, the share would be:

$$\text{Share} = \frac{\text{Number of households tuned to } \textit{American Idol}}{\text{Number of households with a television turned on}} = \frac{17,800,000}{71,000,000} = 25$$

A 16.2 rating would mean that 16.2 percent of all televisions in the United States were tuned to *American Idol*. A 25 share means 25 percent of the households with a television actually turned on were watching the program. Ratings do not guarantee viewers saw the commercial. Ratings and shares only indicate of how well the program fared.

C3 Ratings   Recently, advertisers adopted a new system—the commercial C3 rating—which is a rating for the actual commercial time slot rather than the television program. It calculates commercial's rating plus any viewing of the commercial three days after the original ad ran. Many firms now use the C3 rating to determine national television advertising rates. It is currently calculated by computing the average rating of all commercials within a particular pod, or commercial segment. The criticism advertisers have of the system is that not all ads within a pod create equal exposure. For instance, the first position in a pod generates 28 percent higher awareness than ads in the middle of the commercial sequence. Thus, the position of a particular ad in the commercial break and the length of the pod have no impact on the rates being charged.

Nielsen intends to expand the C3 rating system to correct this problem. Called "On Demand C3" the new system will produce a rating for each commercial. It will include the show's live telecast viewing along with 3-day post viewing period via DVRs.[15]

Figure 8.9 provides the costs of 30-second ads using the C3 system. The higher a show's rating over time, the more that can be charged. The highest costs are for *American Idol* at $467,617 and *Sunday Night Football* at $415,000.[16]

Ratings Providers   ACNielsen is the primary organization that calculates and reports ratings and shares. The company also provides local channel information regarding shares of stations in local markets known as *designated marketing areas* (DMAs). Data-gathering techniques used by ACNielsen include diaries written by viewers who report what they watched, audience meters that record what is being watched automatically, and people meters that allow the viewing habits of individual members of families to be tracked.

These numbers can be further refined to help advertisers understand whether an advertisement reached a target market. Within rating and share categories, viewers can be subdivided by certain demographics, such as age, income, gender, educational level, and race or ethnic heritage. Organizations that prepare this information include Nielsen Media Research; Starch INRA; Hooper, Inc.; Mediamark Research, Inc.; Burke

American Idol	$467,617
Sunday Night Football	$415,000
Glee	$272,694
Family Guy	$259,289
The Simpsons	$253,170
House	$226,180
Grey's Anatomy	$222,113
The Office	$213,617
Desperate Housewives	$210,064

◀ **FIGURE 8.9**

Cost of 30-second advertisements based on C3 ratings

Source: Adapted from Brian Steinberg, "Simon Who? Idol Spots Still Pricest in Primp Time," *Advertising Age*, October 18, 2010, http://adage.com/pring/146495.

Marketing Research; and Simmons Market Research Bureau. Psychographic information can be then be added, such as whether outdoor enthusiasts watch certain program. This gives the advertiser a sense of whether the program provides the best audience for an advertisement or campaign.

Local and Regional Television Advertising For local and regional companies, spot TV may be the best television advertising option. In many cases, national brands supplement national commercials with spot TV purchases in select markets. Media planners do this primarily because of the high cost of national ad time and because 75 to 80 percent of prime-time slots are sold out during the spring, shortly after they go on the market. By selecting local early news, late news, and local prime access, a media planner can generate higher GRP at a lower cost than if only national ad time has been purchased.

Denver local pizza operation Anthony's Pizza & Pasta switched from 90 percent out-of-home to 90 percent television. The company used a concentrated flighting schedule during the fourth and first quarters to build awareness and drive traffic to the restaurants. Spots were run in Denver on all of the national broadcast networks and 14 cable channels including ESPN, Comedy Central, Cartoon Network, Food Network, and AMC. All of the spots featured the key message/tagline "authentic, New York-style pizza." Five spots focused on the crafting of the pizza, and six spots utilized humor. During the 6-months when no ads were run, the company used social media, especially Facebook, to maintain contact with customers.[17]

Effective Television Advertising Choosing the best television advertising outlets starts with finding shows match the firm's target market. Most television programs have well-defined audiences. The media planner looks for the best matches between the product's target market and the television show's audience profile. In a recent advertising and promotions campaign, Oscar Mayer used television to launch the "It doesn't get better than this" campaign on the *Golden Globe Awards*, with supporting print ads.

Social Media and Television With the rise of social media and the Internet, some advertisers have become concerned that television provides less of an impact. While many consumers watch less TV as they spend more time online, for others the opposite takes place. Social media, mobile, and the Internet can enrich television viewing experiences and actually drive consumers to watch more programs. Individuals that spend considerable time with social media tend to watch more TV. Adam Rossow of iModerate notes that these individuals "love the social interaction and frequently add shows to their viewing lineup due to social chatter. More time is spent on social networks and more hours watching television." A Deloitte Research study revealed that 75 percent of consumers multitask while watching TV—42 percent are online, 29 percent are talking on phones, and 26 percent are sending text messages.[18]

As a result of the interaction between social media and television viewing Bluefin Labs began examining online buzz about brands and television shows. People who commented online about Wal-Mart also tweeted or commented about television shows *America's SuperNanny*, *Dallas Cowboys Cheerleaders*, *Wife Swap*, *Cell Block 6: Female Lockup*, and *America's Most Wanted*. In contrast, social media comments about Target were tied to online comments and tweets about *Top Secret Recipe*, *My Yard Goes Disney*, *HGTV'd*, *Fashion Hunters*, and *Free Agents*.[19]

As the amount of time people spend on social media continues to increase, so will the online buzz about television shows. By monitoring this type of online chatter, advertisers and their clients can gain a better perspective on which television shows to place ads.

YouTube and Television Many companies and advertising agencies post television ads on YouTube. Some of the ads are placed on the site simultaneously with the TV launch (called *in-stream*) while others are be submitted to YouTube prior to the national launch (called *pre-roll*). For the Super Bowl, part of the ad, a teaser, appears on YouTube prior to the game.

Google and Ipsos research indicates that YouTube pre-roll of TV ads as well as in-streaming of TV ads result in higher recall. Individuals who watched the ad on You-Tube and on TV had a 200 percent higher recall than individuals who saw the ad only on TV. Those who saw the ad online on YouTube only had a 150 percent higher recall. More than 3 billion consumers watch videos on YouTube daily.[20]

Super Bowl Advertising   The Super Bowl continues to be the biggest television advertising event of the year. Many viewers tune in to watch the game, but a significant percentage of the 110 million also pays close attention to the ads. "We see the Super Bowl as a huge brand-building opportunity," says Paul Chibe, vice-president of marketing at Anheuser-Busch.[21]

In the past, ads were kept under wraps until the moment they appear during the game. With the rise of social media, the trend has changed. Many Super Bowl commercials first appear on YouTube, Facebook, the company's Web site, or the agency's site prior to the game. As noted, teaser ads entice viewers to watch the entire commercial during the game. Another new approach involves the release of extended versions of advertisement with more content or additional information about the ad spot on the Web site. Pre-rolling ads generates excitement and allows viewers to see, share, and discuss the ads before, during, and after the game. Many companies and agencies now spend as much time developing a marketing plan for the pre-roll as they do for the actual Super Bowl commercial.

One teaser ad for Volkswagen released to YouTube three weeks prior to the Super Bowl was viewed 11 million times. An extended version of the sequel was uploaded to YouTube the week prior to the Super Bowl and was viewed over 1.3 million times. A Super Bowl commercial for the Chevrolet Camaro went online 17 days before the Super Bowl. Brian Sharpless, chief executive of HomeAway, stated that "Because social media can build buzz for Super Bowl commercials before, during, and after the game, if you don't take advantage of all that, you're not getting the most bang for your buck."[22]

Super Bowl advertising result in nearly immediate feedback. A number of companies run various types of ad meters during the game and monitor social media buzz to determine the best ads and those that missed the mark. Stan Richards of the Richards Group commented, "You get quick feedback. I have to tell you, when you go to bed right after the Super Bowl, your last thought is, 'What is it going to say in *USA Today* tomorrow morning?'"[23]

RADIO

Despite CDs, iPods, audio books, and other types of audio devices, the vast majority of Americans, approximately 80 percent, still listen to the radio daily.[24] Adverting professional Mary Price stated that, "Right now, on a weekly basis terrestrial radio still reaches 93 percent of everybody. It used to be 96 or 97, but it's still up there. As long as they can create a following for local personalities and local events, you can't get that off an iPod. If you want some kind of commentary about the music you're listening to . . . you can't get that on a pre-recorded iPod."[25]

While radio may not seem as glamorous as television, it remains an effective advertising medium (see Figure 8.10). A well-placed, clever ad results in a one-on-one message (announcer to driver in a car stuck in traffic). Many smaller local companies rely heavily on radio advertising. Most radio ads are produced locally and with small budgets.

Advantages of Radio Advertising   Skillful radio advertisements cause the listener to remember the message by creating powerful images to visualize and by using repetition. This moves the information from the consumer's short-term to long-term memory. Sound effects and lively tunes assist in this process. Through repetition a person hears an advertisement often enough to generate recall.

▶ **FIGURE 8.10**
Radio Advertising

Advantages	Disadvantages
• Recall promoted	• Short exposure time
• Narrower target markets	• Low attention
• Ad music can match audience	• Difficult to reach national audiences
• High segmentation potential	• Target duplication with several stations using the same format
• Flexibility in making ads	• Information overload
• Modify ad to local conditions	
• Intimacy with DJs	
• Mobile – listen anywhere	
• Creative opportunities with sound and music	

A radio station reaches definable target markets based on its format, such as talk radio, lite mix, oldies, or country. A firm can advertise on a specific type of station across the country. Radio advertisers can examine the rating and share of a program as well as the estimated number of people listening. Arbitron calculates these numbers for local stations. Radio's All-Dimension Audience Research (RADAR) reports ratings for national radio networks.

Radio can create intimacy. Listeners often feel personally close to DJs and radio personalities. The attachment grows over time. Listening to the same individual becomes more personal and intimate, especially if the listener has a conversation with the DJ during a contest or when requesting a song. The bond or intimacy level gives the radio personality a higher level of credibility and an edge to goods and services the radio celebrity endorses.

Beachbody, a fitness brand based in Santa Monica, California, used radio as the prime medium to promote its P90X, a home exercise system that promised total body improvements within 90 days. Robinson Radio from Virginia was contracted to develop and manage the radio campaign. Robinson realized the best approach was to use "radio's secret weapon," the DJs, who used the product, documented their successes, and then described their progress on the air. The DJs also posted their photos on the company's Web site, created chat rooms for listeners, and asked listeners to share their success stories. Early in the campaign it became clear that the micro website was a key component of the radio campaign, because it allowed communications between the listeners, customers of the product, and the DJs. The other advantage of using radio was that it was easy and inexpensive to make changes to ads as the campaign progressed. The campaign was highly successful in California. Beachbody expanded the campaign nationally within a few months.[26]

Disadvantages of Radio Advertising   Short exposure time creates one problem for radio. Most commercials last 15 or 30 seconds. Listeners involved in other activities, such as driving or working on a computer, may not pay attention. Further, people often use radio as a background to drown out other distractions, especially at work.

For national advertisers, covering a large area with radio advertisements is challenging. To place a national advertisement requires contacting a large number of companies. Few large radio conglomerates means contacts must be made with multiple stations. Negotiating rates with individual stations based on volume can be difficult. Local businesses can

▼ This advertisement for Mix 95.1 highlights the market niche served by the radio station.

often negotiate better rates than national advertisers because of the local company's relationships with the radio stations.

The four main national radio networks in the United States are Westwood One, ABC, CBS, and Unistar. These are joined by a few other strong networks, such as ESPN radio and CNN. Nationally syndicated programs such as those on the Fox radio network offer some opportunities to national advertisers.

In large metropolitan areas, duplication presents another problem. Several radio stations may try to reach the same target market. Chicago has several rock stations. Advertising on each one may not be financially feasible, yet reaching everyone in that target market will not be possible unless all rock stations are included.

▲ Radio enjoys the advantage of intimacy with the local DJ.

Radio advertising offers a low-cost option for a local firm. Ads can be placed at ideal times and adapted to local conditions. Careful selection of stations, times, and quality construction of the advertisement will be the key. Radio allows local businesses to present remote broadcasts. Remotes can attract attention to a new business (restaurants, retail stores, etc.) or to a company trying to make a major push for immediate customers. Radio promotions can be combined with other media (local television or newspapers) to send more integrated messages.

For business-to-business advertisers, radio provides the opportunity to reach businesses during working hours, because many employees listen to the radio during office hours. Radio can reach businesspeople while in transit to or from work. Both radio and television usage has increased for business-to-business marketing.

OUTDOOR ADVERTISING

Billboards along major roads are the most common form of outdoor advertising; however, there are other forms. Signs on cabs, buses, park benches, and fences of sports arenas are other types of outdoor advertising (also out-of-home advertising, OOH). Some would argue that even a blimp flying above a major sporting event is form of out-of-home advertising. In the past, outdoor advertising was seldom considered in the planning of an integrated marketing communications program or the development of the media plan.

Advances in technology have dramatically changed OOH advertising. Annual expenditures on outdoor advertisements now total more than $5.5 billion. Global positioning systems, wireless communications, and digital display technology have transformed outdoor advertising. LED technology creates animated videos in locations such

◀ This billboard was part of a highly successful campaign for the Snoring Center.

▶ **FIGURE 8.11**
Outdoor Advertising

Advantages	Disadvantages
• Select key geographic areas	• Short exposure time
• Accessible for local ads	• Brief messages
• Low cost per impression	• Little segmentation possible
• Broad reach	• Clutter
• High frequency on major commuter routes	
• Large visuals possible	
• Digital capabilities	

as Times Square in New York and the Strip in Las Vegas. It can present static messages and visuals that change electronically. Figure 8.11 lists the advantages and disadvantages of out-of-home ads and Figure 8.12 shows a breakdown of outdoor spending by categories

A unique billboard campaign was created by Firehouse Agency of Dallas for Stripes Convenience Stores. The campaign invited customers of Stripes to tweet about tacos sold at the convenience stores. The tweets were streamed into digital billboard displays located near traffic lights in 8 different Texas cities where vehicles would stop for a red light. According to Ian Dallimore of Lamar Advertising, "Stripes wanted to do something more than just change the copy a few times a day. It wanted to create the sense of a conversation, and make people feel involved. The idea is to get people more engaged with outdoor advertising and arouse curiosity about the tacos." The tweets ran from lunchtime until midnight daily.[27]

Advantages of Out-of-Home Advertising   Billboard advertising offers long life. For local companies, billboards offer an excellent advertising medium, because the message will primarily be seen by residents. It also provides a low-cost medium in terms of cost per impression. Out-of-home advertising features a broad reach and a high level of frequency if multiple billboards or venues are purchased. Every person who travels past a billboard or sees an advertisement on a taxi may be exposed to the message. Many out-of-home companies provide rotation packages in which an ad moves to different locations throughout an area during the course of the year, thereby increasing

▶ **FIGURE 8.12**
Expenditures on Outdoor Advertising

Source: Adapted from "Outdoor Advertising Expenditures, 2009 January–June, "*TNS Media Intelligence/CMR OAAA,* September 2009.

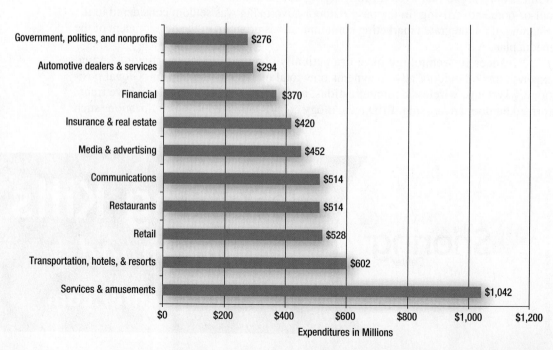

its reach. Digital boards and signs provide higher resolution graphics as well as capabilities of changing messages on demand or on a routine schedule.

Disadvantages of Out-of-Home Advertising

Short exposure time is a major drawback of out-of-home advertising. Drivers must pay attention to the traffic as they travel by a billboard. As a result, messages must be short. Pedestrians often get only a quick look at an advertisement placed on a vehicle. Most either ignore outdoor ads or give them just a casual glance. Ironically, in large cities along major arteries the cost of billboard spots has increased. The reason: traffic jams. People stuck in slow-moving traffic spend more time looking at billboards. If this space is not available, a firm can seek billboard locations where traffic stops for signals or at stop signs.

MAGAZINES

For many advertisers, magazines represented a secondary choice. Recent research indicates that magazines can provide a quality option. An Affinity Research study suggests that half of magazine readers either take action, such as accessing a Web site, or have more favorable opinions about magazine advertisers. Several studies conclude that magazines are a strong driver of purchase intentions and boost the effectiveness of other media.[28]

Nurtured from the start.

Courtesy of Tree Top, Inc.

▲ This Treetop advertisement targets new mothers and appears in magazines such as *Parenting*.

Advantages of Magazine Advertising   Magazines can create high levels of market segmentation by topic area. Even within certain market segments, such as automobiles, a number of magazines exist. High audience interest constitutes another advantage. An individual who subscribes to *Modern Bride* has an attraction to weddings. People reading magazines also tend to view and pay attention to advertisements related to their needs and wants. Often, readers linger over an ad for a longer period of time because they read magazines in waiting situations, such as in a doctor's office, or during leisure time. The high level of interest, segmentation, and differentiation, when combined with high-quality color, are ideal for products with well-defined target markets.

Trade and business journals continue to be the primary choice for business-to-business marketing. Businesses target advertisements to buying center members. The ad's copy can provide a greater level of detail about products. Interested readers take more time to study the information provided in the advertisement. Ads often provide toll-free telephone

Advantages	Disadvantages
• High market segmentation	• Declining readership
• Targeted audience by magazine	• Clutter
• Direct-response techniques	• Long lead time
• High color quality	• Little flexibility
• Long-life	• High cost
• Read during leisure—longer attention to ads	
• Availability of special features	

◀ **FIGURE 8.13**
Magazine Advertising

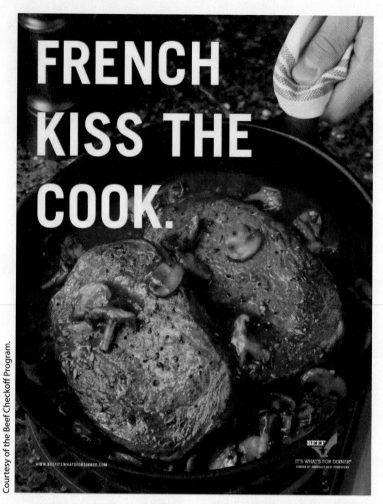

FRENCH KISS THE COOK.

BEEF
IT'S WHAT'S FOR DINNER
WWW.BEEFITSWHATSFORDINNER.COM

▲ Advertisers can target specific market segments with magazines, making it an attractive medium for ads such as this one for the beef industry.

numbers and Web addresses so that interested parties can obtain further information.

Magazines have long lives that reach beyond an immediate issue. An avid magazine reader may examine a particular issue several times and spend a considerable amount of time with each issue. Advertisers know the reader will be exposed to the ad more than once and might be more likely to pay attention. Other individuals may also review the magazine. In the business-to-business sector, trade journals are often passed around to several individuals or members of the buying center. As long as the magazine lasts, the advertisement is still there to be viewed.

In addition to the standard sniff-patches that can be placed in magazines, advertisers can now use QR codes or special mobile apps. DirecTV partnered with *Sports Illustrated* to create a free Android and IOS app for *SI*'s annual swimsuit edition. Individuals downloaded the app to their smartphone could hold the phone over the swimsuit models in the *SI* magazine and watch videos of the model's picture shoot. The magazine had 19 embedded videos, each approximately 30 seconds in length.[29]

Disadvantages of Magazine Advertising While overall readership of magazines has declined, the trend is less evident among "influential Americans." Individuals with incomes of $100,000 or more read an average of 15.3 publications, and individuals with incomes over $250,000 read an average of 23.8.[30] Magazine advertisements require a great deal of lead time and are expensive to prepare. They may be less viable for more general consumption products, such as basic necessities.

At the same time, magazines continue to be an effective medium for advertising. For both consumer and business markets, it appears that magazines, used in conjunction with other media, can enhance the effectiveness of an advertising campaign.

NEWSPAPERS

When *USA Today* was launched, few believed a national daily newspaper could succeed. At the same time, news reporting has changed. Many small local papers no longer exist, and conglomerates, such as Gannett, own most major city newspapers. Still, daily readership continues.

For many smaller local firms, newspaper ads, billboards, and local radio programs represent the most viable advertising options. Newspapers are distributed daily, weekly, or in partial form as the advertising supplements found in the front sections of grocery stores and retail outlets.

▶ **FIGURE 8.14**
Newspaper Advertising

Advantages	Disadvantages
• Geographic selectivity	• Poor buying procedures
• High flexibility	• Short life span
• High credibility	• Clutter
• Strong audience interest	• Poor quality reproduction
• Longer copy	• Internet competition
• Cumulative volume discounts	• Aging readership
• Coupons and special-response features	

Advantages of Newspaper Advertising As noted in Figure 8.14, many retailers rely on newspaper because it offers geographic selectivity (local market access). Promoting sales, retail hours, and store locations is easier. Short lead time permits retailers to quickly change ads and promotions. Such flexibility offers the advantage of allowing advertisers the ability to keep ads current, and the ads can be modified to meet competitive offers or to focus on recent events.

Newspapers retain high levels of credibility. Readers rely on newspapers for factual information. Newspaper readers hold high interest levels in the articles as well as advertisements. Greater audience interest allows advertisers to provide more copy detail in ads. Newspaper readers take more time to read them copy unless simply too much information is jammed into a small space. A recent survey of shoppers revealed that newspapers were the most trusted source of information for purchase decisions.[31]

Recognizing a match between newspaper readers and its customer base, Starbucks launched a unique newspaper campaign designed by the agency Wieden + Kennedy of Portland, Oregon. Starbucks invited coffee drinkers to stop at a local Starbucks for a free cup of coffee on March 15. Four-page full-color ads were placed in daily newspapers of 11 major markets, including New York, Los Angeles, Chicago, Boston, and Dallas. The ads were placed in the newspapers the week before the giveaway and again the day before. Then, on the day of the giveaway, Starbucks hired street vendors to pass out free copies of the newspapers that contained the Starbucks ad. The newspapers were banded with the distinctive Starbuck's coffee cup sleeve. The campaign cost $545,000, but resulted in a half-million customers going into a Starbucks store. In some locations lines wrapped around the block. Starbucks estimated the newspaper campaign resulted in 12 million impressions.[32]

Disadvantages of Newspaper Advertising Newspapers cannot be easily targeted to specific market segments (although sports pages carry sports ads, entertainment pages contain movie and restaurant ads, and so forth). Newspapers have a short life. Once read, a newspaper will be cast aside, recycled, or destroyed. If a reader does not see an advertisement during the first pass through a newspaper, it will go unnoticed. Readers rarely pick up papers a second time. When they do, it is to continue reading, not to reread or rescan a section that has already been viewed.

Newspaper readers continue to age. Younger consumers obtain news either through the Internet or from television; few read a print newspaper. The average age of those who read printed papers is 51 compared to 44 for those who read the digital version. Digital readers are younger, better-educated, and are often more affluent than the print readers.[33]

Baxter Painting. It's *art.*

▲ Newspapers are ideal for advertising local business, such as Baxter Painting, which offers high-end home and commercial painting and decorating.

Courtesy of Baxter Painting Inc.

MEDIA MIX

Selecting the proper blend of media outlets for advertisements is crucial. As campaigns are prepared, decisions are made regarding the appropriate mix of media. Media planners and media buyers are both excellent sources of information about the most effective type of mix for a particular advertising campaign. Figure 8.15 displays the media mix in the

OBJECTIVE 8.6
How can the marketing team use the media mix to increase advertising effectiveness?

▶ **FIGURE 8.15**
U.S. Advertising Expenditures by
Media for Coca-Cola

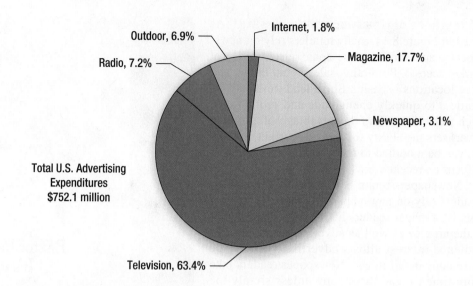

Total U.S. Advertising
Expenditures
$752.1 million

United States for Coca-Cola. Total U.S. spending for advertising by Coca-Cola was $752 million; 63.4 percent went to television advertising. Coca-Cola spent far less on the other media.[34]

Recent studies by Millward Brown and ACNielsen highlight the benefits of combining media.[35] The Millward Brown report states that ad awareness was strongest when consumers were exposed to an advertisement on television and in a magazine. Ad awareness was considerably lower for only those who read the magazine ad and even less for those who only saw the television commercial.

The **media multiplier effect** suggests that the combined impact of using two or more media is stronger than using either medium alone. The British insurance company Churchill discovered that 62 percent of consumers who saw the company's TV commercial and heard its radio ad planned to look into Churchill Insurance, compared to 49 percent who only saw only the television advertisement.[36]

The media multiplier effect is equally important in business-to-business advertising. In a survey conducted by American Business Media, 89 percent of the business respondents indicated that an integrated marketing approach raised their awareness of a company or brand. Seeing advertisements in more than one medium led the company or brand name to become top-of-mind. It also resulted in more businesses making purchases.[37] Finding effective combinations of media is the key to the media multiplier effect. Figure 8.16 displays the process for choosing the best media for a particular advertising message. Media experts decide which go best together for individual target markets, goods and services, and advertising messages.

▶ **FIGURE 8.16**
Developing Logical
Combinations of Media

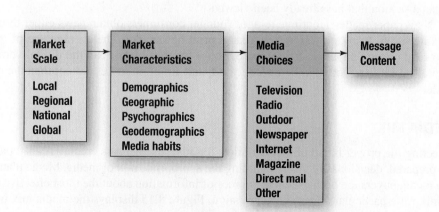

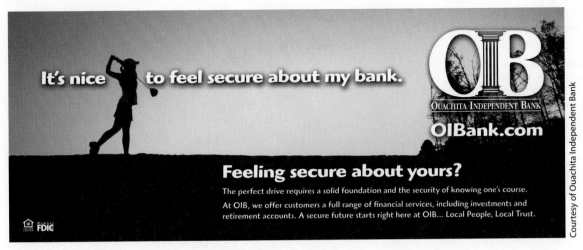

▲ This advertisement for OIBank.com highlights personal security as its key selling point.

Media Selection in Business-to-Business Markets

Identifying differences between consumer ads and business-to-business ads has become more difficult, especially on television, outdoor, and the Internet. In the past, it was easy to spot business-to-business advertisements. The content was aimed at another company. Television, outdoor, and the Internet were seldom used. Currently, over half of all business advertising dollars are now spent in non-business environments.[38]

Several explanations have been offered regarding the shift to non-business media. First, business decision makers also consume goods and services. The same psychological techniques used to influence and gain consumer attention can be used for business decision makers.

Second, business decision makers are difficult to reach at work. Gatekeepers (secretaries, voice mail systems, etc.) often prevent the flow of information to users, influencers, and decision makers. This is especially true in straight rebuy situations in which orders are routinely placed with the current vendor. Any company that is not the chosen vendor finds it difficult to make contact with buying center members. Business-to-business vendors try to reach them at home, in the car, or in some other non-business venue.

Third, clutter among the traditional business media makes it more difficult to get a company noticed. Business advertisers recognize that a strong brand name is a major factor in making a sale. Taking lessons from major giants such as Nike, Kraft Foods, and Procter & Gamble, business marketers seek to develop strong brands because the name helps a company gain the attention of members of the buying center.

In the past, business ads were fairly dull. They now are more likely to resemble ads aimed at consumers. Creative appeals and the use of music, humor, sex, and fear are used. The boldest business ads sometimes include nudity or other more risqué material.

Figure 8.17 identifies the ways business-to-business advertising expenditures are divided among the various media. In the past, business publications would account for most of the expenditures, often assuming half of the dollars. Business publications now represent about one-fourth of the more than $14 billion spent annually on business-to-business advertising. As more dollars are shifted to non-business types of media, the amount being spent on television, newspapers, and consumer magazines has steadily increased.[39]

Although the use of business publications has decreased, trade journals still provide an excellent opportunity to contact members of the buying center whom salespeople cannot reach. Gatekeepers do not prevent trade journals from being sent to members of the buying center. An advertisement has the best chance of success when a firm makes modified rebuy, and the buying center is in the information search stage.

OBJECTIVE 8.7

What are the key issues associated with media selection for business-to-business markets?

▶ **FIGURE 8.17**
Business-to-Business Advertising Expenditures

Source: Based on Kate Maddox, "Top 100 B-to-B Advertisers Increased Spending 3% in '06," *B to B* 92, no. 11 (September 10, 2007).

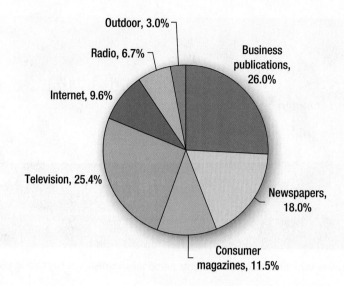

In addition to trade journals, business-to-business advertisers also use business magazines such as *BusinessWeek*. These publications have highly selective audiences, and the ads have longer life spans in print. Business decision makers and members of the buying center spend more working time examining print media than any other medium.

Many goals in business-to-business advertisements are the same as those devoted to consumers. Most of the variables shown in Figure 8.16 apply equally well to business advertising.

International Implications

OBJECTIVE 8.8

What issues are associated with media selection in international markets?

Understanding media viewing habits in international markets remains to be an important part of a successful advertising program. In Japan, television provides a major advertising tool; in other countries, it is not as prevalent. In Europe, a good way to reach consumers is through print media, such as magazines and newspapers.

For several years, reports have surfaced that teenagers are watching less TV and spending more time on the Internet. A study by Forrester Research contradicted that notion, at least in Europe. Thousands of teenagers in Europe were surveyed about their media usage.[40] The general conclusions of the Forrester study are that:

- European teens spend more time watching TV than they do with any other medium, averaging 10.3 hours per week.
- Average personal time on the Internet is 9.1 hours per week.
- Europeans ages 10 to 17 spend less time on the Internet than individuals 18 and older.
- Only 41 percent of European teens visit social networks at least once a week.
- Teenagers like to multitask—watching TV while texting friends or playing video games while listening to music or TV.
- Younger European teens love video games, playing twice as much as individuals 18 and older.
- Most teenagers do not read the paper. They get news from TV or the Internet.

Although there are a large number of media buying agencies throughout the world, nearly three-quarters of all media buying is conducted by only six large global agencies or their holding agencies. The largest global media company is the WPP Group, which holds 22 percent of the market share.[41] To combat these large media networks, a global media consortium has been formed. The consortium consists of a number of smaller independent agencies and offers services in Europe, North America, the Russian

Federation, and Asia. Central offices are located in New York and London to serve business clients and to pitch for regional and national accounts.[42]

The large global media agencies have faced some criticism in recent years from marketing managers. They complain about the inability to provide effective media buys throughout all the countries where the clients operate. Although a few agencies do cover the world, it is difficult to be strong in every country where an agency may have a presence. The global agency may not be the best option in every country. For this reason, local media agencies and the consortium of independent agencies believe they have a chance to increase their market share.

In general, the tactics used to develop advertising campaigns and choose appropriate media in the United States apply to other countries throughout the world. What differs is the nature of the target markets, consumer media preferences, and the processes used to buy media. Company representatives carefully attend to cultural mores to make sure the buying process does not offend the cultural and religious attitudes in any given region. The goal is to fully understand the target market as a company purchases advertising time or space and prepares advertising campaigns.

INTEGRATED CAMPAIGNS IN ACTION

The Snoring Center

In the past decade, the Pink Jacket Creative advertising agency, led by co-owners Bill Breedlove and Elena Baca, helped develop a highly successful advertising program for a medical company—The Snoring Center. According to Breedlove, "When we first started working with The Snoring Center, a physician had an office here in Dallas. He decided he wanted to start treating snoring and sleep apnea. Did you know that 46 percent of adults snore? 25 percent snore habitually? Of that, 23 percent of married couples regularly sleep apart because of sleep apnea."

To develop brand awareness for The Snoring Center, the central component of the advertising program was billboards, with television and print ads as support media. Bill Breedlove recalls, "It was a really simple outdoor campaign. We put up branded billboards that said simply, 'Snoring Kills . . .,' and then underneath it would have something that it kills, such as 'it kills careers' or 'it kills your love life,' or 'it kills your mojo,' or 'your morning quickies,' or 'your afternoon delight,' and so on.

Within a year and a half, the physician shut his ENT practice down and had two locations of The Snoring Center. Within 24 months, The Snoring Center became the world's leading provider of minimally invasive snoring treatment. The company now performs more procedures than any other provider in the world.[43]

The Snoring Center campaign is located at the Pearson Instructor's Resource Center (www.pearsonhighered .com). The campaign has a PowerPoint presentation outlining the details of the campaigns and examples of the collaterals developed by Pink Jack Creative. Also available is video of the creative minds behind the campaign, Bill Breedlove and Elena Baca.

Courtesy of Pink Jacket Creative: A Creative Factory.

▲ Billboard ads were the central component of the campaign for The Snoring Center.

SUMMARY

In traditional advertising, the roles of media planners and media buyers have grown in importance. Bob Brennan, chief operating officer of Chicago-based Leo Burnett Starcom USA, stated that in the past "Ninety-five percent of your success was great creative and 5 percent was great media. Now it's much closer to 50–50."[44]

A media strategy is the process of analyzing and choosing media for an advertising and promotions campaign. Media planners and buyers complete much of this work. The media planner's primary job is to formulate a program stating where and when to place advertisements. Media planners work closely with creatives and account executives. Media buyers purchase the space, and they negotiate rates, times, and schedules for the ads.

The goals of reach, frequency, opportunity to see, gross rating points, effective rating points, cost, continuity, and gross impressions drive the media selection process. Reach identifies the number of people, households, or businesses in a target audience exposed to a media vehicle or message schedule at least once during a given time period. Frequency is the average number of times an individual, household, or business within a particular target market is exposed to a particular advertisement within a specified time period. Gross rating points (GRPs) measure the impact or intensity of a media plan. Cost per thousand (CPM) is one method of finding the cost of the campaign by assessing the dollar cost of reaching 1,000 members of the media vehicle's audience. Cost per rating point (CPRP), a second cost measure, assesses the efficiency of a media vehicle relative to a firm's target market. Ratings measure the percentage of a firm's target market that is exposed to a show on television or an article in a print medium. Continuity sets the schedule or pattern of advertisement placements within an advertising campaign period. Gross impressions are the number of total exposures of the audience to an advertisement.

The three-exposure hypothesis suggests that a consumer must be exposed to an ad at least three times before it has the desired impact; other experts believe even more exposures are necessary. In contrast, recency theory suggests that ads truly reach only those wanting or needing a product and that the carryover effects of advertising diminish rapidly. It is necessary, therefore, to advertise on a continuous basis to ensure that the message is noticed by consumers when a purchase decision is made.

In addition to these basic concepts, advertising experts often utilize the concepts of effective frequency and effective reach. Effective frequency states the number of times a target audience must be exposed to a message to achieve a particular objective. Effective reach identifies the percentage of an audience that must be exposed to a particular message to achieve a specific objective.

In seeking advertising goals, marketing experts, account executives, and others assess the relative advantages and disadvantages of each individual advertising medium. Thus, television, radio, outdoor, magazines, and newspapers should all be considered as potential ingredients in a campaign. Other new media can be used to complement and supplement the more traditional media outlets. Logical combinations of media should be chosen.

In business-to-business settings, companies can combine consumer media outlets with trade journals and other business venues (trade shows, conventions, etc.) to attempt to reach members of the buying center. In many cases, enticing ads using consumer appeals such as sex, fear, and humor have replaced dry, dull, boring ads with an abundance of copy.

International advertising media selection is different in some ways from that which takes place in the United States, because media buying processes differ as do media preferences of locals in various countries. At the same time, the process of media selection is quite similar. Marketing experts choose media they believe will reach the target audience in an effective manner.

Key Terms

media strategy The process of analyzing and choosing media for an advertising and promotions campaign.

media planner The individual who formulates the media program stating where and when to place advertisements.

media buyer The person who buys the media space and negotiates rates, times, and schedules for the ads.

spot ad A one-time placement of a commercial on a local television station.

reach The number of people, households, or businesses in a target audience exposed to a media vehicle or message schedule at least once during a given time period.

frequency The average number of times an individual, household, or business within a particular target market is exposed to a particular advertisement within a specified time period.

opportunities to see (OTS) The cumulative exposures to an advertisement that are achieved in a given time period.

gross rating points (GRPs) A measure of the impact or intensity of a media plan.

cost per thousand (CPM) The dollar cost of reaching 1,000 members of the media vehicle's audience.

ratings A measure of the percentage of a firm's target market that is exposed to a show on television or an article in a print medium.

cost per rating point (CPRP) A measure of the efficiency of a media vehicle relative to a firm's target market.

weighted (or demographic) CPM A measure used to calculate whether an advertisement reached the target market effectively.

continuity The schedule or pattern of advertisement placements within an advertising campaign period.

gross impressions The number of total exposures of the audience to an advertisement.

intrusion value The ability of media or an advertisement to intrude upon a viewer without his or her voluntary attention.

recency theory A theory suggesting that consumer attention is selective and focuses on individual needs and wants and therefore has selective attention to advertisements

effective reach The percentage of an audience that must be exposed to a particular message to achieve a specific objective.

effective frequency The number of times a target audience must be exposed to a message to achieve a particular objective.

media multiplier effect The combined impact of using two or more media is stronger than using either medium alone.

Review Questions

1. What is a media strategy? How does it relate to the creative brief and the overall IMC program?

2. What does a media planner do?

3. Describe the role of media buyer in an advertising program.

⭐ 4. What is reach? Give examples of reach in various advertising media.

5. What is frequency? How can an advertiser increase frequency in a campaign?

6. What are gross rating points? What do they measure?

7. What is the difference between CPM and CPRP? What costs do they measure?

8. What is continuity?

9. Describe the three-exposure hypothesis.

10. How does recency theory differ from the three-exposure hypothesis?

11. What is effective frequency? Effective reach?

12. What are the major advantages and disadvantages of television advertising?

13. What are the major advantages and disadvantages of radio advertising?

14. What are the major advantages and disadvantages of outdoor advertising?

15. What are the major advantages and disadvantages of magazine advertising?

16. What are the major advantages and disadvantages of newspaper advertising?

⭐ 17. Is the strong intrusion value of television an advantage? Why or why not?

18. What special challenges does media selection present for businesses? What roles do gatekeepers play in creating those challenges?

19. What special challenges does media selection present for international advertising campaigns? What differences and similarities exist with U.S. media selection processes?

Critical Thinking Exercises

DISCUSSION QUESTIONS

⭐ 1. To be effective, multiple media should be chosen and integrated carefully. Individuals who are exposed to advertisements in combinations of media selected from television, radio, magazines, newspapers and outdoor are more inclined to process the information than when only a solitary medium is used. For each of the media, what is the probability of you being exposed to an advertisement? The percentages should add up to 100 percent. Discuss which media are most effective in reaching you. Explain.

⭐ 2. Billboard advertising in Times Square has become so popular that space has already been sold for the next 10 years. Coca-Cola, General Motors, Toshiba, Prudential, NBC, Budweiser, and *The New York Times* are paying rates in excess of $100,000 per month to hold these

spaces. Why would companies pay so much for outdoor advertising? What are the advantages and disadvantages of purchasing billboards at Times Square?

3. The Super Bowl is the most watched program on television. Many tune in just to watch the ads. Interview 10 individuals of various ages, genders, and ethnicities. Ask each what they thought of last year's Super Bowl ads. Summarize what you were told. Based on these interviews, how effective is Super Bowl advertising? Is it worth paying $3.5 million for 30 seconds? What about for business-to-business ads? Do you think the Super Bowl is a good venue for business-to-business advertising?

4. Xerox offers a color printer that sells for $1,200. The goal is to market it to business buyers. What media mix would you suggest for a $5 million advertising campaign? Justify your answer.

5. Use the Internet or phone directory to identify all of the radio stations in your area. What type of format does each have (i.e., talk, country, hip hop, rock, etc.)? Is radio a good advertising medium to reach college students at your university? Why or why not? Which of the radio stations on your list would be the most effective in reaching college students?

6. As you drive to school (or home) make a list of all of the billboards and outdoor advertising you see. Which are the most effective? Why? Which are the least effective?

Why? How effective are billboards at reaching you with an advertising message?

⭐ 7. Pick five different magazines on a wide range of topics. For each, describe the types of ads and the number of ads in the issue. Did you see any business-to-business ads? What similarities did you see in the ads across the five magazines? What differences did you notice? Which would be most effective at reaching people in your demographic?

Integrated Learning Exercises

1. Go to the Life Section of *USA Today* (www.usatoday.com/life/default.htm) and locate the Nielsen ratings. What were the top five television shows last week? What other information is available at the Web site about Nielsen ratings?

2. In Canada, a valuable source of information is BBM (Bureau of Broadcast Measurement). Access this Web site at www.bbm.ca. What type of information is available on the site? What media does the BBM cover? How can it be used to develop a media plan for Canada?

3. A trade organization for magazines is the Magazine Publishers of America. Access the association's Web site at www.magazine.org. What type of information is available? How could it be used by a company wanting to advertise in magazines?

4. Two Web sites that are important for radio advertising are the Radio Advertising Bureau at www.rab.com and

the top 100 radio sites at www.100topradiosites.com. Access both sites. What information is available on each site? Discuss how the information can be used to develop an advertising plan using radio.

5. A major company for outdoor advertising is Lamar Advertising Company. Access its Web site at www.lamar.com. Access the outdoor advertising component of the company and locate the rates for your area or another area of interest to you. What type of outdoor advertising is available? What other products does Lamar offer? What services does Lamar offer? Write a short report on what types of advertising Lamar can provide for a company.

⭐ 6. One of the best sources of information for business-to-business advertisers is *BtoB* at www.btobonline.com. What type of information is available at this Web site? How can it be used? What benefits would a business-to-business advertiser derive from the Web site?

Student Project

CREATIVE CORNER

Horse racing has been struggling to maintain attendance at the race tracks. The majority of serious fans of horse racing are older, white males. One challenge in drawing new fans to horse racing is the complexity of understanding the sport. Understanding which horse won a race is easy; however, after that it becomes very complex and difficult to understand horse racing stats. A steep learning curve that requires thoughtful and complex analysis is needed, and many potential fans do not want to invest the time or energy to learn. According to Tim Capps, a professor at the University of the Louisville College of Business, horse racing "has been run more for itself than for its fans. One thing racing has to do is make participation in our sport easier for fans, because the fan has

not come first in our industry." He further adds "people don't want to go to school. They want to be entertained."

While all agree that there is a need to attract new fans, wide disagreement exists regarding the type of fan it should be. Do you market to the individuals who are already going to the track, or do you go after new individuals? Do you go after young people, middle-age individuals, or work harder to reach baby boomers? Which gender—male or female, do you seek?

First, choose the target audience for an advertising campaign. Defend your choice. Second, select the media that would be most appropriate. Third, design a magazine ad for the target market chosen. Fourth, develop a billboard or outdoor ad to accompany the magazine ad.

CASE 1 DOMINO'S *MEA CULPA* AND "NO" CAMPAIGNS

In the past, one classic advertising strategy used by companies involved turning a disadvantage into an advantage. For example, it takes ketchup a long time to pour out of the bottle because it is "thick and rich." A car rental company may be small, but they "try harder."

Recently, the Domino's Pizza chain took such an approach to the extreme. Marketers developed an advertising program to address the problem of slowing sales in a declining economy. Dubbed by some as the *mea culpa* campaign, the first wave of television commercials featured clips of consumers in focus groups, discussing Domino's, providing statements such as "Worst pizza I ever had; totally devoid of flavor," "Domino's pizza crust is to me like cardboard," and "The sauce tastes like ketchup."

Domino's had been able to maintain its market share during the economic downturn. At the same time, employees and company managers were concerned about the quality of the products being offered. The advertising program was created to apologize for poor-quality pizza with the promise to do better by creating pies with improved ingredients and better recipes, which led to a complete menu overhaul during a four year period beginning in 2008. "We think that going out there and being this honest really breaks through to people in a way that most advertising does not," explained new company CEO Patrick Doyle.

Some marketing experts expressed concerns that consumers would not listen carefully to the message. They would hear the part about poor quality but not the part about improving. Doyle believed the risk was worth taking.

When the roll out of new and improved pizzas at bargain prices commenced, a new advertising campaign was launched, featuring the comment, "We're only as good as our last pizza. So tell us how yours was" followed. Domino's had already introduced the Pizza Tracker feature to its Web site, which allows customers placing an online order at the Domino's Web site to follow the progress of the order from the shop to their front door. Users receive an email directing them to the order-tracking page within seconds of placing an order and, without having to refresh the page, are told precisely when their pie is placed in the oven, checked for quality assurance and dispatched to their home. The Pizza Tracker informs the customer who was responsible for an individual pizza during preparation and delivery.

Following the completion of the transaction, the customer can provide feedback directly to the store where the pizza was made, which opens lines of communication with individual stores and managers rather than the larger corporation. The Pizza Tracker program insists that individual store owners will listen when customers are dissatisfied. By naming the actual individual responsible for any service failure, the store's manager can improve operations on an employee-by-employee basis. Over the course of the next apology campaign and new emphasis on customer feedback, sales increased dramatically during the next two quarters.

Later, Domino's introduced a line of Artisan pizza and quickly followed with the "No" campaign, in which customers were advised they could not ask for modifications or changes to the Artisan pizzas. Only those with food allergies could have ingredients removed, but no new ingredients could be added.

The "No" concept was to establish Domino's as a higher end quality pizza provider. Company officials stressed how much energy had been put into creating an exact taste that should not be altered at a person's whim. The company once again was willing to risk customer backlash, even mildly taunting the public with the "Oh yes we did" tagline. Time will tell if these two maneuvers will generate long-lasting, positive effects for the company.[45]

1. What roles would reach, frequency, continuity, and effective reach and frequency play in these campaigns?

2. What advertising objectives were being sought through the *mea culpa* and "No" campaigns?

3. Evaluate the potential the short-term and long-term effects of these two campaigns.

4. Provide alternative methods for presenting the same messages as these to consumers, rather than the *mea culpa* and "No" approaches.

5. For each of the traditional media discussed in the chapter, describe the pros and cons of Domino's Pizza advertising. Which medium is the best? Why? Which is the least effective? Why?

▲ Many consumers enjoy Domino's pizza.

Monkey Business/Fotolia

CASE 2 AFTER UNLEASHING

Dog owners constitute a large target market. Most members share something in common: the desire to let the pet run free and unfettered. If other friendly dogs are nearby and want to play—all the better. The Unleashed Dog Park was created to meet this need.

Out-of-home advertising can be the critical component of an IMC program and, in some cases, the primary medium. To help launch the new business venture, The Pink Jacket Creative advertising agency created a feeling of expectancy and mystery with its "Unleashed Dog Park" campaign, which featured the three successive billboards shown in this section.

The first billboard displays a dog on a leash. The unfinished nature of the image helps capture interest. Next, the dog, now with an unfastened leash, moves to the center of the billboard, and "unleash" appears in the top-right corner. In the final billboard, the dog is on the right side of the billboard, the leash is gone, and the message "Unleashed indoor dog parks" appears. It also displays the services offered, the Web address of the park, and the location of the facility. In addition to billboards, street kiosks and bus wraps were used to get the message out.

The early results of the campaign were positive. Many dog owners became aware of the new indoor dog park. What followed represent common challenges in marketing communications: sustaining initial interest, moving consumers to action, and building repeat business.

In this next phase, dog owners needed to be encouraged to try the facility. They should be led to believe that the price of entry was a value. Then, over time, they can be enticed to make return visits and to offer word-of-mouth referrals to other pet owners. Only if these objectives can be attained will the initial success of the Unleashed campaign become validated.

1. Define the marketing goals for the second phase of the Unleashed Dog Park promotional efforts.

2. How would the three-exposure hypothesis or recency theory apply to this advertising program in its initial stages? What about the second campaign after consumers are aware of the dog park?

3. Which traditional advertising media should the marketing team use for the second campaign? Discuss the pros and cons of each in terms of the Unleashed Dog Park campaign and the desire to stimulate trial usage.

4. How could social media and nontraditional media be used to supplement a traditional media campaign in this circumstance?

5. Design a newspaper ad and an outdoor ad that will be placed at little league baseball parks in the area.

▲ A series of ads for the Unleashed Dog Park was created by Pink Jacket Creative to gain the attention of motorists, causing them to wonder what the total message would be.

MyMarketingLab

Go to **mymktlab.com** for Auto-graded writing questions as well as the following Assisted-graded writing questions:.

8-1. The Super Bowl is the most watched program on television. Many tune in just to watch the ads. Interview 10 individuals of various ages, genders, and ethnicities. Ask each what they thought of last year's Super Bowl ads. Summarize what you were told. Based on these interviews, how effective is Super Bowl advertising? Is it worth paying $3.6 million for 30 seconds? What about for business-to-business ads? Do you think the Super Bowl is a good venue for business-to-business advertising?

8-2. One of the best sources of information for business-to-business advertisers is BtoB at www.btobonline.com. What type of information is available at this Web site? How can it be used? What benefits would a business-to-business advertiser derive from the Web site?

8-3. Mymktlab Only – comprehensive writing assignment for this chapter.

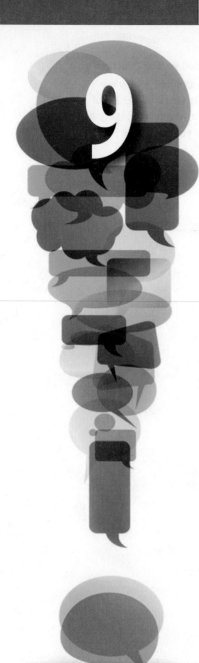

9

DIGITAL MARKETING

CHAPTER OBJECTIVES

After reading this chapter, you should be able to answer the following questions:

1. What is digital marketing?

2. How has the transition to Web 4.0 affected the field of marketing communications?

3. How can e-commerce programs and incentives build a stronger customer base and overcome consumer concerns at the same time?

4. What makes e-commerce a crucial part of business-to-business commerce?

5. How can companies use mobile marketing to reach consumers?

6. What is interactive marketing?

7. What types of online advertising can companies use to reach consumers?

8. How have online social networks, blogs, consumer-generated reviews, e-mail, and viral marketing become key components of market communications programs?

9. How can companies successfully conduct digital marketing programs in international markets?

MARKETING ZEN

magine a situation in which a person walking down a busy street is suddenly handed a bullhorn. The person may or may not have been encouraged to say something and has no idea what to say. In essence, many companies face this dilemma. In the past decade, new megaphones named Facebook, Twitter, Yahoo!, Google, YouTube, MySpace, the blogosphere, and others have emerged., Company leaders wonder if they should use them and, if so, how.

Marketing Zen offers solutions to the social media dilemma. Founder and owner Shama Kabani has been acclaimed one of the "10 Most Influential and Powerful Women in Social Media." She notes, "We take over online marketing for companies; we handle everything from soup to nuts. We handle their Web site, their SEO [search engine optimization], their social media, their e-mail marketing, everything. We are their online marketing department. About 80 percent of our business is essentially taking over online marketing and handling that department for them."

Shama believes that a considerable amount of misunderstanding about social media exists that creates confusion about how a business can use it effectively. She states that one of the biggest misconceptions about social media is "That it's a magic bullet. Companies think or want to believe that social media works differently than offline marketing. They think, 'People are going to find my profile on Twitter and call me and give me their business.' No. It's not a direct route."

Social media also shifts the nature of the communication process. Shama reports, "I did my thesis on why people visit social networking sites and how they utilize their time on those sites. Some interesting results came out of that one. What we found was that people use these sites, more than anything, like a water cooler. Especially for virtual workers."

Consequently, the process goes beyond a company presenting a message to potential customers. Instead, "People don't really want to be on social networks to be fans of something—they don't really care about what a company does. The number one reason why people use social networks, I found in my research, was to showcase their own identities. The companies that are really successful can play into people's identities. So if I say, 'I love Coca-Cola,' that is saying a lot more about me than it is about the company. It takes a certain person to like Coca-Cola and be a fan of their page. If I say, 'I like Pepsi,' that says something about me. I don't really have to care about the brand. I care just about how it tastes, and I'm sticking to it. Companies have to figure out, how can we play into someone's identity? What can we do that is different?"

She continues, "Social media is a megaphone; it's an amplifier, but what are you going to amplify? We talk to most companies about creating their own content. We talk to B2B [business-to-business] companies in terms of, 'How do you establish expertise?' In B2B, the customers want expertise. For B2C [business-to-consumers], the difference is people want free stuff. So, you need something to attract people. There's so much stuff out there."

▲ Shama Hyder Kabani

To assist companies in understanding the nuances of social media, Shama formed Marketing Zen. What at first was primarily a consulting business has evolved into a more full-service company. The organization grew from 4 to over 20 employees in less than a year.

Any new client of Marketing Zen is advised to make sure a bonafide reason exists for becoming involved with social media. In fact, Shama has written and published an article about the 10 reasons why a company should not use the forum. She says, "You use social media when you have something to say. It is a means to an end. If all your customers are on the Web, or people are looking for you on the Web . . . then you should be on the Web."

 The company features two types of metrics to assess the effectiveness of a social media program. "There is a quantitative metric and a qualitative metric," Shama reports. "With social media, often the qualitative can be heavier, because you're looking at what people are saying about the company, and what are they saying about the brand. How are they responding? Are they talking to their friends about it? It's being on the Internet to see what people are saying about them."

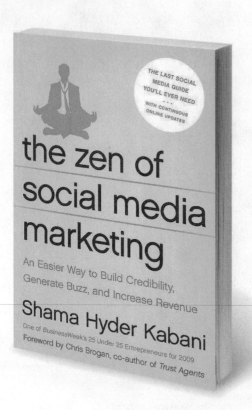

▲ Shama's book *The Zen of Social Media Marketing*.

"The quantitative metrics really depend on what the goals were. We measure things like traffic to the Web site and new visitors. Because social media is a great tool to attract people, we try to send them to the Web site. We try to send them to the hub of what's going on. You look at visitors; you look at how much time they spend on the site. You look at Twitter followers; you look at Facebook fans, and any other tool that we can utilize. We look at how many people left comments on the blog, we look at how many bloggers are talking about them."

In the end, the bottom line is greater traffic to a company's Web site, longer visits while on the site, and ultimately making sales while building loyalty. Marketing Zen stays with a client to update and improve social media efforts over time. Shama notes, "Our business is more than sales. It's relationship-building and networking and marketing and follow up, and keeping in touch." By keeping true to its principles, Shama believes Marketing Zen has a bright future, even as the Internet, social media, and other forms of communication continue to evolve.[1]

OVERVIEW

OBJECTIVE 9.1
What is digital marketing?

The Internet has changed the ways individuals communicate and how the world conducts business. Web 1.0 transformed traditional retailing by selling goods and services over the Internet. A company in practically any location could compete globally, and the size of an organization's operation made little difference. The Internet became an open environment. A buyer could locate numerous sellers offering practically the same merchandise at comparable prices and with similar offers at any time. The Internet offers more than a method to conduct business transactions: it serves as a communication highway. The latest move, to Web 4.0, involves engagement of consumers. It includes interactive Web sites; social media networks, and other communication formats. To survive, businesses use the Internet to interact with customers.

Digital marketing combines all of the components of e-commerce, Internet marketing, and mobile marketing. Digital marketing includes anything with a digital footprint. Today's consumers and businesses rely on the Internet to research products, make comparisons, read comments by other consumers, interact with other consumers and businesses, and make product purchases. An effective IMC program incorporates these new elements into the advertising and promotions plan.

The first part of this chapter examines the evolution to Web 4.0. Next, e-commerce programs, including the incentives used to attract customers as well as consumer concerns with Internet shopping are presented, and business-to-business e-commerce programs are described. The explosion in the use of smartphones also leads to an examination of mobile marketing techniques. The concepts of consumer engagement and interactive marketing are presented. The remaining part of the chapter addresses methodologies being used by companies to create and build Web traffic, including online advertising, offline advertising, online social networks, blogs, e-mail campaigns, and viral marketing are presented. Each may be designed to increase the company's brand presence and influence purchase decisions. International challenges are also described.

Web 4.0

A recent study revealed that many companies have slashed traditional media marketing budgets and moved the funds to online communication. Many marketing experts believe that online searches, e-mail, social media, digital ads, and mobile marketing will soon become a significant portion of marketing expenditures. The transition from Web 1.0 to Web 4.0 changes in the ways consumers communicate and interact with companies. Figure 9.1 displays the characteristics of Web 4.0.

The early stage of the Internet (Web 1.0) in the 1990s was typified by static content provided by a site's creator. Businesses and institutions included little consumer involvement on Web sites. These commercially and technically-based organizations created sites that were crude, simple, and designed to accomplish one specific function.

As Web 2.0 dawned, content became more socially-based and audience generated. Social networking sites such as Facebook and My Space emerged. People wrote blogs. E-commerce expanded greatly. Consumers could purchase almost anything on the Internet. Sites became more appealing and customer-focused as competition drove Web designers to create more customer-friendly sites.

Integration, online metrics, and real-time instant communications characterize Web 3.0. As marketers realized the wealth of online metrics available and the ability to track browser behavior on the Web, content on sites became metric driven. Individuals searching on a site for hiking supplies found that the next time they logged onto that site hiking-related supplies were promoted prominently on the main page. With online metrics came integration of the Web with every aspect of a company's marketing program, both online and offline. What consumers saw online matched what they saw offline.

Web 3.0 online communication channels pushed companies into "real-time" communications. When actor Ed Norton was interviewed in a Times Square studio as part of a Diet Coke promotion, the event was shown live on billboards in Times Square and on the Diet Coke Web site as well as on banner placements on Web sites at E! Online, Cosmopolitan, and Hello. Burger King and Adidas have also presented live feeds. Burger King featured NASCAR driver Tony Stewart, and Adidas ran an online campaign on Justin.tv with Chicago Bulls' star Derrick Rose.[2]

Instant communication meant consumers demanded improved customer service. Apple, Bank of America, and Overstock.com provide live customer service on company Web sites. Verizon offers live chat to contact consumers who access the company's Web

OBJECTIVE 9.2

How has the transition to Web 4.0 affected the field of marketing communications?

- Web 1.0
  - Static content provided by creator
  - Dominated by institutions and businesses
  - Commercially and technically based
- Web 2.0
  - Content is socially-based and audience generated
- Web 3.0
  - Content driven by online metrics
  - Integration of content and communications
  - Instant real-time communications
- Web 4.0
  - Customer engagement
  - Cloud operating systems
  - Web participation a necessity

◀ **FIGURE 9.1**
Primary characteristics of Web 1.0 to 4.0

▲ Many companies now employ individuals to monitor the Web, Twitter, and social media sites.

site. The marketing team knows that when a person spends more than 2 minutes on a step while signing up, the person almost always quits. Verizon can "ping" the customer and offer a live chat with a service representative to guide him through the process.

Consumers also expect instant responses to negative events. When an Internet video showed two Domino's employees doing disgusting things to food, Twitter lit up with chatter and demands that the company address the matter. When Ford's legal department sent a legal notice to a Ford Ranger blogger to surrender his URL, Scott Monty, Ford's social media leader, jumped in and quickly resolved the issue before it went viral.[3]

Now Web 4.0 has emerged, with key characteristics of customer engagement, cloud operations, and Web participation as necessities. Companies cannot just sell products to individuals and then allow customers to post reviews. Engagement is the business model for Web 4.0. Companies that succeed will use the Web to connect customers with the brand through various venues such as social media, blogs, and Twitter. With the rise of smartphones and tablets, consumers have access to thousands of apps and ability to operate using cloud. They can access brands anywhere at any time.

Many companies employ people to monitor Twitter and other social media sites and to develop a Web presence. These activities can be expensive. According to one analyst, a company with 500,000 customers will probably invest about $1.2 million in social networks and online monitoring over the first 3 years.[4]

E-Commerce

OBJECTIVE 9.3

How can e-commerce programs and incentives build a stronger customer base and overcome consumer concerns at the same time?

E-commerce focuses on selling goods and services over the Internet. Many types of e-commerce businesses exist, ranging from click-only operations that sell entirely online to bricks-and-clicks that supplement physical store operations with an online presence. E-commerce involves both businesses selling to consumers (B2C) and businesses selling to other businesses (B2B). Mega-retailers such as Wal-Mart as well as mom-and-pop operations vending merchandise from home engage in e-commerce. Online sales account for nearly 8 percent of all retail activity.[5]

Many consumers that make purchases at retail stores first use the Internet to collect information or read reviews. A Pew Research Center survey revealed that 80 percent of Americans have researched a product online before making a purchase.[6] In Australia, half of the consumers first conduct online research.[7]

BUILDING A SUCCESSFUL E-COMMERCE SITE

E-commerce includes real-time communication and engagement with customers necessitated by Web 4.0. Figure 9.2 offers suggestions for the developing successful e-commerce sites.

E-commerce sites should feature customer-centric designs in which customers can easily locate merchandise. The marketing team arranges and indexes items using terms customers typically use rather than professional or technical language. If a large number of items are sold, then the site needs a drill-down search function that uses customer-friendly terms and allows individuals to find items within one or two clicks.

▶ **FIGURE 9.2**
Characteristics of Web 4.0
E-commerce

● Customer-centric design	● Customization and personalization
● Drill-down search	● Online and offline marketing
● Channel integration	● Search engine optimization (SEO)
● Brand engagement	● Shopping cart abandonment strategies
● Customer interaction	

Channel Integration Channel integration becomes essential when the business sells through additional channels beyond the Web. A company that offers a printed catalog or has a retail store should match the printed catalog with its Web catalog. Victoria's Secret features a "catalog quick order" system that allows customers to enter the product number from the print catalog and then go straight to checkout. The program saves considerable time in trying to find and buy a product on the Web.[8]

Sears Holdings developed the online shopping experience "Shop Your Way" that assists customers by letting them shop in the ways they feel most comfortable. The customer can access Sears.com, Kmart.com, LandsEnd.com, TheGreatIndoors.com, or the new mobile application site Sears2Go. Each offers the consumer the ability to select a product from any retail operation in the manner desired.

To encourage online shopping, Sears Holdings expanded its online offerings to include products not found in the stores or in catalogs. Customers can choose how they shop online: the Web, mobile phone, or at an in-store terminal. A community Web site, MySears.com, presents unbiased customer reviews and assists individuals in getting or giving ideas and sharing knowledge. Online tools such as Quickview, Save for Later, and Wish Lists make the shopping experience convenient for customers. Sears Holdings helps customers purchase products from all of its companies as a single transaction. Sears Holdings provides an example of channel integration and customer-centric Web design.[9]

Courtesy of Skyjacker Suspensions.

▲ Channel integration is an important feature for Skyjacker's Web site.

Brand Engagement E-commerce sites provide opportunities for brand engagement and customer interaction. Blogs, feedback applications, and customer reviews provides ways for e-commerce sites to encourage customers to interact with the Web site. Facebook and Twitter allow customers to like a brand and become fans. Involvement in social causes that involve customers also creates brand engagement.

Many companies remain hesitant about adding reviews and feedback options due to the potential for negative comments, but they represent an emerging trend in the Web 4.0 environment. These venues provide opportunities for active interactions with customers and generate more honest relationships. They encourage customers to become brand advocates and provide a company with insights into customer thoughts and lifestyles.[10]

Review and feedback pages also afford confidence to new customers visiting the site. Best Buy and other retailers include customer reviews on company Web sites regarding the various brands in stock. These programs present opportunities for customer feedback, comments, and interaction. Some e-commerce sites have also added a "tell a friend" function encouraging positive word-of-mouth recommendations.

Part of brand engagement involves personalization and customization. Personalization welcomes individuals by name as they access a site. After an individual registers, cookies recall the person's name and browsing records each time the individual accesses the site. The browsing record and purchase records allow the page to be customized to fit the person's history. Software can suggest additional items based on basket purchases of other customers. For instance, when someone buys a romance mystery novel, the

I remember her in blue jeans and a T-shirt in high school. I remember her in a thrift store leather jacket in college. I remember her in a rain jacket in Oregon. I remember her in a swimsuit on the beach in Florida. I remember her without a swimsuit on the beach in Greece. I remember her in a sleeping bag in a tent in Yellowstone, refusing to come out. But I can't say that I remember ever seeing her in a dress like that.

Date set: _May 20th_

Plan your wedding | Buy a gift | Find your dress | Book your honeymoon | More

Thousands of gowns. And everything else you need to plan the perfect wedding.

WeddingChannel.com™

▲ WeddingChannel.com offers brides a wide array of wedding products, which makes online shopping easy and convenient.

next time she returns to the site it suggests additional titles based on what other customers have purchased.

Most customers enjoy the convenience customization provides. Shoppers do not want to take time to sift through details. They favor the sites that remember them and the merchandise they prefer. Customization features also include the ability to:

- Locate the nearest retail store on a Web site or via mobile phone
- Print coupons or other promotions from the Web site or use a mobile phone to access discounts at the retail store
- Access information on the Web site or via a mobile phone that an item is in stock prior to making a purchase[11]

Successful e-commerce sites require both online and offline marketing to build awareness and to drive traffic to the Web site. Most product purchases begin with someone using a search engine, which means e-commerce sites require a search engine optimization strategy. Both of these topics are discussed in greater detail later in this chapter.

Shopping Cart Abandonment   Online retailers find a higher percentage of online shoppers abandon shopping carts prior to checkout. The reasons vary, but the most common include hidden charges, difficulty in checking out, and requiring customers to register at the site in order to pay. Greg Hintz of Yahoo! Shopping offers these suggestions to keep customers from abandoning a shopping cart:

- Show any additional costs, such as shipping and handling, upfront, so there are no surprises when the customer reaches checkout.
- Make checkout easy and allow customers to make purchases without registering a user name and password.
- Make it easy for customers to enter discount codes from coupons, gift certificates, and other promotions.
- Provide a checkout procedure that is safe and that the customer feels can be trusted.[12]

E-COMMERCE INCENTIVES

Cyberbait includes any lure or attraction that brings people to a Web site. The forms include incentives designed to encourage consumers (or businesses) to visit a Web site and to make online purchases. Cyberbait incentives can be classified into three categories: financial incentives, convenience incentives, and value-added incentives.

Financial Incentives   Financial incentives help persuade an individual or business to make a first-time purchase via e-commerce and encourage customers to return. The incentive may take the form of a reduced price, free shipping, or an e-coupon. These financial enticements can be offered because conducting business online provides cost savings through:

- Reduced shipping costs, because the costs are passed along to the buyer
- Decreased labor costs, because shelves do not have to be restocked or not stocked at all if merchandise is shipped directly from the producer
- Lower personnel costs (sales force), because in-store salespeople are not needed

Once the individual or company takes advantage of the financial incentive and makes the switch, continuing it may not be necessary. At that point, the convenience and added-value features help keep the customer.

Bluefly (www.bluefly.com), a New York–based upscale apparel and home furnishings discounter, sells hard-to-get fashion accessories that even celebrities and socialites wait months to purchase. An online sweepstakes named "30 Bags in 30 Days" focused on this advantage. Customers could enter once per day. The sweepstakes increased site traffic by 100 percent compared to the same month from the previous year. Half of the visitors asked Bluefly to send them a daily reminder to play the sweepstakes. Forty percent referred friends to the site and the sweepstakes. A 62 percent increase in sales from the new customers that the sweepstakes brought in was the result. Existing customers continued to make purchases after the sweepstakes ended.[13]

Typically, the most effective financial incentives offer something free or at a discount. A BizRate Research survey suggested that the most popular online promotion is free shipping.[14] Financial incentives require two ingredients. First, they should be meaningful to individuals visiting the site. Second, they should be changed periodically to entice new visitors to buy and to encourage repeat purchases by current visitors.

Convenience Incentives

Making the shopping process easier creates an incentive that can encourage customers to visit a Web site. Instead of traveling to a retail store, a consumer can place the order in the office or at home. The order can be made at any time, day or night. The convenience and speed of purchasing merchandise online drives many consumers to e-retailers.

Convenience becomes a second advantage when the consumer seeks specific product information. Using the Internet is quicker and easier than reading *Consumer Reports* or talking to a salesperson. Many consumers research major purchases online before going to a store. Most have looked at least once at an online peer review before finalizing a purchase, and roughly 40 percent have compared product features and prices across outlets online before buying.[15]

Value-Added Incentives

Value-added incentives lead consumers to change purchasing habits over the long term. They can make the difference between an ordinary and an exemplary site. The added value may be customized shopping, whereby the software system recognizes patterns in customers' purchasing behaviors and makes offers are matched to past purchasing behaviors or search patterns.

Many e-retailers offer merchandise on the Web site not available in a print catalog in order to add value. Design Within Reach, a modern furniture retailer, advertises, "Our Web site offers

tuesday, 11:15 p.m.
buying a new dress.

bluefly

www.bluefly.com
the outlet store in your home

Courtesy of Bluefly

▲ E-commerce retailer Bluefly often provides financial incentives to encourage online purchases.

▼ This advertisement offers the convenience of making travel arrangements online and paying for them with a credit card.

BOOK A TRIP

Travelocity.com
Powered By SABRE

WITHOUT MAKING ONE

Too busy to book your hotel room, air travel, car rental?
Book your next trip on-line with Visa.
It's fast. It's safe. It's a four-star destination for travelers.

VISA

Worldwide. Webwide. Visa® It's everywhere you want to be®

© 1999 Visa U.S.A. Inc.   www.visa.com

Courtesy of Visa USA, Inc.

Remote Banking

PROGRESSIVE BANK

Progressive Bank offers your business many advantages:

- Save your company's time and money with electronic deposits from your desktop.
- Scan checks received from customers and issue deposits electronically – anytime.
- Improve availability of your deposited funds.
- Cut costly courier fees or trips to the bank.
- Consolidate funds from remote locations.
- Reduce risk of check fraud.

Call us today and let our local Cash Management Team help you effectively manage your time and improve your cash flow.
(318) 651-5049 • progressivebank.com

Member FDIC

▲ Online banking is attractive to consumers because of the convenience incentive.

numerous products not always included in the catalog, as well as weekly features of new items."[16] Sears Holdings uses the same approach.

Frequently, a combination of incentives makes the difference. The cyberbait may include a discount or special price on a pair of jeans (financial-based incentive) and at the same time offer the freedom to place an order at 3:00 a.m. (convenience-based incentive). The same site may feature a game or offer a weekly fashion tip on some topic (value-added incentive). This combination entices consumers and businesses to return to the site. E-shoppers find it easy to surf the Internet and search competing sites. When they do, brand names and particular Web sites are not as important. Consumers need reasons to regularly return to sites.

PRIVACY AND SECURITY ISSUES

Consumer concerns regarding privacy and security are based on past incidents in which credit card numbers have been stolen as well as from cases of identity theft. A Javelin Strategy & Research study estimates retailers lose approximately $21 billion in online sales due to fears about identity and data theft.[17] Although still a concern, worries are declining as more consumers become accustomed to using the Web. Fears about giving out credit card information are no greater now than they are for telephone orders or in-store credit card sales. Consumer confidence in e-commerce Web site security has risen. A recent survey revealed that three-fourths of online shoppers express faith in Web security.[18]

Beyond apprehensions about identity theft and fraud are concerns that firms will sell personal information. Once this information becomes readily available, the individual loses control over who sees it and how it is used. A person might not wish to have his shopping patterns known, especially when the individual buys personal care products such as those for baldness, sexual dysfunction, weight loss, or other private matters. Further, many consumers become frustrated by being bombarded with advertising and marketing messages. Consumers also strongly express the desire to maintain control over personal information. They believe they should decide who should use it and how it should be used.

Trust remains the key to concerns about privacy and security of personal information. A KPMG survey indicates that 62 percent of consumers do not mind being tracked as long as they perceive a benefit in the form of reduced costs or free content. Consumers also want to know a company does with the information it collects. If it is sold, then consumers want the company to request their permission first. Most consumers hate feeling "spied upon: without permission. Tudor Aw of KPMG Europe notes, "People are happy to be tracked but you have to be upfront and explain it."[19]

Business-to-Business E-Commerce

OBJECTIVE 9.4

What makes e-commerce a crucial part of business-to-business commerce?

E-commerce represents a key part of business-to-business operations. In buying situations, many purchasing agents go to the Internet to compare prices and product information. Once a business account has been established, the customer finds it easy to place an order, and the price may be lower than those offered by traditional outlets. Consequently, competing in e-commerce requires an effective e-commerce site and a strong, distinct brand name.

The number of hits on a business-to-business Web site directly relates to the amount spent on advertising and sales promotions. Recently, one large business-to-business company went from 20,000 visits per month to 80,000 visits per month during a 6-month period by doubling the company's annual advertising budget for print, direct mail, and trade shows. A small company went from 2,000 to 6,000 hits per month by increasing the company's budget for print ads from $25,000 to $65,000 per year.[20]

Financial, convenience, and value-added incentives can be offered to business buyers. The iGo Internet advertisement shown in this section offers a 10-percent discount as a financial incentive for orders placed via the Internet at www.igo.com or by telephone.

For businesses, ordering merchandise, supplies, and materials via the Internet can save purchasing agents considerable time. Businesses can check the status of an order, shipment information, and billing data online. In most cases, obtaining information about a purchase online will be considerably faster than making a telephone call. Convenience represents a highly attractive incentive to many companies.

E-commerce programs provide other benefits for business-to-business companies. Online exchanges and auctions offer a growing form of e-commerce in the business-to-business sector. These exchanges allow business buyers to purchase a variety of commodities and goods at lower prices. The Internet enables vendors to speed up time to market, to sell directly to other businesses, and to cut transaction and inventory costs. Buyers can find both nonproduction goods, such as office supplies, as well as production-related supplies, raw materials, and equipment. Sites offering oil, natural gas, electricity, coal, chemicals, steel, and other raw materials are available. Many online markets are operated by intermediary companies that match buyers and sellers.

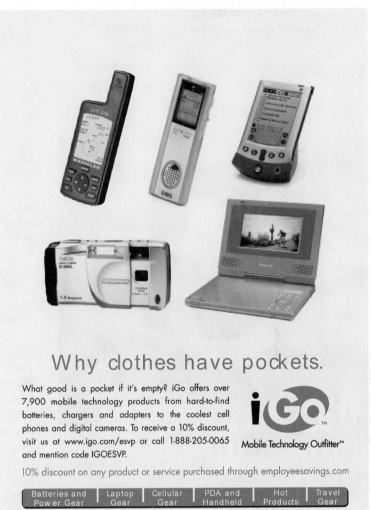

▲ An Internet advertisement for iGo featuring financial incentives to encourage business-to-business purchases.

Mobile Marketing

Although mobile marketing involves various forms of marketing on all mobile cell phone devices, the movement is toward smartphones. Forty-three percent of the U.S. population owns a smartphone. Estimates suggest the figure will rise to almost 60 percent by 2016.[21]

Mobile marketing efficiency improves through an understanding of how individuals use mobile phones, especially a smartphone. It provides a social device that links individuals to social networks, thereby allowing individuals to post comments, pictures, and videos and read the thoughts of others. People can check-in, tweet, and update their status any time and anywhere. They can download deals from companies, read reviews, check prices, and share information.

Further, a mobile device offers a method for shopping. Purchases can be made with a mobile phone. Product information can be obtained and purchases made through a new channel. Consumers are able to check store hours, get directions to a business, and compare prices. This can take place anywhere, including the retailer's store.

Effective mobile marketing involves understanding the social and shopping nature of mobile phones and incorporates it into the firm's mobile marketing strategy. Figure 9.3 identifies various types of mobile marketing. Forms of advertising used on the Internet can be played on smartphone mobile devices such as display ads, search ads, and video ads. All of these will be discussed later in the section regarding the various forms of online advertising.

Companies can take advantage of mobile phones by sending text message ads to consumers. While these may be annoying, they can also be effective when created properly. A text message near lunch or dinner by a restaurant offering a special deal might

OBJECTIVE 9.5

How can companies use mobile marketing to reach consumers?

▶ **FIGURE 9.3**

Types of mobile marketing

- Display ads
- Search ads
- Video advertising
- Text messages
- In-app advertising
- QR codes, digital watermarks, 2D barcodes
- Geo-targeting

pheel
triumphant

Philadelphia is always made with fresh milk and real cream,
to help make the moment a little richer.

Scan this code with your smartphone to get the
Philadelphia Vanilla Mousse Cheesecake recipe

PHILADELPHIA
ORIGINAL   pheel the moment

www.spreadphilly.com

© 2012 Kraft Foods. QR Code is registered trademark of DENSO WAVE INCORPORATED.

Used with permission of Kraft Foods

▲ This advertisement for Philadelphia Cream Cheese has a QR code that provides consumers access to a recipe for cheesecake.

entice a consumer to visit the restaurant. Two keys to text message advertising include gaining the permission of the mobile phone owner and carefully timing when a message is sent.

A new type of mobile advertising gaining popularity is in-app advertisements. Globally, almost 32 billion apps are downloaded to smartphones each year. Advertisers spend $2.9 billion on in-app advertising while consumers spend $26.1 billion buying apps. These apps vary from games to those that check weather, stocks, or recognize songs. This type of advertising will be more effective when it relates to the app's content. For instance, weather-related products should be promoted on a weather app.

QR codes, watermarks, and 2D barcodes directing consumers with a smart phone to a Web site now appear in magazines. Almost every magazine features some type of action code. The codes are especially popular in magazines that focus on home, family, beauty, health, travel, and fashion. A recent issue of *Conde' Nast* magazine provided an action code for Rihanna that took individuals to her Facebook page and to a video of the singer answering questions about her life.

Engaging customers constitutes the primary purpose of action codes in magazines. A Nellymoser study revealed that the greatest usage was for videos (35 percent). These videos may provide a behind-the-scenes look, product demonstrations, a how-to video, or entertainment. Action codes offer an excellent method of collecting data and building opt-in lists for permission marketing. Other uses for action codes are show in Figure 9.4.[22]

The use of smartphones during in-store shopping has increased, with 40 percent of consumers saying they have searched for lower prices while in a retail store.[23] Some retail stores marketers became frustrated and tried to create methods to prevent in-store pricing comparisons. Now, most realize they must adapt. Some stores, such as Best Buy, match any other retailer's price. Other stores have added additional private proprietary brands that reduce price comparisons, because shoppers cannot find the same brand in another store or online and therefore must spend time locating a comparable item. All stores now compare figures with major competitors before pricing items, which reduces in-store price comparisons.

Geo-targeting represents a unique and attractive feature of mobile marketing. By downloading an app, a fast food restaurant such as McDonald's can recognize a person's location and show him how far he is from the nearest outlet and provide walking or driving directions to that unit. Coupled with promoting a special hot beverage or other incentive, the consumer may be enticed to make a purchase.

Many smartphone owners have check-in services at Foursquare, Gowalla, Facebook Places, and Twitter geolocation. Starbuck's, McDonald's, Chipotle, and Burger King provide the largest number of restaurant check-ins. When someone checks in, software can instantly send a special promotion and information about the nearest locations. Marketing experts believe this location-based marketing approach will grow in use in the future. Businesses can harness the ability to drive consumers to retail outlets near where they are located, which can be an effective method to engage consumers with a brand on a one-to-one basis.

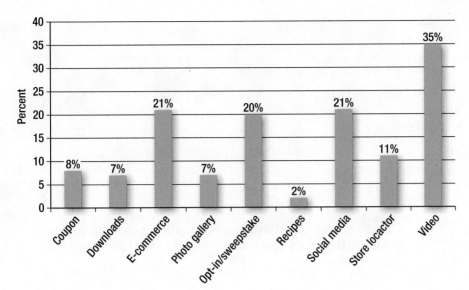

◀ **FIGURE 9.4**
Marketing uses for action codes

Consumer Engagement and Interactive Marketing

The drive to engage consumers with a brand has led to the an increase in **interactive marketing**, which is the development of marketing programs that create interplay between consumers and businesses. The programs feature two-way communication and customer involvement.

The Internet offers the ideal medium for interactive marketing due to the ability to accurately track browser activities and translate the information into instant reactions. Software such as the Relationship Optimizer and Prime Response by NCR provides a powerful data analysis technique to personalize marketing messages. The NCR software analyzes customer interactions such as click-stream data traffic—any type of customer interaction with the firm—and combines it with demographic information from external or internal databases. As the data are being processed, the software can launch complex interactive and personalized marketing materials in real time.

Interactive marketing emphasizes two primary activities. First, it assists marketers in targeting individuals, specifically potential and current customers, with personalized information. Second, it engages the consumer with the company and product. The consumer becomes an active participant in the marketing exchange rather than a passive recipient.Figure 9.5 lists online interactive tactics used by companies and the percentage of companies that utilize each method.

OBJECTIVE 9.6

What is interactive marketing?

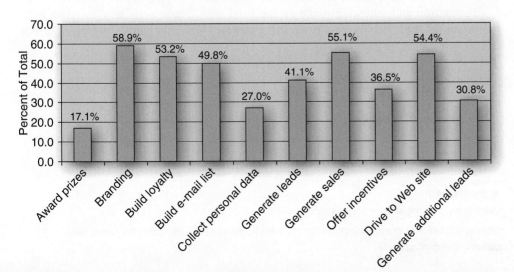

◀ **FIGURE 9.5**
Online interactive tactics

▶ **FIGURE 9.6**
Interactive marketing objectives

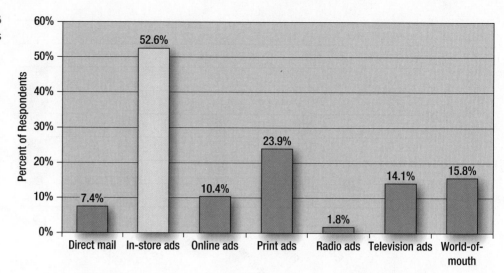

Figure 9.6 identifies marketing objectives and the percentage of companies that use interactive marketing campaigns to accomplish them. As shown, interactive marketing seeks to achieve a wide variety of objectives and serve many purposes.

Marketing Zen's Shama Kabani describes the steps in developing an effective interactive marketing strategy (see Figure 9.7).[24] It starts with cultivating an attitude of giving. Consumers should believe they will receive something in exchange for their involvement. In this two-way interaction, both sides receive something of value. A free gift, such as merchandise or information about some other valuable item, will be the quickest way to capture consumer attention.

The second step is gaining trust involves understanding customers, empathizing with them, and providing solutions to their problems. Consumers engage with companies and brands they trust. The company should be honest, upfront, and cannot pull surprises or use trickery to gain a sale. Otherwise it becomes a one-time transaction.

Shama suggests that companies should synthesize the company or brand down one or two words that best describe what the company offers or stands for. It might be "feminine" or "quality" or "communication" or "innovator" or "passionate." Tied closely with the one-word brand is an ultimate vision. What outcome does the company deliver? For FedEx, provides "overnight delivery." Gatorade delivers energy and refreshment.

Choosing the best communication channels to present messages and to interact with customers and prospects constitutes the next step. As Figure 9.5 shows, several options are available. The best choice depends on the target audience and the message.

Evaluation and adjusting make up the final step. These activities are especially important for digital marketing programs, because the field changes rapidly. Current

1. Cultivate an attitude of giving.	**4.** Define your ultimate vision.
2. Gain trust.	**5.** Choose your communication channels.
3. Identify your one-word brand.	**6.** Evaluate and adjust.

▲ **FIGURE 9.7**

Steps in developing an interactive strategy

Source: Adapted from Shama Hyder Kabani, *Online Marketing Plan,* The Marketing Zen Group (www.marketingzen.com), pp. 9–13.

channels may not exist in 5 years, or even by next year. Different and perhaps better channels may arise.

Online Advertising

Online advertising yields a highly effective method for reaching today's consumers, especially the younger, affluent, and Internet-savvy market. Budgets for online advertising have steadily increased. Funds devoted to online advertising have become a larger portion of overall advertising and marketing expenditures.

Online advertising enjoys the advantage of generating metrics that allow advertisers to measure results, almost instantaneously. This assists agencies in dealing with the accountability pressures they face from clients. Figure 9.8 indicates the percentage of online advertising dollars allocated to each of the primary formats.

BANNER ADVERTISING

The first form of online advertising was a display, or banner, ad. In 1994, AT&T ran one carrying the message "Have you ever clicked your right mouse here? You will." This very basic form of advertising has generated billions of dollars in advertising revenues. Today, banner ads account for 22.6 percent of online advertising.[25]

Currently, banner ads can be embedded with videos, widget applications, or targeted display ads to increase the chances viewers will see and click the icon. The newest online technology, which has been taken from paid search auction systems, allows advertisers to display a banner ad only to individuals the company chooses. This system is built on a vast warehouse of user Internet data and automated auction advertising exchanges, such as Google's Double-Click, Yahoo!'s Right Media ad exchange, and Microsoft's AdECN. Advertisers develop messages for specific audiences and set the price they are willing to pay to reach that audience with a banner ad.

When a consumer, such as a 20- to 25-year-old female, accesses a particular Web site with this new technology, in a microsecond the software searches the ad auction exchange for advertisers matching the profile of the woman who logged onto the page. Once an advertiser has been located, a banner ad instantly flashes on the computer screen. It may be an advertisement for L'Oreal or Liz Claiborne. If a male with an interest in fishing logs on, an advertisement for a boat, fishing supplies, or fishing attire may appear. The automated exchange system grants precise targeting of ads to specific consumers.[26]

Widgets Mini-applications embedded in a banner ad, or **widgets**, permit a consumer access to some form of dynamic content provided by an external source other than the company

OBJECTIVE 9.7

What types of online advertising can companies use to reach consumers?

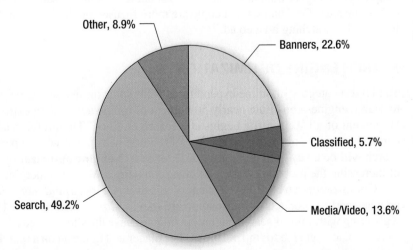

◀ **FIGURE 9.8**
US Online ad spending by format

From de Sede – the DS-51 chair by the de Sede Design Team and DS-9045 modular table designed by Philippe Bestenheider.

IF YOU OWN A
PAIR OF BRASS
MONKEY
LAMPS, KINDLY
IGNORE
THIS AD.

Dallas 1617 Hi-Line Dr. Ste. 100 214.531.3379   Austin 115 W. 8th St. 512.814.8702
Proud member of the TerraPass carbon offset program.

Scott and Cooner Inc. Creative by Gina Cotroneo

▲ Google's Double-Click technology
targets advertisements to consumers
who are browsing the web for stylish
modern furniture.

where the ad resides. Widgets provide individuals personalized access to Web information or functionality from any device connected to the Internet.

Boxcar Creative developed a widget application for ConocoPhillips using RICH expandable banners to create interactive polls, fun facts, and a carbon calculator. The poll and the calculator both collected and produced results without the user ever leaving the banner advertisement. Only when an individual clicked "learn more" was she taken to a micro-site landing page with additional content and data collection opportunities.

Geo-target ads offer another version of banner advertising that have increased in popularity. These ads are presented only to individuals who log on to a Web site in a particular region. It is ideal for retailers and smaller businesses seeking to reach a specific region of the country. As noted earlier, these programs are attractive to mobile marketing and smartphone users.

CLASSIFIED AND MEDIA/VIDEO ADVERTISING

Online classified ads comprise a significant percentage of online advertising budgets. Media/video ads have become the fastest-growing format. This growth will even be greater as mobile phones and other handheld devices develop increased video display capabilities.

An Eyeblaster study revealed that online videos performed best when they appear next to online content or in an e-mail, compared to social network or gaming sites. Eyeblaster examined two metrics: dwell rate and dwell time. **Dwell rate** measures the proportion of ad impressions that result in users clicking an ad or mousing over it. **Dwell time** indicates the amount of time individuals spend engaged with an advertisement. Dwell rate and dwell time were both higher when video ads were placed beside content and in an e-mail as compared to social networks and gaming sites. Ariel Geifman of Eyeblaster explains, "What we found is that people browse social networks really quickly. People spend a lot of time in social networks, but it's not on the same Web page." In terms of gaming sites, Geifman said, "People are more focused on the game" and as a result less interested in watching a video ad.[27]

SEARCH ENGINE OPTIMIZATION

The largest category of online expenditures is for spots on search engines. Funds devoted to search engines constitute nearly 50 percent of online advertising expenditures. About 80 percent of all Web traffic begins at a search engine.[28] Therefore, making sure that a company's name or brand becomes one of the first ones listed when a person performs a search will be a key marketing goal. **SEO**, or **search engine optimization**, is the process of increasing the probability of a particular company's Web site emerging from a search.

Optimization can be achieved in one of three ways. First, a *paid search insertion* comes up when certain products or information are sought. Companies can speed this process by registering with various search engines in order to have the site indexed and also by paying a higher placement fee for top positions. The placement of the ad on a search page depends on the price the company pays and the algorithm a search engine used to determine the advertisement's relevance to a particular search word or phrase.

Second, a company can increase identification through the *natural* or *organic emergence* of the site. This method involves developing efficient and effective organic results that arise from a natural search process. Each search engine uses a slightly different set of algorithms to identify key phrases that match what was typed into the search box. To be listed first in an organic search requires time and effort. Normally, a new website will probably not emerge at the top of the search results. It takes time for the search engine to locate the site.

Some studies suggest that the impact of organic listings can be impressive. For sites that come up on the first page of a search or within the top 10, Web traffic increases nine fold. For second- and third-page listings, Web traffic increases six fold. In terms of sales, being a top 10 listing has resulted in a 42 percent increase in sales the first month and a 100 percent increase the second month.[29]

▲ Search engine optimization leads consumers using search engines to find a company's products and information on the Internet.

The third optimization method, *paid search ads*, includes small text boxes that pop up when a particular word is typed in or it can be paid link boxes at the top or side of a search result. A ComScore study suggests that search ads have a strong positive impact on brand awareness, perception, and purchase intentions, even when consumers do not click the paid search ad.[30] The study revealed that for brands in the top search positions:

- The paid search ads generated a 160 percent increase in unaided awareness.
- Consumers were 20 percent more likely to have a positive perception of the brands.
- Consumers were 30 percent more likely to consider purchasing the brand.

Companies spend large amounts on search engine optimization. The typical click-through rate for online advertising remains around 0.2 percent; for search advertising it is around 5 percent.[31] Although the early results are impressive, marketer should remember that search engine optimization represents a long-term investment. The effects do not occur quickly. Getting into the top 10 listings of a search can take months or years. It requires optimizing content, programming, and finding the codes that will be picked up by search engines.

Search ads can be effective for local businesses. Barbara Oliver owns a boutique jewelry store in Williamsville, New York. She bought $50 per month in Google search ads targeted to an 80-mile radius of her store. It resulted in more customers than all of her offline advertising. With Google Places local directory, someone typing in the keywords designated by Oliver within an 80-mile radius of Williamsville was likely to see her search ad. The effectiveness is also enhanced by smartphones and their GPS capabilities as well as Facebook and Foursquare where people sign-in with their location, which means a visitor to the Williamsville area may see Oliver's search ad.[32]

THE IMPACT OF ONLINE ADVERTISING

As more dollars shift to online advertising, concerns have arisen about the impact of the ads. Web users, just like television viewers, are becoming immune to advertisements. The percentage of people who respond to banner ads steadily shrinks. The click-through rate on major Web destinations has declined to less than 1 percent. A recent measurement showed a response rate of 0.27 percent.[33] For this reason, advertisers have begun banking on new technologies to increase response rates and to deliver targeted messages to the individuals who are most likely to respond.

OFFLINE ADVERTISING

To build a brand's reputation and brand loyalty, online advertising should be integrated with offline branding tactics that reinforce each other to speak with one voice. This process, **brand spiraling**, involves the use of traditional media to promote and attract consumers to a Web site. Marketers design television, radio, newspapers, magazines, and billboards that encourage consumers to visit the firm's Web site in an effort to maintain a uniform brand presence and advertising message.

One recent study indicated that after viewing a magazine advertisement. nearly half of the consumers polled said they might access a Web site or conduct an online search for the product. Over 40 percent are more inclined to visit a Web site after seeing a television or newspaper advertisement.[34] Traditional media can be the driving force behind online branding efforts.

Currently, tailor-made websites accompany many direct and e-mail campaigns. These sites are accessed through **personalized URLs**, called **PURLs**, such as the hypothetical www.kenclow.offer.officedepot.com. A PURL contains a personalized preloaded Web page that contains the customer's personal data, contact information, purchase behavior, and previous interactions with the company. A company such as Ford could display the customer's current vehicle, maintenance record, and other interactions with the company. The PURL creates a one-on-one dialogue with a customer and engages her with the company and provide messages, offers, and incentives tailored to her past data and history.[35]

Although many companies continue to utilize online advertising, a movement into more interactive technologies has taken place. Blogs, e-mail marketing programs, podcasts, social networks, and consumer-generated content are emerging as effective new advertising channels.

▼ Off-line advertising is an important part of building an online presence for Miracle Whip.

Online Social Networks

Online social networks have become popular with people and with companies seeking to communicate with consumers. Forrester Research notes that 75 percent of Internet users participate in some type of social media.[36] A growing percentage of consumer activity on the Internet takes place on social networking or blogging sites. As a result, advertisers spent $7.72 billion on social network advertising which included ads on social sites and in social games and applications. Approximately two-thirds of that amount went to Facebook.[37]

Coca-Cola developed Expedition 206, which involved sending three individuals in their 20s on a 275,000-mile trip to 206 countries where Coca-Cola was sold. Equipped with laptop computers, video cameras, and smartphones the trio set off on their journey, which was tracked on Facebook, Flickr, YouTube, and Twitter. In addition to reading and hearing about the journey, fans could offer suggestions on what the trio should see at each destination.[38]

FACEBOOK

Facebook, the largest social media site, houses over 800 million users worldwide. It presents the largest source of display ads of all social networks, with 17.7 percent share.[39] According to *Adweek*, Facebook's popularity comes from a blend of "sheer size of fan base, record of publishing useful content, and the extent of consumer interaction that is offered." The companies with the most successful Facebook presence, according to *Adweek*, are Starbucks, Coca-Cola, Best Buy, Starbucks, and Microsoft. Starbucks has 3.7 million fans, compared to 3.5 million for Coke. Best Buy has almost 900,000, and Microsoft has just over 300,000.[40] An independent study by WetPaint and the Altimeter Group notes that these companies and others that have high levels of social media activity tend to increase revenues more than companies that lack a social media presence.[41]

Companies that successfully utilize social media offer a discount or special promotion to fans. Of the consumers who follow a brand on Facebook, over one-third cited special deals as the main reason they became fans. When developing a social media strategy, the marketing team attempts to provide content that leads consumers to engage with the brand and ultimately make purchases.[42]

▲ Facebook has become popular with people of all generations.

TWITTER

The Twitter micro-blogging service allows individuals and companies to send out tweets with a maximum of 140 characters per message. Twitter can be an effective method of reaching customers. Marketers may monitor what customers are saying about a company or brand. Software, such as Tweetscan or Summize, locates a brand or company name mentioned in tweets. Company officials are able to respond or gather the information for future use or evaluation. It provides valuable information regarding how customer perceptions of the brand and what they are saying.

JetBlue, Comcast, H&R Block, and Southwest Airlines are just a few companies that monitor tweets. Christopher Hoff tweeted his displeasure with Southwest when his flight was delayed and his luggage was lost. The next day he received a message from Southwest stating, "Sorry to hear about your flight—weather was terrible in the NE. Hope you give us a 2nd chance to prove Southwest = Awesomeness."[43] Some consumers; however, it may find it unnerving to discover that companies can monitor name mentions.

Three weeks after Curtis Kimball opened his crème pastry cart in San Francisco, he noticed a stranger in line to purchase some of his desserts. When quizzed, the man said he heard about the pastry cart from Twitter. Kimball created a Twitter account and now has a fan base of 5,400 customers who wait for him to post his location and list the flavor of the day.[44]

Blogs

Blogs are online musings that cover a wide range of topics. Some permit visitors to post comments; others are just the ramblings of one individual. The power of a blog comes from the new landscape it creates in which one consumer dissatisfied with a particular brand can now tell thousands, and in some cases millions, of others. Previously, a bad shopping experience meant that 12 to 15 people would hear about it. Now an individual's complaint can be sent to more than just friends and family. A discontented consumer speaks to anyone willing to listen (or read about it) via the Internet.

The power of online buzz has grown rapidly. Several unique methods of communication between individuals have emerged. Advertisers now look for ways to tap into these venues. A recent American Marketing Association survey illustrates the growth of these intrapersonal online communication channels. The online survey of 1,174 people revealed that:

- 47 percent go to a social network site to download coupons or to search for information about a product.
- 45 percent go to a social network site to find out about upcoming sales in retail stores and discounts on particular brands of products.
- 22 percent read or write a product review on a blog.[45]

COMPANY-SPONSORED BLOGS

▼ Skyjacker hosts a company-sponsored blog where consumers can discuss suspension systems and lift kits.

Marketing experts have identified methods to use blogs to promote products or to get closer to customers. These include setting up company-sponsored blogs that emulate word-of-mouth communication and engage customers with a company. Fashion retailers entice customers to visit the company's blog to enjoy postings on new styles, upcoming designers, and fashion *faux pas*. In the past, customers may have relied on magazines such as *Vogue* for fashion information. Now, company blogs allow them to obtain information quicker, and, more important, interactively. This helps the marketing team engage with customers and establishes a two-way communication channel.

A company-sponsored blog provides a number of potential benefits; however, analysts stress the importance of identifying a specific reason for the blog before launching it. It may be to make the company more open (Dell), to humanize the company (Microsoft), or to show a fun-and-happy company (Southwest Airlines).[46] When Coca-Cola acquired 40 percent of the Honest Tea company, many customers became unhappy about the move and voiced opinions on the blog. Seth Goldman, CEO of Honest Tea, took time to answer each one. While some customers still did not like the idea, "The blog at least helps people see how we think about it," Goldman said.[47]

Company leaders carefully select methods to respond to negative comments. CEO Bill Marriott of Marriott International hosts a blog for customers and employees. About 20 percent of the blog's readership consists of employees. Marriott employees monitor the comment section. No comment will be posted until it has been approved. The company does not remove comments simply because they are negative. Only those not germane to the discussion or blog are taken down. Those remaining are left up and addressed by Bill Marriott, which provides credibility to the blog through his willingness to hear negative feedback.

GET BENT

Skyjacker's® New 6" TJ Long Arm High Clearance System

The New TJ Long Arm High Clearance Series also includes ¼ wall control arms that are arched (Bent) for ground clearance and increased approach angles.

These Rock Ready Systems are specifically designed with the 'mild to extreme' rock crawler in mind. These Systems have taken the abuse of some of the harshest terrain in the land and came back asking for more.

These Long Arm Kits feature the new "NG" (next generation) rod ends. The lower 1 ¼ forged design heims feature 95,000 psi of strength. They also have an internal rebuildable design with new pivot plus inserts for maximum articulation.

These new TJ Kits feature no welding for easy installation.

Kit Features:
- High clearance skid plate
- Steering box skid plate
- Front and rear track bar
- Front sway bar disconnects
- Transfer case shifter relocation bracket

SKYJACKER SUSPENSIONS®

For an Authorized Skyjacker® Dealer near you call 1.866.4.A DEALER ext.2032 or visit us on the web at skyjacker.com

Courtesy of Skyjacker Suspensions.

For small businesses, blogs provide a relatively inexpensive way to communicate with customers. Robb Duncan began a blog for his Georgetown gelato shop, Dolcezza. When a second store was opened in Bethesda, Maryland, he announced an ice cream giveaway on opening night through the blog. Over 1,000 individuals showed up.[48]

Consumer-Generated Reviews

Word-of-mouth endorsements have changed. Many companies that vend multiple goods or services solicit consumer-generated reviews of those products. Amazon.com stands at the forefront of this approach. Each book offered online holds a space where individual customers can write reviews, both with words and a one- to five-star rating. The site informs the shopper of the number of reviews, the average star rating, and notes if the reviews are written by anonymous critics or those who provide their real names. A person wishing to place his name on a review must authenticate it by presenting Amazon.com with a credit card number. Customers benefit by reading the reviews before making purchases. The system may not be perfect, because an author may use a pseudonym to write a highly favorable review and encourage friends and family members to do the same. At the same time, the author cannot control posts of outside reviews.

Best Buy incorporated consumer feedback into online retailing. The company hosts a blog section for consumers to read about and discuss various topics. In each product category, such as cameras, Best Buy provides a discussion forum on a variety of related topics. In the digital camera discussion forum, consumers can post photos they have taken with various cameras. Best Buy posts customer reviews of each product, both positive and negative. The reviews may influence the brands consumers consider and eventually purchase. By providing blogs, discussion forums, and consumer reviews, Best Buy offers consumers methods to search for and evaluate products and to make purchase decisions without leaving the company's Web site.

Customer-generated reviews should be carefully considered. Reviews provide important information about how company products are evaluated by customers and how the brand compares to the competition. This information becomes critical when developing marketing plans, product modifications, and service strategies. As the usage of consumer-generated reviews continues to rise, the marketing challenge will be managing this aspect of consumer word-of-mouth endorsements in ways that enhance brand equity and increase sales.

E-Mail

E-mail can become an important part of a company's digital marketing strategy. To be successful, companies integrate the e-mail marketing program with other channels. It cannot simply be a program where addresses are purchased and mass e-mails are sent to individuals on the list. Most people resent spam, and response rates are extremely low.

Response rates increase when an e-mail message resembles the information on the company's Web site and in its advertisements and direct mail messages. When Data Inc. introduced new project management software, the marketing team integrated e-mail with a Webinar, direct mail, social media, and telemarketing. The Webinar explained how the new software tool worked.

▲ Best Buy's Web site provides consumer reviews of numerous products, such as video cameras.

▶ Haik Humble can employ various Web analytics to develop a direct e-mail campaign.

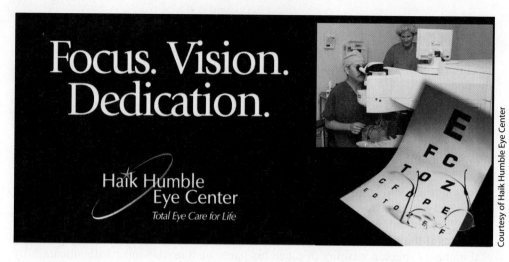

Direct mail, telemarketing, and e-mail were used to reach 600 influential decision makers. For e-mails that were returned undeliverable, Data, Inc. used LinkedIn to locate the contact's correct information. The e-mail integrated approach resulted in a 3 percent response rate.[49]

WEB ANALYTICS

Web analytics allow a company to develop e-mail campaigns that offer the greatest chance of response. E-mails are based on the browsing history of an individual on a particular website. They identify those who made past purchases or items placed in the "wish" list but never purchased.

E-mail campaigns may be directed at consumers who abandon shopping carts without making purchases. About 40 percent of online shoppers abandon the shopping cart just prior to the checkout. Only about 30 percent of these shoppers return to complete the transaction. The IT department can identify the individuals who abandon a shopping basket. Sending an e-mail to these individuals offering free shipping, a discount if they complete the order, or a simple reminder that they have items in their shopping basket can lead to greater sales. Converting these individuals to customers is much easier and more lucrative than sending mass e-mails. Targeted e-mails experience a conversion rate 5 to 10 times higher than mass e-mails sent to the firm's customers. In addition, revenues from these follow-up e-mails are three to nine times higher.[50]

E-MAIL NEWSLETTERS

E-mail newsletters help to create brand awareness, drive traffic to a Web site, and spur sales. Newsletters are especially beneficial when consumers sign up to receive them. The newsletter should offer value to recipients and go beyond providing product information. The more valuable the content is to the recipients, the more likely the newsletter will yield results.

Thrillist (thrillist.com) and UrbanDaddy (urbandaddy.com) send e-mail newsletters to 1.1 million subscribers. Most subscribers are college graduates with median incomes of $88,000. The UrbanDaddy newsletter emphasizes an exclusive and luxurious approach, advising men on where to shop and how to fit in. The Thrillist newsletter features a fun and relaxed tone. Both organize free, heavily-sponsored events for subscribers of the newsletters. The newsletter becomes a means of engaging the subscribers with the Web sites.[51]

- Focus on the product or business.
- Determine why individuals would want to pass the massage along.
- Offer an incentive.
- Make it personal.
- Track the results and analyze the data.

Viral Marketing

Preparing a marketing message to be passed from one consumer to another through digital means, or **viral marketing**, takes the form of an e-mail or a video posted to a personal blog and passed to other blogs or Web sites such as YouTube. It can evolve into a form of advocacy or word-of-mouth endorsement. The term *viral* derives from the image of a person being "infected" with the marketing message and then spreading it to friends, like a virus. The difference is that the customer voluntarily sends the message to others.

Viral marketing messages include advertisements, hyperlinked promotions, online newsletters, streaming videos, and games. For instance, about a dozen videos were posted on YouTube of a man claiming to be the "world's fastest nudist." He streaks through various locations in New York City wearing only tennis shoes, tube socks, and a fanny pack positioned strategically in front. The links to the videos were e-mailed from individual to individual. They were posted on popular blogs such as The Huffington Post and Gawker. One appeared on CNN on *Anderson Cooper 360*. The campaign turned out to be a viral video campaign for Zappos.com, an online shoe and apparel store. The viral campaign highlighted that Zappos was selling clothes, because additional videos were posted that showed a van screeching up to the "fastest nudist" and several people jumping out wearing Zappos T-shirts. As the van leaves, the video shows the nudist dressed in pants and a shirt.[52]

Figure 9.9 provides some suggestions on how to create successful viral campaigns. The viral message should focus on the product or business. In the Zappos.com videos, the nudist receives clothes from a Zappos team. The marketing team determines why an individual would want to pass the message along or tell friends about it.

OfficeMax created a viral campaign for the Christmas holiday season that centered around a quartet of dancing elves with cutout photos pasted on their bodies. Visitors to the special micro-site were encouraged to paste their pictures on the elves and pass it along to friends. The viral campaign drew more than 10 million visitors, because it was unique and it provided something that people wanted to pass along to others. Later, the *Today Show* and *Good Morning America* created their own dancing holiday greetings for viewers.[53]

Individuals should receive an incentive to pass the message along. A message with entertainment value offers one incentive. The incentive may be financial, such as free merchandise or a discount for messages passed along to friends that lead to purchases, logging onto a Web site, or registering for an e-newsletter. The incentive could also found in the campaign's uniqueness. A personalized message has a greater chance of being sent on.

The many forms of digital marketing mean that viral marketing has lost some of its luster. Many consumers have lost enthusiasm and are less willing to pass along messages. The marketing team can take advantage of the ability to track the results of a viral campaign and analyze the resulting data to determine what works and what does not.

il-fede/Fotolia

▲ International shipping is an important component of a global e-commerce business.

International Implications

The ability to reach customers worldwide is one of the major advantages e-commerce holds over brick and-mortar retail stores. Some online companies are still forced to turn away international orders because they do not have processes in place to fill them. This means that while the Internet makes it possible to sell items in an international marketplace, some companies are not prepared to go global. Obstacles to selling across national boundaries include communication barriers, cultural differences, global shipping problems due to a lack of sufficient infrastructure, and varying degrees of Internet capabilities in other countries.[54] Also, Internet companies must follow local exporting and importing laws.

SHIPPING ISSUES

One key to the effective launch of a global e-commerce site is preparing to make international shipments. Air transport may be affordable for smaller products; DHL Worldwide Express, FedEx, and UPS offer excellent shipping options. Larger merchandise normally can be shipped by a freight forwarder that finds the best mode of delivery, from ships to trucks to rail. Air transport companies and freight forwarders both offer specialized logistics software and provide the proper documentation and forms to meet importing and exporting regulations in every country served.

COMMUNICATION ISSUES

Developing a Web site that appeals to the audience in each country will be a key task. It includes adding information that someone in another country would require, such as the country code for telephone numbers. It also requires removing or changing colors, words, or images that might be offensive to a particular group of people in another country.

New globalization software has been developed for companies expanding into other countries. One software package translates an English-language Web site into a large number of foreign languages. Another valuable feature that the software offers is "cultural adaptation," which adjusts a Web site's terminology, look, and feel to suit local norms. The software also has a feature in which the content developed in one location can easily be deployed to all sites around the world. This provides a more consistent look to the Web sites, without someone spending time modifying each foreign site. The software makes it easier to prepare a Web site in the proper native language and also conform to local customs.[55]

TECHNOLOGY ISSUES

The technical side of international e-commerce remains challenging. Software compatibility continues to present an unresolved technical issue. Ideally, these various technologies will eventually be merged into a single system. Currently, the bandwidth for handling Internet traffic varies considerably. Information technology staff members are involved in every step of an internationalization process in order to overcome the potential technical glitches.

A coherent IMC strategy utilizes local input from the various countries involved. The brand on an Internet site should stay consistent from one country to the next and present the company's primary marketing message. For IBM, this meant using local companies in each country to design individual Web sites and provide the information used on each site. To ensure consistency, IBM designs the main marketing messages at its central office, but then local companies translate the messages and add reseller contact and pricing information.

In the future, the growth of international e-commerce will continue to rise. Firms that get in on the ground floor are likely to enjoy a major marketing advantage.

INTEGRATED CAMPAIGNS IN ACTION

Interstate Batteries

Interstate Batteries employed its internal marketing department to launch a geo-targeted online media plan for all company Battery Centers located in cities throughout the United States. The objectives of the campaign were to:

- Increase awareness of all Interstate Battery Centers
- Drive traffic to all Interstate Battery Centers
- Create awareness of key brand messages

Interstate Batteries featured an online display advertising to create awareness and provide information about the location of its stores. The campaign was geo-targeted by each store's market zip codes. Consumers who clicked on the ads were taken to a geo-specific landing page that provided information about the closest All Battery Center. The campaign targeted the 25 to 54 age group with the selected zip codes surrounding each of the battery stores.

Online metrics to measure the success of the campaign were determined prior to the launch. Metrics included click-through, coupon redemption, changes in sales, and the number of transactions at the retail stores. Additional online metrics included the number individuals who enlarged the map, submitted information by e-mail, and printed the coupon.

The Interstate Battery Center digital campaign is located at the Pearson Instructor's Resource Center (www.pearsonhighered.com). The campaign includes a PowerPoint presentation outlining the details of the campaigns and examples of the collaterals. Video by the Interstate Batteries marketing team explaining the campaign is available.

▶ Interstate Batteries launched a geo-targeted online advertising campaign to build awareness and drive traffic to its Battery Centers.

Interstate Battery Systems International, Inc.

MyMarketingLab

Go to **mymktlab.com** to complete the problems marked with this icon .

SUMMARY

Digital marketing includes all of the components of e-commerce, Internet marketing, and mobile marketing. Digital marketing includes anything with a digital footprint. An effective IMC program incorporates these new elements into the advertising and promotions plan.

The transition from Web 1.0 to Web 4.0 changes in the ways consumers communicate and interact with companies. The key characteristics of Web 4.0 include customer engagement, cloud operations, and Web participation as necessities.

An e-commerce Web site includes a catalog, a shopping cart, a payment collection method, and a store locator. Customers should believe the process is secure and be enticed to change buying habits. Three incentives that help people alter buying patterns are financial incentives, greater convenience, and added value.

Interactive marketing is the development of marketing programs that create interplay between customers and businesses. It assists the marketing department in targeting potential customers with personalized information and engages the consumer with the product and company.

Online advertising reaches young, more Internet-savvy consumers. It includes banner advertising, classified and media/video advertising, search engine optimization, and paid search ads.

Brand spiraling may be used to combine the Internet program with advertising in traditional media. Blogs create a new form of word-of-mouth advertising. Blogs can be company-sponsored or posted by individual Internet users.

Online social networks include Facebook, Twitter, and others. Social media have become a major part of the integrated marketing landscape. Consumer-generated advertising includes crowdsourcing and other methods. They represent a new method for engaging customers with a brand or company. Consumer-generated reviews offer the opportunity to create forums for customers to discuss product benefits and problems.

E-mail can supplement an integrated program. Web analytics assist in directing e-mail blasts to the most viable markets. E-mail newsletters help create brand awareness, drive traffic to a Web site, and spur sales.

Viral marketing is preparing a marketing message that will be passed along by consumers. Effective viral programs spur consumer interest and provide rewards for passing messages to others.

International markets may also be served by e-commerce enterprises, especially when cultural differences, shipping problems, and Internet capability problems can be solved. Information technology departments play a key role in solving the Internet problems. Shipping issues and language differences also require attention in this lucrative and growing marketplace.

Key Terms

digital marketing Marketing that incorporates the components of e-commerce, Internet marketing, and mobile marketing.

e-commerce Selling goods and services on the Internet.

cyberbait A type of lure or attraction that brings people to a Web site.

interactive marketing The process of individualizing and personalizing Web content and e-mail messages for various consumers.

widgets Mini-applications embedded in a banner ad that permit a consumer access to some form of dynamic content that is provided by an external source other than the company where the ad resides.

dwell rate Measures the proportion of ad impressions that resulted in users clicking an ad or mousing over it.

dwell time Measures the amount of time individuals spend engaged with an advertisement.

search engine optimization (SEO) The process of increasing the probability of a particular company's Web site emerging from a search.

brand spiraling The practice of using traditional media to promote and attract consumers to a Web site.

personalized URLs (PURLs) A personalized Web page that is preloaded with the customer's personal data, contact information, purchase behavior, and previous interactions with the company.

blogs The online musings of an individual or group; the term is derived from "Web logs."

viral marketing An advertisement that is tied to an e-mail or other form of online communication in which one person passes on the advertisement or e-mail to other consumers.

Review Questions

1. Define digital marketing.
2. How has Web 4.0 influenced the field of marketing?
3. What is e-commerce?
4. What is cyberbait? What are the three main forms of cyberbait?
5. What concerns do some consumers still have about e-commerce?
6. What benefits do e-commerce programs offer to business-to-business operations?
7. What is interactive marketing?
8. What primary forms of online advertising are used by marketing teams?
9. What is meant by the term search engine optimization (SEO)? How can it be accomplished?
10. What is brand spiraling?
11. What is a blog? How can blogs be used in marketing communication programs?
12. How can online social networks be used to supplement advertising and communication tactics?
13. Describe consumer-generated advertising.
14. How can a marketing team take advantage of customer-generated reviews?
15. Identify and describe the elements of an effective e-mail campaign in marketing.
16. What is viral marketing? What is the goal of a viral marketing program?
17. What challenges must be overcome to establish an international e-commerce operation?

Critical Thinking Exercises

DISCUSSION QUESTIONS

1. Examine the characteristics of Web 1.0 to Web 4.0. Discuss how the Internet affects your daily life. Interview individuals in each of the following age categories concerning their use of the Internet: 30-39, 40-59, 60+. Relate their conversations to Web 1.0, Web 2.0, Web 3.0, and Web 4.0.

2. What types of goods or services have you purchased online during the past year? Have your parents or grandparents purchased anything online? If so, compare your purchases and attitudes toward buying via the Internet with theirs. If neither you, your parents, nor your grandparents have used the Internet to make purchases, why not?

3. For what type of products do you conduct Internet searches for information? What factors determine whether you conduct online searches for information? When searching for information, what sites do you use? How effective are each of the following search results in your decision on what sites to access?
   a. Paid search insertions
   b. Organic search results
   c. Paid search ads

4. Are you on Facebook? Why or why not? If you are on Facebook, how much time do you spend online at Facebook? Do you use Twitter? Why or why not? Based on your experience with Facebook and Twitter, how can companies use them to reach you? Are you a fan of any company on Facebook? If so, why did you become a fan? If not, why did you choose not to become a fan?

5. Interview five individuals of different ages about blogs. What percent have read, launched, or participated in blogging on the Internet? What was each person's motivation?

6. Do you use consumer-generated reviews in making purchase decisions? How valuable do you think they are to consumers? What are your thoughts about consumer-generated ads? Is that a trend for the future where companies will use more consumer-generated ads and fewer agency-produced ads? What are the pros and cons, from your perspective, of consumer-generated materials?

7. Have you ever participated in a viral marketing campaign? If so, discuss why you participated and your evaluation of the viral campaign from the company or brand's perspective. If you have not participated in a viral campaign, what type of incentive would it take for you to participate? How effective do you think viral campaigns are with consumers in your market segment?

Integrated Learning Exercises

1. Best Buy was a late e-commerce entrant, but has developed a strong e-commerce component. The key to Best Buy's success, according to Barry Judge, vice president of marketing, is, "We do a lot of one-to-one marketing. We're not overly focused on where the consumers buy." The Web site carries every product that Best Buy stocks. It offers personalized services, along with convenient pickup and fair return policies to entice consumers to shop. Consumers can purchase items on the Internet and either have them shipped directly to them or pick them up at the closest store. Shoppers can use the Internet to see if Best Buy stocks a particular item, to determine what the item costs, and to gather product information. What is the advantage of this strategy? Access the Web site at www.bestbuy.com. Evaluate it in terms of ease of use and product information, and then locate the Best Buy closest to you. Next, access Circuit City's Web site at www.circuitcity.com. Compare it to Best Buy's site. Select a product, such as a camcorder, to compare the two Web sites.

2. Pick one of the following product categories and access the Web sites of two companies that sell the product. What types of financial incentives are offered on each company's Web site to encourage you to purchase? What about the other two types of incentives, greater convenience and added value? What evidence do you see for them? Compare and contrast the two companies in terms of incentives offered.
   a. Contacts or eyeglasses
   b. Water skis
   c. Clothes
   d. Cameras
   e. Camping supplies

3. The three main companies businesses use to ship small packages either overnight or 2-day delivery are FedEx, UPS, and the U.S. Postal Service. Access the Web sites of each shipping solution provider: www.fedex.com, www.ups.com, and www.usps.gov. What delivery guarantees does each offer? Which site is the most user-friendly? Which site appears to offer the best customer service?

4. Pick two of the following e-commerce sites. Discuss each of the characteristics of Web 4.0 e-commerce sites listed in Figure 9.2. Compare and contrast the two sites for each of the characteristics.
   a. Travelocity (www.travelocity.com)
   b. Wells Fargo Bank (www.wellsfargo.com)
   c. WeddingChannel.com (www.weddingchannel.com)
   d. Bluefly (www.bluefly.com)

5. Blogs provide opportunities for both individuals and businesses to share information, thoughts, and opinions. Go to Google Blog Search at http://blogsearch.google.com. Type in a topic that you are interested in exploring that is related to advertising and marketing communications, such as "advertising to children." Locate three blogs on the topic you chose. Discuss who initiated the blog and the value of the information on the blog.

6. Access each of the following search engines. For each one, discuss how it handles paid search advertising when you type in a search, such as "running shoes." What ads do you see as display ads and what ads are part of the search results? Discuss the differences among the five search engines. Which one do you like the best? Why?
   a. Google (www.google.com)
   b. Yahoo! (www.yahoo.com)
   c. AltaVista (www.altavista.com)
   d. AOL Search (http://search.aol.com)
   e. Bing (www.bing.com)

Student Project

CREATIVE CORNER

Bluefly's marketing team wants to enhance the company's brand name and Internet presence. They have asked you to be an Internet advertising consultant. Access the Bluefly Web site at www.bluefly.com. Once you feel comfortable with the company, prepare a banner ad that can be used on the Internet. Design a magazine ad that can be used with the banner advertisement. Then, design an e-mail promotion that can be sent to customers who purchased from Bluefly.com, but it has been at least 90 days since that purchase.

CASE 1 BLACK FRIDAY AND CYBER MONDAY

Each year, as the United States undergoes the traditional Thanksgiving to Christmas holiday season, businesses across the country hope for strong sales. The term "black Friday" resulted from the realization that the Friday following Thanksgiving was the day many retailers moved from the "red" (loss) to the "black" (profit).

Black Friday has evolved over the years. From the traditional rush to shop, retailers began seizing the opportunity by offering special discounts on limited amounts of merchandise, opening stores in the early morning. Bargain hunters lined up in the middle of the night, and more than once physical violence broke out between patrons fighting over the last item on a sales rack. In 2011, some stores actually opened at midnight of Thanksgiving evening, trying to optimize sales.

In the past decade, a new phenomenon emerged. Cyber Monday resulted from shoppers buying online rather than in retail stores. Last year online sales on the Monday following the Thanksgiving weekend topped $1.25 billion, an increase of 39% over the year before.[56] The average order value was nearly $200. Total Internet sales during the holiday shopping season reached $35 billion.

Many consumers did not wait for Cyber Monday. Internet sales on Black Friday were $816 million, also a large increase over the previous year. Shopping patterns also indicate that three additional major spending days were December 17, 23, and 26. Of note, over 10 percent of the orders place came from mobile phone devices.

This annual rush to shop season has its detractors. Some traditionalists decry the overemphasis on materialism. Others note that the holiday shopping season has practically turned into a sporting event, complete with all its corresponding statistics. In addition, cynics note that Black Friday is not the busiest retail shopping day of the year. It actually takes place the weekend before Christmas each year.[57] Critics wonder whether those poor shoppers standing in the cold on the night after Thanksgiving are to be pitied for being exploited or laughed at for going to such extremes to save a few dollars.

In any case, marketers recognize that holiday shopping will likely continue. The methods used to reach customers continue to change. In this dynamic arena, the role of digital marketing will undoubtedly expand.

1. Describe the differences between individuals who shop in retail stores on Black Friday and individuals who participate in Cyber Monday? Are they the same individuals or different? Justify your answer.

2. Discuss for you personally your view of Black Friday and Cyber Monday. Do you participate in both or just one? Why or why not? Do you think retailers take advantage of consumers on these two special days? Why or why not?

3. How can retailers integrate shopping in the store with shopping online?

4. What types of advertising and promotions should be sent out to consumers immediately preceding the Thanksgiving weekend?

5. As some companies now begin Christmas advertising as early as mid-October, how will the roles of Black Friday and Cyber Monday be affected?

6. Design a magazine ad for some type of electronics encouraging consumers to make a purchase on Cyber Monday. Use some other incentive other than a steep price discount.

◀ Many consumers are influenced to make online purchases during Cyber Monday.

Elenathewise/Fotolia

CASE 2 BING CHALLENGES GOOGLE'S SEARCH ENGINE DOMINANCE

Every once in awhile, a product or a company's name becomes so famous it gets added to the national vocabulary. A generation ago, employees started making "xerox" copies. Before that, people started taking "aspirins" instead of "pain medicine" and covering wounds with "band aids" rather than "adhesive strips." Today, it is common to hear someone say she "googled" something.

The basic Google business model organizes a vast amount of information into a system that can be easily accessed using the Web. Google provides information to users for free. The company sells advertising that is linked to the free information. One primary advantage held by Google is that the firm has been able to expand indexing and retrieval searches into nearly 100 languages. Using tools from Basis Technology, Google offers searches in Asian languages as well as other challenging languages. The net result is a global company with a worldwide reach. One industry leader commented that Google has created almost a "new world order" in advertising.

Google's management team remains acutely aware of competitors. Microsoft and Yahoo! are two main search engine providers that could affect Google's share. New competitors emerge every day. In June 2009, Microsoft introduced the search engine Bing in an effort to challenge Google.

Bing replaced Microsoft's Live Search engine. It was started after more than a year of research showing that although users said they were generally satisfied with Web search services there were times when searches became too difficult. In the beginning, Bing received praise from many influential reviewers, increasing the possibility that it could shake up the dynamics

of the search business, which is worth $12 billion in the United States alone.

In July 2009, Microsoft and Yahoo! announced a partnership in Internet search and advertising intended to build on the introduction of Bing and close the gap with Google. By 2012 Google still held 65 percent of the search market, compared with 15 percent for Bing. Both competitors made inroads against Yahoo!

Bing's competition with Google became more direct when the company began running television commercials designed to indirectly hint that Google searches were too complicated, turning users into data-spewing zombies. Bing was offered as the easy-to-use alternative.

Then, Microsoft CEO Steve Ballmer allegedly offered to pay Rupert Murdoch's News Corp. to remove all its content from Google. This would include content from *The Wall Street Journal*, the *New York Post*, and *The Times* of London. The idea was that if Web surfers could not find News Corp. content when they did a Google search, they would be more inclined to use Bing. There were reports that Microsoft offered the same deal to other publishers.

News providers have long been frustrated that stories and materials they create are posted without the news company receiving any compensation, whereas Google and Bing are able to sell advertising beside the stories. Google responded by saying any organization was free to pull content at any time, apparently unfazed by Bing and Microsoft's effort.

Google's power in the marketplace makes company leaders optimistic about the future. Time will tell if Bing can make stronger inroads on what is practically a cultural icon.[58]

▶ Will Bing be able to challenge Google when it comes to search engine dominance?

Adam Borkowsk/Fotolia

1. What tactics should Microsoft and Bing use to gain market share?

2. As an advertiser, does Bing hold an advantage due to lower clutter on the site, or does Google's wider reach offset that advantage?

3. Which site would facilitate a faster search engine optimization effort? Why?

4. Which site, Google or Bing, would be most useful to an international company? Why?

5. Design an advertisement for Bing that would appear in a magazine. Which magazine would you use for the ad? Why?

MyMarketingLab

Go to **mymktlab.com** for Auto-graded writing questions as well as the following Assisted-graded writing questions:.

9-1. For what type of products do you conduct Internet searches for information? What factors determine whether you conduct online searches for information? When searching for information, what sites do you use? How effective are each of the following search results in your decision on what sites to access? a. Paid search insertions b. Organic search results c. Paid search ads

9-2. Have you ever participated in a viral marketing campaign? If so, discuss why you participated and your evaluation of the viral campaign from the company or brand's perspective. If you have not participated in a viral campaign, what type of incentive would it take for you to participate? How effective do you think viral campaigns are with consumers in your market segment?

9-3. Mymktlab Only—comprehensive writing assignment for this chapter.

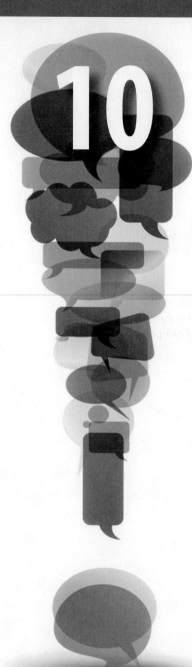

10 ALTERNATIVE MARKETING

CHAPTER OBJECTIVES

After reading this chapter, you should be able to answer the following questions:

1 How can buzz marketing, guerrilla marketing, lifestyle marketing, and experiential marketing enhance a marketing communications program?

2 What methods can be used to effectively employ product placements and branded entertainment?

3 Why has the use of alternative media venues, especially video game advertising, grown in marketing communications programs?

4 How have in-store marketing and point-of-purchase displays evolved into even more effective communication and sales tools?

5 How can brand communities enhance brand loyalty and devotion?

6 What methods are used to adapt alternative marketing programs to international marketing efforts?

MyMarketingLab™

⭐ Improve Your Grade!

Over 10 million students improved their results using the Pearson MyLabs. Visit **mymktlab.com** for simulations, tutorials, and end-of-chapter problems.

THE VIDEO GAME MARKET REACHES A NEW NICHE

Video games offer marketers a popular medium to reach younger consumers as they relax and enjoy free time. Video game marketing reaches a multimillion dollar marketplace. Some companies focus on selling the devices that play the games. Others concentrate on developing new games. More recently, advertisements and product placements provide a lucrative new method for reaching this valuable target market.

Traditionally, mostly teens and young adult males enjoyed video games. Today IDC Research estimates that 40 percent of gamers are females. One recent estimate suggests that more than 130 million females play video games. Another study notes a worldwide growth in the number of female gamers. In India, females make up over 20 percent of all gamers.

The introduction of new games for females has drawn more girls and women into the action. Electronic Arts (EA) introduced *Littlest Pet Shop* for young girls and *Charm Girls* for older girls. Sony created a *Hannah Montana* game. Ubisoft Entertainment launched *Your Shape* and *Just Dance*, and Nintendo offers *Wii Fit Plus*. EA's *Sports Active* became a top 10 title for 3 consecutive months, according to research firm NPD Group. Ubisoft's *Imagine* video game series features games in which girls can play the role of a ballerina or explore female-dominated professions. Ubisoft sold 14 million *Imagine* video games in 3 years.

WomenGamers.com connects with women who enjoy video games. The site offers reviews of games and posts various types of commentary articles. One asks why females who are in a room with men playing a virtual shootout war-type game feel relegated to spectator status; another questions why the most recent list of top 50 game developers did not include one female name.

Some argue that more can be done to entice women into the market. Courtney Simmons, public relations director for Sony Online Entertainment (SOE), recently spoke to an invitation-only crowd at the Game Developers Conference in San Francisco. Simmons was joined by several other women from SOE to announce the details of the Gamers in Real Life (G.I.R.L.) program at the company's San Diego headquarters. The program, which emerged from a partnership with The Art Institutes, was the first of its kind. Female participants, students currently enrolled at an Art Institute school engaged in a game-building contest. The winner received $10,000 toward her tuition and a paid internship at one of SOE's development studios.

Simmons enjoys playing video games with her three children. She argues that women are being "gamed down to," because, she says, "there is a lack of understanding about how women play." Simmons wants "more women making games," she says, "making more games that women want to play."

Studies and sales data indicate that women are more likely to play handheld casual games, such as the Nintendo DS, along with more socially-oriented games, such as *The Sims*, where women represent more than 55 percent of players. Although the number of women who play games continues to grow, women represent less than 12 percent of video game developers, according to the International Game Developers Association. By diversifying the workforce, developers believe they can create products that appeal to a wider audience.

Eléonore H/Fotolia

Some progress has been made. Prior to the *Littlest Pet Shop* release, EA conducted extensive market research about what female users want in a game. The company's marketing team discovered that girls like it better when the pets make eye contact with the player. After testing the game with girls, EA added

Wavebreakmedia Micro/Fotolia

accessories for the pets and gave players the ability to customize them. The *Littlest Pet Shop* became EA's best-selling game in its market.

From a marketing communications perspective, gaming appears to offer great potential for all three aspects of the marketplace. As more females purchase gaming devices and play games tailored to them, sales will likely increase. Further, the ability to reach girls, young women, and mature women with products placed in the games or advertising messages embedded in them presents a potentially powerful new method to develop brand awareness and brand loyalty in an alternative medium.[1]

OVERVIEW

Traditional mass media advertising faces many challenges. Although advertisers are not ready to abandon radio, television, magazines, newspapers, and outdoor programs, they know that many new and valuable media outlets have emerged. As a result, alternative marketing programs and alternative media are on the rise. Marketers spend increasing numbers of dollars finding ways to reach potential customers in new and innovative formats. Successful advertising and promotional programs often utilize these new alternative approaches.

This chapter presents four topics. First, it identifies major alternative marketing programs: buzz marketing, guerrilla marketing, product placements and branded entertainment, and lifestyle marketing. Next, it describes a series of marketing tactics associated with alternative media. Third, in-store marketing will be examined. Finally, brand communities are discussed. The international implications of these new forms of alternative media are also presented.

Alternative Marketing Programs

OBJECTIVE 10.1

How can buzz marketing, guerrilla marketing, lifestyle marketing, and experiential marketing enhance a marketing communications program?

Developing alternative marketing programs requires creativity and imagination. Marketers seek to identify new places where a consumer's path intersects with a brand's presence, or create a new intersection point. Then they can prepare attention-getting marketing messages for those points of contact. This presents the opportunity to supplement or replace mass media advertising with more targeted options.

In essence, the goal remains the same as for traditional media. Marketing professionals continue to look for innovative ways to reach a target audience. Alternative marketing programs and alternative media venues have become widely accepted options. Figure 10.1 lists common alternative marketing choices. These programs seldom operate independently. A guerrilla marketing campaign might also include buzz and lifestyle marketing components. The same campaign may contain digital components and traditional media.

Alternative marketing relies on buzz, word-of-mouth, lifestyles, and times when consumers are relaxing and enjoying hobbies and events. Integrating these venues using one coherent integrated marketing program that speaks with a clear voice and message should be the goal.

▶ **FIGURE 10.1**
Forms of Alternative Marketing

- Buzz marketing
- Guerrilla marketing
- Lifestyle marketing
- Experiential marketing
- Product placement and branded entertainment

Buzz Marketing

Buzz marketing has become one of the fastest-growing areas in alternative marketing. Estimated expenditures for these programs are at $1 billion annually. **Buzz marketing**, or *word-of-mouth marketing*, emphasizes consumers passing along information about a product. A recommendation by a friend, family member, or even an acquaintance carries higher levels of credibility than does an advertisement. It can be more powerful than the words of a paid spokesperson or endorser. Buzz, or word-of-mouth, can be generated by consumers who truly like a brand and tell others, consumers who like a brand and are sponsored by a company to tell others, or by company or agency employees who tell others about the brand.

CONSUMERS WHO LIKE A BRAND

The ideal situation occurs when a consumer truly likes a particular brand and tells others. Enthusiasts deliver these messages in person or via the Internet in chat rooms, blogs, or e-mails. Many musical groups have achieved fame through this type of word-of-mouth support by those who have seen the bands in bars or as part of a small concert or tour.

SPONSORED CONSUMERS

Many companies sponsor individuals as agents or advocates to introduce new products. It works best when these individuals, or ambassadors, also like the brand. An alternative type of sponsorship involves house parties.

Brand Ambassadors Customer evangelists, or brand ambassadors, are typically individuals who already like the products that they are asked to sponsor. The company offers incentives and rewards in exchange for advocacy. Companies select these ambassadors based on their devotion to the various brands and the sizes of their social circles. Once recruited, they deliver messages to their families, friends, reference groups, and work associates. Some are asked to develop grassroots, no- or low-cost marketing events and to promote the brand on the Internet through blogs or on social networks such as Facebook. Brand advocates are told to be upfront and honest about their connections with the brand.

On move-in day at the University of North Carolina, students wearing American Eagle Outfitter shirts volunteered to help new students move into their dorms. They cheerfully unloaded cars and lugged belongings to dorm rooms. They passed out American Eagle coupons, water canisters, and Eagle pens as they helped the students. The helpers were

Courtesy of Kenneth Clow.

▲ The House of Blues in New Orleans benefits from the buzz generated by customers who tell their friends about the music and atmosphere.

▼ Many companies employ college students to pitch products ranging from air filtration systems to cell phones to computer software.

© Andres Rodriguez/Fotolia

student brand ambassadors. An estimated 10,000 college students will be working as ambassadors for a variety of companies, such as American Eagle, Red Bull, NASCAR, Microsoft, and Hewlett-Packard. In exchange for promoting a particular brand, they receive discounts and/or merchandise.[2]

Procter & Gamble took advantage of a similar approach for a series of products through the efforts of Justin Breton, a student at Boston University. He spent about 15-hours per week talking about PUR, a water filtration system from Procter & Gamble. Justin was one of 100 college ambassadors hired by P&G to pitch items ranging from PUR to Herbal Essences hair products. The students created their own marketing plans and earned up to $2,500 per semester. They were required to submit regular reports and were monitored by P&G and RepNation.[3] The approach helped Procter & Gamble place products in the hands of consumers and provided students with opportunities to create unique marketing ideas.

House Parties   Brand ambassadors also host house parties. Nestlé Purina spent $50,000 on 1,000 house parties to market a new line of dog food, Chef Michael's Canine Creations. Purina identified childless individuals with household incomes greater than $60,000, who love to pamper their pets. House Party, a firm that matches brands with party hosts, located the homes for Purina. Dianna Burroughs hosted a party in her Manhattan West Village condo. Fourteen guests and their dogs arrived to sample the filet-mignon-and-potato-flavored kibbles from Chef Michael's Canine Creations. House Party's other clients include Avon, Procter & Gamble, Kraft, Mattel, Hershey's, and Ford.[4]

BzzAgent offers house parties and the ambassador approach for its clients. Suzanne Ermel, a 30-year old unemployed lawyer, is a Bzzagent ambassador for a boxed wine, Black Box. At the grocery store she sees a shopper put a box of wine in her shopping cart. Suzanne stops the shopper declaring "Don't do it! This [Black Box wine] is just a couple of dollars more and you're going to like it a lot more." She adds "I've point Black Box out to random people shopping for wine." She invited friends to her house for a blind tasting part and served Black Box wine without mentioning the brand name. She then solicits comments from her guests and reveals the name of the wine. The Black Box buzz marketing campaign sought to "increase trial, advocacy, and impact sales."[5] The key to these events was that the host was an influencer among his or her friends and associates.

COMPANY EMPLOYEES

A final group of advocates includes company employees. The company or agency decides whether they should pose as customers or identify themselves as being affiliated with the company. The Word of Mouth Marketing Association (WOMMA) argues that individuals should be upfront and clearly identify themselves as being with the company.

A few years ago, Wal-Mart featured a blog about two ordinary people, Laura and Jim, trekking across the Unites States in an RV and staying in Wal-Mart parking lots. The blog appeared to be written by a couple who were avid customers of Wal-Mart. The blog received considerable attention after *BusinessWeek* exposed Jim as a professional photo journalist employed by Edelman, Wal-Mart's public relations firm. Both Wal-Mart and Edelman received considerable criticism regarding the program because of the lack of transparency.[6]

The Word of Mouth Marketing Association provides guidelines for companies seeking to generate word-of-mouth communications through employees, agency employees, or even sponsors or agents. It encourages:

- Honesty of relationship—be honest about the relationship between consumers, advocates, and marketers.

- Honesty of opinion—be honest in presenting opinions about the brand, both good and bad.
- Honesty of identity—identify honestly who you are.[7]

BUZZ MARKETING STAGES

As shown in Figure 10.2 on the bottom of this page, buzz marketing can be compared to how a virus replicates, which consists of three stages: inoculation, incubation, and infection.[8] The inoculation stage corresponds to the product being introduced. During incubation, the product will be tried by a few innovators or trendsetters. In the infection stage, widespread use of the product occurs.

Only a few companies have been successful deploying buzz marketing during the inoculation stage, or product introduction. In most cases, buzz marketing will not be successful at this stage unless the company employs brand agents or brand ambassadors Otherwise, generating word-of-mouth communication can be virtually impossible. Previous research suggests that the true customer-generated buzz occurs only after awareness of the product has developed. That awareness typically requires advertising through traditional channels.[9]

BUZZ MARKETING PRECONDITIONS

Advertising and buzz communication programs from actual customers cannot create a successful buzz by themselves. Other preconditions should be met (see Figure 10.3). The product must be unique, new, or perform better than current brands. It should stand out and have distinct advantages over competitors. Although not essential, memorable advertising helps to generate buzz. Intriguing, different, and unique advertising captures attention and can generate talk among people. Getting consumers involved can enhance the creation of word-of-mouth communications.

Stride Sugarless Gum developed a Web site to complement the company's traditional advertising. The campaign used the tagline "Stride gum lasts a ridiculously long time." The company invited consumers to share what they would like to do for a ridiculously long time and post photographs of these activities on the Stride micro-site developed for the Sugarless Gum.[10]

Buzz marketing works for two primary reasons. First, as noted, people trust someone else's opinion more than paid advertising. Second, people like to render their opinions and share their thoughts. Many people exhibit an innate desire for social interaction and are concerned about the welfare of others. Sharing an opinion can build a person's ego and sense of self-worth, especially when the opinion leads to happiness or satisfaction with a particular product.

- Inoculation—the product is introduced.
- Incubation—the product is used by a few innovators or trendsetters.
- Infection—widespread use of the product occurs.

▲ **FIGURE 10.2**
The Stages of Buzz Marketing

Source: Adapted from Jim Matorin, "Infectious 'Buzz Marketing' Is a Smart Way to Build Customer Loyalty at Your Operation," *Nation's Restaurant News*, Vol. 41, no. 18 (April 30, 2007), pp. 18–20.

- Product must be unique, new, or superior.
- Brand must stand out.
- Advertising should be
  - Memorable
  - Intriguing
  - Different
  - Unique
- Consumer involvement with the brand

◀ **FIGURE 10.3**
Preconditions of Buzz Marketing

▲ After asking someone to take her picture, this individual can then talk about the camera.

STEALTH MARKETING

A special form of buzz marketing, **stealth marketing**, applies surreptitious practices to introduce a product to individuals or fails to disclose or reveal the true relationship with the brand. Someone posing as a tourist might ask people to take a photo with a new camera and then talk to them about the camera. An attractive model ordering a beer or soft drink can tell everyone about how great it tastes. In both instances, the company pays someone to extol the product's benefits.

One stealth marketing ploy that received national attention was a 6-minute video entitled "Bride Has Massive Hair Wig Out" featuring a young bride-to-be who was unhappy with her haircut. In the video, she starts hacking off her hair just prior to the wedding ceremony. Her friends try in vain to stop her. It turns out she was just acting. It was a cleverly produced video ad for Unilever's Sunsilk Haircare brand produced by its advertising agency. Thinking it was a real bride and real situation, the "Wig Out" video attracted millions of online viewers, was tweeted to thousands, appeared on blogs, was featured on CNN, and was the subject of talk shows before Unilever revealed the truth about it being the campaign's stealth marketing campaign.[11]

Stealth marketing thrives in the online world, especially with social media sites due to the ease of creating videos and offering brand endorsements. Most people are not likely to pass on traditional advertisement and clips. The result has been a rise in stealth approaches.

Some argue that stealth marketing represents a shrewd way to reach consumers and generate buzz. At the same time, the Word of Mouth Marketing Association has clearly stated the importance of honesty of relationship and honesty of identity. The Federal Trade Commission (FTC) has issued an opinion letter supporting the Word of Mouth Marketing Association regarding the full disclosure of any paid individuals in ads. The enticement to create stealth marketing campaigns that generate buzz remains, and the debate over the ethical implications will likely continue.

Guerrilla Marketing

Guerrilla marketing programs seek to obtain instant results using limited resources. The concept was developed by Jay Conrad Levinson. Historically, guerrilla marketing offers one of the most successful alternative media marketing programs. Its tactics rely on creativity, quality relationships, and the willingness to try unusual approaches. These programs were originally aimed at small businesses; however, now a wide array of firms use guerrilla marketing tactics. Guerrilla marketing emphasizes a combination of media, advertising, public relations, and surprises to reach consumers.

Guerrilla marketing utilizes alternative tactics and venues and focuses on finding creative ways of doing things. To be successful, the thinking process in the marketing department has to change. Discovering "touch points" with customers constitutes the first step. Touch points include the places where the customers eat, drink, shop, hang out, and sleep. Next, the marketing team identifies ways to reach consumers that are unique and memorable at one of those touch points. To do so requires creativity, imagination, and unorthodox thinking.

Traditional Marketing	Guerrilla Marketing
• Requires money	• Requires energy and imagination
• Geared to large businesses with big budgets	• Geared to small businesses and big dreams
• Results measured by sales	• Results measured by profits
• Based on experience and guesswork	• Based on psychology and human behavior
• Increases production and diversity	• Grows through existing customers and referrals
• Grows by adding customers	• Cooperates with other businesses
• Obliterates the competition	• Aims messages at individuals and small groups
• Aims messages at large groups	• Uses marketing to gain customer consent
• Uses marketing to generate sales	• "You Marketing" that looks at how can we help "You"
• "Me Marketing" that looks at "My" company	

Figure 10.4 compares guerrilla marketing to traditional marketing. Guerrilla marketing tends to focus on specific regions or areas. It is not a national or international campaign, and instead features personal communication. Creating excitement that spreads to others by word-of-mouth is the objective. Guerrilla marketing involves interacting with consumers, not just sending out a message. Building relationships with customers should be the outcome. By getting consumers to react or to do something, the program enhances the chance that the message will hit home. Advertisements reach consumers where they live, play, and work, in ways that are noticed. The eventual relationships that evolve help create brand loyalty and positive recommendations to other consumers. Consequently, guerrilla marketing requires an aggressive, grassroots approach to marketing. It should produce buzz. When carried out properly, guerrilla marketing becomes a powerful marketing weapon. Figure 10.5 on the next page identifies six reasons why companies should use guerrilla marketing.

In the Engobi case described in the Integrated Campaigns in Action segment at the end of this chapter, Pink Jacket Creative generated buzz about Engobi, a caffeine-enhanced snack chip, during the inoculation stage of the buzz process, which can be extremely difficult. As shown in the photo in this section, "Engobi Girls" were employed to distribute free samples of the chips and to generate interest in prospective customers as part of an ingenious guerrilla marketing campaign.

Lifestyle Marketing

Another program companies use to make contacts with consumers in more offbeat and relaxed settings, **lifestyle marketing**, involves identifying marketing methods associated with the hobbies and entertainment venues of the target audience. Lifestyle marketing

▲ Chick-fil-A used a guerilla marketing tactic with this unique cow display.

▶ "Engobi Girls" were a central component of the guerilla marketing campaign created by Pink Jacket Creative for a new form of snack chips.

Pink Jacket Creative, A Creative Factory

▶ **FIGURE 10.5**

Reasons for Using Guerrilla Marketing

Source: Based on Lin Zuo and Shari Veil, "Guerrilla Marketing and the Aqua Teen Hunger Force Fiasco," *Public Relations Quarterly* 51, no. 4 (Winter 2006–2007), pp. 8–11.

- To find a new way to communicate with consumers
- To interact with consumers
- To make advertising accessible to consumers
- To impact a spot market
- To create buzz
- To build relationships with consumers

includes contacting consumers at places such as farmer's markets, bluegrass festivals, citywide garage sales, flea markets, craft shows, stock car races, and other places where large concentrations of potential customers are found.

A wide range of consumer lifestyles create potential target groups, from relatively standard habits to more edgy and extreme behaviors. The energy drink Red Bull and the producers of the energy snack PowerBar gave free samples to people attending sports events, including football and baseball games. The concept was that people who watch sports would be more inclined to try the product.

Toyota gave away t-shirts to young music fans entering and leaving concerts by heavy-metal band Repulsion. On the t-shirts was modern artistic scene and small, boxy Scion car. The company hoped to draw adventurous young customers through this lifestyle marketing approach.[12] Finding a venue where the target market goes for relaxation, excitement, socialization, or enjoyment is the key to lifestyle marketing.

Experiential Marketing

One form of alternative marketing, **experiential marketing**, combines direct marketing, field marketing, and sales promotions into a single consumer experience. It typically involves direct marketing through interactive means such as special events and free samples. Experiential marketing seeks to engage consumers with the brand, rather than just providing a free sample. Bruce Burnett, chief executive of i2i Marketing suggests that experiential marketing, "gives consumers the opportunity to question as well as gain hands-on experience with a brand, allowing them to be more intimate with it, leading to a higher conversion rate."[13]

Cadillac developed a three-part experiential program aimed toward current and perspective buyers. All three events were invitation only. The first element featured a series of 14 golf clinics that paired golf instruction by the David Leadbetter Gold Academy and test drives of the Cadillac. The second element included a culinary tour in 13 different markets paired with the Cadillac SRX model. The third element, a 5-track based event that displayed a souped-up V-Series Cadillac sedan in a half-day of high performance driving and education with Skip Barber Racing School. Invitees participated in three modules: slalom breaking, lane change, and lap driving. GM's head of North American marketing Chris Perry stated that the experiential programs fit the Cadillac brand well because, "The Cadillac customer is one who is more entrepreneurial spirited, perhaps more interested in the latest technology, always looking for the new ideas and thinking, more outer directed.[14]

Jack Morton Worldwide created an experiential marketing campaign for Cotton, Inc. aimed at 18- to 34-year-old women. The traveling mall exhibit presented the songs "The Fabric of Our Lives" and "Dixie" sung by contemporary artists Zooey Deschanel (indie-rock), Miranda Lambert (country), and Jazmine Sullivan (R&B). Mall shoppers were able look into the singers' closets, which were filled with cotton clothes. Shoppers could also record a personal version of "The Fabric of Our Lives." The campaign's budget was $500,000 to $1 million. The exhibit provided mall shoppers with hands on contact with cotton fabrics.[15]

To increase the probability that a positive experience will occur from an experiential marketing event, companies should follow these steps:

Step 1   Choose a clear, concise market segment to target.

Step 2   Identify the right time and place to involve consumers with the brand. Choose opportunities that fit with consumers' lives and when they can engage with the brand emotionally and logically.

Step 3   Make sure the experience reveals clearly the brand's promise and represents the brand well to consumers.

Allowing consumers to enjoy the benefit of a good or service before actually making a purchase gives the program the greatest chance for success.[16]

Courtesy of Oak St. Associates Inc.

▲ The Po-Boy Preservation Festival offers an excellent venue for lifestyle marketing.

▼ Tracy is passing out samples of a new drink at a farmer's market.

JackF/Fotolia

Product Placements and Branded Entertainment

OBJECTIVE 10.2

What methods can be used to effectively employ product placements and branded entertainment?

Most marketers believe getting a product noticed has become increasingly difficult. In response, many firms increased expenditures on product placements and branded entertainment. Each coupled the popularity of an entertainment venue with a product or company.

PRODUCT PLACEMENTS

The planned insertion of a brand or product into a movie, television show, or program in some other, a **product placement**, serves the purpose of influencing viewers. Product placements have been a part of motion pictures since the beginning of the industry in the 1890s. Lever Brothers placed the company's soap brand in some of the early films. In the 1930s, Buick created a 10-picture deal with Warner Brothers for placements. Several tobacco companies paid actors to endorse and use the brands. Early television programs, such as the *Colgate Comedy Hour*, were sponsored by brands.

The biggest surge in product placement occurred in 1982 after Reese's Pieces were used to lure E.T. out of hiding as part of the plot of the movie. The placement of the Reese's Pieces spurred a 65 percent increase in sales following the movie's release.[17] With that surge, product placement continued to grow for both brands and TV shows. During a recent month, American Idol led all television shows with 208 paid product placements. The top brand in terms of product placement was Coca-Cola.[18] Figure 10.6 displays the top six brands and top six television shows for product placements.

Advertisers believe product placements lead to increased awareness and more positive attitudes toward the brand. In a few isolated cases, sales of a brand have increased. In most instances, however, no immediate impact on sales occurs. Research by Nielsen reveals the following about product placements:

- Brands placed within "emotionally engaging" television programs were recognized by 43 percent more viewers.
- Brand recognition increased 29 percent for brands placed in highly enjoyed programs.
- Positive brand feelings increased by 85 percent for brands placed in popular programs.[19]

Brand placement offers the advantage of a low cost per viewer, especially for movies. After a movie has finished at the cinema, it will usually be converted to a DVD for movie rental. From there, the movie may be converted to television for viewing on syndication outlets or one of the premium movie channels. It might also be made available on TV through video-on-demand. This expands a movie's reach beyond the cinema screen to other venues where it may be seen multiple times by individuals.

Harley-Davidson hired Davie Brown Entertainment to locate appropriate product placement opportunities in movies, television, music, and video games. For the first time in Harley-Davidson's history used product placement as its core marketing strategy. According to Dino Bernacchi, director of advertising and promotions for Harley-Davidson, "We want to use [product placement] to socialize Harley-Davidson motorcycling . . . Entertainment can sensationalize the excitement and thrill of riding

▶ **FIGURE 10.6**
Top Television Product Placements

Source: Based on "Product Placement Hits High Gear on American Idol, Broadcast's Top Series for Brand Mentions," *Advertising Age,* April 18, 2011, http://adage.com/print/227041.

Top Brands (Total occurrences/month)		Top Shows (Total occurrences/month)	
Coca-Cola	99	American Idol	208
AT&T	76	Celebrity Apprentice	127
Chevrolet	45	America's Next Top Model	88
Ford	39	Biggest Loser	88
Apple	32	Amazing Race	69
Everlast	32	Shedding the Wedding	40
Nike	32	Dancing with the Stars	38

to the point of moving people to check it out." Only 3 percent of American consumers own a motorcycle, but another 15 to 20 million have the desire to buy one. Harley-Davidson believes strategic product placements will encourage those on the edge to go ahead and make the purchase.[20]

Glamour magazine developed a unique type of product placement. *Glamour* produced four original episodes of a series called *Glamour Girls* exclusively for the iPad. Viewers could pause the program at any time, tap on an item of clothing worn by one of the actresses, and immediately be taken to Gap.com where the person could purchase the clothing. The program integrated the sponsor's brand seamlessly into *Glamour* content.[21]

BRANDED ENTERTAINMENT

The integration of entertainment and advertising by embedding brands into the storyline of a movie, television show, or other entertainment medium, or **branded entertainment** features that are similar to product placements.[22] In an episode of the CTV drama *The Eleventh Hour*, for example, Nicorette was integrated into a story about a character trying to quit smoking.

▲ Harley Davidson emphasized product placement in television shows, movies, music, and video games in a recent marketing campaign.

The movie *Up in the Air* starring George Clooney prominently displayed American Airlines and Hilton Hotels. The movie's plot involves Clooney's character logging 10 million miles on American so he can have his name emblazoned on the plane and ride along with American Airlines' chief pilot. Actual American Airlines planes were used in the film. Many of the hotel scenes were filmed at Hilton locations. Integrating the brands into the story made them much more noticeable to the viewing audience.[23]

The use of branded entertainment has increased with the rise of reality television shows that the focus on creating "real-world" situations. The success of branded entertainment in reality shows has led to its use in scripted television shows. Branded entertainment may also be found in novels, plays, songs, and movies.

ACHIEVING SUCCESS

Figure 10.7 identifies the major factors that influence the success of brand placements and branded entertainment. The media used has an impact on effectiveness. Some television programs have lost clout due to placement clutter. For instance, 4,349 product placements were used during Fox's *American Idol* show from January to May in one season.[24] Only the prominent brands, such as the red plastic cups of Coca-Cola in front of the judges, were noticeable. Most were lost in the clutter of other brands appearing on the show.

- Media
- Supporting promotional activities
- Consumer attitudes toward placements
- Placement characteristics
- Regulations

▲ **FIGURE 10.7**
Key Factors Influencing the Effectiveness of Product Placement and Branded Entertainment

Source: Based on Simon Hudson and David Hudson, "Branded Entertainment: A New Advertising Technique or Product Placement in Disguise?" *Journal of Marketing Management* 22, no. 5/6 (July 2006). pp. 489–504.

Product placements and branded entertainment work because no "call to action" appears. Instead, increasing brand awareness and generating positive feelings toward the brand are the goals. When a consumer's favorite actor enjoys a particular brand or her favorite show contains a particular brand, it becomes more likely that the individual will transfer those positive feelings to the brand. People between the ages of 15 and 34 are more likely to notice brands placed in a movie or show. Also, individuals in North America and the Asia-Pacific area are more receptive than viewers in Europe. When a consumer sees a brand placement of a product that he has purchased, it may reinforce that idea that a wise decision was made, further validating the original purchase decision.[25]

Company Tactics   The actual manner in which a brand is placed into a movie or show is important. Brand insertions work best when they seem logical. In other words, the most effective placements are those woven into the program in such a way that it appears to be a natural part of the story. Brands shown in the background that seem to be artificially inserted are less effective.

For some companies, product placement in movies delivers the advantage of bypassing most of the legislation and guidance intended to control advertising to children and young adults. A study of the top 25 box office movies revealed that 32 percent were rated for viewing by adolescents and contained prominent brand placements for tobacco products. If these companies would have tried to advertise directly to teens, they would have encountered numerous regulations and severe penalties.[26]

Many companies buy advertising spots on television programs that feature product placements of the brand. Additional promotional incentives may also be offered. This helps move the consumer beyond recognition and liking to the actual purchase.

Budgets for product placements and branded entertainment have been increasing for several reasons. First, a brand's appeal may be stronger when it appears in a non-advertising context. Second, the perception of what others think of a brand is important to consumers. For many, it can be more important than how the consumer views the brand. Seeing the brand being used in a television show, a movie, or a book makes the brand look acceptable and even desirable. Third, seeing the brand used by others provides postpurchase reassurance for individuals who already bought the item.

Fourth, for individuals who place little value in brand names and branded products, having a brand placed in a program provides evidence of the brand's advantages. The evidence may be strong enough for them to consider purchasing the brand. In these cases, the brand does not have to directly persuade the consumer of its merits. It does so through the acceptance and use of the brand by the actor or program.

The Media's Perspective   For moviemakers and television producers, money represents the primary motivation behind product placements and branded entertainment. In the past, brand mentions were incidental or used by movie producers to create realism in a film. They now generate additional income. Martha Stewart charges $10,000 for a 30-second placement on her show. For a one-time mention in the show with a product close-up, the price goes up to $100,000. For a 2-minute branded entertainment segment with two or three talking points, the price rises to more than $250,000.[27]

In summary, brand placements present an excellent method to increase share of mind and build brand awareness. Although some are concerned that programs are becoming saturated with product placements, they continue to be utilized. If clutter becomes too severe, usage will be likely to decline, but only if the impact on consumer responses and attitudes also declines.

OBJECTIVE 10.3

Why has the use of alternative media venues, especially video game advertising, grown in marketing communications programs?

Alternative Media Venues

In upper New York, before crossing one of the five bridges operated by the New York State Bridge Authority, a driver must pay a toll or have an EZ-pass. Advertisements now appear on the mechanical arms that come down at the toll booth for a popular tourist attraction called Headless Horseman Hayrides and Haunted Houses. The owner, Nancy

◀ **FIGURE 10.8**
Examples of Alternative Media

- Video games
- Cinema
- Subways
- Street and mall kiosks
- Stairs
- Escalators
- Parking lots
- Airlines
- Shopping bags
- Clothes

◀ **FIGURE 10.8**
Examples of Alternative Media

Jubie, reported "This is so in-your-face advertising we couldn't pass it up." The cost to put the name of her business on a toll booth arm for 3 months was $18,000.[28] Many companies look for unusual and unlikely places to attract attention. Figure 10.8 identifies some of the forms alternative forms of media.

VIDEO GAME ADVERTISING

Product placements in video games have become common. Products can be part of a stand-alone game purchased at a retail store and played on the computer or they can be placed in an Internet video game. In-game brand placement enjoys all of the advantages of brand placements and branded entertainment. Video game advertising reaches young people, who have become more difficult to contact through traditional media. In addition, it has the added feature of interactivity. Advertisers spend approximately $7 billion per year on in-game advertising. It presents an attractive market for the following reasons:

- 75 percent of all U.S. Internet users spend at least 1 hour a month playing online games.
- 27 percent average 30 hours a month playing games.
- The primary game-playing market segment is 16- to 34-year-old males.
- The fastest-growing video game market segment is females.[29]

Video game advertising takes several forms (see Figure 10.9). The original and most widespread form of video game advertising involves locating a brand placement in the game. It can take the form of a billboard in a racing game, a Coke vending machine, or a McDonald's restaurant that is permanently integrated into the game. With the cost of producing a game now in the $20 to $30 million range, game producers welcome product placement advertising as a source of revenue.

The number of game-related Web sites has exploded in recent years. Rather than placing ads in the game itself, advertisers place ads on these gaming Web sites. Although the exact number of gaming Web sites has not been identified, estimates suggest that more than 6,000 exist. Some of these sites receive as many as 7 million visits per year.[30]

Numerous companies offer video games to be played on branded Web sites. These branded video games are called **advergames**. Axe, a brand of men's deodorant, offers an online game for men. The game allows the individual to test their "pickup" skills with 100 different "hot" women. Players collect and use pickup moves to try to woo the women featured in the game.

Other companies vending advergames include Maxwell House, Holiday Inn, Baskin-Robbins, and Suave. Instead of creating a special micros-site for the game, the advergames are placed on free gaming portals, such as Kewlbox (www.kewlbox.com), where 90 percent of the games are advergames, which are offered for free. They are played 500,000 to 700,000 times per day.[31] Blockdot.com research indicates

◀ **FIGURE 10.9**
Video Game Advertising

- In-game advertisements
- Rotating in-game advertising
- Interactive ads
- Game-related Web sites
- Advergames
- Sponsored downloads

that consumers have positive feelings about brands that sponsor advergames. More specifically, 83 percent of consumers think positively about companies that underwrite advergames and 70 percent are more likely to buy products from companies that sponsor the games.[32]

In addition to game-related Web sites, advertisers are attracted to the social gaming market. According to Nielsen, Americans spend nearly 25 percent of the time they are on the Internet on social networking and blogging sites. More exciting to advertisers, gaming has passed email as the second most popular online activity, behind social networking. Of the 800 million individuals on Facebook, 53 percent have played games on the site and 20 percent play them regularly.[33]

Benefits   IGA Worldwide research revealed that the majority of gamers like seeing ads in video games, if they are well done and fit in the scene. The study noted that 82 percent of gamers find the games to be just as enjoyable when ads were present. A 44 percent increase in recall of brands resulted from ads being presented in games when compared to awareness prior to exposure in the video game. Positive brand attribute associations also increased.[34]

Online video games offer advertisers the luxury of using quality Web metrics. Advertisers can track the length of ad exposure in an online game. In most cases, the company can tie in demographic information to find out who views the in-game ad, how long they play, and how often. These metrics then make it possible to target ads specifically to the consumer, demographic group, location profile, or type of player.[35]

New Video Game Technology   Product placement within a game faces the disadvantage of soon becoming static and consequently the player no longer notices it. To combat this problem, Massive, a new media company, has pioneered a technology that rotates or changes ads in online video games in real time. Advertisers can insert new ads and products into the online game each time the person plays it. By changing the ads, the marketing team delivers time-sensitive promotions and the advertising remains current. Massive can make the advertisement interactive, allowing the player to click on it for additional information. Additional technology can measure how much of a billboard or product placement a player sees during the game depending on their in-game actions. Technology can then fine tune the player's surroundings so that the missed ad will reappear later in the game.[36]

CINEMA ADVERTISING

Prior to a movie showing, most theaters present advertisements during pre-feature programming. Some products may have direct relationships with the movie, others are totally unrelated. Although clutter exists in the sense that the commercials often run consecutively and be mingled with new movie previews, they are delivered to what essentially is a "captive" audience waiting for the feature to start.

Cinema advertising rarely appears at the center of an integrated ad campaign, but that was the case with HP's launch of the Photosmart Premium printer with TouchSmart Web. According to Tariq Hassan, HP's vice president of marketing, "We had to create more awareness; we had to touch the consumer. The theater was a natural fit." The cinema campaign included a 30-second spot in the pre-feature programming at 17,300 theaters and 2,600 plasma screens in theater lobbies. It also executed an interactive "lobby domination" strategy in 15 theaters in New York, Chicago, San Francisco, San Diego, Miami, and Houston. Theater lobbies were turned into branded events with banners, signage, holographic 3-D kiosks, and large manned booths where the printer was demonstrated. The campaign delivered 50,000 product demonstrations averaging 6 minutes in length and a total of 700,000 lobby impressions.[37]

OTHER ALTERNATIVE MEDIA

A number of additional media alternatives are available. Ads now appear on subways and other public facilities as local and state governments struggle to balance budgets. Parking lots, stairs, and escalators all feature advertising displays. Airlines increase revenues by presenting advertisements on flight-ticket jackets and using in-plane signage. Shopping bags, clothes, and restaurant menus provide additional advertising venues.

Alternative media was an important component of the advertising campaign for Unleashed Dog Parks created by the Pink Jacket Creative advertising agency. As shown in the two photos in this section, Pink Jacket added a street kiosk ad and a bus wrap ad to reinforce the billboards that were running. The objective was to reach people during routine moments in their daily lives.

The out-of-home component of a recent Kraft Lunchables with Fruit campaign was unique in its use of alternative venues. The company descended on the three largest U.S. markets—Chicago, New York, and Los Angeles with fruit news on about every street corner. In partnership with Feeding America, interactive storefronts were developed. Consumers could engage with the storefronts to contribute to Feeding America. In addition to the interactive storefronts, Lunchables took over bus shelters with dynamic lenticular printing, dominated billboards, sides of buildings, and Time Square.

A new innovative form of alternative media utilizes facial recognition technology. A digital display in a shopping mall with this technology can recognize a female in her 20s standing in front of it. Ads touting makeup, shoes, fashions and ice cream then pop up. If a man in his 50s moves in front of the display a different set of ads appears.

▲ A street kiosk advertisement for Unleashed Dog Parks created by the Pink Jacket Creative advertising agency.

◀ A bus wrap advertisement for Unleashed Dog Parks created by the Pink Jacket Creative advertising agency.

In summary, the popularity of using nontraditional formats to deliver advertising messages continues to increase. Each time an innovative marketing professional identifies a new venue, a segment of the advertising community jumps on board. These methods make it possible to send messages that either cut through or go around clutter to reach people in moments when they may be more receptive to an advertisement's content.

In-Store Marketing

OBJECTIVE 10.4

How have in-store marketing and point-of-purchase displays evolved into even more effective communication and sales tools?

Consumers make approximately 60 percent of all purchase decisions in the retail store.[38] Except for point-of-purchase (POP) displays, many companies do not give much attention to in-store marketing. Funds devoted to it represent a small percentage of advertising and marketing budgets. This may mean companies are missing an opportunity.

To understand the potential of in-store advertising, consider what affects consumers as they purchase clothing. In a survey of about 600 consumers, 52 percent said that in-store signage, displays, or point-of-purchase displays influenced their decisions, far outdistancing print advertising and word-of-mouth communications.[39] Figure 10.10 on the next page displays a complete list of these influences.

IN-STORE MARKETING TACTICS

The in-store shopping experience has a major impact on purchase decisions. In a survey of shoppers, 69 percent called the in-store time the "make or break" experience. "Understanding high potential shopper strike zones has become increasingly critical given the intensified battle for consumer loyalty and share of mind in-store," commented D'Anna Hawthorne, strategic director at Miller Zell, a retail consulting firm. Companies now try to engage consumers, not just merchandise items on a shelf. According to consumers, end-aisle displays and merchandise displays are the most engaging. Ceiling banners and overhead mobiles are the least engaging.[40]

The use of color, light, and sound has long been a part of in-store marketing. Retailers may also add *motion*. Placing and using video screens and television monitors to present messages represents the newest and most expensive in-store marketing tactic. Many static signs have been replaced with high-technology mediums. Also, shopping carts with static signs that are broken or unreadable are being replaced with video screens. Digital media within the store offers retailers the opportunity to customize messages to fit the store and the aisle where the display is located.[41]

Airplay America produces The Salon Channel, a retail television channel and digital signage network for beauty salons. Programming consists of human interest and lifestyle stories. Beauty shop patrons spend an average of 30 to 45 minutes per salon visit. The Salon Channel provides entertainment, including features about nationally-recognized stylists and the latest hairstyles, along with advertisements for products and services, many of which are related to beauty and fashion.[42]

Wal-Mart follows the same path. In the past, Wal-Mart's ads appeared on all in-store televisions at the same time. With new technologies, the marketing department distributes ads geared to each department within a store and for specific aisles. Wal-Mart uses the approach in 1,200 stores on more than 100,000 television monitors. Rather than hanging television monitors from the ceiling, flat-screen panel monitors are placed at eye level in the aisles, which leads to greater ad

pressmaster/Fotolia

▲ Approximately 60 percent of all purchase decisions are made in the retail store.

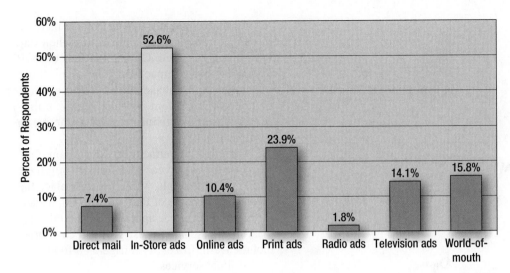

◀ **FIGURE 10.10**

Types of Advertising That Most
Influenced Clothing Purchases

Source: Adapted from Amy Johannes,
"Snap Decisions," *Promo* 18, no. 11
(October 2006), p. 16

recall. Digital monitors are also being installed at end-caps and at point-of-purchase displays. These television monitors contain advertising pertinent to the end-cap or POP display.[43]

To fully appreciate the potential impact of this form of in-store advertising, consider this: Each week 68 million viewers watch the combined national television newscasts of Scott Pelley, Brian Williams, and Diane Sawyer. The number of shoppers at Wal-Mart each week tops 127 million. The potential audience for a commercial on the Wal-Mart television system will be nearly twice as large as an advertisement on the three national newscasts.[44] In addition, the Wal-Mart ad reaches consumers as they shop and as they make purchase decisions.

A final in-store tactic relies on the other senses, *taste* and *smell*. Using scents to enhance a shopping experience is not new. New methods include releasing pheromones into the store's air to make customers feel aroused and sexy. Others retailers rely on less controversial approaches, such as baking and selling pastries and offering specialty coffees and teas. High-end retailers often present patrons with hot tea as part of the shopping experience to personalize the shopping experience and makes it more pleasant, which may cause the customer to return.

Point-of-Purchase Tactics

Traditionally, one of the most important components of in-store marketing has been **point-of-purchase displays (POP)**, which include any form of special exhibit that advertises merchandise. Retailers locate point-of-purchase displays near cash registers, at the end of an aisle, in a store's entryway, or anywhere they will be noticed. Point-of-purchase advertising includes displays, signs, and devices used to identify, advertise, or merchandise an outlet, service, or product. POP displays can serve as an important aid to retail selling.

Point-of-purchase displays remain highly effective tools for increasing sales. Nearly 50 percent of the money spent at mass merchandisers and supermarkets results from unplanned, impulse buys. For food purchases, 88 percent of the decisions about brands are made in the store. Overall, 67 percent of purchase decisions are made in the store. In many instances, point-of-purchase materials and other in-store advertising enticements influenced the decision.[45]

Coca-Cola reports that only 50 percent of soft drink sales are made from the regular store shelf. The other 50 percent results from product displays in other parts of the store. American Express discovered that 30 percent of purchases charged on the American Express card came from impulse decisions by customers seeing the "American Express Cards Welcome" sign.

Courtesy of Bijan Fragrances, Inc.

▲ Point-of-purchase displays help sell products such as cosmetics, perfume, or cologne.

Research indicates that an average increase in sales of about 9 percent occurs when one POP display is used. Only about half of POP display actually impact sales; however, those that increase purchases do so by an average of nearly 20 percent. Consequently, point-of-purchase advertising remains attractive to manufacturers.[46]

Currently, manufacturers spend more than $17 billion each year on point-of-purchase advertising materials. Manufacturers place the greatest percentage of POP materials in restaurants, food services, apparel stores, and footwear retailers. The fastest-growing categories include fresh, frozen, or refrigerated foods and professional services.[47]

Manufacturers view point-of-purchase displays as an attractive method of displaying a brand more prominently in front of customers. Many retailers have a different perspective, believing that POP materials should either boost sales for the store or draw customers into the store. Retailers are not interested in the sales of one particular brand, but instead want to improve overall sales and store profits. Retailers prefer displays that educate consumers and provide information. As a result, retailers are most inclined to set up displays to match the retailer's marketing objectives.

DESIGNING EFFECTIVE POINT-OF-PURCHASE DISPLAYS

To be effective, POP displays should clearly communicate the product's attributes. The price and other promotional information should be included. The display should encourage the customer to stop and look, pick up the product, and examine it. A customer who stops to examine a product on display becomes more likely to buy the item.

© Tyler Olson/Fotolia

▲ Point-of-purchase displays are often located near cash registers.

Effective displays make succinct offers that the customer immediately understands. In most cases, a display has a limited time to capture the customer's attention. If it fails, the customer simply moves on to other merchandise. Colors, designs, merchandise arrangements, and tie-ins with other marketing messages are critical elements of effective POP displays.

The best point-of-purchase displays are integrated with other marketing messages. Logos and message themes used in advertisements should appear on the display. A study by the Saatchi & Saatchi advertising agency revealed that consumers make purchase decisions in just 4 seconds. On average, a consumer only looks at a display or signage for 3 to 7 seconds.[48] Tying a POP display into current advertising and marketing increases the chances of it being noticed. The display should present any form of special

- Integrate the brand's image into the display.
- Integrate the display with current advertising and promotions.
- Make the display dramatic to get attention.
- Keep the color of the display down so the product and signage stand out.

- Make the display versatile so it can be easily adapted by retailers.
- Make the display reusable and easy to assemble.
- Make the display easy to stock.
- Customize the display to fit the retailer's store.

sales promotion that the company offers. Customers quickly recognize tie-ins with current advertising and promotional themes as they view displays. Figure 10.11 lists some additional pointers for point-of-purchase advertising.

MEASURING POINT-OF-PURCHASE EFFECTIVENESS

Manufactures and retailers both seek to measure the effectiveness of POP displays. Linking the POP display into a point-of-sale (POS) cash register makes it easier to gather results. Items on the display are coded so that the POS system picks them up. Then individual stores measure sales before and during a point-of-purchase display program by using cash register data. The data also helps the retailer decide when it is time to withdraw or change a display as sales begin to decline. The technology enables retailers to identify the displays that generate the largest impact on sales. A retailer might deploy this method to test different types of POP displays in various stores. The most effective displays can then be expanded to a larger number of stores.

From the manufacturer's viewpoint, point-of-sale data helps to improve POP displays. The data may also be used to strengthen partnerships with retailers. These bonds help the manufacturer weather poor POP showings. Retailers are more willing to stay with a manufacturer that tries to develop displays that benefit both parties.

Brand Communities

The ultimate demonstration of brand loyalty and brand devotion takes the form of **brand communities**. In most cases, a symbolic meaning behind the brand links individuals to the brand community and other owners of the brand. The identity and belonging are formed through interactions between customers and with the product. A set of shared values and experiences that integrate with feelings about the brand becomes the result.

Brand communities do not always form. They cannot be created by the brand itself; however, a marketing department can facilitate and enhance the community experience. A company with a strong brand community maintains a positive image, has a rich and long tradition, occupies a unique position in the marketplace, and enjoys a group of loyal, dedicated followers.[49] Figure 10.12 highlights some of the reasons that brand communities exist. Most brand communities require some type of face-to-face interactions, although the Internet does provide a venue for members to contact each other and to blog about the product.

Jeep, Harley-Davidson, and Apple all enjoy loyal brand communities. In each case, the brand owners are diverse as evidenced by the Jeep Jamborees and Camp Jeep events. The events allow Jeep owners the opportunity to share driving experiences, tell stories, and share ideas. Most of the interactions among customers occur during the company-sponsored barbecue. They also take place during roundtable discussions hosted by a Jeep engineer or other Jeep employee.

Many, if not most, of the attendees at a Camp Jeep event have no experience driving a Jeep off-road. Among those who have, some use a "tread lightly" ethos, whereas others

OBJECTIVE 10.5

How can brand communities enhance brand loyalty and devotion?

▼ **FIGURE 10.12**

Reasons Brand Communities Form

- Affirmation of the buying decision
- Social identity and bonding
- Swap stories
- Swap advice and provide help to others
- Feedback and new ideas

▶ **FIGURE 10.13**

Ways to Enhance a Brand
Community Spirit

Source: Based on "Brand Communities,"
Bulletpoint, no. 133 (July 2006), pp. 12–16

- Create member benefits to encourage new customers to join a group.
- Provide materials to the group that are not available anywhere else.
- Involve firm representatives in the groups.

- Sponsor special events and regular meetings.
- Promote communications among members of the group.
- Build a strong brand reputation.

have mud-covered vehicles from heavy off-road adventures. First timers at the camp are often timid and afraid they might not fit in, but soon find they do as repeaters fully welcome anyone and everyone to the Jeep community. The vehicle provides the common bond that brings individuals together regardless of demographic and psychographic differences.

Perhaps Harley-Davidson represents the best example of a brand community. The company's leadership team helped create a unique brand community spirit. An organization called HOG has formed around the Harley brand. In return, Harley-Davidson offers benefits, such as information about community gatherings along with special marketing offers for accessories, to HOG members. The benefits are only available to the HOG group. This encourages new Harley-Davidson owners to join the HOG brand community.

Marketers seek to facilitate and enhance the community in which owners can interact. Figure 10.13 provides information on ways a marketing team can assist in creating a brand community.

Building a brand community begins with sponsoring events that bring product owners together. Jeep sponsors both the jamborees and a camp. Harley-Davidson sponsors rides, rallies, and local events. These events are critical in creating a brand community spirit and allow for bonding between owners. Eventually this produces a sense of social identity.

Company representatives should become involved in club events. Jeep engineers attend events and mingle with customers. They provide advice and encouragement to any new owner about to take his or her vehicle off-road for the first time. Harley managers, including the CEO, ride Harleys to rallies to talk with owners.

In addition to company-sponsored events, other venues for interaction can be encouraged. The Internet offers another place for owners to talk. They can visit through blogs, chat rooms, or social network micro-sites. The company can become involved in these exchange venues. Employees should openly identify themselves. Brand communities enjoy company involvement and want an honest exchange of comments.

While providing venues and means for developing a brand community spirit, the company continues other advertising and marketing programs. A brand community normally grows around a brand with a strong image. That image should be maintained. Marketers feature the pride of owning the brand in advertisements, making its uniqueness and position in the marketplace clear.

International Implications

Alternative marketing can be used to reach minority groups within the United States. An example of buzz marketing occurred when the Clamato company sought to increase brand awareness among U.S. Latinos. The firm gave 2,000 agents a 32-ounce

▼ Skyjacker has a brand community consisting of off-road enthusiasts.

bottle of Clamato and 10 coupons. The agents reached 34,000 potential customers, and positive opinions of the drink rose from 32 to 78 percent.[50]

Alternative marketing methods are being tried in other countries. Starbucks and Pepsi combined efforts to produce a movie series called *A Sunny Day*. The film follows a girl from the Chinese countryside to the big city, where she discovers love, blogging, Starbucks, and Pepsi. The series was tailored for Shanghai's subway and the 2.2 million who ride it each day. The story was made into a soap opera-style script featuring short daily segments. A Web site featured story snippets each day for those who missed seeing it on the subway and wanted to know what happened. The Shanghai subway has a network of 4,000 flat-screen monitors that provide train information, clips of soccer highlights, entertainment news, and advertising. Marketers pay to run ads, just like they would on television. *A Sunny Day* was the system's first venture into a short miniseries, with episodes each day for 40 weeks.[51]

Brand communities are developing in other countries. Jeep employed the brand community concept to build a brand presence in China. The first Jeep was introduced in China in 1983 by American Motors through a joint venture in Beijing; however, recent sales of Jeep have slowed. In response, the first 3-day Camp Jeep in China was created. It attracted 700 Jeep owners and 3,000 participants. The event included off-road courses, bungee jumping, a hiking course, wall climbing, a soccer field, and an off-road ATV course. Musical entertainment and time slots for karaoke enthusiasts were provided.[52] The event's purpose was to renew Jeep's strong brand name and to create a strong sense of community among current Jeep owners in China. Through these individuals, Jeep hopes to generate word-of-mouth, or buzz, for the Jeep brand, driving new customers to the Jeep brand.

The clutter problems that plague U.S. advertisers are present around the world. The tactics being used to overcome it domestically will be adapted to international operations. Firms from other nations will adapt alternative media tactics. International conglomerates will also respond with new and creative alternative marketing programs.

OBJECTIVE 10.6

What methods are used to adapt alternative marketing programs to international marketing efforts?

INTEGRATED CAMPAIGNS IN ACTION

Engobi

A notable example of guerrilla marketing is provided by the Engobi campaign created by the Pink Jacket Creative advertising agency. Engobi, the world's first caffeine-infused snack chip, was developed by Rudolph Foods Company. Due to a limited media budget, traditional media were not feasible for the product launch.

Engobi needed to get consumers to both hear about and try the product. This required a unique approach. The team quickly realized that guerrilla marketing was the way to go. A strong device was needed to anchor the brand and portray it as a snack that "hip" individuals would eat. The "Engobi" girl was born. She had cinnamon-and-lemon-colored beehive hair, nerdy glasses, and a sexy lab coat with fishnet stockings. She was impossible to ignore. She was placed inside "vending machines" and provided free samples of the chips.

Courtesy of Pink Jacket Creative, A Creative Factory

▲ The Engobi human vending machine was so captivating it resulted in an average sampling time of 18 to 26 seconds, versus the standard 3 seconds.

MyMarketingLab

Go to **mymktlab.com** to complete the problems marked with this icon .

SUMMARY

Alternative media enjoys many success stories. Well-known brands, such as Ben & Jerry's and Starbucks, have emerged using very little traditional advertising. Each found new methods to establish a brand presence, including alternative media and alternative marketing methods. Starbucks built a community of coffee lovers through local involvement and word-of-mouth.

The four forms of alternative marketing programs are buzz marketing, stealth marketing, guerrilla marketing, and product placements. Buzz marketing, or word-of-mouth marketing, places the emphasis on consumers passing along information about a brand. The consumers can be those who like a brand, sponsored consumers, or company insiders. Some consider using company insiders to be unethical.

Stealth marketing uses surreptitious practices to introduce a product to individuals or fails to disclose or reveal the true relationship with the brand. It also draws ethical criticism.

Guerrilla marketing programs are those designed to obtain instant results with limited resources through creativity, high-quality relationships, and a willingness to try unusual approaches. Lifestyle marketing involves the use of marketing methods associated with the hobbies and entertainment venues of the target audience. Experiential marketing combines direct marketing, field marketing, and sales promotions into a single consumer experience.

Product placements are planned insertions of a brand or product into a movie, television program, or some other media program. Branded entertainment facilitates the integration of entertainment and advertising by embedding brands into the storyline of a movie, television show, or other entertainment medium.

Numerous alternative media venues exist. They include mobile phone advertising, video game advertising and advergames, cinema advertising, airline in-flight advertising, and others. Use of these media has been on the increase.

In-store marketing programs take two forms. New tactics include the use of high-tech video screens and television monitors in new and more visible places. This includes tailoring messages to individual parts of the store. Traditional point-of-purchase advertising continues to be widely utilized. Recently, POP advertising incorporates newer technologies to increase its effectiveness.

Brand communities evolve when consumers feel a great deal of brand loyalty and devotion. They form around events, programs, and exchanges of information. A company with a strong brand and a devoted marketing team can assist in the formation and continuance of brand communities.

Alterative media choices are being utilized to reach minority groups in the United States in unique new ways. They are also expanding into international markets. As advertising clutter increases, the use of these media is likely to grow, and will likely become cluttered as well.

Key Terms

buzz marketing Emphasizes consumers passing along information about a product to others; also known as *word-of-mouth marketing*.

stealth marketing The use of surreptitious practices to introduce a product to individuals without disclosing or revealing the true relationship with the brand.

guerrilla marketing Programs designed to obtain instant results through the use of limited resources by relying on creativity, high-quality relationships, and the willingness to try new approaches.

lifestyle marketing Marketing methods associated with the hobbies and entertainment venues of the target audience.

experiential marketing A program that combines direct marketing, field marketing, and sales promotions into a single consumer experience.

product placement The planned insertion of a brand or product into a movie, television show, or some other media program.

branded entertainment The integration of entertainment and advertising by embedding brands into the storyline of a movie, television show, or other entertainment medium.

advergames Branded video games.

point-of-purchase displays (POP) Any form of special display that advertises merchandise.

brand communities A link that forms due to an association between the brand, a consumer, and others who own or purchase the brand.

Review Questions

1. What are the main alternative media programs described in this chapter?
2. What is buzz marketing?
3. What three types of consumers can pass along buzz marketing messages?
4. Why is buzz marketing effective? What preconditions should be met to ensure its effectiveness?
5. What is stealth marketing?
6. What is guerrilla marketing? How does it differ from traditional marketing?
7. What is lifestyle marketing? What types of locations are suited to lifestyle marketing?
8. What is experiential marketing?
9. What are product placements and branded entertainment? What do they have in common?
10. Identify the alternative media venues described in this chapter.
11. Describe the forms of video game advertising, including advergames.
12. What is in-store marketing? Why is it important?
13. What new in-store marketing tactics are being utilized?
14. What is point-of-purchase advertising? Why is it important?
15. How have new technologies changed some forms of point-of-purchase advertising?
16. What is a brand community?
17. What should a company's marketing team do to assist in the development and growth of brand communities?
18. Is the use of alternative media growing or declining in international markets? Explain why.

Critical Thinking Exercises

DISCUSSION QUESTIONS

1. Consider a set of products to which you feel a strong level of loyalty. Would you consider being a brand advocate, ambassador, or evangelist for a brand? Pick the brand where your loyalty is the highest. What type of offer would it take from the company for you to become a brand ambassador? What would you do to be an effective advocate for that brand?
2. Consider a recent purchase you made at the recommendation of someone else. Why did you trust that person's recommendation? How important is a recommendation by someone else in your purchase decisions?
3. Can you think of a lifestyle marketing program or an experiential marketing campaign that you encountered? What was your reaction? Was the approach effective with you? Why or why not? What about with other consumers? If you have not experience lifestyle or experiential marketing, think of a situation and brand where you think it would be effective. Explain why.
4. Imagine being approached by the owner of a small clothing boutique. She has heard about guerrilla marketing and wants to try it. Why should she use guerrilla marketing? What are the pros and cons? What guerrilla marketing techniques would you suggest?
5. Find a movie that you have already watched and enjoyed. Watch it again, but this time, make a list of all of the product placements in the file. Identify if each was a prominent placement, if the actor used the brand, or if it was just in the background. When you finish, discuss the product placements that were the most effective and those that were the least effective. What made the placement effective? What made it ineffective?
6. Do you play video games? If so, approximately how many hours a month do you play games (including online games)? What advertising have you noticed in the games? How effective was the advertising?
7. Go to a nearby retail store. Examine the point-of-purchase displays in the store. Which ones were the most impressive? Why? Which ones did not succeed at getting your attention? Why not? Go back to the store a week later. How many of the displays have changed? What is your overall evaluation of the point-of-purchase displays used by the retailer?
8. Go to a nearby retail store and talk to the manager or one of the employees. Ask them about the store signage, including point-of-purchase displays. Ask the employee to discuss what signage is effective and why. As a customer, did you agree with the manager's or employee's viewpoint? Why or why not?

Integrated Learning Exercises

1. Access **www.igda.org/women**. What is your overall opinion of this Web site? How can it be beneficial to a marketing manager? How can it be beneficial to females who want to pursue video game design? Go to the parent Web site **www.igda.org**. What types of information is available at this site?

2. Access the Word of Mouth Marketing Association Web site at **www.womma.org**. List the alternative names used for word-of-mouth marketing. Do you think these are good synonyms for word-of-mouth communications? Why or why not? What features did you find on the site? What benefits does the site provide? What value would the site be to a business? Is there any value for a consumer?

3. Type "buzz marketing" into an online search engine. Find two advertising agencies or marketing agencies that offer buzz marketing expertise. Which company do you think offers the best buzz marketing program? Why?

4. Type "guerrilla marketing" into an online search engine. Find two agencies that offer guerrilla marketing services. Describe what type of services each offers. Go to an article database and type in "guerrilla marketing." Find two articles about guerrilla marketing that are of interest to you. Summarize the articles.

5. Online gaming has become very popular, especially with the 16- to 34-year-old demographic. Access the Kewlbox Web site at www.kewlbox.com. Discuss the various games that are available. Locate some advergames. Who were the sponsoring brands? What is your evaluation of the game site?

6. Point-of-purchase displays should be an important component of a firm's IMC program. Research indicates that effective displays have a positive impact on sales. Access the following firms that produce point-of-purchase displays. Which firm's site is the most attractive? Which firm would be the best from the standpoint of developing displays for a manufacturer? Explain.
   a. Acrylic Designs, Inc. (**www.acrylicdesigns.com**)
   b. Vulcan Industries (**www.vulcanind.com**)
   c. Display Design & Sales (**www.displays4pop.com**)

Student Project

CREATIVE CORNER

Ugg is the brand name for an Australian company that sells big, bulky sheepskin boots. The company's marketing team wondered if it would be possible to get fashion-conscious consumers to even consider the boots. Instead of advertising to the fashion-conscious consumer, Ugg's marketing team targeted high-profile fashion influencers. They successfully contacted and convinced Kate Hudson and Sarah Jessica Parker to wear the items. Then Oprah Winfrey praised Uggs on one of her shows. At that point, the boots became fashionable, and retailers couldn't keep them in stock.[53]

Ugg became successful using unique alternative marketing methods. Access Ugg's Web site at **www.uggaustralia.com** to learn about the company's products and the company itself. Suppose Ugg wanted to initiate a buzz marketing campaign at your university and that they contacted you for marketing advice. First, they would like to recruit some brand ambassadors as advocates for their brand. Your first task, therefore, is to design a flyer to post around campus announcing that Ugg wants to hire brand ambassadors. Before you can design the flyer, you must decide on the relationship the ambassador will have with Ugg and the type of reward or payment she will receive. After you design the flyer, your second task is to design a buzz marketing program that you believe Ugg and the new brand ambassador should use on your campus.

CASE 1

AFTER THE RUSH: WHAT'S NEXT FOR RED BULL?

In today's active world, people need help. At least, that would be the position presented by any of the companies that sell energy drinks. Red Bull and other products are designed to jolt a consumer into action.

Red Bull's ingredient list begins with taurine, which occurs naturally in the human body. Red Bull helps to replace the taurine lost during conditions of high stress or physical exertion, which, in turn, helps the person recover more quickly. The carbohydrate glucuronolactone, which also is found naturally in the human body, is added to help with the detoxification processes as well as support the body in eliminating waste substances. The amount of caffeine in a serving of Red Bull is nearly double the amount present in Mountain Dew, a product perceived by many as the highest-energy soft drink. Red Bull also contains acesulfame K, sucrose, glucose, B vitamins, and aspartame, which is well-known as the key ingredient in NutraSweet. The company's marketing materials emphasize that the formula took 3 years to develop. The 8.3-ounce can drink was first launched in Australia in 1984. Red Bull tastes sweet and lemony, and, as one fan put it, "like a melted lollypop." The price of a single can is typically higher than a 16-ounce bottle of soda.[54]

When Red Bull was introduced into the United States, the product clearly struck a chord in some markets. Those pulling all-nighters for school, work, or partying, as well as those engaged in extreme sports, quickly gravitated to Red Bull. By 2010, the drink continued to hold a 60 to 70 percent share of the U.S. market for similar drinks and annual sales.

Red Bull's entry into the United States has been viewed by many marketing experts as one of the first and classic uses of alternative and buzz marketing. Red Bull's brand management team began by identifying a target audience—those who would most likely want the buzz created by an energy drink. One key constituent group would be college students. Consequently, the company provided free samples of the drink to college and university students, who were encouraged to throw big parties where cases of Red Bull would be served.

Red Bull's marketing team created a group of "consumer educators" who traveled to various locations giving out free samples. The brand managers organized and sponsored extreme sporting events, such as skateboarding and cliff diving, for consumer educators to attend. The concept was that the participants and fans of these types of sports had buzz-seeking desires and an interest in products that were positioned as "sleek, sweet, and full-throttle."[55] From the parties and the extreme sports, word-of-mouth communications about the brand spread. The buzz-seeking target audience became Red Bull's first customer base.

The traditional soft-drink companies were slow to react. Eventually, Pepsi created a competing product called Adrenaline Rush; Coca-Cola entered the market with KMX; and Anheuser Busch developed 180, which is supposed to turn a person's energy level around by 180 degrees. Pepsi may be less concerned with Red Bull due to its ownership of Gatorade. Still, both Coke and Pepsi have concentrated efforts on garnering shelf space in convenience stores and superstores.

More recently, Red Bull's marketing efforts have been expanded to include more traditional forms of advertising. At the same time, endorsers tend to be edgier figures, such as famed kayaker Tao Berman, and the commercials themselves remain offbeat. Red Bull creator Dietrich Mateschitz summarized it best, "If we don't create a market, it doesn't exist." And $1.6 billion later, it is clear that he has a point.

Two challenges have begun to emerge. First, Red Bull has been banned in some countries, including France and Canada. Other nations have examined the product and express fears about its impact on health. The second is keeping Red Bull on the cutting edge. A series of new energy formulas are available, including the heavily advertised 5-Hour Energy drinks. Can Red Bull maintain its edgy marketing presence over a sustained period of time?

1. What alternative marketing methods does Red Bull use?
2. Visit Red Bull's Web site (**www.redbull.com**) and identify the alternative media venues used by Red Bull's marketing team.
3. What role should traditional media play in Red Bull's future, especially when compared to alternative media?
4. Are there ways to build brand communities around Red Bull? What role might Twitter, Digg, or Facebook play in supporting such communities?
5. Red Bull believes that staying with alternative approaches best fits its image. As you think about all of the alternative marketing methods and alternative media, what suggestions would you make to Red Bull for the future? Describe a campaign for Red Bull using one or more alternative methods.

▼ Red Bull used alternative marketing to establish a presence in the United States.

© Jeffrey Blackler/Alamy

CASE 2 TANNING AND VOLLEYBALL: REVITALIZING A LIFESTYLE

Jessica Jones faced a difficult challenge as she took control of the Sun Products, Inc., account. As a relatively new account executive, Jessica knew it was important to establish measurable results when conducting various marketing communication campaigns. Sun Products sells items oriented toward beach-related activities, the most successful of which is the company's line of sunscreen products.

The tanning industry faces a unique set of challenges as a new generation of consumers emerges. First, consumers are now more aware of the dangerous long-term effects of tanning than ever before. These include more wrinkles and vastly increased chances of developing skin cancer in later life. In Australia, where the ozone layer is the most depleted, exposure to the sun is even more hazardous. More important, however, is a potential shift in cultural values regarding appearance.

As the new millennium commences, a certain set of consumers might begin to believe that tanning equals "foolishness"—or at least that a suntan is no longer as "sexy" as it has been for many years. Beach bums and bunnies continue to run counter to this trend. The question remains, however, whether being bronze is a good idea.

One way to counter this problem is by developing new products designed to screen out the sun rather than enhance the sun's tanning properties. Lotions with higher SPF (sun protection factor) values generally sell at higher prices. Higher-quality sunscreens do not wash off in a pool or while swimming. Further, items containing herbal ingredients and new aromas are designed to entice new interest. Products with aloe vera and vitamin E may help reduce the pain of and heal sunburns more quickly. Products that "tan" without exposure to the sun are being developed for those who want the beach look without doing time in the sand.

At the same time, to promote more "traditional" products to college students on spring break and others who still enjoy a deep, dark tan requires careful promotion. Advertisements often stress the "fun" aspects of being outdoors.

Hawaiian Tropics, one of the chief competitors in the tanning industry, has taken a unique approach to the promotion of its products. The company holds an annual contest in which the Tropics team of beach girls is chosen to represent the firm. Contestants are female, beautiful, and have good tans. Those who win the contest tour the country promoting Hawaiian Tropics products and appear on television programs. At individual events held at beaches across the United States and in other locations, free samples of Hawaiian Tropics are given out, along with coupons and other purchase incentives. Giveaways of beach towels and other beach equipment are used to heighten interest in the product at various stores.

Beach Volleyball Magazine notes that it features not a sport, but a lifestyle. The activity has the benefit of being included as part of the Summer Olympics. Some women, such as Misty May-Treanor and Kerri Walsh-Jennings, have recognizable names on the national stage and enjoy immense popularity within the

Alvaro German Vilela/Fotolia

▲ Beach volleyball is a natural tie-in with sun tanning products.

women's volleyball fan base. In addition, there are professional beach volleyball tournaments across the United States each year.

Promotion of women's beach volleyball tends to focus on tans, bikinis, and the sexy, athletic competitors. Many of the marketing materials available online, on posters, and in other places, feature photos of beach volleyball players in skimpy swimsuits. Fans also tend to attend events wearing outfits designed to show off a fit body and a great tan.

Jessica suspects there is a natural tie-in available with beach volleyball, especially on the women's side. Instead of tanning for its own sake, getting a tan while doing something healthy seems like a great appeal. The primary issue is whether the appeal can move beyond volleyball fans to the larger public. The secret would be to find a theme for a tie-in that would appeal to a larger audience.

An entire range of promotional items can be utilized. Items include coupons, premiums and giveaways, contests, samples, bonus packs (with various ranges of SPF values in the same pack), and refunds for higher-priced lotions.

Jessica knows the key is to maintain a consistent message and theme for her company. It must stand out in the crowd of Coppertone, Bain de Soleil, and Hawaiian Tropics. She realizes that to succeed she needs Sun Products' point-of-purchase displays placed prominently in as many places as possible, from drugstores to swimming specialty stores.

1. Is a buzz marketing program possible for Sun Products? Why or why not?

2. Design a complete lifestyle marketing program for Sun Products based on a tie-in with women's beach volleyball. Include both traditional and nontraditional advertising venues.

3. Name any opportunities you can identify for product placements or brand entertainment for Sun Products.

4. How could Sun Products use guerrilla marketing? Describe a possible guerrilla marketing campaign.

5. Is there a potential overlap between the brand community that loves beach volleyball and a brand community for Sun Products? Describe the ways that Sun Products' marketing department could build and enhance a connection between the two.

MyMarketingLab

Go to **mymktlab.com** for Auto-graded writing questions as well as the following Assisted-graded writing questions:.

10-1. Consider a set of products to which you feel strong of loyalty. Would you consider being a brand advocate, ambassador, or evangelist for a brand? Pick the brand where your loyalty is the highest. What type of offer would it take from the company for you to become a brand ambassador? What would you do to be an effective advocate for that brand?

10-2. Access Ugg's Web site at www.uggaustralia.com. Evaluate the Web site in terms of its effectiveness, freshness, and the use of alternative marketing methods. What traditional marketing methods did you see? Do you think Ugg has effectively merged traditional and nontraditional advertising methods? Why or why not?

10-3. Mymktlab Only—comprehensive writing assignment for this chapter.

11
DATABASE AND DIRECT RESPONSE MARKETING AND PERSONAL SELLING

CHAPTER OBJECTIVES

After reading this chapter, you should be able to answer the following questions:

1 What role does database marketing, including the data warehouse, data coding and analysis, and data mining, play in creating and enhancing relationships with customers?

2 How can database-driven marketing communication programs help personalize interactions with customers?

3 How do database-driven marketing programs create sales and build bonds with customers?

4 When should direct response marketing programs be used to supplement other methods of delivering messages and products to consumers?

5 What are the tasks involved in developing successful personal selling programs for consumers and businesses?

6 How should database marketing and personal selling programs be adapted to international settings?

MyMarketingLab™

⭐ **Improve Your Grade!**

Over 10 million students improved their results using the Pearson MyLabs.
Visit **mymktlab.com** for simulations, tutorials, and end-of-chapter problems.

SELLING WORDS

PAULA RAMIREZ

O f the many forms of sales that take place in commerce, one of the more complex tasks involves convincing potential clients that a mostly intangible product/service to be delivered in the future offers great value. 1400 Words, a copywriting service housed in Dallas, Texas, features four professional writers and Paula Ramirez, who serves as the company's business development specialist. "We work with advertising firms, marketing firms, and direct loop public relations, human resources, and major corporations. We provide web site content, white papers, case studies, taglines, radio scripts, and annual reports."

Paula has been able to successfully modify the classic steps of selling to business clients for over 5 years. Her approach includes generating prospects, collecting information, qualifying prospects, making the sales call, closing, and following up.

To generate prospects, Paula said, "I go to quite a few networking events. I make sure we are registered with most advertising lists online. I go to the American Marketing Association and Dallas Advertising League, because they usually have lunches and happy hours, and I try to attend both. During the day you get one type of person and at night you get another type. I do a lot of volunteering, because you meet so many people, and usually that's the best because you're meeting people in a relationship and they're not on the defensive. If you can make a friendship connection first, usually the business connection comes after. If you try to create the business connection first, then you have to keep it on a professional level."

Paula notes that, "Word of mouth is a huge factor in our business. 1400 Words obtains clients from people who have worked in advertising agencies and now have opened their own small shops. "We do use social media and we have a YouTube channel as well."

When collecting information about clients, Paula stated, "Right now we're using a program called SUGAR, which is an on-line database that allows me to take the person's business card. I can then upload all the data and information about the person. I go ahead and send an email saying, 'Thanks for meeting with me, and if you need anything let me know.' Then I go to LinkedIn and try to connect with them that way."

For strong prospects, Paula sends the company's newsletter to the contact. Others will wait until a more advantageous situation, so it won't appear like she is bombarding them with spam. The 1400 Words newsletter is sent out about every 6 weeks with stories about the writers. "We call it a 'drip campaign.' It's informational about the industry but also announces, 'We're still here.'" This helps her keep in the contact's mind when it becomes time to look for help with revised web site content, an annual report, or some other document. "It helps keep us top of mind."

Paula does not formally qualify prospects into groups, but she separates them in some way, such as, "These are people I'm going to take Starbucks to and see how they're doing on a monthly basis. The next group gets an email or a phone call conversation. They are more of a reach. For us, a company needs about a $50,000 marketing budget, because they already have a developed brand and voice. A company that will grow to that size will keep getting our newsletter."

The method of sales call to be used depends on each client. Contacts are made by phone, e-mail, and through social media. The SUGAR system allows her to maintain a profile while talking to them by email or on the phone. Paula also keeps personal information about prospects, such as "Kids in Little League," or "from Wyoming" in the client's file in order to maintain more a personal connection. They are a good conversation starter when you meet with a client or when you're finishing a meeting.

Paula uses one of three broad approaches to sales contacts. One is for those already in advertising that know the value of copy-editing. Paula provides this type of prospect with clientele lists in the areas of what the company works on. "The guy in advertising wants to see big names on your client list." The second group, a business customer, receives a more "hands on" presentation, showing them a booklet of the company's works and other items that display the writer's skills. "This type of client wants to see the big names, but doesn't want to pay the high prices. We show that we can adjust to them. The third type of prospect receives a power point presentation that can be shared online, with an invitation to contact Paula for further information.

What does she sell? "We're not the cheapest copy-writers, but we will get the work done faster and more efficiently, and in the long run, our approach saves them money, because a cheaper writer will charge so much per hour, such as $50 per hour, but it's going to take that writer 10 rounds to satisfy the client, to get to what they want. We charge $125 per hour, but when we say, '5 hours', we mean 5 hours and we're done, including the revisions." In essence, she sells a cost to benefit model. She notes, "Experienced, seasoned clients, especially the ones that have had bad experiences with freelancers, understand this; the younger, newer ones just think you're trying to make a sale."

Paula stated, "I make the close with the head creative Margie Bowles. I usually bring her to the meeting. By that time I have what we're going to work on, so the closing involves explaining how the processes is going to work and how long it's going to take." In other words, "We show up with the contract ready to sign." She has already moved incrementally toward the final deal.

"I usually follow up when it's time to pay," Paula noted. "Our service means they will be constantly in contact with our writers throughout the process. When the writer says it is completely done, I call them up to see if there any other final revisions. I contact them when the time is right. I also usually ask about future projects, so I can put that on their SUGAR profile."

Effective use of the steps of selling helps ensure the continued success of 1400 Words. Paula Ramirez is a key part of the success story.

OVERVIEW

Successful businesses continually acquire new customers and work to retain them. Repeat customers purchase more frequently and spend more money. Maintaining repeat business is far less expensive than constantly replacing those who turn to other companies.

This fourth section reviews a variety of promotional tools that are used to acquire and retain customers, as displayed in Figure 11.1. Database programs, direct response marketing, and personal selling are examined in this chapter. Sales promotions, both consumer and trade promotions, are presented in Chapter 12, followed by public relations and sponsorship programs in Chapter 13.

Database marketing provides a new communication link with customers. This, in turn, helps to produce higher levels of customer acquisition, customer retention, and customer loyalty. Database marketing has become increasingly crucial. New technologies associated with the Internet and computer software make it easier to build and develop strong database programs.

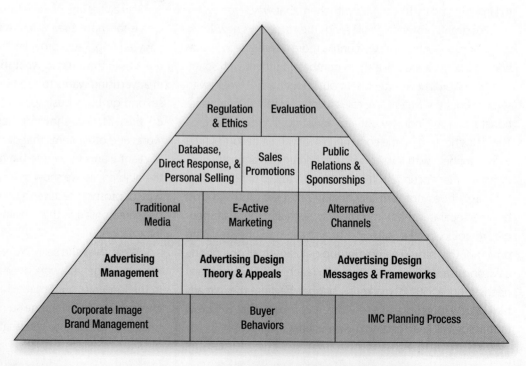

▶ **FIGURE 11.1**
Overview of Integrated
Marketing Communications

The first part of this chapter examines database marketing, including data warehouses, data coding, and data mining, as well as data-driven communications and marketing programs. Three data-driven marketing programs are: permission marketing, frequency programs, and customer relationship management systems. Databases are used for direct response marketing techniques, including direct mail, email, television programs, telemarketing, and traditional and alternative media. Finally, databases are a key component of personal selling.

Today's customers clearly value personalized marketing efforts. Creating programs that individualize messages and marketing materials constitutes the core of successful database marketing, direct response efforts, and personal selling.

Database Marketing

Database marketing involves collecting and utilizing customer data for the purposes of enhancing interactions with customers and developing customer loyalty. Successful database marketing emphasizes identifying customers and building relationships with them. This includes understanding the lifetime values of various customers and the development of customer retention efforts. Enhancing customer loyalty constitutes the primary benefit of database marketing. Although database marketing can be used for selling products, retention and relationships remain the primary focus.

A number of retail boutiques have captured the power of database marketing. When shoppers visit the store, the sales staff can access data regarding their preferences, sizes, previous purchases, and other information. Purchases are followed up with thank-you notes. Customers receive notices when new shipments of clothes arrive and are given invitations to special events. Loyalty to these boutiques remains high. Some customers who have moved away return to buy merchandise. One vital ingredient stands out: Data are used to make customers feel special and develop relationships with them. Although selling occurred, it did not drive the database program.

Figure 11.2 displays the tasks associated with database marketing. Of these, building the data warehouse and data coding are the two key activities described next.

OBJECTIVE 11.1

What role does database marketing, including the data warehouse, data coding, and analysis, and data mining, play in creating and enhancing relationships with customers?

Building a Data Warehouse

Successful database marketing requires a quality **data warehouse**, which holds all of the customer data. In building one, the IT department and marketing team distinguishes between an operational database and the marketing database. The *operational database* contains the individual's transactions individuals with the firm and follows accounting principles. The marketing department manages the *marketing database*, which contains information about current customers, former customers, and prospects. Examples of data and analyses found in a standard marketing data warehouse include:

- Customer names and addresses
- E-mail addresses and digital records of visits to the company's Web site
- History of every purchase transaction
- History of customer interactions, such as inquiries, complaints, and returns
- Results of any customer surveys
- Preferences and profiles supplied by the customer
- Marketing promotions and response history from marketing campaigns

• Building a data warehouse	• Data-driven marketing communications
• Database coding and analysis	• Data-driven marketing programs
• Data mining	

◀ **FIGURE 11.2**

Tasks in Database Marketing

- Appended demographic and psychographic data from sources such as Knowledge Base Marketing or Claritas
- Database coding, such as lifetime value and customer segment clusters

Collecting customer names and addresses is the easiest part of developing the database. Collecting the other information that turns the data warehouse into a powerful marketing and communication tool can be more challenging.

The marketing team typically employs a system for updating addresses, because approximately 20 percent of Americans move each year. When individuals fill out a change of address form with the U.S. Postal Service, the information is sent to all of the service bureaus authorized to sell the information to businesses. A company that sends database names to one of these service bureaus receives address updates for only a few cents per hit, or per individual that moves. Updating mailing addresses occurs at least once each year, depending on how often the database is used and the frequencies of contacts.

E-MAIL AND INTERNET DATA

E-mail addresses are essential elements of a quality database. The Internet and e-mail provide cost-effective channels of communication to be used in building relationships with customers. Most database programs take advantage of digital tracking to register and store Web site visits and browsing patterns. This information allows for personalization of the firm's Web site for each customer. When someone logs onto the site, a greeting such as "Welcome back Stacy" can appear on the screen. The tracking technology makes it possible for the system to recognize that Stacy, or at least someone using her computer, is accessing the Web site. If Stacy has purchased products or browsed the catalog, then the content of the pages can be tailored to contain the products she has an interest in purchasing.

▼ Purchase and communications histories provide important database information for a company such as Scott, which sells and rents power-line and utility equipment.

PURCHASE AND COMMUNICATION HISTORIES

Effective database programs maintain detailed customer purchase histories. The database records every interaction between the company and customer. When a customer sends an e-mail to tech support, the information will be placed in the database. Any person who returns a product or who has called customer service with a complaint has the information documented. Purchases and interaction histories determine future communications with customers and assist the marketing team in evaluating each customer's lifetime value and other customer value metrics.

PERSONAL PREFERENCE PROFILES

Purchase and visit histories do not provide complete information. Quality database marketing programs include profiles with specific information about each customer's personal preferences. These profiles and personal preference files may be constructed in various ways, including customer surveys. Others companies gather information on the Web site or in retail stores.

Every time the company initiates a contact with a customer, the information should be placed in the database, along with the customer's response. This information provides a rich history of what works and what does not. It further allows for customization of communication methods for each customer, which leads to the highest probability of success.

CUSTOMER INFORMATION COMPANIES

Oftentimes, demographic and psychographic information are not available through internal company records. In these cases, the information can be obtained by working with a marketing research firm that specializes in collecting customer data. Knowledge Base Marketing, Donnelly, Dialog, and Claritas are four companies that market this type of information.

Other companies operating Web sites, including Gap and Victoria's Secret, combine online information about customers with offline information provided by firms such as Acxiom and Datran Media. Once merged, this information can be stored in cookies to allow for customization and personalization of Web sites and communications with customers. For instance, based on income level and past purchasing habits, two women in adjoining offices can access the same cosmetics Web site; one might see a $300 bottle of Missoni perfume and the other might see the $25 house brand.[1]

GEOCODING

The process of adding geographic codes to each customer's record so that customer addresses can be plotted on a map, or **geocoding**, helps decision makers finalize placements of retail outlets and directs marketing materials to specific geographic areas. Geocoding allows for combining demographic information with lifestyle data. This assists the marketing team in selecting the best media for advertisements.

▲ Dialog is a marketing research firm that supplies companies with customer information.

One version of geocoding software, *CACI Coder/Plus*, identifies a cluster in which an address belongs. A group such as Enterprising Young Singles in the CACI system contains certain characteristics, such as enjoying dining, spending money on DVDs and personal computers, and reading certain magazines. A retailer could then target this group with mailings and special offers.[2]

Database Coding and Analysis

Database coding and analysis provide critical information for the development of personalized communications. They assist in creating marketing promotional campaigns. Common forms of database coding are lifetime value analysis and customer clusters.

LIFETIME VALUE ANALYSIS

The **lifetime value** figure for a customer or market segment represents the present value of future profits the individual or segment will generate over a lifetime relationship with a brand or firm.[3] Many marketing experts believe a market segment value provides more accurate information, because it sums costs across a market segment. Individual lifetime value calculations normally only contain costs for single customers.

The key figures in calculating the lifetime value of a consumer or set of consumers are revenues, costs, and retention rates. Revenue and costs are normally easy to obtain, because many companies record these numbers for accounting purposes. Retention rates require an accurate marketing database system.

The cost of acquiring a new customer constitutes a key figure. It can be calculated by dividing the total marketing and advertising expenditures in dollars by the number

▲ Knowing the lifetime value of customers helps the marketing team develop useful databases for retailers such as Chic Shaque.

of new customers obtained. As an example, when $200,000 dollars are spent and the company acquires 1,000 new customers as a result, the acquisition cost is $200 per customer ($200,000 divided by 1,000).

The cost of maintaining the relationship represents another key amount. It measures all costs associated with marketing, communicating, and maintaining the database records. These records are more difficult to obtain because such costs are usually for a campaign, which makes allocating costs to a single customer difficult. Computer and database technology can average or allocate a portion of these costs to individual customer records or to a lifetime value segment.

The end product for either individual customers or a customer segment is the lifetime value figure. When the lifetime value of a customer segment is $1,375, the figure represents the amount of income, on average, that each customer will generate over his or her lifetime. By communicating with and marketing to the customer segment, the lifetime value may be increased. Lifetime value analysis notifies the company's customer contact and service personnel about a customer's worth to the company.

CUSTOMER CLUSTERS

Coding can be used to group customers into clusters based on a wide variety of criteria. A bank may group customers based on the number of accounts, types of accounts, and other relationships a customer may have with the organization. For example, customers with a home mortgages above $100,000 with a balance of 30 to 60 percent remaining may be targeted for a home equity loan. A clothing retailer might group customers by the type of clothing each group purchases and then develop marketing programs for the various groups. Teenagers who like Western wear would be in a different cluster than teenagers who like hip, trendy fashions.

Unified Western Grocers, a wholesale cooperative association serving over 3,000 grocery stores, used customer cluster analysis to reduce 19 different advertising campaigns and programs for the various stores it served down to 4, based on customer commonalities. The four clusters that emerged from the analysis were: affluent urban and suburban households; mid-downscale rural seniors; large, low-income urban households; and non-acculturated Hispanics. Advertisements and shelf allocations of brands were then designed for each of the four customer clusters. Advertising design costs were reduced and more effective ads were created.[4]

Data Mining

Data mining involves using computer data analysis software to mine data for meaningful information and relationships. Data mining includes two activities: (1) building profiles of customer segments and/or (2) preparing models that predict future purchase behaviors based on past purchases.

Data mining assists the marketing team in building profiles of the firm's best customers. These profiles, in turn, help identify prospective new customers. They can be used to examine "good" customers to see if they are candidates for sales calls that would move them from "good" to a higher value. Companies offering different types of goods and services develop multiple profiles. The profiles are used to target sales calls and to look for cross-selling possibilities.

The marketing team at First Horizon National Bank used data mining to expand the company's wealth management business by studying consumer groups. Data about existing customers from the mortgage side of the firm's business made it possible to locate the best prospects for investment services. Linking the data mining program with cross-selling resulted in an increase in company revenues from $26.3 million to $33.8 million in just 1 year.[5]

Retailer American Eagle developed a data mining method to study how consumers responded to price markdowns. The information helped the marketing team determine when to cut prices and by how much in order to optimize sales. Markdown programs were geared to individual stores, because consumers responded differently in each outlet.[6]

The second data mining method involves developing models that predict future sales based on past purchasing activities. Staples, Inc. prepared a modeling program to examine the buying habits of the company's catalog customers. The program identified the names of frequent buyers. Customized mailings were then sent to those customers.

The method used to mine the data will be determined based on the specific information that is needed. Once the data have been mined for information, individual marketing programs can be designed. Profiles and models assist in creating effective marketing programs. A direct-mail program to current customers differs from one designed to attract new customers. The data provide clues about the best approach for each customer segment.

Data coding and data mining serve three purposes (see Figure 11.3). First, they can assist in developing marketing communications. The marketing team utilizes the information to choose types of promotions, advertising media, and the message to be presented to each group of customers. Second, they can help in developing marketing programs. Third, companies that employ salespeople can use the information to qualify prospects and make personal sales calls on those individuals or businesses that have the most potential. These activities are discussed in the following sections.

- Develop marketing communications
- Develop marketing programs
- For personal sales
  - ○ Qualify prospects
  - ○ Information for sales calls

▲ **FIGURE 11.3**
Purposes of Data Coding and Data Mining

Database-Driven Marketing Communications

A major reason for building a database, coding the information, and performing data mining is to use the output to establish one-on-one communication with each customer. Personalized communications build relationships and lead to repeat business and customer loyalty. They may help move the company and its products from brand parity to brand equity. A database marketing program contains tools to personalize messages and keep records of the types of effective and ineffective communications. The Internet offers the key technology for database-driven communications. Figure 11.4 highlights the importance of the Internet in customer interactions.

OBJECTIVE 11.2

How can database-driven marketing communication programs help personalize interactions with customers?

◀ **FIGURE 11.4**
Why the Internet is Important in Customer Communications

- It is the cheapest form of communication.
- It is available 24/7.
- Metric analysis reveals that the customer read the message, the time it was read, and how much time was spent reading it.
- Customers are able to access additional information whenever they want.
- It can build a bond with customers.

IDENTIFICATION CODES

A database-driven marketing program starts with assigning individual customers IDs and passwords that allow them to access components of the Web site that are not available to those who simply visit the site without logging on. The IDs and passwords are tied to cookies in order to customize pages and individual offers. When the system works properly, the customer does not have to log in each time. Instead, the cookie automatically does it for the user. For example, each time a user accesses Barnes & Noble, he receives a personalized greeting, such as "Welcome, Jim." Next, when an order is placed, the user does not have to type in address or credit card information. It is in the database and comes up automatically. This saves the customer time and effort and increases the probability he will make a purchase.

Specialized communications should be sent after the sale. A series of communications follows each purchase. First, an e-mail confirming the order and thanking the buyer is sent. An estimate of shipping date will be included. When the order is pulled and shipped, another e-mail containing the tracking number follows. Some companies include an e-mail in the interim stating that the order has reached the warehouse and is being pulled and made ready for shipment.

CUSTOMER PROFILE INFORMATION

▼ Through customer profile information, Columbia can identify individuals with high levels of interest in hiking.

An effective database-driven communication program relies on customer profiles and any other information about customer preferences to help individualize messages. Clothing retailers often send e-mails about new fashions that have arrived. These e-mails do not go to every person in the database. Only to those who have indicated a desire to have access to the information or who have indicated they have an interest in fashion news receive e-mails. Customers should feel they are receiving special "inside" information.

Customer profiles can also be used to send birthday greetings to loyal customers. Recently, a steak and seafood restaurant sent a card and offered a $10 birthday discount to 215,600 customers who provided their birthdates. The cost of mailing the birthday card and discount was $90,000. Approximately 40 percent of the cards were redeemed. Each birthday customer brought an average of 2 other people and those individuals paid full price for their meals. The result was $2.9 million in revenues derived from the program.[7]

The profiles, cookies, and ID numbers are also critical when the customer initiates contact with the company. When a customer contacts the company on the Web or through e-mail, the company's employees already know something about the individual. Responses can then be created that are tailored to that particular individual.

IN-BOUND TELEMARKETING

Contacts made by telephone work the same way as Internet contacts. The service-call operator immediately sees the identity of the person calling. Customer data appears on the screen in front of the in-bound telemarketer. The operator then treats the caller in a personal way. When the company calculates a

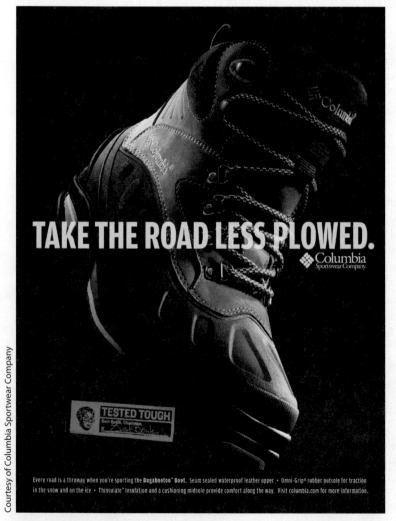

TAKE THE ROAD LESS PLOWED.

◆ Columbia
Sportswear Company.

TESTED TOUGH

Every road is a thruway when you're sporting the **Bugabootoo™ Boot.** Seam sealed waterproof leather upper • Omni-Grip® rubber outsole for traction in the snow and on the ice • Thinsulate™ Insulation and a cushioning midsole provide comfort along the way. Visit columbia.com for more information.

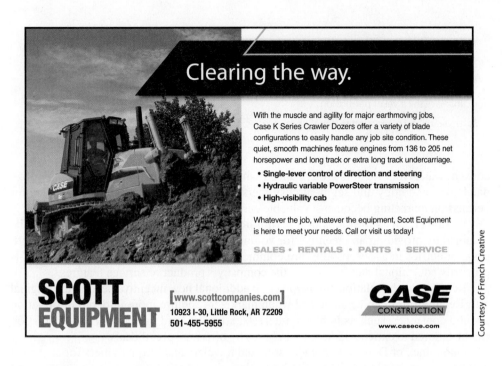

◄ A company such as Scott Equipment can use trawling to correspond with buyers on each yearly anniversary of their purchases.

lifetime value code, the operator knows the customer's value and status. The operator can ask about a recent purchase or talk about information provided on the customer's list of preferences or a customer profile. The operator greets and treats each customer as an individual, not as just some random person making a call.

TRAWLING

Database marketing includes a procedure called **trawling**, or the process of searching the database for a specific piece of information for marketing purposes. Home Depot uses trawling to locate individuals who have recently moved. Home Depot's marketing team knows that when people buy new homes they often need home improvement merchandise. Most of the time these items include merchandise sold at Home Depot.

Other marketers trawl a database to find anniversary dates of a special purchase, such as purchasing a new car. Car dealerships send a correspondence on each year's anniversary of a car purchase to inquire about customer satisfaction and interest in trading for a new vehicle. It can be used to locate individuals who have not made a purchase within the last 3 months or who purchased a lawnmower last year. Trawling presents a wide variety of ways to communicate with specific individuals who meet a particular criterion.

Database-Driven Marketing Programs

Database-driven marketing programs take many forms. They may be undertaken in conjunction with other marketing activities. Some of the more common programs include permission marketing, frequency programs, and customer relationship management efforts.

OBJECTIVE 11.3

How do data-driven marketing programs create sales and build bonds with customers.

PERMISSION MARKETING

A strong backlash by consumers against spam and junk mail exists. Consequently, many marketing departments have turned to **permission marketing,** a program in which companies send promotional information to only those consumers who give the company authorization to do so. Permission marketing programs can be offered on the Internet, by telephone, or through direct mail. Response rates are often higher in permission programs, because customers only receive requested marketing materials or those for which

▶ **FIGURE 11.5**

Steps in Building a Permissions Marketing Program

1. Obtain permission from the customer.
2. Offer the consumer an ongoing curriculum that is meaningful.
3. Reinforce the incentive to continue the relationship.
4. Increase the level of permission.
5. Leverage the permission to benefit both parties.

consent was given. Results are enhanced when permission marketing programs utilize database technology and segment customers; however, not everyone who signs up for permission marketing becomes a valuable customer.

Figure 11.5 lists the steps of a permission marketing program. Permission can be obtained by providing an incentive for volunteering. Information, entertainment, a gift, cash, or entries in a sweepstakes are common incentives. The information provided is primarily educational and focuses on the company's product or service features.

Reinforcing the relationship involves an additional new incentive beyond the original gift. Relationships can be enhanced when marketers acquire more in-depth information about a consumer, such as hobbies, interests, attitudes, and opinions. The information can be tailored to entice additional purchases by offering special deals.

Quris, Inc., of Denver, Colorado, solicited travelers and frequent fliers for an e-mail permissions marketing program. The permission marketing e-mails were opened and read regularly by 54 percent of the program's enrollees. In one year, nearly two-thirds made online purchases that were tied directly to the permission program. Frequent fliers who participated in the e-mail permission program spent an average of an extra $1,210 per year.[8]

Keys to Success in Permission Marketing For a permission marketing program to succeed, the marketing team ensures that the recipients have agreed to participate. Unfortunately, some consumers have been tricked into joining permission marketing programs. One common tactic is to automatically enroll customers in a permission marketing program when they complete an online survey or make an online purchase; opting out of the program requires the individual to un-check a box on the site. Although this approach increases the number of individuals enrolled, the technique often creates bad feelings.

The marketing material should be relevant to the consumer receiving it. Far too many people have joined permission marketing programs that have turned into situations where they provide no input and are bombarded with extraneous marketing messages. This does not create loyalty and runs counter to the purpose of a permission program.

One recent survey revealed that 80 percent of consumers stopped reading permission e-mails from companies because they were shoddy or irrelevant. Another 68 percent said the e-mails came too frequently, and 51 percent said they lost interest in the goods, services, or topics of the e-mails. On the whole, consumers delete an average of 43 percent of permission e-mails without ever reading them.[9]

To overcome these challenges, the marketing team monitors responses and customizes the permission program to meet individual customer needs. Database technology allows for customization by tracking responses. When a customer regularly accesses a Web site through a link in an e-mail sent by the company to read the latest fashion news, the behavior can trigger e-mail offers and incentives on fashions related to the news stories. An individual who does not access the Web site and does not appear to be interested in fashion news receives a different type of e-mail offer. By capitalizing on the power of database technology, a company can enhance the permission marketing program and make it beneficial to the company and the customer.

Permission Marketing Enticements Figure 11.6 notes the top reasons for opting into e-mail programs. Winning a sweepstakes tops the list. Also, when the individual is already a customer of the company, the person feels favorably predisposed to the

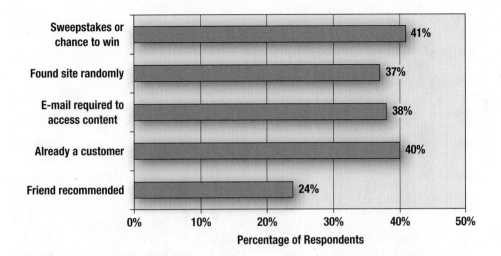

◀ **FIGURE 11.6**
Reasons Consumers Opt into
E-Mail Permission Programs

Source: Joseph Gatti, "Most Consumers
Have Reached Permission E-mail
Threshold," *Direct Marketing* (December
2003), pp. 1–2.

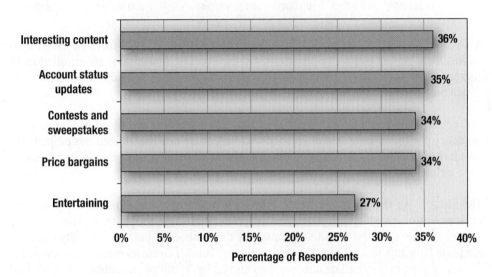

◀ **FIGURE 11.7**
Reasons Consumers Remain in a
Permission Marketing Program

Source: Joseph Gatti, "Most Consumers
Have Reached Permission E-mail
Threshold," *Direct Marketing* (December
2003), pp. 1–2.

company's products.[10] Enticing current customers into the permission marketing program will be easier than attracting new customers.

Figure 11.7 provides a list of motives that help retain customers in a permission marketing relationship. As shown, consumers remain with such programs for many reasons.[11]

Permission marketing programs have the potential to build strong, ongoing relationships with customers when the program offers something of value to them. To optimize permission marketing, firms feature empowerment and reciprocity. **Empowerment** means consumers believe they have power throughout the relationship and not just at the beginning when they agreed to join the program. They can make decisions and have choices about what is received.

To maintain positive attitudes, consumers should be given rewards along the way, not just at the beginning. This creates feelings of **reciprocity**, or a sense of obligation toward the company. Only rewarding customers for joining the program will be a mistake. Empowerment and reciprocity lead the customer to believe the company values the relationship, which increases the chances the consumer will continue to be an active participant.

FREQUENCY PROGRAMS

With a **frequency program** or **loyalty program**, a company offers free merchandise or services for a series of purchases. These efforts encourage customers to make repeat purchases. In the airline industry, frequent-flyer programs offer free flights after a traveler accumulates a certain number of miles. Grocery stores grant special discounts when purchases reach a certain amount within a specified time period.

▶ **FIGURE 11.8**
Benefits of Loyalty Programs
Cited by Customers

Source: Adapted from Mark Dolliver,
"Gauging Customer Loyalty,"
Adweek (**www.adweek.com/aw/
content display/news/agency/
e3i4a73f5d7451749a37c7fca20,**
February 16, 2010).

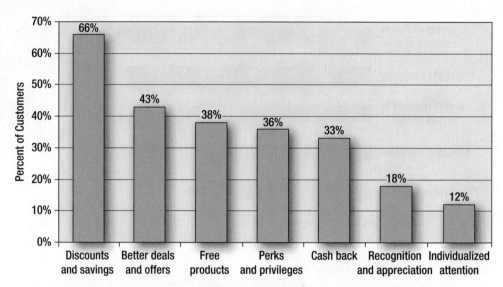

According to research by the Chief Marketing Officer (CMO) Council, two-thirds of consumers belong to loyalty programs. On the average, households are enrolled in 14 programs, but only actively participate in about 6. Figure 11.8 provides a list of benefits of such programs cited by customers.[12]

Goals Various reasons for developing frequency programs are noted in Figure 11.9. Frequency programs were first developed to differentiate one brand from its competition. Now, however, they now tend to be common across all competitors in an industry (credit cards, airlines, grocery stores, hotels, restaurants, etc.).

Principles As shown in Figure 11.10 on the next page, three principles guide the development of a loyalty program. The program adds value to what the product offers or provides a unique new feature. Members of the Outback Steakhouse loyalty club can earn points towards unique items such as winning Tim McGraw memorabilia such as his CDs or cologne or football or cowboy hats signed by McGraw. Members who join and use the card are automatically entered into a contest to win a free trip to Australia to see a Tim McGraw concert.[13]

The more effort a customer expends to participate in a frequency program, the greater the value of the reward. Many consumers are willing to put forth greater effort to obtain luxury rewards as opposed to necessity rewards. Shoppers at a grocery store are more likely to put forth a higher level of effort in order to receive a free overnight stay at a nearby local resort or a free meal at nice restaurant than they would for a $25 gift certificate for food.

Marketers consider the full costs of a loyalty program. If not properly planned, costs can exceed returns. For restaurants, costs to launch a reward program are estimated around 1 percent of sales revenue. The perks offered during the launch can range from 5 percent to 15 percent of sales. The return on this investment is usually around 2 percent of sales, a 100 percent return on the initial expenditure.[14]

Programs should maximize the customer's motivation to make the next purchase. Moderate users of a product are most likely to be enticed by a frequency program. The added incentive encourages loyalty to a particular company or brand. Research suggests that a *variable ratio reward schedule* is superior to regularly scheduled rewards. A *variable ratio* means that customers receive intermittent reinforcements. They do not

▶ **FIGURE 11.9**
Goals of Frequency or
Loyalty Programs

- Maintain or increase sales, margins, or profits
- Increase loyalty of existing customers
- Preempt or match a competitor's offer
- Encourage cross-selling
- Differentiate the brand
- Discourage entry of a new brand

* Enhance the value of the product.
* Calculate the full cost the the program.
* Maximize customer motivation to make additional pruchases.

◀ **FIGURE 11.10**
Goals of Frequency or
Loyalty Programs

know exactly when a reward will be given or the size of the incentive. The random reward schedule, however, should be frequent enough to encourage them to make purchases.[15]

Although consumers have frequency cards, they may not always use them. The marketing manager of a locally-owned restaurant noticed he had a large number of customers who had not recently used their Frequent Diner Club cards. Trawling identified 4,000 Frequent Diner Club members who had not earned any points during the previous 3 months. The restaurant sent a letter to each of the 4,000 offering a $5 discount on dinner. The offer was good for 35 days and the mailing cost $1,800. The results were:

* The average number of member visits per day increased from 25 to 42 during the promotion and to 29 per day after the promotion ended.
* Average visits by individual members holding cards increased both during and after the promotion.
* Incremental sales increased by $17,100 during the promotion and by $4,700 after the 35-day promotion.

By spending $1,800, the promotion led to reactivations by about 600 people who had not dined at the restaurant in 3 months. Of the nearly 600 who came back during the promotion, 147 dined at the restaurant after the promotion was over.[16]

CUSTOMER RELATIONSHIP MANAGEMENT

Customer relationship management programs (CRM) generated a great deal of interest in the 1990s. Several companies invested significant dollars in CRM software, employee training, and implementation. **Customer relationship management (CRM)** programs allow companies to use databases to customize products and communications with customers, with the goals of higher sales and profits. Unfortunately, most CRM endeavors were not successful. Several reasons have been given for the poor results; the central one seems to be that CRM programs focused on making sales rather than on enhancing relationships.

The basic tenets of customer relationship management programs are sound. The objectives of CRM and its implementation are the ingredients that are usually flawed. Successful programs build long-term loyalty and bonds with customers through the use of a personal touch, facilitated by technology. Effective customer relationship management programs are designed to go beyond the development of a database and traditional selling tactics to the mass customization of both communications and products.

Two primary CRM metrics are the lifetime value of the customer and share of customer. The lifetime value concept has already been discussed in an earlier chapter. The second metric, share of customer, is based on the concept that some customers are more valuable than others and that over time the amount of money a customer spends with a firm can increase. **Share of customer** refers to the percentage of expenditures a customer makes with one particular firm compared to total expenditures in that product's category. Share of customer measures a customer's potential value. The question becomes, "If more is invested by the company in developing a relationship, what will the yield be over

Courtesy of the Pasta House, Co.

▲ Many restaurants offer frequency or loyalty programs to diners.

▲ Centric Federal Credit Union can use a CRM program to enhance relationships with its current customers.

time?" When a customer makes only one-fourth of his purchases of a particular product with a specific vendor, increasing the share of the customer would mean increasing that percentage from 25 percent to a higher level, thus generating additional sales revenues. The ultimate goal would be leading the customer to make 100 percent of his purchases with one vendor.[17]

Assuming the tenets of CRM are sound, the question becomes, "Why did so many programs fail?" The Gartner Group, a research and advisory firm, identified four factors. First, the program was often implemented before a solid customer strategy was created. Market segments should be identified first so that customization programs can then proceed. Failing to understand market segments resulted in a "ready, fire, aim" approach.[18]

Second, rolling out a CRM program before changing the organization to match it creates problems. A CRM program affects how customers are viewed as well as the methods used deliver goods and services. A new management philosophy becomes essential. Failing to educate the entire staff about this new perspective and approach quickly leads to difficulties.

Third, some CRM programs failed because they were technology-driven rather than customer-driven. Technology can only assist in record keeping and some aspects of order fulfillment. The rest is the responsibility of the employees, who must understand each customer and develop customized approaches.

Fourth, CRM programs fail when customers feel like they are being "stalked" rather than "wooed." Trying to build a relationship with a disinterested customer will be more annoying to the customer than helpful. A number of companies discovered that telemarketing programs designed to reach customers and expand relationships was annoying people rather than winning them over. These problems led many marketing departments to abandon CRM programs and to search for new and different ways to build relationships with customers.

In general, database-driven marketing programs should be designed to enhance customer loyalty. When a hotel's check-in person knows in advance that a business traveler prefers a nonsmoking room, a queen-size bed, and reads *USA Today*, these items could be made available as the guest arrives. Training hotel clerks and other employees to use the database helps them to provide better service, thereby building loyalty from regular customers. Any organization's marketing department can adapt these techniques to fit the needs of its customers and clients.

In addition to permission marketing, frequency programs, and CRM systems, other marketing programs can result from database analysis. Internet programs, trade promotions, consumer promotions, and other marketing tactics may be facilitated by using the database.

Direct Response Marketing

One program closely tied to database marketing, **direct response marketing** (or **direct marketing**), involves the targeting of products to customers without the use of other channel members. Figure 11.11 identifies the most typical forms of direct marketing and the percentages of companies using them. Notice that direct marketing can be targeted at customers as well as prospects. According to the Direct Marketing Association, about 60 percent of a typical direct marketing budget targets prospecting for new customers; the other 40 percent is spent retaining current customers.[19]

Many pharmaceutical companies employ direct response advertising, especially on television and in magazines. A recent study revealed that this direct response approach works. Ads for prescription medications by pharmaceuticals prompted almost one-third of Americans to ask their doctors about a particular brand of medicine and 82 percent of those who asked doctors received some type of prescription. The prescription was for the advertised brand 44 percent of the time; for another drug, 56 percent of the time. Sometimes doctors prescribed both the advertised brand as well as another brand.[20]

Individuals and companies respond to direct marketing pieces in a number of ways, such as by telephone, e-mail, visiting a retail location, or using a PURL (personalized URL). PURLs offer the advantage of preloading all of the individual's personal data to the site, which can then personalize the information and any offer. It also assists in tracking the individual's onsite activities and to make real-time changes in offers.[21]

DIRECT MAIL

As shown in Figure 11.11, mail remains the most common form of direct marketing. Direct mail targets both consumers and business-to-business customers. The quality of the mailing list determines the success of a direct mail program. Companies have two sources when compiling a mailing list: the firm's internal database or a commercial list.

The company's marketing department parses an internal list and separates active members from inactive members. Prospective new customers receive a different direct mail piece than messages designed to entice repeat purchases. Mailing direct offers to individuals (or businesses) who have not purchased recently but who have purchased in the past often yields a better response rate than cold-call mailing lists from brokers.

OBJECTIVE 11.4

When should direct response marketing programs be used to supplement other methods of delivering messages and products to consumers?

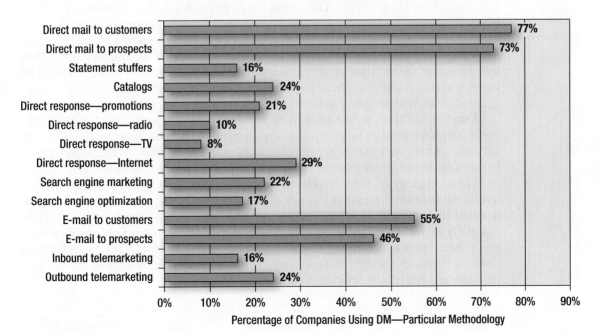

▲ **FIGURE 11.11**

Methods of Direct Marketing

Source: Richard H. Levey, "Prospects Look Good," *Direct* 16 (December 1, 2004), pp. 1–5.

Courtesy of French Creative

▲ Progressive Bank can use direct mail to target specific financial service customers.

Types of Commercial Lists Purchasing a commercial list, either a response list or a compiled list, is the most common approach. A **response list** consists of customers who have made purchases or who have responded to direct mail offers in the past. Brokers selling these lists provide information about the composition of the list and how much was spent by buyers on the list. In addition, a "hot list" can be requested. It contains the names of individuals who have responded within the past 30 days. Individuals on the hot list are the most likely to make purchases. This type of list is more costly: as much as $250 per thousand names. A regular response list may sell for $100 per thousand names.

The second form, a **compiled list**, provides information about consumers who meet a specific demographic profile. The disadvantage of a compiled list is that although someone might fit a demographic category, only about one-half of Americans purchase items by mail.

Caterpillar's marketing team wanted to reach potential buyers in the Southwest as part of its "Eat My Dust" campaign. The company purchased 1,700 names of individuals who had purchased industrial loaders during the past 5 years from Equipment Data Associates, a Charlotte, North Carolina, firm that compiles detailed purchasing histories of more than 870,000 U.S. contractors. Rea & Kaiser's Nichols agency designed a sweepstakes to win a new Cat 414E. An eye-catching direct mail piece urged contractors to sign up either online, by mail, or at a local Caterpillar dealer. Standard response rates are 1 to 3 percent; the response rate for the "Eat My Dust" direct mailer was 18 percent.[22] Using a highly targeted list made the difference.

Advantages of Direct Mail Direct mail can be easily targeted to various consumer and business groups. The impact can easily be measured. The marketing team compares the number of mailings to the number of responses. Every component of a direct-mail campaign may be tested, including the type of offer, the copy in the ad, graphics used, color, and the size of the mail packet. For business-to-business marketing, direct mail will be superior to e-mail and other direct marketing methods, especially when a company seeks to introduce itself to prospects and needs to break through multiple layers of gatekeepers.

Direct mail drives online sales. A recent Pitney Bowes study revealed that direct mail remains the primary tool for promoting company Web sites. Direct mail was used to advertise a firm's Web site by 70 percent of firms with annual sales of at least $1 million. In addition, 43 percent of Internet sales were driven by some type of direct mail.[23]

The technology of direct marketing has greatly improved. Mailings can be customized to the individual recipient through **digital direct-to-press**, a software program that instructs the computer to send a tailor-made message. Digital direct-to-press may be especially useful in the business-to-business sector, where there are fewer total customers to contact than in consumer markets. Sending a customized message to each business customer increases the chance the message will be viewed. The expense of the software limits the number of companies that can afford it.[24]

CATALOGS

Many consumers enjoy catalogs and view them at their leisure. Catalogs have a longer-term impact because they are kept and shared. Catalogs feature a low-pressure direct response marketing tactic that allows consumers time to consider goods and prices.

Many marketers believe that online shopping has replaced catalog mail-order shopping; however, research by the U.S. Postal Service reveals that although the number of consumers purchasing online has increased, consumers continue to prefer to receive catalogs by mail. In many cases, receiving a catalog becomes the first step in the buying cycle.[25]

Successful cataloging requires an enhanced database. Many catalog companies, such as L.L.Bean and JCPenney, create specialty catalogs geared to specific market segments. The specialty catalogs have a lower cost and a higher yield, because they target individual market segments.

Catalogs are essential selling tools for many business-to-business marketing programs. They provide more complete information to members of the buying center as well as prices for the purchasing agent. When combined with the Internet, a catalog program can facilitate a strong connection with individual customers.

DIRECT RESPONSE MASS MEDIA

Television, radio, magazines, and newspapers are additional tools for direct response advertising. Direct response commercials appear on many channels and stations. Often, these commercials are slightly longer (60 seconds), which allows a potential buyer time to find a pen to write down a toll-free number, an address, or a Web site. Catchy, easy-to-remember contact information is often used, such as "1-800-Go-Green" or "**www. gogreen.com**." Repeating the response format helps customers remember how to respond. Often a "call-now" prompt concludes the commercial.

Television also features infomercials for various types of products, such as exercise equipment and cooking tools. Cable and satellite systems have led to the creation of numerous direct response channels. The Home Shopping Network remains one of the most successful. Essentially the channel provides 24-hour infomercial programs. Other channels feature jewelry, foods, and shoes.

Direct response techniques also are presented on radio stations and in magazines and newspapers. Radio does not have the reach of television, but it can be targeted by the type of station format. Radio ads repeat the response number or Web site frequently so consumers can make contacts.

Print media can be sent to various market segments. Newspaper advertisements may feature Web site information and other quick-response formats. The same holds true for magazines. Both contain Web site information and toll-free numbers.[26]

INTERNET

The Internet offers a valuable form of direct marketing. Consumers can respond directly to ads placed on a Web site and direct response advertisements can be placed on search engines and used in e-mails.

As was shown in Figure 11.11, e-mail is a frequently used form of direct response marketing. E-mail provides a cost-effective method of reaching prospects. It helps build relationships with current customers through personalization of communications and by presenting marketing offers tailored to each consumer's needs, wants, and desires. For business-to-business marketers, e-mail works better than postal mail and other direct marketing forms when the recipient is familiar with the company.[27]

By placing ads on search engines and using search engine optimization, firms make direct response offers directly to individuals and businesses in the market for particular products. A direct response ad for fruit trees that appears when a person types in "apple trees" will be more effective than one that appears when a person searches on "iPad" or "office furniture."

DIRECT SALES

In the consumer sector, companies such as Amway, Mary Kay, and Avon rely on direct sales. The salesperson contacts friends, relatives, coworkers, and others and provides them with small catalogs or marketing brochures. Alternatively, individuals host parties and invite friends and relatives to see products.

© SerrNovik/Fotolia

▲ More than 40,000 "Mark Girls" work in the United States for Avon.

Mark is the Avon flanker brand designed for teenagers and women under 30. In launching a new line of cosmetics, Mark brought direct selling into the digital and social media age through the 40,000 "Mark Girls" who work in the United States. They are primarily women between the ages of 18 and 24 who use grassroots methods to sell Mark cosmetics and fashion accessories in dorms, through sororities, and via Facebook. The brand offers personalized e-boutiques, iPhone apps, and a Facebook e-shop. Kristiauna Mangum is a marketing major at Ohio State University. She is also a sales manager for Mark and manages 155 other Mark girls, earning commissions that range from 20 to 50 percent of the product's price.[28]

TELEMARKETING

Telemarketing takes place in two ways: inbound or outbound. *Inbound telemarketing* occurs when an individual initiates a call to a company. When a customer places an order, cross-selling can occur by offering other products or services. At times customers make inbound calls to register complaints or talk about problems. Direct response marketing can give information about how to solve the problem. For example, when a customer calls a mortgage company because of a late fee, the person can be encouraged to sign up for a direct pay program, which means the customer does not have to worry about possible mail delays.

The least popular method for direct marketing is *outbound telemarketing*. Cold-calling of consumers yields few buyers and alienates many people. No-call list legislation, whereby a person or organization can designate a telephone number that may not be contacted by business organizations using telemarketing programs, has been passed. Many people even object to calls from companies with which they do business.

Outbound direct response telemarketing achieves greater success when tied into a database and either customers or prospects are being contacted. An outbound telemarketing program that contacts customers who have not purchased in a year can help bring those customers back. A company that purchased a copy machine can be called to inquire about interest in paper and toner. A vendor can learn why a client has not purchased recently.

Personal Selling

OBJECTIVE 11.5

What are the tasks involved in developing successful personal selling programs for consumers and businesses?

Personal selling offers a face-to-face opportunity to build relationships with consumers. It takes place in both consumer and business-to-business transactions. Personal selling may result in the acquisition of new customers in addition to influencing current customers to increase levels of purchases. It can also be used to service and maintain existing relationships. The goal of personal selling should not be limited to making sales. Developing longer-term relationships with customers represents a second key objective. **Relationship selling** seeks to create a customer for life, not for a single transaction.

Figure 11.12 identifies the standard steps in the selling process. A quality data warehouse accompanied by effective database technologies provides key tools that assist in personal selling.

▶ **FIGURE 11.12**

Steps in the Selling Process

- Generating leads
- Qualifying prospect
- Knowledge acquisition
- Sales presentation
- Handling objections
- Sales closing
- Follow-up

GENERATING LEADS

Producing quality leads will be the first task in personal selling, especially for business-to-business customers. Figure 11.13 identifies some of the most common methods. Personal sales calls are costly, which makes generating quality leads crucial.

Referrals constitute ideal leads, because most recommendations are made by satisfied individuals. Referrals give the salesperson a head start. Making contact with purchasing agents or buyers in business organizations is often difficult. Using the name of the person who gave the referral can help the salesperson get past any gatekeepers. Also, if someone has given a referral, then the potential lead becomes more receptive to the sales call and has a more positive attitude toward the salesperson. The best referrals are from current customers. Referrals from other channel members, vendors, and acquaintances can also be good because they allow the salesperson to get a foot in the door with a potential prospect.

For generating leads, databases provide quality leads, especially internal databases. Most of these leads are generated through some type of advertising or inquiry. Direct response ads in various media, such as television, radio, magazines, or newspapers, can generate leads. Online ads on various Web sites or search engines may also generate leads. Individuals may send an e-mail inquiry or request additional information through the company's Web site.

Databases provide quality leads through trawling and analytical techniques, such as data mining. A company may trawl its database for customers who have not made purchases within the last 6 months or for companies that purchased a particular type of equipment and have not ordered additional parts or supplies. Data mining helps the company's marketing team create a profile of the best customers. Then lists of leads consisting of customers who are not high purchasers may be created. Trawling and data analysis techniques provide leads with higher sales potential.

Other less desirable means of generating sales leads are networking, directories, and cold calls. Although these methods may produce some leads, most are time consuming and less productive. Networking in civic and professional organizations allows salespeople to make personal contacts. Directories may be obtained from the federal government, professional organizations, or research firms that provide the names of companies that purchase specific products or those in a given industry. The challenge is locating quality leads from the list. Cold calls are the worst method of generating leads. The salesperson has no idea whether the company or individual has any interest in the product.

QUALIFYING PROSPECTS

Every name or prospect may not be viable. Also, prospects are not of equal value. With this in mind, qualifying prospects means evaluating leads on two dimensions: (1) the potential income the lead can generate and (2) the probability of acquiring the prospect as a customer. Based on the outcomes of these evaluations, determinations can be made regarding the best methods of contact and what happens with the lead. The high cost of making personal sales calls means that only the best leads warrant personal visits. Some prospects receive telephone calls or e-mails from an inside salesperson. Others may be mailed or e-mailed marketing materials but are not contacted directly by a salesperson.

- Refferals
- Database-generated leads
- Networking
- Directories
- Cold calls

▲ **FIGURE 11.13**
Methods of Generating Sales Leads

▼ Building relationships with customers is an important component of personal selling.

▶ **FIGURE 11.14**
Knowledge Acquisition Information

- Understand the prospect's business.
- Know and understand the prospect's customers.
- Identify the prospect's needs.
- Evaluate the risk factors and costs in switching vendors.
- Identify the decision makers and influencers.

Once the leads are analyzed using the two categories, sales potential and probability of acquisition, they are then placed into categories, or buckets, with the leads high on both dimensions as being the best, or "A" leads. These leads normally receive a sales call from the sales staff. The second best group, or "B" leads, often will be contacted by a telemarketer or through e-mail. "C" leads receive marketing materials and are encouraged to make inquiries if interested. Leads that score low on both dimensions may be kept in a database and monitored for future action in case the lead's situation changes.

KNOWLEDGE ACQUISITION

During the knowledge acquisition phase, the company's salespeople or other members of the sales department gather information about the prospect. Figure 11.14 identifies typical information. The more a salesperson knows about a prospect before making the sales call, the higher becomes the probability of making a sale or gaining permission to demonstrate the company's prospect.

Understanding the prospect's business, customers, and needs will be helpful. When selling janitor supplies to a commercial cleaning company, understanding the commercial cleaning company's customers provides information about the type of cleaning chemicals needed. Cleaning heavy, greasy industrial areas requires different chemicals than those used to clean medical offices or office buildings. A manufacturer that supplies electronic components for high-tech aerospace customers has differing needs than would a company supplying electronics for automobile engines or for televisions and radios.

Changing vendors involves risk and switching costs. From the prospect's perspective, it helps to understand those risks and costs. When switching costs are low and risk is also perceived to be low, convincing a company to change vendors becomes easier.

The final valuable piece of information is a list of the names of decision makers and decision influencers. The names of these individuals are often difficult to obtain prior to the sales call, but getting them should be a high priority during the first meeting. Understanding who will be involved in the decision process is important as the sales process proceeds.

THE SALES PRESENTATION

The initial sales call can be used to gather information, discuss bid specifications, answer questions, or to close the deal with a final pitch or offer.[29] The exact nature of the first sales call depends on the information gathered prior to the call. Also the stage of the buying process affects the presentation. The types of sales presentations used typically fall into one of these categories: stimulus-response, need-satisfaction, problem-solution, and mission-sharing.[30]

A **stimulus-response** sales approach, or a "canned" sales pitch, involves specific statements (stimuli) designed to elicit specific responses from customers. The salesperson normally memorizes the stimulus statement (the pitch). Telemarketers, retail sales clerks, and new field sales reps often rely on this method.

The **need-satisfaction** sales approach strives to discover a customer's needs during the first part of the sales presentation and then to provide solutions. The salesperson should skillfully ask the right questions. She should understand the customer's business

◀ Understanding customer needs provides the basis for the need-satisfaction sales approach.

and customers. Once a need has been identified, the rep then shows how the company's products meet that need.

The **problem-solution** sales approach requires employees from the selling organization to analyze the buyer's business. It usually involves a team of individuals, such as engineers, salespeople, and other experts. The team investigates a potential customer's operations, its problems, and then offers feasible solutions.

In the last approach, **mission-sharing**, two organizations develop a common mission. They then share resources to accomplish that mission. This partnership resembles a joint venture as much as a selling relationship.

HANDLING OBJECTIONS

Companies and individuals seldom make purchases after a sales presentation without raising some objections or concerns. Salespeople anticipate objections and should carefully answer them. Figure 11.15 lists the most common methods of handling objections.

With the *head-on approach*, the salesperson answers the objection directly. Doing so, however, indicates that the customer or prospect is wrong. The salesperson should use tact. No one likes being told he is wrong. The salesperson uses care to not offend the customer.

To avoid a confrontation, some salespeople employ an *indirect approach*. This method allows the salesperson to never really tell the customer he is wrong. Instead, the salesperson sympathizes with the customer's viewpoint and then provides the correct information.

When the customer's objection is partially true, then salesperson may utilize the *compensation method*. With this approach the salesperson replies "yes, but . . ." and then explains the product's benefits or features that answer the customer's objection.

Some customers do not have specific objections, but are anxious or worried about the consequences of switching to a new vendor. For this situation a sales rep can apply the *feel, felt, found* method. The salesperson permits the customer to talk about her fears or worries. In response, the salesperson can relate personal experiences or experiences of other customers who had the same fears and worries and how the product resulted in a positive experience.

- Head-on method
- Indirect method
- Compensation method
- "Feel, felt, found"

▲ **FIGURE 11.15**
Methods of Handling Objections

- Direct close
- Trial close
- Summarization close
- Continuous "yes" close
- Assumptive close

▲ **FIGURE 11.16**
Methods of Closing Sales

CLOSING THE SALE

It may be that the most important part of the sales call is the closing, and it may also be the most difficult part. Salespeople often experience feelings of rejection or failure when prospects or customers say "no." Successful salespeople are masters at making the close. Figure 11.16 identifies some of the most common sales-closing methods. The one to be used depends on the personality of the salesperson, the personality of the prospect, and the situation surrounding the sales call.

With the *direct close*, the salesperson asks for the order outright. The approach may be used when objections have been answered and the salesperson feels confident about the prospect's readiness to buy.

When the salesperson cannot be sure if the prospect is quite ready, the *trial method* can be used. With this approach, the salesperson solicits feedback that provides information regarding the customer's reaction, without asking directly for the sale. A positive reaction leads the salesperson to ask for the order. If not, then the salesperson returns to the sales presentation. The salesperson may also *summarize* the product's benefits and how it meets the customer's needs prior to asking for the order.

Sometimes a salesperson asks a serious of questions along the way, ensuring the customer will *continuously* respond "yes." By answering "yes" to smaller questions about the benefits of a product, when it comes time to ask for the order the customer may be more likely to respond with a "yes."

A salesperson can also *assume* the customer will say "yes." He might ask, "How many cases do you want?" or "How would you like this to be shipped?"

FOLLOW-UP

Keep customers happy after the purchase results in repeat business, customer loyalty, and positive referrals. Quality follow-up programs are cost-effective ways to retain customers, which is much cheaper than continually finding new ones. Unfortunately, following-up may be neglected by the sales staff, especially if the salesperson receives commission on new sales but not on follow-up activities. In this situation, the company must designate other employees to follow-up to ensure that customers are satisfied with their purchases.

International Implications

OBJECTIVE 11.6

How should database marketing and personal selling programs be adapted to international settings?

Database marketing faces the same challenges as other aspects of an IMC program when a firm moves into the international arena. These include differences in technology, which make data collection and analysis more difficult due to issues such as language and Internet availability. Further, local laws may limit the methods by which information can be collected as well as the types of information a company seeks and/or shares with other companies.

In many parts of the world, customers may only live a few miles apart yet reside in different countries. For example, the European Union consists of many nations in close proximity. Therefore, decisions must be made as to whether data will be country specific.

Programs such as permission marketing, frequency, and CRM are subject to legal restrictions as well as cultural differences. In some instances, they may be highly accepted. This is the case for permission marketing in Japan. In many Asian cultures, the giving of gifts takes on added meaning. This may indicate that stronger bonds between customers and companies are important in personal selling.

Direct marketing programs should be adapted to local conditions. Mail delivery systems may be easier to access in some countries than others. The same holds true for telephone systems, Internet access, and other technologies. Infomercials may not be possible in countries with state-run television systems. A company's marketing team considers all local legal, social, cultural, technological, and competitive conditions before embarking on an international database-driven marketing program or direct marketing program.

INTEGRATED CAMPAIGNS IN ACTION

Centric Federal Credit Union

Emogen Marketing was retained by Centric Federal Credit Union to increase new memberships and increase deposit accounts and balances with current members. Centric had a high number of members on its books that had taken advantage of the low interest rates for loans. Some of these members held the minimum required in savings balance and usually had no checking account.

Emogen Marketing developed the "Free-er Than Free Checking" campaign that featured television, radio, and billboard spots. The tagline "just like a bank . . . only better" was adopted.

The entire Centric Federal Credit Union campaign is located at the Pearson Instructor's Resource Center (www.pearsonhighered. com). The campaign contains a PowerPoint presentation outlining the details of the campaigns and examples of the collaterals created by Emogen Marketing.

Courtesy of Emogen Marketing Group.

MyMarketingLab

Go to **mymktlab.com** to complete the problems marked with this icon .

SUMMARY

Database marketing has become a vital element of a complete IMC program. The two key activities involved at the most general level, identifying customers and building relationships with them, have an impact on numerous other IMC tasks. It is more cost-effective to retain customers than to seek out new ones. Further, the actual message may change when communicating with long-time, loyal customers.

Building a data warehouse begins with collecting data to be used by the marketing department. Beyond basic information, such as a customer's name, address, and e-mail address, other key data include the customer's purchase history and preferences. Geocoding involves adding geographic codes to customer records, which assists in selecting media and creating messages targeted to specific groups.

Database coding and analysis leads to either lifetime value analysis of customers or the clustering of customer groups based on customer spending patterns. Data mining programs involve building profiles of customer segments and/or preparing models that predict future purchase behaviors based on past purchases. The information gathered from data coding and data mining leads to the development of data-driven marketing communications and marketing programs.

Database-driven marketing communication programs are facilitated by effective identification codes that allow for personalization of messages and interactions. An effective database-driven communication program relies on customer profiles combined with other information available regarding specific customers. In-bound telemarketing programs, trawling, advertising, and lifetime value segment programs can be fine-tuned for individual customers.

Database-driven marketing programs include permission marketing, frequency programs, and CRM systems. Permission marketing is a selling approach in which the customer agrees to receive promotional materials in exchange for various incentives. Frequency programs are incentives customers receive for repeat business. Both are designed to create customer loyalty over time. CRM is designed to build long-term loyalty and bonds with customers through the use of a personal touch facilitated by technology.

Direct response or direct marketing efforts may be made by mail, catalog, phone, mass media, the Internet, or e-mail. Direct mail programs remain popular as outbound telemarketing programs continue to diminish.

A case can be made that individual consumers desire greater intimacy with the companies that serve them. They are drawn to firms that take the time to build relationships through quality, customized communications and marketing programs. This trend will likely continue. Successful marketing teams should continue to emphasize methods for identifying customers and personalizing relationships.

Key Terms

data warehouse The place where customer data are held.

geocoding Adding geographic codes to customer records to make it possible to plot customer addresses on a map.

lifetime value The present value of future profits a customer generates over his or her life in a relationship with a brand or firm.

data mining The process of using computer data analysis software to mine data for meaningful information and relationships.

trawling The process of searching the database for a specific piece of information for marketing purposes.

permission marketing A form of database marketing in which the company sends promotional materials to customers who give the company permission to do so.

empowerment Consumers believe they have power throughout the seller–consumer relationship, not just at the beginning when they agreed to join a frequency program.

reciprocity A sense of obligation toward a company that results from receiving special deals or incentives such as gifts.

frequency (or loyalty) program A marketing program designed to promote loyalty or frequent purchases of the same brand (or company).

customer relationship management (CRM) Programs designed to build long-term loyalty and bonds with customers through the use of a personal touch facilitated by technology.

share of customer The percentage of expenditures a customer makes with one particular firm compared to total expenditures in that product's category.

direct response (or direct) marketing Vending products to customers without the use of other channel members.

response list A list of customers who have made purchases or who have responded to direct mail offers in the past.

compiled list A list consisting of information about consumers who meet a specific demographic profile.

digital direct-to-press Software that instructs the computer to create a tailor-made direct mail message to a customer.

relationship selling Developing long-term relationships with customers rather than focusing on a single transaction.

stimulus-response A sales approach, often called a "canned" sales pitch, that uses specific statements (stimuli) to elicit specific responses from customers.

need-satisfaction A sales approach in which the salesperson strives to discover a customer's needs during the first part of the sales presentation and then provides solutions to those needs.

problem-solution A sales approach that requires employees from the selling organization to analyze the buyer's operations and offer ways to solve their problems.

mission-sharing A sales approach in which two organizations develop a common mission and then share resources to accomplish that mission.

Review Questions

1. What two activities are parts of a successful database marketing program?
2. What is a data warehouse? What is the difference between an operational database and a marketing database?
3. List the steps involved in building a data warehouse.
4. What is geocoding?
5. Define *lifetime value*. How is it determined?
6. What are the two primary functions of data mining?
7. Explain how identification codes are used in database-driven marketing communications.
8. Explain how consumer profile information is used when sending communications to customers.

9. Describe a permission marketing program. What are the key benefits of this approach?

10. What are the keys to an effective permission marketing program?

11. Describe a frequency program. What three principles should guide the development of a loyalty program?

12. What is customer relationship management? Explain why most CRM programs have not been successful.

13. What is meant by the term *share of customer*?

14. What is direct response marketing?

15. Explain how response lists and compiled lists are used in direct mail programs.

16. Why is digital direct-to-press popular in business-to-business direct marketing?

17. Explain the two ways infomercials are presented as parts of a direct response program.

18. What is relationship marketing?

19. What steps are involved in the personal selling process?

20. Identify the four types of sales presentations typically used by sales reps.

21. What types of closing methods are available to salespeople?

Critical Thinking Exercises

DISCUSSION QUESTIONS

1. Assume that you are the account executive at a database marketing agency. A music retailer has asked you to develop a database for the company. How would you go about building a data warehouse? What information should be in the databases? Where and how would you obtain the data?

2. Hickory Outdoor is a retail store that sells fishing, hunting, camping, and other outdoor equipment and supplies, including various items for a number of outdoor sports. The company has built a database of its customers over the last 5 years. The marketing team can use data mining to improve their marketing efforts. Suggest ways data mining can be used. What type of marketing programs would you suggest based on data mining? What other types of marketing programs can be developed from the database?

3. Karen's Formal Dress is a retailer specializing in formal and wedding wear. She has a database with over 3,000 names of individuals who have purchased or rented formal wear. She would like to develop a permission marketing program. How can the marketing team encourage individuals to give permission to receive marketing materials? Once the company has the customer's permission, how can the relationship be continued to make it beneficial to both the consumer and to Karen's Formal Dress? Describe the methodology Karen should use in her permissions marketing program, including the types of materials, methods of distribution, and incentives.

4. A primary reason for developing a frequency program is to encourage customers to be loyal to a business or brand. For each of the following products, discuss the merits of a frequency program. What types of incentives would individuals need to join the frequency club and then to continue participation in the program?
   a. Local restaurant
   b. Auto repair service
   c. Printing service
   d. Clothing retailer

5. Examine the forms of direct response marketing shown in the graph in Figure 11.11. Which ones have you responded to in the past? Which ones are most likely to influence your purchase decisions? Which ones are the least likely? Explain for each method your personal responses over the last year.

6. The marketing team for Hickory Outdoor (see question 2) is seeking to use direct response advertising to accomplish two goals: (1) to sell specific merchandise and (2) to encourage individuals to visit the store or its Web site. Which types of direct response advertising would be the most effective? Why? What type of direct response offers should Hickory Outdoor make?

7. Examine the direct marketing methods highlighted in Figure 11.11. Evaluate each method for the following types of businesses. Which ones would be the best? Which ones would not work as well? Justify your answers.
   a. Shoe store
   b. Sporting goods retailer
   c. Internet hosiery retailer (sells only via the Internet)
   d. Manufacturer of tin cans for food-processing companies

8. Interview five individuals. Ask each person to list the catalogs they have received during the past month. Have each person discuss why he or she receives certain catalogs. Ask how often each person orders something out of a catalog and how the order is usually placed. Is anyone accessing the Internet for information offered in a catalog or ordering from a catalog after accessing a Web site? Discuss how important the catalog market is today and what you see as the future of catalog marketing.

9. Think about a recent personal purchase experience that involved a salesperson. Describe how the salesperson handled you during the sales call. Which sales presentation approach did the salesperson use? Which methods of handling objections were used? Evaluate how well the objection was handled. Which closing did the salesperson use? How well did the salesperson handle the closing?

Integrated Learning Exercises

⭐ **1.** Pick one company that sells clothing. Go to the company's Web site. What evidence do you see of database marketing and of personalization of the Web site? Describe a database marketing program that the company could use.

2. Go to Web site for Scotts Miracle Gro at **www.scotts.com/smg**. What evidence do you see of database marketing and of personalization? Review the concepts presented in the section "Database-Driven Marketing Communications." What steps should Scotts take to develop data-driven communications with visitors to the Web site as well as individuals who make purchases?

3. A number of companies specialize in database marketing. You are the manager of a small chain of 25 restaurants. Review the Web site of each of the following companies. Outline what each company offers. Which one would be the best for your company? Why?

  a. Database Marketing Group (**www.dbmgroup.com**)

  b. Advanced Marketing Consultants (**www.marketingprinciples.com**)

  c. Dovetail (**www.dovetaildatabase.com**)

4. *DMNews* is a trade journal for database marketing and CRM programs. Access the Web site at **www.dmnews.com**. What types of information are available on the site? How could this help companies with database marketing and CRM programs? Access and read one of the articles from the journal. Write a paragraph about what you learned.

5. CentricData is a database marketing firm that specializes in mid-size to large retailers. Access the Web site at **www.centricdata.com**. What types of services does CentricData offer? How could this company help a retail store develop a database marketing program?

6. The Direct Marketing Association (DMA) is a global trade association of business and nonprofit organizations that use direct marketing tools and techniques. Access the trade organization's Web site at **www.the-dma.org**. What services does the DMA provide its members? What value would this be to a business in developing a direct marketing program?

7. A primary key in successful direct marketing is the quality of the list that is used. One company that specializes in compiling lists is US Data Corporation. Access the company's Web site at **www.usdatacorporation.com**. What types of lists does the company offer? Access one of the lists and describe how that list can be compiled. Discuss how a company could use US Data Corporation for a direct response marketing campaign.

8. Almost all hotels have some type of frequency or loyalty program. Examine the loyalty programs of the following hotels. Critique each one. Which ones are best? Why?

  a. Best Western (**www.bestwestern.com**)

  b. Days Inn (**www.daysinn.com**)

  c. Doubletree Inn (**doubletree.hilton.com**)

  d. Marriott (**www.marriott.com**)

  e. Radisson (**www.radisson.com**)

  f. Wyndham Hotels & Resorts (**www.wyndham.com**)

Student Project

CREATIVE CORNER

Lilly Fashions sells fashionable, trendy clothes. The company's primary target customer is 20 to 30 years old, female, has an average income of $40,000, and has some college. Lilly's marketing team wants to capitalize on the concepts of database marketing and direct response marketing. Design a newspaper advertisement that encourages females in the company's target market to visit the retail store and join Lilly's loyalty program. In addition, design a direct mail piece that would go to individuals who are currently in the database but who have not made a purchase within the last 3 months. Prepare another e-mail that can be sent to members in the database on the person's birthday offering them a free meal at a local restaurant, if they come to the store to pick up the meal voucher. This promotion is a joint promotion with the restaurant, which shares in the cost, which means the restaurant must also be part of the e-mail.

CASE 1 THE TRAVEL AGENCY DILEMMA

Leisure time travel remains a common pursuit across a variety of markets. Numerous forces influence consumers as they seek out restful, adventuresome, romantic, and family-oriented vacations. Factors such as gasoline and airline ticket prices, economic conditions, political unrest, and the changing world of technology factor into personal and family decisions regarding places to go, things to do, people to see, and events to enjoy.

Travel agencies experience the influence of these forces as directly as any other group. When gas prices rise, consumers take shorter trips. When airline tickets are at a premium, travelers look for bargains or seek other alternatives. Unemployment, political turmoil in places such as Mexico and Europe, and other considerations cause people to either stay at home or change travel plans.

The most direct influence on the travel agency business has been the Internet and its popular travel sites. Travelocity, Priceline.com, and other airline booking sites allow consumers to shop online for the best air fares and travel times. Hotels.com plus numerous hotel chain-run booking sites, which also offer frequency programs, make it possible to find the most ideal hotel arrangement without the use of a travel agency. Many Internet-savvy consumers no longer feel the need to call or drive to a local travel agency. These individuals have become convinced that they are able to match any price or travel arrangement that an agency can find.

To compete in this intense environment, agency managers seek ways to deliver value-added services that entice consumers to continue to utilize their companies. Among the potential methods to maintain customer loyalty are offers of convenience, skill at finding better prices than consumers can obtain online, and the ability to package travel into one-price programs. Many travel agencies create agreements with hotels, cruise lines, and airlines to offer better prices than consumers encounter in other ways.

Travel agencies can also offer suggestions regarding combinations of activities, such as fine dining with an elaborate hotel. Many agency employees visit numerous destinations, seeking to obtain better quality information about local attractions that would go unnoticed by travelers to a specific area.

In the future, the question remains as to whether travel agencies will be able to continue to compete. Only with carefully constructed service programs and quality marketing

▲ With access to the Internet, many tourists see little value in the services provided by travel agencies.

efforts will it be possible to maintain a set of clientele as the world of Internet shopping continues to increase.

1. How might database marketing, including the data warehouse, data coding and analysis, and data mining, help a travel agency create and enhance relationships with customers and potential customers?

2. How could data-driven marketing programs including permission marketing, frequency programs, and customer relationship management systems be of use to travel agencies?

3. Discuss each of the direct response marketing techniques in relation to marketing of travel agencies.

4. What personal selling tactics are most important to travel agency employees as they work with customers and potential customers?

5. Discuss the pros and cons of each of the methods of handling objections in personal selling in relation to a couple who are hesitant to purchase vacation to one of the Caribbean islands.

6. Discuss the pros and cons of each of the closing methods in personal selling in relation to a couple who are hesitant to purchase vacation to one of the Caribbean islands.

CASE 2 ANHEUSER-BUSCH: DATABASE MARKETING AND PERSONAL SELLING

Margie Washburn was about to begin an exciting new era in her life. She had purchased the distributorship rights for Anheuser-Busch InBev products in the Denver/Aurora, Colorado area. Even though her company would be standing in the shadow of the Coors Brewing Company, she believed that through effective database marketing and personal selling tactics, Budweiser and Busch products would be widely accepted in the region.

As a distributor, Margie's primary customers are other businesses, specifically, bars, taverns, and restaurants that serve beer to patrons; retail outlets such as grocery stores, convenience markets, and liquor stores; and entertainment venues, including the arena housing the Denver Nuggets. She did not expect to make in-roads selling beer at Coors Field, home of the Denver Broncos.

Anheuser-Busch competes in a highly fragmented market. Major vendors include Miller/Coors, Heineken, Corona, and Guinness. Recently, other beer companies had created buzz and captured some market share, including Dos Equis, Stella Artois, and Samuel Adams. The microbrewery trend that expanded quickly in the 1990s had slowed; however, several popular local companies were doing well in the Denver area.

Anheuser-Busch InBev had endured some negative publicity in the past decade, when the former Anheuser-Busch, owned and operated from the United States, was acquired by Belgian brewer InBev. Some customers feared that popular products such as Budweiser and Bud Light would somehow be changed by an international company.

Advertising and promotional efforts targeted at individual consumers continue. Budweiser's "King of Beers" approach, including commercials featuring the Clydesdales, maintained a strong brand presence. Bud Light's use of comedy had also created positive reactions. A recent campaign emphasizing the romance and marriage of Bud Light with wheat had been used to kick off another variation of Anheuser products, Bud Light Golden Wheat. Anheuser-Busch produces lower-end beers, including Natural Light, as well as the higher-end Michelob line of beers.

One of Margie's challenges was finding out how each type of customer related to her products and brands. She needed to know how many restaurants and drinking establishments prominently displayed her beers. She also was interested in finding out whether her products received good, fair, or poor shelf space in off-sale outlets. From there she might be able to find ways to create bonds with individual consumers that would "pull" Anheuser-Busch brands to the forefront in these locations.

© bst2012/Fotolia

▲ Margie faced a number of challenges with her distributorship.

Margie also knew that her competitors employed brand ambassadors, especially on-campus at the universities in the Denver area. The ambassadors were college students who pitched Miller/Coors products to fellow students and local watering holes. Miller/Coors also sponsored a variety of events targeting college-age students with music and sports.

To compete, the new Anheuser-Busch InBev distributorship required an extensive, coordinated marketing communications program. The objective would be to tie brand loyalty and positive relationships with individual consumers to database programs use personal selling tactics to reach all of the business-to-business customers in the area. Margie looked forward to getting started.

1. What types of data should the distributorship collect about individual consumers? How can it be used?

2. What types of data should the distributorship collect about business customers? How can it be used?

3. Can the distributorship build any frequency or loyalty programs in the area? If so, describe what would work. If not, why not?

4. What sales approach should the sales staff use for the various businesses that sell Anheuser-Busch products, such as nightclubs?

5. What type of sales approach should the company use to entice liquor vendors to carry and emphasize Anheuser-Busch products in both on-sale and off-sale venues?

MyMarketingLab

Go to **mymktlab.com** for Auto-graded writing questions as well as the following Assisted-graded writing questions:.

11-1. Karen's Formal Dress is a retailer specializing in formal and wedding wear. She has a database with over 3,000 names of individuals who have purchased or rented formal wear. She would like to develop a permission marketing program. How can the marketing team encourage individuals to give permission to receive marketing materials? Once the company has the customer's permission, how can the relationship be continued to make it beneficial to both the consumer and to Karen's Formal Dress? Describe the methodology Karen should use in her permissions marketing program, including the types of materials, methods of distribution, and incentives.

11-2. Pick one company that sells clothing. Go to the company's Web site. What evidence do you see of database marketing and of personalization of the Web site? Describe a database marketing program that the company could use.

11-3. Mymktlab Only—comprehensive writing assignment for this chapter.

12

SALES PROMOTIONS

CHAPTER OBJECTIVES

After reading this chapter, you should be able to answer the following questions:

1. What differences exist between consumer promotions and trade promotions?

2. How can the various forms of consumer promotions help to pull consumers into stores and push products onto the shelves?

3. How do different types of customers respond to consumer promotions?

4. What types of trade promotions can help push products onto retailers' shelves and eventually to end users?

5. What concerns exist for manufacturers considering trade promotions programs?

6. What issues complicate international sales promotions programs?

MyMarketingLab™

⭐ **Improve Your Grade!**

Over 10 million students improved their results using the Pearson MyLabs. Visit **mymktlab.com** for simulations, tutorials, and end-of-chapter problems.

SALES PROMOTIONS AND MORE HOOK FANS

"What is your favorite word?" This question was posed by baseball executive Jay Miller at a recent marketing conference. "If you think about it, it might be that one of your favorite words is your own name," he said with a smile. Miller continued, "When you come to our ballpark, we are going to know your name." In truth, Jay Miller is talking about two ballparks, one in Corpus Christi, Texas, and the other in Round Rock, Texas. The ballparks are home to minor league professional baseball teams.

The Corpus Christi team, the Hooks, continues to be a stellar success. The organization, an affiliate of the Texas Rangers, averages more than 7,000 fans per game over 72 home dates each summer. This ranks among the top franchises at the Double-A level of professional baseball. Beyond the statistics, however, is the sense of civic pride that permeates the team, the fans, and the entire organization. In a city with a large Hispanic community, the term *la familia* clearly applies. The Hooks are a family that hosts a large number of guests at each game.

Professional baseball thrives on consumer promotions. For fans, numerous discounts and giveaways are part of the scene. In 2010, the Hooks staged over 30 promotional nights. The free gifts included bobbleheads, baseball card sets, duffle bags, blankets, photos, autographed souvenirs, and more. In addition, the team offers "One Dollar Hot Dog and Soda Night," "Half-Price Group Night," "Thirsty Thursdays," and "Friday Fireworks."

Sponsorships and trade promotion tie-ins are widely utilized. The ballpark is named "Whataburger" field, due to the sponsorship of the popular hamburger chain. Whataburger hosts its own fan day. Other sponsors place advertising on the scoreboard, field, walls, and other places. Corporate box seats are available for entertaining clients and rewarding employees. A video board features various business organizations and items given to fans. In addition, the Hooks maintain ties with several local charities and civic organizations, including the "Get Hooked on Reading" program for young fans.

All of these sales promotions serve to enhance the rest of the organization's marketing efforts. Jay Miller and CEO Reid Ryan strongly emphasize the importance of "awesome customer service." At a Hooks game, everyone from parking attendants to the ticket takers to the ushers and concessions personnel focuses on friendly, first-name care. Miller and Ryan routinely circulate through the stands to mingle with fans, solve any problems, and provide an occasional extra thrill. One of their favorites is finding a family sitting in the cheapest (most distant) seats in the stadium and moving them to the owner's box next to the field.

The team also hosts a "postgame catch" in which many lucky kids are brought down to the field to play catch with players. On Sundays, or "Kids Day," fans are allowed on the field prior to the game. Many times disadvantaged children, Little Leaguers, and others are paired with a player as the game is about to begin to stand on the field during the national anthem. Other attendees participate in the "Dizzy Bat Race" or in races with the Hooks mascot. Even those who stay in the stands may find themselves featured in "Kiss Cam" or "Fan Cam" on the

Courtesy of Ryan Sanders Baseball.

Courtesy of Ryan Sanders Baseball.

▲ Reid Ryan

Courtesy of Ryan Sanders Baseball.

▲ Jay Miller

16-by-22-foot video screen between innings.

Reid Ryan's father, Hall of Fame pitcher Nolan Ryan, is one of the team's principle owners. Reid believes the success of the organization, known as Ryan Sanders Baseball, results from promoting a summer-long experience rather than a single event. Instead of focusing on wins and losses or even on players, the enjoyment of attending a series of games in a low-cost, family friendly environment remains the key to long-term fan loyalty. Players come and go, teams win and lose, but a fun summer evening with family and friends creates a long-lasting impression. The Hooks' advertising tagline, "Catch a Memory-Hooks Baseball," expresses this feeling.

Jay Miller has been associated with professional baseball for over 24 years. He has been named "Executive of the Year" on more than one occasion, and was recently promoted into the front office of the Texas Ranges. He proudly reports that sales of memorabilia for the Hooks are higher than the majority of minor league teams, an indication of the strong loyalty in the community. A walk down the streets of Corpus Christi or a visit to the ballpark confirms the devotion fans show by proudly wearing caps, T-shirts, and jerseys with the Hooks insignia and logo.

Both Miller and Ryan stress the importance of brand and image building. In a marketplace where a wide variety of summertime activities are possible, they emphasize the goal of being top-of-mind, or the family's first choice. A stadium full of happy customers for every home game provides all the evidence they need that their approach works.[1]

OVERVIEW

OBJECTIVE 12.1

What differences exist between consumer promotions and trade promotions?

It may be tempting to think that a high-quality advertising program completes the task of promotion. It does not. An integrated marketing communications program includes additional key activities. This chapter describes sales promotions programs. **Sales promotions** consist of all of the incentives offered to customers and channel members to encourage product purchases.

Sales promotions take two forms: consumer promotions and trade promotions. Companies offer **consumer promotions** incentives directly to customers and potential customers. Consumer promotions are aimed at those who actually use the product, or end users. They may be individuals or households. Another end user may be a business that consumes the product, and the item is not resold to another business. In other words, companies offer consumer promotions in both consumer markets and business-to-business markets.

Trade promotions are only allotted in the distribution channel. **Trade promotions** consist of the expenditures or incentives used by manufacturers and other members of the marketing channel to purchase goods for eventual resale. Trade promotions provided to other firms help push products through to retailers.

In the past, some marketing experts believed that any type of sales promotion, whether consumer or trade, eroded brand equity by shifting the focus to price. Now, however, many company leaders recognize that properly managed promotions differentiate a brand from the competition, helping to build brand awareness and improving a brand's image.[2]

The marketing team designs promotional programs to help the company achieve its IMC objectives and that support a brand's position. In the early stages of a product's life cycle, promotions match advertising and other efforts focused on brand awareness, creating opportunities for trial purchases and stimulating additional purchases. Later, the goal shifts to strengthening a brand, increasing consumption, fending off competition, or finding new markets.

This chapter examines consumer promotions first, followed by trade promotions. Although the presentations are separate, the marketing team designs both at the same time. The adjustments made to sales promotions programs in international markets are also described.

Consumer Promotions

Enticing a consumer to take the final step and make the purchase constitutes a primary goal for a consumer promotions program. Advertising creates the interest and excitement that brings the consumer to the store. Marketers then use other tactics. In addition to leading to the final decision to buy an item, consumer promotions programs help generate store traffic and enhance brand loyalty.

During recent Super Bowls, Denny's offered free breakfast to anyone who came into the restaurant from 6:00 a.m. to 2:00 p.m. on the Tuesday following the game. Roughly 2 million Americans took advantage of the offer each year. Some waited in line for hours for a breakfast. The promotion's goal, according to CEO Nelson Marchioli, was to "re-acquaint America with Denny's." He added, "We've never been thanked this much—and folks are saying they'll come back." The cost of the entire promotion, including food, labor, and the Super Bowl commercial, was about $5 million. In exchange, Denny's earned something money alone cannot buy; a powerful positive public relations blitz. The promotion garnered as much as $50 million in free, positive media news coverage. The company received 40 million hits on its Web site in the week following the Super Bowl, suggesting a highly successful consumer promotions program.[3] Figure 12.1 identifies the most common consumer promotions that will be described next.

Coupons

A coupon offers a price reduction to the consumer. It may be a percentage off the retail price, such as 25 or 40 percent, or an absolute amount, such as 50 cents or $1. Each year companies print almost 300 billion coupons and on average consumers redeem 2.5 billion. The 0.85 percent redemption rate represents approximately $3.87 billion in savings for consumers or around $1.55 per coupon.[4] Nearly 80 percent of all U.S. households use coupons, and almost two-thirds are willing to switch brands with coupons.[5]

COUPON DISTRIBUTION

Manufacturers issue approximately 80 percent of all coupons. Most coupons are sent through print media, with vast majority distributed through **freestanding inserts (FSIs)**, or sheets of coupons distributed in newspapers, primarily on Sunday. FSIs represent almost 90 percent of all coupons distributed, although the percentage has been declined as consumers switch to digitally-delivered coupons.[6] Figure 12.2 identifies the various forms of coupon distribution.

FSIs and print media remain popular for several reasons. First, the consumer makes a conscious effort to clip or save the coupon. Second, coupons create brand awareness. The consumer sees the brand name on the coupon even when it is not redeemed. Third, FSIs encourage consumers to purchase brands on the next trip to the store. Consumers are more likely to purchase a couponed brand and remember the name when they redeem a coupon, which helps move the brand to a consumer's long-term memory.

Digital coupons are growing in popularity. About 15 percent of the U.S. population, or 45 million consumers, redeem digital coupons. Digital coupon users tend to be more affluent and better educated. The average household income for a digital coupon user is $97,000. One-third has earned a college degree. Webs sites make it easy for consumers to find and print coupons, download them onto mobile devices, or transfer them to a loyalty card. Retail stores, including JCPenney, Kroger, and Safeway, feature technologies that permit consumers to redeem coupons from cell phones. CVS Pharmacy customers can

OBJECTIVE 12.2
How can the various forms of consumer promotions help to pull consumers into stores and push products onto the store shelves?

- Coupons
- Premiums
- Contests and sweepstakes
- Refunds and rebates
- Sampling
- Bonus packs
- Price-offs

▲ **FIGURE 12.1**
Types of Consumer Promotions

- Print media
  - Freestanding inserts (FSIs)
- Direct mail
- In- or on-package
- In-store
  - Scanner delivered
- Digital
- Employee delivered

▲ **FIGURE 12.2**
Methods of Distributing Coupons

▲ A manufacturer's coupon for 50 cents off Snax Stix.

▼ A cross-ruffing coupon for Tyson and Betty Crocker.

scan a loyalty card at a kiosk inside the store entrance to receive instant coupon offers and in-store specials based on their purchase histories. Ease of use spurs the growth of digital coupons.[7]

TYPES OF COUPONS

Coupons are distributed in retail stores, offered digitally from the Internet or in a store, such as CVS, and may be placed on or near packages. In each instance, the consumer can immediately redeem the coupon at the store through an *instant redemption coupon* program. The coupons often lead to trial purchases and purchases of additional packages of a product. Many grocery stores sponsor a company to cook a food product and offer free samples along with coupon giveaways, which represents another form of instant redemption couponing.

Coupons can be placed inside packages so that customers cannot redeem them quite as quickly. This encourages repeat purchases. The coupons are called *bounce-back coupons*.

Some retailers issue coupons at the cash register. *Scanner-delivered coupons* are triggered by an item being scanned on the register. The coupon being delivered is often for a competitor's product, thereby which encourage brand switching the next time a consumer makes a purchase.

To encourage purchases of additional products, sometimes manufactures provide *cross-ruffing coupons*, which is placing a coupon on one product for another product. For example, a coupon for French onion dip may be placed on a package of potato chips. Cross-ruff coupons should be for products that logically fit together and that are often purchased and consumed simultaneously. Occasionally, a manufacturer uses cross-ruffing to encourage consumers to purchase another of its products. Kellogg's may place a coupon on a Rice Krispies box for another cereal, such as Frosted Flakes or an oatmeal product. This type of couponing tactic encourages consumers to purchase within the same brand or family of products.

DISADVANTAGE OF COUPONS

Customers who have a brand preference redeem approximately 80 percent of all coupons.[8] Some believe that offering price discounts through coupons to customers who are willing to pay full price does not make sense. Manufacturers, however, argue that these consumers may be willing to stock up on the item, which means they do not buy from the competition. It can also result in the consumer using more of the product. In essence, manufacturers recognize that these brand-preference customer redemptions are a "necessary evil" in mass distribution programs. To avoid sending coupons to current customers, firms may send direct mail coupons to non-loyal customers, thereby targeting nonusers and the competitor's customers.

Premiums

Premiums are prizes, gifts, or other special offers consumers receive when purchasing products. The consumer pays full price vice with a premium. In contrast, coupons grant price reductions.

TYPES OF PREMIUMS

Figure 12.3 identifies four major types of premiums. *Free-in-the-mail premiums* are gifts individuals receive for purchasing products. To receive the gift, the customer mails in a proof of purchase to the manufacturer that then sends the gift to the buyer. More than one purchase may be required to receive some gifts. A premium offer appears in the Fisher Boy advertisement shown in this section. Consumers collect points from the front of Fisher Boy packages to be redeemed for "cool" prizes. To further encourage sales, the advertisement also carries a coupon.

Credit card companies employ premiums to entice individuals to sign up for credit cards. Instead of providing a proof of purchase, the consumer activates the card to receive an incentive, which range from cash back on a purchase to merchandise and frequent-flier miles.

In- or on-package premiums are usually small gifts, such as toys in cereal boxes. The gift may be disguised or packaged so the consumer must buy the product to see the premium. At other times, the gift will be attached to the package, such as a package of blades with the purchase of a razor.

Store or *manufacturer premiums* are gifts given by either the retail store or the manufacturer when the customer purchases a product. Fast-food restaurants lure children a toy that accompanies the purchase of a child's meal. Hyundai recently offered a unique premium. With the purchase of a new Hyundai Equus, with the suggested retail price of $50,000, customers received a free Apple iPad loaded with the 300-page owner's interactive manual. The iPad included a leather slipcase with the car's service appointments preloaded and scheduled.[9]

The fourth type, a *self-liquidating premium*, requires the consumer to pay a small amount of money for the gift or item. The premium may be offered for only $4.99 plus shipping and handling and two proofs of purchase from boxes of Cheerios. The premium is called self-liquidating because $4.99 covers the premium's cost. The manufacturer may also receive money for shipping and handling so that consumers pay for most or all of the expense of the item.

KEYS TO SUCCESSFUL PREMIUM PROGRAMS

Successful premium programs include several common elements (Figure 12.4). First, the premium should match the target market. A target market consisting of older, high-income individuals can be reached with a premium such as china or fine crystal. If the market is children, a cartoon figure or a character from Disney or Sesame Street becomes more attractive.

- Free-in-the-mail
- In- or on-package
- Store or manufacturer
- Self-liquidating

▲ **FIGURE 12.3**
Types of Premiums

Courtesy of Fisher Boy.

▲ A free-in-the-mail premium by Fisher Boy for "cool" prizes and a coupon for 55 cents off.

- Match the premium to the target market
- Carefully select the premiums (avoid fads, try for exclusivity)
- Pick a premium that reinforces the firm's product and image
- Integrate the premium with other IMC tools (especially advertising and POP displays)
- Don't expect premiums to increase short-term profits

◀ **FIGURE 12.4**
Keys to Successful Premium Programs

Source: Based on Don Jagoda, "The Seven Habits of Highly Successful Premiums," *Incentive* 173, no. 8 (August 1999), pp. 104–105.

MENS SUITS & SPORT COATS

BUY 1 GET THE 2ND AT 50% OFF THROUGH OCTOBER

THE TOGGERY

1400 North 18th Street Monroe, LA
388-4939 Mon - Sat 10 am - 6 pm

▲ A newspaper ad by The Toggery offering a premium "Buy 1 get the 2nd at 50% off."

The best premiums reinforce the firm's image. They should not be low-cost trinkets. Giving away cheap merchandise insults customers and damages the firm's image. Premium programs succeed when they tie in with the firm's products to enhance the image of the product and the brand.[10]

Premiums should be integrated with the other components of the IMC program. General Mills recently offered collectable Star War premiums tied in with the recent Star Wars movie. The premium effort was supported by in-store pallet displays, FSIs, and digital efforts on sites such as MyBlogSpark.com, Star-Wars.com, and Lucasfilm's Twitter. In addition, to drive awareness of the promotion, General Mills added a 10-second tag to television spots for the cereal brands with the premiums inside the box.[11]

Some marketing experts believe overusing coupons damages a brand's image. Conversely, premiums might actually enhance an image. Picking the right type of premium becomes the key. Premiums can be used to boost sales; however, they usually are not as successful as coupon sales. Nevertheless, premiums remain a valuable consumer promotional tool.

In the United States, companies spend approximately $24 billion on premiums each year.[12] Although premiums add value and enhance the brand, they are less effective at increasing profits. Therefore, a clear relationship between the premium's intention and IMC goals should be established. Logically, the goal relates to image rather than profit.

Contests and Sweepstakes

Each year, companies spend approximately $1.9 billion on the various games, contests, and sweepstakes, that appear in both consumer and business markets.[13] The prize list largely determines the success or failure of these appeals. Members of the target market for the contest or sweepstakes must desire the prizes in order to entice them to participate.

CONTESTS

The words *contest* and *sweepstakes* tend to be used interchangeably, yet some differences exist, primarily legal. *Contests* normally require the participant to perform an activity. The winner will be selected from the group that performs best or provides the most correct answers. Often, contests require a participant to make a purchase to enter. In some states, however, forcing consumers to make a purchase to enter a contest is illegal. In developing contests, the marketing team first investigates the state and federal laws that apply.

Contests range from the bikini contests at local nightclubs to popular television shows such as *Jeopardy* or *American Idol* in which contestants must answer questions or win competitions to earn prizes. Although some contests are mostly chance, others require skill. For example, Dr. Pepper encouraged visitors to the Web site deviantART.com to submit designs for a Dr. Pepper-themed outdoor mural. The winner, Rey Jawahir of Hillsborough County, Florida, was selected from among 2,105 entries. He won a trip to Brooklyn to see the mural, a $3,000 iPad and various deviantART.com perks. The contest generated 314,000 page views besides mentions on Facebook, Twitter and other social media sites.[14]

SWEEPSTAKES

No purchase is required to enter a sweepstakes. Consumers can enter as many times as they wish, although companies can restrict customers to one entry per visit to the store or location. Probability dictates the chances of winning a sweepstakes. The odds of winning must clearly be stated on all point-of-purchase (POP) displays and advertising materials. In a sweepstakes, the probability of winning each prize must also be published in advance.

PERCEIVED VALUE

People enter contests and sweepstakes that they find interesting or challenging. Consumers do not enter every contest or sweepstakes they encounter. Instead, they selectively choose. The decision will be based on the perceived value of the contest or sweepstakes prize combined with the odds of winning. The greater the perceived odds of winning, the more likely it becomes that a person will participate.

A contest or sweepstakes' perceived value consists of two components: extrinsic value and intrinsic value. The *extrinsic value* represents the actual attractiveness of the prize (a car versus a free sandwich). The greater the perceived extrinsic value, the more likely people will become involved. *Intrinsic values* are those associated with participating. A contest requiring the demonstration of a skill, such as the one with recipes or an essay contest, entices entry by individuals who enjoy demonstrating that skill. Extrinsic rewards become secondary. Instead, participants enjoy competing and demonstrating their abilities. This, in part, explains the popularity of fantasy football and baseball leagues and "pick the winner" sports contests such as the NCAA basketball tournament each spring.

▲ This advertisement for fantasy fishing by Bassmaster is designed to appeal to outdoorsmen.

Sears recently launched a national "More Green Across America" contest that encouraged individuals to nominate baseball fields, playgrounds, and other community green spaces. The contestants sent photos and wrote short essays about why the area deserved a makeover. Baseball Hall-of-Famer Mike Schmidt appeared as the campaign's spokesperson. Sears narrowed the list down to 10 worthy projects and then had the public vote for the winner. The grand prize winner received a new yard tractor, mower, line trimmer, edger, and blower as well as a visit from the Sears Blue Lawn & Garden Crew to help complete the beautification project.[15]

To encourage consumers to continue participating in a contest, the extrinsic values of prizes can be increased by allowing small, incremental rewards. A consumer who wins a soft drink or a sandwich in a sweepstakes at Subway may be more likely to continue participating. Scratch-and-win cards tend to be effective because the reward is instant.

THE INTERNET AND SOCIAL MEDIA

The Internet has become a popular location for contests and sweepstakes. It provides opportunities for individuals to see a prize's intrinsic value by creating interactive games to challenge a contestant's ability. The Internet offers promoters data-capturing capabilities. Internet contests are less costly to set up and run than other types of promotions.

The newest trends in contests and sweepstakes include social media. Microsoft, Sephora, NASCAR, Comcast, Chik-fil-A, and McDonald's have created Twitter sweepstakes or have used Twitter and social media sites to enlist participants for a contest or sweepstakes. The intention is to use the sweepstakes or contest to ignite a viral buzz around the brand.[16]

Courtesy of Skyjacker Suspensions.

▲ This advertisement for Skyjacker offers a $35 rebate on four Skyjacker Hydro or Nitro shocks.

GOALS OF CONTESTS AND SWEEPSTAKES

Contests and sweepstakes encourage customer traffic and can boost sales. Although contests and sweepstakes routinely increase customer traffic, the question remains as to whether they actually boost sales. Some do, others do not. Marketers recognize that intrinsic rewards tend to draw consumers back. This means online games are exciting prospects, because they can be structured to create intrinsic value.

Refunds and Rebates

Refunds and rebates are cash returns offered to consumers or businesses following the purchase of a product. Consumers pay full price for the product but can mail in some type of proof of purchase. The manufacturer then refunds a portion of the purchase price. A *refund* is a cash return on what are called "soft goods," such as food or clothing. *Rebates* are cash returns on "hard goods," which are major ticket items such as automobiles and appliances.

Only about 30 percent of all rebates are claimed. For rebates valued at $50 or more, the percentage of claims rises to about 65 percent. The inconvenience associated with getting the rebate represents the primary reason for low response rates. Too many steps or long waiting times because of "snail mail" are common complaints about rebates. Many consumers wait 2 to 3 months to receive a rebate check.[17]

Rebate programs often suffer from diminished effectiveness because consumers have come to expect them. Car dealers often find that customers wait until rebates are offered. As a result, no new purchase activity takes place without a rebate offer, which delays the purchase process. Further, increasing the amount of a rebate no longer seems to spur additional sales, yet discontinuing or reducing rebate levels tends to have an immediate negative impact.

Refunds and rebates achieve the greatest successes when they are perceived as being new or original. When they become an entrenched part of doing business, they are expected discounts. To be effective, rebates and refunds should change the buyer's behavior, either by leading to a more immediate purchase or by causing the customer to change brands.

Sampling

Sampling is the actual delivery of a product to consumers for their use or consumption. In business-to-business markets, samples of products may be given to potential clients. Sampling also can be featured in the service sector. For example, a tanning salon may offer an initial visit free to encourage new customers to try its facilities. Dentists and lawyers use sampling when they offer an initial consultation free of charge.

In a survey of 1,800 consumers, more than one-third of those who tried a sample purchased the product during the same shopping trip. Fifty-eight percent indicated they would buy the product again. Nearly one-fourth said they bought the product being sampled instead of the brand they intended to purchase.[18] This means sampling constitutes an effective method of getting consumers to try and purchase a particular brand.

SAMPLE DISTRIBUTION

Figure 12.5 lists various methods of samples distribution. The most common consumer method, *in-store distribution*, delivers the sample in the store, such as when a food product is cooked and given to customers on site. *Direct sampling* means items are mailed or

- In-store distribution
- Direct sampling
- Response sampling
- Cross-ruff sampling
- Media sampling
- Professional sampling
- Selective sampling

▲ **FIGURE 12.5**
Methods of Distributing Samples

delivered door-to-door to consumers. In the business-to-business sector, salespeople often deliver direct samples to prospects or to current customers to encourage them to try the company's brand or a new product that just came out.

Response samples are made available to individuals or businesses responding to a media offer on television, on the Internet, from a magazine, or by some other source. *Cross-ruffing* sampling plans provide samples of one product on another. A laundry detergent with a free dryer sheet attached to the package is a cross-ruffing sample.

Media sampling means the sample is included in the media outlet. Recently, samples for Dr. Scholl's Her Open Shoes insoles were affixed to heavy-stock paper in magazines such as *In Style*, *All You*, *Shape*, and *Glamour*. Women could remove the insole and test it on one foot and compare it to the other foot that did not have an insole. Approximately 3 million were distributed. One month after the run, 11 percent of subscribers had purchased insoles and nearly 60 percent said they planned to make purchases. Approximately 57 percent had peeled the sample insole out of the magazine and 37 percent said they actually tested it.[19]

Companies offer *Professional samples* to professionals, such as doctors, who then provide patients with the free drug samples. *Selective samples* are distributed at a site such as a state fair, parade, hospital, restaurant, or sporting event. For instance, Power Bars may be given to people attending football or basketball games. A tie-in exists between the product (nutrition) and the event (athletics).

In recent years, marketers have increased usage of freestanding inserts to distribute samples. A variety of products have been distributed in newspapers, including breakfast bars, coffee, shampoo, snacks, tea, and automotive cleansers. Companies using newspapers employ the FSI insert method because it breaks through the clutter and captures attention. The newspaper is an "invited medium." Therefore, consumers are often more receptive when samples are included in the paper.[20]

▲ This business-to-business Polycom advertisement offers a free 30-day, risk-free trial.

BENEFITS OF SAMPLING

Product sampling offers an effective way to introduce a new item, generate interest in it, and collect information about consumers. Internet-based response sampling programs have become popular with both consumers and manufacturers. Bristol-Myers/Squibb was one of the first companies to utilize the Internet for product sampling. The company offered a free sample of Excedrin to individuals who requested one. They had to be willing to provide their names, addresses, and e-mail information. In addition to the 12-pack sample of Excedrin, consumers received coupons for additional purchases, along with the quarterly *Excedrin Headache Relief Update Newsletter*. This form of response has the advantage of sampling only the consumers who requested the product. Companies normally can gather additional information to be added to a database. Seventy percent of consumers who requested a sample online were willing to complete a survey to receive the item.[21]

SUCCESSFUL SAMPLING PROGRAMS

As with the other consumer promotions, sampling should be related to and based on the IMC plan. Sampling encourages a trial use by a consumer or a business. It will be most effective when it introduces a new product or a new version of a product to a market. Samples also help to promote a current product to a new target market or to new prospects.

Successful sampling means targeting the right audience at the right venue at the right time. Mass sampling will not be nearly as cost-effective as targeted sampling. Chanel sent a sample of its No. 5 fragrance in a package mailer to the 1.2 million subscribers of Vogue magazine. With a median income of $63,000, the readership of Vogue fits the target audience of the affluent Chanel brand. The sample was also sent with the December issue, just in time for making a Christmas gift suggestion. The sample coupled with several ads in the December issue of Vogue created an effective targeted sampling campaign.[22]

Bonus Packs

When an additional or extra number of items are placed in a special product package, it is a bonus pack, such as offering four bars of soap for the price of three. Rayovac recently attached three free AA batteries in a bonus pack containing nine batteries. Typical bonuses range from 20 to 100 percent of the normal number of units in a package. A 30 percent bonus is the most common.

TYPES OF BONUS PACKS

Figure 12.6 identifies the major objectives of bonus packs. Increasing the size or quantity of the package can lead to greater product use. When a package that contains eight small candy bars increases by four more bars, consumers are likely to eat more, because they are readily available. This will not be true for products with more constant consumption rates. If Colgate offers a bonus pack with an additional tube of toothpaste, consumers do not use more of the product. In effect, this delays the next purchase. Manufacturers offer these types of bonus packs because they preempt the competition. A consumer with a large quantity of the merchandise on hand becomes less likely to switch brands.

KEYS TO SUCCESSFUL BONUS PACKS

Bonus packs reward customer loyalty by offering, in effect, free merchandise. Bonus packs can lead to brand switching if the consumer has used the brand previously. Facing purchase decisions, consumers may opt for brands that offer more product at the regular or special price. The packages present an advantage that competitive brands are not offering.

Bonus packs tend to be popular with manufacturers, retailers, and customers. A retailer can build a positive relationship with a manufacturer that features a bonus pack to increase brand switching and stockpiling. Retailers gain an advantage because the bonus pack offers a "bargain" or "value" through the retail outlet. Customers enjoy bonus packs because it feels like they are getting free merchandise. For products with high levels of competition, the bonus pack approach can help maintain brand loyalty and reduce brand switching at a minimal cost.

Bonus packs rarely attract new customers, because they have not previously purchased the brand. Obtaining an extra quantity does not reduce the purchase risk but rather increases its, especially when the customer does not like to waste a product by throwing it away if he is dissatisfied. Marketing research indicates that when the bonus is small (20 to 40 percent), consumers often believe the price per unit has not truly changed. Unfortunately, a large bonus, such as a two-for-the-price-of-one sale, may lead consumers believe that the price was first increased to compensate for the additional quantity. In that instance, increasing the size of a bonus captured the consumer's attention but did not convey the desired message.[23]

▶ **FIGURE 12.6**
Bonus Pack Objectives

- Increase usage of the product
- Match or preempt competitive actions
- Stockpile the product
- Develop customer loyalty
- Attract new users
- Encourage brand switching

Price-Offs

A price-off is a temporary reduction in the price of a product to the consumer. A price-off can be physically marked on the product, such as when a bottle of aspirin shows the regular retail price marked out and replaced by a special retail price (e.g., $6.99 marked out and replaced by $5.99). Producing a label with the price reduction pre-marked forces the retailer to sell the item at the reduced price. This ensures the price-off incentive will be passed on to consumers. At other times, the price-off will not be printed on the actual item, but instead on a point-of-purchase display, sign, or shelf.

BENEFITS OF PRICE-OFFS

Price-offs help stimulate sales of existing products. They entice customers to try new products, because the lower price reduces the financial risk of making the purchase. They encourage customers to switch brands in brand parity situations or when no strong brand loyalty exists. In cases where consumers do have a brand preference, a price-off on a favorite brand encourages stockpiling of the product and possibly increased consumption of the item.[24] A consumer who purchases additional breakfast bars because of a price-off tends to consume more breakfast bars. Again, this will not be true for products such as deodorant or toothpaste. Stockpiling for those types of products only delays the next purchase and does not increase consumption. Similar effects occur in the business-to-business arena when price-offs are offered.

Price-offs have proven to be successful consumer promotions for two reasons. First, the price-off has the appeal of a monetary savings. Second, the reward is immediate. Unlike rebates, refunds, contests, sweepstakes, and other promotional incentives, consumers do not have to wait for the reward.

▲ A bonus pack offer for two packages of Lean Slices by Carl Buddig.

PROBLEMS WITH PRICE-OFFS

Although price-offs are easy to implement and can have a sudden impact on sales, at times they cause problems. Sales may increase, but the program might produce a negative impact on a company's profit margin. It normally takes at least a 20 to 40 percent increase in sales to offset each 5-percent price reduction.

Price-off programs encourage consumers to become more price-sensitive. In the same way that customers respond to rebates, they can either wait for a price-off promotion or choose another brand that happens to be on sale. In addition, when used too often, price-offs can have a negative impact on a brand's image. David Hale, CEO of Good Eats, noted, "Deep discounting doesn't build loyalty or consistency—it's cheapening your brand."[25] Again, price-off programs should be incorporated into the firm's overall IMC program.

Overlays and Tie-Ins

At times companies combine two or more consumer promotions activities into a single campaign, called an *overlay*. To attract Chinese consumers in Canada, Tropicana combined sampling with coupons. Free samples (50,000 cups of orange juice) were given out along with 30,000 coupons at a Chinese New Year's celebration in Vancouver. Asians

▲ A price-off and coupon offer for Eskamoe's Frozen Custard & More.

OBJECTIVE 12.3

How do different types of customers respond to consumer promotions?

who live in the United States and Canada are not typically large users of coupons; however, Tropicana Canada's research indicated that the Chinese consider oranges to be harbingers of good luck. A few weeks after the promotion, 40 percent of the coupons were redeemed, and sales of Tropicana orange juice among the Chinese community in Canada increased considerably.[26]

Developing a consumer promotion with another product or company is another common strategy, called a *tie-in*. Intracompany *tie-ins* are the promotion of two different products within one company using one consumer promotion. An alternative method is partnering with another company, which is an *intercompany tie-in*. Fast-food restaurants often use tie-ins with movies and toys to create attractive children's promotions. Stand-alone, overlay, and tie-in programs deserve careful planning to maximize their effects.

Planning for Consumer Promotions

In planning the consumer promotions component of the IMC, the program should support the brand image and the brand positioning strategy. To ensure this occurs, marketers consider the target audience. Researchers identify the core values present in the target audience, as well as opinions regarding the firm's products, especially as they relate to the competition. After gathering the information, the marketing team finalizes the consumer promotions plan. In terms of promotions, consumers can be divided into the four categories shown in Figure 12.7.

Promotion-prone consumers regularly respond to various consumer promotions and like to purchase products that are on-deal. They tend to clip coupons on a regular basis, enter contests and sweepstakes, purchase bonus packs, and respond to other promotional offers. In contrast, for **price-sensitive consumers**, price remains the primary, if not only, criterion used in making a purchase decision. Brand names are not important, and these individuals will not pay more for them. They take advantage of any type of promotion that reduces the price.

Brand-loyal consumers purchase only one particular brand and do not substitute, regardless of any deal being offered. They make the necessary effort to purchase their chosen brand. More common are **brand-preference consumers**, consider a small set of brands for which they have a strong attachment. When promotions are offered for one of their chosen brands, it becomes the one to be purchased. These

▶ **FIGURE 12.7**

Types of Consumers in Relation to Consumer Promotions

- Promotion-prone
- Brand-loyal
- Brand-preferred
- Price-sensitive

consumers ignore a promotion for brand not in the brand-preferred set, regardless of the size or type of promotion being offered.

Consumers do not fit into one of the four categories for all purchases. They may tend to be one of the four types, but promotion or brand preferences change across product and service categories. A beer drinker may be extremely promotion prone; a wine drinker may be quite brand loyal. The same beer drinker may be extremely loyal to a pizza brand, and the same wine drinker may be price sensitive when it comes to buying potato chips.

In planning promotions, the marketing team understands that promotion-prone consumers look for on-deal brands. Price-sensitive consumers purchase the cheaper brand, regardless if it is on-deal or off-deal. Therefore, these two types of consumers are not highly attractive to pursue with consumer promotions, unless the promotional goal is to increase sales, market share, or customer traffic. There will be little or no future allegiance to the brand.

Brand-loyal consumers only use promotions for their favored brands. Offering a promotion to this group makes little sense, because they will buy the brand anyway. Brand-preferred consumers represent the ideal group to target market, especially when the promotion features a brand in their preference set. This can enhance loyalty toward the brand and prevents them from purchasing a competing brand. It may also move the consumer closer to brand loyalty.

Manufacturers should understand retailer objectives in using promotions. It does little good to create a promotion that will be popular with consumers if retailers are not willing to work with the manufacturer to enhance the promotional offer. Retailers prefer promotions that benefit them. The primary reasons retailers support manufacturer consumer promotions programs are to:

- Increase store traffic
- Increase store sales
- Attract new customers
- Increase the basket size[27]

The promotions program revolve around the theme of the IMC program while keeping in mind where the promotions will be seen by the consumer. Specific goals associated with the product, the target market, and the retail outlets are first formulated. Building-brand constitutes a long-term goal; generating sales

You have been prudent with your finances. Why let the economy determine your lifestyle? **Enjoy the luxury you deserve.**

PLATINUM MOTORCARS

Platinum Motorcars 4514 Cole Avenue, Suite 600 Dallas, Texas 75205 1(888)5-PLATINUM 469.374.9090 469.533.6492 fax platinummotorcars.net

MENTION THIS AD AND RECEIVE 20% OFF A 2 DAY RENTAL

▲ A price-off promotion by Platinum Motorcars offering 20 percent off on a 2-day rental if the consumer mentions seeing this promotion.

▶ Brand-preferred consumers are the ideal group to target.

▲ When developing promotions, Chic Shaque's marketing team first seeks to understand the type of consumers that shop at its retail store.

OBJECTIVE 12.4
What types of trade promotions can help push products onto retailers' shelves and eventually to end users?

is more short range. Price-based offers normally are designed to attract new customers or to build sales. Other consumer promotions such as high-value premiums are used to enhance a firm's image over time.

Trade Promotions

Trade promotions are incentives designed by members of the trade channel to entice another member to purchase goods for eventual resale. Trade promotions are aimed at retailers, distributors, wholesalers, brokers, or agents. A manufacturer offers trade promotions to convince another member of the trade channel to carry its goods. Wholesalers, distributors, brokers, and agents offer trade promotions to persuade retailers to purchase products for eventual resale.

Trade promotions account for a larger percentage of a supplier's gross revenues. Twenty years ago they may have only represented about 25 percent of a manufacturer's marketing budget; today it is nearly 70 percent. Trade promotions often constitute the second largest expense for a manufacturer after the cost-of-goods-sold. Trade promotions account for approximately 17 percent of gross sales revenues for manufacturers.[28]

Trade promotions contribute to many successful IMC programs. Unfortunately, in other companies, the individual handling trade promotions may not be involved in the IMC planning process. Leaders in these firms often view trade promotions as being merely a means for placing products onto retail shelves or satisfying a channel member's request. As a result, little consideration may be given to matching the IMC program when developing trade promotions programs.

A variety of trade promotions tools exist. Individual companies select trade promotions techniques based on several factors. These factors include the nature of the business (manufacturer versus distributor), the type of customer to be influenced (e.g., retailer versus wholesaler), company preferences, and the objectives of the IMC plan. Figure 12.8 lists the primary types of trade promotions.

TRADE ALLOWANCES

Trade allowances provide financial incentives to other channel members to motivate them to make purchases. Trade allowances take a variety of forms, including the ones in Figure 12.9. Each makes it possible for the channel member to offer discounts or other price-reduction deals to customers.

▶ **FIGURE 12.8**
Types of Trade Promotions

- **Off-invoice allowance:** A per-case rebate paid to retailers for an order.
- **Slotting fees:** Money paid to retailers to stock a new product.
- **Exit fees:** Money paid to retailers to remove an item from their SKU inventory.

◄ **FIGURE 12.9**
Types of Trade Allowances

Off-Invoice Allowances   Off-invoice allowances are financial discounts given for each item, case, or pallet ordered. They encourage channel members to place orders. Approximately 35 percent of all trade dollars go to off-invoice allowances, making them the largest expenditure among trade promotions tools.[29] As with refunds, rebates, and price-offs in the consumer sector, many retailers are reluctant to purchase merchandise without some type of trade allowance. In addition, tremendous competitive pressure to offer trade allowances exist, as companies selling the same type of products compete for limited shelf space.

Slotting Fees   The most controversial form of trade allowance, **slotting fees**, are funds charged by retailers to stock new products. Retailers justify slotting fees in various ways.[30] First, retailers spend money to add new products to inventories and to stock merchandise. An unsuccessful product means the retailer's investment in inventory represents a loss, especially when the retailer has stocked the product in a large number of stores. Slotting fees recover some of the loss.

Second, adding a new product in the retail store means providing shelf space. Shelves are already filled. Adding a new product means either deleting brands or products or reducing the amount of shelf space allocated to them. In both cases, the retailer spends both time and money creating space for a new product.

Third, slotting fees make it easier for retailers to make decisions about new products. A typical supermarket carries 35,000 SKUs (stock-keeping units). The supermarket's managers evaluate 10,000 to 15,000 new products per year. Most will fail. Consequently, retailers believe charging slotting fees forces manufacturers to weed out high-risk product introductions. The average total cost in slotting fees for a nationally introduced product ranges from $1.5 to $2 million.[31] Consequently, retailers contend that slotting fees force manufacturers to conduct careful test marketing on products before introducing them. Such testing limits the number of new products offered each year. This, in turn, drastically reduces the number of new product failures.

Finally, slotting fees add to the bottom line. Many products have low margins or markups. Slotting fees provide additional monies to support retail operations. Estimates suggest that between 14 and 27 percent of trade promotion monies given to retailers go directly to the retailer's bottom line.[32]

The other side of the argument comes from manufacturers, who claim slotting fees are practically a form of extortion. Many manufacturers believe slotting fees cost too much and are unfair in the first place. These fees compel manufacturers to pay millions of dollars to retailers that could be used for advertising, sales promotions, or additional marketing efforts.

Slotting fees can prevent small manufacturers from getting products into stores because they cannot afford them. Some large retail operations have small-vendor policies; however, placing merchandise remains extremely challenging.

Exit Fees   Instead of paying a slotting allowance, some retailers ask for **exit fees**, which are monies paid to remove an item from a retailer's inventory. This approach may be used when a manufacturer introduces a new size of a product or a new version, such as a 3-liter bottle of Pepsi or Pepsi Diet Vanilla. PepsiCo already has products on the retailer's shelves. Adding a new-sized container or new variety of the product involves lower risk and is not the same as adding a new product. Rather than charging an up-front fee, such as a slotting allowance, retailers request exit fees if the new version of the product fails or if one of the current versions must be removed from the inventory. Four percent of retailers charge exit fees, compared to the 82 percent using slotting fees.[33]

Trade Allowance Complications   In offering trade allowances to retailers, manufacturers assume that a portion of the price reduction will be passed on to consumers. This occurs only about half of the time. When consumers receive a portion of the price allowance, retailers often schedule competing brands, so they can have at least one special offer going at all times. Thus, one week Pepsi offers a reduced price and the next week Coke offers a discount. The two products are rarely promoted on-deal at the same time. By offering only one on-deal at a time, the retailer always has a reduced priced brand for the price-sensitive consumer. The retailer also can charge the brand-loyal consumer full price 50 percent of the time. While accomplishing these goals, the retailer receives special trade allowances from both Pepsi and Coke.

In an effort to increase profit margins, retailers engage in two activities: forward buying and diversion. *Forward buying* occurs when a retailer purchases extra amounts of a product while it is on-deal. The retailer then sells the on-deal merchandise after the deal period ends, saving the cost of purchasing the product at the manufacturer's full price. *Diversion* takes place when a retailer purchases a product on-deal in one location and ships it to another location where it is off-deal. For example, a manufacturer may offer an off-invoice allowance of $5 per case for the product in France. Diversion tactics mean the retailer purchases an excess quantity in France and has it shipped to stores in other European countries. To do so, retailers first examine the potential profits to be earned, less the cost of shipping the product to other locations. Shipping costs tend to be relatively high compared to trade allowances offered. Consequently, retailers do not use diversion nearly as much as forward buying.

TRADE CONTESTS

To achieve sales targets and other objectives, channel members sometimes provide trade contests. Winners receive prizes or cash, or **spiff money**. A contest can be held at any level within the channel. It can be between brokers or agents, wholesalers, or retail stores. To prevent undue influence of contests on buyers, a number of large organizations prohibit employees from participating in vendor contests. Although influencing salespeople represents exactly what a contest seeks to accomplish, many large retail organizations do not want buyers participating, because these buyers make purchase decisions for as many as 500 to 2,500 stores and participating in a contest may result in poor decisions.

In recent years the demand for cruise ship vacations has steadily decreased. As a result, cruise lines have used a combination of advertising, consumer promotions, and trade promotions to attract patrons. Royal Caribbean International offered travel agents cooperative advertising programs featuring TV commercials, newspaper ads, as well as an e-mail template to contact potential travelers.

Norwegian Cruise Lines enrolled 5,500 agents in a "Sale of All Sails" promotional contest. Prizes were based on bookings. Each agent that set up a Holland America cruise was enrolled in the trade contest. The prizes offered included a free cruise with five veranda staterooms. The Princess Cruise line offered booking agents the chance to win

▼ Trade contests were held among travel agents to increase cruise ship bookings.

© bst2012/Fotolia

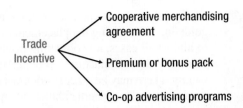

◀ FIGURE 12.10
Types of Trade Incentives

a West Coast sailing cruise with a mini-suite. One cruise was awarded each week during a 90-day period. Offering travel agents the chance to win prizes and cruises for themselves caused many of them to be motivated to book cruises for the lines holding the contests.[34]

TRADE INCENTIVES

Trade incentives are similar to trade allowances. The difference is that **trade incentives** involve the retailer or channel member performing a function in order to receive the funds. The purpose, however, remains the same as for trade allowances: to encourage the channel member either to push the manufacturer's brand or to increase purchases of that brand. Figure 12.10 identifies three major types of trade incentives.

Cooperative Merchandising Agreements   The most comprehensive trade incentive, a cooperative merchandising agreement (CMA), is a formal agreement between the retailer and manufacturer to undertake a two-way marketing effort. The CMA can be for a wide variety of marketing tasks. A CMA may feature the manufacturer's brand as a price leader in an advertisement. A cooperative agreement may be created in which a retailer will emphasize the manufacturer's brand as part of an in-house offer made by the store or a by featuring the manufacturer's brand on a special shelf display.

Cooperative merchandising agreements remain popular with manufacturers because the retailer performs a function in order to receive the allowance or incentive. The manufacturer retains control of the functions performed. Also, if price allowances are made as part of the CMA, the manufacturer knows that the retailer passes a certain percentage or the entire price discount on to the consumer. CMAs allow manufacturers to create annual contracts with retailers. These longer-term commitments reduce the need for last-minute trade incentives or trade allowances.

CMAs also benefit retailers. The primary benefit, from the retailer's perspective, is that the program allows them to develop *calendar promotions*, which are promotional campaigns the retailer plans for customers through manufacturer trade incentives. Signing an agreement means a retailer can schedule the weeks a particular brand will be on sale and offset the other weeks with other brands. Calendar promotions allow the retailer to always have one brand on sale while the others are off-deal and to rotate the brands on sale. By arranging sales through trade incentives, the margins for the retailer stay approximately the same for all brands, both on-deal and off-deal, because they rotate. Retailers can effectively move price reductions given to the customer to the manufacturer rather than absorbing them. A store may feature Budweiser on-deal one week and Heineken the next. Loyal beer drinkers stay with their preferred brand, while price-sensitive consumers can choose the on-deal brand, and the store retains a reasonable markup on all beers sold.

Premiums and Bonus Packs   Instead of giving the retailer a discount on the price, a manufacturer might offer free merchandise in the form of a premium or bonus pack. For example, a manufacturer would offer a bonus pack of one carton for each 20 purchased within the next 60 days. The bonus packs are free to the retailer and are awarded either for placing the order by a certain date or for agreeing to a minimum-size order. Often, to receive the free merchandise the retailer must meet both conditions: a specified date and a minimum order size.

Cooperative Advertising   The final trade incentive, a cooperative advertising program, occurs when the manufacturer agrees to reimburse the retailer a certain percentage of the advertising costs associated with advertising the manufacturer's products in the retailer's

▲ A co-op advertisement for Bob's Furniture Gallery featuring both the Flexsteel and Thomasville brands.

ad. To receive the reimbursement, the retailer follows specific guidelines concerning the placement of the ad and its content. In almost all cases, no competing products can be advertised. Normally, the manufacturer's product must be displayed prominently. There may be other restrictions on how to advertise the product as well as specific photos or copy that must be used.

In most cooperative advertising programs, retailers accrue co-op monies based on purchases, normally a certain percentage of sales. B.F. Goodrich, a manufacturer of automobile tires, offers a 4.5 percent co-op advertising fund on all purchases made by the retailer of Goodrich tires. The money can accrue for one year, and then it starts over. B.F. Goodrich pays 70 percent of the cost of an approved advertisement. Any medium can present the advertisement, including radio, newspaper, magazines, television, and outdoor advertising.

Unlimited media choices are not offered by all manufacturers. Dayton, another tire manufacturer, does not allow co-op dollars to be used for magazine advertising. B.F. Goodrich allows group ads for co-op monies; Dayton does not. Further, Dayton requires preapproval for some of the media buys and advertisements; B.F. Goodrich does not require any preapprovals. Thus, each manufacturer has a unique set of restrictions to be followed by retailers seeking to qualify for co-op monies.[35]

Co-op advertising programs allow retailers to use the manufacturer's dollars to expand advertising programs. In a co-op ad, the retailer gains additional advertising coverage at a reduced cost. Retailers also benefit from the image of a national brand, which can attract new or additional customers to the store. Wal-Mart recently expanded co-op advertising efforts with major manufacturers, who contributed over $400 million toward Wal-Mart's annual advertising budget. In Wal-Mart's system, manufacturers have considerably more creative input into the ads and are prominently displayed in the ad instead of taking minor roles.[36]

Manufacturers also benefit from co-op ads. By sharing advertising costs with retailers, the manufacturer gains additional exposure at a lower cost. More important, almost all co-op advertising programs are tied to sales. The retailer accrues co-op advertising dollars based on a certain percentage of sales. Thus, to get the co-op money, the retailer must promote the brand prominently and purchase the product for resale. As a result, a wide variety of cooperative advertisements appear regularly in every medium, for both consumer and business-to-business products.

TRADE SHOWS

Many business-to-business marketing programs include appearances at trade shows. They benefit both manufacturers and retailers. From a manufacturer's standpoint, a trade show provides the opportunity to discover potential customers and sell new products. Relationships with current customers can be strengthened at the show. A trade show often presents the opportunity to investigate the competition. Many times, trade shows establish a situation in which the manufacturer's sales team meets directly with decision makers and buyers from business-to-business clients. A trade show can strengthen the brand name of a product as well as the company's image.

From the retailer's perspective, a trade show helps buyers to compare merchandise and to make contacts with several prospective vendors in a short period of time. In some cases, the retailers negotiate special deals. Trade shows represent an ideal place for buyers and sellers to meet in an informal, low-pressure setting to discuss how to work together effectively.

Some national and international trade shows are attended by thousands of buyers. To be sure a trade show will succeed manufacturers seek out key buyers and try to avoid

- **Education seekers** Buyers who want to browse, look, and learn but are not in the buying mode

- **Reinforcement seekers** Buyers who want reassurance they made the right decision in past purchases

- **Solution seekers** Buyers seeking solutions to specific problems and are in the buying mode

- **Buying teams** A team of buyers seeking vendors for their business; usually are in the buying mode

- **Power buyers** Members of upper management or key purchasing agents with the authority to buy

◀ **FIGURE 12.11**
Five Categories of Buyers Attending Trade Shows

spending too much time with nonbuyers. Figure 12.11 identifies five categories of buyers who attend trade shows. Many marketers try to weed out the education seekers that are not interested in buying. Manufacturer's agents concentrate efforts on three groups: solution seekers, buying teams, and power buyers. Asking the right questions identifies solution seekers and buying teams. The power buyers are more difficult to find because they do not want to be identified. They often do not wear badges at trade shows, which means vendors are never sure who they are.

In the United States, few deals are finalized during trade shows. Buyers and sellers meet, discuss, and maybe even negotiate, but seldom complete the sale. Instead, manufacturers collect business cards as leads to be followed up later. This procedure varies for international customers. International attendees tend to be senior executives with the authority to make purchases. They fit into the power-buyer category listed in Figure 12.11. U. S. manufacturers know that the international attendee often wishes to conduct business during the show, not afterward. The international attendees spend more time at each manufacturer's booth. They stay longer in order to gather and study information in greater detail. The international guest, who pays more for travel expenses, wants more in-depth information than an American counterpart requires.

The number of international trade show visitors has increased as competition continues to expand globally. The increase in international participants has caused trade show centers to set up more meeting spaces, conference centers, and even places to eat where buyers and sellers meet and transact business.

Trade shows have changed in other ways. Large national and international shows are being replaced by niche and regional shows. For example, in the 1990s many megasports trade shows were attended by everybody in the sporting goods business. The National Sporting Goods Association World Sports Expo in Chicago attracted in excess of 90,000 attendees. That number has dwindled to fewer than 40,000 today. Now manufacturers and retailers attend specialty trade shows featuring only one sport or regional shows that focus on one section of the country. Smaller shows are less expensive to set up. Many company leaders believe they provide higher-quality prospects, better opportunities to bond with customers, and offer more quality one-to-one time with customers and potential customers. In contrast, it is relatively easy to get lost in the crowd at a bigger show.[37]

Concerns with Trade Promotions

Effective marketing teams incorporate trade promotions into the overall IMC effort. In many companies this does not occur, primarily because of employee pay structures. Sales and brand managers face quotas, and when sales fall behind, one quick way to boost them is to offer retailers a trade deal. Further, brand managers are often evaluated based on the sales growth of a brand. Offering trade deals becomes the easiest way to ensure continuing growth. The pattern of using trade deals to reach short-term quotas rather than long-term image and theme-building will not change until top management adopts a new approach. The IMC process succeeds when it emphazies the long-term horizon and the company's compensation structure changes to match.

A strong brand image causes retailers to stock the product even when fewer trade deals are offered, because a strong brand by itself can help pull customers into retail

OBJECTIVE 12.5

What concerns exist for manufacturers considering trade promotions programs?

▲ A trade show provides an excellent opportunity for companies to locate potential customers.

stores. A customer who considers Sony to be a strong brand in the stereo marketplace asks for that brand in an electronics retail store. This makes stocking Sony an advantage, even with limited trade promotions offers.

The cost of trade promotions represents another concern. Manufacturers spend billions of dollars each year on them. These costs are often passed on to consumers in the form of higher prices. Estimates suggest that 11 cents out of every dollar spent for a consumer product goes directly for the cost of trade promotions.[38] The goal should be to keep the cost at a reasonable level. Money should be spent wisely, rather than simply getting into "bidding wars" with competitors. Trade promotions dollars have the greatest long-term impact when they help build relationships and help achieve other key IMC goals.

An unfortunate situation occurs when merchandise does not move until a trade promotion incentive has been offered. In the grocery industry, the majority of all purchases made by retailers are on-deal with some type of trade incentive. The constant use of deals has trimmed manufacturer margins on products and created competitive pressures to conform. If a manufacturer tries to halt or cut back on trade promotions, retailers replace the manufacturer's products with other brands or reduce shelf space to give more room to manufacturers offering better deals.

One way to correct these problems would be to spend more on advertising focused on building or rebuilding a brand's image. Also, the marketing team should be certain promotions fit the brand's image. "If it doesn't fit," writes Brian Sullivan in *Marketing News*, "don't use it."[39] Unfortunately, to spend more on advertising means cutting trade promotions incentives. The risk becomes that other competitors will move in by offering better trade promotions to retailers and gain shelf space as a result. Then, the cycle begins again.

Managing trade promotions programs constitutes a challenging part of the marketing planning process because such a large percentage of the marketing budget goes to trade promotions. Effective IMC programs achieve a balance between all elements of the promotions mix and identify clear goals and targets for trade promotions programs. Only then will the company be able to compete on all levels and not just through a cycle of trade promotions bidding wars.

International Implications

Consumer promotions are adapted to the countries in which they are offered. Two complications occur legal and cultural. Any coupon, premium, contest, sweepstakes, or price change must fit with local legal regulations. The marketing team investigates any potential legal problems before launching an international consumer promotions program.

Culturally, citizens in some countries may take a dim view of some promotions. For instance, in some cultures those who redeem coupons may be viewed as being of lower

◀ Trade promotion expenditures are a major component of the marketing budget for products such as Pennant's pesticides.

socioeconomic status, which may dissuade some from using them. Participation in contests or sweepstakes may violate religious norms in other nations.

The same holds true for trade promotions. Laws vary regarding discounts, spiff money, slotting fees, and exit fees. These issues may also be reflected in cultural values. And, as previously noted, the ways in which managers in companies around the world participate in trade shows varies.

Finally, the emphasis placed on sales promotions will be different, depending on the company involved and the country in which that company operates. Both small companies seeking to do business in foreign countries and large international conglomerates will need to adjust to local conditions when employing these marketing tactics. At the same time, the goal remains to be certain that the efforts match the company's image and overall approach to marketing communications.

OBJECTIVE 12.6

What issues complicate international sales promotions programs?

INTEGRATED CAMPAIGNS IN ACTION

Wayport Austintatious

The Wayport company is the world's largest Internet hotspot provider. Pink Jacket Creative advertising agency executive Bill Breedlove said, "If you're in a Marriott hotel, or a McDonald's, they even have Starbuck's now, you're logging onto their site. They specialize in verticals that are health care, such as regional hospitals and major hospital chains as well hospitality, and QSRs [quick-service restaurants]."

Pink Jacket Creative was able to provide a combination of buzz marketing and trade show expertise in one event. According to Breedlove, "There was a trade show in Austin, Texas. It was for the hospitality industry. They came to us with a challenge. Like any trade show challenge, they wanted to get the top executives from the top hotel chains away from the floor of the trade show and in their own environment, so that their salespeople can work on them, and everybody wants that. "Then we took the folks to this bar that we had redecorated and had a little shindig, and their salespeople got to mingle, and it was quite successful. They were making appointments right and left with their marketing people and technology folks. So it was fun" and highly successful.[40]

The Austintatious trade show campaign is located at the Pearson Instructor's Resource Center (www.pearsonhighered.com). The campaign includes a PowerPoint presentation outlining the details of the campaigns and examples of the collaterals as well as some photos of the event. Also available is video commentary by Bill Breedlove and Elena Baca.

▲ A Willie Nelson impersonator was one of the entertainers at the Austintatious nightclub takeover event.

▲ This Austintatious billboard was seen by trade show attendees at the Austin airport.

MyMarketingLab
Go to **mymktlab.com** to complete the problems marked with this icon .

SUMMARY

An IMC program incorporates all four elements of the promotions mix. Advertising may be considered to be the main "voice" of the IMC message. At the same time, the sales promotion part of the mix, including trade and consumer promotions, plays a crucial role in the success or failure of the overall marketing program.

Attracting customers by using consumer promotions includes the use of coupons, premiums, contests and sweepstakes, refunds, rebates, samples, bonus packs, and price-off deals. These items should be combined with specific promotional goals to have the right impact on customers. Consumer promotions are often used to boost sales and can be an excellent short-term method to increase sales or a firm's market share. They also provide a means of introducing new products. Often, a consumer promotion prompts consumers to at least try the product, where selling it at the regular price will not. Coupons and contests have been successful tactics for gaining new customers. Consumer promotions can boost

sales of a particular brand, and evidence suggests that they increase sales of the overall product category rather than just take sales away from competitors.

Trade promotions complement consumer promotions. The use of trade allowances, trade contests, trade incentives, and participation in trade shows helps the manufacturer or member of the marketing channel maintain positive contact with other organizations and moves products toward the retailer. Trade promotions work best when they are integrated into other IMC efforts rather than being viewed as a necessary evil or simply as a short-term tool to increase sales.

Internationally, sales promotions can be used when they are chosen based on the characteristics, attitudes, laws, regulations, and cultural nuances of a given geographic region. The primary objective of any promotions program must always be to enhance the message sent forth in other aspects of the IMC program in a manner that helps the company reach its long-term marketing objectives in a cost-effective and positive fashion.

Key Terms

sales promotions All of the incentives offered to customers and channel members to encourage product purchases.

consumer promotions Incentives directly offered to a firm's customers or potential customers.

trade promotions Expenditures or incentives used by manufacturers and other members of the marketing channel to purchase goods for eventual sale.

freestanding inserts (FSIs) Sheets of coupons distributed in newspapers, primarily on Sunday.

promotion-prone consumers Consumers who are not brand loyal and regularly respond to promotions, such as coupons, price-off plans, or premiums, only purchasing items that are on-deal.

price-sensitive consumers Consumers for whom price is the primary, if not only, criterion used in making a purchase decision.

brand-loyal consumers Consumers who purchase only one particular brand and do not substitute, regardless of any deal being offered.

brand-preference consumers Consumers who prefer a small set of brands.

trade allowances Financial incentives that are provided to other channel members to motivate them to make purchases.

slotting fees A form of trade allowance in which are funds charged by retailers to stock new products.

exit fees Monies paid to remove an item from a retailer's inventory.

spiff money Rewards given as contest prizes to brokers, retail salespeople, stores, wholesalers, and agents.

trade incentives Funds given that require the retailer to perform a function in order to receive the dollars.

Review Questions

1. Define sales promotion. What are the two main categories of sales promotions?

2. Name and describe the types of coupons. Which is the most popular with manufacturers? Which has the highest redemption rate?

3. What problems are associated with coupon programs?

4. What is a premium? What types of premium programs can companies use?

5. What are the keys to successful premium programs?

6. What is the difference between a contest and a sweepstakes?

7. What are the two main components of prizes rendered in contests and sweepstakes?

8. What role does the Internet and social media play in offering contests and sweepstakes?

9. How is a refund different from a rebate?

10. What are the primary types of samples?

11. What benefits and problems are associated with sampling?

12. What are the benefits of offering bonus packs?

13. What benefits and problems are associated with price-off tactics?

14. What is an overlay? A tie-in?

15. What four categories of consumers can be associated with consumer promotions?

16. What are the major types of trade allowances?

17. What is a slotting fee? An exit fee?

18. What is meant by the term on-deal?

19. What complications are associated with trade allowances?

20. How does the spiff money relate to trade contests?

21. What are the main types of trade incentives?

22. Describe a cooperative merchandising agreement.

23. How are premiums or bonus packs used as trade incentives?

24. How can a cooperative advertising program benefit both a manufacturer and a retailer?

25. Name ways in which trade shows have changed in recent years.

26. Describe how to effectively utilize trade promotions.

27. What problems must be overcome when developing international sales promotions programs?

Critical Thinking Exercises

DISCUSSION QUESTIONS

1. According to Kim James, sales promotion manager for Eckerd Drug, "The teen and preteen segments are important because they (teens) are developing buying habits and loyalties during these ages and are our future loyal consumers." In addition to established brands such as Cover Girl and Maybelline, Eckerd Drug now stocks brands such as Bonne Bell, Jane, and Naturistics.[41] Which consumer promotions would be the best to attract teens and preteens to the cosmetics department of Eckerd Drug? What tie-ins or overlays would you recommend?

2. Refer to the list of consumer promotions in Figure 12.1. Discuss each one in terms of your personal usage. Which ones do you use? How often? Why?

3. Design a magazine advertisement with a detachable coupon or premium for one of the following products. Be sure to put an expiration date and other restrictions on the use of the coupon or premium.
   a. SunBright Tanning Salon
   b. Dixie Printing
   c. Hamburger Haven
   d. Blue Bell Ice Cream

4. The Rawlings Sports Equipment Company plans to increase sales of baseball gloves this season. The company intends to use a coupon program. Discuss the pros and cons of each method of coupon distribution listed in the chapter for Rawlings. Which method or methods should Rawlings use? Why?

5. To maintain a strong brand image, Revlon's marketing team decides to use a premium for each of its lipstick products. What type of premium would you suggest for Revlon for each of the target markets listed here? Which premium would you use? Justify your answers.
   a. Females, ages 60 +
   b. Teenagers, ages 14 to 19
   c. College students, ages 18 to 25
   d. Professional females, ages 30 to 50

6. How often do you enter contests or sweepstakes? What was the last contest you entered? Why did you enter? Discuss the importance of extrinsic and intrinsic rewards to you in entering contests and sweepstakes. If you seldom or never enter contests and sweepstakes, why? What type of intrinsic and extrinsic rewards would it take for you to enter?

7. Video games generate major revenues for many companies. One manufacturer decided to use sampling as a method to reach the primary target market—males between the ages of 15 and 30. The sampling could have been distributed in one of two ways. First, the actual game could be loaded on a computer for targeted individuals. Second, potential customers could be sent an abbreviated version of the game. Which sampling method would be best? Using the list of sampling methods provided in the chapter, discuss the pros and cons of each sampling method in terms of this new video game. Which type and method of sampling would you recommend? Why?

8. Consumers can be divided into four broad categories in terms of how they respond to consumer promotions: promotion prone, brand loyal, price sensitive, and brand preference. Identify two services or goods that would fit into each category for you personally. For example, you may be promotion prone when you buy soft drinks (your favorite brand is "What's on Sale"), but be very brand loyal when you buy shoes (Nike, Reebok). What determines which type of category you fit into for the various products you discussed?

9. Interview three people who have lived in another country about the use of consumer promotions in those countries. Make a list of those promotions that are heavily used and those that are not used. Present your findings to the class.

10. As with the other consumer promotions, international expansion requires understanding the laws and customs of each country and culture. In Saudi Arabia and other Muslim countries, Clinique had to modify its sampling techniques. In the United States and

Western cultures, Clinique provides cosmetics samples in retail outlets for customers to try. In the United States, women normally sell retail cosmetics; in Saudi Arabia, men do. At the same time, Muslim custom prohibits a man from touching a woman if she is not a relative. Female customers must either apply the cosmetics themselves or bring their husbands to the store with them.

Asking a female customer "What color are your eyes?" constitutes a grave offense in Saudi Arabia, because the eyes are believed to be the gateway to the soul. Asking her about skin tone does not make sense because women keep their faces covered. Sampling is important for Clinique in Saudi Arabia.[42]

How would you organize a sampling program in light of these cultural factors? What other consumer promotions could be used? If you have someone in your class from a Muslim country, ask your classmate to discuss the use of consumer promotions in her home country.

Integrated Learning Exercises

1. Coupons are a popular form of consumer promotions. Access three of the following Web sites. What are the advantages and disadvantages of each to a consumer? How do the Web sites impact manufacturers? How do they impact retailers?
   a. Coupon Country (www.couponcountry.com)
   b. CoolSavings (www.coolsavings.com)
   c. SmartSource (www.smartsource.com)
   d. Coupons.com (www.coupons.com)

2. Sweepstakes and contests are excellent methods for building customer traffic to a retail outlet and interest in a brand. Certain firms assist in the development of sweepstakes and contests. This is important due to a variety of legal restrictions imposed by different states. Access the following Web sites. What types of services does each offer? How do the companies assist in developing a contest or sweepstakes? Which firm would you choose if you were responsible for developing a contest or a sweepstakes program?
   a. Promotion Activators, Inc. (www.promotionactivators .com)
   b. Centra360 (www.centra360.com)
   c. Ventura Marketing & Promotion (www.sweepspros .com)

3. Examine the following Web sites. What types of promotions are available? What are the objectives of the various consumer promotions? Do the promotions on the Web sites mesh with the company's advertising and consumer promotions at retail outlets?
   a. Taco Bell (www.tacobell.com)
   b. Hershey's (www.hersheys.com)
   c. Quaker Oats (www.quakeroats.com)
   d. Papa John's (www.papajohns.com/index.shtm)

4. One widely read journal featuring promotional marketing is *Promo*. Access the Web site at http://chiefmarketer.com/promotional-marketing. Examine the table of contents and access the various areas. After exploring the site, write a short report about what is available at the Web site and how it can be used to assist companies wanting to develop various promotions.

Student Project

CREATIVE CORNER

Reread the opening vignette that featured the Corpus Christi Hooks. From the following list of special days, pick two and then design two different ads. Make sure that each advertisement features a consumer promotion that is either mentioned in the vignette or that you come up with on your own.

Opening Day	*Cinco de Mayo*
Mother's Day	Father's Day
Fourth of July	Labor Day
Play-off Games	Championship Celebration

CASE 1 MARKETING SPORTS EQUIPMENT

The term "sports" has many meanings, depending on the context and those involved in a conversation. Some may be inclined to think of college and professional athletes playing games at the highest level in front of large crowds. Others view sports as being related to physical fitness. Other groups think in terms of "leisure time" or "children's recreation."

Regardless of the type of sports one considers, Academy Sports + Outdoors offers the equipment, clothing, and support services consumers need to engage in activities as varied as camping, fishing, boating, barbeques, as well as participating in mainstream sports such as baseball, basketball, soccer, and football, as fans or as participants. Large, brightly lit retail outlets feature a wide variety of merchandise for the majority of sporting and outdoor activities in 130 stores placed in 11 different states in the U.S.

Academy Sports + Outdoor competes with a numerous vendors, including Dick's Sporting Goods, Modell's, Bass Pro Shop, and also big box retailers Wal-Mart, Kmart, and Target. Sports participants can also visit specialty shops, such as golf pro shops and smaller fishing stores and outlets.

Consumer groups range from casual back-yard athletes to serious hunters, fishermen (and women), Little League sponsors and teams, and families looking for equipment to take on a camping expedition. As a result, discovering which target markets are the most lucrative remains an important challenge for each retail chain in this marketplace.

Academy Sports + Outdoor's management team has chosen to offer guns and other types of hunting equipment. Retailers offering firearms often encounter controversy, both from those opposed to guns and members of major gun lobbies.

Recently, an additional challenge faced major sports retailers. A declining economy forced many consumers to consider which purchases were absolutely necessary, and which product purchases could be put on hold. At the same time, some families chose simpler, less expensive vacations and recreational activities, such as camping and home entertainment through games such as badminton and table tennis.

Academy Sports + Outdoor defines itself as "The destination for active-minded families." The company's mission defines the goals of providing an "unparalleled shopping experience," creating a trusting relationship with customers, and promoting a high quality working environment for company associates that includes the opportunity to advance within the company.

It is not surprising that the company receives "an overwhelming volume of requests" for sponsorship activities.

▲ Families are an important target market for Academy Sports + Outdoor.

Company leaders have established well-defined criteria for examining inquiries. Any organization seeking a sponsorship tie-in must make the request 3 months in advance and can expect to wait as long as 5 weeks for a response. A similar backlog exists for its donations and charitable activities.

In the future, Academy Sports + Outdoor will continue to expand. Company policies regarding relationships with suppliers remain an important priority. In any case, as long as people continue to enjoy a wide variety of recreational activities, the potential for further growth remains possible.

1. What are the primary target markets for Academy Sports + Outdoor?

2. For each of the target markets identified in Question 1, what types of consumer promotions should Academy Sports + Outdoor offer? Justify your response.

3. Suppose you are the vice-president of marketing at Academy Sports + Outdoor. Examine the list of consumer promotions shown in Figure 12.1. Discuss the pros and cons of each promotion if the target market is active-minded families with children under 18 and incomes in the $30,000 to $70,000 bracket.

4. From your answer to Question 3, pick one of the promotions that you feel is the best to reach the designated target market. Design a newspaper ad using that promotion. Be sure to include restrictions such as usage and expiration date.

CASE 2   NEWMAN'S OWN ORGANICS: SALES PROMOTIONS AND RETAIL RELATIONSHIPS

Jason David had recently been promoted to Director of Sales Promotions for Newman's Own Organics. He was excited to find ways to expand product offerings into a wider variety of retail stores. His assignment was to fine-tune both the consumer and trade promotions that would be offered in various markets.

Newman's Own Organics is a spin-off from the original Newman's Own company. In the 1980s, celebrity actor Paul Newman and his friend, writer A. E. Hotchner, decided to concoct a batch of salad dressing to be given to their friends for the Christmas holiday season. The dressing became so popular that the two created the Newman's Own company to sell the item. The two agreed that proceeds and profits would be given to charity.

Newman's Own sold over 10,000 bottles of the salad dressing in its first 2 weeks on the market. In the first year, Newman's Own made a profit. The company slowly expanded to a wider variety of salad dressings, and then to salsa, marinara, steak sauce, pizza, and even wine.

Among the more famous charities supported by Newman's Own are the Hole in the Wall Camps, which bring together children with serious and terminal illnesses for a free summer-camp experience. The Newman's Own Foundation had given over $250 million to various charities prior to Paul Newman's death. The figure now approaches $300 million. The company's mission statement reads "Shameless Exploitation in Pursuit of the Common Good."

Newman's Own Organics was founded by Nell Newman, Paul's daughter, in 1993. She became the sole proprietor in 2001. The product line for Newman's Own Organics includes pretzels, chocolate bars, "Fig Newmans," Champion Chip Cookies, Chocolate Cups, Newman O's, Pop's Corn, Alphabet Cookies, coffee, dried fruit, olive oil and balsamic vinegar,, pet food, mints, tea, and soy crisps.

The company's products are certified to be genuinely organic by Oregon Tilth. This means that the ingredients are grown on farms that have not used artificial fertilizers or pesticides for 3 years or more. The farms and processors have been certified by an independent third party. Kosher certification is made by the Union of Orthodox Jewish Congregations.

Newman's Own Organics is described as the "second generation." The company is a for profit, with a royalty paid to the Newman Foundation based on sales and profits. In this way, the organization capitalizes on the popularity of Paul Newman, the strong relationship to charitable giving, and the niche market of organic foods.

Jason's responsibility was to find and develop retail outlets for Newman's Own Organics products. Large retailers that sell food products, such as Target and Wal-Mart, constitute one major marketplace. Small grocery stores that are more upscale and feature organic foods are a second. Third would be any specialty stores that offer organic products.

▲ Jason's challenge was to find and develop retail outlets for the Newman's Own Organics.

Prospects might be developed by identifying the stores that carry Newman's Own products. Further, the Internet offers the potential to sell products directly to consumers without a retail store but also to direct consumers to stores that carry the items. Various types of promotions for the products and various charities, including the Hole in the Wall Camps, could be promoted on the Newman's Own Organics Web site.

Jason knew that he had the advantage of a strong brand, plus connections to the original company that would give him in-roads into meeting with prospective retail customers. He also knew that it would take more than a name to persuade retailers to make room on the shelves for the products. Beyond simple placement, the ultimate goal was to develop bonds and relationships that would lead retailers to feature the products in advertisements and promotions over time.

1. What types of consumer promotions would be best suited to end users of Newman's Own Organics products?

2. What types of trade promotions should Jason offer to retailers?

3. Would you expect Newman's Own Organics products to sell at a higher price than competitors, to match competitor prices, or to compete by lowering prices in various ways, including using sales promotions?

4. Should Jason explore placing Newman's Own Organics in restaurants to gain brand recognition? Why or why not?

5. Can you envision any types of trade shows that Jason should attend on behalf of Newman's Own Organics? Access the Trade Shows News Network at www.tsnn.com and BizTradeShows at www.biztradeshows.com for specific trade shows and locations.

6. Now that Paul Newman has passed away, what challenges will be present as the "second-generation" companies move forward and memories of Paul Newman begin to fade away?

Sources: Lenora Chu, "Newman's Own after Paul," CNNMoney.com (http://money.cnn.com/2008/09/27/smallbusiness/paul_newman.smb/), September 27, 2008; Newman's Own (http://newmansown.com, accessed May 10, 2010); Newman's Own Organics (www.newmansownorganics.com/funfacts.html, accessed May 10, 2010).

MyMarketingLab

Go to **mymktlab.com** for Auto-graded writing questions as well as the following Assisted-graded writing questions:.

12-1. According to Kim James, sales promotion manager for Eckerd Drug, "The teen and preteen segments are important because they (teens) are developing buying habits and loyalties during these ages and are our future loyal consumers." In addition to established brands such as Cover Girl and Maybelline, Eckerd Drug now stocks brands such as Bonne Bell, Jane, and Naturistics. Which consumer promotions would be the best to attract teens and preteens to the cosmetics department of Eckerd Drug? What tie-ins or overlays would you recommend?

12-2. The Rawlings Sports Equipment Company plans to increase sales of baseball gloves this season. The company intends to use a coupon program. Discuss the pros and cons of each method of coupon distribution listed in the chapter for Rawlings. Which method or methods should Rawlings use? Why?

12-3. Mymktlab Only—comprehensive writing assignment for this chapter.

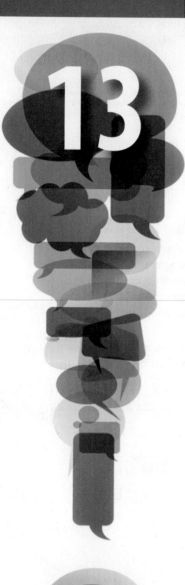

13 PUBLIC RELATIONS AND SPONSORSHIP PROGRAMS

CHAPTER OBJECTIVES

After reading this chapter, you should be able to answer the following questions:

1 What relationships exist between public relations and the marketing activities performed by a company?

2 How can the public relations functions help to build better relationships with all internal and external stakeholders?

3 What types of positive, image-building programs can be used by companies as part of a public relations program?

4 What steps can companies take to prevent or reduce image damage when negative events occur?

5 How can marketers tie sponsorships to public relations efforts to strengthen a customer base?

6 What role can event marketing play in creating customer excitement and brand loyalty?

7 Can public relations programs, sponsorships, and event marketing be adapted to international settings?

MyMarketingLab™

⭐ **Improve Your Grade!**

Over 10 million students improved their results using the Pearson MyLabs. Visit **mymktlab.com** for simulations, tutorials, and end-of-chapter problems.

INTERSTATE BATTERIES

WINNING COLORS

What's in a color? In the world of sprint racing, Interstate Batteries has achieved major notoriety using the colors green, red, and white. When combined with effective sponsorships and other marketing activities, brand recognition, brand loyalty, and brand "fans" have become the result.

Two decades ago, Interstate Battery Chairman Norm Miller and Joe Gibbs began a journey that has taken his company and their partnership to racing victories and marketing success. Interstate Batteries is the number one replacement brand battery in North America. The company consists of three groups: Interstate Battery

System of America, Inc., Interstate All Battery Centers, and Interstate PowerCare. These organizations deliver over 16,000 products related to batteries and battery usage. Automotive batteries represent the Interstate's primary product lines.

The Miller/Gibbs journey began following the sponsorship of the Interstate Batteries Great American Race, which achieved considerable attention as a cross-country driving event designed to build the company's reputation. Stops along the way in 44 cities led to contacts with distributors, dealers, consumers, and media, with the goal of building the brand in the consumer marketplace as a "a real grassroots media program," according to Charlie Brim, Interstate's Manager for Advertising and Sponsorships. Interstate had achieved a favorable rating from *Consumer Reports*, and famous radio commentator Paul Harvey had made note of the rating during one of his programs. Interstate eventually became one of the sponsors of Harvey's show lending additional credibility to the product as a nationally-advertised brand.

As the Great American Race began to wind down, Miller began considering entry into another arena: NASCAR. At first, the races were in smaller venues, with the goal of reaching the target audience of mechanics and part store dealers, which were mostly male.

 At that point, Joe Gibbs had achieved the pinnacle of football coaching prizes—two victories in Super Bowl with the Washington Redskins; however, he had always maintained an active interest (actually a "passion" according to Charlie Brim) in racing. The introduction of Miller with Gibbs led to the highly successful partnership. The team first moved to the Sprint Cup level, which is the top level of NASCAR racing. A relationship with championship driver Dale Jarrett resulted in numerous victories on the track, including an early victory at the Dayton 500, the most famous NASCAR race. The publicity associated with having a successful

Interstate Battery Systems International, Inc.

NFL coach involved in such a win generated substantial positive publicity for the team and for Interstate.

To stand out on television and at the track, the Interstate Battery car was wrapped in a bright, florescent green color with the bright red number 18 featured prominently. Green had been a primary color on the company's batteries. At the time, the color green had been associated with bad luck in racing, so the decision was indeed a bold move. In 2000, a new driver, Bobby Labonte, won the Sprint Cup series championship for the season. Later, Kyle Busch became the primary driver for the team, an affiliation that continues. Busch has become one of the highest winning drivers in the sport.

Interstate participates in NASCAR events through a hospitality tents near the racing venue that will house up to 650 guests. Interstate dealers, wholesale distributors, national account guests such as Honda, Toyota and other automobile manufacturers, retailers such as Firestone and Costco, prospective Interstate All Battery Center retail franchisees, the company's employees, and other company partners are invited to enjoy food, drinks, and mingle with Interstate executives and racing officials. Interstate employees and volunteers manage the tent—it is not farmed out to independent vendors, which is common practice in professional sports. Photos and autographs with Joe Gibbs and Kyle Busch are part of the event. At Texas Motor Speedway, Interstate's home race track, almost 100 guests can watch the race from the company's penthouse level luxury condominium with roof access for a bird's eye view of

Interstate Battery Systems International, Inc.

the event. Joe Gibbs Racing sponsor partners with Mars, Home Depot, and Toyota to tie-in with an Interstate promotion at various tracks, including accommodating each other's customers and guests.

When other racers began using similar green colors, Interstate shifted to a white car with a powerful company graphic in order to recapture attention. The decal displays a battery bursting through the hood, as if the battery is the primary source of the car's energy. The image now appears in a variety of company marketing materials, including route truck back decals, calendars, brochures, retail point-of-purchase signage, business cards, banners at various events, advertising, the company's Web site, and on a show car that travels around the country. If the Kyle Busch number 18 Interstate car wins a race, an e-mail blast is sent out offering an 18 percent discount on various pieces of merchandise at more than 200 Interstate All Battery Centers and on interstatebatteries.com.

Charlie Brim noted that Interstate reached the point at which it made marketing sense to cut back on the number of

racing events and repurpose sponsorship dollars to continue building the brand. Interstate reached an agreement with Mars, Inc through Joe Gibbs Racing to divide the number of annual races between the two companies. For some events, the white hot Interstate Batteries wrap appears on the car; for the others, the same car will be wrapped with an M&M's, Snickers, Doublemint or other Mars' designs. Interstate diverted some of the funding that it saved by cutting back on races into national advertising on TV, radio, digital and mobile media to reach non-NASCAR fans and customers. Other sponsorships include a small position in JGRMX's motocross and super-cross team (owned by Joe Gibbs' son, Coy Gibbs) to target younger patrons and one in NHRA's Pro Stock division with former Champion, Mike Edwards.

 Effective sponsorships and event marketing take advantage of the key strengths of a company and its partners. In the case of Interstate Batteries and NASCAR, the personal connection between Joe Gibbs and Norm Miller has helped the company to grow and achieve success over two decades.

OVERVIEW

The traditional promotions mix consists of advertising, sales promotions, personal selling, and public relations efforts. The first three elements in the mix have been presented. This chapter covers the fourth—public relations. Sponsorship and event programs are also examined.

Public relations efforts, sponsorships, and event programs contribute to the overall IMC approach. The same unified message appears in every marketing endeavor, from the appearance of the company's letterhead and stationery to advertisements, promotional items, information in press releases, and in any sponsorship program. Making sure that each component of a firm's IMC plan speaks with one voice remains the goal. Extending this objective to public relations and sponsorships constitutes an important task for the marketing team.

This chapter begins with a discussion of the nature of a public relations function within an integrated marketing plan. Second, sponsorship programs and event marketing tactics are outlined to show how the company can make quality contacts with existing customers, new prospects, vendors, and others. Successful positive public relations and sponsorship programs enhance the firm's image, and its brands become better known, because they are perceived more favorably in the marketplace.

Public Relations

OBJECTIVE 13.1

What relationships exist between public relations and the marketing activities performed by a company?

In Hollywood, one well-worn phrase is "There's no such thing as bad publicity." This may be true for a bad-boy actor trying to get his name out to the public; however, in the world of marketing and communications bad publicity can be worse than no publicity. Many business organizations spend countless hours fending off negative comments while trying to develop positive and noticeable messages and themes.

The **public relations (PR) department** manages publicity and other communications with every group in contact with the company. Some of the functions performed by the public relations department are similar to those provided by the marketing department. Others are quite different. The two may cooperate with and consult each other, yet each has a unique role. To illustrate, consider the two-pronged approach used by the Mexico Tourism Board to increase tourism. The first component of the campaign was a branding effort carrying the tagline "The Place You Thought You Knew." Second, public relations efforts designed to counter the drug- and violence-related U.S. media take place. Both are necessary to change Americans' perceptions of Mexico.[1]

Some marketing experts argue that public relations should be part of the marketing department, just as advertising, trade promotions, and consumer promotions are under the jurisdiction of the marketing manager. Others suggest that public relations activities are different and cannot operate effectively within a marketing department. Instead, a member of the public relations department should serve as a consultant to the marketing department. Still others contend that a new division, called the "department of communications," should be created to oversee both marketing and public relations activities.

INTERNAL VERSUS EXTERNAL PUBLIC RELATIONS

Deciding who will handle various public relations activities constitutes the first major decision company leaders make. They can be managed by an internal public relations officer or department. Other companies hire public relations firms to complete special projects or all public relations functions. When a company retains a public relations agency, normally an internal company employee takes charge of internal public relations, because most public relations firms deal only with external publics.

The decision criteria used in selecting advertising agencies can be applied to selecting a public relations firm. Developing a trusting relationship with the public relations agency and clearly spelling out what the firm expects from the agency are high priorities.

PUBLIC RELATIONS TOOLS

Public relations employees can utilize a number of tools. These include company newsletters, internal messages, public relations releases, correspondences with stockholders, annual reports, and various special events. Even the bulletin board in the company's break room conveys messages to internal stakeholders.

◀ Company leaders decide who should handle the public relations activities.

Capturing **hits**, or mentions of a company's name in a news story, constitutes one common goal of a public relations firm. Hits can be positive, negative, or neutral in terms of their impact. Each improves the chance that consumers will see the name of a company in a news-related context, which can increase brand or company awareness. This may be true; however, the agency also considers the type of image being portrayed. It may be a more prudent strategy to seek fewer hits and to make sure that each mention of the company in a positive light that reinforces the firm's IMC theme.

When employing a public relations firm, the agency's personnel should be familiar with the client's IMC approach. Then, members of the public relations firm can work on ideas that reinforce the theme. Special events, activities, and news releases may be developed to strengthen the company voice.

Public Relations Functions

OBJECTIVE 13.2

How can the public relations functions help to build better relationships with all internal and external stakeholders?

Public relations activities are not standard marketing functions. The marketing department concentrates on customers and the channel members en route to those customers, such as wholesalers and retail outlets. In contrast, the public relations department focuses on a variety of internal and external stakeholders, including employees, stockholders, public interest groups, the government, and society as a whole.

Figure 13.1 displays five key public relations functions. These tasks are completed by public relations personnel, whether they are internal employees or members of a public relations company hired to perform those functions.

Identifying Stakeholders

Each recipient of company communications is important. Any constituent who makes contact with a company should receive a clear, unified response. A **stakeholder** is a person or group who has a vested interest in the organization's activities. Vested interests include:

- Profits paid as common stock dividends
- Loan repayments that a lending institution seeks to receive
- Sales to the company or purchases made from the company
- Wages paid to employees
- Community well-being
- A special-interest topic

In essence, a wide variety of items can cause people or other companies to believe they hold a stake in the firm's activities. These stakeholders will be monitored and, when appropriate, become targets for public relations communications. Figure 13.2

▶ **FIGURE 13.1**
Public relations functions

- Identify internal and external stakeholders
- Assess the corporate reputation
- Audit corporate social responsibility
- Create positive image-building activities
- Prevent or reduce image damage

▶ **FIGURE 13.2**
Stakeholders

- Employees
- Unions
- Shareholders
- Channel members
- Customers
- Media
- Local community
- Financial community
- Government
- Special-interest groups

identifies the primary internal and external stakeholders that the public relations department monitors.

Communications to each of these stakeholder groups are crucial. To ensure consistency, the company develops a clear communication strategy that fits with the IMC plan and corporate image. The overall message to each stakeholder stays the same. Then, each message can be tailored to meet the different expectations of the various audiences. By customizing the content, style, and channel of communication, each stakeholder group receives a message that best resonates with it, yet it remains consistent with other messages.

In addition to sending communications to individual stakeholders, the public relations department closely monitors the actions and opinions of each group. When changes in attitudes, new views, or serious concerns develop, the public relations department remains ready to respond. The public relations department will be responsible for making certain all communications to each of these publics will consistently present the firm's message and image.

INTERNAL STAKEHOLDERS

Company leaders know the value of quality internal communications. Employees provide a powerful channel of communication to people outside the organization. They can either enhance or damage a firm's reputation. What employees say to others has a much higher level of credibility than what a company says about itself. Word-of-mouth communications, including informal statements by employees, impact purchasing and investing decisions.[2]

Employees receive a constant stream of information from the company. The same holds true for other internal stakeholders, such as corporate shareholders and labor unions. Many of these individuals are away from the marketing and public relations departments. They should still be aware of what the company seeks to achieve with the IMC program, even if this means presenting only basic information. Those closest to the marketing department, such as employees serving customers, will be more acutely aware of the nature of the IMC plan, including how the company's message theme should be transmitted to constituents.

The Motorola advertisement shown in this section states that the company's "Wireless Communications Centers help you stay connected." Employees who are aware of Motorola's theme can communicate the same message when dealing with customers, vendors, and other publics.

To communicate effectively with employees, the public relations department works closely with the human resource (HR) department. Publications and communications aimed at employees should be consistent with the image and message that the firm espouses to customers and others. When a firm advertises that its employees are always ready to assist customers, the public relations team makes sure employees are aware of the message. Employee behaviors should reflect the advertising theme being conveyed to customers. The HR department looks for and hires workers who are attracted to that approach. Performance appraisals and rewards can be structured to favor those who buy into the company's IMC approach. This emphasis on providing quality information about company activities extends to every public relations event and sponsorship program.

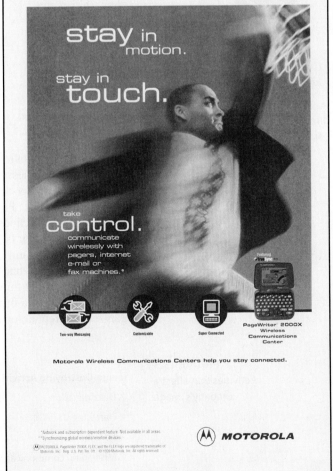

▲ Communications by the employees of Motorola should match the message conveyed in its advertising.

Courtesy of Wal-Mart.

▲ A Wal-Mart advertisement directed to employees, the local community, and other stakeholders.

EXTERNAL STAKEHOLDERS

Overseeing external communications continues to be a daunting task, because the company has little or no influence over how external publics perceive organizational activities. External stakeholders include groups such as the media, the local community, the financial community, the government, and special-interest groups. The company has no control over what these groups say or how information about the company will be interpreted. The public relations agency continually disseminates positive information and quickly reacts to any negative publicity or complaints.

A totally integrated communications program accounts for all types of messages an organization delivers to internal and external stakeholders. Every contact point provides the opportunity for a quality message to be sent. The marketing department tends to create contact points with customers and potential customers. To complement this effort, the public relations department deals with the myriad of contact points that are not created or planned, yet may be just as critical. An unplanned contact point such as a news story or an individual talking to an employee of the firm at a social gathering allows the firm to build a positive image or minimize the impact of any negative messages that are circulating. Dealing with unplanned contact points will be challenging. Constant monitoring of what goes on around the firm is one key to keeping constituents satisfied while insulating the firm from negative publicity.

Assessing Corporate Reputation

A corporation's reputation is both fragile and valuable. Well-received corporate and brand names enhance businesses during the good times and protect them when a crisis or problem occurs. Consumer decisions regarding which brands to purchase are influenced by a company's reputation. People also decide where to invest based on corporate reputations. Potential employees choose where to apply and work based on an organization's reputation.

Corporate scandals, accounting fraud, and the 2008 economic and financial crisis reduced the consumer confidence in the business community. The Edelman's Trust Barometer reported that 56 percent of individuals surveyed said they do not trust businesses to do the right thing.[3] Company actions as well as actions of individuals within an organization impact a firm's reputation. Figure 13.3 identifies activities that can harm an organization's reputation and activities that can enhance a firm's reputation.

▶ **FIGURE 13.3**
Activities that affect a company's image

Image-Destroying Activities	Image-Building Activities
• Discrimination	• Empowerment of employees
• Harassment	• Charitable contributions
• Pollution	• Sponsoring local events
• Misleading communications	• Selling enviromentally safe products
• Deceptive communications	• Outplacement programs
• Offensive communications	• Supporting community events

Assessing and managing a company's reputation will be as important as promoting its products. Yet, with all that is at stake, fewer than half of the companies in the United States have someone assigned to monitor corporate reputation. As a result, many company leaders have little idea what consumers, investors, employees, and the public think or say about the firm. A company cannot effectively pursue a public relations program when company leaders do not know what people believe about the organization.

Assessment begins when surveys and interviews are conducted to reveal perceptions of an organization. Monitoring of online chatter, tweets, and social networks produces additional information. These efforts can be completed internally or are performed by an outside company, such as a public relations firm. Examining both external and internal views of the corporation's reputation produces a complete view of the organization.

Auditing Corporate Social Responsibility

Corporate social responsibility (CSR) is the obligation an organization has to be ethical, accountable, and reactive to the needs of society. It means companies align values for the greater good of society and take actions that have a positive effect. Globalization and increased pressures from the public for corporate transparency have led to an increasing emphasis on social responsibility. Bradley K. Googins, director of the Boston College Center for Corporate Citizenship, stated that "Quality used to be the difference between brands, then it was technology. Now, it really comes back to reputation. It's really the question of who you want to do business with and that relationship with the consumer and the product."[4]

Business experts agree that socially responsible firms are more likely to thrive and survive in the long term. Companies engaged in positive activities generate quality publicity and engender customer loyalty. Firms that work to eliminate unfair practices, pollution, harassment, and other negative activities are more likely to stay out of court, and the company suffers fewer negative word-of-mouth comments by unhappy employees or consumers. Managing these activities properly can lead to a positive corporate image.

The organization's top management team works in conjunction with department managers to oversee the corporate social responsibility audit. Often, external agencies provide guidelines. A social responsibility audit makes sure the organization has clear-cut ethical guidelines for employees to follow and that the company serves the interests of all publics. Guidelines include use of a corporate or professional code of ethics, specifying activities that would be construed as being unethical, and statements about the positive activities a company can pursue. Many firms also offer access to "ethics hotlines," where employees can call or e-mail to discuss specific ethical dilemmas. A firm found to be deficient during a social responsibility audit should take clear steps to resolve the problems.

The public relations department makes sure internal publics are aware of a corporation's social responsibility efforts. The department then informs the general public about these activities while seeking to enhance the firm's image.

Creating Positive Image-Building Activities

In an effort to positively influence the views that consumers and other stakeholders have about a company, many firms engage in cause-related marketing and green marketing. These planned events draw positive attention to the organization as a solid corporate citizen, one committed to social responsibility. The public relations department sends out messages in the form of press releases and holds press conferences to highlight these positive, image-building activities.

OBJECTIVE 13.3

What types of positive, image-building programs can be used by companies as part of a public relations program?

▲ This ad for the Medical Center of Southeast Texas emphasizes water safety.

CAUSE-RELATED MARKETING

A **cause-related marketing** program ties marketing activities with a charity in order to generate goodwill. U. S. businesses pay over $1.5 billion each year for the right to use a nonprofit organization's name or logo in company advertising and marketing programs.[5] This type of partnership agreement between a nonprofit cause and a for-profit business assumes that consumers prefer to purchase from companies that seek to support a good cause. Marketers engage in cause-related marketing to develop stronger ties and to move consumers, as well as businesses, toward brand loyalty. A Cone Communications and Roper Starch Worldwide survey revealed that:

- 78 percent of consumers are more likely to purchase a brand associated with a cause they care about.
- 54 percent would be willing to pay more for a brand that is associated with a cause they care about.
- 66 percent would switch brands to support a particular cause.
- 84 percent indicated that cause-related marketing creates a more positive image of a company.[6]

In the past, some companies donated to causes with little thought to the impact or benefit of such gifts. These philanthropic efforts were expected of big business. Today, most companies try to achieve some type of benefit. Although company leaders view a charity as worthwhile, supporting that charity ought to, in some way, produce a tangible benefit. Possible benefits include:

- Additional customers
- Increased profits
- Consumer goodwill for the future
- Better relations with governmental agencies
- Reduced negative public opinion

These benefits lead companies to get involved. Relationships that do not yield positive benefits to the business sponsor do not last long. In choosing a cause, the marketing team focuses on issues that relate to the company's business. Supporting these efforts makes the activity more credible to consumers. When the company supports an unrelated cause, consumers may conclude that the business merely seeks to benefit from the nonprofit's reputation. This may lead some to stop buying the company's products or to believe the company wishes to cover up unethical behaviors. Many consumers have become even more skeptical about the motives behind giving to various charities. Even though most people understand that a business must benefit from the relationship, they still tend to develop negative views when they believe that the business exploits a relationship with a nonprofit.

When a fit exists, positive reactions emerge. Purina One placed QR codes on the front of select dry cat and dog foods. For each person that scanned the code, Purina One donated $1 to feed shelter pets. The company also placed a 4-question quiz on its Facebook page, challenging people's negative perceptions of adopting shelter pets. For each person that completed the quiz, Purina One donated one bowl of food to a shelter in need.[7]

In addition to social media-based cause-related marketing programs, companies also use games. Social gaming company Zynga produces games such as Farmville, CityVille and Mafia Wars that reach over 230 million players a month. After the earthquake and tsunami hit Japan, Mark Pincus, CEO of Zynga, incorporated cause marketing into 10 of the company's games by creating a virtual fan to blow virtual air. Players could purchase the virtual fan for $5, with all of the proceeds going to relief efforts in Japan. The campaign lasted one week and raised $600,000.[8]

Benefits to Nonprofit Organizations   Cause-related marketing also assists nonprofit organizations. Competition has increased in both the business world and the nonprofit world. An increasing number of nonprofit organizations compete for contributions and gifts. Strategic relationships with businesses can boost contributions to a nonprofit organization. A General Mills Yoplait campaign recently raised over $10 million for the Susan G. Komen Breast Cancer Foundation. Featuring the slogan, "Save Lids to Save Lives," General Mills donated 10 cents for each Yoplait lid that was returned by consumers.[9] The relationship resulted in direct increases in revenues for Yoplait and positive publicity for the foundation.

Most of the time, corporate leaders select the nonprofits they wish to support. Occasionally, the reverse occurs. Alice Berkner, founder of the International Bird Rescue Research Center, obtained a small grant to test major dish soaps for cleaning birds harmed by oil spills.

▲ A Wal-Mart advertisement highlighting a social cause.

Procter & Gamble's Dawn detergent worked the best. When first approached by Berkner about supporting the cause, P&G turned her down. Then, during the 1989 Exxon Valdez oil spill, volunteers used Dawn on the oil-covered birds to remove the black crude. Media coverage was extensive. Now Dawn donates around $100,000 annually to the research center. A television commercial created by Kaplan Thaler Group shows a baby duck, penguin, and seal being washed by Dawn. There is no voice-over, just the song "Wash Away" sung by Joe Purdy. The copy on the screen states that Dawn has helped save thousands of animals caught in oil spills.[10]

A complex linkage exists between public relations and cause-related marketing. To benefit from cause-related marketing, company leaders want publicity. Yet, if the company publicizes too much, people think the cause is only being used for commercial gain. In a survey of British consumers, the vast majority said a company should spend funds on communications about cause-related efforts. The same survey indicated that two-thirds also said the amount spent should not be significant. The majority of those surveyed said their purchase decisions are influenced by the causes a company supports. This makes informing people about a company's activities; however, doing so involves walking a thin line between publicizing and what might be viewed as corporate self-aggrandizement.[11]

GREEN MARKETING AND PRO-ENVIRONMENTAL ACTIVITIES

Green marketing is the development and promotion of products that are environmentally safe. Most consumers favor green marketing. One recent survey indicated that 58 percent of Americans try to save electricity, 46 percent recycle newspapers, 45 percent return bottles or cans, and 23 percent buy products made from or packaged in recycled materials.[12]

Although consumers say they support green marketing and environmentally safe products, actual purchases of such products only occur when all things are considered

The corner office can wait.
Some corners of the world can't.

800.424.8580
www.peacecorps.gov

Life is calling. How far will you go?

PEACE CORPS

Courtesy of Scott Lowden Magnum Photos; Peace Corps.

▲ The Peace Corps is a social cause supported by a number of companies.

equal. Most consumers often will not sacrifice price, quality, convenience, availability, or performance for the sake of the environment. According to David Donnan, a partner with consulting firm A.T. Kearny, "Every consumer says I want to help the environment. I'm looking for eco-friendly products. But, if it's one or two pennies higher in price, they're not going to buy it. There is a discrepancy between what people say and what they do.[13]

To benefit from green marketing, the company identifies the market segments that are most attracted to environmentally-friendly products. In the U.S., consumers can be divided into five segments based on their propensity to use green products and their attitudes about environmental issues. Only 9 percent of American consumers are classified as "True Blue Greens," and another 6 percent are classified as "Greenback Greens." The True Blue Greens are active environmentalists who support environmentally safe products and shop for green brands. The Greenback Greens purchase environmentally safe products, but are not politically active. The other three groups, Sprouts, Grousers, and Basic Browns, are less committed or not committed to environmental protections.[14]

Company leaders choose the green marketing strategy that matches the target market. In making a choice about the degree of emphasis to place on green marketing, managers ask three questions. First, what percentage of the company's customer base fits into the green marketing segments? Second, can the brand or company be differentiated from the competition along green lines in such a way that it can become a competitive advantage? Third, will the company's current target market be alienated by adopting a green marketing approach?

Promoting Green Activities   Almost all firms say they are pro-environment and provide information on company Web sites about environmental activities. The amount of effort given to publicize these activities varies widely.[15] Coca-Cola tries to protect the environment, but most people are unaware of the company's efforts. Coca-Cola has invested in various recycling programs and recyclable package designs but does not publicize the activities, because of concerns that doing so might reduce the product's appeal to some of the company's audience or hurt sales.

Promoting the direct, tangible benefits of a product first, with the environmental benefits presented as secondary factors, can be an alternate approach. The Toyota Prius was launched with an emphasis on fuel efficiency. Consumers were told they would spend less on gas. The fact that the Prius was an environmentally-advanced, fuel-efficient hybrid vehicle was mentioned, but not stressed. The idea was that strong environmentalists would believe buying a hybrid car is important. For those who were not strong environmentalists, it did not matter, because the car delivered fuel efficiency.

For some companies, environmental activities are integrated into the company's business design and marketing approach. This occurs when the primary customer base consists of True Blue Greens and the Greenback Greens. Examples of these types of companies include The Body Shop, Patagonia, Honest Tea, and Seventh Generation. Honest Tea embeds social responsibility into every company activity, from the manufacturing process to the marketing of products. The company features biodegradable tea bags, organic ingredients, and community partnerships. Honest Tea's marketing program focuses on concern for and support of environmental and social issues.

Seventh Generation has produced natural-ingredient cleaning products for 21 years. Although well-known to environmentally-conscious shoppers, including its 27,000 fans on Facebook, few people had ever heard about the Seventh Generation brand. To increase awareness, the company's leaders hired Minneapolis-based Carmichael Lynch to develop a series of print and television commercials about the brand's safety and green ingredients. Print ads appeared in *Good Housekeeping* and *Parents*. TV ads were aired on Bravo, the Food Network, the USA Network, as well as on the *Today Show* and *Ellen*. Video preroll and banner ads appeared on Web sites such as Hulu, iVillage, Yahoo!, Facebook, Lifetime, and Good Housekeeping. The campaign's goal was to educate consumers about the products and the importance of protecting the environment.[16]

Greenwashing   Most business leaders believe their companies should be involved in protecting the environment and creating green products; however, the marketing emphasis varies. Some companies that have claimed to make green products have been exposed by bloggers who point out that the efforts are not truly green. Faking green, or **greenwashing**, damages a company's reputation when such information appears on blogs and other social media. Honesty and transparency are important ingredients in an environmentally-friendly IMC program.

Your daily work will be anything but a chore.

800.424.8580
www.peacecorps.gov

Life is calling. How far will you go?

Courtesy of Scott Lowden Magnum Photos; Peace Corps.

▲ This Peace Corps advertisement asks young adults to join the organization.

OBJECTIVE 14.4

What steps can companies take to prevent or reduce image damage when negative events occur?

Preventing or Reducing Image Damage

One important public relations function, **damage control**, is reacting to negative events caused by a company error, consumer grievances, or unjustified or exaggerated negative press. Bad publicity and negative events quickly damage corporate and brand image. A strong company image that took years to build can be rapidly destroyed. British Petroleum (BP) continues to suffer from the negative publicity surrounding the 2010 spill in the Gulf of Mexico.

Bad news travels fast and hits hard. A Jet Blue incident in which passengers were essentially forced to sit in a plane on the ground for many hours due to bad weather damaged the company's reputation for quality customer service. Company leaders tried to respond rapidly in order to limit the harm to Jet Blue's image.

The media does not generate all negative publicity. Sometimes it comes from word-of-mouth communication from customers, employees, or other individuals connected with the company. With the Internet, bad experiences and negative comments can be posted and spread to thousands in a very short time through social networks, blogs, and Twitter.

Damage control applies to two situations. The first occurs when the firm has made an error or has caused legitimate consumer or public grievances. The second takes place when unjustified or exaggerated negative press appears. Defending an organization's image and handling damage control takes two forms: proactive prevention strategies and reactive damage-control strategies (see Figure 13.4 on the next page).

PROACTIVE PREVENTION STRATEGIES

Proactive prevention means that rather than waiting for harmful publicity to appear and then reacting, many firms charge certain employees with minimizing the effects of any future bad press in advance. These approaches may prevent negative publicity

Fotofreundin/Fotolia

▲ Companies such as Honest Tea and Seventh Generation have demonstrated a concern for the environment.

from emerging in the first place. Two proactive prevention techniques are entitlings and enhancements.[17] **Entitlings** are attempts to claim responsibility for positive outcomes of events. **Enhancements** are attempts to increase the impact of the desirable outcome of an event in the eyes of the public.

Entitling takes place when a firm associates its name with a positive event. For example, being the official sponsor of a U.S. Olympic team that wins a gold medal ties the company's name to the athletic achievements of people who do not work for the firm, yet the firm can claim responsibility for some aspect of their successes.[18]

Enhancements occur when the marketing or public relations department suggests that something relatively small is a bigger deal. Many products that are fat free create the impression that they are diet foods. In fact, many fat-free products have just as many calories as do those that contain fat. Still, a fat-free label might convince customers that the company has tied to help them by offering healthy food that will allow them to watch their weight.

REACTIVE DAMAGE-CONTROL STRATEGIES

Company leaders often must react to unforeseen events. In these instances, managers work diligently to blunt the effects of unwanted bad publicity by every means possible. Crisis management and other techniques help the firm cope with circumstances that threaten its image. Reactive damage-control strategies include Internet interventions, crisis management programs, apology strategies, and impression management techniques.

Internet Interventions Firms combat negative online word-of-mouth with **Internet interventions**. Many new forums for consumers to share negative word-of-mouth and spread bad experiences have emerged, including e-mail, social networks, blogs, and Twitter. Consumers from around the world share horror stories about companies or products. Individuals can say anything online, even when it unfairly portrays various industries, companies, or brands.

These outlets create many venues for people to vent emotions, which can injure a company's reputation. Companies such as Ford, Pepsi, and Southwest Airlines use software and assign employees to monitor Internet postings, blogs, and tweets. Even with these technological tools, monitoring everything said about a company remains a daunting task. It can involve hundreds of posts per day. Employees must quickly decide which to investigate further. Marcus Schmidt, a senior marketing manager for Microsoft suggests, "If you start seeing a lot of people retweeting it, then you know to pay attention."

Last year, Coke's software identified a Twitter post by a frustrated consumer who was not able to redeem a prize from the MyCoke rewards program. The consumer's profile indicated that he had more than 10,000 followers. Adam Brown, Coke's head of social media, posted an apology on the individual's Twitter profile and offered to help. The consumer received the prize. He later changed his Twitter avatar to a photo of himself holding a bottle of Coke. Brown noted, "We're getting to a point if you're not responding, you're not being seen as an authentic type of brand."[19]

• Proactive Strategies
  – Entitlings
  – Enhancements
• Reactive Strategies
  – Internet Interventions
  – Crisis management programs
  – Apology strategy
  – Impression management techniques

▲ **FIGURE 13.4**
Damage-control strategies

Not every activity warrants a formal reaction. Still, monitoring the Internet keeps the company's leadership informed about what people are saying and thinking.

Crisis Management   A company can either accept the blame for an event or offer an apology or refute the charges in a forceful manner in a **crisis management** program. A crisis may be viewed as a problem or an opportunity. Oftentimes, a crisis contains the potential to improve the firm's position and image.

When PepsiCo encountered claims that hypodermic needles were being found in its products, the management team quickly responded with photographs and videos demonstrating that such an occurrence was impossible, because the bottles and cans are upside down before being filled with any soft drink. Next, footage of a con artist slipping a needle into a bottle was shown. This fast and powerful answer eliminated the negative publicity, and Pepsi was able to make a strong statement about the safety of its bottling methods.

Unfortunately, some company leaders only make matters worse, as was the initial reaction of Toyota to quality problems with vehicles. Continual denials of quality problems were not received well when new problems kept emerging. Many consumers became angry when it was revealed that Toyota was aware of the problems for a long time without seeking to correct them. Eventually, the president of Toyota Motors, Akio Toyoda, was summoned to Washington to testify before the House Committee on Oversight and Government Reform.

NOTHING ELSE IS A PEPSI

Courtesy of Pepsi-Cola North America.

▲ When reports surfaced of hypodermic needles in Pepsi products, Pepsi quickly reacted by showing the public how cans and bottles are filled.

Realizing its image was quickly eroding and the outcry against the company was building, Toyota launched a full-scale public relations campaign with print, television, and social media networks. Full-page newspaper ads and several television spots were quickly created in which Toyota announced a temporary halt in production followed by an apologetic, but reassuring, message that Toyota would pull through the crisis.

Toyota's errors in handling mainstream media were apparent to many marketing experts. At the same time, the company did manage social media outlets more effectively. Toyota created a social media response room staffed with individuals who monitored online conversations and responded to consumer concerns. Consumers received answers on Toyota's four Facebook pages and Twitter. Finding brand loyalists online, Toyota asked if they could repost their tweets, blogs, and videos on the Toyota social media outlets. The company then created a series of videos with customers and employees telling their stories that were posted to its YouTube channel and other social media sites. The social media PR effort may have helped save Toyota's brand image, at least in the online world.[20]

Apology Strategies   Another reactive form of crisis management and damage, an **apology strategy**, occurs when an investigation reveals that the firm was at fault. First, a sincere apology should be offered quickly. An apology contains the five elements shown in Figure 13.5.[21]

Apologies are most often used in situations in which the violation is minor or in which the firm or person cannot deny responsibility. It can become an effective strategy

1. An expression of guilt, embarrassment, or regret
2. A statement recognizing the inappropriate behavior and acceptance of sanctions for wrong behavior
3. A rejection of the inappropriate behavior
4. Approval of the appropriate behavior and a promise not to engage in inappropriate behavior
5. An offer of compensation or penance to correct the wrong

for creating a strong emotional bond with the public. Consumers are less likely to remain angry with a company that admits a mistake. When customers believe the apology was sincere and heartfelt, they normally forgive the company and feel more positively toward the organization afterward.

Impression Management   Trying to project a certain type of image, or **impression management**, includes "the conscious or unconscious attempt to control images that are projected in real or imagined social interactions."[22] In order to maintain or enhance an image, individuals and corporations attempt to influence the identities they display to others. Each can be projected in a manner that maximizes positive characteristics while minimizing any negative elements.

Any event that threatens a person's image or a company's desired identity creates a predicament. When faced with one, concerted efforts are made to reduce or minimize the negative consequences. When the predicament cannot be avoided or concealed, then an individual or company engages in any remedial activity that reduces the potentially harmful consequences, including expressions of innocence, excuses, justifications, and other explanations.

An *expression of innocence* approach means company leaders provide information designed to convince others (clients, the media, and the government) that the company was not associated with the event that caused the predicament. In other words, they say, "We did not cause this to happen. Someone (or something) else did."

Excuses are explanations designed to convince the public that the firm and its leaders are not responsible for the predicament or that it could not have been foreseen. Thus, they should not be held accountable for the event that created the predicament. They say, "It was an act of God. It was totally unavoidable. It was the random act of an individual."

Justifications involve using logic designed to reduce the degree of negativity associated with the predicament. Making the event seem minor or trivial is one method. Making the argument that the firm had to proceed in the way it did ("We outsource some of the production process because if we don't we'll be out of business, and our other employees will lose their jobs") is another form of justification.

Other explanations may be created to persuade individuals that the cause of the predicament does not truly represent what the firm or individual is really like. In other words, the case was the exception rather than the rule, and customers should not judge the firm too harshly. You will hear comments such as "This was a singular incident, and not indicative of the way we do business."[23]

Each company's management team, marketing department, and public relations specialists should be acutely aware of the speed with which events can cause great damage to a firm's image. Both proactive and reactive measures can be taken to make sure the firm survives negative publicity with less long-term damage.

Sponsorships

OBJECTIVE 14.5

How can marketers tie sponsorships to public relations efforts to strengthen a customer base?

To build brand loyalty and other positive feelings toward a company, many marketing leaders utilize sponsorships and event marketing. These programs make it possible to meet with prospects, customers, vendors, and others in unique situations. People who attend sponsored activities or special events already have favorable feelings about the activity taking place. These positive attitudes are easily transferred to a company that has provided funding.[24]

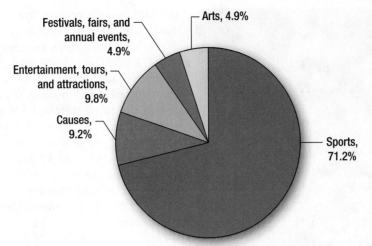

◀ **FIGURE 13.6**
Marketing expenditures on
sponsorships

Sponsorship marketing means that the company pays money to sponsor someone, some group, or something that is part of an activity. A firm can sponsor a long list of groups, individuals, activities, and events. For years, firms sponsored everything from local Little League baseball and soccer teams to national musical tours, NASCAR drivers, and sports stadiums.

FORMS OF SPONSORSHIPS

In North America, companies spend approximately $16.3 billion each year on sponsorships and events.[25] Figure 13.6 provides a breakdown of the spending. Sports represent about 70 percent of all sponsorships. Sporting events are popular and often attract large crowds. In addition to the audience attending the game or competition, many more watch on television. Popular athletes can be effective spokespersons. If possible, the firm should be the exclusive sponsor of the person or team, which makes it easier to remember than when there are multiple sponsors.

Sponsorships were a major part of Ford's integrated advertising and marketing push for the Ford F-Series Super Duty pickup trucks. Although the integrated campaign included television ads, print ads, and online chats, the central component of the campaign was the sponsorship of Toby Keith's concert tour, entitled "America's Toughest Tour." The Ford F-Series trucks were highly visible at the concerts, with truck-themed set pieces on stage and at least one F-Series truck actually on the stage. In addition to the concert tour, Ford also sponsored a Monster Jam truck show and individual professional bull riders. The company sponsors the Future Farmers of America, the American Quarter Horse Association, and the Dallas Cowboys.[26]

Speedo used sponsorships to build customer loyalty and capture over 60 percent of the competitive swimwear market in the United States. Swimmers wearing Speedo's revolutionary LZR Racer swimwear design broke 38 world records. The full-body suit was created with the help of NASA and is worn by competitive swimmers all over the world. By sponsoring the U.S. Olympic trials and athletes, Speedo's market share grew rapidly until it became the swimwear brand of choice for even noncompetitive swimmers.[27]

Some organizations have moved away from sports sponsorships toward cultural events, such as classical music groups and jazz bands, visual art exhibits by noted painters, dance troupes, and actors for various theater performances. Cultural sponsorships are not the best match for every firm. They are most effective for products sold to affluent consumers. Consequently, financial institutions are primary sponsors of these types of performers and performances. In the past, many institutions provided funds without receiving much recognition. Now firms leverage philanthropic efforts by having the name of the company strongly associated with the cultural activity. This includes printing the name of the firm on programs and regularly mentioning the brand or corporate name as being responsible for arranging for the artist to be present at the event. Also,

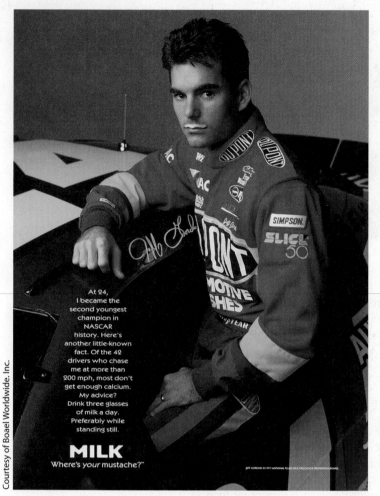

At 24, I became the second youngest champion in NASCAR history. Here's another little-known fact. Of the 42 drivers who chase me at more than 200 mph, most don't get enough calcium. My advice? Drink three glasses of milk a day. Preferably while standing still.

MILK
Where's *your* mustache?™

▲ In addition to milk, notice all of the corporate sponsors on Jeff Gordon's NASCAR uniform.

sponsors usually receive choice seats at performances that can be given to key clients.

Television offers another option for sponsorships. Coca-Cola, Ford, and AT&T chose to sponsor the popular television show *American Idol*. Each company paid $35 million for the right to be part of one of the most watched TV shows, to post online content, and to run off-air cobranded marketing programs. Ford featured its vehicles in music videos sung by the final 12 contestants. Ford also gave away a Ford Escape Hybrid to the top two finalists. Coca-Cola placed branded cups in the center on the judges' table. Coke graphics were also visible behind the contestants when they were being interviewed. AT&T benefited greatly from the sponsorship by being responsible for the text-message voting tabulations each week. AT&T also featured *Idol* downloads, ring tones, and videos of bad auditions and poor performances.[28]

Social Media and Blogs   The newest format is sponsoring bloggers. Colleen Padilla, a 33-year-old mother of two and author of the popular Web site Classy Mommy (www.classymommy.com), has reviewed nearly 1,500 products, including microwave dinners, Nintendo Wii, and baby clothes. Her site attracts 60,000 unique visitors every month. Companies eagerly send her products to test and, if she likes them, to post positive comments on the site. When she does not like an item, nothing will be posted. Padilla tells her readers if the brand was sent to her. She also includes videos of brands, including Healthy Choice, labeled as "sponsored posts."

For some bloggers, such as Drew Bennett, product sponsorships have become a lucrative business. Bennett began with a photo-a-day blog that mushroomed into sponsored products at his site BenSpark.com. He has written more than 600 posts for firms such as X-Shot, a telescope camera extender. Bennett typically earns between $5.35 and $10 per post. Most product sponsors pay Bennett between 11 and 68 cents each time a reader moves from his site to the brand's site.

K-Mart used a similar approach to generate positive buzz. Through 800 blog posts and 3,200 Twitter messages, K-Mart reached 2.5 million people. The campaign began with six popular bloggers receiving a $500 gift card to shop at K-Mart and then writing about their experiences.[29]

SPONSORSHIP OBJECTIVES

It may be hard to measure the direct impact of a sponsorship program. Sponsorships can be designed to accomplish a variety of objectives. They can be designed to:

- Enhance a company's image
- Increase a firm's visibility
- Differentiate a company from its competitors
- Showcase specific goods and services
- Help a firm develop closer relationships with current and prospective customers
- Sell excess inventory

The Green Turtle restaurant built visibility and a positive image through the use of a sponsorship. The company sponsored Amelia's Ace of Hearts Ride to raise money for breast cancer. Approximately 200 of the 400 bike riders registered at the restaurant, and 300 people celebrated at an after-party in the restaurant. The event raised $28,000 for the charity. Leho Poldmae of The Green Turtle reported, "These events and sponsorships put the human aspect into marketing. They are much more powerful than ads in touching and reaching customers."[30]

Event Marketing

Event marketing and sponsorship marketing are similar. The primary difference is that sponsorship marketing involves a person, group, or team. **Event marketing** involves a company in supporting a specific event. Event marketing and lifestyle marketing are closely related. Both often include setting up a booth or display and maintaining a physical presence at an event.

Sponsoring the right event provides a company with brand-name recognition and to develop closer ties with vendors and customers. Events also help boost morale for the employees who participate in or attend them. Sponsoring local events such as the Special Olympics provides a company with the potential to generate free publicity. These events can also be used to enhance the company's image in the local community.

As is the case with sponsorships, many event marketing programs feature sports. Other events are more related to lifestyles. A rodeo sponsored by Lee Jeans, a music concert put on by a local business, or a health fair conducted by a local hospital are all examples of event marketing.

Event marketing has proven to be especially successful with Hispanic consumers. It can be an excellent method of building brand awareness and building brand loyalty. Renata Franco of Cox Communications notes that, "Hispanics are much more community-centered. Events do really well." When Cox Communications sponsors a Hispanic event, the company employs bilingual brand ambassadors who can personally speak to attendees.[31]

Courtesy of French Creative

▲ Non-profits such as Med Camps of Louisiana often pursue corporate sponsors.

OBJECTIVE 13.6

What role can event marketing play in creating customer excitement and brand loyalty?

Selecting Sponsorships and Events

Several key steps are involved in selecting a sponsorship or an event. To ensure the maximum benefit, companies should:

- Determine the objective(s) of the sponsorship or event
- Match the sponsorship or event with the company's customers, vendors, and employees
- Promote the sponsorship or event
- Make sure the company is included in all event advertising and brochures
- Track results

▲ Matching the audience profile with the company's target market is important when selecting sponsorships.

DETERMINING OBJECTIVES

Companies outline communication objectives before becoming involved in a sponsorship or an event. For an objective of rewarding customers, marketers look for sponsorships or events that major customers would enjoy. Some objectives are more internally oriented, especially those designed to increase employee involvement or to boost morale. These can be achieved by finding opportunities internal members will like. Externally-oriented objectives include maintaining market share, building a stronger brand presence, enhancing the product or firm's image, and increasing sales.

MATCHING AUDIENCE TO THE COMPANY'S TARGET MARKET

In choosing a sponsorship or an event, the marketing team matches the audience profile with the company's target market. A firm sponsoring a singer at a music show attended mainly by women works best when the company's primary customers are female. Marketing executives also consider how the individual participant or group image relates to the firm's image. A contestant in an upscale event, such as a piano competition, may be sponsored by a tuxedo or formal gown company. The sponsors of the Women's Bassmaster Tour shown in the advertisement in this section are a good match with the participants in the Tour events.

PROMOTING THE EVENT

Advertising and public relations releases promote sponsorships and events. Special effort will be given to contacting interest groups that would benefit from the event. An event such as a local Special Olympics requires commercials, contacts with the press, and finding ways to reach parents and relatives of those who might participate. Sponsorship of NASCAR by Interstate Batteries involves highlighting the partnership in advertising and public relations efforts.

ADVERTISING AT THE EVENT

Sponsors insist on placement of the company's name and logo and other product information in every advertisement and brochure for the event. Many attendees of games and events keep programs as souvenirs. Placing the sponsor's name and message on the program generates an advertisement with a longer lifespan. The sponsoring business can maximize brand-name exposure by connecting the firm's name with the event's marketing program. The marketing team works closely with the event management team to make sure the company's name receives prominent attention in all materials associated with the occasion.

TRACKING RESULTS

Some events and sponsorships turn out better than others for the sponsor. To determine the best opportunities, the marketing team tracks results. In addition to sales, employees can monitor how many pieces of literature were given to attendees, the number of samples distributed, or the number of visitors to the sponsor's display booth. Further, marketing research measures brand awareness or brand image before and after the event to see if any new level of awareness or higher image emerged.

Tracking results helps the business evaluate its investment. Company leaders and marketing managers then decide if the sponsorship or particular event was beneficial and whether to sponsor the event or similar events in the future.

When Victoria's Secret launched the brand Pink, it was coupled with a unique event marketing promotion during spring break. The goal was to reach 18- to 24-year-old females. The event began with a three-story pink box set up on a beach in Miami. Advertisements, Internet postings, street teams of employees giving out fliers, aerial signs, posters in nearby hotels, and public relations press releases built excitement during the 5-day countdown. Many spring breakers showed up at the pink box. They were treated to a fashion show and a live concert by No Mercy. After the concert, Victoria's Secret Pink gift cards were passed out and the company hosted nightclub parties. The unique marketing event spurred sales of the new Pink brand and the Victoria's Secret brand. The Victoria's Secret marketing team completed the evaluation stage and discovered a big increase in Pink brand sales in the Miami area and that the other Victoria's Secret brand sales also rose dramatically.[32]

▲ Note the sponsors of the Louisiana Fair listed at the bottom of the Web page screen.

Courtesy of Gremillion & Pou.

An Advertising Research Foundation study revealed that intentions to purchase a branded product increased from 11 to 52 percent among consumers who attended a brand-sponsored event. Further research suggests that purchase intentions translate into sales about half the time. The Advertising Research Foundation study investigated events sponsored by Frito-Lay, State Farm, and Coca-Cola. Sports-related sponsorships and events tended to have the best results.[33]

CROSS-PROMOTIONS

Cross-promotions with the event sponsor or other companies involved are often used to boost the impact of the sponsorship. A **cross-promotion** is a marketing event that ties together companies and activities around a specific theme. Recently, eBay partnered with Sony and Baskin-Robbins to create a unique event called "Camp eBay." During the summer months, consumers are typically outdoors enjoying the warm weather and are not logged onto the Internet, so eBay's marketing team decided to go to consumers. Camp eBay was eBay's first attempt at event marketing. The aim was to create awareness in and to educate people who do not use eBay. The program was also designed to encourage existing buyers and sellers to be more active in the summertime.

The Camp eBay program began with the purchase of a refurbished school bus that was sent out on a mobile marketing tour to six high-traffic areas: the Indy 500, CMA Fan Fest, eBay Live, Taste of Chicago, the Ohio State Fair, and the Minnesota State Fair. The school bus classroom drew 52,000 people who attended 30-minute sessions on how to use eBay. Participants earned badges redeemable for prizes that were furnished by Sony and Baskin-Robbins. The prizes were worth a total of $85,000. In addition, eBay pitched tents at 20 Clear Channel Entertainment venues that hosted nearly 400 concerts. The impact of the event marketing program was that 45 percent of existing users increased purchases, leading to an overall increase in sales of 2 percent during the promotion and 9 percent after the event.[34]

Sponsorship programs and event marketing have increased in popularity during the past decade due to the potential to reach consumers on a one-to-one basis. In the future, sponsorships and event marketing tie-ins with other media, especially the Internet, will

Tyler Olson/Fotolia

▲ Sponsoring events such as a rodeo allows companies to reach consumers in a less cluttered environment.

rise. Rock concerts, boat shows, music fairs, and a wide variety of other, more specialized programs are likely to be featured by various companies. Many marketing experts believe that making contact with customers in personalized ways that do not directly involve a sales call are valuable activities. Event marketing and sponsorship programs create that type of contact.

International Implications

The public relations function has become increasingly valuable in the international arena for several reasons. First, the growing number of international firms creates the need to make sure the company will be viewed in a positive light in every country in which it does business.

Second, the impact of terrorism and war over the past decade has heightened sensitivities between many nations. Any company conducting business in a foreign land will have a public relations officer in charge of monitoring news stories and other events so that the firm can react to negative press.

Third, whenever there are differences among cultures, the potential exists to offend without intending to do so. In 2008, when Rocco Mediate was involved in a valiant effort to win a playoff in the U.S. Open golf tournament, sportscaster Johnny Miller made a joke that Mediate looked more like "the guy that would clean your pool" than a professional golfer. A number of Italians took offense, believing it was an ethnic slur. Miller apologized, stating he was referring to the "every man" quality Mediate possessed.

Corporate social responsibility also has no national boundaries. Many heated debates have taken place regarding outsourcing. Critics argue that nations other than the United States have enjoyed the advantages of unfair wage rates and the ability to pollute freely, thereby cutting costs and attracting businesses to them. Any multinational corporation or company conducting business in foreign lands should be aware of these criticisms and find effective ways to respond.

Many sponsorships now include an international events. Some of the more visible ones are found in sports, most notably automobile racing and soccer. Sportswear brand Adidas signed an agreement with the NBA to be the league's official supplier in Europe and worldwide. The sponsorship represents a major effort by Adidas, because NBA merchandise is sold in more than 100,000 stores in 100 countries on six continents.[35]

The principles that guide the development of sponsorships domestically apply equally well to any international involvements. To fully prepare an effective sponsorship program in an international setting, the marketing team will employ a cultural assimilator to ensure correct usage of a foreign language, the legality of the sponsorship, and that it does not violate any local cultural norms. As the world continues to become smaller, with increasing interactions between countries, companies, and individuals, the growth of multinational sponsorships should continue.

OBJECTIVE 13.7

Can public relations programs, sponsorships, and event marketing be adapted to international settings?

INTEGRATED CAMPAIGNS IN ACTION

Curb It

Pratt Industries makes cardboard boxes from recycled paper. The company invested $160 million in a wastepaper recycling mill in Shreveport, Louisiana. Demand was not a problem for Pratt Industries. Wal-Mart, Target, and other large retailers were willing to purchase recycled boxes almost as fast as Pratt could make them. The problem was that Pratt needed recycled materials with which to make the cardboard boxes.

Pratt Industries hired the Gremillion & Pou advertising agency to create an integrated marketing campaign to encourage citizens of Shreveport to recycle their trash. Research showed that people did not like sorting trash and were not willing to go out of the way to drop trash off. The challenges Gremillion & Pou faced were:

- To communicate the ease of curbside recycling
- To leverage environmental concerns to create a desire to recycle materials
- To teach the public how easy it was to recycle

▲ An advertisement encouraging people to recycle.

To meet these challenge, the agency created an animated green frog named "Curb It." This character was used in ads, in PSAs, and on recycling bins. The campaign caught the interest of city officials and the town's citizens. Soon recycling became the easy and popular thing to do.

The Curb It campaign can be found at the Pearson Instructor's Resource Center (www.pearsonhighered.com). The campaign includes a PowerPoint presentation outlining the details of the campaigns and examples of the collaterals including ads and television commercials.

MyMarketingLab

Go to **mymktlab.com** to complete the problems marked with this icon .

SUMMARY

The public relations department plays a major role in an integrated marketing communications program, whether the department is separate from marketing or combined as part of a communications division. Public relations efforts are oriented to making sure that every possible contact point delivers a positive and unified message on behalf of the company.

Any person or group with a vested interest in the organization's activities is a stakeholder. Internal stakeholders include employees, unions, and stockholders. External publics include members of the marketing channel, customers, the media, the local community, financial institutions, the government, and special-interest groups.

To reach all intended audiences, the public relations department has a series of tools available. These include company newsletters, internal messages, public relations releases, correspondence with stockholders, annual reports, and various special events. A bulletin board in the company's break room can be used to convey messages to internal stakeholders.

In the attempt to build a favorable image of the company, the public relations department develops special events such as altruistic activities and cause-related marketing programs. Care must be taken to make certain that these acts are not perceived with cynicism and skepticism. This means being certain that any good deed matches with the company's products and other marketing efforts. A natural fit between an altruistic event and the company's brand is more readily accepted by various members of the public.

The public relations team tends to damage control when negative publicity arises. Proactive and reactive tactics help maintain a positive image for the company. Damage-control tactics include Internet interventions, crisis management programs, and impression management techniques.

Sponsorship programs enhance and build the company's image and brand loyalty. A sponsorship of an individual or group involved in an activity—whether a sporting event, a contest, or a performance by an artistic group—can be used to link the company's name with the popularity of the player involved. Sponsorships should match with the firm's products and brands.

Event marketing occurs when a firm sponsors an event. A strong physical presence at the event is one of the keys to successfully linking an organization's name with a program. To do so, the firm determines the major objective of the sponsorship, matches it with company customers and publics, and ensures that the firm's name is prominently displayed on all event literature.

Managing public relations, sponsorships, and event marketing programs requires company leaders to assess the goals and the outcomes of individual activities. A cost–benefit approach may not always be feasible, but the marketing team should be able to track some form of change, whether it is increased inquiries, the number of samples passed out at an event, or a shift in the tenor of news articles about the organization. The public relations department serves as the organization's "watchdog," making sure those who come in contact with the company believe the firm is working to do things right and to do the right things.

Key Terms

public relations (PR) department A unit in the firm that manages items such as publicity and other communications with all of the groups that make contact with the company.

hit The mention of a company's name in a news story.

stakeholder A person or group with a vested interest in a firm's activities and well-being.

corporate social responsibility An organization's obligation to be ethical, accountable, and reactive to the needs of society.

cause-related marketing Matching marketing efforts with some type of charity work or program.

green marketing The development and promotion of products that are environmentally safe.

greenwashing Activities that are presented as being green or environmentally friendly that are not.

damage control Reacting to negative events caused by a company error, consumer grievances, or unjustified or exaggerated negative press.

entitlings Attempts to claim responsibility for positive outcomes of events.

enhancements Attempts to increase the impact of a desirable outcome of an event in the eyes of the public.

Internet interventions Confronting negative publicity on the Internet, either in Web site news releases or by entering chat rooms, blogs, or social networks.

crisis management Either accepting the blame for an event and offering an apology or refuting those making the charges in a forceful manner.

apology strategy Presenting a full apology when the firm has made an error.

impression management The conscious or unconscious attempt to control images that are projected in real or imagined social situations.

sponsorship marketing When the company pays money to sponsor someone or some group that is participating in an activity.

event marketing When a company pays money to sponsor an event or program.

cross-promotion A marketing event that ties together companies and activities around a specific theme.

Review Questions

1. Describe the role of the public relations department. How is it related to the marketing department? Should both departments be called the "department of communications?" Why or why not?

2. What is a stakeholder?

3. Name the major internal stakeholders in organizations. Describe each one's major interests in the company.

4. Name the major external stakeholders in organizations. Describe each one's major interest in the company.

5. What is corporate social responsibility? How is it related to public relations activities?

6. What is cause-related marketing? How can company leaders create effective cause-related marketing programs?

7. What is green marketing? How do different companies promote environmentally-friendly activities?

8. What reactive damage-control techniques are available to the public relations team?

9. What four forms of impression management are used to combat negative events?

10. What is sponsorship marketing? Name a pro athlete, musician or musical group, or performer of some other type who has been featured in a sponsorship program. Was the program effective or ineffective? Why?

11. Describe an event marketing program. What must accompany the event in order to make it a success?

12. What are cross-promotions? How are they related to event marketing programs?

13. How are public relations programs and sponsorship adapted to international companies?

Critical Thinking Exercises

DISCUSSION QUESTIONS

1. Watch the news on television, read a local news story, or access the Internet for a story about a local or national business. Was the report positive or negative toward the firm? Did the news report or article affect your attitude toward the company? Watch one of the many special investigative shows, such as *60 Minutes*. What companies did it investigate? If your firm was being featured, what would you do to counteract the bad press?

2. One of the vice presidents of a small but highly respected bank in a local community was charged with sexual harassment by a female employee. What types of communications should be prepared for each of the constituencies listed in Figure 13.2? Which of the constituencies would be the most important to contact?

⭐ 3. Is the local community important to a manufacturing firm that sells 99 percent of its products outside the area? Does it really matter what the local people say or believe about the manufacturer as long as the firm's customers are happy? Explain your answer.

4. What causes do you support or are special to you? Do you know which corporations sponsor or support the causes? If not, see if you can find literature or Web sites that contain that information. Why do you think the corporations choose a particular cause to support? What benefits do corporations receive from sponsorships?

⭐ 5. When Starbucks opened its first coffee shop inside a public library, 10 percent of all coffee proceeds went to support the operation of the library. Do you think a public library should allow a for-profit organization such as Starbucks to sell products inside the building? Is this a conflict of interest for government-sponsored organizations, such as libraries? What if the local doughnut shop wanted to sell doughnuts at the library? Should it be allowed to do so? How does a head librarian decide?

6. Managers often are the most difficult group for the public relations department to reach. To entice employees to reach departmental goals, managers often communicate using memos or verbal messages. These messages may conflict with the IMC theme. For example, in an effort to trim costs a manager may send a memo to all employees telling them to use only standard production procedures. Through verbal communications, employees learn that anyone caught violating or even bending the policy to satisfy a customer will be immediately reprimanded. The manager's action suggests that even though he wants employees to provide customer service, in actuality they had better not do anything that is not authorized. Employees soon get the message that management cares only about costs, not the customer. Employees will perceive any advertising message about customer service as a big joke. Write a memo to employees that supports the IMC goal of high customer service, yet alerts them to the need to follow standard operating procedures. Is there anything else you would do to ensure that employees do not receive conflicting messages?

⭐ 7. Sponsorships are now a major component of professional sports. Football, basketball, baseball, and golf all have sponsors. Many stadiums are now named for companies. Why do you think companies spend millions on these sponsorships? What impact does it have on you? What sponsorships do you notice? Which ones do you not notice? Why?

8. Because of the shortage of state funds for universities and colleges, many are considering using sponsorships as a means of generating revenue. What would you think about your university having the stadiums and different sports being having corporate names? Discuss the pros and cons of your school using corporate sponsors to fund athletics.

Integrated Learning Exercises

1. Although some firms handle public relations activities internally, many firms retain public relations firms to work on special projects and to handle unique situations. The Public Relations Society of America (PRSA) is one of the major associations for PR practitioners. In Canada, the primary association is the Canadian Public Relations Society (CPRS). Access the Web sites of these two organizations at www.prsa.org and www.cprs.ca. What types of information does each provide? What types of services are offered? How would these organizations be beneficial to various companies?

2. Access the online version of *PRWeek* at www.prweek.com. What type of information is available? How would this site be valuable to a PR practitioner? How could it be used by a firm seeking a public relations agency? How could it be used by a marketing manager?

3. The American Institute of Philanthropy ranks many charities. Access the Web site at www.charitywatch.org. How does the Institute rate the charities? How can this information be used by a company to determine which charities to support?

4. A number of companies offer services to help firms plan and develop sponsorships. One company is IEG. Access the Web site at www.sponsorship.com. Review the site. Identify the various services offered by IEG. If you were the marketing manager for a company that wanted to develop a sponsorship program, how could IEG help? Be specific.

5. Many companies participate in event marketing to accomplish various objectives. Access the following companies that assist firms with event marketing. What type of services does each offer? What is your evaluation of each of the companies? If you were hosting an event, which company would you hire? Why?

   a. Advantage International, LLC (www.advantage-intl. com)

   b. Fuse Youth Marketing Agency (www.fusemarketing. com)

   c. RPMC Event and Promotion Agency (www.rpmc.com)

6. Corporate sponsorships are important to nonprofits. Without the financial assistance provided, many nonprofits would not exist. Look up two organizations from the following list of nonprofits. Who are their corporate sponsors? What benefits do the profit-seeking companies receive from these sponsorships?

   a. American Cancer Society (www.cancer.org)

   b. Arthritis Foundation (www.arthritis.org)

   c. Multiple Sclerosis Society (www.mssociety.org.uk)

   d. United Cerebral Palsy (www.ucp.org)

   e. Alliance for the Wild Rockies (www.wildrock iesalliance.org)

   f. National Wildlife Federation (www.nwf.org)

   g. Trout Unlimited (www.tu.org)

Student Project

CREATIVE CORNER

Circle K Ranch has been selling, training, and boarding horses for almost 20 years. With the recent downturn in the economy, however, Circle K has experienced a decline in all facets of its business. In talking with some marketing students at the local university, the owner of Circle K Ranch, Kathy Kroncke, wondered about using cause-related marketing, sponsorships, and even event marketing to boost the awareness and image of her business. She recently added horseback riding to her list of services and developed a 10-mile ride that goes through a local state park. So far, business has not been what she expected, despite research that indicated a high level of interest in riding, especially by 15- to 40-year-old females. Design a cause-related marketing program, a sponsorship program, and an event marketing program for Circle K Ranch. After you have designed each of the programs, choose the one you think would be the best for Circle K Ranch. Design a newspaper ad featuring the program. What other methods would you use, both traditional and nontraditional, to publicize the program you chose?

CASE 1 OLIVE GARDEN: MEET THE GIRLS NEXT DOOR

Public relations challenges come in many forms, some expected and others that could never be imagined. The Olive Garden has developed a strong brand and corporate image focused on family, friends, and fun. The company was launched as a subsidiary of General Mills as an entry into the casual Italian restaurant marketplace. The initial success and growth led to a spin-off, and Darden Restaurants has directed the chain since the early 1990s.

Olive Garden restaurants are distinctive, featuring a casual Italian decor. The menus have been upgraded to move beyond more basic dishes to include items such as Mediterranean Garlic Shrimp and Capellini Pomodoro. Chefs continue to look for ways to treat regular customers to new and exciting dishes to accompany old favorites. All the while, endless bowls of salad and servings of breadsticks, along with tasty servings of soup, are part of the regular fare.

The wholesome family atmosphere projected in the Olive Garden's marketing communications includes the term "Hospitalino," which suggests the commitment to a warm, comfortable environment for dining. Commercials and advertisements carrying the tagline "When you're here, you're family" have helped Olive Garden establish a strong brand presence in a highly competitive marketplace.

The Girls Next Door has become a popular television program on E! Entertainment Television. The show features three beautiful young women who live in Hugh Hefner's exotic Playboy Mansion. In 2008, over 1.4 million viewers watched the antics of the young women in various stages of dress and settings. One of the three, Kendra Wilkinson happens to be a genuine fan of the Olive Garden. During one program, she mentioned how much she loved the artichoke dip and breadsticks. She quickly became known as practically a "new spokesperson" for the company.

Without question, Kendra's affection for the Olive Garden was sincere. As she noted, "I love the Olive Garden, because I grew up going there. That used to be the place we would go for Mother's Day, for birthdays. My grandpa just died, and right after his funeral, we went to the Olive Garden." She pointed out when asked that she received no compensation for mentioning the restaurant on *The Girls Next Door*.

Ms. Wilkinson did, however, convince Hefner to create a contest. Women were invited to compete for a chance to become one of the "Sexiest Girls of Olive Garden." The winner was to receive a Playboy photo shoot conducted by Kendra Wilkinson for an upcoming edition of the magazine.

Olive Garden's management and marketing team faced a dilemma. On the one hand, a surprising overlap exists between the types of individuals who dine at the Olive Garden and those who watch *The Girls Next Door*. Many are college educated, affluent, and enjoy upscale dining. More women watch the television program than men, and more women dine at the Olive Garden than men.

At the other extreme, protests have been lodged against the television show. The Florida Family Association had

▲ The Olive Garden has communicated an image of being a "wholesome family restaurant."

encouraged advertisers to stop buying spots for the show. Playboy has long been a source of controversy in the United States.

From the Olive Garden's perspective, the publicity generated by the linkage between the two organizations could have been viewed as a blessing or a curse. At first, the company did not make official statements about the contest. Undoubtedly, the marketing and public relations teams believed the company was navigating through some very choppy waters.[36]

1. Who are Olive Garden's internal and external stakeholders that have been affected by this turn of events?

2. For casual observers of media, would the "Sexiest Girls of Olive Garden" appear to be a sponsorship?

3. Is this event an instance in which damage-control programs were in order? If so, which one(s)?

4. Kendra Wilkinson said she believed Olive Garden could afford to appear to be a little "edgy" without detracting from its family-friendly brand. Do you agree or disagree? Why?

5. If you were the public relations agency for the Olive Garden, how would you handle this situation? What steps would you take and what tactics would you use to ensure Olive Garden's image is not adversely affected.

CASE 2   NEW DRUG FACES PUBLIC RELATIONS AND MARKETING CHALLENGES

It is unusual for a new product to create a vehement public response with both supporters and detractors. One such product, which was approved by the FDA in 2006 and made widely available in 2007, is Gardasil. The drug was developed by Merck and Company.

Gardasil is provided in the form of a vaccine. It was developed to prevent cervical cancer by blocking infection from human papillomavirus, which is spread through sexual contact. The Food and Drug Administration permits Gardasil to be used by females ages 9 through 26, with the goal of inoculating girls before they become sexually active. Although the vaccine does not prevent every form of papillomavirus, it does treat four of the most common, including 100 percent prevention of the most common type and 70 percent of the four most common types combined.

Nearly half a million women are diagnosed with cervical cancer each year. According to some experts, Gardasil might make it possible to eliminate cervical cancer within a generation. It is also a victory for Merck, the fourth-biggest U.S. drug maker, which has focused increasingly on vaccines and may generate $3 billion in annual sales from Gardasil alone. "It's important from a public health perspective because you're eliminating a cancer," said Les Funtleyder, an analyst in New York for Miller Tabak & Co. "The subtle point is these guys are creating new drugs for important health problems, which is what a pharma is supposed to do."

Gardasil requires three doses to be given over 6 months. In 2007, each dose cost around $120. Consequently, affordability may determine how effective the drug is in quelling cervical cancer. About 80 percent of cases are in poorer countries. "Critical to success will be ensuring that women in the world's poorest countries—where cervical cancer hits hardest—have rapid and affordable access to this lifesaving new tool," said Gabriel N. Hortobagyi, a physician at the University of Texas M.D. Anderson Cancer Center in Houston and president of the American Society of Clinical Oncology, in a statement. Human papillomavirus, or HPV, is one of the most common sexually transmitted viruses in the world, and it causes genital warts as well as cancer. About 20 million people in the United States are infected, according to the U.S. Centers for Disease Control and Prevention (CDC).

Why the controversy? Many social conservatives fear that providing the vaccine may provide subtle approval for young women to engage in sex, much in the same way as providing birth control information and condoms are sometimes condemned. Some of the response was in regard to the recommendations from a panel of experts assembled by the CDC. The panel issues widely followed guidelines, including recommendations for childhood vaccines that become the basis for vaccination requirements set by

© Deklofenak/Fotolia

▲ Many young girls could benefit from the HPV virus vaccine Gardasil.

public schools. The panel recommended that the vaccine be required.

Merck company officials and others noted that research indicates the best age to vaccinate would be just before puberty to make sure children are protected before they become sexually active. The vaccine would probably be targeted primarily at girls, but could also be used on boys to limit the spread of the virus. "If you really want to have cervical cancer rates fall as much as possible as quickly as possible, then you want as many people to get vaccinated as possible," said Mark Feinberg, Merck's vice president of medical affairs and policy, noting that "school mandates have been one of the most effective ways to increase immunization rates." That is the view being pushed by cervical cancer experts and women's health advocates.

Not surprisingly, a major clash emerged, mostly notably when the state of Texas made it a requirement to have the vaccine in order to be admitted to school. The battle lines were primarily drawn over girls being forced to take a medicine, with or without parental consent, along with the concerns expressed about sexual activity.

Company officials from Merck worked carefully with both governmental agencies and other groups to reduce concerns. In 2008, the company began advertising Gardasil in television commercials entitled "One Less" and "Guard Yourself." A powerful point is made: by taking the medicine, one less person will become infected.

1. Describe the stakeholders and the positions of each group involved in this controversy.

2. Outline the positive public relations opportunities available to promote Gardasil.

3. Describe how Merck should respond to negative publicity and complaints about the product.

4. Could Merck use cause-related marketing effectively, or would it be construed as a means of marketing the drug?

5. What sponsorships and event marketing programs should be used to promote Gardasil?

Sources: Angela Zimm and Justin Blum, "FDA Approves Merck's Cervical Cancer Vaccine," *Boston Globe* and *Bloomberg News* (www.boston.com/business/healthcare/articles, accessed January 28, 2008), June 9, 2006; Rob Stein, "Cervical Cancer Vaccine Gets Injected with a Social Issue," *Washington Post* (www.washingtonpost.com/wp-dyn, accessed January 28, 2008), October 31, 2005.

MyMarketingLab

Go to **mymktlab.com** for Auto-graded writing questions as well as the following Assisted-graded writing questions:.

13-1. When Starbucks opened its first coffee shop inside a public library, 10 percent of all proceeds from coffee sold there went to support the operation of the library. Do you think a public library should allow a for-profit organization such as Starbucks to sell products inside the building? Is this a conflict of interest for government-sponsored organizations, such as libraries? What if the local doughnut shop wanted to sell doughnuts at the library? Should it be allowed to do so? How does a head librarian decide?

13-2. Sponsorships are now a major component of professional sports. Football, basketball, baseball, and golf all have sponsors. Many stadiums are now named for companies. Why do you think companies spend millions on these sponsorships? What impact does it have on you? What sponsorships do you notice? Which ones do you not notice? Why?

13-3. Mymktlab Only—comprehensive writing assignment for this chapter.

14 REGULATIONS AND ETHICAL CONCERNS

CHAPTER OBJECTIVES

After reading this chapter, you should be able to answer the following questions:

1 Which agencies and laws regulate marketing communications?

2 What are the relationships between puffery, deception, and substantiation?

3 What legal remedies can be used to correct deceptive communications practices?

4 How do the three major industry regulatory agencies help keep advertising and business practices from injuring customers or other businesses?

5 What ethical criticisms have been registered against advertising and marketing practices?

6 What marketing tactics raise ethical concerns?

7 How can marketers apply the various ethical frameworks and ethics programs to their activities and actions?

8 What international issues influence the discussion of legal and ethical marketing activities?

MyMarketingLab™

⭐ **Improve Your Grade!**

Over 10 million students improved their results using the Pearson MyLabs.
Visit **mymktlab.com** for simulations, tutorials, and end-of-chapter problems.

REEBOK PAYS $25 MILLION SETTLEMENT

The running shoe and sport shoe industry has dealt with criticism and concern for many years. Complaints have been made regarding the high prices of shoes, the foreign labor used to produce them, and the strong amount of social pressure parents and children face to buy the most fashionable and cutting edge models, at the expense of other, more practical and necessary merchandise.

In 2011, Reebok encountered a new controversy. The company's Easy Tone and Run Tone product lines in the toning shoes market are designed with a rounded or otherwise unstable sole. Companies including Reebok, New Balance, and Skecher make such shoes and claim they force wearers to use more muscle to maintain balance while working out. The different shoe styles for running, walking, and training, sell for about $100 per pair. Reebok has sold more than five million pairs in the US and 10 million abroad. Toning shoes became a $1.1 billion market in just a few years.

In ads for the Easy Tone and Run Tone lines, Reebok made specific claims. One commercial featured a super fit women who assures viewers that Easy Tone sneakers strengthen hamstrings and calves by up to 11 percent and tone one's butt (e.g, one's gluteus maximus muscles) "up to 28 percent more than regular sneakers, just by walking." And, as Ellie Krupnick from the Huffington Post noted, "How was Reebok planning on backing that up, exactly?"

The Federal Trade Commission (FTC) stepped in. The agency announced that Reebok must pay $25 million in a settlement over the Easytone and RunTone products, which fail to fulfill the body-shaping promises claimed in the ads. According to the FTC complaint, Reebok was making made unsupported claims in advertisements. David Vladeck, director of the FTC's Bureau of Consumer Protection, said, "The FTC wants national advertisers to understand that they must exercise some responsibility and ensure that their claims for fitness gear are supported by sound science."

Reebok maintained its stance regarding the shoes, stating that "We stand behind our Easy Tone technology—the first shoe in the toning category that was inspired by balance-ball training. Settling does not mean we agree with the FTC's allegations; we do not. We have received overwhelmingly enthusiastic feedback from thousands of Easy Tone customers, and we remain committed to the further development of our Easy Tone line of products. Our customers are our number one priority, and we will continue to deliver products that they trust and love."

Reebok International Ltd. continues to make a range of toning products, including its Run Tone running shoes, Easy

Piotr Marcinski/Fotolia

Tone walking shoes and flip flops and some clothing. The company, which is owned by Adidas AG, claims that its toning shoes were one of its most popular product launches ever when they debuted in 2009. The company marketed them heavily with ads featuring women in shorts and with shapely bottoms; one ad even said the shoes would "make your boobs jealous".

Reebok was not the only company admonished by the FTC. Skechers agreed to pay $41 million regarding advertising and marketing of a similar product. In both situations, the Federal Trade Commission concluded that the claims being made were not in the best interests of consumers because they were misleading.[1]

OVERVIEW

The final level of an IMC program includes making certain the communications program meets ethical and legal requirements and is properly evaluated. These topics are examined in this part of the text. Figure 14.1 displays the completion of an IMC program.

The fields of marketing and marketing communications have long been the subject of scrutiny from the general public, special interest groups, and the government, which may not be surprising. In marketing and sales, money is involved as people make purchases.

▶ **FIGURE 14.1**
Integrated marketing
communications

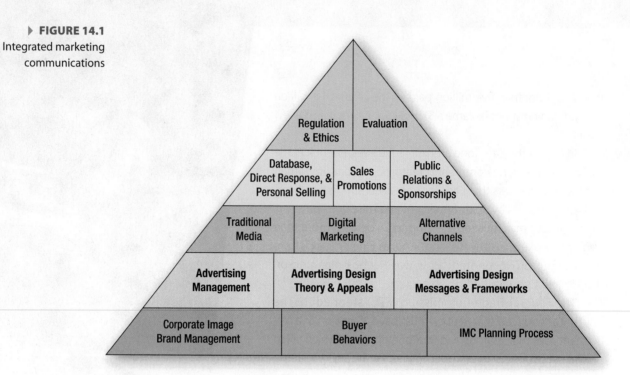

Many people and organizations express concern about the public trust and the well-being of the community. When companies sell goods and services that can injure people or cause harm in some other way, criticisms and legal actions likely will follow.

This chapter examines two interrelated topics. The first is a description of the legal environment surrounding marketing and marketing communications. The second part features views of ethics, morals, and social responsibility as they relate to marketing, advertising, and promotions.

In essence, those involved in marketing programs should consider both the letter of the law—regulations and other legal limitations—as well as the spirit of the law. Guided by both personal principles and organizational guidelines, marketing professionals can try to ensure that their actions are both legal and ethical.

Marketing Communications Regulations

OBJECTIVE 14.1

Which agencies and
laws regulate marketing
communications?

The U.S. federal government has passed considerable legislation designed to keep companies from taking unfair advantage of consumers and other businesses. Various states also regulate for-profit companies and other organizations. Many of these federal and state laws are enforced by regulatory agencies. This section reviews governmental actions in the areas of legislation and regulation of company marketing practices.

GOVERNMENTAL REGULATORY AGENCIES

Governmental agencies serve as watchdogs to monitor for potential violations of the law, some of which are only partially related to marketing. For example, the Food and Drug Administration (FDA) regulates and oversees the packaging and labeling of products. The FDA also monitors advertising on food packages and advertisements for drugs, yet its primary responsibilities are ensuring food quality and drug safety.

The Federal Communications Commission (FCC) regulates television, radio, and the telephone industry. The FCC grants (and revokes) operating licenses for radio and television stations. The FCC also holds jurisdiction over telephone companies. The FCC does not have jurisdiction over the content of advertisements transmitted by mass media. Further, the FCC does not control which products may be advertised. The organization

- Food and Drug Administration (FDA)
- Federal Communications Commission (FCC)
- U.S. Postal Service (USPS)
- Bureau of Alcohol, Tobacco and Firearms (ATF)
- Federal Trade Commission (FTC)

◀ **FIGURE 14.2**
Government regulatory agencies

monitors advertising directed toward children. Under FCC rules, TV stations are limited to 12 minutes per hour of children's advertisements during weekdays and 10 minutes per hour on weekends. Recently, Viacom agreed to pay $1 million for programming on Nickelodeon that violated the time limitation 600 times in the span of 1 year.[2]

The U.S. Postal Service (USPS) has jurisdiction over all mailed marketing materials. The USPS also investigates mail fraud schemes and other fraudulent marketing practices. The Bureau of Alcohol, Tobacco and Firearms (ATF) rules when the sale, distribution, and advertising of alcohol and tobacco are at issue. Ordinarily, the governmental agency that examines incidents involving deceptive or misleading marketing tactics is the Federal Trade Commission (FTC). These agencies are listed in Figure 14.2.

THE FEDERAL TRADE COMMISSION

The **Federal Trade Commission**, or **FTC**, which was created in 1914 by the passage of the Federal Trade Commission Act, presides over marketing communications. The act's original intent was to create a federal agency to enforce antitrust laws and to protect businesses from one another. It had little authority over advertising and marketing communications except when an advertisement was considered to be unfair to the competition, thereby restricting free trade.

UNFAIR AND DECEPTIVE MARKETING PRACTICES

In 1938, Congress passed the Wheeler–Lea Amendment to Section 5 of the Federal Trade Commission Act to increase and expand the authority of the FTC and to prohibit false and misleading advertising. The agency was granted the authority to stop unfair or deceptive advertising practices and to levy fines when necessary. The law also provided the FTC access to the courts to enforce the law and ensure that violators abide by FTC rulings.

A firm can violate the act even when the company did not expressly intend to deceive. An advertisement or communication is deemed to be deceptive or misleading when:

1. A substantial number of people or the "typical person" is left with a false impression or misrepresentation that relates to the product.
2. The misrepresentation induces people or the "typical person" to make a purchase.

Consumers may be misled by advertisements, mailings, corporate literature, labels, packaging, Web site materials, and oral and written statements made by salespeople. This gives the government a great deal of latitude in dealing with deceptive practices.

DECEPTION VERSUS PUFFERY

Puffery can be used in advertisements and marketing messages. **Puffery** exists when a firm makes an exaggerated statement about its goods or services. The key difference, in terms of the FTC and the courts, between puffery and a claim is that puffery does not constitute a *factual statement*. In contrast, a *claim* makes a factual statement that can be proven true or false. Firms may make puffery statements without proving them; claims must be substantiated or proven in some manner.

Terms normally associated with puffery include words such as *friendliest*, *best*, *greatest*, and *finest*. A firm can advertise "our brand is the best" or "our signature dishes use only the finest ingredients." Courts and the regulatory agencies view these statements as puffery and believe that consumers expect firms to use them routinely in their

OBJECTIVE 14.2

What are the relationships between puffery, deception, and substantiation?

▲ This Interstate Batteries billboard advertisement provides an excellent example of using puffery by stating its products are "outrageously dependable."

advertisements. An advertisement for Flair Jewelers stating that "Nobody does 'I do' like we do," a form of puffery. The tagline makes no statement of fact that can be proven true or false.

The word *best* will normally be accepted as puffery. The word *better* has been construed to imply a comparison. The term has recently been tested through the FTC, the National Advertising Division of the Better Business Bureau, and the courts. Papa John's use of the phrase "Better Ingredients, Better Pizza" was found to be puffery, as was the phrase "Only the best tomatoes grow up to be Hunt's."

In another situation, Progresso made the statement "Discover the Better Taste of Progresso" in company advertisements. The slogan was challenged by Campbell's Soup Company, which argued that Progresso's "better taste" phrase was not puffery. Representatives for Campbell's contended that taste tests can be used to determine if one food product tastes better than other brands. The courts agreed and ordered Progresso to either modify the phrase or prove that Progresso soups do taste better.[3]

▲ Southwest General Hospital uses puffery in this advertisement stating its heart care is first, and "second to none."

Quick service restaurants and other food providers have begun using words such as "wholesome, fresh, natural, and local" to avoid scrutiny by the FTC that was created by ads making health-related claims. The words are vague and have no specific marketing-related meaning. In addition, they are accepted by consumers. Darren Tristano, V.P. at Technomic, commented, "More traditional health claims on the menu tend to get adverse reactions by the customer because they associate healthy claims with less taste. The newer descriptors are designed around the idea that the food is better for you."[4]

SUBSTANTIATION OF MARKETING CLAIMS

The concept of substantiation applies to claims that are not puffery. **Substantiation** means that an advertising claim or promise must be proven with data, facts, or through competent and reliable evidence. Failure to do so can result in a lawsuit or governmental action.

An advertisement featuring an endorser must contain truthful statements representing the person's experiences or opinions. When a commercial uses an expert endorsement, the statements must be based on legitimate tests performed by professionals in the field.

All marketing claims must reflect the typical experience that a customer would expect to encounter from the use of a good or service, unless the advertisement clearly and prominently states otherwise. A few years ago a Kleenex Cottonelle advertisement made the claim that the product was softer. Kleenex provided actual touch tests by consumers as evidence. The company then used engineering and lab tests to show that Kleenex tissue consists of 24 percent more cottony, soft fiber. Thus, Kleenex was able to substantiate the claim. Substantiation may not always be easy. To increase the probability the substantiation will be accepted by the FTC and courts, company leaders use the following principles:[5]

1. The federal government assumes consumers read ads broadly and do not pay much attention to fine print and qualifying language. Thus, hiding a qualifier at the bottom of the ad or using words such as *usually*, *normally*, or *under typical situations* somewhere in the ad is not normally accepted as substantiation.

2. The evidence has to be for the exact product being tested, not for a similar product, regardless of the similarity.

3. Evidence should come from or be accepted by experts in the relevant area of the product and would be considered valid and reliable by the experts. Studies conducted by the company or something found on the Internet is not acceptable.

4. The FTC and courts will consider the totality of the evidence. If the company has one study that supports the claim but there are four studies by other independent organizations that indicate something different, then the evidence will not be accepted as valid substantiation.

It's softer.
It's thicker.
It's from Kleenex.

650 sheets of Kleenex Cottonelle UltraSoft.

650 sheets of the leading premium brand.

Here's how
Kleenex Cottonelle UltraSoft
stacks up against
the leading bath tissue.

In actual touch tests, people say Kleenex Cottonelle UltraSoft is *softer* than the leading premium brand. In fact, it's the softest bath tissue of all. And it's thicker, too. It's made with 24% more cottony, soft fiber. If you want to make the comfortable choice in bath tissue, remember three words of comfort: "Soft. Thick. Kleenex."

▲ An advertisement for Kleenex Cottonelle with a claim that must be substantiated.

▼ Cruex states that nothing else stops itching better or faster, which would be considered a claim by the FTC and therefore would require substantiation.

JOCK ITCH JUST GOT
A ONE-TWO KNOCKOUT.
INTRODUCING PRESCRIPTION
STRENGTH CRUEX.

1 *Nothing stops the itching better.*

2 *Nothing cures jock itch better.*

You know how annoying the constant itching of jock itch can be. New Prescription Strength Cruex both stops the itching and cures the jock itch that causes it. Its new formulas are so effective they were formerly available only with a doctor's prescription.

*Among OTC antifungals only. Use only as directed.

NEW PRESCRIPTION STRENGTH
Cruex
CURES JOCK ITCH
RELIEVES THE ITCH
FORMERLY SOLD ONLY BY PRESCRIPTION
PRESCRIPTION STRENGTH **Cruex** CREAM

NEW
PRESCRIPTION STRENGTH
Cruex
SPRAY POWDER
CURES JOCK ITCH
RELIEVES THE ITCH

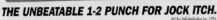

THE UNBEATABLE 1-2 PUNCH FOR JOCK ITCH.

Regardless of the type of communication, the FTC prohibits unfair or deceptive marketing communications. Marketers must substantiate claims through competent and reliable evidence. Unfortunately, a great deal of gray area exists between puffery and a claim that must be substantiated. Consequently, lawsuits are filed and governmental agencies are required to address complaints and suspected violations of the law. These agencies and their rulings strongly affect individual marketing practices as well as company actions.

HOW INVESTIGATIONS BEGIN

OBJECTIVE 14.3
What legal remedies can be used to correct deceptive communications practices?

An investigation into misleading or deceptive advertising can be triggered in a number of ways. Sources of complaints can be:

- Consumers
- Businesses
- Congress
- The media

Each can raise questions about what appears to be an unfair or deceptive practice. Investigations by the FTC remain confidential at first, which protects the agency and the company being investigated.

CONSENT ORDERS

▼ An advertisement for Progresso Soup with a testable claim that must be substantiated.

When the FTC believes a law has been violated, a **consent order** will be issued. Company leaders that sign consent orders agree to stop the disputed practice without admitting guilt.

Kentucky Fried Chicken (KFC) signed consent agreements with the FTC concerning two ads the FTC investigated and concluded they were not adequately substantiated. In the first, the FTC held that KFC made false claims in an advertisement that stated eating two Original Recipe fried chicken breasts had less fat than the Burger King Whopper. It was true that the chicken did have slightly less total fat and saturated fat than the Whopper; however, the chicken had more than three times the trans fat and cholesterol, more than twice the sodium, and more calories. Thus, the FTC ruled the claim was inadequately substantiated.[6]

FTC SETTLEMENTS

Occasionally, rather than agreeing to a consent order, company leaders accept a settlement with the FTC. Such a situation occurred at Facebook with regard to its privacy practices. The settlement required Facebook to take a number of steps to improve its privacy policies and practices. In addition, Facebook agreed to FTC monitoring for the next 20 years. The FTC had charged that Facebook "deceived consumers by telling them they could keep their information on Facebook private, and then repeatedly allowing it to be shared and made public." The challenge Facebook now faces is that the information about its members that makes Facebook attractive to advertisers because they can target ads to specific market segments based on their profiles. It is this very issue that led the FTC to require monitoring of Facebook for 20 years as part of the settlements.[7]

THIS SOUP'S GOT FEWER NET CARBS THAN THE CRACKERS FLOATING ON TOP.

INTRODUCING PROGRESSO CARB MONITOR™ SOUPS, WITH 6-7g NET CARBS* PER SERVING.

Discover Progresso's Carb Monitor™ soups: Chicken Vegetable, Beef Vegetable, Chicken Cheese Enchilada Style, and Tuscan-Style Meatball. They're a great way to cut the carbs without cutting the taste.

ADMINISTRATIVE COMPLAINTS

Most FTC investigations end with the signing of a consent order or settlement. When a one cannot be reached, the FTC issues an **administrative complaint**. At that point, a formal proceeding similar to a court trial will be held before an administrative law judge. Both sides submit evidence and render testimony. At the end of the administrative hearing, the judge makes a ruling. When the judge concludes a violation of the law has occurred, a *cease and desist order* is issued. The order requires the company to stop the disputed practice immediately and refrain from similar practices in the future. When a company is not satisfied with the decision of the administrative law judge can be appeal the case to the full FTC commission.

The *full commission* holds hearings similar to those before administrative law judges. Rulings are made after hearing evidence and testimony. Companies that are dissatisfied with the ruling of the full FTC commission can appeal the cases to the U.S. Court of Appeals and further, to the highest level, the U.S. Supreme Court. The danger for companies that appeal cases is that consumer redress can be sought at that point. This means companies found guilty of violating laws can be ordered to pay civil penalties.

COURTS AND LEGAL CHANNELS

Occasionally, the FTC uses the court system to stop unfair and deceptive advertising and communications practices. This take place when a company violates previous FTC cease and desist orders or when the actions of a company are so severe that immediate action is needed. The latter occurred in a case involving the National Consumer Council (NCC), a debt reduction and negotiation firm based in Santa Ana, California. The FTC investigation found that the National Consumer Council encouraged consumers to stop paying their debts once they signed up with NCC for debt reduction. At the same time, NCC did not normally start negotiation with debtors for 6 months. By then, the customer's debtors were irate and not willing to negotiate. In the meantime, the NCC customer had been making payments into a fund at NCC. Charges and monthly fees were being withdrawn for payment to NCC. Many customers did not know NCC was making the charges. Eventually, the customers discovered that not only did NCC ruin their credit ratings, but they were also deeper in debt than when they signed on. Almost all of them were forced to declare bankruptcy. Due to the severity of NCC's activities, the FTC obtained a restraining order from a federal court to immediately close NCC's operation. The FTC also obtained a restraining order against the London Financial Group, which provided telemarketing, accounting, and management services to NCC.[8]

The FTC also works with other legal entities, such as state and federal attorneys general. The FTC, Orange County (CA) district attorney, and the California State Attorney investigated Body Wise International, Inc., for false and deceptive advertising and for violating a consent agreement between Body Wise International and the FTC that was signed previously. The complaint against Body Wise involved the alleged medical benefits of a product called "AI/E-10." Body Wise International advertised that AI/E-10 could prevent, treat, and cure diseases such as cancer, HIV/AIDS, and asthma. Body Wise supported these claims through the expert testimony of

▼ The FTC would consider the statement "Twice as Good" to be puffery, but the statement "Tree Top puts 2 apples in every glass" would have to be substantiated.

Twice as Good

Tree Top puts 2 apples in every glass. And nothing else.

Every delicious glass of Tree Top apple juice is made from the juice of two fresh, Washington state apples. Nothing added (not a single granule of sugar). And nothing taken away. It's simply pure apple juice. Pasteurized. And naturally sweetened by the sun.

a physician, Dr. Stoff. The FTC investigation revealed that Stoff received royalties for every bottle sold and that he could not provide medical substantiation for any of the claims. The FTC order banned Body Wise International from making the claims and prohibited Stoff from misrepresenting the tests and studies of AI/E-10. In the final settlement, Body Wise International agreed to pay $2 million to the FTC in civil penalties and $1.5 million in civil penalties. The final agreement also contained a $358,000 monetary judgment against Dr. Stoff.[9]

CORRECTIVE ADVERTISING

In the most severe instances of deceptive or misleading advertising, the FTC orders a firm to prepare **corrective advertisements**. These rare situations occur when the members of the FTC believe that discontinuing a false advertisement will not be sufficient. When the FTC concludes that consumers believed the false advertisement, it can require the firm to produce corrective ads to bring consumers back to a neutral state. Consumers should return to the beliefs they had prior to the false or misleading advertising.

The FTC ordered corrective advertising for the Novartis Corporation. The judgment was based on false and deceptive advertisements of a product called Doan's analgesic. During the investigation, members of the FTC concluded that Doan's claim of greater efficiency than competing products was not substantiated. The FTC ordered Novartis to immediately cease comparative advertising and to make this statement in corrective ads: "Although Doan's is an effective pain reliever, there is no evidence that Doan's is more effective than other pain relievers for back pain." Novartis was ordered to spend $8 million advertising the statement and include it for 1 year in all advertisements, except for 15-second broadcast ads. Unhappy with the order, leaders at Novartis filed a lawsuit in federal court against the FTC, but the federal court upheld the FTC order.[10]

TRADE REGULATION RULINGS

The final type of action the FTC takes, a **trade regulation ruling**, applies to an entire industry. Normally, the commission holds a public hearing and accepts both oral and written arguments. The commission then makes a ruling that applies to every firm within an industry. As with other FTC rulings, decisions can be challenged in the U.S. Court of Appeals.

The recent rise in personal blogs led to an explosion of product reviews by bloggers. Often bloggers are paid or received free merchandise to post positive comments. Blogger Jessica Smith was given a Ford Flex to use for 1 month plus a free gas card in exchange for a positive review. Microsoft sent bloggers a free laptop loaded with the newest Microsoft operating system. After investigating these practices, the FTC issued a ruling that bloggers who review products must disclose any connection with the advertiser or product, whether the product provided was free or if they were compensated in any way. The ruling also applies to celebrities who promote products on talk shows or on Twitter.[11]

A similar industry trade ruling occurred with gift cards issued by retailers. Many retailers were charging dormancy fees for cards that were not used immediately and many had expiration dates. This information was not conveyed to consumers at the time of purchase. The FTC issued a ruling that any merchant issuing a gift card must "boldly" display any fees or expiration dates on the card.[12]

Industry Oversight of Marketing Practices

OBJECTIVE 14.4

How do the three major industry regulatory agencies help keep advertising and business practices from injuring customers or other businesses?

Federal regulatory agencies cannot handle all industry activity. Although industry regulatory agencies have no legal power, they can reduce the load on the FTC and the legal system. The three most common and well-known industry regulatory agencies are all a part of the Council of Better Business Bureaus: the National Advertising Division, the Advertising Self-Regulatory Council, and the Children's Advertising Review Unit (Figure 14.3).

- National Advertising Division (NAD)
- Advertising Self-Regulatory Council (ASRC)
- Children's Advertising Review Unit (CARU)

◀ **FIGURE 14.3**
Regulatory agencies

COUNCIL OF BETTER BUSINESS BUREAUS

The Council of Better Business Bureaus provides resources to either consumers or businesses. Consumers and firms can file complaints with the bureau about unethical business practices or unfair treatment. The bureau compiles a summary of all charges leveled against individual firms. Customers seeking information about the legitimacy of a company or its operations can contact the bureau. The bureau provides a carefully worded report containing any complaints against the company and reveals the general nature of customer concerns. The Better Business Bureau helps individuals and businesses make sure they are dealing with a firm with a low record of problems.

National Advertising Division Complaints about advertising or some aspect of marketing communications are referred to the National Advertising Division (NAD) of the Council of Better Business Bureaus for review. The NAD reviews the specific claims. NAD lawyers collect information and evaluate data concerning the complaint to determine whether the advertiser's claim is substantiated. If it is not, the NAD negotiates with the advertiser to modify or discontinue the advertisement. When the firm's marketing claim can be substantiated, the NAD dismisses complaint.

▼ Most of the cases reviewed by the NAD are from comparative ads, such as this one by Miller Life claiming it has "Half the Carbs of Bud Light."

Individuals and companies can file complaints about unfair ads. Most complaints are from competing brands and deal with comparative ads. A few do not deal directly with a competitor but are the result of advertising that is viewed as misleading. Such was the case with a print ad for CoverGirl NatureLuxe Mascara featuring singer Taylor Swift that was investigated by the NAD. After reviewing the claims and photos in the advertisement, the NAD ruled that Swift's eyebrows had been digitally enhanced to make them look fuller and as a result were misleading. In response, Procter & Gamble (owner of the CoverGirl brand) discontinued the ads and the use of any photographs of Swift that had been enhanced in production. Procter & Gamble stated, "As soon as we were aware that the NAD had concerns, we voluntarily discontinued the advertising—a move that the NAD itself regarded as entirely proper."[13]

The CoverGirl decision illustrates the power of the NAD and is typical of NAD recommendations. In 95 percent of the cases when the NAD recommends an ad be discontinued or modified, the company voluntarily complies with the decision. The NAD is not a legal entity, which means companies do not have to abide by a decision.[14]

Advertising Self-Regulatory Council When a complaint cannot be resolved by the NAD or the advertiser appeals the NAD's decision, it goes to the Advertising Self-Regulatory Council (formally the National Review Board). The Advertising Self-Regulatory

GREAT TASTE.
LESS FILLING.
HALF THE CARBS OF BUD LIGHT.

BEFORE, DURING AND AFTER
THE CARB CRAZE.

Great Taste. Less Filling.   *Miller* Good call.

Council (ASRC) is composed of advertising professionals and prominent civic individuals. When the ASRC rules that the firm's advertisements are not substantiated, it orders the firm to discontinue the advertisements in a manner similar to a consent order by the FTC. The ASRC is a private board. When the business or firm being accused refuses to accept the ASRC ruling, the matter will be turned over to the FTC or the most appropriate federal regulatory agency.

The ASRC has been involved in numerous business-versus-business disputes. Minute Maid was recently ordered to modify ads because the copy claimed that consumers preferred Minute Maid orange juice to Tropicana by a 2:1 margin. Tropicana lodged a complaint and won when it was heard by the NAD. Minute Maid disagreed with the NAD ruling and appealed to the ASRC. Minute Maid complained that the decision by the NAD placed an unnecessary and unfair burden on comparative advertising, because all claims relative to a competitor must be substantiated. The ASRC supported the NAD and issued an order for Minute Maid to comply with the ruling.[15]

The ASRC seldom refers a case to the FTC. Such an action has been taken only four times in the past 25 years. The last was a case dealing with Winn-Dixie, which made direct price comparisons with competitors. The ASRC found that Winn-Dixie was using prices that were up to 90 days old. The ASRC ruled that any price comparisons made in an advertisement by Winn-Dixie must use prices that are no more than 7 days old. The decision to forward the case to the FTC was made when Winn-Dixie refused to modify the ads and accept the ASRC ruling.[16]

Children's, Advertising Review Unit
The Children's Advertising Review Unit (CARU) investigates and monitors all forms of advertising in all media directed toward children younger than 12 years of age. It also monitors online privacy practices of Web sites targeted at children younger than 13 years of age. The CARU operates in a manner similar to the NAD.

In addition to handling complaints about advertising to children, CARU began prescreening ads directed to children in 2005. CARU now examines more than 300 ads per year. The prescreening allows CARU to highlight any potential problems with an advertisement before it goes into production. CARU has also issued a series of guidelines to help advertisers prepare ads for children. Figure 14.4 highlights these guidelines.[17]

Children younger than age 12 do not have the same reasoning abilities as adults. Consequently, the CARU stresses the importance of advertisers acting responsibly. Advertisements must show a toy as if a child were playing with it. It must convey the difference between any fantasy used in a commercial and the reality when the child plays with the toy. When accessories are shown, the commercial must clearly state that the accessories do not come with the original toy so the child will not be disappointed. If an item such as a trampoline is advertised, then adult supervision must also be shown in the advertisement.

Advantages to Using Self-Regulation
These industry-based actions are designed to control the marketing communications environment and limit legal actions that will be required by the courts or a governmental agency. As highlighted in Figure 14.5, industry

▶ **FIGURE 14.4**
CARU guidelines for advertising to kids

- Ads for toys should not create unreasonable expectations. Toys shown in acts should lock and act as they would if a child were playing with it.
- Ads should not blur the line between fantasy and reality.
- Ads should have clear and visible disclosures about what items come with a toy and what items do not.
- Items that require adult supervision must be shown with adults supervising the child.
- Products and ad content should be appropriate for children.

◀ **FIGURE 14.5**
Using the CBB's regulatory agencies

- Lower cost
- Faster resolution
- Heard by attorneys and business professionlas with experience in advertising

regulatory agencies offer several benefits over FTC and legal remedies. The cases are normally heard sooner and are less costly for the companies involved. Further, complaints are heard by attorneys and business professionals with experience in advertising. Although FTC judges may have knowledge of the advertising industry, it is not normally as extensive as the individuals involved in the CBBB's agencies.

Effective management, however, will be proactive rather than reactive. Company leaders can work to create an image of a socially responsible firm. This creates a far better approach than reacting to the constant scrutiny of angry consumers and regulatory agencies.

IMC and Ethics

In many instances, an advertising or marketing practice may be legal but be ethically suspect. This section considers various marketing and advertising tactics. Then ethical frameworks and responses involving them are described.

Ethics and morals are key principles that can be used to guide a person's activities in the world of commerce. **Morals** are beliefs or principles that individuals hold concerning what is right and what is wrong. **Ethics** are moral principles that serve as guidelines for both individuals and organizations. Many ethical and moral concerns affect the fields of marketing, advertising, and marketing communication. At the most general level, several major concerns and criticisms have arisen. They include the items shown in Figure 14.6.

OBJECTIVE 14.5

What ethical criticisms have been registered against advertising and marketing practices?

Ethics and Advertising

Some critics complain that advertisements cause people to *buy more than they can afford*. It is closely connected to the comment that advertising *overemphasizes materialism*. A case can be made that many commercials do indeed stress luxury, social standing, and the prestige of being first to purchase an item. At the same time, the messages are still just commercials. Those who defend advertising point out that consumers should be responsible for spending money wisely.

Advertising has been alleged to *increase the costs of goods and services*. This debate has been waged for many years. Advertising professionals note that without consumer awareness, products would not be purchased, because consumers would not know of their existence. Further, advertising widens the base of potential customers and may increase repeat business. Additional sales lead to economies of scale and lower, rather than higher, prices.

◀ **FIGURE 14.6**
Concerns regarding advertising

1. Advertisements cause people to buy more than they can afford.
2. Advertising overemphasizes materialism.
3. Advertising increases the costs of goods and services.
4. Advertising perpetuates stereotyping of males, females, and minority groups.
5. Advertisements often make unsafe products, such as alcohol and tobacco, seem attractive.
6. Advertisements often are offensive.
7. Advertising to children is unethical.

iofoto/Fotolia

▲ Elderly people are sometimes stereotyped in advertising.

PERPETUATING STEREOTYPES

Many social commentators suggest that advertising and other forms of media perpetuate stereotyping of men, women, and minority groups. This leads to several questions. For instance, is segmentation the same as stereotyping? In an era in which the term *political correctness* routinely appears, debate defining "acceptable" continues. In marketing, some of the categories in which market segments are identified include age, race, gender, social status, and income. When marketing to or portraying different individuals from these categories, do advertisers use clichés that are no longer appropriate?

Advertisements often portray a market segment as one-dimensional figures rather than reflecting the complexities of specific gender, racial, or age segments. Teens are depicted as rebellious, carefree, and sexually starved. Asian Americans are shown in advertising as technological experts—knowledgeable, savvy, and even mathematically adept or intellectually gifted. They are usually shown in ads for business-oriented or technical products. From a marketing perspective, it is much easier to group people into smaller subgroups with common interests. Is it unethical, bad business, or simply a practical matter to represent or misrepresent consumers in these ways?

ADVERTISING UNSAFE PRODUCTS

Marketing has been associated with unsafe products, such as alcohol, cigarettes, and other potentially harmful items. By the age of 18, the average American teen has viewed more than 100,000 beer commercials. The use of sexuality and social acceptance combined with humor makes the products in commercials appear desirable. Critics of the brewing industry and marketing agree: Many beer commercials encourage underage drinking and build brand loyalty or brand switching in a population that should not even use the product. Occasional underage drinking can lead to an addiction in a few months, because underage drinkers are less developed mentally, physically, and emotionally. The question becomes: Do a few public relations advertisements represent a real attempt to reduce underage drinking, or are they designed to placate the government and critics?

The same holds true for tobacco products. Many charges have been made arguing that tobacco companies focus on reaching young people through characters such as Joe Camel. Any marketing professional entering the field should consider his or her comfort level with such approaches.

After tobacco advertising on television was banned by the government, marketers created a series of tactics to make certain company products are mentioned on the air. Sponsorships of the Virginia Slims Tennis Tournament and Marlboro Cup Racing have come under scrutiny, because sportscasters state the names of the products while reporting scores and results. Is this ethical?

OFFENSIVE ADVERTISEMENTS

Many adult products require tasteful advertising and marketing programs, even when they are free to be shown through any medium. Feminine hygiene products, condoms, and other personal adult products may be featured in practically any venue. Marketing professionals should select media that are appropriate as well as to create ads that will not offend.

In the international arena, the responsibility becomes even greater. In many Islamic countries, advertisements for personal hygiene or sexually-related products are offensive. Company leaders should explore cultural differences before undertaking any kind of marketing campaign.

Another ethical issue that has arisen concerns the use of nudity and sexuality featuring children. In recent years, an increase in sensitivity to issues of child molestation, child pornography, and related sexual issues has emerged. Marketing professionals must carefully consider what the limits should be. Suggesting that sex sells is simply not enough, nor is making a defensive claim about freedom of speech or freedom of expression. Ethics, morals, and a clear conscience should serve as additional guides when a company pushes the limits of sexuality when using young people as models.

▲ From a social perspective, advertising to children remains a controversial issue.

ADVERTISING TO CHILDREN

A continuing controversy in the field of marketing is the ethical acceptability of advertising to children. Children represent a tremendous level of spending and buying power, over $20 billion annually. Critics question the tactics used to reach them.

Mary Pipher, clinical psychologist and author of *The Shelter of Each Other*, suggests that "No one ad is bad, but the combination of 400 ads per day creates in children a combination of narcissism, entitlement, and dissatisfaction."[18] Ads targeted to children employ multiple tactics, including building brand awareness through images and logos, featuring toys and collectibles, and developing tie-ins with television programs and movies, including the *Hannah Montana* phenomenon. Characters such as Barney, Ronald McDonald, and Harry Potter vend everything from food to toys to clothes.

With so many potential venues to sell directly to children and to put pressure on their parents, many company leaders believe it is best to "get them while they're young." From a societal perspective, however, the question remains as to whether such impressionable young minds should be subjected to so many messages.

Marketing and Ethics

Ethical dilemmas are present in places other than advertisements. Many times, however, a connection exists between a marketing program and what takes place in the marketing communications area. A review of some of these issues follows (see Figure 14.7).

OBJECTIVE 14.6
What marketing tactics raise ethical concerns?

BRAND INFRINGEMENT

Numerous ethical challenges have been associated with brand management. One continuing problem, **brand infringement**, occurs when a company creates a brand name that closely resembles a popular or successful brand, such as when the Korrs beer company

- Brand infringement
- Professional services marketing
- Gifts and bribery
- Spam and cookies
- Ambush marketing
- Stealth marketing

◄ **FIGURE 14.7**
Ethical issues in marketing

was formed. In that case, the courts deemed the brand an intentional infringement, and the name was abandoned. Another brand-infringing company ordered by the courts to give up the name was Victor's Secret.

The brand infringement issue becomes more complex when a brand becomes so well-established that it may be considered a generic term, such as a Kleenex tissue or a Xerox copy. Band-Aid encountered the problem in the 1970s, forcing the marketing team to make sure the product was identified as "Band-Aid Brand Strips" rather than simply "band aids," to keep the competition from being able to use the name. The most vulnerable new brand name may be Google, as in "I Googled myself" or "I Googled it."

A newer form of unethical behavior, *domain squatting* or *cyber squatting* on the Internet, is the controversial practice of buying domain names (barnesandnoble.com, kohls.com, labronjames.com, etc.) that are valuable to specific people or businesses in the hopes of making a profit by reselling the name. At the extreme, whitehouse.com was a pornographic Web site. Any new company trying to build a presence in the marketplace may find itself stifled by domain squatters. Names matter, and cyber squatters are willing to take advantage of these activities to make profits at some else's expense.[19]

MARKETING OF PROFESSIONAL SERVICES

Is it ethical to advertise a physician's services or new drugs? For many years, attorneys, dentists, and physicians did not advertise for fear of being viewed as "ambulance chasers." Recently the trend has gone in the opposite direction. For example, a dermatologist will advertise a "skin rejuvenation" practice with only a bare mention that it is also part of a medical practice. Critics argue that this takes medicine into the area of merchandising and suggest that doing so is deceptive.

People injured by accidents, poor medical care, or bad medications are encouraged to call a toll-free number for information on how they can obtain compensation. Other ads encourage people to get rid of bad debts by filing bankruptcies. Critics of medical advertising have suggested attorneys are now chasing the same ambulances, hoping for large settlements of which they receive a substantial portion.

▼ Attorneys, dentists, and physicians who advertise have been criticized as "ambulance chasers."

© CandyBox Images/Fotolia

Pharmaceutical companies now spend millions advertising new drugs. A great deal of discussion has taken place with regard to sexual dysfunction products. Unfortunately, many young men are buying and using the drugs for recreational purposes. Marketing critics complain that advertising and promotional tactics encourage this type of misuse.

The marketing of herbs, supplements, and other untested products has also created concern. Claims are made regarding their contributions to energy level, sexual stamina, and mental acuity. Other products are marketed using unsubstantiated reports about weight loss.

Physicians, pharmaceutical companies, and attorneys have the right to market their services. The ethical questions deal with how these services are presented to the public.

GIFTS AND BRIBERY IN BUSINESS-TO-BUSINESS MARKETING PROGRAMS

When marketing to other businesses, close personal contacts are often common, both in personal sales calls and in other venues such as trade shows. Among the more serious ethical issues are gifts and bribery.

To influence sales, purchasing agents and other members of the buying company are often the recipients of gifts, meals, entertainment, and free trips. From a personal ethics standpoint, many concerned leaders question accepting personal gifts that are designed to influence business decisions. The International Olympics Committee wrestles with this issue when selecting sites for games. Exorbitant gifts, meals and entertainment have been used by various cities in an effort to sway the selection process.

Closely tied with the issue of receiving gifts is offering or accepting bribes. These can be related to gaining governmental contracts or making business contacts. Without them, permits may not be granted or can be very difficult to obtain. In Germany and France, the government actually allows companies to write off bribes as tax deductions.

SPAM AND COOKIES

Technology creates a double-edged sword in the area of marketing. On the one hand, it leads to ingenious new ways to quickly reach a set of consumers with a key message and to keep in continuous contact with those customers. On the other hand, it can be invasive and intrusive and presents ethical dilemmas for those working on the Web.

Numerous complaints about spamming have been raised. Even with anti-spam legislation, individuals continue to receive unwanted e-mails. One university in the Midwest receives about 100,000 e-mails a day, of which approximately 95,000 are spam. Should this be considered an ethical issue or simply a practical matter? Either way, the marketing team should assess the viability of spam programs.

Cookie technology allows a company's Web site to track a browser's activities and other Web sites a consumer has visited. The technology allows a firm to customize and personalize Web content to match a consumer's interest. A Harris Interactive survey revealed that 95 percent of consumers believe it is at least somewhat important that companies know "who I am, my buying history, past problems or complaints, preferences, and billing record."[20] At the same time, many consumers express concerns about privacy issues and what firms do with the information collected. Primary questions that are raised are:

- Should an Internet company be allowed to gather this information?
- Should the company be allowed to sell the information to other companies?

Answers fall into two categories: legal and moral. Although it may be legal to collect and transfer consumer information in this manner, the ethical issue remains. Marketing professionals continue to experience the need for quality information. They should try to balance this need with the ethical ramifications of invading privacy rights. Failure to do so may result in long-term implications for both the company and those who use the Internet to shop for products.

AMBUSH MARKETING

The rise of dollars spent on sports sponsorships and the use of athletes as endorsers has been accompanied by a rice in **ambush marketing**, which is "a brand's attempt to associate itself with a team or event without buying the rights to do so."[21] Official sponsorships often cost millions, so firms have looked at alternative methods of capitalizing on a major sporting event without paying for the rights to be an official sponsor.

To appreciate the potential impact of ambush marketing, consider Figure 14.8. Chadwick Martin Bailey of Boston surveyed individuals asking them to recall the official sponsors of the Winter Olympics. In Figure 14.8, the bars in blue represent the $40 million companies paid to become official sponsors. The companies indicated by red were not official sponsors, but consumers thought they were. Some of this confusion was deliberately created. Figure 14.9 identifies the primary categories of ambush marketing.

▶ **FIGURE 14.8**
Recall of Olympic sponsors

Source: Adapted from Aaron Baar, "Olympics Sponsors Benefit, As Do Competitors," *Marketing Daily* (www.mediapost.com/publications/?fa=Articles.printFriendly&art aid=122665), February 17, 2010.

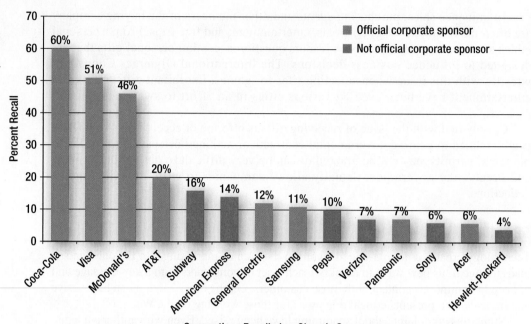

Direct ambush marketing occurs when firms intentionally design advertising or marketing campaigns to capitalize on a major sporting event. The firm seeks to appear to be an official sponsor without stating whether it is or is not a sponsor. VISA was the official credit card sponsor of the Olympics. American Express was not; however, during, and after the Olympics American Express ran television commercials with scenes of Barcelona, Spain (the site of the Summer Olympics) and a message that said, "You don't need a visa" to visit Spain.

Verizon was also not an official sponsor of the Olympics, but the company ran ads stating that it was a sponsor of the U.S. speed skating team. The result of the campaign was that 7 percent of viewers of the Olympics thought Verizon was a sponsor, more than some of the companies that paid the $40 million sponsorship price tag.[22]

Indirect ambush marketing occurs when a firm suggests or hints it is associated with a sporting event when it is not. With **allusion ambushing**, an organization creates an impression that is a sponsor, when it is not. During a recent Summer Olympics, Nike ran a series of ads centered on the number 8, which is a symbol of good luck in China, where the games were being held. Nothing was said about the Olympics or even the athletes competing in the events. **Distractive ambushing** involves a company designing a promotion or event near a major sporting event. At a recent Winter Olympics, MasterCard, which was not an official sponsor, sent two catering trucks to busy intersections in Vancouver every day to distribute cups of coffee and cocoa. As a result, MasterCard's logo was seen all over downtown Vancouver on cups and napkins. **Saturation ambushing** happens when a firm increases advertising and marketing during a major event, such as the NCAA basketball tournament. No mention is made of the event, but the brand will be seen numerous times by viewers of the event not only during but also before and after

▶ **FIGURE 14.9**
Types os ambush marketing

Source: Adapted from Simon Chadwick and Nicholas Burton, "Ambushed!" *The Wall Street Journal* (http://online.wsj.com/article/SB10001424052970204731804574391102699362862.html). January 25, 2010.

the event. This method works best when an event lasts several days, such as the NCAA basketball tournament or the Olympics.[23]

Incidental ambushing takes place when a brand is associated with an event without any intentional or indirect effort on the part of the company. At recent collegiate swimming events as well as the Olympics, announcers have mentioned Speedo's LZR Racer swimsuit worn by swimmers. Speedo gained considerable brand exposure, but it was incidental and not planned by Speedo's marketing team.

None of these ambushing strategies are illegal; however, some question whether such approaches are ethical. Clearly, direct and indirect ambush marketing approaches capitalize on the popularity of the event without paying the price to be an official sponsor.

STEALTH MARKETING

Some companies have used the buzz method of **stealth marketing**. The approach entices consumers to look at a product through a personal contact without them realizing the person making the pitch is actually being paid or compensated in some way.

Jonathan Margolis, CEO of the Michael Alan Group and co-author of the book *Guerilla Marketing for Dummies*, believes the risks of stealth marketing outweigh the benefits. He says, "It might work if the product is good enough, but ultimately the consumer is being duped. It's risky to stage something that people think is a natural occurrence. There is a potential for backlash. Consumers don't like being deceived, and brands don't want to look bad."[24]

▲ Stealth marketing involves pitching the benefits a brand without revealing you area paid to do so.

A recent event illustrates why Margolis believes stealth marketing borders on being unethical. An attractive 26-year-old woman was paid by BlackBerry to go to nightclubs and bars and flirt with well-dressed men. She enticed the men to pay attention to her, handed them her BlackBerry, and asked them to put their phone numbers in the phone, with the promise she would call. She had no intention of calling; rather she sought to show them the phone, get them to hold it, and use it while she talked about how much she loved it. Many view that level of deception as unethical.

Not all marketers agree. Jason Van Trentlyon, president of Street Guerilla Marketing, argued, "Stealth marketing has a greater potential to make a more sincere impact on the public as opposed to a TV or billboard ad. People are inundated with so many blatant advertisements on TV and in magazines that they don't pay attention anymore. This is a way of creating buzz, and any buzz is good buzz."[25]

Responding to Ethical Challenges

The foundation and frameworks for ethical guidelines are derived from several sources. These include philosophy, law, religion, and common sense.

One *philosophy of life* involves maximizing pleasure and minimizing pain. This idea represents **hedonism**. Critics note that life is often more than the simple pursuit of pleasure and avoidance of pain. **Homeostasis** is the natural craving for balance. People balance a variety of urges throughout life.

OBJECTIVE 14.7

How can marketers apply the various ethical frameworks and ethics programs to their activities and actions?

The **law** offers guidelines regarding right and wrong as well as what is acceptable and what is not within a geographic area. Legal systems are designed to tell people what they can and cannot do. Remember, however, that not all legal systems are the same.

Many **religions**, or belief systems, profess a version of the philosophy that is summarized by the *Golden Rule*: Do unto others as you would have them do unto you. Acting in a morally acceptable manner starts with treating others well. Still, specific religious ideologies vary widely. Many disagreements about what is right or wrong exist. Respect, tolerance, discussion, compromise, and accommodation should become ethical guidelines when the religious views of others contradict your own.

At the end of the day, one overriding constant may be that ethical actions, moral correctness, and social responsibility all boil down to *common sense*. Two processes can be used to analyze an ethical concept. The first is logic and reasoning, which leads to common sense conclusions. One's conscience may become muted over time if it is continually ignored; however, most people know when they are doing something right or wrong. The second element of common sense is gut instinct. Deep down inside, most people know when something is appropriate or inappropriate. A person's inner thoughts and gut reaction should never be ignored in an ethical reasoning process.

ETHICAL FRAMEWORKS

The building blocks and personal ethical systems noted in the previous sections help to define various approaches to ethical reasoning. As shown in Figure 14.10, several frameworks have been proposed for the analysis of ethical issues, including utilitarianism, individualism, the rights approach, and the justice approach.

Utilitarianism is a means of making decisions based on what is the greatest good for the greatest number of people. Utilitarianism is referred to as the "calculus of pain," because it tries to minimize pain and maximize pleasure for the greatest number of people.

Unfortunately, utilitarianism perspectives may overlook the rights or needs of the minority. As an extreme example, the use of slaves may create greater well-being for a vast majority of slaveholders, but at the same time the rights of the few, the slaves, are being destroyed.

Ethicists may conclude that utilitarianism involves a judgment call as to what is "good" as well as considering that "good" in light of its effects on both the majority and the minority. Care should be given in deciding how much "pain" to others is acceptable.

Individualism represents the degree to which a society values personal goals, personal autonomy, privacy over group loyalty, commitments to group norms, involvements in collective activities, social cohesiveness, and intense socialization. Therefore, ethical decisions are based on personal self-interests, so long as one's actions do not harm others.

The individualism approach may cause the weakest members of society to suffer the most. In health care, individualists favor systems in which those with money are able to retain the best medical professionals. The individualist position has been used to criticize programs such as socialized medicine. It suggests that those who contribute to society's well being, by being employed and paying taxes, have earned greater access to health care, and others should have less access.

The **rights approach** is a means of making decisions based on the belief that each person has fundamental rights that should be respected and protected. These rights include freedom of speech, privacy, and access to due process, plus the right to a safe and healthy environment at work and at home. Rights to free speech include the rights of companies to advertise any kind of product, even those that make people uncomfortable or ones they object to.

The difficulty with the rights approach is that many times the rights of one group, or a certain type of right, may impede on others. For example, conflict between rights

- Utilitarianism
- Individualism
- Rights approach
- Justice approach

▲ **FIGURE 14.10**
Ethical frameworks

to privacy versus freedom of speech arises when the issue is a job reference. Someone who has been fired for being incompetent, unreliable, or unethical may wish to keep that information confidential. Freedom of speech, however, should protect the rights of a former employer who simply tells the truth about why the person was terminated. As an ethical framework, the balancing act is present in defining what rights apply to a situation and which rights take precedent.

The **justice approach** is a method of decision making based on treating all people fairly and consistently. *Distributive justice* concentrates on the fairness of rewards, punishments, and outcomes. *Procedural justice* focuses on fair and consistent application of rules and protocols.

▲ The rights approach is based on the belief that each person has the fundamental rights that should be protected.

The justice approach suggests that when someone is hurt by another's actions, as an individual or collectively, there should be consequences. These consequences are supposed to punish the perpetrator for the misdeeds and serve as a deterrent to others. Also, when one's actions help others or lead to a greater good, the consequences should be in the form of a reward. In both circumstances (harm or good), the methods by which rewards are granted or negative sanctions are imposed should be based on an impartial, reasonable, and constant program of judgment and justice.

One problem with the justice approach is that what one person considers a proper reward or punishment may not seem fair to another. Many people believe that capital punishment is a just outcome for some crimes. Others believe it is never justified. The same holds true regarding those who make the judgments. What may seem like a fair procedure to one could appear to be totally biased to another.

Ethics Programs

Various individuals and groups have responded to the need for a more ethical environment by creating ethics training programs, codes of ethics, and ethics consulting systems. These attempts are designed to assist individual employees, managers or supervisors, and others within a company facing ethical challenges or dilemmas.

ETHICS TRAINING PROGRAMS

Ethics training can take place at several points. Early moral training occurs in many families as part of growing up, both in secular settings and in religious organizations. Those attending college receive further instruction. The Association to Advance Collegiate Schools of Business (AACSB), a major accrediting body for schools of business, places a strong emphasis on ethics instruction for over a decade.

Many corporations now add ethics topics into new-employee training programs as well as manager training systems. Some are self-created; others are developed in conjunction with professional organizations and nearby colleges and universities.

CODES OF ETHICS

Codes of ethics are created in two ways. The first appears within professional organizations. In marketing, two key organizations are the American Marketing Association (AMA) and the American Academy of Advertising (AAA). The AMA code of ethics may be found on the organization's Web site (www.marketingpower.com).

▶ **FIGURE 14.11**
Components of codes of ethics

- The purpose of the code, including (1) regulation of behaviour and (2) inspiration to employees.
- A statement of aspirations often included in a preamble that outlines the ideals a company aspires to for its employees. The statement should include the values and principles of the organization.
- A list of principles.
- A list of rules, if needed.
- A statement regarding how the code was created.
- How the code will be implemented.
- How the code will be publicized internally to employees.
- How the code will be publicized externally to constituents and publics.
- How the code will be embraced.
- A statement regarding how and when the code will be revised.
- Most of the time, values, principles, and rules are listed in order of importance.

The second way ethical codes are developed is within business organizations. Many firms have written and revised ethical codes. Figure 14.11 displays some common components of codes of ethics.

ETHICS CONSULTING SYSTEMS

Numerous individuals and organizations are willing to provide counsel regarding ethical dilemmas. Some employ "ethics hotlines" through which a concerned employee can make contact to discuss an ethics problem. The services offered by such organizations vary. Some provide additional instruction, whereas others offer ethical consultations designed to build in-house ethics advisors as well as formulate codes of ethics.

Ethics and social responsibility concerns all boil down to the actions and decisions made by individuals and groups. Any person entering the fields of marketing and advertising should carefully consider what he or she considers to be acceptable and unacceptable acts prior to taking a position as well as while working within any role. The term *whistle-blower* describes an individual who is willing to go public with charges about an organization doing something that is illegal or unethical. Making the choice to be a whistle-blower is difficult; it can cause a career setback and make the individual vulnerable to lawsuits and other retaliatory actions. Failure to take action is also a choice. One's conscience and belief system provide the ultimate guides as to when and how to respond to moral issues.

International Implications

OBJECTIVE 14.8

What international issues influence the discussion of legal and ethical marketing activities?

Each individual country has its own set of laws regarding what is legal and what is not in the areas of marketing, promotions, and advertising. The role of the marketing department is to make sure these laws and regulations are clearly understood. The company should make every effort to comply with them. For instance, in China it is important to remember the Communist Party is always in charge. Censorship rules are vague, but enforced by the Communist Party. Rules governing the Internet are also vague, but again can be censored and enforced by the Communist Party. Finally, trademarks belong to the first entity that registers it, not the first person or company that uses it. While pro-business, China creates ethical and legal challenges for U.S. companies.

Legal systems vary. In the United States and many Western countries, *common law* is based on local customs, traditions, and precedents. Legal history, previous cases, and national customs serve as guides, and judges typically have more discretion in making legal decisions.

Civil law, which is present in many European countries, is based on a broad set of legal principles, and decisions are made based on legal codes that have been written over time. This gives judges less flexibility.

Theocratic law is based on religious teachings. The most common form of theocratic law, Islamic law, is based on the *Koran* and *Sunnah*. In many Islamic countries, transactions are regulated in different ways. For instance, charging interest is not permitted in the Islamic system.

Moral reasoning follows a similar pattern in international marketing. One cannot assume that a given system of ethics and morals is completely acceptable in another country. For example, views of the roles of men and women in society vary widely. Any marketing program with an international outreach should employ a cultural assimilator to help individuals understand ethical principles present in other nations.

MyMarketingLab

Go to **mymktlab.com** to complete the problems marked with this icon .

SUMMARY

To enforce fair standards in the areas of advertising and marketing communications, a number of governmental agencies are ready to take action when needed. These include the Federal Trade Commission, the Food and Drug Administration, the Federal Communications Commission, and others. Each tries to keep unfair marketing activities from taking place.

The primary agency regulating marketing communications, the FTC, makes special efforts to stop instances of unfair or deceptive practices. In conjunction with the courts, the FTC and other governmental agencies regulate the majority of companies and industries in the United States. The FTC regulates cases of fraudulent practices targeted at individual consumers as well as conflicts between businesses. Through the use of consent orders, administrative complaints, cease and desist orders, and full commission hearings, the FTC is able to make its findings and rulings known to the parties concerned. Court actions and corrective advertising programs are utilized in more severe cases. Trade regulation rulings apply when an entire industry is guilty of an infraction.

Ethics and morals are key principles that can be used to guide a person's activities in the world of commerce. Morals are beliefs or principles that individuals hold concerning what is right and what is wrong. Ethics are moral principles that serve as guidelines for both individuals and organizations. Marketing and marketing communications activities are affected by ethical and moral concerns.

Some of the more common complaints about advertising include issues of materialism and overconsumption. Also, there are criticisms that advertising perpetuates stereotypes, features unsafe products, sends out offensive messages, is deceptive, and unfairly targets children. Each of these issues requires consideration by anyone entering the profession.

Marketing programs are also subject to ethical concerns. Brand infringement, questionable medical marketing and advertising programs, business-to-business tactics, and Internet marketing programs have all come under scrutiny. Responses to these criticisms are the responsibility of top management, the marketing department, and those associated with public relations.

A number of ethical frameworks and guidelines are available. Those in the field of marketing may be guided by concepts regarding social responsibility. Also, ethics programs consisting of ethics training, codes of ethics, and ethics consulting systems are available to those facing dilemmas or wishing to pose questions.

The issues of legality and morality are present in the international arena as well. Each is complicated by different bodies of law and views of ethics in various nations. Companies seeking to expand internationally should be aware of these differences in order to find ways to respond to them.

Key Terms

Federal Trade Commission (FTC) A federal agency that presides over marketing communications.

puffery When takes place when a firm makes an exaggerated claim about its products or services without making an overt attempt to deceive or mislead.

substantiation Firms must be able to prove or back up any claims made in their marketing communications.

consent order A directive issued when the FTC believes a violation has occurred.

administrative complaint A formal proceeding similar to a court trial held before an administrative law judge regarding a charge filed by the FTC.

corrective advertisements Ads that bring consumers back to a neutral state, so consumers once again hold beliefs they had prior to being exposed to a false or misleading advertisement.

trade regulation ruling Findings that implicate an entire industry in a case of unfair or deceptive practices.

morals Beliefs or principles that individuals hold concerning what is right and what is wrong.

ethics Moral principles that serve as guidelines for both individuals and organizations.

brand infringement Occurs when a company creates a brand name that closely resembles a popular or successful brand.

ambush marketing A brand's attempt to associate itself with a team or event without buying the rights to do so.

direct ambush marketing When a firm intentionally designs advertising or marketing to capitalize on a major sporting event without becoming a sponsor.

indirect ambush marketing When a firm suggests or hints that it is associated with a sporting event when it is not.

allusion ambushing When a firm creates an impression that it is a sponsor, when it is not.

distractive ambushing When a firm designs a promotion or event near a major sporting event without sponsoring the event.

saturation ambushing When a firm increases advertising and marketing during a major event without mentioning or sponsoring the event.

incidental ambushing A brand is associated with an event without any intentional or indirect effort on the part of the company.

stealth marketing A tactic in which consumers are enticed to look at a product through a personal contact without them realizing that the person making the pitch is being paid or compensated.

hedonism Maximizing pleasure and minimizing pain.

homeostasis The natural craving for balance.

law Governmental guidelines for what is right and wrong as well as what is acceptable and what is not within a geographic area.

religions Belief systems.

utilitarianism A means of making decisions based on what is the greatest good for the greatest number of people.

individualism The degree to which society values personal goals, personal autonomy, privacy over group loyalty, commitments to group norms, involvements in collective activities, social cohesiveness, and intense socialization.

rights approach A means of making decisions based on the belief that each person has fundamental rights that should be respected and protected.

justice approach A method of decision making based on treating all people fairly and consistently.

Review Questions

1. Name the governmental agencies that oversee marketing programs.

2. What role did the Wheeler–Lea Amendment play in regulating advertising practices?

3. When does an ad or message become false or misleading?

4. What is puffery? When is puffery legal?

5. What does substantiation mean? How does a company know that the substantiation test has been passed?

6. What four groups can trigger an investigation by the FTC?

7. What are the steps of the process when the FTC investigates a claim of false or misleading advertising?

8. What is a consent order?

9. What is an administrative complaint?

10. What is the purpose of a corrective advertisement?

11. What is a trade regulation ruling? How does it differ from other Federal Trade Commission rulings?

12. What is the relationship between the Council of Better Business Bureaus and the National Advertising Division?

13. What is the primary function of the National Advertising Review Board?

14. How does the Children's Advertising Review Unit operate?

15. Define *ethics* and *morals*.

16. Identify the types of ethical complaints that are raised regarding advertising.

17. What is brand infringement?
18. What types of ethical issues have been raised regarding medical marketing and advertising?
19. Describe the ethical issues associated with Internet marketing.
20. Describe all of the forms of ambush marketing.
21. What is stealth marketing? How does it create an ethics debate?
22. Describe four ethical frameworks noted in this chapter.
23. Name the three types of ethics programs that can be used to help marketing professionals cope with moral challenges.

Critical Thinking Exercises

DISCUSSION QUESTIONS

1. In labeling of food products, companies walk a fine line between promoting the product and truth in content. Phrases such as "low sodium," "fat free," "no sugar added," and "light" may give the impression that a food is healthful, but not reveal the entire truth. How often do you read package labels and make purchases based on their content? On your next trip to the grocery store, examine various labels that have one of the words identified earlier in this question and compare them to other brands. Do those brands actually contain less than competing brands?

2. Reread the section "Deception Versus Puffery." Find three advertisements that you think are examples of either deception or puffery. How difficult is it to differentiate between the two? When does an ad cease to be puffery and become deceptive?

3. One of the industries closely watched by the FTC is the weight-loss industry. Find three advertisements from magazines, newspapers, or television that deal with weight loss. What claims were made? Do you believe the claims are truthful and legitimate? How do you, as a consumer, distinguish between what is truthful and what is deceptive?

4. Advertising directed toward children remains a hot topic among parents and educators. Many feel that advertising unfairly targets children and creates materialistic desires. By the time a child is 3 years old she already knows many brands of products, such as McDonald's. What is your opinion of advertising to children? Is the current regulation enough, or should it be more stringent?

5. One of the criticisms of advertising is that it causes people to buy more than they can afford. Each year a large number of people in United States declare bankruptcy, often because they have overspent. Do you agree that advertising causes people to buy more than they can afford, or is advertising just responding to the materialistic desire of individuals? Defend your response.

6. Advertising does increase the cost of goods and services, but a common defense is that advertising provides people with knowledge about availability of products, which allows consumers to make more intelligent decisions. Do you think this is a valid defense of advertising? Why or why not? What other defense could you offer to support why advertising is important?

7. Think about advertisements you have seen or heard recently and identify one that you believe is offensive. Why was it offensive? Why do you think the advertiser ran the ad if it is offensive? Do you think offensive ads can be effective? Why or why not?

8. What is your opinion of alcohol and tobacco advertising? Should alcohol and tobacco companies have the same freedom to advertise as other product manufacturers? Do you think it is a danger for children to see alcohol or tobacco ads? Does it influence their desire to use these products?

9. Using sex to sell products is another area that many consumers find offensive. Locate two print ads or ads on television that are highly sexual in nature, one that you consider offensive and one that you consider is appropriate. What makes the difference? Are there too many ads that use sexual themes?

10. You undoubtedly have seen advertisements by attorneys and medical professionals. Discuss your opinion about these advertisements? Do you think ads by attorneys just increase the number of lawsuits and bankruptcies? Why do medical professionals such as doctors and dentists advertise? Does it affect your opinion of their professionalism? Why or why not?

11. The textbook identifies four ethical frameworks. Although each framework has its merits, which one do you lean toward or believe in the most? Why? Discuss all four frameworks in terms of your personal philosophy of life.

12. Do you believe that ethics can be learned, or is it something an individual has internally? What can companies do, if anything, to make their employees more ethical? Why has America seen so much corruption in the corporate world? What steps would you suggest to curb this corruption?

Integrated Learning Exercises

1. The Federal Trade Commission (FTC) is the primary federal agency that oversees advertising and other marketing-related communications. Access its Web site at www.ftc.gov. What type of information appears on the Web site for consumers? For businesses? Pick one of the headlines and write a brief report about the article's contents.

2. The FTC's Bureau of Consumer Protection works for the consumer to prevent fraud, deception, and unfair business practices in the marketplace. Access the FTC's Web site at www.ftc.gov and go to the Consumer Protection section of the site. What information is available? Find an article or recent event from the Web site and write a short report. How does the FTC's Bureau of Consumer Protection safeguard consumers?

3. Access the FTC's Web site at www.ftc.gov. Access each of the following components of the Web site. What type of information does each section contain? Why is it important?
   a. Competition
   b. Economics
   c. Policy

4. One of the primary functions of the FTC is to investigate possible false and deceptive advertising and marketing practices. Access the FTC Web site at www.ftc.gov. Go to the "Actions" section of the site. Read through the list of recent actions. Find two that are interesting. Review the cases and write a brief report on each case. What were the results of the FTC investigation?

5. Access the FTC Web site at www.ftc.gov. Go to the "News" section of the Web site. Read through the list of recent actions. Find two that are interesting. Review the cases and write a brief report on each case. What were the results of the FTC investigation?

6. The Council of Better Business Bureaus is an important industry organization for businesses as well as consumers. Access the Web site at www.bbb.org. What types of information are available on the Web site? Go to the "Consumer" section of the Web site. How can the BBB assist consumers? What types of information is available to consumers?

7. Access the Web site of the Council of Better Business Bureaus at www.bbb.org. Go to the "Business" section of the Web site. What types of information are available? Briefly describe each component of the "Business" section of the Web site and how it is beneficial to businesses.

8. The National Advertising Division (NAD) of the Council of Better Business Bureaus can be found at www.nadreview.org. Access the site. Look through the recent cases the NAD has investigated. Find two of interest to you. Write a report about each case, discussing the issues and the findings of the NAD.

9. The Children's Advertising Review Unit (CARU) of the Better Business Bureau can be found at www.caru.org. Access the site. Look through the recent cases the CARU has investigated. Find two of interest to you. Write a report about each case discussing the issues and the findings of the CARU.

10. Protecting the privacy of children is an important function of the Children's Advertising Review Unit (CARU). Access the CARU Web site at www.caru.org. Go to the "Privacy Program" component of the site. Discuss the information that is available on the site. How does this protect children? How is it beneficial to parents?

Student Project

CREATIVE CORNER

Solidax ADX was developed in the United States in 2005 and was recently rated by the Weight Loss Institute to be the best weight-loss product on the market. Solidax ADX is based on synephrine, chromium picolinate, and pyrovate and is designed to suppress appetite and increase metabolism and calorie expenditure. Unlike other diet pills, it does not have negative central nervous effects. The ingredients found in Solidax have been proven to be effective in controlled, laboratory-based human weight-loss studies.[26]

Concerned about recent FTC investigations of false and deceptive advertising of competing brands, the makers of Solidax ADX want a print ad that will be effective but not subject to FTC investigation. Based on the information provided, design a print advertisement for Solidax ADX.

CASE 1 A SALTY SITUATION

How much sodium should an adult consume per day? According to the National Research Council of the National Academy of Sciences, 1,200 to 1,500 milligrams per day is sufficient. The body needs sodium for a number of key functions, including regulation of blood pressure and blood volume as well as muscle and nerve functioning. A tablespoon of table salt, which is 40 percent sodium, contains 2,300 milligrams of sodium.

Many health care professionals are concerned with the amount of sodium in food products, especially processed foods. Overconsumption of sodium is related to numerous health problems, including high blood pressure, which can lead to strokes and heart attacks. Further, excess sodium is connected to fluid build-up, which aggravates cirrhosis and kidney problems, and can contribute to congestive heart failure.

These concerns have been well known for many years, yet the food industry has been slow to respond. Why? Essentially, there are two answers. First, salt gives food flavor. Everything from meats, such as bacon, sausage, and ham, to canned soups and vegetables use salt to add taste. A serving of Van Camp's Baked Beans contains over 390 milligrams of sodium (a 15-ounce can contains more than three servings of sodium). Products such as Worcestershire sauce, soy sauce, and bouillon cubes also contain high levels of salt. Typical diet-food frozen dinners average between 510 and 590 milligrams per serving. Even cookies and cakes contain surprisingly large amounts of sodium.

The second reason for high sodium content is food preservation. Salt placed into food draws away moisture so that bacteria do not grow. Salt also kills existing bacteria that might cause spoilage. At one time, salting was one of the only methods available to preserve food. Currently, many other methods are available, which leads back to the taste issue.

Fast-food companies and other restaurants are notorious for using high levels of sodium in the items sold. For example, a McDonald's Big Mac contains 1,040 milligrams of sodium (the number rises when a soft drink and fries are added). A Burger King Whopper contains nearly 1,500 milligrams.

The net result is that consumers, unless they are very careful, typically consume as much as 3,000 milligrams of sodium per day. The negative health effects of sodium overconsumption are well documented. Yet Congress and the Food and Drug Administration do little more than require the amount of sodium contained in products to be reported, with no attempts to limit amounts.

Some companies have begun to respond. In 2008, Lays launched a new line of products with the label "Pinch of Salt." A 1-ounce serving of these potato chips contains 75 milligrams of sodium (a bag is typically 12 ounces). In contrast, a 1-ounce serving of regular Lays chips contains 270 milligrams of sodium.

In 2006, Campbell's began selling soup flavored with sea salt, which reduces the sodium content. Campbell's is also looking for ways to reduce sodium in V8 drinks. Numerous companies specialize in low-sodium foods.

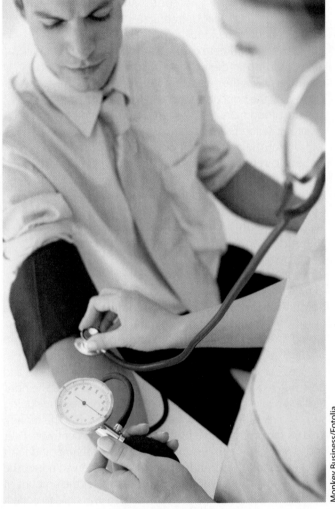

▲ Salt is a major contributor to high blood pressure.

Monkey Business/Fotolia

The sodium content of food products provides an example of the intersection between what is legal and what is ethical. Time will tell if various organizations respond in ways that benefit profits or society, and whether the government will respond with legislation.[27]

1. What are the ethical issues in this case?
2. What ethical frameworks should guide companies as they consider sodium content in foods?
3. What, if any, are the potential legal aspects of sodium content in foods? Explain your answer.
4. Compare sodium content in food to nicotine content in cigarettes and alcohol content in beer. What are the ethical and legal similarities? Differences?
5. What role should advertising and marketing communications play in explain sodium content levels to consumers?

CASE 2 ASSESSING SMART CHOICES

One continuing trend in the United States is an interest in the content of food products. Many consumers want to buy foods that promote good health and nutrition. One recent effort that generated a substantial amount of controversy was the Smart Choices Program, which was created by the nonprofit American Society of Nutrition. Ten large food manufacturers enrolled in the program, including Kellogg's and Kraft.

Under the system, a food product had to meet a specific set of guidelines to qualify for the Smart Choices endorsement. The system was based on the federal Dietary Guidelines for Americans developed by a conglomerate of food industry leaders, academics, nutritionists, and public interest organizations. Accepted products received permission to print a front-of-package or front-of-box label, in the form of a large green checkmark, with the phrase "Smart Choices Program and Guiding Food Choices" underneath. The logo clearly suggested an endorsement of a nutritional program, and many critics believed consumers would interpret the label as carrying a governmental stamp of approval.

Any company wishing to place the Smart Choices label and logo was required to pay up to $100,000 per year for the right to do so. Quickly, manufacturers of a series of foods, including sugary cereals, snacks, and sandwich spreads, paid the money. Among the products that featured the endorsement were Fruit Loops, Kid Cuisine Cheeseburgers, Teddy Grahams, and Kraft Macaroni and Cheese. And as one industry observed noted, the more products receiving the label, the greater the amount of money the American Society of Nutrition was able to collect from a food producer.

It did not take long for the reactions to grow strong. Following a *CBS Evening News* report and other exposures in various media, companies began to withdraw support for the Smart Choices Program logo. Charges were raised that conflicts of interest could not be avoided using the system as it had been implemented. The Food and Drug Administration (FDA) issued a Guidance for Industry letter in October of 2010. The agency announced that it would analyze food labels with the intent of identifying any that might be misleading. The FDA also announced it would develop a universal front-of-packaging labeling system that all food manufacturers must follow. The FDA did not name the Smart Choices Program specifically in the letter, but the program subsequently decided to suspend the use of the logo.

▲ The Smart Choice endorsement suggests a nutritional healthy product.

Monkey Business/Fotolia

The Friedman Sprout, which is the official student newspaper for the Friedman School for Nutrition Science and Policy, published an article wondering if the school's reputation had been damaged by the involvement of the school's dean with The American Society of Nutrition.

The American Society of Nutrition continues operations. Its chief officer remains with the organization. The organization has announced intentions to follow new FDA guidelines for labels on packages and to become re-involved with the food manufacturers that had originally participated in the program.[28]

1. Why would the FDA become involved in this situation? What legal standard might have been violated?

2. What actions could the FDA have taken beyond writing a Guidance for Industry letter?

3. Do you believe the American Society of Nutrition violated any ethical standards? If so, which ones?

4. Do you believe the food manufacturers that sold sugary cereals and junk food carrying the Smart Choices Program label violated any ethical standards? If so, which ones? Explain.

5. Should the food manufacturers continue associating with the American Society of Nutrition? Why or why not?

6. Do you believe the dean of the School for Nutrition Science and Policy violated any ethical standards? If so, which ones? Explain.

MyMarketingLab

Go to **mymktlab.com** for Auto-graded writing questions as well as the following Assisted-graded writing questions:.

14-1. Do you believe that ethics can be learned, or is it something an individual has internally? What can companies do, if anything, to make their employees more ethical? Why has America seen so much corruption in the corporate world? What steps would you suggest to curb this corruption?

14-2. Protecting the privacy of children is an important function of the Children's Advertising Review Unit (CARU). Access the CARU Web site at www.caru.org. Go to the "Privacy Program" component of the site. Discuss the information that is available on the site. How does this protect children? How is it beneficial to parents?

14-3. Mymktlab Only—comprehensive writing assignment for this chapter.

15 EVALUATING AN INTEGRATED MARKETING PROGRAM

CHAPTER OBJECTIVES

After reading this chapter, you should be able to answer the following questions:

1 What are the three broad categories of evaluation tools used to evaluate IMC systems?

2 How do marketing teams match evaluation methods with IMC objectives?

3 What forms of message evaluations can be conducted to assess IMC programs?

4 Which evaluation criteria are suggested by the positioning advertising copytesting (PACT) system?

5 How do online evaluation systems assist advertising managers in assessing the quality of a firm's Internet activities?

6 What types of behavioral evaluations can be employed to assess IMC programs?

7 What criteria should be used to assess the overall IMC program?

8 How are evaluation programs adjusted to match international operations?

MyMarketingLab™

⭐ **Improve Your Grade!**
Over 10 million students improved their results using the Pearson MyLabs.
Visit **mymktlab.com** for simulations, tutorials, and end-of-chapter problems.

SANDS RESEARCH, INC.
NEUROMARKETING ON THE CUTTING EDGE

f any one theme emerges from the interviews with members of the various advertising agencies featured in this textbook, it would be that company executives demand clear and convincing evidence that marketing and advertising actually work. Tangible measures such as increases in store traffic, Web site hits, coupons redeemed, and sales provide behavioral evidence. Many times, of course, other factors influence these outcomes, and a time lag, from when the ad ran to when the behavior occurred, also become involved.

Advertising agencies continue to look for methods to refine the development and delivery of marketing messages. Many techniques are available, including day-after-recall tests and studies of brand perceptions and loyalty. What remains is finding real-time data suggesting that an advertisement has captured and kept a viewer's attention.

Sands Research, Inc., led by its chairman and chief science officer, Dr. Steve Sands, is a leading neuromarketing firm. The company pioneered developments in applications that draw on cognitive neuroscience technology to provide unique insights into consumer responses to television and print advertisements, product packaging, and digital media. By combining its technology with before- and after-questionnaires, Sands Research provides a comprehensive, objective analysis of the viewer's engagement in the marketing material being presented by an advertiser.

Recently, Dr. Sands announced a breakthrough in the rapidly growing area of applying neuroscience to market research. Sands Research uses high-density arrays of EEG (electroencephalograph) sensors to capture brainwave activity across the full brain at 10,000 times a second, per sensor. In essence, this means the firm has the ability to study the impact a message has on capturing a person's attention and track times of peak interest as the person stays engaged with that message.

Traditional methods of analyzing the impact of an advertisement use rating statements and open-ended questions that tend to be verbally biased. They may also fail to completely measure the impact of the nonverbal components of commercials, including music and visuals. Creative people have long suspected that traditional research approaches, such as day-after-recall testing, unfairly reward overly rational advertising and penalize emotional executions.

Research suggests that when commercials quickly capture attention, they tend to generate more "peak" moments during the run. Peak moments of attention increase positive feelings toward commercials and potentially influence recall. Peaks are likely to occur when:

- Important news, such as the announcement of a strong price promotion, is provided.

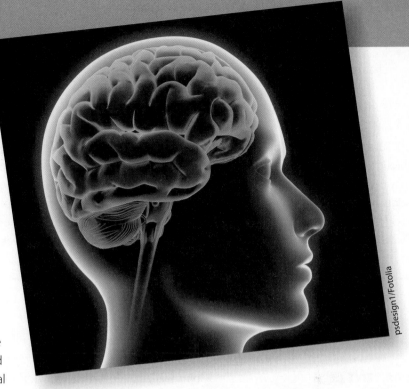

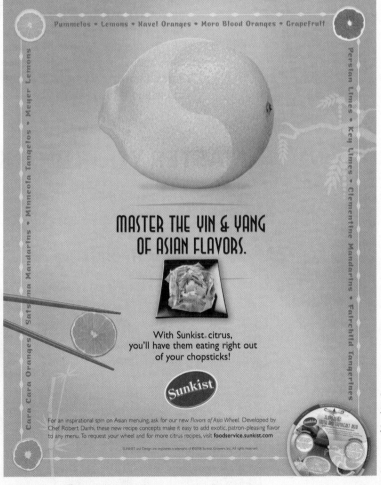

MASTER THE YIN & YANG OF ASIAN FLAVORS.

With Sunkist. citrus, you'll have them eating right out of your chopsticks!

Sunkist

- Inciting incidents, typically involving a moment strongly charged with negative emotion to set up a joke or story-line, appear.
- Surprising moments or turning points in stories take place.
- The delivery of climatic moments or punch lines occurs.

The value of these new techniques may be enhanced through the understanding that three different memory systems may be involved in developing a person's view of a brand: knowl-edge memories, emotion or episodic memories, and action or pro-cedural memories of bodily experiences and physical sensations. Evidence from these studies suggests that these memories might be stored in different parts of the brain. Consequently, a rational and verbal memory might be reported but emotional or episodic memories may not. This would explain the under-reporting of the impact of musical and visual cues in advertisements.

The full impact of these new technologies has yet to be realized. At the least, Sands Research sug-gests the company can help an advertiser create an advertisement with the greatest potential for capturing attention from storyboard to the run of the commercial. And, an exciting new era in mar-keting measurement may be well underway.[1]

OVERVIEW

OBJECTIVE 15.1

What are the three broad categories of evaluation tools used to evaluate IMC systems?

John Wanamaker, a well-known nineteenth-century department store owner, was one of the first to use advertising to attract customers to his store. He once remarked, "I know half the money I spend on advertising is wasted, but I can never find out which half." Evaluating the effectiveness of advertising has become increasingly difficult. In today's environment, company executives demand measurable results because of the high costs of advertising campaigns. The challenge for advertising account executives and others who prepare ads continues to be offering evidence that those campaigns are successful.

To meet the growing insistence for accountability, research and media experts spend time and energy seeking to develop new and accurate measures of success. These mea-sures, known as **metrics**, should accurately portray the effectiveness of a marketing com-munications plan, which may not be easy.

▶ This advertisement for the Scott Equipment could be evaluated using respondent behavior techniques by the number of inquiries and purchases.

This final chapter considers the methods available for evaluating components of an IMC program. Three broad categories of evaluation tools can be used to evaluate IMC systems: message evaluations, online evaluations, and respondent behavior evaluations.

Message evaluation techniques examine the message and the physical design of the advertisement, coupon, or direct marketing piece. Message evaluation procedures include the study of actors in advertisements as well as the individuals who speak in radio ads. A message evaluation program reviews the cognitive components associated with an ad, such as recall and recognition, as well as emotional, attitudinal, and behavioral intention responses.

Online evaluation metrics examine online advertising and marketing campaigns. The Internet provides a unique set of metrics not available with traditional media. In addition to click-throughs, companies can track such metrics as dwell rate and dwell time. The Internet provides highly accurate, real-time measures of consumer reactions.

Respondent behavior evaluations address visible customer actions, including store visits, inquiries, or actual purchases. This category contains evaluation technique measures that use numbers, such as the number of coupons redeemed, the number of hits on a Web site, and changes in sales.

The emphasis on providing compelling proof that advertising actually works has led to a greater emphasis on respondent behaviors. Higher sales, increases in store traffic, a greater number of daily Internet hits on a Web site, and other numbers-based outcomes appeal to many managers. At the same time, message evaluations, online metrics, and behavioral responses help the marketing manager and advertising team build short-term results and achieve long-term success.

Matching Methods with IMC Objectives

OBJECTIVE 15.2

How do marketing teams match evaluation methods with IMC objectives?

Marketers choose methods of evaluation that match the objectives being measured.[2] An advertising campaign with the objective of increasing customer interest in and recall of a brand will be measured using the level of customer awareness as the metric. Normally, this means the marketing team measures awareness before, during, and after the ads have run. At other times, objectives vary. Redemption rates measure the success of a campaign featuring coupons, which means behaviors (purchasing) rather than cognitive processes (recall) are being tested. Redemption rates reveal the number of items purchased, with and without coupons.

Several levels are used to analyze an advertising or IMC program. They include the following:

- Short-term outcomes (sales, redemption rates)
- Long-term results (brand awareness, brand loyalty, or brand equity)
- Product- and brand-specific awareness
- Awareness of the overall company
- Affective responses (liking the company and a positive brand image)

The temptation may arise to overemphasize the first factor, short-term outcomes, without considering the long-term impact of a campaign or marketing program. The company endeavors to maintain a voice that carries across campaigns over time.

In light of the overall marketing and advertising goals, the marketing manager then considers the various options for evaluating advertising. Selection of evaluation procedures takes place prior to launching a campaign. An ad placed in a trade journal can contain a code number, a special telephone number, or a special Internet microsite to track responses. For coupons, premiums, and other sales promotions, code numbers are printed on each item to identify the source.

In general, careful planning prior to initiating an IMC program allows the evaluation of the campaign to be easier and more accurate. At the same time, the evaluation of

YOU CAN'T RIDE OFF INTO THE SUNSET IF YOUR NEST EGG WON'T CARRY YOU. We're big believers in a long-term retirement plan based on objective financial advice. And in having a financial consultant who can help you every step of the way. To see whether your nest egg could benefit from such Midwestern horse sense, visit agedwards.com or call 866-379-4243.

A.G. EDWARDS.
FULLY INVESTED IN OUR CLIENTS.

Courtesy of A.G. Edwards

▲ Careful planning prior to launching a campaign can help a company such as A.G. Edwards better evaluate the effectiveness of advertising.

OBJECTIVE 15.3

What forms of message evaluations can be conducted to assess IMC programs?

a specific advertisement or marketing piece may be difficult, because many factors affect the outcome being measured. For instance, a retailer may run a series of newspaper and radio ads to boost store traffic. In order to measure the impact of the ads, the retailer keeps records of store traffic before, during, and after the campaign. Unfortunately, the traffic count might be affected by other factors, even something as simple as the weather. If it rains for 2 days, the traffic count will probably be lower. Further, the store's chief competitor may run a special sale during the same time period, which also affects traffic. A TV program, such as the season finale of a major series, or even a special program at the local high school (commencement, school play), could have an impact. In other words, many extraneous factors could affect results. When reviewing an advertising program, these factors should be considered.

Performing one analysis normally does not adequately assess the influence of the impact of an advertisement on a company's image. Even though store traffic was low, the ad may have been stored in the buyer's long-term memory, which may make a difference later. Conversely, the same ad may have been awkward or offensive in some way. The store owner may believe the weather affected the outcome instead of a poor advertising design. Consequently, company leaders consider short- and long-term implications when assessing an IMC program.

Message Evaluations

Evaluation or testing of advertising communications occurs at every stage of the development process. This includes the concept stage before an advertisement is produced. Testing at that stage often involves soliciting the opinions of a series of experts or from "regular" people. Ads can be tested after completion of the design stage but prior to development. Television commercials can be designed using a **storyboard**, such as the one shown in this section for Maidenform. Print ads can be analyzed using artist sketches.

Although ads and marketing pieces can be tested prior to production, most advertising agencies perform a small amount of pretesting, primarily due to the lack of reliable test results. Elena Petukhova from The Richards Group advertising agency notes that, "We really don't trust the results of pretests using boards, because the format makes a difference. Consumers are used to seeing the finished product, so when you show them a mockup or sketch they tend not to see it very positively. It is difficult for them to make the transition to what the ad will look like after production, and in their minds they compare it to finished ads, which produce low evaluation scores. Whenever possible, we wait until after production to test ads."[3]

As shown in Figure 15.1, the primary methods currently used by companies and advertising agencies to evaluate advertising and ad campaign messages are advertising tracking research and copytesting. Each fits with different circumstances, advertising methods, and IMC objectives. For the future, a promise method of advertising evaluation involves cognitive neuroscience.

ADVERTISING TRACKING RESEARCH

A common method of evaluation involves tracking an advertisement by one of the major advertising research firms, such as Nielsen IAG or Millward Brown. Tracking research examines ads that have launched. This in-market research method monitors a brand's performance and advertising effectiveness. Tests can be performed at specific times or intervals or continuously. Ad tracking provides a general measure of the effect of the media weight (i.e., spending level), the effectiveness of the media buys, and the quality of the ad's message and execution. Ad tracking examines the relative impact of a message compared to the competition and over time.

Nielsen IAG provides ad tracking. The company offers a syndicated database of real-time brand and ad performance tracking based on more than 210,000 program television episodes and 250,000 commercials. In addition to television ads, the service can be used to evaluate Internet ads and in-cinema campaigns. Nielsen conducts thousands of surveys daily measuring viewer engagement with TV programs and the effectiveness of each advertisement on network and cable television channels.[4]

Ad Tracking Methodology With ad tracking, research respondents are usually shown a brief portion of an advertisement or a few stills from a TV ad with the brand name removed or not visible. Respondents are asked if they recognize the company, which measures brand and ad recognition. They are then asked to identify the brand being advertised, which measures unaided brand awareness. When they are unable to correctly identify the sponsor, they are given a list of brands and asked to identify the correct brand, which measures aided brand awareness. In addition to recognition and unaided and aided brand awareness, tracking research also measures:

* Memorability
* Likability
* Unaided and aided message recall
* Unaided and aided campaign recall

Similar techniques are available for magazines. Mediamark Research & Intelligence's AdMeasure tracks recall and response to advertisements in every issue of 200 magazine titles. Affinity has produced a competing service, the American Magazine Study Print Ad Ratings, which tracks ad measurements across 125 magazine titles.[5]

When mcgarrybowen advertising agency created a campaign for Burger King, the agency used ad tracking to measure the brand's impression score. Both Burger King and its primary rival were measured using YouGov Brandindex's impression score which asks respondents "Do you have a general positive feeling about the brand?" Prior to the campaign launched, Burger King's impression score was 24.4 compared to McDonald's score of 48.9. During the campaign Burger King's score rose to a high of 45.1 then dropped at the end to 38.4. At the same time McDonald's impression score fell to 34.8. By tracking these results before, during, and after the campaign, marketers from Burger King and mcgarrybowen were able to obtain accurate measures on the campaigns effectiveness in creating a more positive impression of the restaurant chain.[6]

▲ A storyboard for a Maidenform TV advertisement.

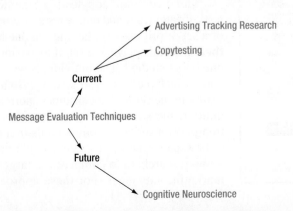

◀ **FIGURE 15.1**
Evaluating advertising messages

Show Your True Colors.

Flair JEWELERS

Monroe • West Monroe

▲ Tracking measures can now be used to evaluate print ads in magazines, in addition to television and the Internet.

▼ Copytesting provides valuable input for advertising agencies and clients such as 3M about the effectiveness of ads.

Report Cards and Benchmarks   Dave Snell of The Richards Group reported the tracking by Nielsen IAG offers a continuous "report card" as well as a "benchmark." Within the second or third week of a new campaign, the ad tracking research provides two types of information about a new advertisement's performance. First, it shows how the new ad performs in comparison to the brand's competitors. Second, it indicates show how well the advertisement performed in relation to those from previous campaigns.

Nielsen IAG also builds a benchmark for a company as it measures ad performance over months and years. These benchmark data are especially valuable when a new campaign launches. New ads can be compared to previous ones along various dimensions to ensure the ads performed as expected. The benchmark from previous ads provides a better indicator of performance than would comparisons with competitors or ads for similar products.

Tracking services can also "help us to know when wear-out is beginning to set in," says Dave Snell. Measuring the advertisement's effectiveness on a biweekly basis and graphing those measures indicates when an advertisement starts to lose its impact. At that point, the agency and client can switch to a new campaign, bring back a previous ad, or modify the current commercial.

The Richards Group's Elena Petukhova notes that ad tracking includes the disadvantage of failing to provide any diagnostics. The data indicate how the ad performs in relation to the competition, against previous ads, and over time. They do not provide information about why an advertisement did not perform well. Other types of research are explores the reasons why an advertisement failed. In essence, ad tracking research indicates when an advertisement has worn out or is not performing, but it does not tell the agency what to do.

COPYTESTING

The second form of message evaluation, **copytests**, assesses the finished marketing piece or one in the final stages of development. **Copytesting** elicits responses to the main message of the ad as well as the presentation format. Television and print ads have long been tested using copytesting procedures. Online print and video ads were seldom copytested, but that trend is changing. According to Jeff Cox, CEO of ARSgroup which performs copytesting, about 75 percent of the firm's clients now test at least some of their digital ads during development.[7]

Three common copytesting techniques are portfolio tests, theater tests, and online tests. A **portfolio test** displays of a set of print ads containing the one being evaluated. A **theater test** displays of a set of television ads including the one being studied. The individuals who participate do not know which piece is under scrutiny. Both techniques mimic reality in the sense that consumers normally are exposed to multiple messages, such as when a radio or television station plays a series of commercials in a row or when a set of newspaper ads appears on a single page. The tests also allow researchers to compare the target piece with other marketing messages. For these approaches to yield the

3M

Growth through education

Post-it® Products for Kids are creating new learning opportunities in classrooms everywhere. Post-it® Education Notes aid reading readiness and can be produced in literally any language. 3M's commitment to new products for education markets is helping develop young minds. One more reason why Post-it® and Scotch® are among the world's most recognized brands. Visit Post-it.com/kids.

高

stera

La pelota

球

Post-it **Scotch**

3M, Post-it and Scotch are trademarks of 3M. © 3M 2006

optimal findings, all of the marketing pieces shown must be in the same stage of development, such as preproduction ads or finished ads.

Internet copytesting can replace both the portfolio and theater tests for copytesting. Online copytesting costs less and produces more immediate results. One of the advertising firms featuring online testing procedures, including copytesting is Millward Brown. Typically, an agency client will perform copytests five to eight times per year. Copytests provide an advertising agency with the in-depth potential of an ad under ideal circumstances. When tests take place online, consumers pay more attention to the ad than they would for a television show, radio program, or while reading a magazine. Therefore, copytesting results offer a measure of the ad's potential when it receives the viewer's complete, 100 percent attention.

Copytesting are used for finished ads that have already been launched. Millward Brown typically copytests the ad using 150 respondents. Quantitative questions address issues such as:

- Breakthrough ability
- The brand message and image
- The level the ad and brand memory
- Levels of enjoyment
- What the ad communicates
- How well the intended message was communicated
- Potential responses (i.e., likelihood of making a purchase)
- Persuasive power of the advertisement
- Engagement of the viewer with the ad and brand

Testing Emotional Reactions In addition to these measures, Millward Brown provides a second-by-second emotional reaction chart that indicates how viewers feel about an advertisement to be shown on television. As they watch the commercial on a computer screen, respondents move the computer mouse to indicate their feelings, one direction for positive feelings the other direction for negative feelings. By superimposing these 150 emotional reaction tests onto one graph, the client sees how the feelings and emotions of the respondents change throughout the advertisement. This information has value valuable because it indicates when emotions change. Although the test does not measure the level of emotion but rather changes in emotion, these data provide sufficient evidence for the agency to develop hypotheses or best practice ideas to assist in making future advertisements.

Verbatim Comments The final pieces of information provided to clients by Millward Brown and other agencies are the verbatim comments of the respondents. Each respondent is asked to present, in his or her own words, thoughts about the advertisement. According to Dave Snell from the Richard's Group, "These verbatim comments are extremely valuable to us because it provides a written commentary on what people think about the ad and what thoughts are foremost from watching the ad."[8] Millward Brown asks a number of open-ended questions to engage respondents and gain a deeper understanding of their thought processes. The research team also asks respondents to tell the story of the ad, which provides additional valuable insights. The Richard's Group's Elena Petukhova commented that, "It can tell you a lot about the ad, both

▼ Verbatim comments obtained through copytesting can be valuable when evaluating advertisements, such as this one featuring Spike Lee.

Here's the direction. You thought milk was just a kid thing. But the plot thickens and you discover your bones are still growing until you're 35. You're on a mad quest for calcium. AND... ACTION. You open the fridge, you grab the lowfat milk, you drink it. CUT. Not from the carton. TAKE 2. Let's use a glass.

MILK
Where's your mustache?

Courtesy of Bozell Worldwide, Inc.

positive and negative. It tells you what the customer sees and thinks and how the ad story came across to them."[9]

As noted, ad tracking does not generate information regarding the reasons an ad did not perform well or what to do to correct it. Copytesting procedures can provide some of this information. Advertising creatives can then determine what to do next. By using continuous ad tracking and copytesting, an agency can build a benchmark for a particular client on an advertisement's performance. The agency can also gain ideas on what works and what does not for consumers for that particular product category and brand.

Copytesting Controversies   Some controversy regarding copytesting remains. A number of advertisers and marketers strongly believe that copytesting favors rational approaches over affective and conative (action-inspiring) methods. To correct this potential deficiency, some research firms have added emotional tests to copytesting procedures.

Further, some marketers believe copytesting prior to production stifles the creativity needed to produce ads that will stand out in the clutter. Recently, creatives working for brands including Nike, Volkswagen, Budweiser, and Target have been allowed to skip the copytesting phase of advertising design and move straight into production. When the agency Wieden + Kennedy created "the man your man could smell like" campaign for Old Spice cologne, the brand's parent firm Procter & Gamble allowed Wieden to skip the concept testing stage completely. Also, the approval process for the Old Spice campaign was streamlined to just one P&G executive.[10]

Unless the client insists on preproduction copytests, agencies are now moving directly into production and perform them after the ad launches. Many advertisers believe copytests are likely to lead to ad messages about the product benefits that are believable and understandable to members of a focus group or copytest panel. Most consumers in focus groups will know little, if anything, about how to create an effective advertisement. Most creatives believe it does not make sense to have them serve as final judges of an advertisement's quality.

Although a number of marketing professionals do not favor using copytests at all, the majority believe they are necessary, primarily due to accountability issues. Jeff Cox, CEO of ARSgroup a copytesting agency argues that, "Copytesting can squelch creative, but the marketplace and the world's largest advertisers see value in doing this."[11] When the time comes to support a decision for a high-dollar advertising campaign, advertising agency and company executives want evidence that supports the investment. Also, advertising agencies can use the results of copytesting to perfect future ads and campaigns by understanding what works and what does not work in a given marketplace.

EMOTIONAL REACTION TESTS

Many advertisements seek to elicit emotional responses from consumers. Emotional ads are based on the concept that messages eliciting positive feelings are more likely to be remembered. Also, consumers who have positive attitudes toward ads develop more positive attitudes about the product. This, in turn, should result in increased purchases.[12]

Measuring the emotional impact of an advertisement can be difficult. The simplest method involves asking questions about an individual's feelings and emotions after viewing a marketing communication piece. An alternative method, a **warmth monitor**, relies on the concept that feelings of warmth are positive when they are directed toward an ad or a product. To measure warmth, subjects are asked to manipulate a joystick or the mouse on a computer while watching a commercial, moving one direction for warmer and another for cooler.[13]

The warmth meter was developed at the University of Hawaii. Individuals viewed advertisements in a theater-type lab featuring a big-screen television. Those who felt negatively about what they were watching pulled a joystick downward. Those who felt more positively pushed the joystick in the opposite direction. As they watched a commercial, the subjects constantly moved the joystick, thereby conveying their feelings during every moment of the ad. The results of the 20 participants were tallied into one graph and then placed over the commercial. This technology allowed the advertiser to see the parts of the commercial that elicited positive emotions and which parts elicited negative emotions.[14]

A similar technology has been developed by Reactions & Opinions, Inc., for use on the Internet. The company can easily poll 1,000 or more people who view an advertisement online. As individuals watch the ad on streaming video, the participants use a mouse to move a tab on a sliding scale from 1 to 10. When they like what they see, they slide the tab toward the 10. Those who do not like what they see slide the tab toward the 1. After the data have been collected, a graph will be superimposed over the advertisement to indicate the likable and dislikable parts of the commercial. The Internet offers the advantage of allowing subjects to provide ratings at their convenience. If the agency needs a focus group to discuss the ad, subjects can be selected from the participants. The focus group session can even be held online.[15]

Courtesy of The Family Circle Inc.

▲ Conducting emotional reaction tests or biometrics would help Family Circle determine viewer's reaction to this advertisement.

Another approach to measuring emotional reactions is **biometric research**, which involves measuring physiological reactions to advertisements and marketing messages. The Innerscope company specializes in biometric research. Carl Marci, CEO and chief science officer stated that, "Innerscope strongly believes that unconscious emotional responses direct attention, enhance learning, and memory, and ultimately drive behaviors that our clients care about." Innerscope puts test subjects in a living room setting. A device on the television tracks eye movement to track the subject's attention to stimuli. At the same time a special belt worn by the subject collects data about the person's heartbeat, perspiration levels, respiration, and body movements. By integrating all of these biological measures, Innerscope measures the level of emotional engagement of viewers during every second of the ad via their emotional, unconscious responses to what they see.[16]

Time Warner built a 9,600 square foot media lab in Manhattan for its own operation but also leases to clients for biometric research. The cost is $50,000 for basic focus groups to $120,000 for research using biometrics. Similar to Innerscope, biometric belts are available to measure physiological reactions to ads. Cameras can measure eye movements and two-way mirrors allow for client observation.[17] Rather than rely on consumers telling researchers how they are reacting via some type of warmth meters, biometrics measure actual emotional reactions. Individuals can lie about how they feel with a warmth meter, but bodily reactions to ads are difficult to fake.

COGNITIVE NEUROSCIENCE

In recent years, significant advances have occurred in **cognitive neuroscience**, a brain-image measurement process that tracks brain activity. As noted in the opening vignette for this chapter, it tracks the flow and movement of electrical currents in the brain. One study using cognitive neuroscience (psychophysiology) demonstrated that the currents in a subject's brain indicated a preference for Coke or Pepsi that are the same as for the product a person chooses in a blind taste test. According to neuroscientist Justin Meaux, "Preference has measurable correlates in the brain; you can see it." Richard Siberstein, an Australian neuroscientist, used physiological measurements of the brain to show that successful ads tend to generate higher levels of emotional engagement and long-term memory coding.[18]

Consider a sexually provocative advertisement under development. Members of a focus group may enjoy the ad but cover up these feelings by saying it was sexist and inappropriate. These responses may be due to the desire for social acceptance. In a copytest for the same ad, a respondent may also offer socially acceptable answers even though he is not face-to-face with the researcher. The individual may not move

Courtesy by permission of Maidenform, Inc.

▲ Cognitive neuroscience tests can be used to study the impact of this advertisement for Maidenform.

the computer mouse to report his true feelings in a study using an emotional monitor. The negative stigma attached to sex in advertising often affects self-reported reactions. A physiological arousal test, such as cognitive neuroscience, may provide a better indicator of a person's true response. Many advertising researchers believe physiological arousal tests are more accurate than emotional reaction tests because physiological arousal cannot easily be faked.[19]

The most recent research in this area has been undertaken by companies such as EmSense, Neuro-Focus, Sands Research, and OTX Research. These companies experiment with portable devices that measure both brain waves and biologic data. Coca-Cola employed this methodology to select ads to run on the Super Bowl. Coke produced a dozen ads that were evaluated by the EmSense device. The EmSense device measures brain waves and monitors breathing, heart rates, blinking, and skin temperatures as consumers watch ads. Through these physiological measurements, Coca-Cola researchers were able to determine which ads to run during the Super Bowl. Some Super Bowl commercials were modified to produce higher levels of emotions.[20]

Frito-Lay used neuroscience to test product packaging. The company discovered that matte beige bags of potato chips picturing potatoes and other healthier ingredients did not trigger anterior cingulated cortex activity (the area of the brain associated with guilt) as much as shiny potato chip bags.

Frito-Lay's chief marketing officer, Ann Mukherjee, said, "Brain-imaging tests can be more accurate than focus groups." After a focus group rejected a Cheetos advertisement, Frito-Lay tested the commercial using neuroscience methods. The ad featured a woman taking revenge on someone in a Laundromat by putting orange snack food in a dryer that was full of white clothes. The focus group participants felt the prank made Frito-Lay look mean-spirited. The neuroscience test showed women loved the commercial.[21]

Cognitive neuroscience reveals physiological reactions to a message. It shows where brain activity occurs and, to some extent, the level of activity. It can identify times when a test subject becomes enthralled with a message. It also indicates when the person merely focuses on the logo or an attractive woman in the commercial. The methodology identifies positive and negative emotions and the intensity of the emotions by the amount of neurons firing. This methodology enables scientists (and marketers) to understand the information being processed, where it is being processed, and how the individual reacted to the ad or marketing piece. Although still in its infancy, cognitive neuroscience offers great potential for evaluating advertising and marketing.

Evaluation Criteria

OBJECTIVE 15.4

Which evaluation criteria are suggested by the positioning advertising copytesting (PACT) system?

Each of the evaluation programs mentioned thus far require quality evaluation criteria. One helpful program, **positioning advertising copytesting (PACT)**, was created to evaluate television ads. It was formulated by 21 leading U.S. advertising agencies.[22] Even though PACT examines the issues involved in copytesting television ads, the principles can be applied to any type of message evaluation system and all types of media. Figure 15.2 lists the nine main principles to follow when testing a written or verbal marketing communication piece.

Any advertising procedure should be *relevant to the advertising objective being tested*. For a coupon promotion designed to stimulate trial purchases, marketers should evaluate coupon's copy in order to determine its ability to stimulate those purchases. An evaluation of attitudes toward a brand requires a different instrument.

Researchers should agree on how the results are going to be used when selecting test instruments. They should also agree on the design of the test in order to obtain the desired results. This will be especially important during the preparation stage in an advertisement's development, because many tests are used to determine whether the advertisement eventually will be created.

- Testing procedure should be relevant to the advertising objectives.
- In advance of each test, researches should agree on how the results will be used.
- Multiple measures should be used.
- The test should be based on some theory or model of human response to communication.
- Tha testing procedure should allow for more than one exposure to the advertisement, if necessary.
- In selecting alternate advertisements to include in the test, each should be at the same stage in the process as the test ad.
- The test should provide controls to avoid biases.
- The sample used for the test should be representative of the target sample.
- The testing procedure should demonstrate reliability and valldity.

◀ **FIGURE 15.2**

Copytesting principles of PACT

Source: Based on PACT document published in the *Journal of Marketing* 11, no. 4 (1982), pp. 4–29.

The research team should also select a *cutoff score* to be used following the test. This prevents biases from affecting findings about the ad's potential effectiveness. Many advertising agencies use test markets for new advertisements before they are launched in a larger area. A recall method used to determine if people in the target market remember seeing the ad should have a prearranged cutoff score. In other words, the acceptable percentage may be established so that 25 percent of the sample should remember the ad in order to move forward with the campaign. An advertisement that does not achieve the percentage has failed the test.

Using multiple measures allows for more precise evaluations of ads and campaigns. A well-designed ad may fail one particular testing procedure yet score higher on others. Consumers and business buyers who are the targets of marketing communications are complex human beings. Various people perceive individual ads differently. As a result, advertisers usually try to develop more than one measure to be certain greater agreement can be reached about whether the ad or campaign will succeed and reach its desired goals.

The test to be used should be *based on some theory or model of human response to communication*, which makes it more likely that the test will accurately predict the human response. Enhancing the odds that the communication will produce the desired results (going to the Web site, visiting the store, or making a purchase) when an ad launches becomes the objective.

Many testing procedures are based on a single exposure. Although in many cases this may be sufficient for research purposes, sometimes *multiple exposures* are necessary to obtain reliable test results. For complex ads, more than one exposure may be needed. The human mind comprehends only so much information in one viewing. The marketing team should make sure a person can and will comprehend the ad to determine whether it achieve the desired effects.

Often ads are tested in combination with other ads to disguise the one being examined. Placing the test marketing piece in with others means the test subjects do not know which ad is being evaluated. This prevents personal biases from affecting judgments. To ensure valid results, *the alternative ads should be in the same stage of process development*. When ad copy is being tested prior to ad development, then the alternative ads should also be in the ad copy development stage.

Next, adequate controls are put in place to *prevent biases and external factors from affecting*

▼ Following the principles of PACT will ensure a better evaluation of this ad for Chic Shaque.

results. To help control external factors, researchers often use experimental designs. When conducting experiments, researchers hold as many things as constant as possible and manipulate one variable at a time. With a theater test, the temperature, time of day, room lighting, television program, and ads shown can all be the same. Then, the researcher may display the program and ads to an all-male audience followed by an all-female audience. Changing a single variable (gender) makes it possible to see if the ad, in a controlled environment, was perceived differently by men as opposed to women.

Field tests can also be effective. Testing marketing communications in real-world situations offers value, because they approximate reality. When conducting field tests, such as mall intercepts, those performing the testing seek to control as many variables as possible. Thus, the same mall, same questions, and same ads are shown. Then, researchers manipulate age, gender, or other variables one at a time.

As with any research procedure, sampling procedures are important. The *sample being used should be representative of the target population.* A print ad designed for Spanish-speaking Hispanic Americans should be tested using a Spanish questionnaire or interview format.

Finally, researchers continually try to make tests *reliable and valid.* Reliable means "repeatable." In other words, if the same test were given five times to the same person, the individual should respond in the same way each time. If a respondent is "emotional" on one iteration of a warmth test and "neutral" when the ad is shown a second time, the research team will wonder if the test is reliable.

Valid means "generalizable." Valid research findings can be generalized to other groups. For instance, when a focus group of women finds an ad to be funny, and then a group of men reacts in the same way, the finding that the humor was effective becomes more valid. This would be an increasingly valuable outcome if the results were generalizable to people of various ages and races. Many times an ad may be reliable, or repeatable in the same group, but not valid or generalizable to other groups of consumers or business buyers.

The PACT principles are useful when designing tests of short-term advertising effectiveness. They are also helpful when seeking to understand larger and more long-term issues such as brand loyalty and identification with the company. Generating data that document what a company is doing works should be the objective. When this occurs, the company and its advertising team have access to valuable information.

Online Evaluation Metrics

OBJECTIVE 15.5

How do online evaluation systems assist advertising managers in assessing the quality of a firm's Internet activities?

To evaluate digital marketing communications from the Internet, a number of metrics are available that provide hard and soft data. Figure 15.3 identifies methods of measuring digital marketing and the percentage of companies using each method.

Click-throughs remain the primary method used to measure the impact of online advertising. The number of click-throughs provides an idea of how many people who see an online ad click it and go to the Web site. Once there, additional metrics, such as

▶ **FIGURE 15.3**
Measuring effectiveness of interactive marketing

Source: Based on Larry Jaffe, "Follow the Money." *Promo* 20, no. 11 (November 2007 Sourcebook), pp. 5–10.

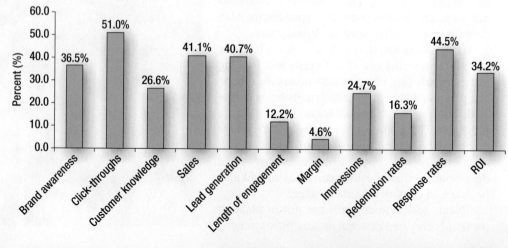

length of engagement, dwell rate, dwell time, redemption rates, response rates, and sales, become available. Redemption rates and response rates occur when visitors to the site take an action. Sales occur when the individual makes the purchase online. *Dwell rate* measures the proportion of ad impressions that resulted in a user engaging with the ad, such as clicking it or just mousing over it. *Dwell time* measures the amount of time users spend engaged with a particular advertisement. *Length of engagement*, a newer metric, measures how long the person stays at a Web site. It offers a surrogate of a person's interest in the product and the site being visited.

AdKnowledge introduced an online management tool called MarketingMatch Planner to evaluate Internet advertising campaigns. MarketingMatch Planner software includes two components: Campaign Manager and Administrator. Campaign Manager records traffic to a site and performs postpurchase analysis. Administrators integrate Web ad-buy data and performance analysis with the firm's accounting and billing systems. In addition, MarketingMatch Planner can integrate third-party data, including audience demographics, from the following sources:

- MediaMetrix for basic demographics
- NetRatings for gross rating points (GRP) and other ratings instruments
- Psychographic data from SRI Consulting
- Web site ratings and descriptions from NetGuide
- Web traffic audit data from BPA Interactive[23]

▲ By using technology such as MarketMatch Planner, the McCormick company can track who went to the Web site to see recipes.

Marketers view digital data results in light of the company's IMC objectives. An IMC objective of building brand awareness requires something other than Internet sales data to be assessed. An Internet ad might bring awareness to a brand but not lead to an online purchase. This may occur when a consumer or business uses the Internet to gather information but then makes the actual purchase at a retail store or by telephone. In that situation, the analysis of an Internet advertising campaign may not reflect all of the brand awareness or sales that the campaign generated.

One of the newest forms of online evaluations is measuring and monitoring *Web chat*. A company called WiseWindow developed software (Mass Opinion Business Intelligence, MOBI) that can swiftly analyze large numbers of opinions on the Web, blogs, Twitter, and social networking sites such as Facebook. MOBI can provide continuous, real-time information concerning consumer sentiment about a brand, business, or advertising campaign from millions of sites virtually instantaneously. Companies including Kia, Best Buy, Viacom, Cisco Systems, and Intuit utilize the software to analyze how customers, employees, and investors feel.

Gaylord Hotels applied sentiment analysis software called Clarabridge to determine how customers feel about the company's network of upscale resorts. From the sentiment analysis Gaylord concluded that the first 20 minutes of a guests visit were the most critical and there was five ways the company could increase the likelihood that guests would recommend the hotel to others. For instance, the web chat analysis revealed it was important to take a new guest to a location rather than just point out where it was or show them on a map. Before this sentiment analysis, Gaylord believed there were 80 things it had to do. David C. Kloeppel, chief operating officer for Gaylord Hotels, stated, "We learned that the first 20 minutes of the hotel experience was of vital importance to our guests. Our hypothesis became, if we could prefect the first 20 minutes of the experience, we could drive positive overall guest satisfaction."[24]

Behavioral Evaluations

▲ **FIGURE 15.4**
Behavioral measures

The first part of this chapter regarding message evaluations focuses on insights into what people think and feel. Some marketers contend that sales represent the only valid evaluation criterion. An advertisement may be fun and enjoyable, but if sales do not increase sales, it was ineffective. The same reasoning applies to other marketing communication tools, such as consumer promotions, trade promotions, and direct marketing tactics.

It may be true that tangible results should be the bottom line of any marketing program; however, not all communication objectives can be measured using sales figures. Leaders of companies with low brand awareness may be most interested in the visibility and memorability aspects of a communication plan, even though a marketing program designed to boost brand awareness does not result in immediate sales.

Measuring the results of a consumer promotion campaign featuring coupons using sales figures is easier than measuring the results of a television advertising campaign. Consequently, effective promotions evaluations involve the study of both message and behavioral elements. This section describes behavioral measures (see Figure 15.4).

SALES AND RESPONSE RATES

Measuring changes in sales following a marketing campaign is relatively simple. Retailers collect information from universal product codes (UPCs) and scanner data. These data are available on a weekly and, in some situations, daily basis for each store. Many retail outlets have access to real-time sales information that can be accessed at any point during the day.

Scanner data make it possible for companies to monitor sales and help both the retailer and the manufacturer discover the impact of a particular marketing program. At the same time, extraneous factors can affect sales. In a multimedia advertising program, it would be difficult to know which ad moved the customer to action. A company featuring a fall line of jackets may be affected by a cold snap. If so, what caused the customer to buy—the ad or the weather? Firms utilizing trade and consumer promotion programs must account for the impact of both the promotion and the advertising when studying sales figures. Sales provide one indicator of effectiveness; however, they may be influenced by additional factors.

As highlighted in Figure 15.5, advertisements may be the most difficult component of the IMC program to evaluate, for several reasons. As just noted, distinguishing *the effects of advertising from other factors* may be difficult. Advertisements create short- and long-term effects, and consumers and businesses see them in many different contexts. The direct impact of one advertisement or one campaign on sales will be difficult to decipher.

Advertising often has a delayed impact. Many times consumers encounter ads and are persuaded to purchase the product, but will not actually make the buy until later, when they actually need the item. A woman may be convinced that she wants to buy a new pair of jeans in response to a sexy and effective advertisement by Calvin Klein. Still, rather than buying them herself, she leaves several well-placed hints for her husband before her next birthday, which could be several months later. The problem could be that her husband purchased another brand or a different gift. So, she either waits for another special occasion for her husband to buy the jeans or she makes the purchase herself at a later time.

Many times consumers may decide to make purchases based on an advertisement but *change their minds when they arrive at the retail store*. A competing brand may be on sale, the store could be out of the desired brand, or the salesperson could persuade the customer that another brand is better. In each case, the ad was successful on one level but another factor interfered before the purchase was made.

Further, *the brand being advertised may not be part of the consumer's evoked set*. Upon hearing or seeing the ad, however, the brand moves into the evoked set. Thus, even

- influence of other factors
- Delayed impact of the ads
- Consumers changing their minds while in the store
- Whether the brand is in the consumer's evoked set
- Level of brand equity

▲ **FIGURE 15.5**
Advertising is difficult to evaluate

when the brand is not considered at first, it will be in the future when the need arises or when the consumer becomes dissatisfied with a current brand.

Advertising helps generate brand awareness and brand equity. Although sales may not be the result immediately, *the ad may build brand equity*, which, in turn, will influence future purchases.

Measuring the effects of trade and consumer promotions, direct marketing programs, and personal selling on actual sales is easier. Manufacturers can study the impact of trade promotions by observing changes in sales to the retailers at the time the promotions are being offered. The same holds true for consumer promotions, such as coupons, contests, and point-of-purchase displays. Many manufacturers' representatives push hard to get retailers to use the company's POP displays. At the same time, the retailer might be more interested in the effects of the display on sales. Using scanner data, both the retailer and the manufacturer can measure the impact of a POP display. Retailers normally use POPs that have demonstrated the ability to boost sales.

POPAI   To track the impact of POP displays, Anheuser-Busch, Frito-Lay, Procter & Gamble, and Warner-Lambert joined together as initial sponsors of a program developed by Point-of-Purchase Advertising International (POPAI). In the initial study, POPAI tracked 25 different product categories in 250 supermarkets nationwide. Sponsors paid between $50,000 and $75,000 to receive customized data about the POP displays featuring particular brands. Using POPAI data holds an advantage in that that each firm sees the impact of the POP for its brand and also receives comparative data showing how well the display fared against other displays. The POPAI program features a low cost. Sponsors of the POPAI program attained valuable data at a much lower cost than if they had sought the information on their own.[25]

A wide variety of responses to marketing communications programs are available besides sales. Figure 15.6 lists some of the responses that can be tracked.

Toll-Free Numbers   One method of measuring the impact of an advertisement, direct mailing piece, TV direct offer, or price-off discount to a business customer involves assigning a toll-free number to each marketing piece. A great deal of information

- Changes in sales
- Telephone inquiries
- Response cards
- Internet responses
- Direct-marketing responses
- Redemption rate of sales promotion offers—coupons, premiums, contests, sweepstakes

▲ **FIGURE 15.6**
Tracking marketing responses

◀ One measure of effectiveness of this O'Nealgas advertisement is the increase in the number of phone calls made for pricing and scheduling.

Courtesy of Alliance One Advertising

▲ Kraft Foods can measure how many individuals access the QR code contained in this advertisement for Parmesan cheese.

can be collected during an inbound call. Sales data can be recorded and demographic information gathered. Psychographic information then can be added by contacting various commercial services.

In business-to-business situations, a toll-free number provides contact names to help the vendor discover who performs the various functions in the buying center. As a result, a toll-free number provides sales data to determine which marketing program would be best and generate valuable information that can be tied to the sales data. Knowing who responds to an offer helps a firm better understand its customers and the right approach for each target group.

QR Codes and Facebook Likes   Two new methods of evaluation are QR code responses and Facebook "likes." Many ads now have a QR code that consumers can access with their mobile phones. Some are to a company's website while others are for special deals or information. The advertisement for Kraft Parmesan Cheese in this section includes a QR code consumers can access. A company can count how many individuals access the QR code. It is even possible to gather information about individuals who access the QR code.

With the increased popularity of Facebook, a new measure of a brand's popularity is the number of individuals who "like" a brand. Companies can count the number of likes but also correlate the likes to special offers that are made on the brand's Facebook. Many marketers consider fans "liking" a brand or something a brand does is a surrogate for word-of-mouth endorsement.

Response Cards   Response cards collect customer information as the forms are filled out at the time of an inquiry. Response cards carry the disadvantage of providing less data. Consequently, commercial sources are needed to obtain additional demographic and psychographic information, because response cards solicited from current customers contain information the firm may already have in its database.

Internet Responses   Internet responses provide quality behavioral measures. By using cookies, a marketing team obtains considerable information about the person or business making the inquiry. In addition, many times the person or business responding voluntarily provides a great deal of helpful information. Responses to direct advertising through Internet views may also be tracked.

The Canadian Tourism Commission tested direct-response ads that were placed on television, radio, direct mail, and online. Each ad used a different URL for viewers to access for additional information. To the tourist, there was no perceivable difference, because each URL took the person to the designated Canadian Tourism site. The Tourism Commission could track which ad the person viewed and which URL the person used. This made it possible to count the number of visitors from each of the direct-response advertisements.[26] The next section of this chapter presents more detail about online evaluation methods.

Redemption Rates   Various kinds of redemption rates are used as behavioral effectiveness measures. Coupons, premiums, contests, sweepstakes, and direct-mail pieces can be coded to record redemption rates. Comparing a current campaign with previous campaigns makes it possible for a firm to examine changes made in the design or advertisement's execution. Marketers review the results in light of positive or negative changes in redemption rates.

Immediate changes in sales and redemptions are offer form of behavioral evaluation. An advertiser or company may use them and fail to see "the forest for the trees." One campaign, advertisement, or promotions program should be viewed in the context of all other marketing efforts. Behavioral measures are best when the team sees them as part of the bigger picture.

TEST MARKETS

Test markets allow company leaders to examine the effects of a marketing effort on a small scale before launching a national or international campaign. An organization can examine several elements of a marketing communication program in one setting. If the test market achieves success, the likelihood that the national campaign also will be effective increases. Test markets measure the effects of a campaign in a new country before launching a full-scale international effort. Test market programs are used to assess:

- Advertisements
- Consumer and trade promotions
- Pricing tactics
- New products

Test markets provide cost-effective methods to analyze and then make changes in marketing efforts before millions of dollars are spent on something that will not accomplish its objectives. Ads can be modified, promotions revised, and pricing policies revisited before undertaking a more widespread program. For example, McDonald's tested new ads that touted cleaner restaurants and friendlier service. The goal of the commercials was to test a campaign emphasizing McDonald's effort to improve in-store and drive-through service. Two television spots and one radio spot were produced and aired in Tampa and Seattle. Reactions from the test markets provided McDonald's marketing team and the advertising agency information about the impact of the ad campaign, the parts of the message that should be modified, and whether the campaign should be launched nationally.[27]

Test markets hold the advantage of resembling an actual purchasing situation more than any of the other tests discussed thus far. Making sure that the site selected for the test market strongly resembles the target population will be the key. A product targeted toward senior citizens should be studied in an area with a high concentration of seniors.

The test market campaign should resemble the national or full marketing plan, if possible. A lengthy time lapse may cause a company to experience differing results. Marketers try to make sure the test market provides a mirror image of the actual marketing program.

A test market can be as short as a few days or as long as 2 to 3 years. A test that is too short may yield less reliable results. If the test market is too long, the national market situation may change and the test market may no longer be a representative sample. The greater drawback is that the competition can study what is going on, which gives them time to react to the proposed marketing campaign.

Competitive Responses   Competing companies can respond to a test market program in one of two ways. First, some firms may introduce a special promotion in the test market area in order to confound the results. This may reduce sales for the product, making the

Andrey Bandurenko/Fotolia

▲ Marketers can use scanner data to measure the results of a test market.

campaign appear to be less attractive than it actually was. The second approach involves not intervening in the test market, but instead using the time to prepare a countermarketing campaign. Firms that use this tactic are ready when the national launch occurs, and the impact may be that the test market results are not as predictive of what will happen.

Scanner Data Scanner data make it possible for results from test market campaigns to be quickly available. The figures help determine the acceptability of test market results. A firm can design several versions of a marketing campaign in different test markets. Scanner data assist marketers in comparing the sales from each test market to determine which version works best. For example, in one test market the firm may present an advertising campaign only. In the second test market, coupons may be added to the ad program. In the third test market, a premium will be combined with advertising. The results from each area help the marketing team understand which type of marketing campaign to use.

Test markets provide the opportunity to test communication ideas in more true-to-life settings. Test markets can examine trade and consumer promotions, direct marketing, and other marketing communication tools. They are not quite as accurate when assessing advertising, because changes in sales take longer and the test market program may not be long enough to measure the full impact. In any case, test markets are valuable instruments when examining specific marketing features and more general communications campaigns.

PURCHASE SIMULATION TESTS

Instead of test markets, marketing researchers employ purchase simulation tests. *Simulated purchase tests* present a cost-effective approach to examine purchase behaviors. Research Systems Corporation (RSC) specializes in purchase simulation studies. RSC tests the impact of commercials by studying consumer behaviors in a controlled laboratory environment.

Consumers are asked if they would be willing to buy products in a variety of ways, using various methods. They might be asked about purchase intentions at the end of a laboratory experiment. In this situation, however, intentions are self-reported and may be a less accurate predictor of future purchase behaviors. RSC does not request consumer opinions, ask them to describe their attitudes, or even ask if they plan to purchase the product. Instead, RSC creates a simulated shopping experience. Subjects choose from a variety of products they would see on a store shelf. After completing a simulated shopping exercise, the subjects are seated and watch a television preview containing various commercials. The participants are asked to view the TV program as they would watch any TV show at home. The test ad is placed in with other ads, and the subjects do not know which ad is being tested.

After completing the preview, the subjects participate in a second shopping exercise. Researchers then compare the products chosen in the first shopping trip to those selected in the second. Shifts in brand choices are at least partly due to the effectiveness of the advertisement, because it was the only variable that changed.

This methodology provides the advantage of using test procedures that do not rely on opinions and attitudes. Among other things, this means that RSC's procedure would work in international markets as well as domestic markets.[28] In some cultures, subjects tend to seek to please the interviewer who asks questions about opinions and attitudes. As a result, the answers are polite and socially acceptable. The same subjects may also seek to provide answers they think the interviewer wants to hear. By studying purchases instead of soliciting opinions, subjects are free to respond in a more accurate fashion.

Any methodology designed to tap into behaviors rather than emotions and feelings features a built-in advantage. Opinions and attitudes change and can be quickly affected by other variables. Observing behaviors and changes in behaviors gets more quickly to the point of the experiment, which is whether the buyer can tangibly influenced by a marketing communications tool.

In summary, the systems that are available to examine respondent behaviors are response rates, online metrics, test markets, and purchase simulation tests. Marketers employ programs in conjunction with one another and also with the message evaluation techniques described earlier. None of these approaches is used in a vacuum. Instead, the data generated and findings revealed are tested across several instruments and with numerous groups of subjects. In that manner, the marketing department manager and the advertising agency can try to heighten the odds that both short- and long-term goals can be reached through the ads, premiums, coupons, and other marketing communications devices used. Even then, the job of evaluation is not complete.

▲ Rather than field test markets, researchers can use simulated shopping exercises.

Evaluating the Overall IMC Program

As has been noted throughout this textbook, the expenditures companies make for marketing communications has led CEOs and other executives to continue to push for greater accountability. These individuals, as well as stockholders and boards of directors, want to know what type of return results when a firm spends a large sum of money on an advertising campaign or other marketing activity. The idea is to try to discover the *return on investment (ROI)* of an advertising and promotions program.

Little agreement can be found regarding what "ROI" means when applied to a marketing program. No consensus exists regarding how to measure marketing ROI. In one study, more than 70 percent of marketers said it would be difficult to measure the impact of advertising and marketing on sales. The same number predicted that it would be extremely difficult for the marketing industry to reach any agreement on what constitutes ROI for marketing. The most common are behavioral responses, such as incremental sales, total sales, and market share.[29]

This confusion will likely continue, even as company executives try to justify advertising and marketing expenditures. This means those in the marketing profession will keep trying to identify ways to measure the impact of marketing communications, ultimately in dollars and cents.

Many years ago, Peter Drucker outlined a series of goal areas that are indicative of organizational health. These goals listed in Figure 15.7 match well with the objectives of an IMC program.[30] As marketers struggle to find a way to measure ROI of marketing communication expenditures, understanding the various measures of overall health of an organization can provide valuable insight on how marketing communications contributes.

Market share has long been linked to profitability. It demonstrates consumer acceptance, brand loyalty, and a strong competitive position. The IMC planning process should help the marketing team understand both market share and the relative strengths and weaknesses of the competition. IMC programs are designed to hold and build market share.

Innovation includes finding new and different ways to achieve objectives. This applies to many marketing activities, including new and unusual trade and consumer promotions, public relations events and sponsorships, e-commerce and e-active programs, and the firm's advertising efforts.

Productivity reflects the industry's increasing emphasis on results. IMC experts are being asked to demonstrate tangible results from IMC campaigns. Both short- and long-term measures of the effects of advertisements and promotions demonstrate the

OBJECTIVE 15.7
What criteria should be used to assess the overall IMC program?

- Market share
- Level of innovation
- Productivity
- Physical and financial resources
- Profitability
- Manager performance and development
- Employee performance and attitudes
- Social responsibility

▲ **FIGURE 15.7**
Overall health of a company
Source: Based on Pater Drucker, *Management: Tasks, Responsibilities, Practices* (New York: Harper and Row, 1974).

Yuri Arcurs/Fotolia

"productivity" of the organization in terms of gaining new customers, building recognition in the marketplace, determining sales per customer, and through other measures.

Physical and financial resources are important to an IMC program. Physical resources include the most up-to-date computer and Internet capabilities. The firm must provide sufficient financial resources to reach this goal. Scanner technologies and other devices that keep the firm in contact with consumers are vital elements in the long-term success of an IMC plan.

Profitability remains vitally important to the marketing department and the overall organization. Many IMC managers know that more than sales are at issue when assessing success. Sales must generate profits in order for the company to survive and thrive.

Manager performance and development is possibly an overlooked part of an IMC program. Effective marketing departments and advertising agencies must develop pipelines of new, talented creatives, media buyers, promotions managers, database Webmasters, and others in order to succeed in the long term. Also, new people must be trained and prepared for promotion for more important roles.

Employee performance and attitudes reflect not only morale within the marketing department, but also relations with other departments and groups. An effective IMC plan consists of building bridges with internal departments so that everyone is aware of the thrust and theme of the program. Satisfied and positive employees are more likely to help the firm promote its image.

Social responsibility can be linked to the long-term well-being of an organization. Brand equity and loyalty are hurt when the firm is known for illegal or unethical actions. Therefore, marketing leaders should encourage all of the members of an organization to act in ethical and socially responsible ways.

When these goals are reached the firm's IMC program works well. Beyond these targets, IMC plans should continually emphasize the evolving nature of relationships with customers. Retail consumers and business-to-business buyers should be constantly contacted to find out how the company can best serve their needs.

Simply stated, every chapter in this book implies a series of key performance targets for IMC programs that can guide the actions of the marketing department and the advertising agency both in the short term and for the long haul. Firms that are able to maintain one clear voice in a cluttered marketplace stand the best chance of gaining customer interest and attention as well as developing long-term bonds with all key publics and stakeholders. An effective IMC program helps set the standards and measure performance and, in the end, becomes the model for marketing success for the entire organization.

International Implications

OBJECTIVE 15.8

How are evaluation programs adjusted to match international operations?

Many of the techniques described in this chapter are available worldwide. IMC programs should be assessed in several ways, including: domestic results, results in other countries, and as an overall organization.

Individual advertisements and promotional programs are examined within the countries in which they appear. Due to differing standards regarding advertising content, they must be evaluated in light of local cultures and purchasing habits.

Many times, advertising and promotional programs are assessed across national boundaries. For example, a campaign launched in Europe leads to evaluations in individual countries such as France, Spain, and Italy, but also as a collective, such as the European Union. Measures of attitudes are difficult to collect. Sales are easier to assess due to the use of the Euro in all of these nations; however, inflation rates and other statistics are affected by local conditions.

It is advisable to contract with local advertising agencies to discover which techniques are most viable in other countries. In some nations using coupons may be viewed as a sign of poverty, and users are either secretive or embarrassed about redeeming them. In those situations it helps to study results in light of the cultural norms that are present.

Numerous multinational conglomerates assess advertising and promotional efforts through regional offices. Pacific Rim information will be combined with information from Europe, Africa, and other places. The goal is to make sure an overall image and theme is projected worldwide.

MyMarketingLab

Go to **mymktlab.com** to complete the problems marked with this icon .

SUMMARY

Assessing an IMC program often involves examining the effects of individual advertisements. These efforts are conducted in three major ways: message evaluations, online evaluation metrics, and evaluating respondent behaviors. A wide variety of techniques can be used. Most of the time, marketing managers and advertisement agencies apply several different methods in order to get the best picture of an ad's potential for success. Advertisements are studied before they are developed, while they are being developed, and after they have been released or launched.

The guiding principles for any marketing tool include agreement on how test results will be used, pre-establishing a cutoff score for a test's results, using multiple measures, basing studies on models of human behaviors, creating multiple exposures, testing marketing instruments that are in the same stage of development, and preventing as many biases as possible while conducting the test. Many times, certain members of the marketing team may not be objective, especially when they had the idea for the ad or campaign. In these instances, companies retain an outside research agency to study the project.

Message evaluations take place at every stage of the development process. Methods that may be employed include advertising tracking research, copytesting, emotional reaction tests, and cognitive neuroscience.

Positioning advertising copytesting (PACT) is primarily used to evaluate television advertisements. Nine key principles are involved. The principles may be applied to any type of message evaluation system and all types of media.

Online evaluation metrics include the use of click-throughs, dwell rates, dwell time, and length of engagement. Interactive data are carefully evaluated in light of the company's IMC objectives. The newest form of evaluation is measuring and monitoring Web chat.

Behavioral evaluations consist of sales and response rates, toll-free number responses, response cards, Internet responses, and redemption rates. Test markets assess advertisements, consumer and trade promotions, pricing tactics, and acceptance of new products. Purchase simulation tests offer cost-effective methods to analyze the impact of advertising and promotion on immediate consumer purchase responses.

IMC plans guide the entire company. Therefore, more general and long-term criteria should be included in any evaluation of an IMC program. When the IMC theme and voice are clear, the company is achieving its long-range objectives, the principles stated in this book are being applied efficiently and effectively, and the company is in the best position to succeed at all levels, including in all international operations.

Key Terms

metrics Measures that are designed to accurately portray the effectiveness of a marketing communications plan.

message evaluation techniques Methods used to examine the creative message and the physical design of an advertisement, coupon, or direct marketing piece.

online evaluation metrics Methods used to examine online advertising and marketing campaigns.

respondent behavior evaluations Methods used to examine visible customer actions, including making store visits, inquiries, or actual purchases.

copytests Tests that are used to evaluate a marketing piece that is finished or is in its final stages prior to production.

portfolio test A test of an advertisement using a set of print ads, one of which is the ad being evaluated.

theater test A test of an advertisement using a set of television ads, including the one being evaluated.

warmth monitor A method to measure emotional responses to advertisements.

biometric research A method to measure physiological reactions to advertisements and marketing messages.

cognitive neuroscience A brain-image measurement process that tracks brain activity.

positioning advertising copytesting (PACT) Principles to use when assessing the effectiveness of various messages.

Review Questions

1. What are the three categories of evaluation tools that can be used to evaluate IMC systems?

2. What common IMC objectives are matched with methods of evaluation?

3. What are message evaluations?

4. What is advertising tracking research? What does it help the marketing team assess?

5. Describe the use of portfolio tests and theater tests in copytesting programs.

6. What is a warmth monitor? What does it measure?

7. Describe the advantages and uses of cognitive neuroscience as a method for evaluating advertising and marketing programs.

8. What are the positioning advertising copytesting principles that are used to help advertisers prepare quality ads and campaigns?

9. Define the terms click-throughs, dwell rate, dwell time, and length of engagement. How are these measures used to evaluate marketing communications?

10. What are the primary forms of behavioral evaluations that can be used to test advertisements and other marketing pieces?

11. How are behavioral responses to marketing messages measured?

12. What items can be evaluated using test markets?

13. Describe a purchase simulation test.

14. Name and describe the criteria that can be used to assess the impact of the overall IMC program, as noted in this chapter.

15. What differences occur when international marketing programs are assessed?

Critical Thinking Exercises

DISCUSSION QUESTIONS

1. Create an advertising approach for one of the following products. Put the idea down in three or four sentences. Organize a small focus group of four other students in your class or individuals you know. Ask them to evaluate your advertising concept. What did you learn from the exercise?
   a. Retail pet store
   b. Baseball caps
   c. Computers
   d. Sweaters
   e. Watches

2. Pick out five print advertisements. Organize a small focus group of four to five other students in your class or individuals you know. Ask the group to discuss the ads. What do they like? What do they dislike? Write a summary of the evaluation of the ad and the process you used.

3. Form a group of five other students or individuals. Ask each person to write down two advertisements they enjoyed and their reasons. Ask individuals to write down two advertisements they dislike and their reasons. Finally, ask them to write down an advertisement they believe is offensive and their reasons. Ask each student to read his or her list comparing ads that were liked, disliked, or were considered to be offensive. What common elements did you find in each category? What were the differences?

4. Are sales figures important when evaluating integrated marketing communications? How should hard data such as redemption rates and store traffic be used in the evaluation of marketing communications? In terms of accountability, how important are behavioral measures of IMC effectiveness?

5. From the viewpoint of a marketing manager of a large sporting goods manufacturer, what types of measures of effectiveness would you want from the $5 million you pay to an advertising agency for an advertising campaign? Knowing that evaluation costs money, how much of the $5 million would you be willing to spend to measure effectiveness? What type of report would you prepare for your boss?

6. A clothing manufacturer spends $6 million on trade promotions and $3 million on consumer promotions. How would you measure the impact of these expenditures? If an agency was hired to manage these expenditures, what type of measures would you insist the company utilize?

7. Look through a magazine. Make a record of how many advertisements include methods for measuring responses. How many list a code number, a toll-free number, or a Web site? Just listing a toll-free number or a Web site does not ensure that the agency or firm will know where the customer obtained that information. How can the advertising agency or firm track the responses from a specific advertisement in the magazine you examined?

8. In some Asian countries, it is improper to talk about oneself. Therefore, people often are too embarrassed to answer questions about feelings and emotions. Those who do answer the questions would tend to provide superficial answers. Explain the advantages of a simulated purchasing test methodology in this situation. What other methods of evaluating feelings and emotions could an agency use in Asian countries?

Integrated Learning Exercises

1. Pick three print or television advertisements that give Web site URLs. Visit each site. Was the Web site a natural extension of the advertisement? What connection or similarities did you see between the Web site and the advertisement? Do you think your response was tracked? How can you tell?

2. Decision Analysts, Inc. is a leading provider of advertising and marketing research. The company's Web site is www.decisionanalyst.com. Access the site and investigate the various services the company offers. Examine the advertising research services that are available. Write a short report about how advertising research services provided by Decision Analysts could be used.

3. Ipsos-ASI (www.ipsos-asi.com) is an advertising research firm with a high level of expertise in ad testing and measurements. Access the company's products and services. What services are offered? When would the various services be used? How would each be used?

4. AdKnowledge is a firm that excels at measuring Internet traffic and Internet advertising. Access the Web site at www.adknowledge.com. What services does the company offer? Describe a research project that you feel this company could do successfully to assist in advertising or Internet research.

5. ComScore is a firm that measures Internet traffic and Internet advertising. Access the Web site at www.comscore.com. What services does the company offer? Describe a research project that you feel this company could do successfully to assist in advertising or Internet research.

6. Millward Brown provides marketing and advertising evaluations. Access the company's Web site at www.millwardbrown.com. Describe the various services offered by the company. Suppose you want to evaluate an advertising campaign for Sunkist. Identify and discuss what Millward Brown tools you would use.

Student Project

CREATIVE CORNER

After leaders at PepsiCo and Starbucks became concerned about the diminishing supply of fresh, clean water, they teamed together to sell Ethos Water. The product's distribution has expanded, and it is now sold in major grocery stores, convenience stores, and drug stores. The goal of Ethos Water is to ensure that children throughout the world have clean water.

Access the Ethos Water Web site at www.ethoswater.com. After reviewing the site, design a print ad for a magazine aimed at college students in your area. When you have finished designing the ad, trade your ad with another student or ask him or her to show it to 10 students not enrolled in this class. Explain to the student how to conduct a copytest to gather attitudes and opinions about the ad. Before conducting the copytest, make a list of questions that you want to ask. Some suggestions are:

1. Have you ever heard of Ethos Water?
2. What do you think is the primary message of this advertisement?
3. Does the copy make sense? Is it understandable?
4. Does the visual attract your attention?
5. What types of feelings does the ad elicit?
6. How likely would you be to access the Ethos Water Web site for more information?
7. What is your overall evaluation of the advertisement?

It is important that someone else conduct the copytest for you to gain honest answers. Respondents are less likely to be honest, especially about any negative feedback, if you show them the advertisement and they know you designed it.

CASE 1   SPYCH MARKET ANALYTICS

A new age of marketing communication evaluation may be under way. Spych Marketing Analytics, which was founded in 2008, provides innovative solutions for companies seeking a better understanding of the future market environments, including the Gen Y and Millennial consumer segments, the advancement of technology, and the quickly evolving world of customer experience. The company tries to delve into the insights and emotions of these groups, providing an innovative portal into the psyches of these markets through its program called Empathic Youth Research and other mixed methodological approaches to consumer insights. CEO Benjamin Smithee argues that, "You have to look at the foundations and fundamentals of the advertising industry, and right now we are seeing a dramatic paradigm shift in the ways marketing communications are delivered and consumed." The media include traditional advertising venues, public relations, but also social media and mobile technologies, utilized by an evolving set of consumers.

Company employees work to enhance every aspect of the market research process. On its web site, the organization proclaims, ". . . we create natural environments for our respondents, evoking rich insights and opinions that surface only through truly natural and empathic interactions." Further, "The Spych Experience maximizes the return your team obtains from each project overcoming fallacies often associated with traditional youth research."

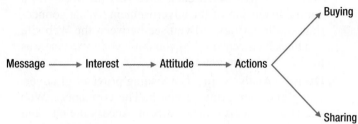

▲ **FIGURE 15.8**
Moving from message to buying/sharing

To achieve these ideals, the company employs innovative concepts regarding marketing metrics and consumer understanding. The concepts are based on the importance of going beyond simply engaging customers to include "re-advertising." CEO Benjamin Smithee notes a new model in which "sharing" becomes a second important outcome from a marketing effort as shown in Figure 15.8.

Spych seeks to identify levels of engagement in terms of "intensity," in which a message is shared with friends and others. The concepts of "share-ability" and "virality" take on particular importance in Spych parlance. As Spych Marketing Analytics brand strategist Landon Ledford notes, "We ask the question, does this pass the traditional advertising test and then lead to sharing?" He notes that in previous times an ad might be shared

◀ Spych Brand Strategist Landon Ledford and CEO Ben Smithees.

with one or two other people, such as when a person would tear an advertisement out of a newspaper or magazine and give it to a friend. Now, a message can quickly be re-posted to 200-plus Facebook friends.

In essence, Spych bases its conclusions regarding a message's success with "engagement" with an advertisement being measured first by "click commitment," which is the willingness of a person to click on an ad on a medium such as Twitter, making that decision in 3 seconds or less, and second by "socialization" or passing the advertisement on to others.

Taking the next step, new technologies allow for tracking of shares and targeted marketing capabilities unlike anything we have ever possessed. Beyond simply counting the number of times a marketing message has been passed along to others, the company can examine the "social profiles" of those receiving re-advertisements and focus on the influences most relevant to a brand, rather than the generic traditional means of targeting. The reasoning behind such tracking goes to the heart of the target market. A new generation of consumer shops in a new manner, communicates through channels that have not been previously available, and responds to companies and marketing messages in ways which we have never seen.

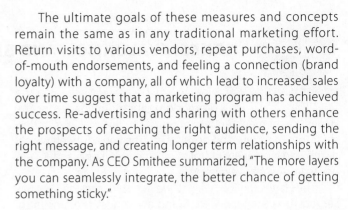

The ultimate goals of these measures and concepts remain the same as in any traditional marketing effort. Return visits to various vendors, repeat purchases, word-of-mouth endorsements, and feeling a connection (brand loyalty) with a company, all of which lead to increased sales over time suggest that a marketing program has achieved success. Re-advertising and sharing with others enhance the prospects of reaching the right audience, sending the right message, and creating longer term relationships with the company. As CEO Smithee summarized, "The more layers you can seamlessly integrate, the better chance of getting something sticky."

1. Would the concepts used to measure marketing success match with the message evaluation methods presented in this chapter? Why or why not?

2. Compare the concepts used by Spych with the terms "behavioral response" and "attitudinal response."

3. What roles do "emotions" and "logic" play in the Spych approach to marketing communications?

4. What roles to social media and hand-held technologies such as smart phones play in today's marketing environment? How will they evolve in the future?

CASE 2   HANES: EVALUATION AND BRAND LOYALTY

Kelsey Van Sickle proudly accepted the promotion to brand manager for the Hanes line of men's undergarments. The line includes undershirts, briefs, boxers, and boxer briefs. The line has been widely distributed in a variety of stores, ranging from Kohl's and JCPenney to less expensive retailers.

The Hanes tagline "Wait 'til we get our Hanes on you" has served the company well. Brand awareness remains high. Kelsey was interested in enhancing or improving brand loyalty. She had all of the marketing tools at her disposal, including bonus packs, coupons, contests or sweepstakes, price-off deals, plus several incentives to be offered to retail stores, most notably cooperative advertising.

The advertising agency employed by Kelsey had recently encountered a public relations problem. Celebrity endorser Charlie Sheen had run into legal problems and was dropped. Sheen and basketball legend Michael Jordan appeared in a series of humor-based commercials for Hanes products.

The agency and Kelsey viewed the moment as an opportunity. Kelsey suggested that a new campaign should be developed, perhaps one more focused on product quality. She wondered whether greater long-term loyalty emerges from perceptions of quality as opposed to simply competing based on price or consumer promotions. She concluded that a well-designed consumer promotions program might enhance an advertising campaign.

The primary competitors for Hanes men's underwear may be found in three areas. First, higher-priced products designed to entice wealthy or fashion-conscious consumers are available in stores such as Saks Fifth Avenue. Second, comparable products, especially those produced by Fruit of the Loom, are on the market. Hanes competes for both consumer loyalty and shelf space with these items. Third, lower-end and generic undergarments are often sold side-by-side with Hanes and Fruit of the Loom.

Kelsey charged the advertising agency with engaging in some basic product and brand research. She wanted focus groups with members that purchase Hanes to tell her why they buy the items. She also wanted them to explain whether they were brand loyal or if buying Hanes was simply a habit that could be influenced by consumer promotions. Finally, she wanted to know what kinds of advertisements would cause them to take the time to watch the commercial and pay attention to its content.

Pricing was an additional concern. In 2008, a major recession had begun that reached many countries. Kelsey had heard that consumers had trended to more cost-conscious purchases, even for basic clothing necessities such as underwear.

She wondered if an optimal price-quality perception could be established for Hanes.

1. What IMC objectives are important to Kelsey?

2. What types of message evaluation techniques should Hanes and the advertising agency use when developing the next set of commercials for television and print (magazines)?

3. Are there any online evaluation metrics that would be valuable to Kelsey's efforts?

4. What types of respondent behavior evaluations should Hanes and the advertising agency employ for the next set of commercials?

5. Which consumer promotions should Hanes use? How should they be evaluated?

6. What long-term IMC criteria should be used to assess the Hanes men's underwear brand?

gosphotodesign/Fotolia

▲ Kelsey suggested a new campaign for the Hanes line of men's underwear she now managed.

MyMarketingLab

Go to **mymktlab.com** for Auto-graded writing questions as well as the following Assisted-graded writing questions:.

15-1. Are sales figures important when evaluating integrated marketing communications? How should hard data such as redemption rates and store traffic be used in the evaluation of marketing communications? In terms of accountability, how important are behavioral measures of IMC effectiveness?

15-2. ComScore is a firm that measures Internet traffic and Internet advertising. Access the Web site at www.com- score. com. What services does the company offer? Describe a research project that you feel this company could do successfully to assist in advertising or Internet research.

15-3. Mymktlab Only—comprehensive writing assignment for this chapter.

ENDNOTES

Chapter 1

1. Based on T. L. Stanley (2011). Miracle Whip ads: Love Them or Hate Them? *Adweek*, February 24, http://www.adweek.com/adfreak/miracle-whip-ads-love-them-or-hate-them-127028, accessed February 20, 2012.
2. Donald Baack, "Communication Processes," *Organizational Behavior* (Houston: Dame Publications, Inc., 1998), pp. 313–37.
3. Brian Morrissey, "Chick-fil-A's Strategy: Give Your Fans Something to Do," *Brandweek* 50, no. 35 (October 5, 2009), p. 40.
4. James G. Hutton, "Integrated Marketing Communications and the Evolution of Marketing Thought," *Journal of Business Research* 37 (November 1996), pp. 155–62.
5. Diane Brady, "Making Marketing Measure Up," *BusinessWeek* (December 13, 2004), pp. 112–13; "Top 10: Issues Facing Senior Marketers in 2007," *Advertising Age* 78, no. 17 (April 23, 2007), p. 23.
6. "Unilever Cuts Agency, Production Spending Even as Ad Costs Rise," *Advertising Age*, February 2, 2012, http://adage.com/print/232485 .
7. Andrew McMains, "Ad Spending Trends Reveal No Surprises," *Adweek* 48, no. 44 (December 3, 2007), p. 9.G14
8. Bob Liodice, "Essentials for Integrated Marketing," *Advertising Age* 79, no. 23 (June 9, 2008), p. 26.
9. Alison Circle, "Marketing Trends to Watch," *Library Journal* 134, no. 16 (October 1, 2009), pp. 26–29.
10. Lauren Keller Johnson, "Harnessing the Power of the Customer," *Harvard Management Update* 9 (March 2004), pp. 3–5; Patricia Seybold, *The Customer Revolution* (London: Random House Business Books, 2006).
11. Lauren Indvik, "U.S. Online Retail Sales to Reach $327 Billion by 2016, http://mashable.com/2012/02/27/ecommerce-327-billion-2016-study, accessed March 9, 2012.
12. Dominic Carey, "Global Mobile-Phone Sales and Market Share: Summary," *Bloomberg*, www.bloomberg.com/news/2011-11-15/global-mobile-phone-sales-and-market-share-summayr, November 15, 2011; "Wireless/Mobile Statistics"(**www.mobileisgood .com/statistics.php**, accessed November 13, 2009).
13. M. N. Tripathi, "Customer Engagement—Key to Successful Brand Building," *The XIMB Journal of Management* 6, no. 1 (March 2009), pp. 131–40.
14. Jean-Noel Kapferer, "The Roots of Brand Loyalty Decline: An International Comparison," *Ivey Business Journal* 69, no. 4 (March–April 2005), pp. 1–6.
15. Debbie Howell, "Today's Consumers More Open to Try New Brands," *DSN Retailing Today* 43, no. 20 (October 25, 2004), pp. 29–32.
16. Jana Lay-Hwa Bowden, "The Process of Customer Engagement: A Conceptual Framework," *Journal of Marketing Theory & Practice* 17, no. 1 (Winter 2009), pp. 63–74.
17. Arundhati Parmar, "10 Minutes with Rex Briggs," *Marketing News* 42, no. 6 (April 1, 2008), pp. 24–27.
18. Don E. Schultz and Philip J. Kitchen, "Integrated Marketing Communications in U.S. Advertising Agencies: An Exploratory Study," *Journal of Advertising Research* (September–October 1997), pp. 7–18.
19. Stephen J. Gould, Dawn B. Lerman, and Andreas F. Grein, "Agency Perceptions and Practices on Global IMC," *Journal of Advertising Research* (January–February 1999), pp. 7–26.
20. Ibid.
21. Jane L. Levere, "A Campaign from Jaguar to Show its Wild Side," *The New York Times*, February 26, 2012, http:///www .nytimes.com/2012/02/27/business/media/jaguar-ad-campaign.
22. Parekh Rupal, "Febreze Sniffs Out New Target: Dorm Dwellers," *Advertising Age* (April, 2004), pp. 34–35.
23. "1 on 1 with Twitter's Co-Founder," *CNNMoney.com* (http://money.cnn.com/video/technology/2009/07/24/f_bst_twitter_biz_stone.fortune/); "Rumor: Twitter's Worth $1B," *CNNMoney.com* (http://money.cnn.com/video/technology/2009/09/25/f_tt_twitter_valuation.fortune/).

Chapter 2

1. V. Mabrey and S. Rosenberg (2008). Can Julia Stewart Save Applebee's?, ABC Nightline, April 2, http://abcnews.go.com/Business/CEOProfiles/story?id=4573076&page=1, retrieved July 25, 2011; Jeff Bailey, "Reinventing Applebee's," *Forbes Women: Power Women*, December 2, 2009, http://www.forbes.com/2009/12/02/restaurant-business-applebees-ihop-julia-stewart.html, accessed March 5, 2012; Applebee's, IHOP Parent Say Sales are Up, *U.S. Equities, Forbes.com*, September 23, 2010, http://www.forbes.com/2010/09/23/applebees-ihop-parent-says-sales-are-up-marketnewsvideo.html, accessed March 5, 2012; Applebee's Girl's Night Out: http://technorati.com/social-media/article/applebees-using-social-media-to-bring/#ixzz1oMGa6Jp7
2. Arun Sudhaman, "Brand Quality Still Key to Corporate Reputation: Edelman," *Media Asia* (November 19, 2004), p. 8.
3. Kari Greenberg, "Mazda, Subaru Racing to Upgrade Dealerships," *Brandweek* 45, no. 39 (November 1, 2004), p. 10.
4. Joan Voight, "The Lady Means Business," *Adweek* 47, no. 15 (April 10, 2006), pp. 32–36.
5. Based on "2011 Ranking of Top 100 Brands," *Interbrand*, www .interbrand.com/en/knowledge/best-global-brands, accessed October 5, 2011
6. Brad Dorfman, "Exclusive: Kraft's New Marching Orders: Make Today Delicious," *Reuters* (http://uk.reuters.com/articlePrint?articleID=UKN15243520090217), February 17, 2009.
7. Interview with Anne Gremillion, Gremillion & Pou Advertising Agency, Shreveport, Louisiana, December 10, 2009.
8. "Comeback Kids: Haggar, Keds Stage Brand Revival," *Advertising Age*, October 30, 2011, http://adage.com/print/230721.

9. Stuart Elliott, "L'eggs Returns to TV Advertising," *The New York Times Media Decoder*, April 7, 2011, http://mediadecocer.blogs.nytimes.com/2011/04/07.

10. "How PMH Gave Target Its Signature Look," *Advertising Age*, March 18, 2012, http://adage.com/print/233378.

11. Paul McNamara, "The Name Game," *Network World* (April 20, 1998), pp. 77–78.

12. Max Du Bois, "Making Your Company One in a Million," *Brand Strategy*, no. 153 (November 2001), pp. 10–11.

13. Michael J. De La Merced, "Kraft, Mondelez and the Art of Corporate Rebranding," *The New York Times*, March 21, 2012, http://dealbook.nytimes.com/2012/03/21.

14. Pamela W. Henderson and Joseph A. Cote, "Guidelines for Selecting or Modifying Logos," *Journal of Marketing* (April 1998), pp. 14–30.

15. Natalie Zmuda, "What Went into the Updated Pepsi Logo," *Advertising Age* (http://adage.com/print?article_id=132016), October 27, 2008.

16. Elaine Wong, "New Hormel Campaign Beefs Up Portfolio Strength," *Brandweek* (**www.brandweek.com/bw/content_display/news-and-features/direct/e3ia613cdbc5ebe**), February 8, 2010.

17. Natalie Zmuda, "What Went Into the Updated Pepsi Logo."

18. "Branding Isn't Just for Large Companies with Deep Pockets Anymore," *Smart Business* 4, no. 2 (May 2009), pp. 20–21.

19. Andrew Ehrenberg, Neil Barnard, and John Scriven, "Differentiation or Salience," *Journal of Advertising Research* (November–December 1997), pp. 7–14.

20. Stuart Elliott, "A Campaign Linking Clean Clothes with Stylish Living," *The New York Times* (**www.nytimes.com/2010/01/08/business/media/08adco.html**), January 8, 2010.

21. "How PMH Gave Target Its Signature Look," *Advertising Age*, March 18, 2012, http://adage.com/print/233378.

22. Karlene Lukovitz, "Brand Experience, Values Increasingly Drive Loyalty," *Marketing Daily*, February 6, 2012, www.mediapost.com/publications/article/167095.

23. "Brandz Top 100 Most Valuable Global Brands 2010," Millward Brown Optimor, www.millwardbrown,com, accessed March 16, 2012.

24. Kusum L. Ailawaldi, Scott A. Neslin, and Donald R. Lehman, "Revenue Premium as an Outcome Measure of Brand Equity," *Journal of Marketing* 67, no. 4 (October 2003), pp. 1–18; Don E. Schultz, "Understanding and Measuring Brand Equity," *Marketing Management*, Spring 200, Vol. 9, No. 1, pp 8–9; Tanya Irwin, "Apple, Hershey's, Sprite Top Youth Brands," *MedaiPost News*, October 26, 2011, www.mediapost.com/publications/article/161108.

25. John N. Frank, "Walking the Private Label – National Brands Tightrope," *Buyer*, Vol. 25, No. 5 May 2011, pp. 16-21.

26. Stephanie Hilderbrandt, "What's in Store for Private Label," *Beverage Industry*, Vol. 102, No. 9, September 2011, pp. 18-22.

27. Terri Goldstein, "Battling Brand Malpractice," *BrandWeek* (**www.brandweek.com/bw/content_display/news-and-features/direct/e3i422dde68f61e91f2f602f6a04ac4d207**), November 2, 2009; Ellen Byron, "At the Supermarket Checkout, Frugality Trumps Brand Loyalty," *The Wall Street Journal* (http://online.wsj.com/article/SB122592835021203025.html), November 6, 2008.

28. Jack Neff, "Study: Cutting Spending Hurts Brand Long Term," *Advertising Age* (http://adage.com/print?article_id=135790), April 6, 2009.

29. Dongdae Lee, "Image Congruence and Attitude Toward Private Brands," *Advances in Consumer Research* 31 (2004), pp. 435–41.

30. Rusty Williamson, "Penney's Launching New Line," *Women's Wear Daily (WWD)* 191, no. 83 (April 19, 2006), p. 2.

31. Kelly Nolan, "Apparel & Accessories: A Label for Every Style at JCP," *Retailing Today* 45, no. 14 (August 7, 2006), pp. 27, 36.

32. John Kalkowski, "Private Labels Are Booming."

33. Vanessa L. Facenda, "A Swift Kick to the Privates," *Brandweek* 48, No. 31 (September 3, 2007), pp. 24–28.

34. Kris Perry, "Do You Help Your Customers Sell or Market?" *Paperboard Packaging* 89, no. 11 (November 2004), p. 8.

35. "Packaging Affects Brand Loyalty," *Supermarket News* 53, no. 45 (November 7, 2005), p. 36.

36. Andrea Zoe Aster, "Good Drinks Come in Smart Packaging," *Marketing Magazine* 109, no. 32 (October 4–11, 2004), pp. 13–15.

37. Stuart Elliott, "A Redesigned Brand Hopes to Avoid Tropicana Storm," *The New York Times, Media Decoder*, August 31, 2011, http://www.mediacoder.blogs.nytimes.com/2011/08/31.

38. Heidi Tolliver-Walker, "The Top Five Most Effective Ways to Use QR Codes on Packaging," *Seybold Report: Analyzing Publishing Technologies*, Vol. 12, No. 1, January 9, 2012, pp. 2–6

39. Johnny K. Johansson and Ilkka A. Ronkainen, "Consider Implications of Local Brands in a Global Arena," *Marketing News* 38 (May 15, 2004), pp. 46–48.

40. Ibid.

41. Andrew McMains, "To Compete Locally, Global Brands Must Adapt," *Adweek.com* (http://adweek.com/pt//cpt&title=To+compete+locally.html), September 25, 2008.

42. Johnny K. Johansson and Ilkka A. Ronkainen, "Consider Implications of Local Brands in a Global Arena."

43. Material furnished by Gremillion & Pou Marketing, August 2010.

Chapter 3

1. "Chipotle Mexican Grill, Inc." (**www.fundinguniverse.com/company-histories/Chipotle-Mexican-Grill-Inc-Company-History.html**, accessed November 3, 2009); "Happy Pig, Happy Customer," ABC News "Nightline" (http://abcnews.go.com/video/playerIndex?id=8018211), July 6, 2009.

2. Jeffrey B. Schmidt and Richard A. Spreng, "A Proposed Model of External Consumer Information Search," *Journal of Academy of Marketing Science* 24, no. 3 (Summer 1996), pp. 246–56.

3. Merrie Brucks, "The Effect of Product Class Knowledge on Information Search Behavior," *Journal of Consumer Research* 12 (June 1985), pp. 1–15; Schmidt and Spreng, "A Proposed Model of External Consumer Information Search."

4. Laura M. Buchholz and Robert E. Smith, "The Role of Consumer Involvement in Determining Cognitive Responses to Broadcast Advertising," *Journal of Advertising* 20, no. 1 (1991), pp. 4–17; Schmidt and Spreng, "A Proposed Model of External Consumer Information Search"; Jeffrey J. Inman, Leigh McAllister, and Wayne D. Hoyer, "Promotion Signal: Proxy for a Price Cut," *Journal of Consumer Research* 17 (June 1990), pp. 74–81; Barry J. Babin, William R. Darden, and Mitch Griffin, "Work and/or Fun: Measuring Hedonic and Utilitarian Shopping Value," *Journal of Consumer Research* 20 (March 1994), pp. 644–56.

5. Schmidt and Spreng, "A Proposed Model of External Consumer Information Search."

6. M. Fishbein and Icek Ajzen, *Belief, Attitude, Intention, and Behavior: An Introduction to Theory and Research* (Reading, MA: Addison-Wesley, 1975).

7. Richard P. Bagozzi, Alice M. Tybout, C. Samuel Craig, and Brian Sternathal, "The Construct Validity of the Tripartite Classification of Attitudes," *Journal of Marketing* 16, no. 1 (February 1979), pp. 88–95.

8. Stuart Elliott, "Levi's Courts the Young with a Hopeful Call," *The New York Times* (**www.nytimes.com/2009/06/30/business/media/30adco.html**), June 30, 2009.

9. Discussion of cognitive mapping based on Anne R. Kearny and Stephan Kaplan, "Toward a Methodology for the Measurement of Knowledge Structures of Ordinary People: The Conceptual Content Cognitive Map (3CM)," *Environment and Behavior* 29, no. 5 (September 1997), pp. 579–617; Stephan Kaplan and R. Kaplan, *Cognition and Environment, Functioning in an Uncertain World* (Ann Arbor, MI: Ulrich's, 1982, 1989).

10. Discussion of heuristics and multiattribute model based on William L. Wilkie and Edgar A. Pessemier, "Issues in Marketing's Use of Multiattribute Models," *Journal of Marketing Research* 10 (November 1983), pp. 428–41; Peter L. Wright, "Consumer Choice Strategies: Simplifying vs. Optimizing," *Journal of Marketing Research* 11 (February 1975), pp. 60–67; James B. Bettman, *An Information Processing Theory of Consumer Choice* (Reading, MA: Addison-Wesley, 1979).

11. Mark Sneider, "Create Emotional Ties with Brand for Sales," *Marketing News* 38 (May 15, 2004), pp. 44–45.

12. Peter Leimbach, "Role Reversal: Mr. Mom Goes Shopping," *Adweek.com* (**www.adweek.com/aw/content_display/news/agency/33i1a1890f91e4cda9a5b3c3348b4c85509**), July 1, 2009.

13. "The Domestication of Man: More Men Taking on Cleaning Chores," *Quirk's Marketing Research Review*, August 2011, Article 20110826-3.

14. Mark Dolliver, "Alas, Free Time Comes at a Price," *Adweek* 45, no. 34 (September 13, 2004), p. 42; Mark Dolliver, "More Money or More Time?" *Adweek* 42, no. 11 (March 12, 2001), p. 44.

15. Discussion of second-chancers based on Richard Halverson, "The Customer Connection: Second-Chancers," *Discount Store News* 37, no. 20 (October 26, 1998), pp. 91–95.

16. "LGBT Consumers Warm to Ads Targeted to Gays," *eMarketer Digital Intelligence*, September 1, 2011, www.emarketer.com/articles/print.aspx?1008571.

17. Stuart Elliott, "Luxury Hotels Market the Memories They Can Make," *The New York Times*, September 13, 2011, www.nytimes.com/2011/09/14.

18. "Boomers Bend the Trends," *Private Label Buyer* 21, no. 4 (April 2007), p. 14.

19. Allison Linn, "Companies Are Under Pressure to Reduce Sodium, But Americans Love Salty Taste," *MSNBC*, May 26, 2011, www.msnbc.com/id/43143369/ns/business-us_business.

20. Discussion based on Frederick E. Webster, Jr., and Yoram Wind, "A General Model for Understanding Organizational Buyer Behavior," *Marketing Management* 4, no. 4 (Winter–Spring 1996), pp. 52–57; Patricia M. Doney and Gary M. Armstrong, "Effects of Accountability on Symbolic Information Search and Information Analysis by Organizational Buyers," *Journal of the Academy of Marketing Science* 24, no. 1 (Winter 1996), pp. 57–66; Rob Smith, "For Best Results, Treat Business Decision Makers as Individuals," *Advertising Age's Business Marketing* 84, no. 3 (1998), p. 39.

21. Patricia M. Doney and Gary M. Armstrong, "Effects of Accountability on Symbolic Information Search and Information Analysis by Organizational Buyers," *Journal of the Academy of Marketing Science* 24, no. 1 (Winter 1996), pp. 57–66.

22. Herbert Simon, *The New Science of Management Decisions,* rev. ed. (Upper Saddle River, NJ: Prentice Hall, 1977).

23. Webster and Wind, "A General Model for Understanding Organizational Buyer Behavior"; Doney and Armstrong, "Effects of Accountability on Symbolic Information Search and Information Analysis by Organizational Buyers"; James A. Eckert and Thomas J. Goldsby, "Using the Elaboration Likelihood Model to Guide Customer Service-Based Segmentation," *International Journal of Physical Distribution & Logistics Management* 27, no. 9–10 (1997), pp. 600–15.

24. Patrick J. Robinson, Charles W. Faris, and Yoram Wind, "Industrial Buying and Creative Marketing," *Marketing Science Institute Series* (Boston: Allyn & Bacon, 1967).

25. Adapted from Webster and Wind, "A General Model for Understanding Organizational Buyer Behavior."

26. Eugene F. Brigham and James L. Pappas, *Managerial Economics,* 2d ed. (Hinsdale, IL: Dryden Press, 1976).

27. Charles A. Weber, John R. Current, and Desai Anand, "Vendor: A Structured Approach to Vendor Selection and Negotiation," *Journal of Business Logistics* 21, no. 1 (2000), pp. 134–69.

28. Discussion of dual channel marketing is based on Wim G. Biemans, "Marketing in the Twilight Zone," *Business Horizons* 41, no. 6 (November–December 1998), pp. 69–76.

29. Ibid.

30. Ibid.

31. Robert Duboff, "True Brand Strategies Do Much More Than Name," *Marketing News* 35, no. 11 (May 21, 2001), p. 16.

32. Interview with Brian and Sarah Warren, Emogen Marketing Group, February 15, 2010; Emogen Marketing Group (**www.emogenmarketing.com**, accessed May 22, 2010).

Chapter 4

1. Tanya Irwin (2012). Pet Products Poised for Continued Growth, editorial@mediapost.com, accessed April 11, 2012.

2. **www.petsmart.com** (accessed November 26, 2007); Elizabeth Weise, "We Really Love—and Spend On—Our Pets," *USA Today* (December 11, 2006), p. 1-D.

3. Nancy Pekala, "Marketing to Today's Women: Focus on Life Stages, Not Ages," *Marketing Matters Newsletter*, American Marketing Association, November 10, 2009.

4. Ibid.

5. Cecilia King, "Marketers Target Moms Armed with Smartphones," *The Washington Post*, June 24, 2011, www.washingtonpost.com/business/economy/marketers-target-moms-armed-with-smartphones/2011/06/24

6. Simon Goodall, "How to Connect with the Heart and Mind of the Male Shopper," *Advertising Age*, March 29, 2011, http://adage.com/print/149623.

7. Andrew Adam Newman, "Orthodontists Market to Adults Seeking Prettier Smiles, *The New York Times*, February 1, 2012, www.nytimes.com/2012/02/02/business/media/orthodontists-market-to-adults-seeking-prettier-smiles.

8. Brian Braiker, "The Next Great American Consumer," *Adweek*, September 26, 2011, www.adweek.com/print/135207.

9. Gary Evans, "This Consumer Has Cash, But She's Tired," *Furniture Today* 31, no. 50 (August 27, 2007), pp. 1, 42.

10. Gavin O'Malley, "Marketers Advised to Target Ethnic Preferences," *Online Media Daily*, November 29, 2011, www.mediapost.com/publications/article/153175.

11. Tanya Irwin, "Ram Truck Hispanic Effort Most Comprehensive," *Media Post News Marketing Daily*, September 28, 2011, www.mediapost.com/publications.

12. Rebecca Piirto Heath, "Psychographics," *Marketing Tools* (November–December 1995), pp. 74–81.

13. SRI Consulting Business Intelligence (**www.sric-bi.com**, accessed January 3, 2008); Dana-Nicoleta Lascu and Kenneth E. Clow, *Marketing Principles*, Textbook Media, 2012.

14. Jane L. Levere, "We Have Dinner, Drinks, Swimming … Oh, and Gambling, Too," *The New York Times*, April 2, 2012, www.nytimes.com/2012/04/02/business/media. .

15. David Feldman, "Segmentation Building Blocks," *Marketing Research* (Summer 2006), pp. 23–29.

16. PRIZM, "My Best Segments" (**www.claritas.com/MyBestSegments/Default.jsp**, accessed January 3, 2008).

17. Ronald L. Zallocco, "Benefit Segmentation of the Fitness Market," *Journal of Health Care Marketing* 12, no. 4 (December 1992), p. 80.

18. Susan Pechman, "Custom Clusters: Finding Your True Customer Segments," *Bank Marketing* 26, no. 7 (July 1994), pp. 33–35.

19. Andrew Adam Newman, "Carnival Cruise Campaign Focuses on the First-Timers," *The New York Times*, December 20, 2011, www.nytimes.com/2011/12/21/business/media.

20. Gene Koprowski, "Bovine Inspiration," *Marketing Tools* (October 1996), pp. 10–11.

21. Andrew Adam Newman, "SnackWell's Nudges Up the Portion Pack," *The New York Times*, April 20, 2011, www.nytimes.com/2011/04/02/business/media/21adco.html.

22. Andrew Adam Newman, "Yes, the Diner's Open. How About a Seat at the Counter?" *The New York Times*, February 1, 2011, www.nytimes.com/2011/02/02/business/media/02adco.html.

23. Gerard J. Tellis, "Study: Advertising Half as Effective as Previously Believed," *Advertising Age*, June 26, 2011, http://adage.com/print/228409.

24. Margaret Henderson Blair, "An Empirical Investigation of Advertising Wearin and Wearout," *Journal of Advertising Research* 40, no. 6 (November–December 2000), pp. 95–100.

25. Ibid.

26. Gerard J. Tellis, "Study: Advertising Half as Effective as Previously Believed," *Advertising Age*, June 26, 2011, http://adage.com/print/228409.

27. Lionell A. Mitchell, "An Examination of Methods of Setting Advertising Budgets: Practice and Literature," *European Journal of Marketing* 27, no. 5 (1993), pp. 5–22.

28. Gregory Bresiger, "It's Ad Infinitum," *New York Post*, May 1, 2011, www.nypost.com/f/print/news/business/it_ad_infinitum_3ThF9rxodhlKnSkcIjdTPK.

29. James E. Lynch and Graham J. Hooley, "Increased Sophistication in Advertising Budget Setting," *Journal of Advertising Research* 30, no. 1 (February–March 1990), pp. 67–76.

30. James O. Peckham, "Can We Relate Advertising Dollars to Market Share Objectives?" *How Much to Spend for Advertising,* M. A. McNiver (ed.) (New York: Association of National Advertisers, 1969), p. 30.

31. "Higher Gear," *Promo Industry Trends Report* (**www.promo-magazine.com**, accessed January 2, 2008).

32. "2004 Advertising to Sales Ratios for 200 Largest Ad Spending Industries," *Adage* (**www.adage.com**, accessed February 26, 2005).

33. "U.S. Ad Expenditures," *2008 Marketing Fact Book, Marketing News* (July 15, 2008), p. 22.

34. "U.S. Alternative Media Spending," *2008 Marketing Fact Book, Marketing News* (July 15, 2008), pp. 18, 22.

35. Shannon Dortch, "Going to the Movies," *American Demographics* 18, no. 12 (December 1996), pp. 4–8.

36. Interview with Benny Black, February 18, 2010, by Donald Baack and Kenneth E. Clow.

Chapter 5

1. Interview with Stan Richards by Donald Baack and Kenneth E. Clow, January 20, 2010. Marketing materials provided by The Richards Group, including excerpts from "It's Been a Rocket Ride," an article reprinted from the *Dallas Business Journal.*

2. Rupal Parekh, "Thinking of Pulling a CareerBuilder? Pros and Cons of Bringing an Account In-House," *Advertising Age* (http://adage.com/print?article_id=136701), May 18, 2009.

3. Bruce Horovitz, "Amateur Doritos Ad Maker Could Win $1M… and a Job," *USA Today, Money*, accessed November 27, 2011, www.usatoday.com/money/media/story/2011-09-26.

4. Eric Pfanner, "When Consumers Help, Ads Are Free," *The New York Times* (**www.nytimes.com/2009/06/22/business/media/22adco.html**), June 22, 2009.

5. G+G Advertising (**www.gng.net**, accessed January 16, 2010); "G&G Advertising," *Agency Compile* (**www.agencycompile.com/factsheet/factsheet.aspx?agency_id=7823**, accessed January 16, 2010).

6. Beth Snyder and Laurel Wentz, "Whole Egg Theory Finally Fits the Bill for Y&R Clients," *Advertising Age* 70, no. 4 (July 25, 1999), pp. 12–13.

7. E.J. Schultz and Rupal Parekh, "Behind Kraft's Seismic Shift: Why It's Shaking Up Its Shops," *Advertising Age*, November 15, 2010, http://adage.com/print?article_id=147105.

8. Suzanne Vranica and Daniel Fitzpatrick, "BofA Reviews Ad Strategy," *Wall Street Journal*, January 12, 2012, http://online.wsj.com/article/SB10001424052970204257504577115050.

9. Heather Jacobs, "How to Make Sure Your Pitch Is Heard," *B&T Weekly* 57, no. 2597 (February 8, 2007), pp. 14–16.

10. Interview with Jane Hilk, Senior Vice-President of Marketing, Oscar Mayer, January 28, 2010.

11. Emily Bryson York, "Behind Kraft's Marketing Makeover: From New Ad Agencies to New Attitude," *Advertising Age* (http://adage.com/article?article_id=141943), February 8, 2010.

12. Jacobs, "How to Make Sure Your Pitch Is Heard."

13. Rupal Parekh, "Want More Out of Your Agencies? Write Better Briefs," *Advertising Age* (http://adage.com/print?article_id=138468), August 17, 2009.

14. Laura Petrecca, "Agencies Urged to Show the Worth of Their Work," *Advertising Age* 68, no. 15 (April 14, 1997), pp. 3–4.

15. Stuart Elliott, "Playing UP a Scotsman's Lawn Expertise," *The New York Times*, March 12, 2012, www.nytimes.com/2012/03/13/business/media/playing-up-a-scotmans-lawn-expertise.

16. Interview with Stan Richards, The Richards Group, February 5, 2010.

17. Robert J. Lavidge and Gary A. Steiner, "A Model for Predictive Measurements of Advertising Effectiveness," *Journal of Marketing* 24 (October 1961), pp. 59–62.

18. Steve Miller, "VW is Going Outdoors, Literally," *Brandweek.com* (http://brandweek.com/VW+IS+Going+Outdoor), June 23, 2008.

19. Jack Neff, "The Newest Ad Agencies: Major Media Companies," *Advertising Age* (http://adage.com/print?article_id=140712), November 3, 2008.

20. "Media Agencies Make Mark as Content Creators," *Advertising Age*, April 24, 2011, http://adage.com/print/227163.

21. Rupal Parekh, "Want More Out of Your Agencies? Write Better Briefs," *Advertising Age* (http://adage.com/print?article_id=138468), August 17, 2009.

22. Henry A. Laskey and Richard J. Fox, "The Relationship Between Advertising Message Strategy and Television Commercial Effectiveness," *Journal of Advertising Research* 35, no. 2 (March–April 1995), pp. 31–39.

23. Herbert E. Krugman, "Memory Without Recall, Exposure Without Perception," *Journal of Advertising Research* 40, no. 6 (November– December 2000), pp. 49–55; David Kay, "Left Brain Versus Right Brain," *Marketing Magazine* 108, no. 36 (October 27, 2003), p. 37.

24. "Picking up the Pace," *Marketing News* 36, no. 7 (April 1, 2002), p. 3.

25. Laurel Wentz and Bradley Johnson, "Top 100 Global Advertisers Heap Their Spending Abroad," *Advertising Age* (http://adage.com/print?article_id=140723), November 30, 2009.

Chapter 6

1. Mark Dolliver, "Assessing the Power of Ads," *Adweek.com* (http://adweek.com/aw/content_display/news/agency/e3i34e2ede5adb7e1e8aa21d1f4fa3b2d0b), June 22, 2009.

2. Jerry Olson and Thomas J. Reynolds, "Understanding Consumers' Cognitive Structures: Implications for Advertising Strategy," *Advertising Consumer Psychology*, L. Percy and A. Woodside, eds. (Lexington, MA: Lexington Books, 1983), pp. 77–90; Thomas J. Reynolds and Alyce Craddock, "The Application of the MECCAS Model to Development and Assessment of Advertising Strategy," *Journal of Advertising Research* 28, no. 2 (1988), pp. 43–54.

3. Interview with Jane Hilk, Sr. Vice-President of Marketing, Oscar Mayer, January 28, 2010.

4. Laurie A. Babin and Alvin C. Burns, "Effects of Print Ad Pictures and Copy Containing Instructions to Imagine on Mental Imagery That Mediates Attitudes," *Journal of Advertising* 26, no. 3 (Fall 1997), pp. 33–44.

5. Marc Bourgery and George Guimaraes, "Global Ads: Say It with Pictures," *Journal of European Business* 4, no. 5 (May–June 1993), pp. 22–26.

6. Based on Rosemary M. Murtaugh, "Designing Effective Health Promotion Messages Using Components of Protection Motivation Theory," *Proceedings of the Atlantic Marketing Association* (1999), pp. 553–57; R. W. Rogers and S. Prentice-Dunn, "Protection Motivation Theory," *Handbook of Health Behavior Research I: Personal and Social Determinants*, D. Gochman, ed. (New York: Plenum Press, 1997), pp. 130–32.

7. Ibid.

8. Michael S. Latour and Robin L. Snipes, "Don't Be Afraid to Use Fear Appeals: An Experimental Study," *Journal of Advertising Research* 36, no. 2 (March–April 1996), pp. 59–68.

9. Martin Eisend, "A Meta-Analysis of Humor Effects in Advertising," *Advances in Consumer Research–North American Conference Proceedings* 34 (2007), pp. 320–23.

10. James J. Kellaris and Thomas W. Cline, "Humor and Ad Memorability," *Psychology & Marketing* 24, no. 6 (June 2007), pp. 497–509.

11. Theresa Howard, "Windex Birds Make Clean Sweep as Most-Liked Ads," *USA Today* (December 18, 2006), p. 7B (Money).

12. Jeremy Mullman, "How Bud Light Lost the Sense of Humor—and Subsequently, Sales," *Advertising Age* 80, no. 27 (August 10, 2009), pp. 1, 21.

13. Matthew Creamer, "Marketing's Era of Outrage," *Advertising Age* 78, no. 7 (February 12, 2007), pp. 1, 26.

14. Jimmy Yap, "McDonald's Finds Humor a Hit with Singapore Viewers," *Media Asia* (February 7, 2004), p. 22; Bill Britt, "Ford Tries Witty, Edgy Advertising to Promote the Kia," *Automotive News Europe* 9, no. 2 (January 26, 2004), p. 4.

15. "Sex Doesn't Sell," *The Economist* 373, no. 8399 (October 30, 2004), pp. 62–63.

16. Andrew Adam Newman, "Selling a Household Cleaning Product on Its…Sex Appeal?" *The New York Times* (**www.nytimes.com/2009/11/13/business/media/13adco.html**), November 13, 2009.

17. Sandra O'Loughlin, "Hanes Shows Some 'Love' in Battle for Intimates," *Brandweek* 48, no. 9 (February 26, 2007), p. 11.

18. Based on G. Smith and R. Engel, "Influence of a Female Model on Perceived Characteristics of an Automobile," *Proceedings of the 76th Annual Convention of the American Psychological Association* 15, no. 3 (1968), pp. 46–54; Leonard Reid and Lawrence C. Soley, "Decorative Models and the Readership of Magazine Ads," *Journal of Advertising Research* 23 (April–May 1983), pp. 27–32; R. Chestnut, C. LaChance, and A. Lubitz, "The Decorative Female Model: Sexual Stimuli and the Recognition of Advertisements," *Journal of Advertising* 6 (Fall 1977), pp. 11–14.

19. Bob Garfield, "Dentyne Spot Makes It Seem That Naysayers Have a Point," *Advertising Age* 76, no. 5 (January 31, 2005), p. 41.

20. Jessica Severn, George E. Belch, and Michael A. Belch, "The Effects of Sexual and Non-Sexual Advertising Appeals and Information Level on Cognitive Processing and Communication Effectiveness," *Journal of Advertising* 19, no. 1 (1990), pp. 14–22.

21. Tom Reichart, "Sex in Advertising Research: A Review of Content, Effects, and Functions of Sexual Information in Consumer Advertising," *Annual Review of Sex Research* 13 (2002), pp. 242–74; D. C. Bello, R. E. Pitts, and M. J. Etzel, "The Communication Effects of Controversial Sexual Content in Television Programs and Commercials," *Journal of Advertising* 3, no. 12 (1983), pp. 32–42.

22. "Note to Chrysler: Gutter Humor Has No Place in Ads," *Automotive News* 78, no. 6064 (October 27, 2003), p. 12.

23. Tom Reichart, "Sex in Advertising Research: A Review of Content, Effects, and Functions of Sexual Information in Consumer Advertising," *Annual Review of Sex Research* 13 (2002), pp. 242–74; Andrew A. Mitchell, "The Effect of Verbal and Visual Components of Advertisements on Brand Attitude and Attitude Toward the Advertisement," *Journal of Consumer Research* 13 (June 1986), pp. 12–24.

24. Bruce Horovitz, "Risqué May Be Too Risky for Ads," *USA Today* (April 16, 2004), p. 1B.

25. Julie Naughton and Amy Wicks, "Eva's Seduction: Calvin Klein Stirs Controversy with Mendes Ads," *Women's Wear Daily* 196, no. 25 (August 4, 2008), p. 1.

26. Bruce Horovitz, "Super Bowl Ads Get Racier, But Does Sex Really Sell?" *USA Today, Money*, January 19, 2012, www.usatoday.com/money/advertising/story/2012/01/19.

27. Kate Lunau, "Study Finds Real Women Don't Sell," *Maclean's* 121, no. 33 (August 25, 2008), p. 34.

28. Howard Levine, Donna Sweeney, and Stephen H. Wagner, "Depicting Women as Sex Objects in Television Advertising," *Personality and Social Psychology Bulletin* 25, no. 8 (August 1999), pp. 1049–58.

29. Daniel A. Joelson, "Rebel Sell," *Latin Trade* 12, no. 8 (August 2004), p. 16.

30. Elizabeth Bryant, "P&G Pushes the Envelope in Egypt with TV Show on Feminine Hygiene," *Advertising Age International* (December 14, 1998), p. 2.

31. Gerard Stamp and Mark Stockdale, "Sex in Advertising," *Advertising Age's Creativity* 7, no. 6 (July–August 1999), pp. 35–36; Bob Garfield, "Pushing the Envelope: The Performing Penis," *Advertising Age International* (July 12, 1999), p. 4; Jean J. Boddewyn, "Sex and Decency Issues in Advertising: General and International Dimensions," *Business Horizons* 34, no. 5 (September–October 1991), pp. 13–20.

32. Boddewyn, "Sex and Decency Issues in Advertising: General and International Dimensions."

33. Steve Oakes, "Evaluating Empirical Research into Music in Advertising: A Congruity Perspective," *Journal of Advertising Research* 47, no. 1 (March 2007), pp. 38–50.

34. Andrew Hampp, "A Reprise for Jingles in Madison Avenue," *Advertising Age*, September 6, 2010, http://adage.com/pring?article_id=145744.

35. Felicity Shea, "Reaching Youth with Music," *B&T Weekly* 54, no. 2491 (October 1, 2004), pp. 16–17.

36. Brian Steinberg, "The Times Are a-Changin' for Musicians and Marketers," *Advertising Age* 78, no. 43 (October 29, 2005) p. 43.

37. Nicole Rivard, "Maximizing Music," *SHOOT* 48, no. 4 (February 23, 2007), pp. 17–21.

38. Douglas Quenqua, "What's That Catchy Tune? A Song for Car Insurance Makes the Charts," *The New York Times* (**www.nytimes. com/2007/12/31/business/media/31 allstate.html**), December 31, 2007.

39. Stuart Elliott, "Godiva Rides in a New Direction," *The New York Times* (**www.nytimes.com/2009/11/16/business/media/16adnewsletter1.html**), November 16, 2009.

40. Joanne Lynch and Leslie de Chernatony, "The Power of Emotion: Brand Communication in Business-to-Business Markets," *Journal of Brand Management* 11, no. 5 (May 2004), pp. 403–420; Karalynn Ott, "B-to-B Marketers Display Their Creative Side," *Advertising Age's Business Marketing* 84, no. 1 (January 1999), pp. 3–4.

41. "Bloomberg Business Week Ad Campaign Pitching Consumers on Personality," *Advertising Age*, November 1, 2011, http://adage.com/print/230757.

42. Stephanie Thompson, "Big Deal," *Mediaweek* 7, no. 44 (November 24, 1997), p. 36; Judann Pollack, "Big G Has Special Cheerios for Big '00,'" *Advertising Age* (June 14, 1999), pp. 1–2.

43. Gregg Cebrzynski, "Teachers Hot about Hot Teacher Dancing in 'Sexually Exploitive' Hardee's TV Spot," *Nation's Restaurant News* 41, no. 37 (September 17, 2007), p. 12.

44. Rob Walker, "Cul-de-sac Cred," *New York Times Magazine*, July 10, 2005.

45. www.amazon.com (accessed January 5, 2008); Kevin Maney, "A Book That Never Ends?" *USA Today,* December 6, 2007, p. 19A.

Chapter 7

1. Melinda Brodbeck and Erin Evans, "Dove Campaign for Real Beauty Case Study," http://psucomm473.blogspot.com/2007/03/dove-campaign-for-real-beauty-case.html, March 5, 2007; Burt Helm, "Surprise! Dove's "Campaign for Real Beauty" ads actually kind of fake, Brand New Day, Bloomberg Business Week, http://www.businessweek.com/the_thread/brandnewday/archives/2008/05/surprise_doves.html, May 7, 2008; Rebecca Winters Keegan, "Top 10 TV ads" (www.time.com/specials/2007/top10/article, accessed January 9, 2008).

2. Henry A. Laskey, Ellen Day, and Melvin R. Crask, "Typology of Main Message Strategies for Television Commercials," *Journal of Advertising* 18, no. 1 (1989), pp. 36–41.

3. David Aaker and Donald Norris, "Characteristics of TV Commercials Perceived As Informative," *Journal of Advertising Research* 22, no. 2 (1982), pp. 61–70.

4. **www.campbellsoupcompany.com/atw_usa.asp** (accessed January 12, 2008).

5. Wolfgang Gruener, "Nintendo Wii Surrenders Market Share in Weak Game Console Market," *TG Daily* (**www.tgdaily.com/trendwatch-features/43289**), July 17, 2009.

6. Tony Smith, "Intel Extends Market Share Gains," *Register Hardware* (**www.reghardware.co.uk/2007/04/20/intel_vs_amd_q1_07/print.html**), April 20, 2007.

7. Shailendra Pratap Jain and Steven S. Posavac, "Valenced Comparisons," *Journal of Marketing Research* 41, no. 1 (February 2004), pp. 46–56.

8. Dhruv Grewal and Sukumar Kavanoor, "Comparative Versus Noncomparative Advertising: A Meta-Analysis," *Journal of Marketing* 61, no. 4 (October 1997), pp. 1–15; Shailendra Pratap Jain and Steven S. Posavac, "Valenced Comparisons," *Journal of Marketing Research* 41, no. 9. (February 2004), pp. 46–56.

9. Joseph R. Priester, John Godek, D. J. Nayakankuppum, and Kiwan Park, "Brand Congruity and Comparative Advertising: When and Why Comparative Advertisements Lead to Greater Elaboration," *Journal of Consumer Psychology* 14, no. 1/2 (2004), pp. 115–24; Grewal and Kavanoor, "Comparative Versus Noncomparative Advertising: A Meta-Analysis."

10. Aaron Baar, "Subaru Taps Nostalgia for the First Car," *Marketing Daily*, February 26, 2012, www.mediapost.com/publications/article/168531.

11. Stuart Elliott, "In New Ads, Stirring Memories of Commercials Past," *The New York Times*, January 12, 2012, www.nytimes.com/2012/01/13/business/media/stirring-memories-of-commercials-past.

12. Joanne Lynch and Leslie de Chernatony, "The Power of Emotion: Brand Communication in Business-to-Business Markets," *Journal of Brand Management* 11, no. 5 (May 2004), pp. 403–420.

13. Jim Hanas, "Rotoscope Redux," *Creativity* 10, no. 1 (February 2002), pp. 40–41.

14. Interview with Stan Richards by Donald Baack and Kenneth E. Clow, January 20, 2010.

15. Aaron Baar, "For Stein Mart, It's Love At First Find," *Marketing Daily*, September 10, 2011, www.mediapost.com/publications.

16. Matthew Warren, "Do Celebrity Endorsements Still Work?" *Campaign (UK)* 44 (November 2, 2007) p. 13.

17. "Angelina Joli to be $10m face of Louis Viutton," *Marketing*, www.marketingmagazine.co.uk/news/1067170, accessed May 3, 2011.

18. "Highest Paid Athletes," *Buzzle.com*, www.buzzle.com/articles/highest-paid-athletes.htmil, accessed April 16, 2012.

19. Jonathan Wexler, "Who Is the Athlete With the Most Endorsements?" Playing Field Promotions (**www.playingfieldpromotions.com/blog/438/who-is-the-athlete-with-the-most-endorsements**), June 9, 2009.

20. Interview with Stan Richards by Donald Baack and Kenneth E. Clow, January 20, 2010.

21. Laura Petrecca, "Small Companies Seek Publicity from Celebrities," *USA Today*, www.usatoday.com/cleanprint/?1296061644796, accessed January 26, 2011.

22. Claire Murphy, "Stars Brought Down to Earth in TV Ads Research," *Marketing* (January 22, 1998), p. 1.

23. Kamile Junokaite, Sonata Alijosiene, and Rasa Gudonaviciene, "The Solutions of Celebrity Endorsers Selection for Advertising Products," *Economics & Management* 12, no. 3 (2007), pp. 384–90.

24. Stuart Elliott, "La-Z-Boy, Meet Brooke Shields," *The New York Times*, November 29, 2010, www.nytimes.com/2010/11/29/business/media/29adnewsletter1.html.

25. "Betty White Voted America's Most Trusted Celebrity: Poll," *Reuters*, August 18, 2011, www.reuters.com/assets/print?aid=USTRE77H2WE20110818.

26. Roobina Ohanian, "Construction and Validation of a Scale to Measure Celebrity Endorsers' Perceived Expertise," *Journal of Advertising* 19, no. 3 (1990), pp. 39–52.

27. Cathy Yingling, "Beware the Lure of Celebrity Endorsers," *Advertising Age* (**www.adage.com/print?article_ide=120560**), September 24, 2007.

28. Kenneth Hein, "Danica Patrick Talks GoDaddy, Pepsi," *Brandweek* (**www.brandweek.com/bw/content_display/news-and-features/direct/e3i7a35e791d5c**), November 30, 2009.

29. Lee Hawkins, "Taking a Flier on Michael Vick," *The Wall Street Journal*, April 14, 2011, http://online.wsj.com/article/SB100014 24052748704336504576258610982097444.html.

30. Dipayan Biswas, Abhijit Biswas, and Neel Das, "The Differential Effects of Celebrity and Expert Endorsements on Consumer Risk Perceptions," *Journal of Advertising* 35, no. 2 (Summer 2006), pp. 17–31.

31. "Priceline Kills the Messenger Because Ads Worked Too Well," *Advertising Age*, January 29, 2012, http://adage.com/print/232409.

32. "Look Which NBA Finals Winner Could Score Some Endorsement Deals," *Advertising Age*, June 13, 2011, http://adage.com/print/228168.

33. David J. Moore and John C. Mowen, "Multiple Sources in Advertising Appeals: When Product Endorsers Are Paid by the Advertising Sponsor," *Journal of Academy of Marketing Science* 22, no. 3 (Summer 1994), pp. 234–43.

34. Raymond R. Burke and Thomas K. Srull, "Competitive Interference and Consumer Memory for Advertising," *Journal of Consumer Research* 15 (June 1988), pp. 55–68.

35. Karen Robinson-Jacobs, "With Employees in Ads, Pizza Hut Goes for Slices of Life," *The Dallas Morning News*, November 17, 2010, www.dallasnews.com/sharedcontent/dws/bus/stories.

36. "Francois: The Fiat 500 Brand Brief Was Wrong," *Advertising Age*, January 10, 2012, http://adage.com/print/232011.

37. A. W. Melton, "The Situation with Respect to the Spacing of Repetitions and Memory," *Journal of Verbal Learning and Verbal Behavior* 9 (1970), pp. 596–606.

38. H. Rao Unnava and Deepak Sirdeshmukh, "Reducing Competitive Ad Interference," *Journal of Marketing Research* 31, no. 3 (August 1994), pp. 403–411.

39. Naveen Donthu, "A Cross-Country Investigation of Recall of and Attitudes Toward Comparative Advertising," *Journal of Advertising* 27, no. 2 (Summer 1998), pp. 111–21.

40. Grewal and Kavanoor, "Comparative Versus Noncomparative Advertising: A Meta-Analysis."

41. Michael L. Maynard, "Slice-of-Life: A Persuasive Mini Drama in Japanese Television Advertising," *Journal of Popular Culture* 31, no. 2 (Fall 1997), pp. 131–42.

42. Information and materials supplied by Emogen Marketing, Ruston, Louisiana, February 2010.

43. Grewal and Kavanoor, "Comparative Versus Noncomparative Advertising: A Meta-Analysis."

44. Stuart Elliott, "With Economy Volatile, Financial Firms Start to Stress Stability," *The New York Times* (**www.nytimes.com/2007/09/19/business/media/19adco.html**), September 19, 2007.

Chapter 8

1. Steve McClellan, "SB TV Advertisers See Online Gains," *Adweek Media* (**www.adweek.com/aw/content_display/custom-reports/superbowl/e3ib96053a9e47796d76708c1d3b173fc76**), February 8, 2010; Jack Neff, "Future of Advertising? Print, TV, Online Ads," *Advertising Age* (**www.adage.com/print?article_id=136993**),
June 1, 2009; Aishwarya Bhatthttp, "GoDaddy.com–Lola Super-Bowl Ad Controversy," Thaindian News (**www.thaindian.com/newsportal/tech-news/godaddycom-lola-superbowl-ad-controversy_100316040.html**, accessed May 19, 2010), February 6, 2010; Peter Hartlaub, "The Sleaziest Super Bowl Commercials of all Time," MSNBC.com (**www.msnbc.msn.com/id/22871730/**, accessed May 18, 2010); GoDaddy.com (accessed May 18, 2010).

2. Mickey Marks, "Millennial Satiation," *Advertising Age* 14 (February 2000), p. S16; J. Thomas Russell and W. Ronald Lane, *Kleppner's Advertising Procedure,* 15th ed. (Upper Saddle River, NJ: Prentice Hall), 2002, pp. 174–75.

3. Larry Percy, John R. Rossiter, and Richard Elliott, "Media Strategy," *Strategic Advertising Management* (2001), pp. 151–63.

4. Kate Maddox, "Media Planners in High Demand," *BtoB* 89, no. 13 (November 8, 2004), p. 24.

5. Arthur A. Andersen, "Clout Only a Part of Media Buyer's Value," *Advertising Age* 70, no. 15 (April 5, 1999), p. 26.

6. Ibid.

7. Herbert E. Krugman, "Why Three Exposures May Be Enough," *Journal of Advertising Research* 12, no. 6 (1972), pp. 11–14.

8. Erwin Ephron and Colin McDonald, "Media Scheduling and Carry-over Effects: Is Adstock a Useful Planning Tool," *Journal of Advertising Research* 42, no. 4 (July–August 2002), pp. 66–70; Laurie Freeman, "Added Theories Drive Need for Client Solutions," *Advertising Age* 68, no. 31, p. 18.

9. Larry Percy, John R. Rossiter, and Richard Elliott, "Media Strategy," *Strategic Advertising Management* (2001), pp. 151–63.

10. Ibid.

11. Jack Loechner, "TV Advertising Most Influential," *Media Post Research Brief*, March 23, 2011, www.mediapost.com/publications/?fa=articles.printfriendly&art_aid=147033.

12. Diane Holloway, "What's On? Ads, Ads, and Maybe a TV Show," *Austin American Statesman* (**www.austin360.com/tv/content/movies/**television/2005/10/11tvcolumn.html, accessed January 17, 2008), October 11, 2005.

13. Jack Neff, "Future of Advertising? Print, TV, Online Ads," *Advertising Age* (**www.adage.com/print?article_id=136993**), June 1, 2009; Gregory Solman, "Forward Thought: Ads A-Ok on DVRs," *Hollywood Reporter* (http://hollywoodreporter.com), December 27, 2007.

14. Steve McClellan, "Audit Finds Nielsen's C3 Ratings Hurt Advertisers," *Media Daily News*, September 19, 2011, www.mediapost.com/publications/article/158818.

15. Brian Steinberg, "Simon Who? Idol Spots Still Pricest in Prime Time," *Advertising Age*, October 18, 2010, http://adage.com/pring/146495.

16. Adapted from Brian Steinberg, "Sunday Night Football Remains Costliest TV Show," *Advertising Age* (http://adage.com/article?article_id=139923), October 26, 2009; "List of Top 20 Prime-time Programs in the Nielsen Ratings for Sept. 28–Oct. 4," *Entertainment Daily* (http://blog.taragana.com/e/2009/10/06/list-of-top-20-prime-time-programs-in-the-nielsen-ratings-for-sept28-oct4), October 6, 2009.

17. Karlene Lukovitz, "Regional Gain Uses TV To Take On Big Pizza Brands," *Marketing Daily*, November 15, 2011, www.mediapost.com/publications/article/162392.

18. Gavin O'Mally, "Social Media Chatter Ups Live TV Stats," *MediaPost News*, March 22, 2012, www.mediapost.com/publications/articl/170743; Jack Loechner, "TV Advertising Most Influential," *Media Post Research Brief*, March 23, 2011, www.mediapost.com/publications/?fa=articles.printfriendly&art_aid=147033.

19. Ki Mae Heussner, "Social Data Uncovers Brand, TV-Show Affinity," *Adweek*, December 22, 2011, www.adweek.com/print/137243.

20. Susan Kuchinsakas, "Brands Increase Recall with TV/Digital Mix, Google Says," *ClickZ*, December 6, 2011, www.clickz.com/print_article/clikz/stats/2130484.

21. Stuart Elliott, "Mainstays Will Reappear in the Big Game Again," *The New York Times*, January 27, 2012, www.nytimes.com/2012/01/27/business/media/mainstays-will-reappear-in-the-big-game-once-again.

22. Stuart Elliott, "Before the Toss, Super Bowl Ads," *The New York Times*, February 2, 2012, www.nytimes.com/2012/02/03/business/media/before-the-toss-super-bowl-ads; Stuart Elliott, "Before Sunday, A Taste of the Bowl," *The New York Times*, February 3, 2012, www.nytimes.com/2011/02/04/business/media/04adco.html. G28

23. Interview with Stan Richards, The Richards Group, February 4, 2010; Rupal Parekh, "Behind the Scenes of Bridgestone's Super Bowl Spots," *Advertising Age*, February 8, 2010, pp. 4–5.

24. Doug McPherson, "Into Thin Air," *Response* 18, no. 5 (February 2010), pp. 40–45.

25. Interview with Mary Price by Donald Baack and Kenneth E. Clow, January 20, 2010.

26. Doug McPherson, "Into Thin Air," *Response* 18, no. 5 (February 2010), pp. 40–45.

27. Sarah Mahoney, "Taco Tweets Fuel Texas C-Store's Advertising," *Media Post News, Marketing Daily*, February 9, 2011, www.mediapost.com/publications/?fa=Articles.print_aid=144522.

28. Morianna Morello, "Why Print Media—and Why Now?" *Response* 17, no. 8 (May 2009), p. 77.

29. Edward C. Baig, "DirecTV Takes the Dive with SI's Swimsuit Issue," *USA Today Money*, February 1, 2012, www.usatoday.com/money/media/story/2012-02-01/directv-takes-the-dive-with-sis-swimsuit-issue.

30. Nat Ives, "If You're Rich, You Still Have Time to Read," *Advertising Age* (**www.adage.com/print?article_id=130685**), September 2, 2008.

31. Erik Sass, "Newspaper Ads Still Guide Shopping," *Media Daily News*, April 13, 2011, www.mediapost.com/publications/?fa=Articles=148632.

32. Bill Gloede, "Best Use of Newspapers," *Adweek* 48, no. 25 (June 18, 2007), pp. SR22–23.

33. Erik Sass, "Newspaper's Digital Audience Skews Younger, More Affluent," *Media Daily News*, December 13, 2011, www.mediapost.como/publications/article/164161.

34. *"Marketer Trees 2009"* (http://adage.com/marketertres09), December 28, 2009.

35. Lindsay Morris, "Studies Give 'Thumbs Up' to Mags for Ad Awareness," *Advertising Age* 70, no. 32 (August 2, 1999), pp. 16–17; Rachel X. Weissman, "Broadcasters Mine the Gold," *American Demographics* 21, no. 6 (June 1999), pp. 35–37.

36. Stacey Pratt, "Planning Casebook," *Mediaweek,* no. 1230 (October 20, 2009), p. 17.

37. "ABM Releases Harris Study Data: B2B Advertising Highly Effective," *Min's B2B* 9, no. 26 (June 26, 2006), p. 8.

38. Kate Maddox, "Top 100 B-to-B Advertisers Increased Spending 3% in '06," *BtoB* 92, no. 11 (September 10, 2007), pp. 25–30.

39. Kate Maddox, "Top 100 B-to-B Advertisers Increased Spending 3% in '06."

40. Eric Pfanner, "TV Still Has a Hold on Teenagers," *The New York Times* (**www.nytimes.com/2009/12/14/business/media/14iht-cache14.html**), December 14, 2009.

41. Joe Mandese, "Power Shift," *Broadcasting & Cable* 135, no. 53 (December 12, 2005), p. 12.

42. Martin Croft, "Media Indies Take on Networks with Consortium," *Marketing Week* 29, no. 28 (July 13, 2006), p. 13.

43. Interview with Bill Breedlove by Donald Baack and Kenneth E. Clow, January 21, 2010.

44. Jack Neff, "Media Buying & Planning." *Advertising Age* 70, no. 32 (August 2, 1999), pp. 1–2.

45. N. Skid. (2010). Ad campaign boosts Domino's Pizza revenue in the third quarter, Crain's Detroit Business, http://www.crainsdetroit.com/article/20101019/FREE/101019856/ad-campaign-boosts-domino-8217-s-pizza-revenue-in-the-third-quarter#

46. P. Farhi (2010). Behind Domino's mea culpa campaign, The Washington Post, January 13, http://www.washingtonpost.com/wp-dyn/content/article/2010/01/12/AR2010011201696.html, retrieved August 21, 2011.

Chapter 9

1. Interview with Shama Kabini by Donald Baack and Kenneth E. Clow, January 19, 2010.

2. Brian Morrissey, "Marketers Get Real," *Adweek* (**www.adweek.com/aw/content_display/news/agency/e3i26911e62celee0f7ela76831**), November 2, 2009.

3. Brian Morrissey, "Real Time: The Web's New Prime Time," *Adweek* (**www.adweek.com/aw/content_display/news/digital/e3i15f4e2b3b4a487b3b5cd5347ebd07cbf**), May 25, 2009.

4. "The Decline of 'Old Media' and the Rise of Web 2.0," *Trends E-Magazine* 6, no. 11 (November 2009), pp. 33–36.

5. Cate T. Corcoran, "Delivering the Goods: E-tailing Sales to Rise But Gains Seen Slowing," *Women's Wear Daily* 197, no. 94 (May 5, 2009), p. 94.

6. Michael Stich, Jim Leonard, and Jennifer Rooney, "Ring Up E-Commerce Gains with True Multichannel Strategy," *Advertising Age* 79, no. 10 (March 10, 2008), p. 15.

7. "Consumers Embrace Internet as Regular Shopping Tool," *Australian Giftguide* (October–December 2009), p. 10.

8. David Sparrow, "Get 'em to Bite," *Catalog Age* 20, no. 4 (April 2003), pp. 35–36.

9. Amanda Gaines, "Leading the Charge," *Retail Merchandiser* 49, no. 6 (November–December 2009), pp. 16–19.

10. Mike Fletcher, "How to Create the Perfect E-Commerce Website," *Revolution* (March 2009), pp. 60–63.

11. Joab Jackson, "E-Consumers Get Smart," *CIO* 23, no. 7 (February 1, 2010), p. 18.

12. Gwen Moran, "Check Out Your Checkout," *Entrepreneur* 38, no. 1 (January 2010), p. 38.

13. Maya Dollarhide, "Bluefly Buzz Bags Shoppers," *Incentive* 180, no. 1 (June 2006), p. 10.

14. Lisa Cervini, "Free Shipping Offers Fueling Online Sales," *This Week in Consumer Electronics* 20, no. 24 (November 21, 2005), p. 16.

15. Nanette Byrnes, "More Clicks at the Bricks," *BusinessWeek,* no. 4063 (December 17, 2007), pp. 50–52.

16. Mark Del Franco, "Mailers Say, Webward Ho!" *Catalog Age* 19, no. 4 (March 15, 2002), pp. 1–3.

17. "Data-Insecurity Fears Said to Hamper Online Shopping," *Card-Line* 9, no. 13 (March 27, 2009), p. 34.

18. Suzanne Beame, "Consumer Confidence in Online Shopping Sites Is on the Rise," *New Media Age* (November 15, 2007), p. 15.

19. "Online Consumers Happy to Be Tracked," *The Wall Street Journal*, December 5, 2011, http://blogs.wsj.com/tech-europe/2011/12/05/online-consumers-happy-to-be-tracked.

20. Carol Patton, "Marketers Promote Online Traffic Through Traditional Media," *Advertising Age's Business Marketing* 84, no. 8 (August 1999), p. 40.

21. "Black Consumers Active, Engaged on Mobile," *eMarketer*, April 24, 2012, www.emarketer.com/articles/print. aspx?R=1008994.

22. Roger Matus, "Mobile Action Codes in Magazine Advertising," Whitepaper from Nellymoser,Inc (www.nellymoser.com), p. 4.

23. Dana Mattioli, "Retailers Try to Thwart Price Apss," *Wall Street Journal*, December 23, 2011, http://wsj.com/article/SB10001424 0529702036862045771149.

24. Shama Hyder Kabani, "Online Marketing Plan," The Marketing Zen Group (**www.marketingzen.com**), pp. 9–13.

25. "Online Ad Spending Consolidates Among Search, Banners, Video," *eMarkter Digital Intelligence*, February 3, 2012, www .smarketer.com/articles/print.aspx?R=1008815.

26. Brian Morrissey, "Beefing Up Banner Ads," *Adweek* (**www .adweek.com/aw/content_display/news/digital/e3if-04360897e1103df4b92464543af6649**), February 15, 2010.

27. Mike Shields, "Social Sites Not as Video Ad Friendly as Content, E-mail," *Mediaweek* (**www.mediaweek.com/mw/content_display/news/digital-downloads/metrics**), November 18, 2009.

28. "Problem Solved," *BtoB* 92, no. 15 (November 12, 2007), p. 21; "Online Ad Spending Consolidates Among Search, Banners, Video," *eMarkter Digital Intelligence*, February 3, 2012, www .smarketer.com/articles/print.aspx?R=1008815

29. "Problem Solved," *BtoB* 92, no. 15 (November 12, 2007), p. 21

30. Jack Neff, "Why CPG Brands Better Buy Paid Search," *Advertising Age* (http://adage.com/print?article_id=130353), August 18, 2008.

31. Josh Quittner, Jessi Hempel, and Lindsay Blakely, "The Battle for Your Social Circle," *Fortune* 156, no. 10 (November 26, 2007), pp. 11–13.

32. "Google Searches for Success in Local Ads," *Advertising Age*, March 1, 2011, http://adage.com/print/149140.

33. Josh Quittner, Jessi Hempel, and Lindsay Blakely, "The Battle for Your Social Circle," *Fortune* 156, no. 10 (November 26, 2007), pp. 11–13.

34. Michael Fielding, "We Can All Get Along," *Marketing News*, May 15, 2007, p. 4.

35. Paula Andruss, "Personalized URLS," *Marketing News*, September 1, 2008, p. 10.

36. Brian Morrissey, "Forrester: Social Web Now Mainstream," *Adweek.com* (http://adweek.com/aw/content_display/news/digital/e3icc3b73373ecfd4b35823e7a5e43da05), October 24, 2008.

37. "Total Worldwide Social Network Ad Revenues Continue Strong Growth," *eMarketer Digital Intelligence*, February 24, 2012, www.emarketer.com/articles/print.aspx?R=1008862.

38. Natalie Zmuda, "Behind Coca-Cola's Biggest Social-Media Push Yet," *Advertising Age* (http://adage.com/print?article_id=140591), November 17, 2009.

39. Daniel Frankel, "Report: Facebook, Google Overtake Yahoo in Display Ad Market Share," *PaidContent.org*, February 22, 2012, http://cnt.to/pUc.

40. Brian Morrissey, "Brands Seek Fans on Facebook," *Adweek .com* (http://adweek.com/aw/content_display/news/digital/e3id3d058ba458918f0fc8ec45), October 12, 2009.

41. Mark Walsh, "Study: Social Media Pays," *Media Post News, Online Media Daily*, (**www.mediapost.com/publications/?fa=Articles_aid=110120**), July 20, 2009.

42. Mark Walsh, "Razorfish Study: Special Offers Drive Engagement in Social Media," *Media Post News, Online Media Daily* (**www.mediapost.com/publications/?fa=Articles_aid=117008**), November 8, 2009.

43. Rachael King, "How Companies Use Twitter to Bolster Their Brands," *BusinessWeek* (**www.businessweek/com/print/technology/content/sep2008/tc2008095_320491.htm**), September 6, 2008.

44. Claire Cain Miller, "Marketing Small Businesses with Twitter," *The New York Times* (**www.nytimes.com/2009/07/23/business/smallbusiness/23twitter.html**), July 23, 2009.

45. Rory J. Thompson, "Study: Chat Rooms Influence Holiday Purchases," *Marketing Power* (**www.marketingpower.com/content/OPTEDRELEASE12–06.pdf**), December 13, 2007.

46. Beth Snyder Bulik, "Does Your Company Need a Chief Blogger?" *Advertising Age* 79, no. 15 (April 14, 2008), p. 24.

47. Sarah Halzack, "Marketing Moves to the Blogosphere," *Washingtonpost.com* (**www.washingtonpost.com/wp-dyn/content/article/2008/08/24/AR20080824051517**), August 25, 2008.

48. Ibid.

49. Karen J. Bannan, "The Mandate to Integrate," *BtoB* 94, no. 12 (September 28, 2009), p. 23.

50. "Re-Marketing Helps Boost Online Shoppers' Baskets," *Data Strategy* 3, no. 7 (May 2007), p. 9.

51. Basil Katz, "Email Newsletters Aim for Inbox and Wallet," *Reuters* (**www.reuters.com/articlePrint?articleId=USTRE589 4XI20090910**), September 10, 2009.

52. Andrew Adam Newman, "A Campaign for Clothes by a Guy Not Wearing Any," *The New York Times* (**www.nytimes.com/2009/10/29/business/media/29zappos.html**), October 29, 2009.

53. **www.elfyourself.com**, accessed August 30, 2010.

54. Lynda Radosevich, "Going Global Overnight," *InfoWorld* 21, no. 16 (April 19, 1999), pp. 1–3.

55. "The Worldly Web," *CFO* 19, no. 7 (June 2003), p. 30.

56. "Black Friday and Cyber Monday Sales Break Holiday Records, Magic Logix Digital Marketing Solutions, http://www.magiclogix.com/blog/ecommerce/record-holiday-sales-in-2012-for-black-friday-cyber-monday-and-ecommerce/, December 30, 2011.

57. "Lies, damned lies, and Black Friday Sales Statistics," Constantine Von Hoffman, CBS News, http://www.cbsnews.com/8301-505123_162-57342402/lies-damned-lies-and-black-friday-sales-statistics/, December 13, 2011.

58. Heidi Gautschi, "Search in Any Language," *EContent* 28, no. 5 (May 2005), p. 29; "Google Is Standing on the Brink of Global Dominance," *Marketing Week* (April 28, 2005), p. 31; Thomas Claburn and Tony Kontzer, "Google Wants a Piece of the Business Market," *InformationWeek*, no. 1040 (May 23, 2005), p. 29; Mathew Creamer and Kris Oser, "Google Breaks Down and Decides to Advertise," *Advertising Age* 76, no. 18 (May 2, 2005), p. 3; Daniel Lyons, "Google This: The Tech Giants Duke It Out—Again" (www.newsweek.com/id/224597/page/1, accessed March 29, 2010), November 28, 2009; "Microsoft Corporation" (http://topics.nytimes.com/top/news/business/companies/microsoft_corporation/index.html?scp=1&sq=bing%20versus%20google&st=cse, accessed March 29, 2010).

Chapter 10

1. WomenGamers.com (**www.womengamers.com/news/2010/03/11/breaking-down-female-demographic**), May 3, 2010; Yukari Iwatani Kane, "Videogame Firms Make a Play for Women," *The Wall Street Journal* (http://online.wsj.com/article/SB1000142405274870488240457446365277785 432.html), October 13, 2009; CNN.com (**www.cnn.com/2008/TECH/ptech/02/28/women.gamers/index.html**), May 3, 2010.

2. Natasha Singer, "On Campus, It's One Big Commerical," *The New York Times*, September 11, 2011, www.nytimes.com/2001/09/11/business-at-colleges-the-marketers-are-everywhere.

3. Laurie Burkitt, "Procter & Gamble Taps Co-Eds to Sell Products," *Forbes.com* (**www.forbes.com/2009/09/09/procter-gamble-repnation-cmo-network-readyu_print.html**), September 9, 2009.

4. Laurie Burkitt, "Marketers Break Into Homes By Sponsoring Parties," *Forbes.com* (**www.forbes.com/2009/08/19/purina-house-party-cmo-network-houseparty_print.html**), August 19, 2009.

5. Andrew Adam Newman, "Putting Boxed Wine to the Taste Test," *The New York Times*, October 11, 2011, www.nytimes.com/2011/10/12/business/media-boxed-wine-firms-claim-theyll-pass-the -taste-test.

6. Angelo Fernando, "Transparency Under Attack," *Communication World* 24, no. 2 (March–April 2007), pp. 9–11.

7. Ibid.

8. Jim Matorin, "Infectious 'Buzz Marketing' Is a Smart Way to Build Customer Loyalty at Your Operation," *Nation's Restaurant News* 41, no. 18 (April 30, 2007), pp. 18–20.

9. Kate Niederhoffer, Rob Mooth, David Wiesenfeld, and Jonathon Gordon, "The Origin and Impact of CPG New-Product Buzz: Emerging Trends and Implications," *Journal of Advertising Research* 47, no. 4 (December 2007), pp. 420–26.

10. Ibid.

11. Chris Powell, "The Perils of Posing," *Profit* 26, no. 2 (May 2007), pp. 95–96.

12. Ben Sisario, "Backing Indie Bands to Sell Cars," *The New York Times*, September 27, 2011, www.nytimes.com/2011/09/28/media/toyota-scion-is-backing-indie-bands-to-sell-cars.

13. Becky Wilkerson, "Bringing Brands to Life," *Marketing* (**www.marketingmagzine.co.uk**), February 18, 2009, pp. 35–38.

14. "Karl Greenberg, "Cadillac in the Performance Swim Lane With V-Centric Events," *MediaPost News, Marketing Daily*, April 20, 2011, www.mediapost.com/publications/?fa=articles.printfriendly&art_aid=149076. .

15. Stuart Elliott, "King Cotton Goes on Tour," *The New York Times* (**www.nytimes.com/2009/08/24/business/media/24adnewsletter1.html**), August 24, 2009.

16. Derek Drake, "Prove the Promise of Your Brand," *Adweek* 50, no. 35 (October 5, 2009), pp. S11–S12.

17. Simon Hudson and David Hudson, "Branded Entertainment: A New Advertising Technique or Product Placement in Disguise?" *Journal of Marketing Management* 22, no. 5/6 (July 2006), pp. 489–504.

18. "Product Placement Hits High Gear on American Idol, Broadcast's Top Series for Brand Mentions," *Advertising Age*, April 18, 2011, http://adage.com/pring/227041.

19. Linda Moss, "Nielsen: Product Placements Succeed in 'Emotionally Engaging' Shows," *Multichannel News* (**www.multichannel.com/index.asp**), December 10, 2007.

20. Stacy Straczynski, "Harley-Davidson Revs Product Placement," *Adweek* (**www.advweek.com/aw/content_display/news/agency/e3i84436228620cd549875945**), November 12, 2009.

21. Jeremy Peters, "Glamour's iPad Series to Let Viewers Buy Clothes from Gap," *Media Decoder*, March 6, 2011, www.mediadecoder.blogs.nytimes.com/2011/03/06-galmours-ipad-series-to-let-virewers-buy-clothes-from-gap.

22. Simon Hudson and David Hudson, "Branded Entertainment: A New Advertising Technique or Product Placement in Disguise?" *Journal of Marketing Management* 22, no. 5/6 (July 2006), pp. 489–504.

23. Andrew Hampp, "How American Airlines Got a Free Ride in 'Up in the Air,'" *Advertising Age* (http://adage.com/print?article_id=141059), December 14, 2009.

24. Cecily Hall, "Subliminal Messages," *Women's Wear Daily* 195, no. 2 (January 3, 2008), p.12.

25. Marc Graser, "More Ads Set for Videogames," *Variety*, September 13, 2011, www.variety.com/article/VR1118042795; Simon Hudson and David Hudson, "Branded Entertainment: A New Advertising Technique or Product Placement in Disguise?" *Journal of Marketing Management* 22, no. 5/6 (July 2006), pp. 489–504.

26. Raj Persaud, "The Art of Product Placement," *Brand Strategy*, no. 216 (October 2007), pp. 30–31.

27. Burt Helm, "Marketing: Queen of the Product Pitch," *BusinessWeek* (April 30, 2007), pp. 40–41.

28. "Hey, Advertisers: New York Has a Bridge to Sell You," *Advertising Age*, October 26,2011, http://adage.com/print/230643.

29. Theresa Howard, "As More People Play, Advertisers Devise Game Plans," *USA Today* (July 11, 2006), p. Money, 3b.

30. Ibid.

31. Ibid.

32. Rita Chang, "Advergames a Smart Move, If Done Well," *Advertising Age* (http://adage.com/print?article_id=131786), October 16, 2008.

33. Heather Chaplin, "Players Lend a Helping Hand or Thumb," *Adweek*, April 20, 2012, www.adweek.com/print/139461; "Brands Friending Social Gaming Amid New Web Craze," *The Wall Street Journal*, August 8, 2010, http://online.wsj.com/article/SB10001424052748704657504575411804125832426.html.

34. Mike Shields, "IGA: Most Gamers Cool with In-Game Ads," *Mediaweek.com* (http://mediaweek.com/mw/content_display/news/digital-downloads/gaming/e3i8d91a7147083886bf-b91a8ee5978c1a7), June 17, 2008.

35. Susan Catto, "Are You Game?" *Marketing Magazine* (November 26, 2007, Supplement), pp. 18–19.

36. Ibid.

37. Katy Bachman, "HP Employs Cinema Experience to Push Printer," *Mediaweek* (**www.mediaweek.com/mw/content_display/news/out-there/place-based/e3i4cb8ab6**), November 29, 2009.

38. Kenneth Hein, "Study: In-Store Marketing Beats Traditional Ads," *Sales & Marketing Management* 161, no. 6 (November 2009), p. 57.

39. Amy Johannes, "Snap Decisions," *Promo* 18, no. 11 (October 2005), p. 16.

40. Kenneth Hein, "Study: In-Store Marketing Beats Traditional Ads," *Sales & Marketing Management* 161, no. 6 (November 2009), p. 57.

41. Tim Dreyer, "In-Store Technology Trends," *Display & Design Ideas* 19, no. 9 (September 2007), p. 92.

42. Ibid.

43. Steve McClellan, "Wal-Mart Takes Its Ads to a New Level: The Aisle," *Adweek* 47, no. 38 (October 16, 2006), p. 9.

44. Michael Bellas, "Shopper Marketing's Instant Impact," *Beverage World* 126, no. 11 (November 15, 2007), p. 18.

45. Ibid.

46. "POP Sharpness in Focus," *Brandweek* 44, no. 24 (June 6, 2003), pp. 31–36; David Tossman, "The Final Push—POP Boom," *New Zealand Marketing Magazine* 18, no. 8 (September 1999), pp. 45–51.

47. Betsy Spethmann, "Retail Details," *Promo SourceBook 2005* 17 (2005), pp. 27–28.

48. RoxAnna Sway, "Four Critical Seconds," *Display & Design Ideas* 17, no. 11 (November 2005), p. 3.

49. Catja Prykop and Mark Heitmann, "Designing Mobile Brand Communities: Concept and Empirical Illustration," *Journal of Organizational Computing & Electronic Commerce* 16, no. 3/4 (2006), pp. 301–23.

50. Sinclair Stewart, "More Marketers Using Word of Mouth to Whip Up Sales," *Seattle PI* **www.seattlepi.com/business/344656_wordofmouth24.html**, December 23, 2007.

51. James T. Areddy, "Starbucks, PepsiCo Bring 'Subopera' to Shanghai," *The Wall Street Journal Online* (http://online.wsj.com/public/article_print/SB119387410336878365.html), November 1, 2007, p. B1.

52. Thomas Clouse, "Camp Jeep Comes to China," *Automotive News* 82, no. 6281 (November 12, 2007), p. 48.

53. Jeff Weiss, "Building Brands Without Ads," *Marketing Magazine* 109, no. 32 (October 4–11, 2004), p. 22.

54. "Red Bull's Good Buzz," *Newsweek* (May 14, 2001), p. 83.

55. Jeff Weiss, "Building Brands Without Ads," *Marketing Magazine* 109, no. 32 (October 4–11, 2004), p. 22.

Chapter 11

1. Stephanie Clifford, "Ads Follow Web Users, and Get More Personal," *The New York Times* (**www.nytimes.com/2009/07/31/business/media/31privacy.html**), July 31, 2009.

2. Leo Rabinovitch, "America's 'First' Department Stores Mines Customer Data," *Direct Marketing* 62, no. 8 (December 1999), pp. 42–45.

3. Jason Q. Zhang, Ashutosh Dixit, and Roberto Friedman, "Customer Loyalty and Lifetime Value: An Empirical Investigation of Consumer Packaged Goods," *Journal of Marketing Theory & Practice* 18, no. 2 (February 2010), pp. 127–139.

4. Elliot Zwiebach, "Wholesalers Segment Shoppers Using Lifestyle Clusters," *Supermarket News* 55, no. 7 (February 12, 2007), p. 23.

5. Howard J. Stock, "Connecting the Dots," *Bank Investment Consultant* 13, no. 3 (March 2005), pp. 28–31.

6. Jordan K. Speer, "Digging Deep: Extreme Data Mining," *Apparel Magazine* 45, no. 12 (August 2004), p. 1.

7. Arthur M. Hughes, "The Importance of Customer Communications," *Database Marketing Institute* (**www.dbmarketing.com/articles/ART233.htm**), August 23, 2007.

8. "High-Fliers Are Attractive Buyers," *Marketing News* 38, no. 1 (September 15, 2004), p. 2.

9. Joseph Gatti, "Poor E-Mail Practices Provoking Considerable Customer Defection," *Direct Marketing* (December 2003), pp. 1–2.

10. Joseph Gatti, "Most Consumers Have Reached Permission E-Mail Threshold," *Direct Marketing* (December 2003), pp. 1–2.

11. Ibid.

12. Mark Dolliver, "Gauging Customer Loyalty," *Adweek* (**www.adweek.com/aw/content_display/news/agency/e3i4a73f-5d7451749a37c7fca20**), February 16, 2010.

13. Julie Jargon, "Restaurants Serve Perks for Loyalty," *The Wall Street Journal*, August 9, 2010, http://online.wsj.com/article/SB10001424052748704271804575405363647189110.html.

14. Julie Jargon, "Restaurants Serve Perks for Loyalty," *The Wall Street Journal*, August 9, 2010, http://online.wsj.com/article/SB10001424052748704271804575405363647189110.html.

15. Mark A. Santillo, "Active Engagement," *Greater Games Industry Catalog* 12 (Spring 2010), p. 14.

16. Arthur M. Hughes, "The Importance of Customer Communications," *Database Marketing Institute* (**www.dbmarketing.com/articles/ART233.htm**), August 23, 2007.

17. "CRM Metrics," *Harvard Management Update* 5, no. 3 (March 2000), pp. 3–4.

18. Darrell K. Rigby, Frederick F. Reichheld, and Phil Schefter, "Avoid the Four Perils of CRM," *Harvard Business Review* 80, no. 2 (February 2002), pp. 101–108.

19. Richard H. Levey, "Prospects Look Good," *Direct* 16, no. 6 (December 1, 2004), pp. 1–5.

20. Julie Appleby, "As Drug Ads Surge, More Rx's Filled," *USA Today* (**www.usatoday.com/news/health/2008–02–29-drugs-main_N.htm**), February 29, 2008.

21. Paula Andruss, "Personalized URLs," *Marketing News* , September 1, 2008, p. 10.

22. Jeff Borden, "Eat My Dust," *Marketing News* 42, no. 2, February 1, 2008, pp. 20–22.

23. Cara Beardi, "E-Commerce Still Favors Traditional Techniques," *Advertising Age* 71, no. 43 (October 16, 2000), pp. 2–3.

24. Patrick Totty, "Direct Mail Gets a New Lease on Life," *Credit Union Magazine* 66, no. 4 (April 2000), pp. 36–37.

25. Carol Krol, "USPS Magazine Touts Direct Mail," *BtoB* 90, no. 3 (March 14, 2005), p. 20.

26. Based on Jay Kiltsch, "Making Your Message Hit Home: Some Basics to Consider When…," *Direct Marketing* 61, no. 2 (June 1998), pp. 32–34.

27. Daniel B. Honigman, "Sweet Science," *Marketing News* 41, no. 16 (October 2, 2007), pp. 16–17.

28. Camille Sweeney, "Avon's Little Sister Is Calling," *The New York Times* (**www.nytimes.com/2010/01/14/fashion/14SKIN.html**), January 14, 2010.

29. Ken Le Meunier-FitsHugh and Nigel F. Piercy, "Does Collaboration Between Sales and Marketing Affect Business Performance,"*Journal of Personal Selling & Sales Management* 27, no. 3 (Summer 2007), pp. 207–220.

30. Patricia R. Lysak, "Changing Times Demand Front-End Model," *Marketing News* 28, no. 9 (April 25, 1994), p. 9.

Chapter 12

1. Personal interview of Reid Ryan and Jay Miller by Donald Baack, March 12, 2008 **www.cchooks.com**, accessed June 20, 2008).

2. Mariola Palazon-Vidal and Elena Delgado-Ballester, "Sales Promotions Effect on Consumer-Based Brand Equity," *International Journal of Market Research* 47, no. 2 (2005), pp. 179–205.

3. Bruce Horovitz, "2 Million Enjoy Free Breakfast at Denny's," *USA Today* (**www.usatoday.com/money/industries/foo.2009/02/03-denny's_N.htm**), February 10, 2009.

4. Patricia Odell, "Now in Vogue," *PROMO* (http://promomagazine.com/incentives/marketing_vogue/index.html), December 1, 2009.

5. Joe Mandese, "Marketers Hold the Promo Line in 2011, Coupon Volume Drops for First Time in Years," *Media Daily News*, January 4, 2012, www.mediapost.com/publications/article/165125; "Do Coupons Make Sense," *Incentive* 177, no. 5 (May 2003), p. 19.

6. Erik Sass, "Is Digital Coupons' Rise Print Insert's Demise?" *MediaPost News* (**www.mediapost.com/publications/?fa=Articles.showArticle&art_aid=122690**), February 18, 2010; Patricia Odell, "Now in Vogue." *PROMO* (http://promomagazine.com/incentives/marketing_vogue/index.html), December 1, 2009.

7. Erik Sass, "Is Digital Coupons' Rise Print Insert's Demise?" *MediaPost News* (**www.mediapost.com/publications/ ?fa=Articles.showArticle&art_aid=122690**), February 18, 2010; Allen Adamson, "CMOs: Your Brand Is on Digital Time," *Forbes* (**www.forbes.com/2010/02/02/digital-branding-apple-ipad-cmo-network-allen-adamson**), February 2, 2010.

8. Elizabeth Gardener and Minakshi Trivedi, "A Communication Framework to Evaluate Sales Promotion Strategies," *Journal of Advertising Research* 38, no. 3 (May–June 1998), pp. 67–71.

9. "Hyundai Adds Luxury Glitz with iPad-based Owner's Manual," *PROMO* (http://promomagazine.com/incentives/news/0407-hyundai-adds-ipad-manual/index.html), April 7, 2010.

10. Don Jagoda, "The Seven Habits of Highly Successful Promotions," *Incentive* 173, no. 8 (August 1999), pp. 104–105.

11. Karlene Lukovitz, "General Mills Ties Into 3D Star Wars Release," *Marketing Daily*, January 23, 2012, www.mediapost .com/publications/article/166262.

12. "Prizewinning Growth," *PROMO* (http://promomagazine.com/ contests/marketing_prizewinning_growth/index.html), July 1, 1998.

13. Patricia Odell, "Spending up by a Nose," *PROMO* (http://promo-magazine.com/contests/marketing_spending_nose/index.html), December 1, 2009.

14. Christopher Heine, "Dr Pepper's Outdoor Mural Contest Thrives Online," September 15, 2001, www.clickz.com/news/2109658/ dr-peppers-outdoor-mural-contest-thrives-online.

15. Sarah Mahoney, "Sears Launches Yard Guru Campaign," *Marketing Daily* (**www.mediapost.com/publications/?fa=Articles. printFriendly&art_aid=125255**), March 31, 2010.

16. Brian Morrissey, "Brand Sweepstakes Get Twitterized," *Adweek* (**www.adweek.com/aw/cn\content_display/news/digital/ e3ied5661580e6e68a1834a7e3**), November 22, 2009.

17. Sandra Block, "Rattled About Rebate Hassles? Regulators Starting to Step In," *USA Today* (March 22, 2005), p. 3b.

18. Kenneth Hein, "Study: Sampling Works," *Brandweek.com* (**www.brandweek.com/bw/content_display/news-and-features/shopper- marketing/e3i32e9c3e84ea86c79e-3ae157688c1ad0a**), September 29, 2008.

19. Andrew Adam Newman, "Dr. Scholl's Widens Its Insole Campaign," *The New York Times* (**www.nytimes.com/2010/04/01/ business/media/01adco.html**), March 31, 2010.

20. Pete Wetmore, "Inserts Branch Out Beyond Print Fliers," *Advertising Age* 75, no. 16 (April 19, 2004), p. N-6.

21. Betsy Spethman, "Introductory Offer," *PROMO* 16 (2004), p. 27; Jennifer Kulpa, "Bristol-Myers Squibb Breaks Ground with Direct Response Product Sampling Website," *Drug Store News* 19, no. 7 (April 7, 1997), p. 19.

22. Rachel Lamb, "Chanel Taps Vogue Supplement to Spark Holiday Gift-Giving," *Luxury Daily*, November 23, 2011, www.luxurydaily.com/ chanel-taps-vogue-supplment-to-spark-holiday-gift-giving.

23. Beng Soo Ong and Foo Nin Ho, "Consumer Perceptions of Bonus Packs: An Exploratory Analysis," *Journal of Consumer Marketing* 14, no. 2–3 (1997), pp. 102–12.

24. David R. Bell, Ganesh Iyer, and V. Padmanaghan, "Price Competition Under Stockpiling and Flexible Consumption," *Journal of Marketing Research* 39, no. 3 (August 2002), pp. 292–304.

25. "Papa John's Tries to Hold the Price of its Pies," *Advertising Age*, March 4, 2012, http://adage.com/print/233109.

26. Showwei Chu, "Welcome to Canada, Please Buy Something," *Canadian Business* 71, no. 9 (May 29, 1998), pp. 72–73.

27. Walter Heller, "Promotion Pullback," *Progressive Grocer* 81, no. 4 (March 1, 2002), p. 19.

28. Miguel Gomez, Vithala Rao, and Edward McLaughlin, "Empirical Analysis of Budget and Allocation of Trade Promotions in the U.S. Supermarket Industry," *Journal of Marketing Research* 44, no. 3 (August 2007), pp. 410–24.

29. Ibid.

30. K. Sudhir and Vithala Rao, "Do Slotting Allowances Enhance Efficiency or Hinder Competition?" *Journal of Marketing Research* 43, no. 2 (May 2006), pp. 137–55.

31. Paula Bone, Karen France, and Richard Riley, "A Multifirm Analysis of Slotting Fees," *Journal of Public Policy & Marketing* 25, no. 2 (Fall 2006), pp. 224–37.

32. "Study: Trade Dollars Up," *Frozen Food Age* 50, no. 2 (September 2001), p. 14.

33. Walter Heller, "Promotion Pullback," *Progressive Grocer* 81, no. 4 (March 1, 2002), p. 19.

34. "Cruise Selling Season Kicks Off with Agent Promotions and Optimism," *Travel Agent* 319 (January 3, 2005), p. 9.

35. Roger A. Slavens, "Getting a Grip on Co-Op," *Modern Tire Dealer* 75, no. 3 (March 1994), pp. 34–37.

36. Jack Neff, "Wal-Mart Ups the Ante with Brand Co-op Ads—in More Ways than 37.ne," *Advertising Age* (http://adage.com/ article?article_id=140743), November 30, 2009.

37. Jennifer Gilber, "The Show Must Go On," *Sales & Marketing Management* 155, no. 5 38. May 2003), p. 14.

38. Walter Heller, "Promotion Pullback," *Progressive Grocer* 81, no. 4 (March 1, 2002), p. 19.

39. Brian Sullivan, "Make Sure Promotional Items Fit Brand Perfectly," *Marketing News* 35, no. 19 (September 10, 2001), p. 15.

40. Personal interview with Bill Breedlove by Kenneth E. Clow and Donald Baack, January, 2010.

41. Liz Parks, "Chains See Today's Wealthy Teens as Tomorrow's Loyal Customers," *Drug Store News* 21, no. 15 (September 27, 1999), p. 84.

42. Donald Baack, *International Business* (New York: Glencoe McGraw-Hill, 2008), pp. 28–49.

Chapter 13

1. "Mexico Leans on PR to Lure Back Tourists," *Advertising Age*, June 26, 2011, http://adage.com/pring/228385.

2. Jenny Dawkins, "Corporate Responsibility: The Communication Challenge," *Journal of Communication Management* 9, no. 2 (November 2004), pp. 106–17.

3. Heather Chaplin, "Players Lend a Helping Hand – or, Thumb," *Adweek*, April 10, 2012, www.adweek.com/print/139461.

4. Michael Fielding, "Companies that Behave Responsibly Earn Good Rep, Consumers' Attention," *Marketing News* 41, no. 8 (May 1, 2007), pp. 17–18.

5. Suzanne Vranica, "NBC Universal Tees Up Cause-Related Shows," *The Wall Street Journal* (http://online.wsj.com/article/ SB10001424052748704112904574477872926288910.html), October 19, 2009.

6. Larry Chiagouris and Ipshita Ray, "Saving the World with Cause-Related Marketing," *Marketing Management* 16, no. 4 (July–August 2007), pp. 48–51.

7. Tanya Irwin, "Purina Launches Initiatives Benefiting Shelters," *Marketing Daily*, December 7, 2011, www.mediapost.com/ publications/article/163693.

8. Heather Chaplin, "Players Lend a Helping Hand – or, Thumb," *Adweek*, April 10, 2012, www.adweek.com/print/139461.

9. Nan Xiaoli and Heo Kwangiun, "Consumer Responses to Corporate Social Responsibility (CSR) Initiatives," *Journal of Advertising* 36, no. 2 (Summer 2007), pp. 63–74.

10. Andrew Adam Newman, "Tough on Crude Oil, Soft on Ducklings," *The New York Times* (**www.nytimes.com/2009/09/25/business/media/25adco.html**), September 25, 2009.

11. Dawkins, "Corporate Responsibility: The Communication Challenge."

12. Jill Meredith Ginsberg and Paul N. Bloom, "Choosing the Right Green Marketing Strategy," *MIT Sloan Management Review* 46, no. 1 (Fall 2004), pp. 79–84.

13. Stephanie Clifford and Andrew Martin, "As Consumers Cut Spending, Green Products Lose Allure," *The New York Times*, April 21, 2011, www.nytimes.,com/2011/04/22/business/energy-environment/22green.html.

14. Jill Meredith Ginsberg and Paul N. Bloom, "Choosing the Right Green Marketing Strategy, *MIT Sloan Management Review* 40, no. 1 (Fall 2004) pp. 79–84.

15. Examples based on Ginsberg and Bloom, "Choosing the Right Green Marketing Strategy."

16. Tanya Irwin, "Seventh Generation Debuts First National Campaign," *Marketing Daily, MediaPost News* (**www.mediapost.com/publications/?fa=Articles.printFriendly&art_aid=120626**), January 14, 2010.

17. Marvin E. Shaw and Philip R. Costanzo, *Theories of Social Psychology,* 2nd ed. (New York: McGraw-Hill, 1982), p. 334.

18. Rich Thomaselli, "New Orleans is a Super Bowl Winner," *Advertising Age* (http://adage.com/superbowl10/article?article_id=141988), February 8, 2010.

19. Sarah E. Needleman, "For Companies, A Tweet in Time Can Avert PR Mess," *The Wall Street Journal* (http://online.wsj.com/article/SB1249258302403003.html), August 3, 2009.

20. Michael Bush, "The Cult of Toyota," *Advertising Age* (http://adage.com/print?article_id=142335), March 1, 2010; Rich Thomaselli, "Toyota Sends in Jimi Lentz for Cross-Media Saatchi-Led PR Control," *Advertising Age* (http://adage.com/print?article_id=141856), February 1, 2010; Laurie Burkitt, "From Trusted to Busted: Brands Have a Credibility Crisis," *Forbes* (**www.forbes.com/1010/02/25/toyota-tiger-consumer-faith-cmo-network-trusted-to-be-busted**), February 25, 2010.

21. Shaw and Costanzo, *Theories of Social Psychology,* 2nd ed., p. 334.

22. Ibid, p. 329.

23. Ibid, p. 333.

24. Nigel Pope, Kevin E. Voges, and Mark Brown, "Winning Ways," *Journal of Advertising* 38, no. 2 (Summer 2009), pp. 5–20.

25. "Events & Sponsorships," *2008 Marketing Fact Book, Marketing News* 42, no. 12 (July 15, 2008), p. 26.

26. Karl Greenberg, "Ford Intros Integrated Push for F-Series," *Marketing Daily, MediaPost News* (**www.mediapost.com/publications/?fa=Articles.printFriendly&art_aid=125753**), April 8, 2010.

27. Natalie Zmuda, "Speedo Makes a Splash with LZR Racer Suit," *Advertising Age* (http://adage.com/print?article_id=128002), June 25, 2008.

28. Gail Schiller, "Idol Sponsors Coke, Ford, AT&T Paying More," *Brandweek.com* (http://login.vnuemedia.com/bw/esearch/article_display.jsp?vnu_content_id=1003696656), January 15, 2008.

29. Pradnya Joshi, "Approval by a Blogger May Please a Sponsor," *The New York Times* (**www.nytimes.com/2009/07/13/technology/internet/13blog.html**), July 13, 2009.

30. Patricia Cobe, "Working the Neighborhood," *Restaurant Business* 108, no. 11 (November 2009), pp. 20–26.

31. David Tanklefsky, "Events-based Campaigns, Experiential Marketing Prove Successful Among Hispanic Consumers," B&C (**www.broadcastingcable.com/article/print/355270-Hispanic_TV_Summit_Promotion**), September 24, 2009.

32. Betsy Spethmann, "A Winning Season," *PROMO* 18, no. 1 (December 2004), pp. 32–41.

33. Kenneth Hein, "Study: Purchase Intent Grows with Each Event," *Brandweek* 49, no. 4 (January 28, 2008), p. 4.

34. Diane Anderson, "eBay's Campy Road Tour: One on One, No Mosquitoes," *Brandweek* 46, no. 10 (March 7, 2005), p. R6.

35. Jonathan Clegg, "NBA, Adidas Shoot for Europe," *The Wall Street Journal* (http://online.wsj.com/article/SB100014240527487048961045751400325745513978.html), March 23, 2010.

36. R. Dana, "When You're Here, You're Family—But What About a Playboy Model?; Olive Garden Has Mixed Feelings About Its Biggest Celebrity Fan," *Wall Street Journal* (August 13, 2008). p. A.1; "Playboy.com features 'The Girls of Olive Garden,'" The Bryant Park Project, National Public Radio (www.npr.org/templates/story/story.php?storyId=92544599, accessed May 13, 2010); Korin Miller, "Playboy Dishes up 'Girls of Olive Garden,'" *New York Daily News* (http://www.nydailynews.com/gossip/2008/07/16/2008-07-16_playboy_dishes_up_girls_of_the_olive_gar.html, accessed May 13, 2010), July 16, 2008; www.olivegarden.com (accessed May 13, 2010).

Chapter 14

1. Sarah Skidmore, "Reebok to Pay $25 Million over Toning Shoe Claims," Business Week, September 28, 2011, http://www.businessweek.com/ap/financialnews/D9Q1P9PG0.htm, accessed March 16, 2012.

2. Ellie Krupnick, "Reebok Reaches $25 Million Settlement over Toning Sneakers," The Huffington Post, November 28, 2011, http://www.huffingtonpost.com/2011/09/28/reebok-settlement-toning-sneakers_n_985141.html, accessed March 16, 2012.

3. "Broadcasters Breach Kids Rules," *Marketing Magazine* 109, no. 35 (November 1, 2004), p. 4.

4. Bart Lazar, "This Column Is the Best One You'll Ever Read," *Marketing News* 38, no. 13 (August 15, 2004), p. 8.

5. "Fast Feeders Serve Up Fresh Buzzwords," *Advertising Age*, March 7, 2011, http://adage.com/print/149264.

6. Gary D. Hailey and Jeffrey D. Knowles, "Claiming Sufficient Substantiation Is No Easy Task," *Response* 13, no. 4 (January 2005), p. 50.

7. "KFC's Claims That Fried Chicken Is a Way to 'Eat Better' Don't Fly," *Federal Trade Commission* (**www.ftc.gov/opa/2004/06/kfccorp.htm**, accessed June 30, 2002).

8. Robert Hof, "What Facebook's FTC Privacy Settlement Means to Marketers," *Forbes*, November 29, 2011, www.forbes.com/sites/orberthof/2011/11/29/what-facebook-ftc-privacy-settlement-means-to-marketers.

9. "FTC Takes Aim at Another Credit Counseling Firm," *Mortgage Servicing News* 8, no. 7 (August 2004), p. 21.

10. "Body Wise International to Pay $3.5 Million to Settle Federal and State Deceptive Advertising Charges," Federal Trade Commission (**www.ftc.gov**, accessed September 20, 2005).

11. Debbi Mack, "FTC Use of Corrective Advertising Upheld," *Corporate Legal Times* 10, no. 108 (November 2000), p. 80.

12. Tim Arango, "Soon, Bloggers Must Give Full Disclosure," *The New York Times* (**www.nytimes.com/2009/10/06/business/media/06adco.html**), October 6, 2009; Douglas MacMillan, "Blogola: The FTC Takes on Paid Posts," *BusinessWeek* (**www.businessweek.com/print/technology/content/may2009/tc20090518_532031.htm**), May 19, 2009.

13. Loraine Debonis, "FTC Sends Issuers a Message: Adequately Disclose Card Fees," *Cards & Payments* 20, no. 5 (May 2007), pp. 16–17.

14. Tanzina Vega, "CoverGirl Withdraws Enhanced Taylor Swift Ad," *Media Decoder*, December 21, 2011, http://mediadecoder.blogs.nytimes.com/2011/12/21/covergirl-withdraws-enhanced-taylor-swift-ad.

15. Seth Stevenson, "How New Is New? How Improved Is Improved?" *Slate* (**www.slate.com/toolbar.aspx?action=print&id=2221968**), July 13, 2009.

16. "Minute Maid Complains, but NARB Forces Change," *Advertising Age* 68, no. 15 (April 14, 1997), p. 51.

17. "NARB Sends Winn-Dixie Complaint to FTC," *Advertising Age* 67, no. 52 (December 23, 1996), p. 2.

18. Wayne Keeley, "Toys and the Truth," *Playthings* 106, no. 2 (February 2008), p. 8.

19. Mary Pipher, *The Shelter of Each Other* (New York: Ballentine Books, 1996).

20. Internet Marketing Register (**www.marketing-register.com**, accessed February 28, 2005).

21. Beth Snyder Bulik, "Consumers to Providers: Do You Know Who I Am?" *Advertising Age* 79, no. 10 (March 10, 2008), p. 8.

22. Simon Chadwick and Nicholas Burton, "Ambush!" *The Wall Street Journal* (http://online.wsj.com/article/SB10001424052970204731804574391102699362862.html), January 25, 2010.

23. Ibid; Aaron Baar, "Olympics Sponsors Benefit, As Do Competitors," *Marketing Daily* (**www.mediapost.com/publications/?fa=Articles.printFriendly&art_aid=122665**), February 17, 2010.

24. Chadwick and Burton, "Ambush!"; Anne Kingston, "The Outlaws," *Maclean's* 123, no. 8 (March 8, 2010), pp. 48–49.

25. Jacob E. Osterhout, "Stealth Marketing: When You're Being Pitched and You Don't Even Know It," *NY Daily-News* (**www.nydailynews.com/lifestyle/2010/04/19_stealth_marketing**), April 19, 2010.

26. Ibid.

27. Weight Loss Institute (**www.weight-loss-institute.com/products/solidax_adx.html**, accessed March 23, 2008).

28. **www.nutrition.about.com**, **www.conagrafoods.com**, **www.mcdonalds.com**, **www.foodproductdesign.com**, **www.fritolay.com**, and **www.nlm.nih.gov**, all accessed March 13, 2008.

29. Kelly Dumke and Rachel Zavala, "The Controversy Surrounding Smart Choices," *The Friedman Sprout* (http://friedmansprout.wordpress.com/2009/12/02/the-controversy-surrounding-smart-choices/), December 2, 2009; Randall Pinkston, "Experts Say Industry Food Labels Deceptive," *CBS Evening News* (www.cbsnews.com/stories/2009/09/06/eveningnews/main5291352.shtml), September 6, 2009; "Smart Choices?" *CBSNewsOnline* (www.youtube.com/watch?v=dWMVcURE-eE, accessed May 18, 2010); Rebecca Ruiz, "Eight Puzzling Food Labels," *Forbes* (www.forbes.com/2009/09/23/food-labels-healthy-lifestyle-health-smart-choices-nutrition.html), September 23, 2009.

Chapter 15

1. http://www.sandsresearch.com/, accessed September 14, 2010.

2. Gordon A. Wyner, "Narrowing the Gap," *Marketing Research* 16, no. 1 (Spring 2004), pp. 6–7.

3. Interview with Elena Petukhova, The Richards Group, May 17, 2010, by Kenneth E. Clow.

4. "Nielsen IAG" (http://en-us.nielsen.com/tab/product_families/iag, accessed May 19, 2010).

5. Lucia Moses, "Publishers Offer TV-Like Metrics, But Will Buyers Bite?" *Mediaweek*, (**www.mediaweek.com/mw/content_display/news/magazines-newspapers/e3ieea0d35**), January 17, 2010.

6. "Has Burger King's First Mcgarrybowen Ad Helped the Brand?" *Advertising Age*, September 19, 2011, http://adage.com/print229832.

7. "Copy Testing Coming to Digital Marketing," *Advertising Age*, February 27, 2011, http://adage.com/print/149100.

8. Interview of David Snell by Kenneth E. Clow, May 17, 2010.

9. Interview with Elena Petukhova, The Richards Group, May 17, 2010, by Kenneth E. Clow.

10. Andrew McMains, "P&G Does Dan Wieden's Bidding," *Adweek*, June 27, 2011, www.adweek.com/print/132903.

11. "Copy Testing Coming to Digital Marketing," *Advertising Age*, February 27, 2011, http://adage.com/print/149100.

12. Steven P. Brown and Douglas M. Stayman, "Antecedents and Consequences of Attitude Toward the Ad: A Meta-Analysis," *Journal of Consumer Research* 19 (June 1992), pp. 34–51.

13. Douglas M. Stayman and David A. Aaker, "Continuous Measurement of Self-Report or Emotional Response," *Psychology and Marketing* 10 (May–June 1993), pp. 199–214.

14. Freddie Campos, "UH Facility Test Ads for $500," *Pacific Business News* 35, no. 23 (August 18, 1997), pp. A1–A2.

15. Patricia Riedman, "DiscoverWhy Tests TV Commercials Online," *Advertising Age* 71, no. 13 (March 27, 2000), pp. 46–47.

16. Jon Lafayette, "Biometric Study: Broadcast Ads Make Web Work Better," May 9, 2011, www.broadcastingcable.com/article/print/467935.

17. Amy Chozick, "These Lab Specimens Watch 3-D Television," *The New York Times*, January 24, 2012, www.nytimes.com/2012/01/25/business/media/a-media-lab-will-test-consumers-reactions.

18. Bruce F. Hall, "On Measuring the Power of Communications," *Journal of Advertising Research* 44, no. 2 (June 2004), pp. 181–88.

19. Hall, "On Measuring the Power of Communications."

20. John Capone, "Microsoft and Initiative Strive for Better Advertising Through Neuroscience," *Online Media Daily* (**www.mediapost.com/publications/?fa=Articles.printFriendly&art_aid=118835**), December 9, 2009; Steve McClellan, "Mind Over Matter: New Tools Put Brands in Touch with Feelings," *Adweek* (http://www.adweek.com/aw/content_display/news/media/e3i975331243e08d74c5b66f857ff12cfd5), February 18, 2008.

21. Laurie Burkitt, "Battle for the Brain," *Forbes* 184, no. 9 (November 16, 2009), pp. 76–78.

22. Based on PACT document published in *Journal of Marketing* 11, no. 4 (1982), pp. 4–29.

23. http://www.adknowledge.com/usa/index.php, accessed September 14, 2010.

24. Rachel King, "Sentiment Analysis Gives Companies Insights into Consumer Opinion," *Bloomberg Business*, March 1, 2011, www.businessweek.com/print/technology/content/feb2011/tc20110228_366762.htm. .

25. Amanda Beeler, "POPAI Initiates Study Tracking Effectiveness of Displays," *Advertising Age* 71, no. 15 (April 10, 2000), p. 54.

26. Chris Dillabough, "Web Lets Canadian Tourism Test Media Effectiveness," *New Media Age* (October 31, 2002), p. 12.

27. Kate MacArthur, "McDonald's Tests Ads That Focus on Service," *Advertising Age* 74, no. 1 (January 6, 2003), p. 3.

28. Tim Triplett, "Researchers Probe Ad Effectiveness Globally," *Marketing News* 28, no. 18 (August 29, 1994), pp. 6–7.

29. Paul J. Cough, "Study: Marketers Struggle to Measure Effectiveness," *Shoot* 45, no. 29 (August 20, 2004), pp. 7–8.

30. Peter Drucker, *Management: Tasks, Responsibilities, Practices* (New York: Harper & Row, 1974).

SUBJECT INDEX

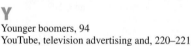